Relax.

You've opened the right book.

Once upon a time, people were wrong. They thought the automobile was an electric death trap that would never replace the buggy, the Internet was only for academic shut-ins, and people who used study guides were simply *cheaters*. Then cars stopped exploding every time you started the engine, people realized you could use computers for more than just calculating the digits of *pi,* and the "cheaters" with the study guides ... well, they started getting it. They got better grades, got into better schools, and just plain ol' got better. Times change. Rules change. *You snooze, you lose, buggy drivers.*

SparkNotes is different. We've always been thinking ahead. We were the first study guides on the Internet back in 1999— you've been to SparkNotes.com haven't you? If not ... why?! You'll find busy message boards, diagnostic test prep, and all kinds of tools you'll need to get your act together and your grades up. And if your act's already together, SparkNotes will help you brutalize the competition. Or work for peace. Your call.

We're inexpensive, not cheap. Not only are our books the best bang for the buck, they're the best bang, period. Our reputation is based on staying smart and trustworthy—one step ahead, making tough topics understandable. We explain, we strategize, we translate. We get you where you want to go: smarter, better, faster than anyone else.

If you've got something to say, tell us. Your input makes us better. Found a mistake? Check www.sparknotes.com/errors. Have a comment? Go to www.sparknotes.com/comments. Did you read all the way to the bottom? Awesome. We love you. You're gonna do just fine.

SPARKNOTES™

SPARKNOTES®

GUIDE TO THE
NEW
LSAT®

by Eric Goodman

SPARK PUBLISHING

Spark Publishing
A Division of Barnes & Noble
120 Fifth Avenue
New York, NY 10011
www.sparknotes.com

Library of Congress Cataloging-in-Publication Data

Goodman, Eric (Eric Craig), 1966–
  SparkNotes guide to the new LSAT / Eric Goodman.
    p. cm.

 ISBN-13: 978-1-4114-9968-3
 ISBN-10: 1-4114-9968-9
 1. Law School Admission Test—Study guides. 2. Law schools—United States—Entrance examinations. I. Title.

KF285.Z9G667 2007

340.076—dc22

                                    2007011725

Please submit changes or report errors to www.sparknotes.com/errors.

Printed and bound in Canada.

10 9 8 7 6 5 4 3 2 1

ACKNOWLEDGMENTS

I would like to thank Doug Tarnopol for recommending me to SparkNotes; Jessica Allen for getting the ball rolling; my agent, Janice Sharifi, for her representation and advice; and Ben Paris for reprising his role as expert reviewer in our long-time LSAT collaboration.

I especially want to thank Laurie Barnett for her support during the challenging phases of this project and her invaluable hands-on contributions to the manuscript.

Finally, love and gratitude go to Cathy, Memphis, and Dasha for keeping me grounded and in excellent spirits during this outpouring of language and logic.

Eric Goodman
New York City

Contents

Introduction: Meet the LSAT 1

First Things First: The New LSAT .1

Three LSAT Myths Dispelled 1

LSAT by the Numbers 2

LSAT Minutiae 5

Master Gameplan 8

Chapter 1: Logical Reasoning 11

Overview 12

Gameplan 13

X-ray of a Typical Logical Reasoning Question 14

Essential Concepts. 15

An Integrated Approach. 22

Essential Strategy 22

Question Types 23

The Real Deal: Practice Set 97

Logical Reasoning Summary 113

Chapter 2: Logic Games 115

Overview 116

Gameplan 117

X-ray of a Typical Logic Game 117

Game Types 119

Essential Strategy 122

The Real Deal: Practice Set 153

Logic Games Summary 177

Chapter 3: Reading Comprehension 179

Overview 180

Gameplan 181

X-ray of a Typical Reading Comprehension Passage 182

Essential Elements. 184

Mining the Essential Elements 187

Essential Strategy 193

Question Types 195

The New Paired Passages 222

Paired Passages Essential Strategy 223

The Real Deal: Practice Set 232
Reading Comprehension Summary 260

Chapter 4: The Writing Sample 261
Overview 261
Gameplan 262
X-ray of a Typical Writing Sample Prompt 263
Essential Strategy 265
Essay Practice 268
Writing Sample Summary 272

Chapter 5: LSAT Practice Test 273
Section Management 273
How to Use This Test 275
LSAT Practice Test 277
Logic Games Hints 306
Answer Key 308
Section I: Answers & Guided Explanations 310
Section II: Answers & Guided Explanations 362
Section III: Answers & Guided Explanations 395
Section IV: Answers & Guided Explanations 442

Chapter 6: Top 15 LSAT Test Day Tips 493
Final Thought 495

About the Author 497

Meet the LSAT

You, LSAT . . . LSAT, You.

Now that we've dispensed with the formalities, let's get down to business.

FIRST THINGS FIRST: THE NEW LSAT

For a standardized test that's remained relatively constant since 1991, any change in structure or content is big news. And that's exactly what the LSAT creators announced beginning with the June 2007 administration. The changes aren't major, but they do include a new Reading Comprehension question type and the elimination of one kind of Writing Sample essay prompt. Rest assured that this book will give you the lowdown on these changes. But first let's continue with your introduction to the test.

We're going to begin by pointing out a few things about the LSAT in order to dispel some myths right off the bat.

THREE LSAT MYTHS DISPELLED

Myth #1: The LSAT is like any academic test you've taken before.

Most tests are created to determine what you know. The LSAT is constructed to determine *how you think*. The LSAT is a skills test—specifically, a test of the reading, critical thinking, and analytical reasoning skills that you've acquired from your years as a conscious person on this planet. If you're taking a graduate entrance exam and your attitude is "it's mostly just an updated version of the SAT . . . ," you'd better be taking the GMAT or GRE, since three-quarters of the LSAT doesn't fit that description (although the other quarter, Reading Comprehension, is pretty much ubiquitous throughout Testing Land).

The good news is that the LSAT contains no science, math, or grammar. The bad news is that the LSAT contains no science, math, or grammar—things that are easily accessible for review. Your major concerns will be logic and comprehension, areas you can't improve on by memorizing geometric formulas or the periodic table. If you consider reading a torture, logic a luxury, and debate a distraction, you're probably headed for the wrong line of work. But if you relish these intellectual challenges, then the LSAT is for you. It is unique among standardized tests. We challenge you from the start to *embrace* that uniqueness, recognizing that you may already possess many of the skills that the LSAT requires. This book will teach you what those skills are, how to sharpen the ones you have, and how to develop the ones you're lacking. It is intended to guide you along the most direct path to LSAT success.

Myth #2: The LSAT is a predictor of how good a lawyer you'll be.

The LSAT does not predict your starting salary. It does not predict your ending salary. It does not predict your legal specialization or clientele or chances of arguing a case in front of the Supreme Court. The LSAT is created to predict one thing and one thing only: *your chances of success in the first year of law school.* This is, cleverly enough, exactly the kind of thing that law school admissions officers want to know.

Myth #3: The LSAT is just another factor among many in law school admission decisions.

Many admissions officers believe in the LSAT so much that they count LSAT scores *equally* with college GPAs when deciding who to let through their pearly gates. Talk about a "high stakes" test—the stakes don't get much higher than equating a three-hour performance with a four-year college career. Certainly there is variability in how schools factor the LSAT into the admissions equation, but no one denies that the LSAT is usually one of two major factors (the other being GPA) that determine where law school applicants wind up.

Now that we've exposed some general myths about the LSAT, let's take a look at the specifics.

LSAT BY THE NUMBERS

Structure

There are four scored multiple-choice sections on the test, one unscored multiple-choice section (some call it the "experimental"), and one unscored written essay. Here's how it breaks down.

Section	Number of Questions	Time	Scored
Logical Reasoning	24–26	35 minutes	✓
Logical Reasoning	24–26	35 minutes	✓
Logic Games	22–24	35 minutes	✓
Reading Comprehension	26–28	35 minutes	✓
Writing Sample	n/a	35 minutes	✗
Experimental	22–28	35 minutes	✗

As you can see, two of the four scored sections are Logical Reasoning, which means that *Logical Reasoning accounts for approximately half of your score*. Got that? Half your score. This is the section that we deal with extensively in Chapter 1. The Logic Games section accounts for a bit less than one-quarter of your score, while Reading Comprehension accounts for a bit more than one-quarter. We cover those in Chapters 2 and 3, respectively. The Writing Sample is *unscored*, but we give you the lowdown on that in Chapter 4.

Here are a few more tidbits that may interest you about the LSAT testing experience.

- The multiple-choice sections may appear in any order, but the Writing Sample is always last. There is a 10-minute break that usually falls between the third and fourth sections of the test.

- The unscored experimental section can take the form of any one of the scored sections—Logical Reasoning, Logic Games, or Reading Comprehension. You won't know (and shouldn't try to guess) which one it is. It's used to test out questions for future exams, so consider yourself a guinea pig or a very temporary unpaid employee of LSAC, the folks who create the test (more on them later).

- The 35 minutes allotted for each multiple-choice section is for that section only. You must turn to the next section (or close your test booklet for the 10-minute break) when instructed to do so. That means that you cannot bounce between the sections. For example, if you finish the Logic Games section in only 30 minutes, you can't spend the remaining 5 minutes finishing a previous section or getting a head start on the next one. The proctors are very strict about this, and there are large printed numbers distinguishing each section on the top of every page to help them spot offenders.

- The LSAT must be completed entirely in pencil, including the Writing Sample. Ink or ballpoint pens are not allowed. You may, however, bring a highlighter, which some people use to mark up Reading Comprehension passages.

THE NEW LSAT

- Everyone taking the LSAT is thumbprinted on the day of the exam. This is standard operating procedure to ensure that test takers are who they say they are.

Scoring

Yeah, we saw that—that little eyebrow-raise upon spying this header. And why not? Your final score is understandably your primary focus, so let's talk a bit about how it's calculated.

All Questions Are Created Equal

There are usually 101 scored multiple-choice questions on the LSAT. Each question is worth exactly one point. There is no penalty for guessing, so fill in an answer for every question. If you don't know the answer or don't get to some questions at the end of a section, fill in answers anyway; you have nothing to lose. Some tests, like the SAT for example, subtract a quarter of a point for each wrong answer, so a bit of strategy regarding whether to guess is in order. Not so for the LSAT. To repeat: Never leave an answer blank.

Additionally, hard questions count the same as easy ones. Therefore it makes no sense to get bogged down on hard questions when easier ones beckon. In other words, if you find yourself struggling, guess and move on to the next question. Almost everyone misses at least some questions, but those who don't overly obsess over the tough stuff do better in the long run.

From Raw to Ranking

The total number of questions you answer correctly is called your "raw score." The test makers then wave their magic scoring wand, which sets in motion a nifty but complicated formula that converts the raw score to a score between 120 and 180. This computation includes adjustments to equalize scores on each test with scores on all other LSATs so that no one has an unfair advantage. In other words, the test is scored such that a 160 on one test, for example, is equal to a 160 on any other administered LSAT. This is necessary because LSATs vary slightly in difficulty level from test to test; it's just impossible to avoid. This equalization method, called "equating," is used to adjust for this variability.

The scaled score is further assigned a percentile ranking, which shows at a glance how that test taker did compared to all other test takers from the previous three years. A test taker who scores in the 90th percentile, for example, did better than 90 percent of LSAT test takers from the previous three years. Note that this means that you won't be competing directly against the people taking the test on the same day as you but with everyone who took the test in the past three years. This greater sample size allows for more consistency in the percentile rankings.

Scoring Patterns

The scoring distribution resembles a typical bell curve, with most people bunched in the middle and far fewer at the extremes. The number of scores in the 120s and 170s is relatively low, whereas roughly 70 percent of test takers score between 140 and 160. Although it varies from test to test, getting half the questions right (roughly 50 out of 101) results in a scaled score of around 145, or somewhere near the low 30th percentile. The 90th percentile corresponds approximately to a scaled score of 163, and the 99th percentile clocks in around 172. You can miss about 10 questions and still get a 172, which shows you that no one expects you to get every question right. The LSAT is a difficult test, but the scoring formula allows you to get a number of questions wrong and still receive a very respectable score.

LSAT MINUTIAE

Okay, we could have said "details," but that's kind of boring. "Ins and outs"? That's a little better, but you are, after all, heading to law school, where you'll be deluged with minutiae, or "small, minor details," as it's commonly defined, so why not? This section contains a combination of information and advice that answers common questions often asked by those new to the LSAT.

Meet Your Hosts

So who throws this LSAT shindig, anyway? It's a group of people from New-town, Pennsylvania, known as the Law School Admission Council, or LSAC. You can familiarize yourself with the entire LSAT universe at the LSAC web-site. We provide the essentials of the LSAT experience right here, but if you have additional issues just go to www.lsac.org and get your information right from the horse's mouth. (That's just an expression. The LSAT is not really written by horses.) If person-to-person communication is your thing, call LSAC with any questions at (215) 968-1001. You should also download a copy of the *LSAT Information Book*, which is chockablock with useful information. If your computer is on the fritz, you should be able to find a copy at any college career-counseling office.

Registering for the Test

The fastest way to register for the LSAT is to create an online account at www. lsac.org. The immediate advantage is that you can find out whether the testing center closest to you is available. Some testing centers fill up quickly, so you'll want to register as early as you can to reserve a space in your testing center of choice. The last thing you need on test day is a three-hour journey into the unknown, so plan ahead. Other advantages of registering online include print-ing your LSAT ticket yourself instead of waiting for it in the mail, receiving your LSAT score early via e-mail, and quicker processing if you need to change your test date or test center. If you can't register online, call LSAC at (215) 968-1001 to find out how to register by phone or mail.

Test dates and registration deadlines are listed on the LSAC website and printed in the *LSAT Information Book*. There's a fee for late registration, and there is no walk-in registration on the day of the test. That is, you can't just show up without a ticket and hope to sit for the exam. As of this publication, the LSAT registration fee is $123 in the United States, which is of course subject to change. Check the LSAC website for the most up-to-date information on test dates, fees, and registration policies.

Testing Locations

There are hundreds of LSAT testing sites scattered throughout all 50 states and the District of Columbia, not to mention many international locations, as well. However, not every test site is available for every LSAT administration. Go to www.lsac.org, click on "LSAT," and check out the "Test Locations" and "Test Center Availability" links to find the location closest to you and to check whether it has space available on your preferred test date. If you sign up for a testing center, you may, for a fee, change it, provided you submit your request by the appropriate deadline and there is space in the center where you wish to take the test. If it is impossible for you to get to a test center and there are no available testing locations within 100 miles of where you live, you can request that LSAC create what they call a "nonpublished test center." Information on this option can be found at the LSAC website and in the *LSAT Information Book*.

What Is LSDAS?

Beside the LSAT, LSAC's other claim to fame is LSDAS, which stands for Law School Data Assembly Service. If you want to apply to American Bar Association–accredited law schools in the United States, you'll need to register with LSDAS. LSDAS compiles all of the relevant application materials (your college transcripts, LSAT score, and letters of recommendation) into law school reports and sends them along to any law schools to which you apply. You don't have to register for LSDAS at the same time that you register for the LSAT.

When to Take the LSAT

The LSAT is offered four times a year: February, June, October, and December. (The October exam occasionally falls in late September.) Most law school programs begin in the fall, so the best time to take the LSAT is usually the October before you wish to start. That gives you plenty of time to include your score in your applications, and even enough time to take the test again in December if need be and still start law school the following fall. But June or February may work best for you, depending on your timing. If you're still in college, you can take it any time during your four-year undergrad experience, but most college students find the opportune time is June of their junior year or October of their senior year.

Retesting and Canceling

What if you're unhappy with your score? You can take the test again if you think there is a significant chance that you'll do better. Some schools average the scores of candidates who have taken the LSAT multiple times, and others simply take the highest score. If you're concerned about how multiple scores will be handled by specific schools, contact them to find out their policies. You can also cancel your score immediately following the test or send a cancellation form to LSAC, which must be received within nine calendar days of the test. Canceling the day of the test is not recommended, considering that most test takers are in a bit of a daze following the ordeal and may not have the proper perspective to make that decision. Besides, you have more than a week to think about it, so you're probably best off sleeping on it at least a couple of nights.

Prep Smart

The LSAT universe is populated by "PrepTests"—actual LSATs sold by LSAC dating back to June of 1991. There are over 50 such tests, which means more than 5,000 real LSAT questions are available for practice. These tests are so important that we've gone and integrated actual questions from them into the content chapters of this book under the heading "The Real Deal." You'll find them with Real Deal icons and citations telling you which PrepTests they're from. This is to give you an appreciation of how the strategies and techniques we lay out in the book pertain to the actual kinds of questions you'll see.

Of course, with such a mountain of practice materials available to you, it would be foolish not to make use of them. But there's no reason to do 5,000 questions. Sure, if you have months to prepare and steadily work through every available PrepTest, you may get around to all that material. But simply getting through every available question won't guarantee success on the test. Taking a practice test doesn't mean anything unless you apply consistent strategies, reinforce solid approaches, and learn as much as you can from each correct *and incorrect* choice. This book was written to provide you with the framework you need to do just that. It will help you get as much as possible out of each PrepTest you take and reach your LSAT potential without having to burn through 50 or more practice tests. Because, let's face it, you have better things to do.

Get in Shape

The LSAT is an endurance test—a marathon, not a sprint. There are three and a half hours of actual testing, a 10-minute break in the middle, and plenty of administrative chores up front. Count on being at the test site for at least five hours; the *LSAT Information Book* advises budgeting up to *seven hours* for the entire experience. Many a promising test taker has been done in by fatigue, so keep in mind from the very beginning that stamina will be an issue. If you find yourself nodding off after two paragraphs of political analysis or current events, what do you think will happen when you're faced with four paragraphs on Navajo weaving patterns, followed by three more reading passages equally

as deadly, and five more *entire sections* on top of that? Do everything you can to increase your mental toughness and physical fortitude.

One thing you can do immediately is begin reading difficult text—often, and with intense concentration. Don't sequester yourself in an air-tight, noise-free chamber to do this, because your testing center may be crowded and filled with distractions. Train yourself to concentrate on difficult material in difficult situations—on the bus, in crowded cafeterias, during loud gatherings, and so on. Read articles, editorials, and other analyses from the *New York Times*, *Washington Post*, *Wall Street Journal*, science magazines (for the dreaded Reading Comp science passage), and whatever other challenging prose you can find. Get your brain working, and keep it working throughout your preparation. Don't neglect your physical being, either. Exercise helps the mind stay sharp and allows the necessary downtime for your brain to recover and process the information you're learning. There's no sugarcoating it: The LSAT dishes out some heavy-duty mental and physical punishment. You need to know that from the start so you can prepare for the battle.

What's a Good Score?

No one can tell you what a "good" LSAT score might be—only you can decide that. But keep in mind that the only reason you take this test in the first place is to find yourself one day at a law school that will serve as a springboard to a satisfying legal career. Many schools and many scores are consistent with that goal. So while a 180 and a scholarship to Yale would be nice, that's not your only ticket to future success and happiness. It's a good idea to take a full practice test early on to see where you're scoring at the beginning of your preparation and set realistic improvement goals from there. It's fine to set your sights high, but setting them *unrealistically* high, especially in the beginning, could lead to frustration and impede your improvement. As Socrates implored thousands of years ago, "Know Thyself!" And he should know: Most law schools today employ the Socratic method, whereby professors grill students as mercilessly as Socrates grilled fellow citizens in the town square of Athens.

MASTER GAMEPLAN

The following master gameplan will help you envision your overall path to success and make the most of your total preparation.

- **Work Through the Scored Section Chapters.** In Chapters 1–3, you'll study and practice every nuance of the three scored multiple-choice sections: Logical Reasoning, Logic Games, and Reading Comprehension. Take your time and work diligently with the material in these chapters to form the foundation of your LSAT approach.

We've included "Take Away" boxes throughout the book that look like this and contain nuggets of LSAT wisdom derived from the numerous practice examples we provide. As the name suggests, these bits of LSAT wisdom represent the concepts that you should *take away* from each specific practice example you work through. Internalizing the Take Aways will be an important part of your LSAT success.

- **Practice the Writing Sample.** Work through the Writing Sample material in Chapter 4 during downtime from your primary preparation. Because this section of the test is unscored there's no great urgency to get to this chapter, but you should certainly read it at some point and be sure to practice writing at least a few additional sample responses prior to test day.

- **Take and Review the Practice Test.** Reinforce what you've learned throughout the book by taking the practice test in Chapter 5 and reviewing the answers and explanations thoroughly. Use the practice test to highlight your strengths and weaknesses and to guide you to the relevant sections of the book that address your problem areas.

- **Work with PrepTests.** After assimilating the strategies and techniques in this book, cement your approach by applying everything you've learned to recent PrepTests purchased from LSAC. In your final phase of preparation, you should take at least three full-length timed tests. That means that for each of these practice tests you should work through two Logical Reasoning sections, one Reading Comprehension section, one Logic Games section, and one unscored section of any of the three types. (You can, if you wish, cut yourself some slack and omit the unscored section and the Writing Sample, but if you want to create a fully simulated experience, include these as well.) Try, if you can, to schedule these simulated test runs at the same time of day as your actual test. It's important to build up your stamina even after you've mastered the material, and having full-length test experiences under your belt will help you avoid test day burnout and will make the real thing seem that much more familiar. Continue to delineate areas of concern and return to this book to reinforce the skills you need to turn weaknesses into strengths. Scan the Take Aways scattered throughout the book to gear yourself up for your simulated test runs, and as a last-minute review in the days before the real thing.

- **Succeed on Test Day.** Knowledge, practice, and experience will pay off when it counts as you confidently knock back this first challenge of your legal career.

No doubt, mastering the LSAT is a major undertaking. As you'll soon see, however, the test is extremely systematic, coachable, and conquerable. Ready to get started?

Okay, let's do it.

## Chapter 1

LOGICAL REASONING

or

How to Increase Your LSAT Score *and* Annoy Your Friends

Preparing for the Logical Reasoning section can be hell on your social life. No, not just because you'll be spending solitary hours mastering and applying the techniques in this section—that's to be expected, and no one will give you grief for that. But as you begin to internalize the thought processes outlined in the following pages and learn to spot flaws in a large assortment of arguments, you might just find yourself incorporating a new way of thinking into your everyday interactions in a way not likely to be appreciated by those around you.

When you find yourself saying things like . . .

"No Uncle Charlie, arguing that 'because drinking makes Aunt Selma loopy, she must therefore be drunk right now because she's acting loopy' shows your obvious inability to differentiate between necessary and sufficient conditions . . ."

. . . you'll know you're ready to do battle with Logical Reasoning on test day.

Much to the chagrin of unsuspecting friends and family, this chapter will enable you to:

- Develop the ability to spot logical errors

- Recognize subtle assumptions

- Make deductions

- Mimic reasoning patterns

- Break down arguments

Is this a good thing? Absolutely. You can afford a bit of unpopularity and endure a few nasty looks, at least until your LSAT is over. Just think how popular you'll be when you've aced the test and are heading off to the law school of your dreams—unless of course your friends are envious, in which case they'll hate you even more.

So bid farewell to the lazy linguistic conventions and infuriating imprecision that often dominate advertising, journalism, letters to the editor, and plain old everyday written and verbal communication. Say hello to a thorough analysis of evidence, conclusions, assumptions, and logical flaws.

Embrace your inner Spock. Let's get logical.

OVERVIEW

What It Is

There are two Logical Reasoning sections on the LSAT, each consisting of short passages and 24 to 26 multiple-choice questions. There is no difference between the two Logical Reasoning sections, other than the questions, of course. Each section lasts for 35 minutes, which means you'll have roughly a minute and a quarter per question. Most of the passages that make up these sections contain some kind of argument—that is, a conclusion backed up by evidence. Logical Reasoning questions test your ability to assess the validity, recognize the strengths and weaknesses, mimic the logic, and grasp the structure of these arguments. Some passages do not contain arguments but rather a set of facts from which you are to derive inferences or draw conclusions. There are 11 kinds of Logical Reasoning questions, and in this chapter you'll learn how to handle each one.

Why It Is

Why not? Seriously, the kinds of thought processes tested in this section represent the skills that law students and lawyers employ all the time. Law is empowered by logic and language, and lawyers must be able to rigorously apply standards of logic to the facts of the cases they handle, be it in a courtroom or corporate boardroom. As we go along, we'll comment more specifically on the relevance of various elements of this section to the study and practice of law.

Your Motivation

Logical Reasoning accounts for half of your total LSAT score. If that doesn't motivate you, we don't know what will.

GAMEPLAN

We want to maximize your score on the Logical Reasoning section, and we have created an effective gameplan to ensure that your study time is efficient and to allow you to approach each question with the best possible mindset. Here's how we organized the chapter to guarantee that your test preparation is in fact useful:

- **X-ray of a Typical Logical Reasoning Question:** First, we'll get familiar with the basics of a typical Logical Reasoning question and its answer choices.

- **Essential Concepts:** Six core concepts are presented next, as they are integral to mastering the Logical Reasoning section.

- **Essential Strategy:** This is an important method for approaching all of the questions you'll encounter in this section.

- **Question Types:** There are 11 question types for this section, and we will go over every one and detail all the specific patterns, issues, and traps you could encounter on test day. We will then show you how to tailor the Essential Strategy, tackling each kind of question and working through examples of each with a specific "battleplan."

- **The Real Deal:** Finally, we will give you *real LSAT practice questions* so you can apply what you've learned to the full practice test, including the two full Logical Reasoning sections, at the end of this book.

Let's get started.

X-RAY OF A TYPICAL LOGICAL REASONING QUESTION

Below is a typical Logical Reasoning question. Don't worry about working through it just yet—we'll do that later. For now, just take a quick look so we can establish some terminology.

> Incompetence causes workers to perform inferior work. In addition, some incompetent people do not recognize their own incompetence, which causes them to reject the feedback and assistance that would enable them to improve the quality of their work.
>
> The situation described above conforms most closely to which one of the following propositions?
>
> (A) A behavior that causes negative repercussions may sometimes bring about positive outcomes that outweigh the negative repercussions of the behavior.
>
> (B) A consequence of a phenomenon may in some cases be compounded by a secondary effect of that same phenomenon.
>
> (C) The rejection of valuable recommendations may prove to be the difference between a negative outcome and the best possible outcome.
>
> (D) When a character trait of a particular worker results in the performance of inferior work, that worker should be assigned less demanding responsibilities.
>
> (E) An inferior project based on a faulty premise will be made worse by any attempt to incorporate a conflicting premise into the project.

The "passage" is the short paragraph in the beginning. The "question stem" is the question you'll need to answer regarding the passage—in this case, the text beneath the passage beginning "The situation described above . . . " The "choices" are the five statements labeled (A) through (E) from which you'll select your answer.

Most passages contain some kind of argument—that is, a conclusion backed up by evidence. The conclusion is the point the author is trying to establish, and the evidence is anything the author provides to back up that point. The conclusion answers the question "*What* does the author say?" while the evidence answers the question "*Why* does the author say that?" For example, consider the following statement:

My breakfast was terrible.

On its own, this statement has no context, so we can't rightfully call it evidence or conclusion—it's simply a declarative statement. However, let's say we add the following sentence to it:

My breakfast was terrible. The eggs were overcooked, the cereal was stale, and the coffee was weak.

Now we have a proper argument. The facts in the second sentence answer the question *"Why* was your breakfast terrible?" which means that the breakfast being terrible is the conclusion and that bad eggs, bad cereal, and bad coffee are the evidence for that conclusion.

Of course, the arguments in LSAT Logical Reasoning questions are generally more complicated, but the format is essentially the same: a conclusion backed up by evidence. The questions test your ability to assess the validity of these arguments, recognize their strengths and weaknesses, mimic their logic, and grasp their structures.

Some passages do not contain arguments but rather a set of facts from which you are to derive inferences—that is, make deductions. You'll learn all about that later in the chapter.

So now you know what a typical question looks like, but what are you supposed to do with one? The directions to the section spell that out. The directions will always be the same, so don't waste valuable time reading them on test day. Read through them carefully now so you'll never have to read them again.

> Directions: The questions in this section are based on the reasoning contained in brief statements or passages. For some questions, more than one of the choices can conceivably answer the question. However, you are to choose the best answer; that is, the response that most accurately and completely answers the question. You should not make assumptions that are by commonsense standards implausible, superfluous, or incompatible with the passage. After you have chosen the best answer, blacken the corresponding space on your answer sheet.

One interesting thing to notice about these directions is that the test makers admit there may be more than one choice that could "conceivably" answer the question. However, only one choice is considered the most "accurate" and "complete." The techniques you learn in this chapter will help you to distinguish between the credited answer and what many consider to be the "next best" choice. Also note that although the questions are geared toward the application of strict logic, a bit of common sense comes into play as well. If you've got some street smarts, use 'em.

ESSENTIAL CONCEPTS

Skateboarders use vocabulary unique to them. So do professional kangaroo wrestlers. Not to be left out, there is vocabulary to express core concepts in LSAT Logical Reasoning that is fundamental and will lay the foundation for your success.

The purpose of this section is to establish the right frame of mind to tackle the Logical Reasoning section. To that end, we'll introduce six important concepts that will appear in some form on your test:

1. Necessary and sufficient conditions

2. Cause and effect

3. Alternatives

4. Bait and switch

5. Unknowables

6. Loose ends

Essential Concept #1

Necessary and Sufficient Conditions

LSAT test makers are especially enamored with the distinction between what's *required* to bring about a result (a necessary condition) and what by itself is *enough* to bring about a result (a sufficient condition). It's not hard to figure out the relevance of this distinction to the study and practice of law. Say, for example, that the Duke of Gloom Manor was found murdered in the night, the autopsy revealing death by strangulation. In keeping with mystery folklore, Jeeves, the butler, is the primary suspect. Now if the police determine that Jeeves possesses *sufficient* strength to strangle the Duke, that's not enough to implicate him in the crime; just because he *could* have done it doesn't mean he did. But if Jeeves's power is found to be *necessary* for the murder to have occurred (that is, no one else possessed sufficient strength to strangle the Duke), that's a different story—it strongly suggests that Jeeves is in fact the culprit.

Necessary and sufficient conditions are an important subset of formal logic, which we'll discuss in greater depth later. The tricky thing is that these conditions are often hidden in seemingly ordinary language, and it's up to you to recognize statements of necessity and sufficiency no matter what form they take. Consider the following:

Logical Reasoning success is contingent upon your ability to recognize and understand the common logical structures, elements, and nuances that appear in the section test after test, year after year.

"Contingent upon your ability" means that the ability described is required—that is, *necessary* for Logical Reasoning success. In other words, without such ability, one will *not* achieve Logical Reasoning success. But does that mean that possessing such ability will *guarantee* success? No, and that's the distinction you're expected to understand. Familiarity with common Logical Reasoning elements is not, by itself, *sufficient* to guarantee success, even though it is one necessary requirement. That's because there may be other requirements as well, such as the ability to read quickly under time pressure. Take a look at this statement:

If Martin recognizes and understands the common logical structures, elements, and nuances that consistently appear in the Logical Reasoning section, then he will attain Logical Reasoning success.

This is *not* inferable from the statement before it—it represents a classic case of mistaking something that's *required* to bring about a result for something that's *enough* to make it happen. Stay alert to this distinction; you're likely to see it in many forms. In fact, you've seen it once already—go back and reread "Uncle Charlie and Aunt Selma" on the first page of this chapter. If it confused you then, it should make more sense now.

Essential Concept #2
Cause and Effect

Lawyers are naturally very preoccupied with the issue of cause and effect. When untangling matters ranging from traffic quarrels to billion-dollar disputes, it pays to understand what causes what, what *could not* have caused what, what might have been caused by something else, and so on. Cause and effect is a particularly common source of misunderstanding and thus finds itself at the heart of some Logical Reasoning questions. What claims of causation do you notice in the following scenario? Might there be other possibilities?

From September through December of this year, Amalie had been very shy and self-conscious around her classmates, causing her to shun social interaction. In March, however, she began displaying noticeable confidence and sociability, which was also the month she began to participate in a very popular after-school drama workshop. Clearly, the workshop has worked wonders for Amalie's self-esteem.

Ironically, the cause-and-effect relationship that's suspect here does *not* concern the statement with the word *causing* in it, as there's no reason to doubt that the self-consciousness that Amalie exhibited could lead her to shun social interaction. There's greater room for debate regarding the author's conclusion that the workshop has increased Amalie's self-esteem. Why? Because it's also reasonable to suppose that a boost in self-esteem may have caused Amalie to participate in the workshop. Or, perhaps, there's no relationship between her confidence and her workshop participation; maybe the workshop is required and the timing is entirely coincidental. In any case, it's by no means clear that the workshop *caused* an improvement in Amalie's self-esteem, and a number of possible questions could focus on this ambiguity.

You'll see numerous examples of causation along the way, but for now, keep in mind that just because something precedes something else doesn't mean that the first necessarily *caused* the second, and just because two things are *correlated* in some way doesn't necessarily mean they're *causally* linked.

Essential Concept #3

Alternatives

Elwood Blues: What kind of music do you usually have here?
Bartender: Oh, we got both kinds—we got country *and* western!

Regardless of your opinion of country western music, it should be fairly obvious that the bartender in this scene from the movie *The Blues Brothers* suffers from an acute case of tunnel vision. The structure of her statement—in particular, her use of the word *both*—suggests that she believes there exist in the world only two kinds of music. Your ability to recognize plausible alternative explanations or possibilities that the author overlooks will help you with the various question types.

You'll soon see how recognizing alternatives leads directly to points. Meanwhile, maintain a healthy skepticism. To treat the arguments in the Logical Reasoning section as gospel is the kiss of death, considering how many of them contain flaws and omissions and allow for alternative explanations or possibilities. Keep your guard up, especially when an author states unequivocally how something *has to be*. As the old, somewhat sadistic saying goes, "There are many ways to skin a cat." (Not that we can figure out why anyone would want to.)

Essential Concept #4

Bait and Switch

You may be familiar with the age-old scam "bait and switch," whereby something turns out not quite as promised. For example, you see a sign advertising a dozen donuts for $2.99 and go to the store only to find that you have to buy four dozen donuts to get that price. In general terms, some aspect of the offer is altered in its fulfillment. The same can be said of Logical Reasoning arguments in which some aspect of the evidence is altered (often subtly) when it appears as part of the conclusion. The authors of such passages proceed down one logical path, only to end somewhere slightly unrelated—sometimes intentionally, but often unintentionally. Take the case of Johnson and Brown:

Johnson: Due to an extreme aversion to the cold, Mr. Brown almost never ventures out of his apartment when the temperature feels below freezing to him. Since the thermometer I passed in the park yesterday read 31 degrees Fahrenheit, one degree below freezing, the person I briefly glimpsed at the other end of the park could not have been Mr. Brown.

There are actually two bait and switches in this argument: Evidence that Brown "almost never" goes out under certain conditions is used to conclude that the person Johnson spots "could not have been" Brown. This is a fairly common bait and switch, featuring a mismatch in degree. The evidence better supports a conclusion that the person glimpsed was *probably* not Brown, but as stated the conclusion is too definitive to be drawn from the evidence presented. That's because "*almost* never" is not, in fact, the same as "never." If a question asked for the flaw in the reasoning, the answer could read "the author treats a probable result as a definite result," or something along those lines. Noticing this bait and switch should make the correct choice stand out.

But did you notice the other inconsistency between the first part of Johnson's argument and his conclusion? It's a bit trickier and concerns the difference between "the temperature feels below freezing to him" and "the thermometer . . . read 31 degrees Fahrenheit." First, we don't know that the thermometer is accurate; it would be better to explicitly state that it *was* in fact 31 degrees. Even if we assume that it definitely was just below the freezing point, we don't know what actual temperature *feels below freezing to Brown*. The "freezing" element of the evidence does not match the way this element is presented in the conclusion. Such switches en route from evidence to conclusion are notoriously subtle, which is why we're warning you about them up front.

You'll see many cases such as this as we journey forward. And you'll see more of quirky Mr. Brown, as well, when we take up our discussion of Flaw questions. Can't wait until then? Not a problem—Johnson and Brown make a cameo in the next Essential Concept, a little something we call "unknowables."

Essential Concept #5

Unknowables

There's enormous pressure in our media-saturated society to be "in the know"—that is, to be up on recent events lest we be considered, at best, behind the times, or at worst a total fool. In the face of this expectation, we have a tendency to pretend to possess knowledge we don't actually have. Exploring this phenomenon, a media critic once regaled fellow professors with bogus claims supposedly reported in reputable journals. For example, he relayed the "widely reported study" that proved that eating three chocolate éclairs a day would actually make people lose weight—to which some of his overeager colleagues, in an attempt to hide their shameful ignorance of said study, responded "Yeah, I think I heard something like that . . ."

As far as the LSAT goes, a position of humility with respect to knowledge is in order. While most exams you've taken in your life have tested *what* you know—the capital of Wyoming, the twelfth president of the United States, the atomic weight of helium, for example—the LSAT, to an astounding degree, tests your power to recognize what you *don't* know. No standardized test is more interested in evaluating your ability to comprehend the logical boundaries of statements and the limitations on inferences derived from a set of facts. Again, this corresponds to the requirements of legal study and practice, disciplines that highly prize a capacity for recognizing the irrelevant and unknowable.

Logical Reasoning questions (as well as Reading Comprehension questions) thus are littered with traps, wrong answer choices that are either irrelevant to the passage or out-and-out unknowable based solely on the information given. Later in the chapter you'll learn to adopt an appropriate "don't know, don't care" attitude toward such choices. Right now, let's consider the case of Pepe's and Pablo's eateries:

Pepe's Café, located in the northeast corner of the Riverside Quadrangle, closed last July. The same month that Pepe's Café closed, Pablo's Cantina experienced a 7% increase in revenues compared to its revenues the previous month.

What *don't* we know about this situation? Plenty. *Why* did Pepe's Café close? Who knows? Is Pablo's Cantina in the Riverside Quadrangle? In the same neighborhood as Pepe's Café? In the same state even? Does Pepe know Pablo? Are Pepe and Pablo even real people (and not just brand names, for instance)? All unknowable. All excellent fodder for wrong answer choices.

Just about the only thing we *can* deduce for sure from the facts in the passage is that Pablo's Cantina must have had higher revenues in July than in June. Still, it's mighty tempting to concoct our own scenarios. For example, Pepe's customers must have flocked to Pablo's Cantina after Pepe's closed, right?—that would explain the rise in Pablo's July revenues. No, that *could* explain the rise. It's certainly a reasonable possibility, but there's absolutely no evidence for it. Maybe it's the other way around—maybe Pablo's successful month put the nail in Pepe's coffin. Harking back to the Amalie example, we have no way of knowing whether the two events described are causally related. These events are *correlated* because they happen to occur in the same month and both concern the performance of restaurants, but that's not nearly enough to determine that one was caused by the other. If the author did conclude a causal connection, we would be wise to recognize what we *don't* know and envision alternatives.

Ah, but what about the increased revenue? Doesn't this mean that Pablo's turned a greater profit in July than it did in June? Again, no way to tell—in fact, this smacks of the old bait and switch discussed earlier, because "revenue" does not equal "profit." We know nothing about the expenses at Pablo's Cantina; maybe its increase in revenue resulted from a 50 percent increased outlay for advertising and the restaurant is actually *losing* money overall. Here, a good ear for bait and switches allows us to recognize something we can't possibly know and dismiss an unsupported inference out of hand.

Want a bit more practice in *not* knowing stuff? Consider again, if you will, the case of thin-blooded Brown in Essential Concept #4—we can fill a canyon with all the things we *don't* know about that deal:

- Does Brown *ever* go to that park? DON'T KNOW.

- Do Brown and Johnson live near that park? Or near each other? Does Brown even know Johnson? DON'T KNOW, DON'T KNOW, DON'T KNOW.

- Does Brown go out in warm weather? DON'T KNOW—perhaps he's a hermit and never goes out at all!

"That's silly," you might say. No, it's not. It may be unfortunate, unusual, even unbelievable, but it's not *illogical* in the sense that it doesn't directly contradict any aspect of the stated situation. Think of it this way: The fact that Noah never plays baseball in the winter does *not* imply that he *does* play baseball in the summer. The same applies to Mr. Brown. Go on, try it. It's easy—you may even surprise yourself with the depth of your ignorance regarding the Johnson/Brown universe. Don't get offended—it's *good* ignorance, *useful* ignorance, as long as you're mindful of it.

Embrace the unknowable. When it comes to eliminating choices out of left field (and there are plenty of those on the LSAT), the less you know, the better—*as long as you know what you don't know.*

Essential Concept #6

Loose Ends

A "loose end" is something that appears out of nowhere in the conclusion or that appears in the evidence and disappears in the conclusion. Always be on the lookout for aspects of the passage's conclusion that are insufficiently or ambiguously related to the evidence. Loose ends must be tied up in order for the argument to work.

Loose ends in real life are pretty obvious; they're things that make you say, "Where did *that* come from?" Say, for example, your mother calls and tells you that the New York Philharmonic is performing Mozart this weekend, so your brother Brian will soon eat Chinese food. Your most likely response would be "Okay, crazy lady—*whatever* . . . " Obviously, there's at least one missing piece to this puzzle. Brian's impending Chinese feast comes out of nowhere and is therefore a loose end that needs to be tied somehow to the Mozart concert for your mother's statement to make sense. If you cared enough to ask, you might find out that your brother goes to every Mozart performance by the New York Philharmonic, and whenever he attends the Philharmonic he makes a point to visit his favorite Chinese restaurant a few blocks away. This, or some other kind of similar explanation, is necessary to make your mother's conclusion understandable based on the evidence she presents for it.

Loose ends in LSAT Logical Reasoning arguments are more subtle, but the same principle applies. Consider the following:

Virtue is not a self-sustaining attribute. To be considered virtuous, one must habitually display exemplary behavior not only in familiar but also in novel situations. Dede is virtuous, so she must be well disciplined.

Abstract concepts such as "virtue" and "discipline" may not be as easy to grasp as Mozart and Chinese food, but if you look carefully the argument above suffers from the same type of disjunction exhibited in the concert example. It too contains a term in the conclusion ("well disciplined") that appears out of nowhere and needs to be tied in some way to what precedes it for the argument to work. The habitual adherence to exemplary behavior may *seem* like something

LOGICAL REASONING

Essential Concepts

1

THE NEW LSAT

The habitual adherence to exemplary behavior may *seem* like something that naturally requires discipline, but lacking an *explicit* connection between these concepts, the argument is incomplete. The test makers could ask what is assumed by the argument, in which case the answer might be:

Habitually exhibiting exemplary behavior requires much discipline.

Or they could ask for something that weakens the argument, in which case severing the tie between these concepts would suffice. Something along the lines of:

Undisciplined people are often capable of habitually demonstrating exemplary behavior.

In both cases, the answer hinges on recognizing "well disciplined" as a loose end that needs to be tied up for the argument to be complete.

You'll get plenty of opportunities to spot loose ends in the pages to come, as well as numerous chances to employ the other Essential Concepts we've covered in this section.

AN INTEGRATED APPROACH

So there you have it: a foundation of Essential Concepts to give you a head start with Logical Reasoning. You've probably noticed by now that these concepts are not mutually exclusive—for example, spotting a bait and switch can alert you to unknowables; recognizing a claim of cause and effect can lead you to consider alternatives; formal logic statements (which we'll discuss later) may key you in to necessary and sufficient conditions, and so on. Understanding the Essential Concepts and the connections between them is all part of our integrated approach to Logical Reasoning. That integrated approach extends to the question types too, as you'll see that those are interconnected in many important ways as well. Meanwhile, if you've seriously thought through these examples, excellent!—now you're beginning to think like a lawyer (or at least the way the LSAT creators believe a first-year law student should think).

ESSENTIAL STRATEGY

Let's now turn our attention to our general strategy for approaching all types of Logical Reasoning questions. As we said previously, we will later tailor this method to tackle specific question types. For now, let's get the Essential Strategy under wraps.

It's not brain surgery, so we feel no need to dazzle you with some flashy method consisting of a mixture of biorhythms, astrology, and Eastern meditation. There are passages, questions, and choices, so we're going to focus on what you should do with these passages, questions, and choices. Just not in that order.

Step 1: Grill the Interrogator. In other words, read the question first! An LSAT instructor once sent a student down to the corner of a busy metropolitan street and instructed him to wait there for five minutes and then come back to class. After the student had gone, the teacher ordered another student to camp out for five minutes on a different corner and told her to count the number of people she saw wearing white sneakers. After the students returned, the instructor asked them how many people they saw wearing white sneakers. The answers were predictable: Student 1 said "Uh, I dunno . . ." and student 2 said "Seven." When looking for the answer to a question, you're in much better shape if you know in advance *what the question is*. So *read the question stem first*; it will put you in the right frame of mind to scope out the information you need.

Step 2: Attack the Passage. Many test takers think their job is simply to "read" the passage, but that's not enough. The goal is not merely to get from the first word to the last but to understand and extract from the passage the information and concepts that will lead you to the correct choice. Reading the stem comes first because the specific question you face will dictate how you attack the passage and what you'll look for in it. You'll learn in this chapter how to perform a targeted passage analysis for each of the 11 question types you'll face.

Step 3: Work the Choices. Depending on the question type and your success with the passage, there will be a number of possible ways you interact with the choices. Sometimes you'll have a viable prediction in mind, in which case you'll scan the choices for that idea. Other times, you'll need to fully evaluate each choice, eliminating common wrong answer types. In other cases, you'll work backward from the choices, meticulously comparing every element of each to the specifics of the passage. Often, a combination of approaches will prevail. Again, it all depends on the context, but the goal is the same: one choice—the correct one—left standing.

Step 4: Mine the Experience. We've included this fourth step as a vehement reminder to review every practice question to reinforce what each one teaches for test day. "Well duh," you're probably thinking, "of course I'm going to see if I got it right, and check what I did wrong if I didn't." But you've got to go beyond that: Did you get it right *for the right reason*? Did you just get lucky, or is the process you used repeatable in the future? If you got it wrong, was your mistake simply careless, or does it indicate a lack of understanding regarding a particular concept? Each question offers a wealth of information, and the more you get out of each one, the fewer questions you'll need to do in the long run.

QUESTION TYPES

The table on the next page summarizes the 11 question types you'll encounter in the two Logical Reasoning sections. As you'll see, the question types fall under specific categories and are arranged by these groups. We'll cover each question type in depth, in the order in which they appear in the table. Take a few minutes to familiarize yourself with them now.

Category/ Question Type	Your Task	Percentage of Section
Critique		
1. Assumption	Recognize essential but unstated parts of arguments.	17%
2. Strengthen/Weaken the Argument	Recognize statements that support or damage the reasoning in arguments.	17%
3. Flaw	Recognize logical mistakes and common erroneous forms of reasoning.	15%
4. Paradox	Recognize factors that would resolve discrepancies or contradictions.	5%
Deduction		
5. Inference	Make deductions and infer conclusions from a set of statements.	14%
Matching		
6. Disagreement	Identify the point at which the opinions of two people diverge.	4%
7. Method	Understand the techniques used by passage authors.	2%
8. Principle	Match specific situations to general propositions, and vice versa.	10%
9. Parallel Reasoning	Recognize different situations that have the same underlying logical structure.	7%
Construction		
10. Main Point	Differentiate conclusions from supporting evidence.	3%
11. Role	Discern the function of statements in the context of logical arguments.	6%

Note: Percentages are accurate at the time of publication and may vary slightly from test to test.

You will soon see that there are specific challenges posed by each kind of question you face and that you will need to shift into the proper frame of mind—hence, the first step of our Logical Reasoning Essential Strategy. You'll learn to approach the passages in some questions with skepticism, an approach that's not warranted in other cases. Moreover, you'll find that the Essential Concepts discussed earlier play a larger role in some question types than in others, another point of differentiation that will help you focus on the right issues at the right time. Finally, while you'll learn different approaches to the different question types, you'll find there's a great deal of synergy among them, and you'll learn how skills developed to handle one question type may often be applied to other question types as well.

The first four questions types make up the "Critique" category and require you to assess the validity of arguments and note breakdowns and weaknesses in the reasoning process—that is, the way in which an argument's evidence fails to fully establish its conclusion. Each question type in this category involves some sort of validity crisis.

Assumption is up first, so let's get to it.

1. Assumption (Critique)

An assumption is a *required* but *unstated* part of an argument. It is something that is necessary for the argument to work. Many test takers confuse assumptions with inferences. Keep these two important points in mind:

- An *inference* is something that must logically *follow from* the premises of an argument.

- An *assumption* is a premise that must be *added to* the argument if the conclusion is to stand.

Let's take a simple example.

Saffron and all of Saffron's siblings, ages four to nine, are the only people at a sleepover. Therefore, only girls are at the sleepover.

Ah, if they were only this easy . . . Don't worry, we'll get to the tough stuff soon enough, but sometimes it's best to introduce difficult concepts with straightforward examples. It's likely that you immediately recognized the assumption here—namely, that Saffron has no brothers. Why must that be assumed? Because if Saffron *does* have one or more brothers, the conclusion (all-girl sleepover) doesn't follow logically from the evidence (Saffron and *all* Saffron's siblings are there). There's a gap between the evidence and the conclusion that must be bridged for the argument to stand. "No Saffron brothers" bridges that gap.

Tackling the Assumption Argument

When a question stem includes some form of the word *assumption* or asks what is "presupposed" in the argument, expect there to be a gap between evidence and conclusion. Wrap your mind around the idea that the *argument is incomplete* as presented. Here are our strategies for attacking the Assumption argument.

Use the Essential Concepts. Did you recognize the bait and switch in the Saffron example? The author started with "siblings" but ended with "girls." Not necessarily the same, right? This bait and switch creates the gap in the argument. You may, instead, have recognized an alternative: that Saffron does have one or more brothers, which would make the argument collapse. If you see a plausible alternative that would sink the argument, the correct assumption might be something that discounts that possibility. When considering alternatives, ask yourself "But what if . . . ?"—a healthy skepticism triggered by this seemingly innocuous phrase goes a long way toward helping you sniff out the gaps in arguments.

Loose ends is Essential Concept #6 and endemic to Assumption questions. Loose ends must be tied up for the argument to work, so if you notice one, chances are good that the assumption will have something to do with that. Also be on the lookout for necessary and sufficient conditions; this too will appear at the heart of Assumption questions.

Reword the Passage. If the passage is complex, *reword* it in simpler language: "The author says this (conclusion) because of that (evidence)." That should help you see how the evidence and conclusion diverge. Again, remember your Essential Concepts, such as alternatives, bait and switches, and loose ends. These concepts will give you a clearer sense of what's required to bridge the gap.

Tackling Assumption Answer Choices

Optimally, your targeted passage analysis will yield clues as to what the correct assumption might look like, or at least what gap it must close. If so, scan the choices to see if one jumps out. Are you expected to predict word for word what the right answer will say? Of course not—but it helps if you can get in the ballpark. In the sleepover example, you might simply sense that there's something funky going on with the sibling/girl thing and scan for something related to that.

Negate and Destroy. This is a unique strategy specific to Assumption questions. We've stated that the correct assumption must be *necessary* to the argument. How do you know if something is necessary? Take it away, and see what happens. For example, what happens if you take the cathode ray tube out of your TV? The picture goes blank, which means the tube is necessary for the TV to function properly. Take away the idea in the correct answer to an Assumption question, and the argument falls apart, which demonstrates that that idea is necessary for the proper functioning of that argument. We can therefore test any Assumption choice *by seeing if negating it kills the argument.* Here, negating the idea "no Saffron brothers" *does* wreck the reasoning: If all of Saffron's siblings are present, and Saffron has at least one brother, it cannot be true that only girls are at the sleepover. That confirms "no Saffron brothers" as a necessary assumption. We'll use this test often both to kill wrong choices and to confirm correct ones.

Spot the Traps. You also need to be able to spot some common traps in Assumption choices. Let's get to know some of the common ways in which Assumption choices go astray:

- **Irrelevant:** Some wrong choices involve issues that have nothing to do with the situation at hand.

- **Overreach:** Some wrong choices extend the parameters of the situation in a way not required for the argument to stand—that is, they go too far to be required by the argument.

- **Unnecessary Clarification:** Some wrong choices clarify issues that require no clarification. A choice must address the specific gap in the passage to qualify as the assumption.

Practice: Rockin' (Maybe) with the Muddles

You'll get plenty of practice recognizing these wrong answer types as we go along. For now, let's drill a bit more on assumptions. See how many assumptions you can spot in the following passage. (Hint: There are many.)

An amplification system is dependable if all of its speakers can withstand the constant wear and tear of a lengthy rock-and-roll tour without damage to their woofers and tweeters. These two speakers used for the Muddles' tour sounded as good at the last show of the tour as they did at the first, which clearly shows that the amplification system used on the Muddles' tour is dependable.

The Muddles argument is a loose ends tour de force, containing no fewer than *five assumptions*. The heading here is meant to suggest one gap in the argument— we're not told that the Muddles is in fact a rock band. Rock, funk, blues, what's the difference? It matters because the evidence clearly states the ability to endure the "constant wear and tear of a lengthy *rock-and-roll* tour" as the condition on which the designation of dependability is based. But what if the Muddles is *not* a rock band (the negate and destroy test)? Then the evidence presented is irrelevant to the claim it's intended to justify, and the argument falls apart.

For the "dependable" label to hold based on the condition of these specific speakers from this specific tour, *the Muddles must be a rock band*. And speaking of which, what *kind* of rock tour does the author believe is necessary to test the mettle of speakers? That's right, a "lengthy" one. But what if the Muddles' tour is *not* lengthy? Again, a feature of the tour in question would not match the requirements of the dependability test as stated, which means that the condition of the Muddles' speakers could not serve as the basis by which to deem the system dependable. So the argument must assume that *the Muddles' tour is lengthy*.

In the same vein, the author of this argument also assumes the following: *Damage to a speaker's woofers and tweeters would be noticeably reflected in the sound of the speakers*. If not, then it's possible that the speakers have not withstood the wear and tear of the tour even though they still *sound* good, and the claim of dependability would be compromised. Sound quality is a loose end that must be tied back into the concept of damage for the argument to work. The statement above does the trick.

Want more assumptions? Try these:

The two speakers in question are the only two speakers in the Muddles' amplification system.

If there are more speakers, is it still possible that the system is dependable? Sure, but not based on the stated criteria, which state that *all* the speakers withstand the tour. If there are more speakers, then the condition of these two speakers alone would not suffice to establish the conclusion because we'd have no way of knowing the condition of the others.

The speakers were used throughout the tour.

This assumption is derived from the Essential Concept bait and switch: The evidence speaks of "*constant* wear and tear"; the conclusion refers only to the first and last show. For all we know, the speakers were only used during the first and last show. Or maybe they broke down after the first show, so a related assumption would be that *the speakers have not been repaired during the tour.* If repairs were necessary, then the speakers did not "withstand" the constant wear and tear of the tour.

No doubt this is an extreme example; most arguments you'll face won't contain this many loose ends and bait and switches. But if you can understand everything we've said to this point, you should have a fine grasp of the inner workings of Assumption questions and the kinds of things you need to notice in order to tackle them successfully. Nothing to sneeze at either, because this question type tends to give test takers fits, particularly those who don't grasp the mechanism at work. But you do now. If not, review these examples again until it clicks. When you're ready, it's time to apply these concepts to actual LSAT questions. Review the Assumption Battleplan that follows and then see how you do with the first two of the 24 actual LSAT questions in this chapter, "Employee Reductions" and "Bird Energy."

Assumption Battleplan

Step 1: Grill the Interrogator. When a question stem includes some form of the word *assumption* or asks what is "presupposed" in the argument, expect there to be a gap between evidence and conclusion. Wrap your mind around the idea that the *argument is incomplete* as presented.

Step 2: Attack the Passage. Rephrase the passage in your own words, if necessary. Isolate and compare the evidence and conclusion, looking for the gap between them. Look for loose ends, bait and switches, and anything else that might separate the evidence from the conclusion. Try to envision alternatives that would sink the argument. Ask "But what if . . .?"

Step 3: Work the Choices. If you have seen a possible gap in the argument, scan for something that bridges or at least addresses it in some way. Apply the negate and destroy test to confirm your choice. Did you come up with a "But what if . . .?" alternative that would sink the argument? Look for a choice that discounts that possibility and thus allows the conclusion to stand. No clues? Delete any Irrelevant, Overreach, or Unnecessary Clarification wrong choices. Apply the negate and destroy test to the remaining choices and make your final selection.

Step 4: Mine the Experience. One last reminder to get as much as possible out of every practice question you do. The wisdom you extract from the practice questions will form the basis of your Logical Reasoning mastery. Don't skip this crucial step!

Practice: Assumption

Now we'll show you some real LSAT questions. Try to do them on your own before you check the answers and explanations on the next page. Remember to use the Battleplan and keep the Essential Concepts in mind.

EMPLOYEE REDUCTIONS

(PrepTest 29, Section 1, Q. 5)

> Barnes: The two newest employees at this company have salaries that are too high for the simple tasks normally assigned to new employees and duties that are too complex for inexperienced workers. Hence, the salaries and the complexity of the duties of these two newest employees should be reduced.
>
> Which one of the following is an assumption on which Barnes's argument depends?
>
> (A)   The duties of the two newest employees are not less complex than any others in the company.
> (B)   It is because of the complex duties assigned that the two newest employees are being paid more than is usually paid to newly hired employees.
> (C)   The two newest employees are not experienced at their occupations.
> (D)   Barnes was not hired at a higher-than-average starting salary.
> (E)   The salaries of the two newest employees are no higher than the salaries that other companies pay for workers with a similar level of experience.

BIRD ENERGY

(PrepTest 30, Section 4, Q. 19)

> Birds need so much food energy to maintain their body temperatures that some of them spend most of their time eating. But a comparison of a bird of a seed-eating species to a bird of a nectar-eating species that has the same overall energy requirement would surely show that the seed-eating bird spends more time eating than does the nectar-eating bird, since a given amount of nectar provides more energy than does the same amount of seeds.
>
> The argument relies on which one of the following questionable assumptions?
>
> (A)   Birds of different species do not generally have the same overall energy requirements as each other.
> (B)   The nectar-eating bird does not sometimes also eat seeds.
> (C)   The time it takes for the nectar-eating bird to eat a given amount of nectar is not longer than the time it takes the seed-eating bird to eat the same amount of seeds.
> (D)   The seed-eating bird does not have a lower body temperature than that of the nectar-eating bird.
> (E)   The overall energy requirements of a given bird do not depend on factors such as the size of the bird, its nest-building habits, and the climate of the region in which it lives.

Guided Explanations: Assumption

EMPLOYEE REDUCTIONS

Step 1: Grill the Interrogator. This question contains the standard Assumption question stem, specifically asking for the assumption on which the argument depends. This allows you to quickly shift into assumption mode from the get-go.

Step 2: Attack the Passage. The passage hinges on a bait and switch between "newest employees" and "inexperienced workers." Just because the two employees in question are new to the company doesn't mean that they're necessarily inexperienced or that conditions that "normally" apply to new workers necessarily apply to them.

Step 3: Work the Choices. Apply the negate and destroy test. Negating choice **C** destroys the argument: If these two employees are in fact experienced at their jobs, then it makes no sense to say their jobs should be dumbed down and their salaries should be cut. **C** is correct.

A basically says that no one in the company has more complex jobs than the two employees in question. This needn't be assumed because the issue is not how their job complexity compares to that of others but rather how it stacks up against their status as newbies. Test it with negate and destroy if you're not sure: What if their duties *were* less complex than the duties of some others in the company (the CEO, for example)? Does that destroy the author's argument? No—he could still maintain that as new employees, the complexity of their assigned tasks should be reduced.

B, if anything, tends to go against the reasoning in the argument. The author can't argue that the newest employees' pay and responsibilities should be reduced and at the same time assume that the current complexity of their duties justifies their high salaries.

D: What does *Barnes's* salary have to do with anything? A quick kill due to irrelevancy.

> ## TAKE AWAY
>
> Don't overthink! You might figure that **D** suggests the real reason behind Barnes's broadside: sour grapes. But that's taking things too far. Barnes's salary then, now, in the future, whatever, has nothing to do with the *logic* here. You've got to make quick kills when possible; it's the only way to get through the section in time.

E: How the salaries of these two workers compare to the salaries of workers at *other* companies is irrelevant to whether their status as new employees justifies their demotion at this particular company.

Often, multiple choices can be eliminated for virtually the same reason. There are two job factors discussed here—complexity and salary. **A** presents an irrelevant comparison regarding the first, while **E** does the same for the second.

Step 4: Mine the Experience. We won't repeat this step again, but you should always remember to employ it.

BIRD ENERGY

Step 1: Grill the Interrogator. The question stem not only alerts us to the fact that we need to scope out an assumption but also tells us that the assumption is *questionable*. In such cases, the skills you develop handling Flaw questions (which we'll discuss later in the chapter) may very well come into play.

Step 2: Attack the Passage. The passage contains a classic loose end—or a bait and switch, if you see it that way. There's no need to get hung up on the terminology, as long as you see that the evidence is all about *energy* while the conclusion concerns a prediction about *time*. That disjunction forms the gap in the argument. For the argument to work, we've got to tie the two together.

Step 3: Work the Choices. If you recognized that the gap is between energy and time, **C** is the only possibility because it's the only choice that deals with time at all. Even if this question baffled you, noticing "time" as a loose end should have put you on the right track. Sure, nectar may yield more energy than the equivalent quantity of seeds, but what if it takes a really long time to imbibe that amount of nectar as compared to ingesting seeds? That would throw the whole time conclusion into disarray, as it would raise the possibility that the seed eaters *wouldn't* have to spend more time fulfilling the same energy requirement. Knowing whether the statement in **C** is "questionable" requires knowledge of the relative time it takes to consume nectar and seeds—maybe the test makers know something we don't. That the notion in **C** *must be assumed*, however, is confirmed by an examination of what happens if it is false—the author would have no grounds to argue that the seed-eating species will spend more time eating based solely on the energy evidence presented. **C** is correct.

A: So what? The birds in question *do* have the same energy requirements, and that's all that matters here.

B: The negate and destroy test is the easiest way to discard this one. So what if nectar-eating birds do occasionally chow down on some seeds? Would that be in place of nectar? Don't know. How would it affect the energy/time equation? Don't know. Would this fact *destroy* the argument? That we do know—no. So there is no necessary assumption here.

TAKE
AWAY Remember Essential Concept #5, unknowables? Recognizing what you *don't* know doesn't just help you understand the boundaries of the passage—it's a powerful skill that helps you work the answer choices too.

D: Body temperature is presented more as background information than as a primary consideration. It is involved in the explanation of why birds need to eat so much. That's as important as body temperature gets here, so no further clarifications are necessary to make the argument work. Call it irrelevant, or an unnecessary clarification, or whatever you want, but the relative body temperatures of the birds in question play no necessary role in this argument.

TAKE
AWAY What we call a "loose end" might have struck you as a bait and switch, which might have caused an alternative possibility to pop into your head. The terms are not mutually exclusive—they're merely aids to help you recognize the logical patterns that appear in the section. As long as you have the tools you need to pick up the point, it doesn't matter what you call these things, *or that you call them anything at all*. Names are simply a way for us to convey to you what you need to succeed. Make use of them in your own way.

E: The size of the *bird*? What about the size of *this choice*? Like the fluff in choice **A**, the factors determining energy requirements are all irrelevant since all we need to know is that the birds in this argument have the same requirements, period. How that state of affairs came about has nothing to do with the time it takes to satisfy their energy needs.

TAKE
AWAY Let go of the idea that you need to understand everything about a question to get it right. Sometimes, all you need is to get in the ballpark. Sure, **C** is no cakewalk, but it is the only choice that deals with the issue left hanging (time), and even if you didn't think through the precise reason why **C** is necessary to the argument, it would still make for the best guess on the loose ends front alone. A big part of increasing your LSAT score is *honing your hunches*.

Thus concludes our discussion of Assumption questions . . . or does it? Actually no, not by a long shot. The good news is that everything you've learned about spotting assumptions will help you directly with most of the other question types in this Critique category, and in other places as well. In fact, the "Bird Energy" argument, based around a questionable assumption, would be perfectly suited as a Strengthen/Weaken the Argument passage. It is to that question type that we turn our attention now.

2. Strengthen/Weaken the Argument (Critique)

Strengthen/Weaken the Argument questions test your ability to understand the effect that new information has on an argument. Weaken question stems generally ask:

> Which one of the following, if true, most seriously weakens/undermines the argument?

Strengthen stems usually sound something like:

> Which one of the following, if true, most strengthens/provides the most support for the argument?

The "if true" part tells you you're not to determine the validity or "truth" of the choice itself but rather the *effect* that statement has on the reasoning employed in the argument. Here's the effect we're talking about:

- A weakener is a statement that makes one *less likely* to believe the conclusion.

- A strengthener is a statement that makes one *more likely* to believe the conclusion.

A valid weakener need not utterly destroy the argument. Conversely, a valid strengthener need not prove the argument beyond a shadow of a doubt. They both just need to push our believability level in the right direction.

Tackling the Strengthen/Weaken Argument

Here are some strategies for attacking Strengthen/Weaken passages:

Reword the Passage. Same advice as for Assumption questions: If you're having trouble spotting the gap, ambiguity, or weakness in an argument, rephrase it in simpler terms: "The author says this (conclusion) because of that (evidence)." You need to understand the reasoning employed if you're to recognize a statement that makes it better or worse.

Look for Ambiguities. An argument that can be strengthened or weakened cannot, by definition, be airtight—there must be some ambiguity, some weakness to either exploit (in the case of weakening) or rectify (in the case of strengthening). Often the ambiguity takes the form of an assumption that, once recognized, can lead you to the right answer. That means that all of the techniques you learned on the previous pages regarding Assumption questions are relevant here. Remember the Muddles? The evidence spoke of damage, the conclusion spoke of sound. We tagged this as a loose end and from it derived a necessary assumption. But the test makers may not have asked you for an assumption; they could easily have asked for a strengthener instead. No problem—we'd then look for a choice that *makes the assumption go away*; the less ambiguity, the better the argument. Here's one that would work:

The sound of a speaker always indicates whether damage has occurred to the speaker's woofers and tweeters.

Because this statement ties up one of the argument's loose ends, it qualifies as an idea that, when added to the argument, makes the conclusion seem more plausible.

Look for Alternatives. Sometimes the most obvious thing to strike you about an argument will be an alternative possibility or explanation that the author overlooks. Remember, recognizing alternatives is a crucial skill that's included in our list of six Essential Concepts. In regard to this question type, the existence of a plausible alternative to the author's reasoning weakens the argument. *Discounting* such a plausible alternative strengthens the argument.

Tackling Strengthen/Weaken Answer Choices

Now some ideas for working with the choices:

Accept. We can all stand to be a bit more accepting, right? Remember, "if true" in Strengthen/Weaken question stems means you are to accept the choices as true and see what happens when you bounce them off the information in the passage. Focus on the *effect*.

Scan. Optimally your passage analysis will yield an assumption, or a bait and switch, loose end, alternative, or some other Essential Concept that you're learning to spot, in which case you should scan for the choice that addresses that issue. Often, however, nothing will jump out—these arguments are, after all, created to sound very persuasive as written. In those cases . . .

Define the Objective. Formulate the specific task the correct answer must perform. For example: "Convince me that the fossil record *really does prove* that those birds didn't live during that period . . . " Or: "Convince me that James *didn't* actually work overtime on Thursday, as the author says." Then test each choice in light of this specific objective, seeing how each measures up to the task. See how each choice makes you feel about the conclusion. Better? Worse? No change? In the case of the latter, you've hit upon a classic wrong answer type. Let's have a look at some of those now.

Spot the Traps. Like Assumption questions, Strengthen/Weaken questions contain common types of wrong answer choices. Don't let these trip you up:

- **Irrelevant:** The most common wrong answer type in these questions provides useless comparisons, meaningless background information, and things that simply have no effect on the conclusion. You'll get plenty of mileage out of the question "So what?" Also beware of . . .

- **Opposites:** Be careful—those tricky test makers sometimes plant strengtheners among the choices of Weaken questions, and vice versa. Pay careful attention to the question asked.

Practice: Evaluating Effects

Determine whether each statement below the following passage *strengthens, weakens,* or is *irrelevant* to it:

Mrs. Sholskie's third-grade class will have six more students this upcoming school year than were in her previous third-grade class. Wexler Elementary will therefore have to order more third grade–level math books this year than it did last year.

1. The third-grade population of Wexler Elementary has decreased every year since Mrs. Sholskie last taught third grade four years ago.

2. A teacher assistant has been added to Mrs. Sholskie's class to accommodate the greater number of students.

3. Mrs. Sholskie teaches at Wexler Elementary.

4. Wexler Elementary orders more math books than reading books each year.

5. Mrs. Sholskie's class was the only third-grade class at Wexler Elementary last year and will be the only third-grade class this year.

6. An unusually high percentage of students entering third grade at Wexler Elementary have been preselected to study math above their grade level.

7. Wexler Elementary does not have a surplus of third-grade math books left over from last year.

Compare your thinking to the following explanations:

1: Weakens. From evidence comparing the number of upcoming students to the number in Mrs. Sholskie's *previous* third-grade class, the author draws a conclusion about how this year's book requirement will differ *from last year's.* But we don't know that Mrs. Sholskie last taught third grade last year, qualifying this as a bait and switch (hey, we said they were subtle). For the evidence to be relevant to the conclusion, *the author must assume that Mrs. Sholskie taught her previous third-grade class last year.* Statement 1 goes against this central assumption. Moreover, it also suggests that compared to last year, the number of third graders is actually dwindling. Under such circumstances, the case for a greater number of third-grade math books required this year does not seem as persuasive.

2 and 4: Irrelevant. The addition of an extra teacher, and the comparison between math and reading books, are both issues that have no bearing on whether more math books are required based on the extra students in Mrs. Sholskie's upcoming class. *So what* that an assistant has been hired—what does that have to do with the number of third-grade math books needed? And *so what* if there are more math than reading books; we don't know how many reading books there are, so this has no bearing on the argument either. Since so many wrong choices are irrelevant, a hearty, well-placed "so what!" will be an extremely important component of your Strengthen/Weaken technique.

3: Strengthens. Yeah, it definitely helps if Mrs. Sholskie is indeed a teacher at the school in question, something never stated outright. Does this fact *prove* that more books will be needed? No—but it makes the claim more believable because it binds the evidence to the conclusion in a way that's necessary for the argument to stand. In other words, it shores up a central assumption.

5: Strengthens. Statement 5 affirms the central assumption that Mrs. Sholskie was in fact teaching third grade last year, which by itself helps the argument. At the same time, it also addresses the assumption that the situation in this single third-grade class is enough to determine the math book needs *of the entire third grade*. It discounts the possibility that the head counts in *other* third-grade classes might lead to fewer third grade math books required than last year. For both reasons, statement 5 makes us more likely to believe the stated conclusion.

6: Weakens. Statement 6 breaks down another assumption in the argument; namely, that all third graders use third-grade math books. If a much greater percentage than usual has been chosen to study math beyond the third-grade level, the school may not actually need more third-grade math books just because of the six extra students cited in the evidence.

7: Strengthens. Perhaps the following "But what if . . .?" struck you: *But what if there are some extra third-grade math books lying around from previous years?* If true, that would certainly increase the ambiguity regarding the number of books the school must order. Statement 7 discounts this possibility and in so doing strengthens the argument.

Now review the tailored Battleplan, and then try your hand at "Math Principles" and "Power, Pleasure, and Pain."

Strengthen/Weaken Battleplan

Step 1: Grill the Interrogator. "If true" in the question stem reminds you to accept the choices and focus on the effect they have on the argument. Expect some kind of deficiency or ambiguity in the argument that will be addressed (one way or the other) by the correct choice.

Step 2: Attack the Passage. Rephrase the passage in your own words, if necessary. Look for bait and switches and loose ends that may indicate assumptions or other ambiguities in the argument. Keep your eye out for plausible alternatives or explanations that the author overlooks that might compromise the argument. Ask "But what if . . .?" to help spot these.

Step 3: Work the Choices. See an assumption in the argument? For Weaken questions, scan for something that attacks the validity of that assumption. For Strengthen questions, scan for something that bolsters the validity of that assumption. Did you come up with an alternative that would compromise the conclusion? For Weaken questions, scan for a choice that speaks to the plausibility of that alternative. For Strengthen questions, scan for a choice that discounts that possibility. No clues? Define the objective of the correct choice in simple language and test each choice rigorously against that objective. Ask "So what?" to help you spot and delete Irrelevant choices. Beware of Opposite choices that do the reverse of what the question seeks.

Practice: Strengthen/Weaken

MATH PRINCIPLES

(PrepTest 30, Section 2, Q. 1)

More and more computer programs that provide solutions to mathematical problems in engineering are being produced, and it is thus increasingly unnecessary for practicing engineers to have a thorough understanding of fundamental mathematical principles. Consequently, in training engineers who will work in industry, less emphasis should be placed on mathematical principles, so that space in the engineering curriculum will be available for other important subjects.

Which one of the following, if true, most seriously weakens the argument given for the recommendation above?

(A) The effective use of computer programs that provide solutions to mathematical problems in engineering requires an understanding of mathematical principles.

(B) Many of the computer programs that provide solutions to mathematical problems in engineering are already in routine use.

(C) Development of composites and other such new materials has meant that the curriculum for engineers who will work in industry must allow time for teaching the properties of these materials.

(D) Most of the computer programs that provide solutions to mathematical problems in engineering can be run on the types of computers available to most engineering firms.

(E) The engineering curriculum already requires that engineering students be familiar with and also able to use a variety of computer programs.

POWER, PLEASURE, AND PAIN

(PrepTest 30, Section 4, Q. 18)

People who have political power tend to see new technologies as a means of extending or protecting their power, whereas they generally see new ethical arguments and ideas as a threat to it. Therefore, technical ingenuity usually brings benefits to those who have this ingenuity, whereas ethical inventiveness brings only pain to those who have this inventiveness.

Which one of the following statements, if true, most strengthens the argument?

(A) Those who offer new ways of justifying current political power often reap the benefits of their own innovations.

(B) Politically powerful people tend to reward those who they believe are useful to them and to punish those who they believe are a threat.

(C) Ethical inventiveness and technical ingenuity are never possessed by the same individuals.

(D) New technologies are often used by people who strive to defeat those who currently have political power.

(E) Many people who possess ethical inventiveness conceal their novel ethical arguments for fear of retribution by the politically powerful.

Guided Explanations: Strengthen/Weaken

MATH PRINCIPLES

Step 1: Grill the Interrogator. The conclusion may be the recommendation itself, but the question stem helps us to focus on the exact issue at hand—the reason underlying this recommendation. So even before delving into the passage, we already have a sense of its structure. Of course, we know our task: to weaken the reason given.

> The question stems often provide lots of valuable information. Milk them for all they're worth.

TAKE AWAY

Step 2: Attack the Passage. The recommendation is that the training of industrial engineers should focus less on math principles. The "why" of this is provided in the first sentence: Computers can do the math, so practicing engineers don't need a thorough math background. You want to find a weakener to this argument, so define your objective: You're looking for something that suggests that math training *is* actually pretty important for engineers, despite the new fancy computers. By phrasing it this way, you're essentially looking for a direct alternative to the author's support for the recommendation. And that's really as far as you need to go with the passage. At this point, you can simply test each choice against this objective.

Step 3: Work the Choices. **A** says you need to know math pretty well to use the computers.

> It often helps to paraphrase the choices in simpler words, especially when you need to evaluate their effects on the argument.

TAKE AWAY

Does that meet our objective? In other words, does that make us more likely to believe that math skills are still important to engineers despite the new number-crunching computers? Sure—if you need math skills to operate the thing that supposedly obviates the need for those very math skills, it looks like cutting math from the curriculum is a bad idea. **A** is therefore the weakener we seek. But let's quickly check the others to make sure **A** is the best weakener of the bunch.

> Should you check the other choices once you've found one that seems to work? That depends on your confidence level and your place in the section. If you're facing a time crunch at the end of a section, you might want to choose **A** and move on. But in general you should take at least a quick look at the others to make sure they're as bad as they need to be. In your practice stage, of course, you should analyze and review *every* choice to get the hang of what wrong choices typically look, feel, sound, and smell like (well, maybe not that last one, but you get the idea).

TAKE AWAY

If anything, all of the wrong choices lean in the other direction. They all, in some way, support the idea that the use of computers could or should supplant math training for engineers. The fact that the computers intended to render math skills largely obsolete are already being used (**B**), and the fact that they're compatible with current engineering hardware (**D**), shows that the proposal endorsed by the author is currently viable. Moreover, the fact that time for teaching specific new engineering subjects is needed (**C**) speaks to the author's contention that the time normally devoted to math can be used in better ways. Finally, while by no means a definitive strengthener, it can only help that engineers are required to be computer literate (**E**), since that makes it more likely they'll be able to manipulate the highly touted math crunching programs. Now, we can quibble with how strong a strengthener each of these wrong choices would make, but it's hard to see how the author would object to admitting any one of these facts as supporting evidence for her case. If, on the other hand, the fact in choice **A** were to come to light, the author would have every incentive to cover it up.

TAKE AWAY

Opposite choices in a Weaken question actually strengthen the argument, while Opposite choices in a Strengthen question weaken the argument. It's not unusual to see one or more Opposite choices in these question types; here, *all four* wrong choices lean in the wrong direction.

POWER, PLEASURE, AND PAIN

Step 1: Grill the Interrogator. This one contains the prototypical Strengthen the Argument question stem. Be prepared to see lots of these.

Step 2: Attack the Passage. The structure is crystal clear: The second sentence is the author's conclusion, nicely highlighted by the signal word *Therefore,* which makes the assertion in the first sentence the evidence for that conclusion. Paraphrasing, we can spit the argument back to the author like so: "You say certain people enjoy benefits while others suffer pain because of the way the powerful see certain advantages and threats." Stating the case in such a way may help you to see that the benefit/pain issue is a loose end, since attitudes, by themselves, don't bring benefits and pain—attitudes *put into action* can bring benefits and pain. This argument therefore relies on the assumption that the worldview of the politically powerful is somehow enacted in a form that benefits tech geniuses while hurting ethical visionaries.

Step 3: Work the Choices. Choice **B** strengthens the argument by providing a concrete example of this phenomenon. If you defined the correct choice objective as "show me that tech people really do benefit and that ethical people really do suffer based on the way powerful people see things," it would be hard to deny that **B** does the trick.

Our earlier assertion that Strengthen/Weaken questions are very closely tied to Assumption questions is highlighted nicely by this example. A major assumption in a Strengthen/Weaken argument will almost always be tied to the right answer.

A: If we assume that those justifying power in this choice do so via innovative ethical arguments, **A** could weaken the argument by suggesting that ethical innovators might be rewarded by the powerful under certain circumstances. However, the choice as written is probably too vague for this interpretation. In any case, it's no strengthener.

C: The fact that these traits are mutually exclusive has no bearing on whether the techies prosper and the ethicists suffer. What happens to these different groups of people under these circumstances is unaffected by the fact that no one person happens to possess both talents.

D, if anything, goes against the argument by suggesting that technology is a threat to those in power, whereas the author thinks that the powerful view technology as a means of extending or protecting their power.

E suggests that the creative ethicists are afraid of voicing their theories, which is, at least, along the right lines. But it doesn't go far enough to indicate that ethical visionaries who do go public actually suffer for it—for all we know, the concealers' fears are misguided. **E**, at best, merely hints at what **B** says outright.

Always keep the range of the argument in mind. This one focuses squarely on two issues: benefits for tech innovation and suffering for ethical innovation. Notice how **B** covers all the bases, while **A, D,** and **E** fail to take the whole story into account.

Okay, let's move on to our third question type, Flaw.

3. Flaw (Critique)

In the classic detective satire *Murder by Death*, master sleuth Sidney Wang (played by Peter Sellers), in response to another detective's explanation of a murder, utters something to the effect of, "Very interesting theory, but it leaves out one important point:

IT'S STUPID! IT'S THE STUPIDEST THEORY I EVER HEARD!!"

It is in this spirit that you're to approach Flaw questions. Whereas some passages are salvageable through strengtheners, and others can be weakened by the addition of extra information, the passages in Flaw questions are *logically hopeless*—the flaws are inherent in the arguments, and you're asked to recognize the ways in which the evidence fails to establish the conclusion. Here are some tips to get you started.

Tackling the Flaw Argument

Use the Essential Concepts. Essential Concepts come up big in Flaw questions. If a passage contains a bait and switch, the right answer to a Flaw question might simply point out the disconnect between evidence and conclusion. If there's a central assumption, the right answer might point out that the author has taken something for granted without justification. A good "But what if . . ." might suggest that an argument is faulty because it overlooks a plausible alternative or explanation—in fact, many question stems actually contain the phrase "overlooks the possibility that . . . " Confusion regarding cause and effect (remember Amalie?) and the difference between necessary and sufficient conditions also provides fertile ground for flaws, so keep your eyes peeled for those situations too. Consider again, if you will, the strange case of thin-blooded Brown, the guy who doesn't go out when it feels freezing to him:

Johnson: Due to an extreme aversion to the cold, Mr. Brown almost never ventures out of his apartment when the temperature feels below freezing to him. Since the thermometer I passed in the park yesterday read 31 degrees Fahrenheit, one degree below freezing, the person I briefly glimpsed at the other end of the park was most likely not Mr. Brown.

The correct answer to a Flaw question based on this passage might read: "The argument contains an ambiguity concerning the meaning of a key term." This is based on our earlier observation that we don't know what temperature "feels below freezing" to Brown; maybe it's not exactly 31 degrees Fahrenheit. Recognizing this bait and switch would lead you to the point.

Spot the Classic Flaws. Certain flaws appear regularly in Logical Reasoning. We can't predict which ones you'll see on your test, but think of the advantage every time you read a passage and say, "Yeah, I know this one. I've seen it tons of times." Since logical flaws are characterized by a disjunction between evidence and conclusion, it's not surprising that so many of them contain some form of bait and switch. Confusing cause and effect, and confusing necessary and sufficient conditions, fall into this category and are common sources of flaws. We've seen examples of these already, and you'll see more as we go along. The passages below contain other kinds of bait and switch flaws that have regularly appeared on the test over the years. See if you can spot the problem with each:

Practice

SMOKING BAN

The members of the Parents' Association of the Valley Brook school district voted unanimously to petition the city council to ban smoking in indoor public spaces. Since the association must act in the interests of a majority of its constituency, it is evident that the majority of Valley Brook residents are in favor of the ban.

THE DETERMINED MAYOR

Political commentator: Publicly, Mayor Ellison claims to remain steadfast in his determination to appoint a new police commissioner. However, no determination has yet been made regarding the appointment, so Mayor Ellison's vow is clearly disingenuous.

NEW ENGLAND TRANSCENDENTALISTS

Ten percent of the adult population of a New England town, when surveyed in 1835, defined themselves as Transcendentalists, while in 1845 a full 50 percent of adults in the same town defined themselves as Transcendentalists. Thus, more adults in the town defined themselves as Transcendentalists in 1845 than did so in 1835.

SMOKING BAN

Classic Flaw: **Nonrepresentative Sample**

When evidence regarding a particular person or group is generalized to draw a conclusion regarding a larger group, the group in the evidence must be representative of the group in the conclusion for the argument to stand. Here, evidence concerning the interests of the Parents' Association—and by extension their constituency, *other parents*—is used to support a conclusion concerning the opinion of *the majority of town residents*. The bait and switch between "parents" and "majority of residents" is at the heart of the flaw.

THE DETERMINED MAYOR

Classic Flaw: **Equivocation**

Equivocation is a special form of bait and switch whereby a single word or phrase is used in two different ways yet treated as if the same. In this example, the mayor has expressed "determination"; that is, has claimed to be resolved, motivated, determined to appoint a commissioner. The author then takes the fact that no "determination" has been made to conclude that the mayor is lying. But there's no contradiction, because "determination" in this second case refers to a "choice" or "decision." It is in fact possible that the mayor *is* genuinely determined while at the same time no determination has yet been made. Equivocation is the culprit here.

NEW ENGLAND TRANSCENDENTALISTS

Classic Flaw: **Confusing Percents and Numbers**

A percentage represents the ratio between a part of a group and the total group to which that part is compared. The total in this case is the number of people in the town. The logic would hold if we knew that the town had the same adult population in 1835 and 1845; since we don't know that, the conclusion is improperly drawn. Consider: If there were 1,000 adults in the town in 1835, then 10 percent of that would be 100 professed Transcendentalists. If there were only 100 adults in the town in 1845, then there would only be 50 professed Transcendentalists (50 percent) that year. Without information regarding the number of adults in the town, the conclusion is unverifiable. Don't lose sight of the numbers from which percentages are calculated.

More Classics. Other classic forms of flawed reasoning have shown up on the LSAT since time immemorial, and you should be familiar with them. You may come across these classics in passages or see references to them among the answer choices. These oldies but goodies, straight out of Logic 101, include:

- **Ad Hominem Attack:** attempts to support a claim by railing against the character of supporters of an opposing position.

- **Appeal to Emotion:** attempts to convince by engendering pity for a person or thing rather than by supplying evidence to back up the position argued for.

- **Appeal to Authority:** attempts to convince based on the credentials of an expert.

- **Part to Whole, Whole to Part:** inappropriately uses evidence about part of a group to infer a conclusion about the whole group, or vice versa.

- **Circular Reasoning:** evidence and conclusion are functionally identical, even though they may be phrased in different ways. The problem is that no distinct evidence backs up the conclusion.

Keep your eyes open for all of the classic flaws discussed above, not only in LSAT material but in real life too—they've been known to pop up in newspaper articles, on TV, and in everyday conversation. Note them, study them, internalize them. Correct them when uttered by friends and family. Get yourself into trouble—it's for a good cause.

Tackling Flaw Answer Choices

Now let's talk about how to approach the choices.

Scan. Optimally, you'll recognize an Essential Concept or classic flaw that you've seen before, enabling you to scan the choices for it. It's important to familiarize yourself with the various ways these flaws may be described. For example, a correct choice may read: "The argument confuses a condition sufficient for a result with a condition necessary to bring about that result." It might instead employ the specific terminology of the passage: "The author fails to establish that drinking is required for Aunt Selma to act loopy." (You knew we'd make our way back to loopy Aunt Selma at some point, right?) Learn to recognize both the flaws themselves and the common ways the test makers refer to them.

Spot the Traps. Also beware of common wrong answer types:

- **Does No Such Thing:** blames the author for doing something he or she does not do.

- **Not a Problem:** blames the author for doing something he or she *does* in fact do but that poses no logical problem for the argument.

- **Not Obligated:** blames the author for not doing something he or she is not logically obligated to do. Don't fault the author for leaving things out that need not be there in the first place.

- **Irrelevant:** nothing irrelevant to the argument can illuminate the flaw in it.

Now review the Flaw Battleplan and then try "Heart Disease" and "Corporate Boardrooms."

Flaw Battleplan

Step 1: Grill the Interrogator. Phrases like "flaw in the argument," "vulnerable to criticism," "error in reasoning," and "questionable technique" tell you that a flaw is at hand. Give the passage no respect—there *is* a mistake in it, so get ready to find it.

Step 2: Attack the Passage. Keep your eyes peeled for Essential Concepts and classic flaws. Look for bait and switches, assumptions, and alternatives that the author overlooks. If you can't spot the flaw directly, at least try to get a sense of where the problem lies. That will help you quickly cut through the dead wood and put you on the scent of the best candidate among the choices.

Step 3: Work the Choices. See a classic flaw, Essential Concept, or plausible alternative that the author overlooks? Scan the choices for something that addresses the relevant issue. No clues? Rigorously evaluate each choice, eliminating the common wrong answer types: Does No Such Thing, Not a Problem, Not Obligated, and Irrelevant.

Practice: Flaw

HEART DISEASE

(PrepTest 30, Section 2, Q. 25)

Physician: Heart disease generally affects men at an earlier age than it does women, who tend to experience heart disease after menopause. Both sexes have the hormones estrogen and testosterone, but when they are relatively young, men have ten times as much testosterone as women, and women abruptly lose estrogen after menopause. We can conclude, then, that testosterone tends to promote, and estrogen tends to inhibit, heart disease.

The physician's argument is questionable because it presumes which one of the following without providing sufficient justification?

(A) Hormones are the primary factors that account for the differences in age-related heart disease risks between men and women.

(B) Estrogen and testosterone are the only hormones that promote or inhibit heart disease.

(C) Men with high testosterone levels have a greater risk for heart disease than do postmenopausal women.

(D) Because hormone levels are correlated with heart disease they influence heart disease.

(E) Hormone levels do not vary from person to person, especially among those of the same age and gender.

CORPORATE BOARDROOMS

(PrepTest 30, Section 2, Q. 17)

Only a very small percentage of people from the service professions ever become board members of the 600 largest North American corporations. This shows that people from the service professions are underrepresented in the most important corporate boardrooms in North America.

Which one of the following points out a flaw committed in the argument?

(A) Six hundred is too small a sample on which to base so sweeping a conclusion about the representation of people from the service professions.

(B) The percentage of people from the service professions who serve on the boards of the 600 largest North American corporations reveals little about the percentage of the members of these boards who are from the service professions.

(C) It is a mistake to take the 600 largest North American corporations to be typical of corporate boardrooms generally.

(D) It is irrelevant to smaller corporations whether the largest corporations in North America would agree to have significant numbers of workers from the service professions on the boards of the largest corporations.

(E) The presence of people from the service professions on a corporate board does not necessarily imply that that corporation will be more socially responsible than it has been in the past.

Guided Explanations: Flaw

HEART DISEASE

Step 1: Grill the Interrogator. The word "questionable" tips us off that a flaw is present in the argument. The end of the stem tells us the reason is that the author presumes (another word for "assumes") something without sufficient justification. These are the things to keep in mind as you venture into the passage.

> Notice the extremely close bond between Flaw and Assumption questions; this one's literally a combination of both.
>
> **TAKE AWAY**

Step 2: Attack the Passage. The conclusion in the final sentence sounds reasonable, as long as we overlook the fact that the supposed causal mechanism described is not backed up by any actual evidence. Other than the fact that heart disease and high levels of testosterone seem to go together, and lack of heart disease and high levels of estrogen seem to be linked as well, there is nothing to suggest that either hormone in fact causes or inhibits heart disease. What we have here are classic cases of correlation: things that tend to occur together. Just because two events, conditions, or factors are *correlated* does not mean they are *causally* linked.

Step 3: Work the Choices. As soon as you spot a cause and effect relationship, you should examine (especially in a Flaw or Weaken question) whether the proposed causality is justified. In the Amalie example earlier in the chapter, you learned to question the *direction* of the presumed causality; maybe instead of X causing Y, Y actually caused X. This heart disease example illustrates another common flaw: confusing correlation for causation. This flaw is elucidated quite nicely in correct choice **D**.

> Learn to recognize the various ways in which authors say or imply that one thing causes another. The phrases "tends to promote" and "tends to inhibit" essentially indicate that the author believes the hormones discussed cause heart disease to occur or not—or as **D** puts it, "influence" heart disease.
>
> **TAKE AWAY**

The wrong choices all fall within the Does No Such Thing category, as the author simply does not make any of the presumptions discussed in those choices. **A** and **B** are far too extreme to match the argument. Sure, the author discusses only testosterone and estrogen. However, saying that two things have an effect on a condition is not the same as presuming that they are the *only* or *primary* things associated with that condition. The phrases "primary factors" and "only hormones" reveal **A** and **B** as good candidates for quick kills.

C presents a comparison that the author never touches, and **E**, the unusual notion that everyone has the same level of hormones, plays no part in the argument, explicitly or otherwise.

This question was the 25th of 26 questions in the actual LSAT section in which it appeared. For those versed in the distinction between causation and correlation, this question was among the easiest of the section. Easier questions often appear toward the end of the section to test your time-management skills. If you make quick kills of certain questions and choices and refuse to get bogged down in the most difficult material, you should be able to reach the end of every Logical Reasoning section and give yourself a chance to bag all the easy stuff along the way.

CORPORATE BOARDROOMS

Step 1: Grill the Interrogator. The word *flaw* in the stem leaves no doubt as to your task in this one. Prepare to be seriously underwhelmed by the logic in the argument and to home in on the problem.

Step 2: Attack the Passage. The argument is short but likely confusing to those unfamiliar with Logical Reasoning classic flaws. We hope this one smacked enough of "New England Transcendentalists" to remind you to investigate statistical evidence carefully. Every Flaw question stem should put you in a skeptical frame of mind, but the word "percentage" should put you on double alert. Is it valid to conclude that there aren't enough service professionals in corporate boardrooms just because a large "percentage" of service people don't become board members? The pool of service professionals may be huge, vast, gigantic—well you get the idea. There may be millions and millions of these people running around, so even if only a small percentage of them end up in important boardrooms, that may still constitute a significant, healthy percentage of corporate boardrooms since we have no idea of the composition of these boards in general. Maybe they're fragmented into so many small groups that service professionals actually constitute a majority. A small percentage of one group need not constitute a small percentage of another group that you know nothing about.

Remember: What you *don't* know can *help* you, if you understand what it is that you can't possibly know. A keen grasp of unknowables can go a long way. Of course, arguing from a percentage in one case to a percentage in an unrelated case qualifies as a bait and switch. Call it what you want, as long as you know it's a no-no and why.

Step 3: Work the Choices. So, inappropriately applying a statistical percentage is the flaw here, a common mistake. But we're not home free yet. Even when you know the problem, choosing the correct choice is no picnic. It takes some additional translation to see that **B** points out that the percentage cited in the evidence does not establish the percentage implied in the conclusion. **B** is correct.

A: *Six* companies may be too small, but *600*? One hundred more than the Fortune 500? The author is simply not obligated to provide a more robust sample.

C: Corporate boardrooms across the board (so to speak) are irrelevant to an argument concerning the composition of the 600 largest corporations in the land. That is to say, with regard to the accusation in **C**, the author Does No Such Thing. He never insists that anything concerning the 600 biggies applies throughout all of corporate land.

D: Now that's the pot calling the kettle black! Smaller corporations are irrelevant to the argument, so what's *irrelevant to them* is like, what, irrelevant *squared*? (Which we think equals something like a billion, give or take. Good thing there's no actual math on the LSAT . . .)

E: Keep your focus. The argument is about nothing more than the composition of certain corporate boards with regard to service professionals. The *effect* of having service professionals on corporate boards is irrelevant to the argument. Perhaps your quick kill radar went bananas at the phrase "socially responsible"— if so, bravo. If not, think about what you need to do to make sure you recognize this same kind of wrong choice in the future.

Okay, it's time to move on to our fourth question type, Paradox.

4. Paradox (Critique)

In one of the earliest episodes of *The Simpsons*, Bart, after switching test booklets with the brainy Martin, is mistakenly placed into a school for geniuses. When the teacher asks for examples of paradoxes, one student replies "without law and order, man has no freedom"; another intones "if you want peace, you must prepare for war." Bart's offering? "Well . . . you're damned if you do, and you're damned if you don't."

Alas, none of the examples quite fit the test makers' conception, since LSAT Paradox questions don't in fact contain *genuine* paradoxes but rather "seeming" paradoxes and "apparent" discrepancies. In the final analysis, situations that appear at first glance to be surprising or unusual, or to contain discrepancies or contradictions, are not in fact paradoxical at all but merely require a correct choice to resolve them. Identifying the proper resolution is your task.

In a sense, then, Paradox questions are offshoots of Strengthen the Argument questions because in both cases you're looking for the choice that solidifies the connection between the facts in the passage. This question type falls into the Critique category because the author's claim of mysterious goings-on turns out to be invalid. The supposedly contradictory elements of the passage peacefully coexist after all.

Because this question type makes up roughly only 5 percent of the Logical Reasoning section, and because it's so similar in nature to Strengthen the Argument, let's, without further ado, get right to the Paradox Battleplan. Check that out, and then see what you can make of "The Case of the Mysterious Symptoms."

Paradox Battleplan

Step 1: Grill the Interrogator. The word *paradox* or the phrase "apparent discrepancy" is a sure tip-off. When you see these, or are asked to find the choice that "resolves" or "explains" some situation, prepare to first encounter and then help solve a mystery.

Step 2: Attack the Passage. Identify the "paradox" or "discrepancy"; it's hard to recognize a resolution if you don't understand the mystery at hand. Be on the lookout for assumptions, bait and switches, loose ends, and overlooked alternatives, any of which may lead you to the resolution.

Step 3: Work the Choices. As in Strengthen questions, define the objective of the correct choice in simple language, and test each choice rigorously against that objective. Ask yourself, "If this choice is true, does everything now make sense?" Ask, "So what?" to help you delete Irrelevant choices that have no bearing on the paradox. Beware of Unnecessary Clarification choices that explain aspects of the situation that require no explanation and Opposite choices that actually deepen the mystery.

Practice: Paradox

THE CASE OF THE MYSTERIOUS SYMPTOMS
(PrepTest 29, Section 1, Q. 10)

The symptoms of hepatitis A appear no earlier than 60 days after a person has been infected. In a test of a hepatitis A vaccine, 50 people received the vaccine and 50 people received a harmless placebo. Although some people from each group eventually exhibited symptoms of hepatitis A, the vaccine as used in the test is completely effective in preventing infection with the hepatitis A virus.

Which one of the following, if true, most helps resolve the apparent discrepancy in the information above?

(A) The placebo did not produce any side effects that resembled any of the symptoms of hepatitis A.

(B) More members of the group that had received the placebo recognized their symptoms as symptoms of hepatitis A than did members of the group that had received the vaccine.

(C) The people who received the placebo were in better overall physical condition than were the people who received the vaccine.

(D) The vaccinated people who exhibited symptoms of hepatitis A were infected with the hepatitis A virus before being vaccinated.

(E) Of the people who developed symptoms of hepatitis A, those who received the vaccine recovered more quickly, on average, than those who did not.

Guided Explanation: Paradox

THE CASE OF THE MYSTERIOUS SYMPTOMS

Step 1: Grill the Interrogator. "Resolve the apparent discrepancy" tells us that something in the passage might seem paradoxical but really is not. Gear yourself for scoping out and debunking this pseudo mystery.

Step 2: Attack the Passage. The first step in a Paradox question is to define the mystery. It's certainly understandable that some of the placebo folks ended up with the disease; after all, the whole point of a placebo is that it does nada even though the people taking it think it's real. But why did some of the people who received the actual vaccine exhibit hepatitis symptoms if the vaccine is "completely effective in preventing infection"? Well, you may have reasoned that the solution must have something to do with the "60 days" thing that the author mentioned right up front. In fact, there's nothing else here that can solve our little mystery, so that must be it.

TAKE AWAY

The Essential Concept loose ends often plays a role in Critique questions because problems (flaws, assumptions, weaknesses, seeming discrepancies, etc.) emerge when things are mentioned up front and are then ignored later on, or when new things unrelated to the first part of an argument suddenly appear in the conclusion. Hone your ability to spot these logical vagrants.

Step 3: Work the Choices. If the infected people got the disease before taking part in the study, and then the symptoms showed up after the vaccination (notice the very vague "eventually" employed by the author), then it's no real surprise that people who got the vaccine also began to show symptoms since the symptoms never appear earlier than 60 days anyway. If they got the disease before the vaccination—choice **D**—everything makes perfect sense.

TAKE AWAY

Remember, LSAT "paradoxes" are paradoxical in name only. There will always be a viable resolution, so keep that in mind from the get-go.

A: Placebo side effects (or lack thereof) tell us nothing about why the real-deal vaccine apparently failed in some instances when its effectiveness has supposedly been guaranteed.

B: Group member awareness is irrelevant to the mystery at hand, as is any comparison of same between the members of the two groups. This clarification is entirely unnecessary.

C and E: Again, so what? So some people were in better shape than others, and some recovered faster. Who cares! The fact remains that some people who shouldn't have gotten the disease did. *That's* the mystery. And nothing in any choice but **D** addresses it.

>
> Remember to define the objective that the correct choice must satisfy and stick to it as you evaluate each answer choice. The choices will no doubt present interesting, sometimes even confusing information. If you focus on the objective at hand, you should be able to chop solution imposters with confidence. And keep it as simple as possible: Here, the correct choice must show how some people exhibited symptoms of a disease after taking a drug said to be *completely effective* in preventing that disease. Side effects, awareness of symptoms among the infected, the shape of the test subjects, and recovery time have no bearing on this question.

That finishes our preliminary discussion of Critique questions. You'll have more chances to practice with these in the practice set at the end of this chapter and the full-length test at the end of the book. For now, let's move on to our next category, Deduction, and the fifth question type, Inference.

5. Inference (Deduction)

As you've seen, the passages in Critique questions are always *trying* to get somewhere, no matter how successful the result. The fifth major Logical Reasoning question type—Inference—is another animal altogether. If in the first four question types you mainly played the role of critic, then in these you get to play detective. Many Inference passages have no overriding "point" per se, and for this reason they often have a different feel to them. An Inference passage may leave you with the sense that you've been left hanging. Unlike the previously discussed question types, it is *not* necessary to focus primarily on the stated conclusion and how the author got there; in some cases there *is no* conclusion to speak of. In fact, Inference passages consist of statements from which *you* are to derive reasonable deductions or conclusions.

Inference is the only question in the Deduction category because it is the only Logical Reasoning question type that requires you to connect statements in such a way. It also comes in a few different varieties, and we'll show you how to handle each. Plenty to cover, so let's get to it.

>
> Inference is important not only because there are many of these questions in the two Logical Reasoning sections but also because one type of Inference question involves formal logic, a perennial bane of LSATers' collective existence and a major component of Logic Games.

Clapton is God.
—*Anonymous, England, 1968*

God is dead.
—*Friedrich Nietzsche, Germany, 1882*

Whereas in Strengthen/Weaken questions you must accept the choices as given, in Inference questions you must accept the passages' *premises* as true and focus on what can be deduced from them. Well, if indeed Clapton is God (a slogan scrawled on English walls intended as praise for Eric Clapton's guitar playing), and indeed God is dead, it follows that Clapton is dead. It may not be what the ancient Greeks, the inventors of logic, had in mind, but it does qualify as an example of the age-old deductive syllogism:

X is Y.
Y is Z.
Therefore, X is Z.

Of course, you won't see subject matter like this on the LSAT, which tends to be a fairly RC (Religiously Correct) affair, and actual people rarely appear on the test outside of the Reading Comp section. But if we accept the statements as true and at face value, a logical deduction follows from them, and that's the kind of thing that's tested in Inference questions. Simple, right? Not necessarily. The test makers often disguise the logic under a thicket of complex terminology, making it difficult to spot the proper inference.

Moreover, there are two main types of Inference questions, each requiring its own approach. First we'll look at Standard Inference questions, and then move on to everyone's favorite (not!), Formal Logic Inference questions.

Tackling the Standard Inference Argument

We call these "standard" to differentiate them from questions involving formal logic. They ask you to recognize which statement among the choices is best supported by the information in the passage. Here are a few tips to guide your work.

Shift Gears. The four most popular Logical Reasoning question types are Assumption, Strengthen/Weaken, Flaw, and Inference. These types make up close to 65 percent of the Logical Reasoning sections, which means you'll be seeing a lot of each. The first three we grouped in the Critique category and taught you how to dissect and evaluate their arguments. But it bears repeating that Inference is another story entirely. In these, you're not looking for a missing piece, or a flaw, or ways to make the conclusion stronger or weaker—you're looking for something additional that's suggested by the statements in the passage. You must shift gears from evaluating the argument to seeing where the pieces of it lead.

Focus on Relevant Essential Concepts. For the reasons stated earlier, you shouldn't expect Inference passages to hinge on bait and switches, loose ends, or alternatives. These are things that generally come into play in Critique situations. However, you may see statements containing necessary and/or sufficient conditions or elements of cause and effect that yield valid inferences. For example:

If X is necessary for Y, and Y is necessary for Z, then it's inferable that X is necessary for Z.

If X is sufficient for Y, and Y is sufficient for Z, then it's inferable that X is sufficient for Z.

If X causes Y, and Y causes Z, then it's inferable that X causes Z.

As for the other Essential Concept, recognizing unknowables is a valuable tool for eliminating wrong choices, as we'll discuss below.

Tackling Standard Inference Answer Choices

Negate and Destroy. The negate and destroy test that's used to confirm or eliminate choices in Assumption questions generally works for Standard Inference questions as well. If negating the choice you believe to be correct causes a serious problem for the argument, chances are that choice is correct. Conversely, if nothing happens to the argument when you negate a choice, then that choice is probably wrong. This is useful because sometimes it is hard to tell that something must be true but easier to tell that its opposite conflicts with the passage.

Spot the Traps. Standard Inference questions contain very formulaic wrong choices:

- **Twister** choices inappropriately distort the information contained in the passage. These may be tricky because they employ the language of the passage but twist its ideas in a way that results in an unsupportable statement.

- **Unknowable** choices focus on issues not discussed in the passage and propose things we simply cannot speculate on based on the passage's information. Unknowables is also an Essential Concept.

- **Overreach** choices take the passage's information too far—for example, something that is *probably* the case is taken as a *definite*. Like Twister choices, these play off the language of the passage but fail because they go to extremes.

- **Opposite** choices directly contradict the passage. When searching for a choice that's strongly supported by the passage, don't be surprised to come across choices that are highly improbable or out-and-out false.

You'll see examples of these traps as we go along. Keep in mind that there may be some overlap among these categories. In the end, it doesn't matter what you *call* a wrong choice, as long as you know it's wrong.

Okay, let's see how these Inference tips play out in the context of an actual problem. First study the Battleplan, and then work your deductive magic in "Endangered Species."

Standard Inference Battleplan

Step 1: Grill the Interrogator. The question stems for these usually ask you to find the choice that is "most strongly supported" by the information in the passage. Not only does that tell you you're dealing with an Inference question, but it also tells you that you probably don't need to manipulate complex formal logic statements or deal with the kind of logical elements featured in Critique questions.

Step 2: Attack the Passage. Don't be surprised if there is no major conclusion—or, in cases where there *is* a conclusion, if the correct choice has little or nothing to do with it. If a connection strikes you, certainly note it, but don't expect the inference to necessarily jump out at you—often, the bulk of work in these involves analyzing the choices. The correct inference can be derived from any part of the passage, so look to combine related statements no matter where they appear.

Step 3: Work the Choices. The correct choice must be relevant, and it must be appropriately limited in scope to fall within the passage's parameters. If not, chances are it's an Overreach. Also beware of the other common Inference traps: Unknowable, Twister, and Opposite. Rigorously test your selection against the passage to confirm that it is indeed supported by it, and use negate and destroy to further confirm it if necessary.

Practice: Standard Inference

ENDANGERED SPECIES
(PrepTest 30, Section 2, Q. 16)

Zoos have served both as educational resources and as entertainment. Unfortunately, removing animals from their natural habitats to stock the earliest zoos reduced certain species' populations, endangering their survival. Today most new zoo animals are obtained from captive breeding programs, and many zoos now maintain breeding stocks for continued propagation of various species. This makes possible efforts to reestablish endangered species in the wild.

Which one of the following statements is most strongly supported by the information above?

(A) Zoos have played an essential role in educating the public about endangered species.

(B) Some specimens of endangered species are born and bred in zoos.

(C) No zoos exploit wild animals or endanger the survival of species.

(D) Nearly all of the animals in zoos today were born in captivity.

(E) The main purpose of zoos has shifted from entertainment to education.

THE
NEW
LSAT

Guided Explanation: Standard Inference

ENDANGERED SPECIES

Step 1: Grill the Interrogator. "Most strongly supported" is classic Standard Inference wording, so when you see a stem like this, recognize that you're not expected to spot assumptions, weaknesses, flaws, and so on, but rather must put two and two together.

Step 2: Attack the Passage. This passage has a typical Standard Inference feel to it: a bunch of statements, which are related but not seeming to lead toward any kind of grand conclusion. Also, no major deduction jumps off the page, so the battle is best fought among the choices.

Step 3: Work the Choices. **A** is a Twister choice, combining two elements of the passage—education and endangered species—in a way not suggested by the author. (In Reading Comp, we call this a "Mish-Mash.") Sure, both things are in there, but whether zoos actually teach about endangered species is unknowable.

B is inferable. Since most new zoo animals come from zoo breeding stocks intended to propagate various species, and this effort "makes possible efforts to reestablish endangered species in the wild," then it must be true that some of the animals born and bred in zoos as part of their maintenance effort belong to endangered species. If that *weren't* the case, why would the author say that the zoo breeding programs are helping the replenishment of endangered species in the wild? It makes sense too: If the zoos propagate these species for their own needs, then fewer animals need to be removed from their natural habitats. **B** is correct.

C overreaches: "Many" zoos have breeding programs, and "most" zoo animals are obtained from these programs. But that's not enough to say that "no zoos" exploit animals or endanger species.

TAKE AWAY

> Be alert to the degree of certainty surrounding the statements in Inference passages. Words like *most, many, some, usually,* and *probably* denote more leeway than their more extreme brethren such as *no, none, all, never,* and *always*. Here, the qualified language of the passage renders the unqualified assertion in choice **C** unacceptable.

D overreaches as well, but not as badly as **C** because it is qualified somewhat by "nearly." Still, we have no way of determining the makeup of current zoos. All we know is that while zoos used to get their animals from the wild, today most *new* zoo animals are bred in captivity. How many of these newly bred animals there are compared to ones taken from the wild is unknowable.

E: The test makers couldn't resist one more Twister choice distorting the education/entertainment thing. We're told that zoos have served both educational and entertainment functions. Fine. Which have they done more? DON'T KNOW. Which costs more money? DON'T KNOW. Which do they do more of now? DON'T KNOW. Is either one the "main purpose" of zoos? If so, has this main purpose *shifted* over time? DON'T KNOW, DON'T KNOW.

Now let's take a look at the second kind of Inference challenge: questions involving formal logic.

Tackling the Formal Logic Inference Argument and Answer Choices

It's very likely that at least some Logical Reasoning questions will require you to recognize the proper implications of *if, only, all, some, none, unless,* and others of their ilk. It's dead certain you'll need to know how to interpret these words in Logic Games. So it's all good that we take the time to run through some key formal logic concepts. Let's begin with the most widely tested formal logic construction, the "if/then" statement.

If you've eaten your pudding, then you've eaten your meat.

Assuming the truth of the statement above, what can you deduce from the following? Take the statements below one at a time and see if each can combine with the statement above to lead to a new deduction.

If you also know . . .	Then you can deduce . . .
1. Naomi has eaten her pudding.	
2. Naomi has not eaten her pudding.	
3. Naomi has eaten her meat.	
4. Naomi has not eaten her meat.	

Reverse and Negate. Here's how to form valid deductions from an "if/then" statement: Reverse and negate the "if" and the "then" clauses to come up with a logical equivalent. Let's see how this works. The "then" part is "you've eaten your meat." To reverse the full statement, put that first, and to negate it, turn it into its opposite: "You *haven't* eaten your meat . . ." Now finish this new statement with the opposite of the original "if" clause—you *haven't* eaten your pudding. Reversing and negating the clauses of the if/then statement thus yields another statement that is logically equivalent to the original:

If you haven't eaten your meat, you haven't eaten your pudding.

Given the original statement and the logical equivalent we formed by reversing and negating, let's look at what can be deduced from the statements above:

1. Naomi has eaten her pudding.

Deduction: *Naomi has eaten her meat.*

This one isn't too tough. The original rule tells us anyone who has eaten his or her pudding has eaten his or her meat. So Naomi the pudding eater must also have eaten her meat.

2. Naomi has not eaten her pudding.

Deduction: *Nothing!*

Here's where it gets a little trickier. Eating pudding means you ate your meat, but *not* eating pudding triggers nothing. Imagine that you knew that everyone who ate blue popsicles got blue tongues. What happens when someone *doesn't* eat blue popsicles? We don't know. Maybe their tongues are normal color (that is, not blue), but maybe their tongues are blue for another reason. This brings us into unknowable territory.

> ## TAKE AWAY
>
> A rule that tells us the consequences of X happening doesn't tell us anything about the consequences of X *not* happening.

3. Naomi has eaten her meat.

Deduction: *Nothing!*

Eating her meat is required for eating her pudding, but it isn't sufficient to prove that she has. See the necessary/sufficient Essential Concept at play here? Eating meat makes Naomi *eligible* to eat pudding, but we don't know if she has.

4. Naomi has not eaten her meat.

Deduction: *She hasn't eaten her pudding.*

Here we go! This is the deduction we formed from reversing and negating the original statement. Anyone who has eaten pudding has eaten meat, so if Naomi *hasn't* eaten her meat, she can't have eaten her pudding. How could she have had any pudding if she hasn't eaten her meat?

Do the Math. Translation: Figure it out. Of course, we don't mean to *actually* do any math, since there is no math on the LSAT. But we can state the essence of reverse and negate in general algebraic terms:

> If X, then Y
> means the same thing as
> If NOT Y, then NOT X.

Try it out:

If Sam goes to the beach, then Ashley will go to the beach.

If Ashley goes, Sam may or may not go; we can't tell. But one thing's for sure: If NO Ashley, then NO Sam. This, like the pudding example, is similar to a Logic Games rule. Logical Reasoning formal logic tends to be wordier, but it works in exactly the same way.

Practice: Salonian Economy

Reverse and Negate. Now try using the reverse and negate technique to extract a valid deduction from this mess:

Whenever the economy of Salonia retreats into recession, the unemployment level rises in direct proportion to the decrease in government subsidies to high-tech industries.

Does this passage make immediate sense? Not particularly. Does it need to? Not particularly. It's merely a disguised if/then statement (note that "whenever" functions the same as "if") that must follow the law of reverse and negate:

If unemployment is NOT rising in direct proportion to decreases in high-tech subsidies, then the economy of Salonia has NOT retreated into recession.

Many test takers would get bogged down in the wordiness without realizing that understanding the if/then formal logic structure and applying reverse and negate *are all that's required.*

Practice: Sebastian's Caffeine

Now see what you can make of the following passage involving another formal logic concept. What can you deduce for sure?

Only by imbibing caffeine in the morning will Sebastian be fully awake by 8:00 A.M. But Sebastian will not imbibe caffeine unless his wife is not present.

The word "only" denotes "necessity": Caffeine in the morning is *necessary* for Sebastian to be fully awake by 8:00. No morning caffeine, no full wakefulness by 8 A.M. for Sebastian. Does morning caffeine *guarantee* full wakefulness by 8:00 A.M.? No—it's not sufficient, merely required. Maybe Sebastian hasn't slept all night, or maybe he's ill, or some other reason has conspired to keep him tired with or without morning caffeine. Moreover, he *can* be fully awake any time *after* 8:00 A.M., as nothing forbids that. Notice the very precise and strict boundaries created by formal logic statements. Now let's add the "unless" part to the mix: No caffeine for Sebastian *unless* his wife's not present means that his wife's absence is *required* for Sebastian to imbibe caffeine. So if his wife is with him up until 8:00 A.M., we know for a fact that Sebastian will not be fully awake by then.

Practice: Authors and Majors

Here's another passage with a formal logic concept. What issue is left up in the air?

Many authors who write about cultural studies majored in communications in college. However, no one who majored in communications or philosophy in college has been published by Zenith Press. Some of the authors published by Zenith Press have written about both cultural studies and the civil rights movement, and Zenith Press has published books on both of these subjects.

Work in Groups. Think of this as a "groups" passage, testing your ability to understand who's in which group and which groups can and cannot overlap. Notice the plethora of groups represented here: authors, cultural studies authors, civil rights authors, Zenith Press authors, communications majors, non–communications majors, philosophy majors, and non–philosophy majors. There's a decent amount of wiggle room when it comes to figuring out who can, cannot, and must be associated with each group, and the ambiguities inherent in the passage create more than enough material for wrong choices. For example, just because some Zenith Press authors have written on both cultural studies and the civil rights movement doesn't mean they haven't written on *other* topics—or, for that matter, that they have. Even trickier, it doesn't necessarily mean that these are the authors of the books Zenith has published on these topics; perhaps these authors wrote magazine articles on these subjects but published books on different topics for Zenith.

TAKE AWAY

Read very carefully! Remember the Unknowables drill from the Essential Concepts section? The ability to recognize Unknowables definitely comes into play here.

So what *can* be deduced for sure, then? On the test, you wouldn't try to make a prediction—the passage is far too complicated. Instead, you'd look at the choices and consider them one by one. But for practice, let's try to make a deduction without the choices to help us. The trick is to focus on the most *concrete* facts, in this case represented by the phrase "no one" and the statement in the final clause of the passage. Working backward, we know that Zenith definitely published books on both cultural studies and the civil rights movement. We also know for a fact that no Zenith author was a communications or philosophy major in college. So it must be true that some cultural studies writers, and some civil rights movement writers, were neither communications nor philosophy majors in college. Some form of that idea would appear as the right answer. The rest is all a matter of conjecture—and, not surprisingly, perfect fodder for many would-be wrong choices.

Okay, now check out the Battleplan and then pit your skills against "Concert Rules."

Formal Logic Inference Battleplan

Step 1: Grill the Interrogator. Whereas Standard Inference questions usually contain some form of the phrase "most strongly supported," questions containing formal logic almost always ask for the choice that "*must* be true" or is "most properly" or "most logically inferred." When you see wording like this in a question stem, there's a good chance that the passage contains formal logic. Words in the passage like *if, only, many, all, some, none, never,* and *always* confirm it.

Step 2: Attack the Passage. Take note of statements containing words such as *if, only, unless, all, some,* and *none* and their equivalents, such as *whenever, each, every, never, most,* and *many.* Translate such statements into simpler language when necessary, and treat these statements as hard-and-fast rules. Reverse and negate if/then statements (or any statements that can be translated into if/then statements) to form valid deductions. Look to combine statements, especially those containing repeated words or phrases. When attempting to form deductions, focus on the most concrete information first. Take note when different groups appear in the passage, and do your best to keep track of who belongs where.

Step 3: Work the Choices. If you've successfully combined statements to form a new deduction, scan for it among the choices. If you can't form a deduction, evaluate the choices one by one, searching for the statement that absolutely must be true.

Practice: Formal Logic Inference

CONCERT RULES

(PrepTest 30, Section 2, Q. 18)

If there are any inspired musical performances in the concert, the audience will be treated to a good show. But there will not be a good show unless there are sophisticated listeners in the audience, and to be a sophisticated listener one must understand one's musical roots.

If all of the statements above are true, which one of the following must also be true?

(A) If there are no sophisticated listeners in the audience, then there will be no inspired musical performances in the concert.

(B) No people who understand their musical roots will be in the audience if the audience will not be treated to a good show.

(C) If there will be people in the audience who understand their musical roots, then at least one musical performance in the concert will be inspired.

(D) The audience will be treated to a good show unless there are people in the audience who do not understand their musical roots.

(E) If there are sophisticated listeners in the audience, then there will be inspired musical performances in the concert.

Guided Explanation: Formal Logic Inference

CONCERT RULES

Step 1: Grill the Interrogator. The stem here strongly suggests that formal logic is in play. The test makers don't ask you for something that is "most strongly supported" if in fact the correct choice must absolutely be true. When that's the case, you'll usually see a stem like this one, and you should prepare for the strong possibility of encountering formal logic elements in the passage.

Step 2: Attack the Passage. "Good show" is more than just a British way of saying "Way to go!"—it's a term contained in each of the first two sentences, which is a clue that the inference we seek will hinge on this term. Translating the "not . . . unless" construction of the second sentence yields the following: "If there are no sophisticated listeners, there will not be a good show." By using reverse and negate, the first sentence yields "If there is not a good show, then there will not be inspired performances." Combining the two results in correct choice **A.**

Step 3: Work the Choices. The correct answer is derived by combining statements as described above.

>
>
> **TAKE AWAY**
>
> Notice the difference in your approach to a Formal Logic Inference question and a Standard Inference question. On Standard questions, you'll often need to focus on the choices and work backward from them to the information in the passage, eliminating common wrong answer choices as you go. This doesn't work as well for Formal Logic questions because the answer choices usually contain the same terms combined in different ways. If you don't know what to look for, the choices are all likely to look the same. So when formal logic is included in the passage, your best bet is to be proactive. Try to translate and manipulate the statements to form at least one solid deduction before hitting the choices.

As for why the others are wrong:

B and **C:** Understanding musical roots is *necessary* for sophistication, which in turn is *necessary* for there to be a good show. But these are not sufficient conditions—understanding roots does not *guarantee* sophistication, nor do sophisticated listeners *guarantee* a good show. So it's possible for people who understand their musical roots to be present at a crappy show with no inspired performances, contrary to the assertions in **B** and **C**.

D makes it sound as if a good show is inevitable as long as all the audience members understand their musical roots. As we've seen, the presence of people who understand their musical roots makes a good show *possible* but does not by itself guarantee a good show.

> **TAKE AWAY**
>
> One way to wrap your mind around necessary and sufficient conditions is to think in terms of "triggers." A sufficient condition *definitely* triggers a result, while a necessary condition makes a result *possible* but not inevitable.

E: The presence of sophisticated listeners means only one thing for sure: the presence of at least some people who understand their musical roots. Again, as we've seen, neither of these things guarantees a good show or inspired performances, although they make them possible. You'd need to switch this choice around to make it work: If there are inspired performances, there must be sophisticated listeners.

That does it for our sole Deduction question type for now. Let's move on to our next category, Matching, and our sixth question type, Disagreement.

6. Disagreement (Matching)

The most important thing about questions in the Matching category, and the reason we call it "Matching" in the first place, is that the questions in this group often are best approached by matching each element of the choices to the elements of the passage. You'll find that the wrong answer types you've studied so far—Irrelevant, Overreach, Opposite, etc.—are less important for the questions in this category. Although some wrong choices may certainly be characterized as such, you'll learn to work the choices in these questions in a more directed manner based on the matching mechanism noted above; you'll see what we mean in the context of each question type. You should also expect to make a few "quick kills" in Matching questions—that is, to knock off one or more choices very fast based on a single word or short phrase contained in the choice.

Debate is the name of the game in Disagreement questions. Consider the following:

First Man: Argument is an intellectual process. Contradiction is just the automatic gainsaying of any statement the other person makes.

Second Man: No it isn't.

This exchange from the Monty Python sketch "Argument Clinic" parodies the contentious and litigious nature of our society by portraying a place where people pay a fee solely for the opportunity to argue with someone. Naturally, disagreement plays a large part in legal proceedings, and it therefore stands to reason that law schools would be interested in your ability to recognize the point at issue when people don't see eye to eye. We include this question type in the Matching category because your task is to match each answer choice to the dialogue in the passage, looking for the choice containing the issue that encapsulates the diverging viewpoint. Perhaps the chorus from Dave Mason's 1970's hit "We Just Disagree" best captures the spirit of this question type: "There ain't no good guys, there ain't no bad guys. There's only you and me and we just disagree." Now consider the following exchange:

Tess: As digital video cell phones become more sophisticated and affordable, they will revolutionize the field of journalism because they will enable ordinary bystanders to feed breaking stories in real time to news organizations.

Moe: But news organizations have a vested interest in maintaining the privileged status of their field reporters, so it's more likely that bystander involvement will be forbidden and the new technology will be used by reporters to submit their footage faster than is currently possible.

Tackling the Disagreement Argument

Identify the Crux. In Matching questions, much of the work takes place in evaluating the answer choices by matching them to the debate in the passage. But there is one important step you should perform as you familiarize yourself with the disagreement, and that is to see whether you can scope out the point that seems to be at the heart of the matter. You need not put it into words; the choices do that for you. But you should try to get a sense of the overlapping and debatable issue—the sticking point, so to speak—so you'll recognize that issue when it appears in the choices.

Tackling Disagreement Answer Choices

Scan if Possible. If you have a firm grasp of the debate and have successfully identified the crux of the matter, the right answer might jump out at you, so a quick scan may be in order. This may help you to single out the right answer faster, but you'll still need to confirm your choice by matching it to the specifics of the dialogue.

Embrace the Unknowable. Your job is to recognize where the disagreement lies; one major key is to understand where it *doesn't*. Our Essential Concept unknow-ables thus plays a large role here, for we have to *know* each speaker's opinion on an issue before we conclude that they disagree on that matter. Many wrong an-swer choices will center around issues that one or both speakers don't address. Consider the following choice:

Cell phones will cause a revolution in journalism.

This can't be the answer since we don't know Moe's opinion on this issue. He does believe cell phones will speed things along, but whether he thinks this will spur a journalistic *revolution* is anyone's guess. What about:

Bystander involvement in documenting breaking news stories will jeopardize the status of current field reporters.

Moe says yes; Tess says . . . well, we don't know what Tess says. The effect on field reporters is not part of her argument. Her opinion on this is therefore an unknowable, so a choice focusing on this issue can't be correct either.

Eliminate Points of Agreement. The disagreement obviously can't center around a point of *agreement,* so any choice containing an issue that the two speakers agree on should be quickly chopped. For example, in the Tess/Moe standoff, an answer choice reading "video cell phones will affect journalism" would have to be rejected, since both would vote yes on this count, although for different reasons.

Test for Relevance. Some choices focus on issues that simply are irrelevant to the topic under discussion, and you should make quick kills out of these. In *Tess v. Moe,* for example (may as well start getting down with legal lingo, right?), future improvements in cell phone technology is beyond the scope of both arguments and cannot be the point of disagreement we seek.

Quiz the Speakers. The process described above involves asking how each speaker would respond to the issue contained in each choice. Doing this allows us to discover choices containing Unknowables and points of agreement that we can cross off with confidence. Quizzing the speakers also helps us to confirm the right answer, because the opinions we get from the two speakers in response to the issue in the correct choice will be at odds. In the Tess/Moe debate, the point at issue concerns the question of *how* video cell phones will affect journalism. Having identified that as the crux of the argument, we may find it a simple matter to ascertain the speakers' positions on a choice like the following:

Bystanders will play a role in the improvement of journalism through cell phones.

Put the issue to our arguers: Tess says yes, Moe says no. When quizzing the speakers leads to different answers, we've found our winner.

> **TAKE AWAY**
>
> Notice that the issue of "bystanders" is part of both arguments—the right answer must revolve around an issue that both speakers care about.

Keep these points in mind as you check out the Disagreement Battleplan, and then apply what you've learned to the fascinating debate in "Oceans and Eccentricity."

Disagreement Battleplan

Step 1: Grill the Interrogator. Sometimes you'll see the phrase "point at issue" in the stem; other times, some form of the word "disagreement." You generally won't have to engage in the kinds of logical gymnastics described earlier in this chapter, so prepare instead to perform a rigorous comparison of the choices to both sides of the dialogue to locate the sticking point.

Step 2: Attack the Passage. Identify the crux of the argument—the issue that seems relevant to both speakers' statements. Note points of agreement, if any (it's likely that some wrong choices will center around those), and see if you can sniff out the source of the disagreement.

Step 3: Work the Choices. If the point at issue jumps out at you, scan for your idea. Match the choices to the argument. To test a choice, first test whether it is relevant to both speakers' comments. If it's irrelevant to either or both, or if either speaker's opinion on the matter in the choice is unknowable, cross that choice off. If the issue in a choice *is* relevant to both statements, Quiz the Speakers to analyze each one's take on that issue, searching for a point of conflict. Ask yourself, "What would speaker 1 say about this? What would speaker 2 say about this?" If different answers come back, you'll know you've found the winner.

Practice: Disagreement

OCEANS AND ECCENTRICITY

(PrepTest 30, Section 4, Q. 21)

Tina: For centuries oceans and human eccentricity have been linked in the literary and artistic imagination. Such linkage is probably due to the European Renaissance practice of using ships as asylums for the socially undesirable.

Sergio: No. Oceans have always been viewed as mysterious and unpredictable—qualities that people have invariably associated with eccentricity.

Tina's and Sergio's statements lend the most support to the claim that they disagree about which one of the following statements?

(A) Eccentric humans were considered socially undesirable during the European Renaissance.
(B) Oceans have always been viewed as mysterious and unpredictable.
(C) The linkage between oceans and eccentricity explains the European Renaissance custom of using ships as asylums.
(D) People have never attributed the same qualities to oceans and eccentrics.
(E) The linkage between oceans and eccentricity predates the European Renaissance.

Guided Explanation: Disagreement

OCEANS AND ECCENTRICITY

Step 1: Grill the Interrogator. The word *disagree* is the clear tip-off here that tells you to be on the lookout for the point at issue in the two arguments.

Step 2: Attack the Passage. Tina and Sergio go at it in this debate about the possible relation between oceans and human eccentricity. Zeroing in on the crux of the matter, you may have recognized that the combatants seem to agree that there's some kind of connection, but they disagree about what that connection is. Let's try out our Matching method by meticulously comparing each choice to the specifics of the dialogue, looking for the one that adequately captures the point at issue.

> **TAKE AWAY**
>
> You don't have to spend a lot of time on your initial run through the dialogue itself, since you're going to return to it often when you check the choices. Getting the gist of the debate is good enough.

Step 3: Work the Choices.

A: Sergio says nothing about eccentrics or social undesirables during the Renaissance, so this choice can't be correct since his opinion on these things is an Unknowable.

B captures Sergio's first point verbatim, but we don't know what Tina thinks about the issue of oceans and mysteriousness/unpredictability. Tina speaks of oceans and eccentricity, which is different, so we can't say she'd disagree with him on this point. This choice fails because of an Unknowable on Tina's end.

C focuses on the Renaissance "Ships of Fools" (as they were called back in the day), something Sergio never discusses. Moreover, this choice appears to switch cause and effect. Tina says that the custom of using asylum ships probably explains why people associate oceans with eccentricity. **C** says it happened the other way around.

> **TAKE AWAY**
>
> Notice how Essential Concepts (in this case, cause and effect) tend to sneak into unexpected places. The LSAT functions as a totality, testing your reading and reasoning skills across a broad spectrum of topics but in ways that overlap considerably, both within sections and throughout the test as a whole—which is a fancy way of saying that what you learn in one place will help you in others, if you see and embrace the underlying synergy of the test.

D: We know that Sergio's point is diametrically opposed to the assertion in **D**, so if we determine that Tina *agrees* with **D**, we'd have a winner. But Tina sees a link between oceans and eccentrics too, so we'd have to say that **D** represents a point of agreement—Tina and Sergio would agree that the statement in this choice is false.

> **TAKE AWAY**
>
> Don't lose sight of what you're looking for! Tina and Sergio both disagree with choice **D**, but we're looking for them to disagree *with each other.*

E: Having dismissed the others, **E** must be correct, but let's play Quiz the Speakers to check it anyway. Tina believes that the link between oceans and eccentricity dates back to the Renaissance, so she would disagree with the assertion that the link *predates* the Renaissance. Sergio takes the long view of things, maintaining that oceans have *always* been associated with qualities that *invariably* (also meaning "always") have been linked to eccentricity. So we can infer that Sergio agrees with **E.** One yea, one nay, so we've got our answer to this Disagreement question.

Next let's take a look at Method questions.

7. Method (Matching)

Method questions ask what the author is *doing* in the passage. For example, perhaps the author cites a relevant source to dispute the evidence for a claim. Or maybe the author agrees with a conclusion but offers alternative evidence for it. Perhaps he or she employs an analogy to counter or confirm a point or rejects a recommendation on the basis of an alternative interpretation. You'll notice the abstract nature of Method arguments; this abstraction is reflected in the answer choices, and this will be challenging for some.

We place Method questions in the Matching category because you need to meticulously compare the specific elements of each choice to the information in the passage. For instance, using the last example cited above, you'll ask yourself, "Is there *really* a recommendation here?" and will look back at the passage to find out. If not, you can cross that choice off without reading another word—*every* element must match for a choice to be correct. If there *is* a recommendation, you then have to see whether it is in fact rejected by the author, and if so whether an alternative interpretation is involved. Only when *all* elements are present and accounted for should you deem a choice worthy. The trick is to become adept at recognizing the very precise usages of the kinds of words that appear in the answer choices—not any old thing will count as a "hypothesis," for example.

> **TAKE AWAY**
>
> Don't let lofty-sounding language just wash over you. Put the choices through their paces to see if the elements they contain really exist in the passage or just in the test makers' active imaginations.

There are two kinds of Method questions: Stand-alone and Dialogue.

Stand-alone Method Questions. These contain a single passage accompanied by a question asking how the author makes her point. In this type, you generally need not worry whether the logic is *sound*; you merely need to understand what the author is *trying* to do. Common stems for Stand-alone Method questions include the following:

The author's **method** in the argument can best be described as . . .

The argument **proceeds by** . . .

The author **does** which one of the following . . .

The author **employs** which one of the following **techniques/argumentative strategies** . . .

Dialogue Method Questions. These are based around conversations like the ones you just saw in the Disagreement discussion, with one speaker responding to the argument of another. The stems for these usually look something like this:

Person X uses which one of the following **techniques** in **countering** Person Y's argument?

Person X **responds** to Person Y **by doing** which one of the following?

Which one of the following most accurately describes how Person X's **response is related to** Person Y's argument?

Tackling the Method Argument

Take a Step Back. Method questions, especially the stand-alone variety, often test your ability to generalize from a specific situation. For example, an argument in which the author states that something should be done would match the word "recommendation" if that word showed up in a choice but not the word "prediction" or "phenomenon." A series of causal factors might rightfully qualify as a "process" but not an "occurrence." An argument that features a counter to a position would nicely match the word "refutation" but not the word "propagation." Many big words may sound alike if you let them just wash over you; it's likely that you'll be tested to see whether you know the difference between them. So as you read through Method passages, keep one eye on what the author is doing *in general*, because you'll often encounter generalizations in the choices that you'll need to match to the specifics of the passage. The better you extract the gist of the passage in general terms, the better off you'll be when you get to the choices.

Go with What You Know. Since the second speaker in dialogue Method questions often attempts to point out a weakness or an error in the first person's argument, the things you dealt with in Weaken the Argument and Flaw questions, including Essential Concepts, may very well come in handy. For example, say the Aunt Selma story from earlier was presented in the form of the following exchange.

Uncle: Your Aunt Selma is acting loopy, and since drinking always makes Aunt Selma loopy, it follows that she is drunk right now.

Nephew: But surely there are other things besides intoxication that might cause Aunt Selma to act loopy, so I disagree with the basis of your claim.

TAKE AWAY

A quick flashback to Disagreement questions: What's the point at issue in the Uncle-Nephew dialogue? One choice would almost certainly refer to the issue of *whether Selma is in fact drunk.* Clearly the uncle believes she is. And the nephew thinks she's not, right? Wrong! We don't know for sure that he thinks she's sober in this instance; he's merely objecting to the process by which his uncle reaches his conclusion (i.e., objecting to "the basis" of his claim). Recognizing the uncle's confusion between what's sufficient and what's necessary to bring about Selma's loopiness, as we've discussed earlier, the nephew essentially points out that Selma need not *necessarily* be drunk based on the evidence cited by the uncle. He's therefore saying that his uncle's conclusion doesn't make logical sense; he doesn't, however, argue that his aunt is actually sober. The disagreement therefore centers on whether loopiness ensures drunkenness. The uncle evidently believes it does; the nephew says it need not.

What might a Method question based on this scenario look like? Something like this:

The nephew's response is related to the uncle's argument in which one of the following ways?

Your recognition that the nephew is in some way invoking our necessary and sufficient conditions Essential Concept gets you more than halfway there.

Tackling Method Answer Choices

Use Essential Concepts and Scan. If you notice an Essential Concept at work during your attack on the passage, scan for it among the choices. In regard to the nephew's response to his uncle's argument, an answer choice could read:

It challenges the support for his main assertion by pointing out that a factor that guarantees a behavior need not be required to produce that behavior.

Sounds like gobbledygook to the untrained ear. To you it should sound like a description of the necessary/sufficiency flaw, the very thing you'd be scanning for among the choices. This illustrates how recognizing an Essential Concept would help you solve a Method question.

Make the Match. Notice how the general wording of the choice above accords perfectly with the specifics of the dialogue: "challenges the support for his main assertion" matches "I disagree with the basis of your claim," and "a factor that guarantees a behavior need not be required to produce that behavior" is a fancy way of pointing out the necessary/sufficient error in the uncle's reasoning. And rest assured that some wrong choice in this Method question would assert that the nephew takes issue with the uncle's main point, period, when, as we've seen, he doesn't directly challenge the actual conclusion that she's drunk but rather the uncle's support for that conclusion.

So the trick is to match the choices to the situation meticulously, using your Essential Concepts and full arsenal of strategies to help you when possible. Having worked through the dialogue Method exercise above, get some practice with the Stand-alone variety on the following page. Review the Method Battleplan and then check out the wonderful world of "Species Alterations."

Method Battleplan

Step 1: Grill the Interrogator. When the stem indicates Method is your concern, adopt a generalist frame of mind that will help you to match the choices to the passage. Maintain a generalist perspective, but remember that strategies adopted for other question types may come into play.

Step 2: Attack the Passage. In Stand-alone Method questions, translate the specifics of the passage into general terms such as *prediction, recommendation,* and *analogy*—these are the kinds of terms you'll often encounter in the choices. Take special note of whether the author is arguing for or against a specific position, and whether the author offers an explanation or alternatives to an explanation or proposal. If the question is in dialogue form, look for the responder to point out alternatives to or assumptions and flaws in the other speaker's reasoning.

Step 3: Work the Choices. Match the elements in the choices to the passage or, in a dialogue situation, to the comment in question. Look for "quick kills"—choices that you can axe quickly thanks to an obvious wrong word or phrase. Remember, you only need one good reason to get rid of a choice. If you find a good reason, eliminate that choice and move on. On the other hand, the correct choice is correct in all its elements. Meticulously sign off on every aspect of the choice before making your selection.

Practice: Method

SPECIES ALTERATIONS

(PrepTest 29, Section 1, Q. 12)

It is well known that many species adapt to their environment, but it is usually assumed that only the most highly evolved species alter their environment in ways that aid their own survival. However, this characteristic is actually quite common. Certain species of plankton, for example, generate a gas that is converted in the atmosphere into particles of sulfate. These particles cause water vapor to condense, thus forming clouds. Indeed, the formation of clouds over the ocean largely depends on the presence of these particles. More cloud cover means more sunlight is reflected, and so the Earth absorbs less heat. Thus plankton cause the surface of the Earth to be cooler and this benefits the plankton.

Which one of the following accurately describes the argumentative strategy employed?

(A) A general principle is used to justify a claim made about a particular case to which that principle has been shown to apply.
(B) An explanation of how a controversial phenomenon could have come about is given in order to support the claim that this phenomenon did in fact come about.
(C) A generalization about the conditions under which a certain process can occur is advanced on the basis of an examination of certain cases in which that process did occur.
(D) A counterexample to a position being challenged is presented in order to show that this position is incorrect.
(E) A detailed example is used to illustrate the advantage of one strategy over another.

Guided Explanation: Method

SPECIES ALTERATIONS

Step 1: Grill the Interrogator. The question asks about the "argumentative strategy," which tells you that Method is the name of the game. Immediately let go of validity issues (such as those you deal with in Critique questions) and concern yourself with *how* the author goes about making his or her point.

Step 2: Attack the Passage. The passage begins with a theory (species adapt) and an assumption associated with that theory (only the most evolved species adapt to aid their survival).

TAKE AWAY

> Think in general terms in Method questions. The questions "What is this?" and "Why is it here?" should be at the forefront of your mind as you make your way through the passage.

Then the word "however" strikes like a lightning bolt, strongly suggesting that the author is going to take exception to the theory or the assumption. The latter is the case, as the author goes on to say that this "characteristic" (adapting to survive) is quite common and *not* relegated only to the most highly evolved species. The phrase "For example" tells us that an example of this assertion is upcoming, and the case of plankton is outlined to complete the story.

TAKE AWAY

> Don't obsess over details in Method questions. All you need to do is figure out why the details are there—in other words, what the author is using them for. Seventy-six out of the 116 words in this passage are devoted to describing the process by which a kind of plankton evolves. If this were an Inference question, for example, you'd certainly be interested in the specifics. But you're being asked about the author's *method;* none of the choices requires you to understand the process laboriously put forth in 65 percent of the passage. All you need to understand is that it's a process meant to corroborate the author's assertion that some non–highly evolved species adapt to survive. It bears repeating: *Understanding your task in each question type you face puts you at an **enormous** advantage.*

Step 3: Work the Choices. We've generalized enough of the passage, so we should be ready to consider the choices in search of the perfect match.

A: Knowing the difference between a principle and an example makes quick work of this one. The author's trying to justify a claim, certainly, but doesn't resort to a "general principle" to do so. A principle, as you'll see in the next question type, is a general proposition that informs how a specific situation should be viewed. That's not what we get here. The support for this argument comes in the form of a concrete example—all that specific stuff about plankton.

B: Is the author concerned with the origin of a phenomenon? We'd have to go a long way indeed to make the passage fit this description, and on top of that to argue that the support she provides is there to show that the phenomenon really did arise. The author's contention might be considered controversial by the "assumers" cited in the first sentence, but that's too far afield to serve our purposes here.

TAKE AWAY

You may have found yourself thinking, "Well, maybe there's, like, *kind* of a controversy in here somewhere . . ." Nip such meandering speculations in the bud. Hold your answer choices to the highest possible standards. As soon as you find yourself rationalizing why a choice *might* be reasonable, you're probably on the wrong track. Save your rationalizations for why you skipped the gym six weeks straight. (Here's one: "I was studying for the LSAT . . .") Correct choices on the LSAT rationalize themselves—they need no help from you.

C: Aaahh!! What does all that mean? It sounds awfully official, but hopefully you found a way to reduce it to just plain awful. The phrase "examination of certain *cases*" is one ticket to a quick kill here, as we've already labeled the majority of the passage as simply a description of one specific process. If you wished to wade into the "generalization about the conditions . . ." morass, you wouldn't have found that in the passage either, since the whole "a process did occur, therefore it *can* occur" thing has no parallel in the passage.

D, finally, provides matching elements—in normal language, to boot. Is there a "position being challenged"? Yes, the theory that only high-level species adapt to survive. Is there a "counterexample . . . presented"? Yes—the whole plankton saga (the specifics of which, we remind you, we need not bother to analyze). Is this counterexample presented to show that the position about high-level adaptations is incorrect? Sure: The word "however" tipped us off to that early on. Everything present and accounted for, so **D** contains the method we seek and is correct. For practice, let's see where the last one goes astray.

E: Is there a "detailed example"? Yeah, you could say that—so detailed we don't even want to touch it. So far so good. In fact, this choice is fine all the way up to word 8. Words 9 through 14 . . . not so good. No strategies, no *comparison* of strategic advantages, no point.

TAKE AWAY

The "benefits" to the plankton *kind of* sounds like an "advantage," though, right? See the previous Take Away, and look back at choice **D** to see what a dead-on correct Method answer choice looks like.

So will you see as many Method questions in Logical Reasoning as Assumption, Flaw, or Inference questions, for example? Probably not. But learning to generalize from the text is sure to help you significantly in Reading Comprehension as well, especially in what we refer to as "Big Picture" questions.

Okay, we'll move on to our third kind of Matching question: Principle.

8. Principle (Matching)

A principle is a general proposition that informs how specific situations that fall within its domain should be viewed. Consider the following excerpt from the Declaration of Independence:

All experience hath shewn that mankind are more disposed to suffer, while evils are sufferable than to right themselves by abolishing the forms to which they are accustomed. But when a long train of abuses and usurpations, pursuing invariably the same Object evinces a design to reduce them under absolute Despotism, it is their right, it is their duty, to throw off such Government, and to provide new Guards for their future security.

Translation: People tend to put up with sucky situations, but when a government tries to enslave its own people, the people are justified in overthrowing it.

Why did Jefferson and Co. bother to delineate this principle? Because they themselves had a bit of overthrowing on their minds, and they wanted to justify the split from England that this famous document was created to declare. The general proposition—the principle—was established, followed by the announcement of an upcoming event to be justified by the principle invoked. The appearance of Principle questions on the LSAT is certainly no mystery, since general principles form the foundation of law, which is inherently concerned with the establishment of guidelines by which to interpret behavior and events.

Principle questions generally come in two varieties: supporting and conforming.

Supporting Principle Questions. This kind of Principle question asks for a principle that would "best support" or "most help to justify" a situation described in the passage. These work very much like Strengthen the Argument questions, except that the answer choices are principles that you have to accept as *valid* instead of facts that you have to accept as *true*. The mechanics are the same, however, as your task is still to evaluate the *effect* of the choices on the scenario in question.

Conforming Principle Questions. This kind of Principle question asks you to match a situation in the passage to the principle in the choices to which it conforms, or vice versa: to match a principle in the passage to a situation among the choices that best accords with the stated principle.

Let's discuss how to handle each type.

Tackling the Supporting Principle Argument and Answer Choices

Go with What You Know. For Supporting Principle questions, use all of the strategies you learned to handle Strengthen the Argument questions. As with all Strengthen questions, the passage may hinge on an assumption, or one of the Essential Concepts, such as a bait and switch or loose end. If that's the case, the correct principle will function much like a typical strengthener, solidifying the argument by closing gaps and helping the evidence lead more smoothly to the conclusion. You should also rely on another Strengthen the

Argument technique: Define the objective of the correct answer, and then meticulously adhere to that objective while investigating the general propositions set out in each choice. No matter how you come to it, the correct choice will be the one containing a principle that makes you *more likely to believe* the argument put forth in the passage.

Spot the Traps. Since Supporting Principle questions share so much in common with Strengthen questions, the common traps from the Critique world apply. Beware of principles that are Irrelevant to the argument and Opposite choices that actually weaken the argument.

(**Note:** You may occasionally see a question that asks for the principle that most *weakens* or *damages* an argument. No problem—just adopt a Weaken the Argument mentality instead.)

Tackling the Conforming Principle Argument and Answer Choices

Avoid Distractions. Conforming Principle questions generally don't involve assumptions, inferences, flaws, or the Essential Concepts, so don't get bogged down looking for these. Home in on the principle or situation described in the passage, and then meticulously test the answer choices to find the proper match that "accords with" or "conforms to" it.

Obey the Rule. If the principle appears in the passage, treat that principle as a rule and look for the choice containing the specific situation that satisfies that rule. Expect the wrong choices to either break or be irrelevant to the rule.

Make the Match. No matter where the principle appears—in the passage or in the choices—the elements of the correct choice must perfectly match up with the elements of the passage. If anything in an answer choice seems mislabeled, or out of kilter in any way with what you see in the passage, chop it.

As always, the strategy points are distilled in the Battleplan. Review that now, and then see what you can make of "Charity Scam."

Principle Battleplan

Step 1: Grill the Interrogator. Some variation of the phrase "Which principle, if established/valid, would support the position above" is your clue that you're dealing with a Supporting Principle question. (Sometimes they'll use the word "generalization" or "proposition," but it basically means the same thing.) If the question takes this form, shift into Critique mode with your Strengthen the Argument techniques and Essential Concepts at the ready. If, however, you're asked to find the choice that most closely conforms to a principle stated in the passage, or a principle that best accords with a situation described in the passage, shift *out* of Critique mode—don't expect to see gaps in logic or much in the way of Essential Concepts.

Steps 2/3: Attack the Passage/Work the Choices. We treat these two steps together because sometimes the principle in Conforming Principle questions appears in the passage, while other times a specific situation is described in the passage and principles appear in the choices. In the first case, treat the principle as a rule and look for the choice that contains a situation that satisfies that rule. In the second case, get the gist of the specific situation in the passage, and then meticulously compare its elements with the principle in each choice, looking for the perfect match. In Supporting Principle questions, use the Essential Concepts and look for assumptions that the correct principle may shore up. In all cases, meticulously match the choices to the passage and sign off on every element of a choice before making it your selection.

Practice: Principle

CHARITY SCAM

(PrepTest 30, Section 4, Q. 23)

When investigators discovered that the director of a local charity had repeatedly overstated the number of people his charity had helped, the director accepted responsibility for the deception. However, the investigators claimed that journalists were as much to blame as the director was for inflating the charity's reputation, since they had naïvely accepted what the director told them, and simply reported as fact the numbers he gave them.

Which one of the following principles, if valid, most helps to justify the investigators' claim?

(A) Anyone who works for a charitable organization is obliged to be completely honest about the activities of that organization.

(B) Anyone who knowingly aids a liar by trying to conceal the truth from others is also a liar.

(C) Anyone who presents as factual a story that turns out to be untrue without first attempting to verify that story is no less responsible for the consequences of that story than anyone else is.

(D) Anyone who lies in order to advance his or her own career is more deserving of blame than someone who lies in order to promote a good cause.

(E) Anyone who accepts the responsibility for a wrongful act that he or she committed is less deserving of blame than someone who tries to conceal his or her own wrongdoing.

Guided Explanation: Principle

CHARITY SCAM

Step 1: Grill the Interrogator. The phrase "most helps to justify" tells us we're up against a Supporting Principle question, which means that our Strengthen the Argument strategies may come into play in helping us to match the situation in the passage to the correct supporting principle among the choices.

Steps 2/3: Attack the Passage/Work the Choices. The investigators' claim concerns the appropriate way of assigning blame among various parties responsible for the creation and perpetuation of a lie. Although the director lied and admitted it, the investigators think the journalists who reported the lie are "as much to blame." There's no major logical element to exploit here—just the opinion of the investigators. But we can still define the objective of the correct choice: Make us more likely to agree that the journalists are "as much to blame as the director."

A basically says the director shouldn't have lied in the first place. Very noble, but it does nothing for the whole "placing equal blame" thing.

B: There's no evidence that the journalists "knowingly" aided the lying director—in fact, the phrases "naïvely accepted" and "simply reported" suggests that they were not in the know. So **B** doesn't contain the match we seek.

C pans out, word-by-word, phrase-by-phrase—exactly what you should demand in a correct answer to any Matching question. The journalists *did* present as factual something that turned out to be untrue, before they tried to verify the story. According to **C**'s principle, such people are "no less responsible" for the results than anyone else. This therefore supports the investigators' central claim that the journalists are "as much to blame as the director." **C** is correct.

D: "Advance his or her own career"? Nothing about the director's or journalists' motivations is discussed in the passage, so this phrase doesn't match up with any character in the story. Moreover, "*more* deserving of blame" actually overstates the case, which concerns the placing of *equal* blame. Finally, "promote a good cause" can only be the test makers' feeble attempt to play off the notion of charity in general, but it has nothing to do with the actions of anyone in the passage. So take your pick. Any one of these reasons suffices to chop this choice.

E: We should give this one the benefit of the doubt up to the word "committed," since it does decently describe the director taking responsibility for the deception. The rest is a bit of a train wreck, however: The phrase "less deserving of blame" misses the mark (as we've seen, equal blame is the name of this game), and no party in the passage tries to conceal wrongdoing.

Stay true to the passage's essence. As discussed, "equal blame" is the central issue in the investigators' claim. The correct principle here must therefore support the idea that placing equal blame is appropriate in this case, so choices that ignore or distort the issue of blame should be quick kills. Only choice **C** addresses the equal blame issue straight on.

That does it for this Supporting Principle question. You'll have a chance to try your hand at the Conforming variety in the practice set at the end of this chapter and the practice test at the end of the book. We turn now to the last of the Matching question types, the granddaddy of Matching, as it were, Parallel Reasoning.

9. Parallel Reasoning (Matching)

Parallel Reasoning questions contain the most obvious matching element of the question types in this category, since they ask you flat-out to find an argument among the choices that mimics or parallels the logical structure of the argument in the passage. The correct choice must therefore be a perfect match of the original, with no omissions or extraneous elements. Note that you're asked to mimic the *logic,* not the *content* of the original.

Parallel Reasoning questions are among the most intimidating on the LSAT: They're long, they appear complicated, and the fact that the choices usually differ in subject matter from the passage tends to throw test takers for a loop. However, these can be cut down to size if you know what to look for and how to match the choices against the elements of the original.

Standard and Parallel Flaw. Most Logical Reasoning sections contain two Parallel Reasoning questions, which means that you'll likely face four of these overall. Moreover, the two per section usually include one Standard Parallel Reasoning question and one Parallel Flaw question. In Standard Parallel Reasoning questions, the reasoning in the original argument and the correct choice is valid, while in Parallel Flaw questions it's not. That's the only difference between these two Parallel Reasoning varieties. You'll learn an effective approach to each.

Tackling the Standard Parallel Reasoning Argument and Answer Choices

Eliminate the Flaws. If the question stem doesn't explicitly indicate that there's a flaw in the passage argument, then we're dealing with a standard Parallel Reasoning question. Since the logic of the original argument and the correct choice must both be valid, you can eliminate any choice containing faulty reasoning.

Do the Math. Some passages are amenable to symbolic representation, in which case blocking the passage out in X's and Y's may help you to reword the passage and recognize the logically equivalent argument. For example, consider the following adaptation of the Zenith Press argument introduced in the Inference section:

No one who majored in communications in college has been published by Zenith Press. Since some of the authors published by Zenith Press have written about the civil rights movement, some people who have written about the civil rights movement have not majored in communications.

Could be pretty confusing, even though you've seen a form of this argument before. But since we're concerned only about its logical *structure*, nothing stops us from breaking the argument down like so:

No X (college communication majors) are Y (authors published by Zenith Press). Since some Y (authors published by Zenith Press) are Z (people who have written about the civil rights movement), some Z (people who have written about the civil rights movement) are not X (college communication majors).

Of course, you wouldn't repeat the passage wording; we've just done that to illustrate the technique. Your algebraic representation would look like this:

No X are Y. Since some Y are Z, some Z are not X.

Make the Match. You would then match this structure to each choice, looking for the one that perfectly conforms. And don't expect the right answer to be about authors and publishers! Remember, that's the *content*; you need to mimic the *logic*. For kicks, see if you can mimic this very structure using "dogs obtained at the pound," "dogs who have received shots," and "dogs who are housebroken" as the passage elements.

Here's one possibility:

No dogs obtained at the pound (no X) have received shots (are Y). Since some dogs who have received shots (some Y) are housebroken (are Z), some housebroken dogs (some Z) were not obtained at the pound (are not X).

Note that while the logic must be identical, the sequence of statements need not be. In other words, the next argument would be parallel as well.

Some housebroken dogs were not obtained at the pound since some dogs who have received shots are housebroken and no dogs obtained at the pound have received shots.

Different order, same logic.

If you're comfortable with this approach, use it when possible. However, understand that often an algebraic treatment is not viable. In those cases, rely on the following technique.

Characterize the Conclusion and Scan. When it's not possible to break the argument down into symbols, your best bet is to characterize the conclusion of the original argument and scan the conclusions in the choices, eliminating those that don't match up. That will usually allow you to eliminate at least one, often two, and sometimes even three choices right off the bat. Then you can dig deeper among the remaining choices to spot other points of inconsistency, but the point is that you should never have to read and reread *every word of every choice*; that's what drives people crazy in Parallel Reasoning questions, and it eats up a ton of clock, to boot.

After eliminating choices containing flawed logic and choices with dissimilar conclusions, you should only have to fully analyze a few choices—that's what cuts these down to size. But what do we mean by "characterizing the conclusion"? We mean you should put the conclusion into general terms, much like we discussed in Method and Principle questions. For example, "The judge should therefore dismiss the witness's testimony" can be simply characterized as a "recommendation." It's guaranteed that at least one choice, and maybe more, will not conclude with a recommendation, so you can cross those off on that count alone. Maybe the original conclusion contains a "refutation," or "prediction," or "proposition," or whatever—figure out what it is and then scan for the same kind of conclusion among the choices. Then find the choice that backs up that conclusion with the same kind of evidence as in the original.

Tackling the Parallel Flaw Argument and Answer Choices

In this kind of Parallel Reasoning question, you're told right in the question stem to find the choice that mimics or parallels the "flawed" or "erroneous" reasoning in the original. The techniques described above for standard questions, especially characterizing the conclusion, will usually work for this type as well. However, in this case you have even more to work with: your understanding of common and classic flaws that you picked up from our earlier discussion of Essential Concepts and Flaw questions. Here's how that knowledge can pay off here.

Generalize the Flaw. If you can characterize the flaw, all you need to do is find the choice that contains the same flaw in the context of a different scenario. For example, to call on loopy Aunt Selma yet again, if the uncle's argument was found in the original passage, you'd say to yourself, "Okay, he's confusing necessary and sufficient conditions." If you spot this from the get-go, finding the choice that contains the same mistake shouldn't be too difficult, especially when usually one choice, and sometimes more, won't be flawed at all. The key is to *generalize* the flaw, whether you've seen it before or not. If you can't generalize the flaw, you can still eliminate the arguments that seem valid and then compare conclusions using the Characterize the Conclusion and Scan technique to narrow down the rest.

All of these approaches are best understood in context. Between the questions in this chapter and those on the practice test at the end of the book, you'll get practice with both kinds of Parallel Reasoning questions and each of the techniques discussed above. Of course, you should hone your approach with many real practice questions as well. Begin with the Battleplan and then test out its strategies on "First-time Authors."

Parallel Reasoning Battleplan

Step 1: Grill the Interrogator. Words like *parallel*, *most similar*, and *mimic* are your clues that you're up against Parallel Reasoning. Note whether the question stem indicates that the reasoning in the passage is flawed. If so, prepare to scope out the flaw. If not, prepare to chop any choice that does contain a flaw.

Step 2: Attack the Passage. In Parallel Flaw questions, try to determine the flaw in the passage's reasoning. Keep your eye out for flaws related to the Essential Concepts, such as confusing necessary and sufficient conditions and reversing cause and effect. Also be on the lookout for the classic flaws you learned about in our earlier discussion of Flaw questions. If the passage contains formal logic elements, consider "doing the math," rewording the statements using algebraic variables. If the passage is not ripe for symbolization, characterize the conclusion in general terms so you can search for the same kind of conclusion among the choices.

Step 3: Work the Choices. If you spotted the flaw in the original, scan for the choice that exhibits the same faulty reasoning. If you "did the math," match your algebraic symbolization to the choices to find the perfect match. If neither approach applies, compare the conclusions in the choices to that of the original, crossing off those that don't match. Don't be influenced by the *sequence* of statements in the choices. The *logic* of the correct choice must match the original, but the order need not. Narrow the choices down as far as you can, and then rigorously match every element of each remaining choice to every element of the original until the one truly parallel argument emerges.

Practice: Parallel Reasoning

FIRST-TIME AUTHORS

(PrepTest 30, Section 4, Q. 9)

REAL DEAL

Manuscripts written by first-time authors generally do not get serious attention by publishers except when these authors happen to be celebrities. My manuscript is unlikely to be taken seriously by publishers for I am a first-time author who is not a celebrity.

The structure of which one of the following arguments is most similar to the structure of the argument above?

(A) Challengers generally do not win elections unless the incumbent has become very unpopular. The incumbent in this election has become very unpopular. Therefore, the challenger may win.

(B) Fruit salad that contains bananas is ordinarily a boring dish unless it contains two or more exotic fruits. This fruit salad has bananas in it, and the only exotic fruit it has is guava. Thus, it will probably be boring.

(C) Thursday's city council meeting is likely to be poorly attended. Traditionally, council meetings are sparsely attended if zoning issues are the only ones on the agenda. The agenda for Thursday is exclusively devoted to zoning.

(D) The bulk of an estate generally goes to the spouse, if surviving, and otherwise goes to the surviving children. In this case there is no surviving spouse; hence, the bulk of the estate is likely to go to the surviving children.

(E) Normally about 40 percent of the deer population will die over the winter unless it is extremely mild. The percentage of the deer population that died over the recent winter was the normal 40 percent. I conclude that the recent winter was not unusually mild.

Guided Explanation: Parallel Reasoning

FIRST-TIME AUTHORS

Step 1: Grill the Interrogator. The phrase "structure is most similar" is a clear indication that this is a Parallel Reasoning question. Since it says nothing about erroneous or flawed logic, this is a Standard Parallel Reasoning question so you should expect the logic of the original and the correct choice to be sound.

TAKE
AWAY

> Remember, the reason it's so important to read the question stem before reading the passage is that doing so puts you in the best frame of mind to capture the point. When you see a Standard Parallel Reasoning question, for example, you do not enter Critique mode or Deduction mode, but instead adopt a Matching mentality.

Step 2: Attack the Passage. Since there's no flaw to scope out and no overriding formal logic elements present, it's best to proceed with this Standard Parallel Reasoning question by first "characterizing the conclusion" to narrow down the choices. The signal word "for" most often indicates evidence, so the phrase "I am a first-time author who is not a celebrity" is support for the conclusion that precedes it: "My manuscript is unlikely to be taken seriously by publishers."

So, how can we characterize the conclusion in general terms? Basically, it's a statement of a probable result. The right answer must therefore conclude with a statement of what probably will happen—not something that absolutely *will* happen, or definitely *won't* happen, or anything other than the exact thing we've identified.

Step 3: Work the Choices. Scanning the choices with this thought in mind, we can immediately eliminate choice **E**, which concludes not with something that will likely *happen*, but with a judgment regarding how something probably *was*.

To move forward, we now need to examine the evidence. Why is the result likely? Because of the combination of two factors. The situations in choices **A** and **C** cite only one factor leading to the probable result, so we can cross those off. That leaves **B** and **D**. **D** sets up a choice between two options, eliminates one, and settles on the other. That's not parallel to the original, which settles on a probable result from a combination of two things. Which means that's what we must find in **B**, and indeed we do: The fruit salad has bananas (condition #1) and does not have two or more exotic fruits (condition #2), so it will probably be boring. Notice how even the positive/negative dynamic of the original is matched in choice **B**: Condition 1 is positive (I am a first-time author/the fruit salad has bananas), and condition 2 is negative (I am not a celebrity/the fruit salad does not have two or more exotic fruits). A perfect match, so **B** is correct!

> Characterizing the conclusion and matching it to the choices will usually knock out one or two choices. Comparing the type of evidence that leads to that conclusion will knock out the rest.

TAKE AWAY

And that finishes up our discussion of Matching questions, so let's move on to our final Logical Reasoning category, Construction, and our next question type, Main Point.

10. Main Point (Construction)

> To construct is to put something together, and accordingly both Main Point and Role questions focus on how the authors of Logical Reasoning arguments combine their thoughts to create a desired effect.

TAKE AWAY

Construction questions could just as easily be called Dissection questions, since one way to understand how something is constructed is to take it apart. Remember dissecting pigs and frogs in eighth grade science class, with that horrible-smelling stuff called formaldehyde and that one future surgeon ripping out organs and guts, holding stuff up asking "What's this thing for?!?" That, minus the gore, is the mindset you need to adopt for the final two question types we'll consider, Main Point and Role questions.

Dissecting written text is an important skill we'll explore in more depth in Reading Comprehension when we work on deconstructing the passages to form paragraph synopses. Just as formal logic Inference questions are closely related to the formal logic challenges in the Logic Games section, Construction questions are similar to certain Reading Comprehension question types. Both test your ability to extract the main points from written passages, to understand what an author is *doing* as opposed to what she's *saying,* and to recognize how certain statements function in the context of the passage.

Don't expect to see a lot of these in Logical Reasoning, but you don't want any surprises on test day, and the skills and techniques that come into play here are, as we've said, extremely relevant to Reading Comprehension. So let's get to the point with Main Point.

Tackling the Main Point Argument

Think Globally. In these questions you're asked to locate the choice that best expresses the overriding idea of the passage. Sometimes the test makers will ask you for the main point, other times for the conclusion, and still other times simply for what the author is arguing. Specifically, they want to see whether you can differentiate between the thing the author is ultimately getting at and the other stuff in the passage that's used to back that point up. The conclusion is in there somewhere—you just have to recognize it for what it is. The conclusion answers the question "*What* does the author say?" while the evidence answers the question "*Why* does she say that?"

Let Context Be Your Guide. The meaning of a statement depends on the context in which it is found. Consider the following two arguments:

Nunez is the best sales representative in the Northwest region. He has secured the most new accounts in each of the previous three quarters and earned the highest customer satisfaction rating of all the reps in the region.

Nunez is the best sales representative in the Northwest region. Nunez will be out of town on a sales call next Friday. We should postpone the employee awards ceremony until next week.

The bolded statement is the same in each case, but its function in the two arguments differs. Think about the main point of each argument and the evidence that backs it up. (As you'll soon see, this kind of drill is very applicable to handling Role questions as well.)

Get to the Point. Okay, let's consider Nunez of the North. If the author was given only one sentence to convey her main concern, what would it be? Would the author of the first argument be satisfied if a listener walked away knowing only that Nunez has gotten the most accounts in each of the last three quarters? No; her point would be incomplete. She might say, "No, I told you *that* for a reason— to prove that Nunez is the best rep in the Northwest." That confirms the bolded sentence in the first argument as the conclusion.

If we gave the author of the second passage one chance to get to the point, we'd see that the bolded sentence is *not* that argument's main point. A listener leaving the conversation only with the knowledge "Nunez is the best" is not going to do anything about postponing the awards ceremony, which is, after all, the thing that second author is after. No doubt he'd rather have the ceremony postponed, without anyone knowing *why*, than convince a listener of Nunez's superiority and yet have nothing done about rescheduling the ceremony. Given one chance to convey his thought, he'd have to go with "postpone the ceremony." The fact that the rest of the argument answers the question "*Why* should we do this?" further confirms that the last sentence in argument two is the main point, and the rest merely evidence for it.

Use the Clues. Speaking of evidence, you should stay attuned to evidence keywords such as *because, for,* and *since.* Passage ideas highlighted by these words usually denote *support* for the main point and thus won't be reflected in the correct choice. The test makers usually don't give away the main point by prefacing it with common conclusion signal words (e.g., *consequently, so, therefore,* and *thus*), but if they do, take careful note. Also keep an eye out for contrast signal words such as *but* and *however,* which tell you some sort of shift is upcoming. Often, the new idea is part of the main point.

Take Care of Business. Now perhaps you're wondering about the assumptions underlying the second argument. Don't! That's not your job here. Does the author assume that the ceremony is currently scheduled to take place on Friday? Yeah—but so what? Does he presuppose the principle that top employees should be present at awards ceremonies? Sure—but who cares? The reasoning in Main Point questions may be valid, and it may not—*but that doesn't matter.* Don't get distracted by logical nuances—simply look to extract the major point the author is *trying* to make. There's no need to *evaluate* that point; save that for Critique questions.

Tackling Main Point Answer Choices

Hear Ye, Hear Ye . . . The correct choice to a Main Point question should make for a decent headline if the passage were a newspaper article. It may not be as exciting and snappy as a typical headline, but the idea contained in it should represent the essence of the passage well enough to be condensed into headline material. If, on the other hand, an answer choice doesn't even seem like it belongs in the same article as the passage text, chances are that choice is wrong.

Spot the Traps. Some wrong choices in this question type speak to evidence for the conclusion instead of the conclusion itself; others try to blow up a minor side issue into the central focus of the passage. The latter we've already dubbed Overreach choices, and don't be surprised to see other classic wrong choice types you've encountered to this point such as Twister, Irrelevant, and Opposite.

That should be more than enough to get you started. Review the Main Point Battleplan, and then see how you do with "Earthquake Theory."

Main Point Battleplan

Step 1: Grill the Interrogator. When asked for the main point, the conclusion, or what the author is arguing overall, prepare for picking out the dominant idea the author is trying to convey by focusing on the structure of the passage, not the merits of the reasoning.

Step 2: Attack the Passage. Consider each statement in the context of the overall argument. Imagine the author had one sentence to express the gist of the argument—what would it be? Stay alert to signal word clues that might help you to separate the passage's evidence from its conclusion, and don't be distracted by whether the argument is valid—that's not your concern.

Step 3: Work the Choices. Use the "headline test" to see if the choice you favor would serve as a proper synopsis of the argument. Spot the traps to dismiss common wrong answer types. Remember that anything that leads to a larger issue cannot be the *main* point. The correct choice should have a satisfying, "end of story" feel to it; settle for nothing less.

Practice: Main Point

EARTHQUAKE THEORY

(PrepTest 30, Section 4, Q. 2)

The current theory about earthquakes holds that they are caused by adjoining plates of rock sliding past each other; the plates are pressed together until powerful forces overcome the resistance. As plausible as this may sound, at least one thing remains mysterious on this theory. The overcoming of such resistance should create enormous amounts of heat. But so far no increases in temperature unrelated to weather have been detected following earthquakes.

Which one of the following most accurately expresses the main point of the argument?

(A) No increases in temperature have been detected following earthquakes.
(B) The current theory does not fully explain earthquake data.
(C) No one will ever be sure what the true cause of earthquakes is.
(D) Earthquakes produce enormous amounts of heat that have so far gone undetected.
(E) Contrary to the current theory, earthquakes are not caused by adjoining plates of rock sliding past one another.

Guided Explanation: Main Point

EARTHQUAKE THEORY

Step 1: Grill the Interrogator. This standard Main Point question stem leaves no doubt as to your task. There's no need to analyze the validity of the argument or match its elements to the choices. Read the passage with the intention of extracting a headline from it.

Step 2: Attack the Passage. The first sentence merely presents a theory, but it's the second sentence that provides the clue as to where this whole thing is going. The theory is plausible, the author says, but something remains mysterious. We're then told about a consequence that should result if the theory is correct, and that no evidence of that consequence has yet surfaced. No doubt the wrong choices will deal with the various specifics of the passage, but the one overriding issue seems to concern the fact that the theory is not fully complete. *Why* it's not fully complete—all that stuff about resistance and temperature increases—supports the idea that a mystery remains concerning an otherwise plausible theory.

Step 3: Work the Choices. B comes closest to capturing this idea. "Earthquake Theory Missing Crucial Data" would make for a fine headline of a newspaper blurb consisting of the passage text. **B** is correct.

TAKE AWAY

> Envisioning the choices as headlines can help you to recognize the one that adequately captures the main point and those that do not.

A is not even inferable, let alone the main point of the passage. No temperature increases "unrelated to weather" have been detected, but that's not to say there have been no observed temperature increases overall. Still, this is part of the evidence that suggests that the theory is incomplete.

C is a classic Overreach choice. The fact that the author points out a mystery related to the theory doesn't suggest that she believes the cause of earthquakes will *always* remain mysterious. All she says is that this particular theory has at least one unresolved issue.

D assumes the current theory is correct, something the author herself never does. It's possible that the theory is incorrect and the reason no earthquake-related heat increases have been detected is because there are none. Conversely . . .

E: The author never goes so far as saying that the theory is false. She merely raises one issue concerning the theory that has yet to be validated. The title "Earthquake Theory Proven Wrong" would seem at odds with the cautious, nonconclusive tone of the passage.

11. Role (Construction)

In Role questions, you're asked to determine the function of a specific passage element—that is, you're directed right to a specific part of the passage and asked to figure out what purpose that thing serves. Here are some strategies to help you handle these.

Tackling the Role Argument

Know the Common Roles. You may be asked the role of a claim, statement, assertion, proposition, or some other aspect of the argument. It may seem wide open, but there are only so many functions that a statement can serve in the context of a Logical Reasoning passage. Here are some examples of the kinds of roles you should expect to see:

- **Conclusion.** Same as Main Point: the overriding idea that the author is attempting to establish.

- **Intermediate Conclusion.** A bit trickier. An "intermediate" conclusion is something that results from information in one part of the passage but itself leads to a larger point that the author is trying to make.

- **Evidence.** As we've seen many times before, evidence is any point the author uses to back up his or her main conclusion.

- **Specific Support.** Some passage elements are used to specifically help the author achieve what he or she is trying to accomplish. While this falls under the general category of "evidence," it's a special kind of evidence that may be described in a very specific way in a correct answer choice. For example, instead of saying "it is evidence for the main conclusion," a correct choice may say "it provides a reason for questioning the claim that early dinosaurs were water dwellers." Try to get as specific as possible when evaluating the role of the statement in question.

- **Example/Illustration.** Some passage elements are included primarily to provide examples or illustrations of the point the author is trying to make.

- **Refutation.** Some passage elements are included to refute or counter some other claim or position cited in the passage.

This list is not all-inclusive; there are other roles you may come across in the course of your preparation. The more roles you're familiar with, the greater the chance that you'll breeze through any Role question they throw at you.

Go with What You Know. Role questions tie in quite nicely with Main Point questions, since both types require you to figure out what the various statements are doing in the passage. In Main Point questions, you take it upon yourself to determine the function of each element of the passage so that you can isolate the conclusion, the passage's overriding idea, from its supporting evidence. Since conclusion and evidence are two of the common functions tested in Role questions, use everything you learned in the Main Point discussion on pages 87–91 to help you determine whether the featured statement in Role questions fits in either of these main categories.

Tackling Role Answer Choices

Predict and Scan. If, as recommended above, you use what you know to determine that the statement in question functions as the argument's evidence or conclusion, make that your prediction and scan for it among the choices. If you believe the featured statement is evidence for the conclusion, scan for that. If you think it's the passage's conclusion itself, scan for that. Logical Reasoning choices are written to sound very convincing, so if you know what you're looking for, respect no choice until it matches the thought you have in mind.

Spot the Traps. In questions in which the featured statement is *not* the passage's evidence or conclusion, the test makers often include evidence and conclusion answer choices to distract you from the actual role the statement plays. It's tempting to choose one of these choices because evidence and conclusion are the most well-known features of arguments. If you become adept at dissecting passages and locating the actual evidence and conclusion, you may be able to make some quick kills when the featured statement serves a different function. Also, beware of Irrelevant and Twister choices, which pop up in Role questions too. Anything that doesn't pertain to the passage as a whole can't pertain to an individual part of the passage, and anything that distorts the passage's information can't be correct, either.

Now analyze the Battleplan, and then give "Homelessness and Profit Motive" a whirl.

Role Battleplan

Step 1: Grill the Interrogator. Role question stems are recognizable by the words "role" or "function" or the phrase "figure in the argument in which one of the following ways?" When you see any of these things, orient your thinking toward the issue of *why* the element in question is included in the passage. Take special note of the featured element before moving on to the passage.

Step 2: Attack the Passage. Focus on the relevant element in the context of the passage's other statements. Ask yourself: "Is this the conclusion?" If not, "Is this evidence for the conclusion?" If not, check to see if it serves one of the other common roles listed on page 92 or some other role you've encountered in a practice question. Get a general sense, but rest assured that the choices will give you ideas to test.

Step 3: Work the Choices. If you've determined that the element in question is the conclusion or evidence for it, scan for the choice that reflects that. If not, scan for evidence and conclusion choices anyway *so you can cross those off.* Eliminate Twister choices that distort the featured element's relation to other elements of the passage or that focus on issues irrelevant to the passage entirely. Narrow the choices down in this manner, and then rigorously test the ones that remain to find the one that best accords with the element cited in the stem.

Practice: Role

HOMELESSNESS AND PROFIT MOTIVE

(PrepTest 29, Section 4, Q. 2)

Economist: To the extent that homelessness arises from a lack of available housing, it should not be assumed that the profit motive is at fault. Private investors will, in general, provide housing if the market allows them to make a profit; it is unrealistic to expect investors to take risks with their property unless they get some benefit in return.

Which one of the following most accurately describes the role played in the economist's argument by the phrase "To the extent that homelessness arises from a lack of available housing"?

(A) It limits the application of the argument to a part of the problem.
(B) It suggests that the primary cause of homelessness is lack of available housing.
(C) It is offered as evidence crucial to the conclusion.
(D) It expresses the conclusion to be argued for.
(E) It suggests a possible solution to the problem of homelessness.

Guided Explanation: Role

HOMELESSNESS AND PROFIT MOTIVE

Step 1: Grill the Interrogator. We're asked for the role that a specific phrase plays in the argument, so note that phrase and move on to the passage.

Step 2: Attack the Passage. The phrase in question may be a bit abstract, but guess what—that's a good thing because it allows us to eliminate **C** and **D** right off the bat. Whatever this phrase represents, by itself it's an incomplete thought that therefore cannot be the author's conclusion or his evidence for it. It *prefaces* the author's conclusion, which comes later in the same sentence, but nothing that fails to express a full thought can be the conclusion by itself.

> **TAKE AWAY**
>
> Answering Logical Reasoning questions correctly is a multi-tier process. Sometimes you'll be able to paraphrase an answer beforehand and then zero right in on the correct choice. Other times you'll test the choices individually without having any preconceived notion as to what's in them. Still other times, you may have an idea of specific types of wrong answer choices to scan for and eliminate. As you've seen already, different techniques apply in different situations. Practice with each kind of approach, where applicable, so you have as many weapons as possible in your Logical Reasoning arsenal come test day.

In general, the phrase "to the extent that . . ." serves to qualify something that's upcoming, and in this case that something—the idea that profit motive is not at fault—is the conclusion, supported by the bit about investor behavior. So with **C** and **D** out, we can analyze the remaining choices to see what best describes the function of this clause.

Step 3: Work the Choices. Consider **A**. Homelessness may have many causes, but this author wishes to restrict his argument to one specific cause: lack of housing. He does not wish his argument to be applied to scenarios involving *other* causes of homelessness and thus attempts to limit his reasoning by use of the "extent to which" phrase. He therefore argues that profit motive is not to blame for homelessness caused by lack of housing. He says nothing about other possible ways in which profit motive may affect the problem. Should anyone question his defense of the profit motive in other areas concerning homelessness, he would rightfully respond that he limited his argument by use of the highlighted phrase to apply only to one specific aspect of the homelessness problem. **A** is correct.

B: The primary cause of homelessness is not an issue addressed in the passage, by the phrase in question, or by anything else the author offers.

E: If it were only that easy! No solution to homelessness is attempted in any part of the passage, least of all in the incomplete, preparatory phrase in question. This author is all about defending profit motive in the face of the homelessness problem. Solutions to homelessness would constitute a different passage.

THE REAL DEAL: PRACTICE SET

So, how are you feeling about Logical Reasoning? A bit overwhelmed, perhaps? Don't worry, that's natural. For one thing, there's lots of information to digest with 11 distinct question types, especially since we've provided you with specific Battleplans for each.

How can you be expected to memorize all that stuff?

Simple—you're not. In the context of practice, the steps we've discussed will make sense, as long as you get as much as you can out of every question you face. So it shouldn't be a matter of robotic memorization but rather of *internalization*—something we've reminded you of in Step 4 of the Essential Strategy. Get to know the strategies for each question type to the point where they not only make sense to you but occur to you unconsciously, automatically. As you internalize the Take Aways, you will also internalize the ways to approach each question. The Essential Concepts and Battleplans are your tools, but these tools will be no good to you unless you sharpen them with directed practice. The practice set that follows is your first opportunity. Then you'll have two full Logical Reasoning sections—50 more questions—to hone your approach. And then of course you should practice with real LSAT questions to reinforce your understanding and apply the finishing touches.

So, let's get to the practice set, which contains nine more Logical Reasoning questions from previous LSATs. If you're in the beginning stages of your preparation, don't obsess over timing; cut yourself a bit of slack to focus on the concepts we've thrown at you. If you're further along, and your test is approaching soon, then try to do each question in roughly a minute and a quarter, give or take. Of course, spend an ample amount of time with the explanations following the set. We'll catch up with you on the other side.

1. Despite the fact that antilock brakes are designed to make driving safer, research suggests that people who drive cars equipped with antilock brakes have more accidents than those who drive cars not equipped with antilock brakes.

    Each of the following, if true, would help resolve the apparent discrepancy described above
    EXCEPT:

    (A) Most cars equipped with antilock brakes are, on average, driven more carelessly than cars not equipped with antilock brakes.
    (B) Antilock brakes malfunction more often than regular brakes.
    (C) Antilock brakes require expensive specialized maintenance to be even as effective as unmaintained regular brakes.
    (D) Most people who drive cars equipped with antilock brakes do not know how to use those brakes properly.
    (E) Antilock brakes were designed for safety in congested urban driving, but accidents of the most serious nature take place on highways.

2. Opponents of peat harvesting in this country argue that it would alter the ecological balance of our peat-rich wetlands and that, as a direct consequence of this, much of the country's water supply would be threatened with contamination. But this cannot be true, for in Ireland, where peat has been harvested for centuries, the water supply is not contaminated. We can safely proceed with the harvesting of peat.

    Which one of the following, if true, most strengthens the argument?

    (A) Over hundreds of years, the ecological balance of all areas changes slowly but significantly, sometimes to the advantage of certain flora and fauna.
    (B) The original ecology of the peat-harvesting areas of Ireland was virtually identical to that of the undisturbed wetlands of this country.
    (C) The activities of other industries in coming years are likely to have adverse effects on the water supply of this country.
    (D) The peat resources of this country are far larger than those of some countries that successfully harvest peat.
    (E) The peat-harvesting industry of Ireland has been able to supply most of that country's fuel for generations.

(PrepTest 29, Section 1, Q. 9)

3.   Jean: Our navigational equipment sells for $1,100 and dominates the high end of the market, but more units are sold by our competitors in the $700 to $800 range. We should add a low-cost model, which would allow us to increase our overall sales while continuing to dominate the high end.

     Tracy: I disagree. Our equipment sells to consumers who associate our company with quality. Moving into the low-cost market would put our competitors in the high-cost market on an equal footing with us, which could hurt our overall sales.

Jean's and Tracy's statements most strongly suggest that they disagree over which one of the following propositions?

(A)   There is a greater potential for profits in the low-cost market than there is in the high-cost market.

(B)   The proposed cheaper model, if it were made available, would sell to customers who would otherwise be buying the company's present model.

(C)   The company could dominate the low-cost market in the same way it has dominated the high-cost market.

(D)   The company would no longer dominate the high-cost market if it began selling a low-cost model.

(E)   Decreased sales of the high-cost model would result in poor sales for the proposed low-cost model.

(PrepTest 29, Section 4, Q. 21)

4.   All too many weaklings are also cowards, and few cowards fail to be fools. Thus there must be at least one person who is both a weakling and a fool.

The flawed pattern of reasoning in the argument above is most similar to that in which one of the following?

(A)   All weasels are carnivores and no carnivores fail to be nonherbivores, so some weasels are nonherbivores.

(B)   Few moralists have the courage to act according to the principles they profess, and few saints have the ability to articulate the principles by which they live, so it follows that few people can both act like saints and speak like moralists.

(C)   Some painters are dancers, since some painters are musicians, and some musicians are dancers.

(D)   If an act is virtuous, then it is autonomous, for acts are not virtuous unless they are free, and acts are not free unless they are autonomous.

(E)   A majority of the voting population favors a total ban, but no one who favors a total ban is opposed to stiffer tariffs, so at least one voter is not opposed to stiffer tariffs.

(PrepTest 29, Section 4, Q. 10)

5. Parents should not necessarily raise their children in the ways experts recommend, even if some of those experts are themselves parents. After all, parents are the ones who directly experience which methods are successful in raising their own children.

Which one of the following most closely conforms to the principle that the passage above illustrates?

(A) Although music theory is intrinsically interesting and may be helpful to certain musicians, it does not distinguish good music from bad: that is a matter of taste and not of theory.

(B) One need not pay much attention to the advice of automotive experts when buying a car if those experts are not interested in the mundane factors that concern the average consumer.

(C) In deciding the best way to proceed, a climber familiar with a mountain might do well to ignore the advice of mountain climbing experts unfamiliar with that mountain.

(D) A typical farmer is less likely to know what types of soil are most productive than is someone with an advanced degree in agricultural science.

(E) Unlike society, one's own conscience speaks with a single voice; it is better to follow the advice of one's own conscience than the advice of society.

(PrepTest 29, Section 1, Q. 18)

6. Some planning committee members—those representing the construction industry—have significant financial interests in the committee's decisions. No one who is on the planning committee lives in the suburbs, although many of them work there.

If the statements above are true, which one of the following must also be true?

(A) No persons with significant financial interests in the planning committee's decisions are not in the construction industry.

(B) No person who has a significant financial interest in the planning committee's decisions lives in the suburbs.

(C) Some persons with significant financial interests in the planning committee's decisions work in the suburbs.

(D) Some planning committee members who represent the construction industry do not work in the suburbs.

(E) Some persons with significant financial interests in the planning committee's decisions do not live in the suburbs.

(PrepTest 29, Section 4, Q. 4)

7. Political opinion and analysis outside the mainstream rarely are found on television talk shows, and it might be thought that this state of affairs is a product of the political agenda of the television stations themselves. In fact, television stations are driven by the same economic forces as sellers of more tangible goods. Because they must attempt to capture the largest possible share of the television audience for their shows, they air only those shows that will appeal to large numbers of people. As a result, political opinions and analyses aired on television talk shows are typically bland and innocuous.

An assumption made in the explanation offered by the author of the passage is that

(A) most television viewers cannot agree on which elements of a particular opinion or analysis are most disturbing

(B) there are television viewers who might refuse to watch television talk shows that they knew would be controversial and disturbing

(C) each television viewer holds some opinion that is outside the political mainstream, but those opinions are not the same for everyone

(D) there are television shows on which economic forces have an even greater impact than they do on television talk shows

(E) the television talk shows of different stations resemble one another in most respects

(PrepTest 30, Section 4, Q. 16)

8. Sales manager: The highest priority should be given to the needs of the sales department, because without successful sales the company as a whole would fail.

    Shipping manager: There are several departments other than sales that also must function successfully for the company to succeed. It is impossible to give the highest priority to all of them.

    The shipping manager criticizes the sales manager's argument by pointing out

    (A) that the sales department taken by itself is not critical to the company's success as a whole
    (B) the ambiguity of the term "highest priority"
    (C) that departments other than sales are more vital to the company's success
    (D) an absurd consequence of its apparent assumption that a department's necessity earns it the highest priority
    (E) that the sales manager makes a generalization from an atypical case

(PrepTest 29, Section 4, Q. 14)

9. Plant manager: We could greatly reduce the amount of sulfur dioxide our copper-smelting plant releases into the atmosphere by using a new process. The new process requires replacing our open furnaces with closed ones and moving the copper from one furnace to the next in solid, not molten, form. However, not only is the new equipment expensive to buy and install, but the new process also costs more to run than the current process, because the copper must be reheated after it has cooled. So overall, adopting the new process will cost much but bring the company no profit.

    The plant manager's argument is most vulnerable to criticism on which one of the following grounds?

    (A) The overall conclusion is about a new effect but is based solely on evidence about only some of the factors that contribute to the effect.
    (B) The support for the overall conclusion is the authority of the plant manager rather than any independently verifiable evidence.
    (C) The overall conclusion reached merely repeats the evidence offered.
    (D) Evidence that is taken to be only probably true is used as the basis for a claim that something is definitely true.
    (E) Facts that are not directly relevant to the argument are treated as if they supported the overall conclusion.

Question 1: Guided Explanation

The Mystery of the Failing Brakes

Step 1: Grill the Interrogator. This one's a Paradox EXCEPT question, which means that all of the choices but one are capable of clearing up the apparent discrepancy. So expect the upcoming mystery to be "debunkable" in numerous ways.

TAKE AWAY

You may encounter Assumption EXCEPT, Strengthen/Weaken EXCEPT, Inference EXCEPT, even rare Parallel Reasoning EXCEPT questions, among others. In EXCEPT questions, the same principles apply but in reverse: The right answer will be the one that *doesn't* satisfy the requirement of the question stem. Since EXCEPT questions switch things around, the credited choice will usually fall into one of the common wrong answer categories.

Step 2: Attack the Passage. It does seem odd that people who drive cars with antilock brakes have more accidents than those who don't drive such cars, in light of the fact that these kinds of brakes were specially designed for safety. There's no overriding logical element to break this thing wide open, so we should simply evaluate the choices with an eye out for factors that make this situation less mysterious.

Step 3: Work the Choices. **A** and **D** shift the focus to drivers. If drivers of cars with antilock brakes drive more carelessly and don't know how to use these brakes, it's much easier to understand why more accidents occur with these cars than cars without antilock brakes. Antilock brakes may be *designed* to be safer, but there's no reason to think they will be if the people who drive them are boneheads.

B and **C** present factors regarding the brakes themselves that help do away with the apparent discrepancy. If they malfunction frequently and require special maintenance to perform even up to the standard of regular brakes, it's not so surprising that these cars are involved in more accidents.

E does not help clear things up, and is therefore the correct choice in this EXCEPT question. The *nature* of accidents is irrelevant to a mystery concerning the *number* of accidents, so this choice does nothing to explain why antilock brakes seem more dangerous despite being specifically designed for safety. In a standard Paradox question, this choice would be crossed off as Irrelevant. In an EXCEPT question, however, it's the credited choice, so **E** is correct.

TAKE AWAY

Cut to the heart of the matter. The mystery centers around the concept of "more accidents," and choices **A** through **D** provide information that relates well to this issue. Compared to these, the "nature" of accidents in choice **E** should stick out like a sore thumb.

Question 2: Guided Explanation

Peat Harvesting

Step 1: Grill the Interrogator. We're presented with a standard Strengthen stem, which tells us to switch into a critical mode as we attack the passage.

Step 2: Attack the Passage. A fairly blatant bait and switch lies at the heart of this argument, since there's no indication that what applies to Ireland applies to "this country."

TAKE
AWAY

> Continually hone your ability to recognize bait and switches—instances in which a key element of the evidence and a key element of the conclusion are mismatched. When the switch is obvious, the question will generally not be very hard. It's when the switch is *subtle* that things can get hairy.

The conclusion "we can safely proceed" is unequivocal and unqualified—no buts about it. Perhaps this helped you spot the author's assumption that the ecological ramifications of peat harvesting in the country in question would exactly match the effects of peat harvesting in Ireland, a questionable assumption at best since the author provides zero evidence that the two situations are similar. Strengthening the argument merely entails shoring up this questionable assumption.

Step 3: Work the Choices. If, as **B** has it, the Irish ecology was virtually identical to that of the wetlands in this country, it's easier to believe that the opponents are wrong and that it's safe to harvest peat, as the author of the passage maintains. **B** is correct.

A: If the author deemed to add the fact in **A** to her argument, what do you think the opponents' reaction would likely be? A big fat "So what!" perhaps? And rightfully so: Slow changes, possible advantages, *flora and fauna* . . . huh? This is all too vague and removed from the argument to be of any help here.

TAKE
AWAY

> You may have noticed that we refer to the choices in Strengthen/Weaken questions as "facts." And it's correct to treat them as facts because of the phrase "if true" in the stems. One important part of Logical Reasoning success is an ability to accurately and quickly understand what the answer choices in each question type represent. Only then will you be able to deal with them efficiently.

C: *Other* industries? Irrelevant. Quick kill.

D: The magnitude of the peat resources is irrelevant to whether peat harvesting will harm the water, since we have no way of knowing how size affects the process, if at all. Still, insofar as this represents a difference between the peat industry in this country and that in most others, including Ireland for all we know, **D** may, if anything, work to the advantage of the opponents' argument by suggesting that what works in some places may *not* work here.

E: "So what?" is once again the proper response, as the *use* of peat harvesting in Ireland is irrelevant to whether peat harvesting in this country will contaminate the water.

> ### TAKE AWAY
>
> An argument based around a questionable assumption can be featured in an Assumption, Strengthen, or Weaken question. Assumption is the most straightforward, where the right answer is simply the assumption itself. The right answer to a Weaken question will show that the assumption isn't all that reasonable, while a valid strengthener will be the choice that in some way demonstrates that the assumption is in fact well founded.

Question 3: Guided Explanation

Equipment Sales

Step 1: Grill the Interrogator. The stem clearly indicates that Disagreement is the question type here, so read the dialogue with an eye out for the point at issue.

Step 2: Attack the Passage. You may be on your way to law school, but you've got a typical business school dilemma to consider in this one. Tracy pulls no punches, flat-out intoning "I disagree." Since a recommendation lies at the heart of Jean's argument, we can infer that Tracy disagrees with this recommendation, but we need to read on to figure out exactly what part of Jean's argument she finds objectionable. As always in Matching questions, let's let the choices do our work for us. Some will skew one way, some the other. Some will concern only one arguer, while others may be irrelevant to both or even represent points of agreement. Keep these possibilities in mind as you hit the choices.

Step 3: Work the Choices.

A: Neither combatant compares the profitability of different markets. Both focus solely on how the company will fare against the competition if they pursue various strategies. Jean thinks the company can venture into a new market and help overall sales, but that doesn't tell us which market she believes is bigger. Similarly, Tracy *might* believe that the new market is too small to be worth worrying about, but nothing in the passage shows that she has this belief or any other on the subject. Also (and this is subtle), while overall sales is relevant to both arguments, *profit* per se is not, so again there's no source of disagreement here.

B speaks to the issue of the cheaper model cannibalizing sales of the present model, an issue not touched by either speaker. Again, they are interested in how the new model might affect market share and overall sales.

C: Jean thinks the low-cost model will add to sales while allowing the company to continue its *high-end* dominance. Tracy believes that entering the low-end market will threaten the company's high-end dominance. If you look carefully, you'll see that low-end market domination is not addressed by either argument, which means the disagreement cannot center on this issue.

D: Does Jean have an opinion on the proposition in **D**? Sure: She thinks the company can add the low-cost model and still continue to dominate the high end. So Jean would disagree with **D**. Tracy thinks moving into the low-end market will allow high-end competitors to gain an equal footing with the company, so she would agree with the proposition in **D**. That means we've found our source of disagreement. **D** is correct. For the record, let's evaluate the last choice.

E: Neither speaker considers the effect high-cost sales might have on low-cost sales—both speculate how high-end prospects might influence the company's overall sales in the event that the low-cost model is introduced. They disagree over *that* but not over the proposition in **E**.

> Sometimes it's tough to spot irrelevancies because they spring not from new and obvious extraneous subject matter but rather from subtle distortions of the information that exists in the passage. High-cost, low-cost, cheaper model, present model . . . all of the wrong choices here play off these terms, only not to the effect we seek. Learn to recognize the ways in which passage information is twisted or combined inappropriately. "Twister" choices play a large role in both Logical Reasoning and Reading Comprehension.

TAKE AWAY

Question 4: Guided Explanation

Cowards, Weaklings, and Fools

Step 1: Grill the Interrogator. The terms "flawed reasoning" and "most similar" tell us not only that we're up against Parallel Reasoning but also that the logic in the passage and the correct choice will be flawed in the same exact way. So prepare to find the error in the original that will be replicated in the correct choice.

Step 2: Attack the Passage. The formal logic element should jump out at you, but watch out: Some careful translation is required. If you can get through that, and then successfully compare conclusions, you'll find you can cut this tough question down to size. The key is properly translating the "All too many" and "few fail" phrases. "All too many" does *not* necessarily mean "all"—it means "some." "All too many weaklings are cowards" means that it can't be true that no weakling is a coward, yet we don't know enough to say that *all* weaklings are cowards. So we must settle for what we absolutely know to be true from that statement, which is "some weaklings are cowards."

On the LSAT, "some" is translated strictly as "at least one." "Some" is not inconsistent with "all." For example, if we say "some ninth graders went to the museum," no rule is violated if in fact *all* the ninth graders went to the museum. But if that were the case, why wouldn't we say "all" instead of "some"? We probably would, in real life. But if you haven't noticed yet, the LSAT is not real life. It's much more precise, and you have to play by its strict rules to succeed.

Similarly, "few cowards fail to be fools" is a fancy way of saying that "some cowards are fools." Based on our definition of "some" in the Take Away above, "At least one person is both a weakling and a fool" simply means "some weaklings are fools." So we can translate the passage into a much more manageable form: "Some weaklings are cowards, and some cowards are fools. Therefore, some weaklings are fools." In algebraic terms, that's "Some X are Y, and some Y are Z. Therefore, some X are Z." The flaw should be much more noticeable with the argument stated in this form. Do you see it? The author assumes that some of the X that are Y are also Z. But for all we know the X's that are Y do not overlap with the Y's that are Z.

Our formal logic Work in Groups strategy specifically encourages you to understand how the members of groups *must, could,* and *cannot* overlap. As you'll see in the next chapter, this skill is crucial for Logic Games success.

Step 3: Work the Choices. Zeroing in on the "some X are Z" conclusion allows us to eliminate any choice whose conclusion doesn't match.

B breaks down to "few can do both X and Y." **D** takes the form "if X, then Y." **E**'s "some X believe Y" doesn't match either. We could arguably go out on a limb for **E**, translating it as "some X (voters) are Y (people not opposed to stiffer tariffs)," but even then it breaks down in the evidence stage of our analysis because it contains a definite "no one," while the original argument is based exclusively around "some" statements.

A's "all weasels are carnivores" fails to match the original argument on the same count. You may also notice that the logic in **A** is technically not flawed. Even though we could go further to conclude that "all weasels are nonherbivores," that's not inconsistent with the statement "some weasels are nonherbivores."

In Parallel Flaw questions, the argument in the right answer must meet two criteria: It must be flawed, and it must be flawed in the same way as the original. You'll often find at least one choice with a valid argument, and if you recognize its validity you can eliminate it for that reason alone.

That leaves **C** as the winner, and a quick check reveals the same logical elements as the original, despite the fact that the conclusion comes first followed by the evidence at the end. **C** is correct.

TAKE AWAY

Remember that in Parallel Reasoning questions, the elements of the passage and the correct choice must match logically, but not necessarily *sequentially*. The order doesn't matter as long as the reasoning is the same.

Question 5: Guided Explanation

Parents vs. Experts

Step 1: Grill the Interrogator. The stem tells us that the principle is illustrated in the passage, which means that you should first distill it as a general rule and then see which of the scenarios in the choices conforms best to that rule.

Step 2: Attack the Passage. The general rule illustrated by the passage goes something like this: People in a situation should not necessarily listen to the advice of experts who, while qualified in their own right, aren't familiar with the specifics of the situation the people face. Okay, let's find the best match.

Step 3: Work the Choices.

A: No experts here. Quick kill.

B: There are experts in this scenario to which one should not pay much attention, so that part matches, but the reason given differs from the principle illustrated in the passage. There, the reason is that people have greater specific knowledge of the situation at hand than do the experts. Here, the experts *don't care* about issues important to the people.

C matches in all respects. Mountain climbing experts are authorities in their own right (just like parenting experts are authorities on their own kids), but if they're unfamiliar with a specific mountain (like the parenting experts unfamiliar with another parent's child), it's proper to ignore their advice. **C** is correct.

TAKE AWAY

Distilling the principle as a rule means factoring out the specific topic—in this case, parenting. Why do we do this? Because we're interested in the principle underlying the situation in the passage. But when testing the choices, it may still help to relate them back to the original situation to confirm that the principle illustrated there is a good match for your selection. Here, the relationship between the mountain climbers and the experts in choice **C** matches the relationship between the parents and the experts in the passage.

D suggests that the expert knows more than the person with direct experience, which is the opposite of what we seek. It also omits the central issue of ignoring advice.

E creates an opposition between singular and collective advice but does not address the specific notion of "expertise" in a given area. **E** therefore doesn't help the principle illustrated in the passage.

Question 6: Guided Explanation

Committee Members

Step 1: Grill the Interrogator. The phrase "must also be true" suggests a Formal Logic Inference challenge, so keep your eyes peeled for traditional formal logic elements.

Step 2: Attack the Passage. The word *members* suggests that this is a "groups" type of problem, and the words *some, no one,* and *many* confirm that formal logic is present. Much like the Zenith Press example from earlier in the chapter, we're interested in figuring out who's in what group, who can't be in what group, and so on. Also like Zenith Press, the most concrete piece of information is indicated by the words *no one.*

> **TAKE AWAY**
>
> Words like *some* and *many* are not nearly as definitive as *no one,* because while we know that some people must be included in the groups prefaced by *some* and *many,* we don't know which ones. *No one,* on the other hand, absolutely excludes certain people from a particular group. In this case, planning committee members cannot be in the suburban living group, and vice versa. Always begin with the most definitive information.

So, we see that the suburban living group cannot overlap with the planning committee members group. But there are planning committee members who represent the construction industry and who have financial interests in the committee's decisions. So there must be some people in each of these two groups (representatives of the construction industry and people with financial interest in the committee's decisions) who do not live in the suburbs, since the people in these groups are committee members and no committee members are suburbanites.

Step 3: Work the Choices. Scanning the choices with these deductions in mind, **E** is the one that must be true.

A: Translating the double negative into something more manageable, **A** essentially says that everyone with significant financial interests in the planning committee's decisions is in the construction industry. But nothing forbids people outside the construction industry from entertaining such interests.

B: Any number of people besides the ones mentioned in the passage may have significant financial interests in the planning committee's decisions, and these people can live anywhere they want—even in the suburbs. If the first word of the passage was *only* instead of *some*, **B** would be inferable. But it's not. So it isn't.

C and **D**: Tricky, right? These two choices try to get you to connect the "some" and "many" statements, but if you think about it, there need not be any overlap between the planning committee members with financial interests and the planning committee members who work in the suburbs. Who's in this latter group of "many" committee member suburb workers? *We don't know*—could be anybody. Maybe none of the construction industry reps with the financial interests are among the many planning members who work in the suburbs, eliminating **C**, or maybe all of the construction industry reps with the financial interests work in the suburbs, eliminating **D**.

As is common in Formal Logic questions, the choices are a bit nightmarish—similar-sounding combinations of the same terminology with a double negative thrown in, to boot. In Standard Inference questions, it pays to focus heavily on the choices, which are often chock-full of common wrong answer types to eliminate. In Formal Logic questions, however, try to piece deductions together yourself before venturing off into the choices. Developing this ability will help you immensely in Logic Games as well.

Question 7: Guided Explanation

TV Politics

Step 1: Grill the Interrogator. The stem tells us what to look for (an assumption), and where to look for it (the author's explanation). All your Assumption strategies are in play as you head into the passage.

Step 2: Attack the Passage. The question stem has put you into a bait and switch, loose end frame of mind, and the final three-word phrase of the passage—"bland and innocuous"—is your ticket to success. This characterization of TV political analyses comes out of nowhere and thus constitutes a classic loose end that needs to be tied back into the rest of the passage for the argument to be complete. "As a result" is a common signal for a conclusion, while the "Because" beginning the next-to-last sentence is a sure sign that that sentence contains evidence for the upcoming conclusion.

TAKE AWAY

Because, for, and *since* are common evidence signal words. Conclusion signal words include *as a result, consequently, therefore, thus,* and *so. However* and *but* are the most common words signaling that a contrast is upcoming. Signal words and phrases that clearly denote evidence, conclusion, or contrast are especially important tools for following the author's train of thought in both Logical Reasoning and Reading Comprehension passages.

Since we're looking for the gap between the evidence and conclusion, and these signal words clearly indicate which is which, we can paraphrase the argument like so: You say X (TV politics is boring and harmless) because of Y (TV shows must suck in the maximum audience possible). What goes unsaid is that "boring and harmless" is the way to achieve maximum audience. Perhaps you formed a valid "But what if . . .?" based on this reasoning: "But what if lots of people like TV politics that's *not* boring and harmless?" Then the progression from evidence to conclusion—that is, the argument—would make much less sense.

Step 3: Work the Choices. The realizations above allow us to see how **B** must be assumed. The author must believe that controversial and disturbing TV political analyses (the opposite of "bland and innocuous") would turn some people off (who would respond in kind by turning *them* off). As we've already demonstrated with our "But what if . . .?" example, the negation of choice **B** destroys the argument. If *no one* refused to watch controversial and disturbing programming, one can't argue that the mandate to bring in the largest possible audience requires airing bland and innocuous analyses. **B** is correct.

A: Viewer agreement is Irrelevant to the argument. As long as many viewers are disturbed in some way by controversial analyses, it makes no difference to the author's reasoning whether they agree on what are the *most* disturbing aspects.

C: The argument holds up fine even if some TV viewers don't have non-mainstream views. This precise clarification concerning the "outside the mainstream" reference is unnecessary, as it has no bearing on the specific argument laid out in the final two sentences.

D, like **C**, focuses on a minor issue—the thing about economic forces. But what really makes this one a quick kill is the reference to *other* TV shows. What does that have to do with the idea that bland and innocuous programming is necessary to capture *talk show* market share? Nothing.

E Overreaches, big time. Presumably, TV talk shows across the board (or the dial, as the case may be) resemble each other in at least one respect: They're all beholden to economic forces and thus try to capture the largest possible audience. But why must they resemble each other in other respects, let alone *in most respects,* for this argument to work? What if, in accordance with the negate and destroy test, we say that TV talk shows on different stations are *not* the same as one another in most respects? Does that change anything in the final two sentences? No, which means we can cross off **E** with confidence.

TAKE AWAY

You can use the negate and destroy test to both confirm the answer you think is right and eliminate wrong choices. Notice how negating correct choice **B** sinks the argument, while negating wrong choice **E** has no effect on the issue at hand.

Question 8: Guided Explanation

Company Infighting

Step 1: Grill the Interrogator. The question stem alerts us to the fact that a criticism is present in the second argument, so our task is to discover the way in which the second speaker disagrees with the first.

Step 2: Attack the Passage. The sales manager's conclusion stems from a statement of necessity. Success in sales is *necessary* for the company's overall success, he says. Therefore, the sales department should get *top priority*. A bona fide bait and switch.

> Essential Concepts appear in numerous questions and in various forms. Be on the lookout for them throughout the Logical Reasoning sections.

 TAKE AWAY

If you had trouble spotting the suspect reasoning here, the shipping manager helps you out: Other departments are necessary for the company to succeed, he says, but not *every* department can get top billing. So the shipping manager, recognizing a bait and switch when he sees one, attacks the sales manager's idea that *necessity* leads to *highest priority*. That's enough to get us going, so let's match the choices against that issue.

Step 3: Work the Choices.
A: The shipping manager does not contest the assertion that the sales department is necessary for the company's success. He contests the conclusion the sales manager derives from this fact.

B: There's no ambiguity surrounding the term "highest priority." Nothing suggests that either speaker understands "highest priority" to mean anything other than "the top concern."

C: "*More* vital"? That's not what the shipping manager says. He merely points out that other departments are vital as well and suggests a counter-conclusion based on that.

D: As we've seen, the shipping manager does take the sales manager to task for the assumption that a department's necessity grants it the highest priority. So the second half of the choice seems on target, but the first part requires some investigation. Does the shipping manager point out an "absurd consequence"? In a backhanded way, he does, by saying that it's impossible for every department to be the company's highest priority. A company can have only one "highest" priority. The absurd notion of "multiple highest priorities" (an oxymoron, in fact, like "escaped inmate" and "government intelligence") is thus what the shipping manager believes would result from the sales manager's reasoning. **D is correct.**

E: What's the atypical case? What's the generalization? Both the sales manager's recommendation and the evidence provided for it deal specifically with the sales department.

Question 9: Guided Explanation

The Profitless Process

Step 1: Grill the Interrogator. The phrase "most vulnerable to criticism" puts us squarely in the Flaw camp, so be on the lookout for Essential Concepts and classic flaws.

Step 2: Attack the Passage. Remember Pablo's Cantina from the Essential Concepts section earlier in the chapter? In our discussion of unknowables, we pointed out how we can't know anything regarding profit just from evidence concerning revenues since profit is, after all, a two-way street consisting of costs and revenues. We saw the same issue arise in choice **A** of question 3 earlier in this practice set. And we see it here again, which qualifies this argument as another bait and switch special. While it's reasonable for the author to infer the first half of the conclusion beginning with the helpful signal word "So" in the final sentence—that is, that the process will cost much—he has no business taking the final leap to "no profit." This is especially true considering that the author conveniently forgets about a factor that might mitigate at least some of the increased cost: the great reduction in sulfur dioxide brought about by the new process.

Step 3: Work the Choices. The fact that the benefit of the process is relegated to a loose end points the way toward correct choice **A**: The conclusion *is* about the effect of the new process (no profit) but is based only on one side of the story: the cost situation. Benefits of the new process—including but not necessarily limited to the reduction in sulfur dioxide—aren't considered, and that's what's wrong with the argument. **A** is correct.

B and **C** refer to a couple of "oldies but goodies," but the plant manager does not appeal to the authority of her position in making her case, nor does she merely repeat the evidence she cites. She supplies information about the process that is in fact verifiable (what the new process involves, what it costs, etc.), and never simply suggests "Trust me on this one, I'm the head honcho." And circular reasoning, which is the atrocity invoked in choice **C**'s accusation, is off the mark too. "No profit" is the conclusion, skyrocketing costs is the evidence. This evidence may not be *complete,* but it's not *identical* to the conclusion.

TAKE
AWAY

> Keep track of the types of flaws that you come across in your practice. The "oldies but goodies" we mentioned earlier in the chapter usually come up in wrong answer choices, but don't be surprised if an occasional argument centers around one of these as well.

D accuses the author of relying on indefinite information to form a definite conclusion, but he Does No Such Thing. There is no ambiguity in the evidence. We have no reason to doubt that the process is what it is and costs what it costs, in accordance with the author's description. The problem lies elsewhere.

E is another Does No Such Thing choice: The facts (how the new process works and how it increases costs) are entirely relevant to a conclusion regarding profit. The problem is they don't go far enough to tell the full story.

> No doubt you see by now how words are used very precisely on the LSAT. *Irrelevant* and *incomplete* are both negative, but they're not the same thing. Only one of them can be used to properly describe the facts presented in this passage.

TAKE AWAY

LOGICAL REASONING SUMMARY

The point of this chapter is to establish a foundation from which to tackle Logical Reasoning questions with speed, confidence, and accuracy. On top of the Essential Concepts and the Essential Strategy, you've learned how to recognize and handle every question type that's likely to appear on your test. Not just the three or four most common ones, but *all 11*. Are you expected to be an expert now? No—you'll need to apply what you've learned to many practice questions. The 24 questions in this chapter provide an excellent start. Later you'll see another 50 Logical Reasoning questions in the practice test at the end of the book, which will help reinforce what you've learned already as well as illuminate further nuances.

"But all this logic stuff is totally nitpicky . . ." you may be thinking at this point. Well guess what?—so is the law. Professional billiards players don't need to think like this. *You do*. You chose this path. Precision is what it's all about; this section *is* called "Logical Reasoning," after all. You can rail against a form of thinking you consider cruel and arcane, or you can relish the challenge it presents. Let's just say that the latter is more pleasing to the LSAT gods. Consider Logical Reasoning questions as mini mysteries, and the Essential Concepts, Essential Strategy, Battleplans, and techniques discussed in this chapter your tools for solving them.

## Chapter 2

LOGIC GAMES

or

What Three Hyenas and a Mountain Lion Have to Do with Your Future

If you're wondering what in the world the Logic Games section is doing on the LSAT, you're not alone. Why do they torture you with these silly puzzles that seemingly have nothing to do with being a lawyer? Here you are, Mr. or Ms. Serious Aspiring Law Student, ready to take on the world and stamp out injustice (or make billions brokering corporate mergers), and what do they throw in your way? *Bears. Jugglers.* Seven snot-nosed kids at some stupid birthday party where *you,* of all people, have to figure out the order for pin-the-tail-on-the-donkey. And what about those scenarios they dream up? Sounds like a bad joke: *Three rabbis, a priest, and an elephant walk into a bar . . .*

Guess what? No joke. Fast forward to the future . . .

Packed courtroom. Palms sweating. Your client's fate hanging in the balance. And suddenly it dawns on you that if you combine the testimony offered by witnesses 1 and 7 with the testimony offered by witness 3, there's no way that key witness 4 can be telling the truth. Two things become immediately clear to you: First, you're going to win this case. Second, the LSAT Logic Games section is more than the mere sadistic ritual you thought it to be.

Sure, not every law career involves dramatic courtroom scenes, but the relevance of Logic Games extends to many aspects of legal study and practice—we'll talk more about the "why" of this section later. The good news is that logic games, like all puzzles, get easier with practice and familiarity. So buckle up for a heaping helping of drills and games as we dissect this formidable challenge and cut it down to size.

OVERVIEW

What It Is

The Logic Games section—officially called "Analytical Reasoning" by the testmakers—makes up one of the four scored sections of the LSAT. The Logic Games section accounts for a little less than one quarter of your LSAT score. The section contains four games, each usually containing 5 or 6 questions for a total of 22 to 24 questions overall. You'll have 35 minutes to complete the four games. Each game contains an introductory paragraph, which we'll refer to as the "introduction." This is followed by a number of rules. The introduction and the rules taken together we'll call the "setup." Multiple-choice questions come next, each based on the parameters set forth in the setup.

Why It Is

The skills that enable one to successfully handle not only one logic game but *four* games in 35 minutes are indeed skills prized by the legal profession. By means of the Logic Games section, prospective law schools can gauge your ability to:

- Compile numerous pieces of information into one coherent framework

- Keep multiple entities and the relationships between them in mind simultaneously

- Recognize numerical limitations imposed on a situation

- Understand, interpret, translate, and apply complicated rules

- Spot connections between pieces of evidence

- Draw deductions from two or more interrelated statements

- Focus on a relevant question and answer the precise question asked

- Work quickly and accurately under strict time pressure

So while you probably won't run into three hyenas and a mountain lion, the mental gymnastics required in the Logic Games section will come in handy. When you're analyzing statutes, regulations, and judicial decisions you'll need to interpret the same logical terms you'll see on the LSAT. The good news is you won't have a 35-minute time limit. In fact, if you're paid by the hour, taking more time is encouraged. But that's another story.

Your Motivation

To outfox that damn mountain lion. Seriously: Logic Games accounts for just under one quarter of your total LSAT score, so you can't ace the test without kicking butt on this section. Bragging rights around the law library water cooler wouldn't hurt, either.

GAMEPLAN

Once again we'll follow a specific gameplan intended to maximize your study time. Here are the topics we'll cover in this chapter:

- **X-ray of a Typical Logic Game:** First we'll take a look at what a logic game looks like so that we're on the same page regarding terminology and the nature of your task. We'll introduce the directions, the setup, the rules, and a typical Logic Games question.

- **Game Types:** Each logic game generally falls into one of four basic game types. You'll learn about these game types early on so that you'll recognize them in the examples to come.

- **Essential Strategy:** Next you'll learn a general strategy to follow for every logic game you face. We'll practice employing each step of this strategy with drills and exercises, which will sharpen your skills to tackle each game type.

- **The Real Deal:** Finally, you'll have a chance to test out all of your new knowledge and skills on four actual logic games from previous LSATs. When you've gotten everything out of those that you can, four more games await you in the practice test at the end of the book.

X-RAY OF A TYPICAL LOGIC GAME

So what does one of these things actually look like? Glad you asked. Take a brief look through the following, but don't worry about working through the setup or answering the question just yet—we'll get to that later on, promise. For right now, just take a minute to get the lay of the land.

Seven works of art—P, Q, R, S, T, V, and W—will be exhibited at a local gallery opening. A short lecture will be delivered by the creator of each work during the gallery opening. No two lectures will be delivered at the same time. The sequence of lectures must satisfy the following requirements:

>   The lecture on artwork R is delivered second or sixth.
>   The lecture on artwork T is delivered fourth.
>   The lecture on artwork S is delivered at some point after the lecture on artwork V.
>   The lecture on artwork P is delivered either immediately before or immediately after the lecture on artwork W.

1.   Which one of the following could be an accurate list of artwork lectures delivered in order from first to last?

(A)   Q, V, P, T, W, R, S
(B)   Q, V, W, P, T, R, S
(C)   S, R, Q, T, P, W, V
(D)   V, R, S, T, W, P, Q
(E)   W, P, R, T, V, Q, S

The first paragraph lays out the basic parameters of the game: what's being done, who or what it's being done to, and who's doing it. This, cleverly enough, we call the "introduction," and in this case it tells us that lectures on specific works of art will be delivered in some order. The indented statements following the introduction are the "rules," which further define how the action outlined in the introduction will play out. The introduction and the rules taken together we call the "setup." The setup is followed by five to seven multiple-choice questions, an example of which is provided in question 1 above. (In a real game, there would be four to six more questions to round out the question set.) The setup applies to every question in the question set unless otherwise noted—occasionally, an individual question will add, subtract, or change a rule, but for the most part the questions will be solved according to the information provided in the setup.

You'll learn much more about these components when we discuss game types and demonstrate the Essential Strategy later on. But before we get to that, let's round out our X-ray with a quick scan through the directions.

<u>Directions:</u> Each group of questions in this section is based on a set of conditions. In answering some of the questions, it may be useful to draw a rough diagram. Choose the response that most accurately and completely answers each question and blacken the corresponding space on your answer sheet.

Pretty cut-and-dried: The "set of conditions" you'll soon recognize as the "setup" described just above. The "rough diagram" refers to scratchwork you may jot down next to individual questions, and the final sentence is just test-prep boiler-plate: Don't forget to blacken in your answer on the answer sheet.

Notice what's conspicuously absent here—the statement found in both the Logical Reasoning and Reading Comprehension directions that says there is more than one choice that *could conceivably answer the question,* but only the *best* answer will be credited. That disclaimer is missing in these directions because credited Logic Games answers are objectively correct; that is, there's no two ways about it. When you do a Sudoku (Japanese number game), for example, you can't enter a wrong number and still solve the puzzle. Similarly, every wrong choice in a logic game can be proven wrong, and the correct choice can be proven right. As in any logic puzzle, there's absolutely no wiggle room corresponding to the tiny bit of leeway inherent in the other sections.

Okay, that completes our X-ray, so let's talk a bit about what kinds of games you're likely to see.

GAME TYPES

The table below summarizes the four main game types, each characterized by a different game action. They are as follows:

Game Type	Your Task
1. Ordering	Arrange characters in a sequential order.
2. Choosing	Select a smaller group of characters from a larger group.
3. Placing	Distribute characters into different groups.
4. Linking	Match up two or more characteristics of the characters in the game.

In addition, a single game may involve multiple game actions—for example, you may be asked to choose a smaller group from a larger set and then arrange the selected entities in order. We'll call these Combination games.

Either way, you'll always see four games, and there's no way to tell what mix of games you'll get. Perhaps you'll get two Ordering games, a Choosing game, and a combination Placing/Linking game. Or you may get two Placing games and no Choosing games as part of the four-game set. You won't, however, see a section consisting entirely of one game type, such as four Choosing games. They usually mix it up pretty well, so your best bet is to get comfortable with all types.

Your first order of business for tackling any logic game is to recognize the game type—that is, determine the action of the game. Now that we've identified the four basic game types, let's get some practice doing just that.

Every logic game begins with a solid understanding of the game's action. Without this, you'll just get more and more lost as you venture further into the game, so make sure not to skimp on your initial analysis of the situation.

Examine the game introductions below. Note that rules are not included here. You should be able to determine a game's action from the introduction alone. Let's take a look.

1. Ordering Games

> Seven works of art—P, Q, R, S, T, V, and W—will be exhibited at a local gallery opening. A short lecture will be delivered by the creator of each work during the gallery opening. No two lectures will be delivered at the same time. The sequence of lectures must satisfy the following requirements:

The phrases "at the same time" and "sequence of lectures" are sure giveaways that this is a straightforward Ordering game. The goal is to put the characters in sequential order in accordance with the rules.

Ordering games, whether the characters are in a line, in a circle, or otherwise, involve the following issues:

- Where characters must be in the ordering

- Where characters can be in the ordering

- Where characters cannot be in the ordering

- Which characters can or must be next to which other characters in the ordering

- Which characters cannot be next to which other characters in the ordering

- Which characters come before and after which other characters in the ordering

- How many spaces apart two characters are in the ordering

2. Choosing Games

> Maggie must select exactly three introductory courses for the upcoming semester. The available introductory courses are biology, communications, English, French, history, literature, and philosophy. Her selection must accord with the following conditions:

Here we're presented with seven courses and the requirement to choose exactly three. Whenever you begin with a group of characters and are asked to form a smaller group from that initial group, you're dealing with a Choosing game.

Choosing games involve the following issues:

- Which characters must be chosen

- Which characters can be chosen

- Which characters cannot be chosen

- Which characters must be chosen with which other characters

- Which characters cannot be chosen with which other characters

- How many characters may be chosen under various circumstances

3. Placing Games

The participants of two economic seminars, one on free trade and one on venture capital, are to be assigned from among six company employees—Jobson, King, Lee, Manute, Nora, and Orson. King and Nora are vice presidents; the rest of the employees are middle managers. Each employee must participate in at least one seminar. The following rules govern the assignment of employees to seminars:

The fact that each character must participate in at least one seminar means that we're asked to take six people and split them in some way into two groups. We can't leave anyone out, so distributing the characters among the groups is the action here. That means this is a Placing game.

Placing games involve the following issues:

- Which characters must be placed in which groups

- Which characters could be placed in which groups

- Which characters cannot be placed in which groups

- How many characters are placed in each group

- Which characters must, could, or cannot be placed with which other characters

4. Linking Games

> Six children—Edel, Francie, Gillian, Holly, James, and Kayli—attend a birthday party.
> Three of the children are in nursery school, two are in first grade, and one is in second grade.
> Each child eats either pizza or a sandwich at the party. No child eats both kinds of food. The
> following must obtain:

In this one there are two things we need to figure out about the children: the
grade they're in and the food they eat. So this is a Linking game in which children, grades, and food items will be matched up according to the rules. We have
six characters (the children) and two characteristics (grades and food) to assign
them. That's how Linking games work: You need to figure out who the characters are and what characteristics those characters have.

Linking games involve the following issues:

_____

- Which characters must be matched to which characteristics

- Which characters can be matched to which characteristics

- Which characters cannot be matched to which characteristics

- Which characters must, can, or cannot have which characteristics in common

_____

Now that you're familiar with the kinds of games you'll see, let's move on to the
method you'll use to solve them.

ESSENTIAL STRATEGY

Logic Games, perhaps more than any other LSAT section, is amenable to a
precise, methodical approach. We'll briefly introduce the steps below, and then
we'll delve into each one in depth in the next section.

Step 1: Create a Blueprint. A blueprint is a foundation—something you use to accomplish a task. Here, the task is to knock down Logic Games questions, and the
blueprint phase of the operation takes you from your initial assessment of the
game type up through creating a simple sketch of the situation at hand. A big
part of this step is "shorthanding" (that is, abbreviating in an efficient manner)
the introductory information provided in the setup—something we'll be discussing shortly.

Step 2: Get the Specs. After you've blueprinted the situation, you'll use the
game's specific rules to figure out how it works. Some rules are fairly simple,
while others are more complex. We'll discuss many types in both categories and
give you practice interpreting all the varieties of rules you're likely to see.

Step 3: Search for Game Breakers. After creating a blueprint and using the rules to nail down the specs of the game, many test takers proceed right on to Step 4, attempting to cash in from the work performed in Steps 1 and 2. This is a grave mistake, since many games are crafted to contain key deductions that can be deduced from the setup alone—deductions that break the game wide open. Some games are nearly impossible to complete in the time allotted without noticing such "Game Breakers." You probably won't find earth-shattering deductions in every game you face, but discovering Game Breakers in one or two instances is often the key to a successful Logic Games performance. We'll teach you what to look for and how to make and use such deductions to ease your burden and pick up some quick and easy points.

Step 4: Cash In. When you've done all you can do, it's time to cash in and pick up as many points as you can, as fast as you can. If you skimp on the steps described above and go to the questions right out of the box, each question is likely to be its own struggle. However, if you organize your attack and uncover Game Breakers when possible, some questions will fall in a matter of seconds, leaving enough time to work through the more complicated challenges. Don't be surprised when certain questions seem very easy—they're easy only because you've already done the necessary work up front. When you've done the right preparatory work, don't hesitate to cash in on your efforts.

Now that you understand the general concept behind our four steps of the Essential Strategy, it's time to learn how to employ them. Let's take a deeper look.

Create a Blueprint:
Tackling the Introduction

We've already covered the initial stage of this step: determining the game type by analyzing the action set forth in the introduction. Your next task is to determine who or what that action is to be performed on. In other words, you need to identify the "characters."

Meet the Characters

Let's take our example from the first paragraph of this chapter: "Three rabbis, a priest, and an elephant walk into a bar . . ." It's a good idea to write the characters down, in shorthand form, somewhere on your page. No need for formality; we'd simply label these characters as "R R R P E."

> You are NOT allowed to use scrap paper on any section of the LSAT except for the Writing Sample. On that section, you'll be provided with scrap paper to plan out your written response. For Logic Games, you must do ALL of your work in the test booklet itself.

TAKE AWAY

Not all characters are created equal. There are generally two types:

1. **The Stars** of the game are featured heavily in the game's action or the rules. These are the characters you'll return to again and again when looking for ways to begin and proceed through each question.

2. **Free Agents** are characters featured in few or even no rules at all. Free agents usually won't be the focus of your attention unless specifically mentioned in a question stem. Stars, however, will often come into play whether a question mentions them or not.

In straightforward games, there's nothing particularly fancy about the characters, and you can simply abbreviate them on your page much as we did above. But for more complicated games, the characters themselves are sometimes broken up into different groups, in which case you need to keep track of who's who *to start with*, on top of everything else you'll need to do with them.

Sketch It Out

The final result of Step 1 is a sketch on the page that accurately and efficiently represents the scenario and puts you in a position to manipulate the information to come.

TAKE AWAY

Shorthand is abbreviated writing you use to help you manage the information provided. You can use shorthand to

- Represent the game's action
- Note the game's characters
- Abbreviate the rules
- Note any further deductions you derive from the rules

Now let's see what a blueprint would look like for the situations described in the four game introductions discussed earlier:

ART LECTURES: ORDERING

Seven works of art—P, Q, R, S, T, V, and W—will be exhibited at a local gallery opening. A short lecture will be delivered by the creator of each work during the gallery opening. No two lectures will be delivered at the same time. The sequence of lectures must satisfy the following requirements:

This is clearly a standard Ordering game; for these games, it's best to create an initial list of time slots, with the characters off to the side:

PQRSTVW

    1   2   3   4   5   6   7

> **TAKE AWAY**
>
> It's fairly easy to shorthand characters already presented in abbreviated form, but don't forget to do so when the characters are represented by full names too.

MAGGIE'S COURSES: CHOOSING

> Maggie must select exactly three introductory courses for the upcoming semester. The available introductory courses are biology, communications, English, French, history, literature, and philosophy. Her selection must accord with the following conditions:

Here our characters are the seven courses. Don't get distracted by Maggie! She's just there to add some flavor to the game, which works the same whether she or a Martian or a hyena chooses the courses. Your blueprint would therefore begin with getting the characters down on the page and a reminder of how many letters you're to select from this roster. Three dashes illustrate this fine and at a glance remind us that our job is to choose exactly three courses to fill in those dashes.

BCEFHLP

____ ____ ____

ECONOMIC SEMINARS: PLACING

> The participants of two economic seminars, one on free trade and one on venture capital, are to be assigned from among six company employees—Jobson, King, Lee, Manute, Nora, and Orson. King and Nora are vice presidents; the rest of the employees are middle managers. Each employee must participate in at least one seminar. The following rules govern the assignment of employees to seminars:

Here, the characters themselves are broken up into two groups (vice presidents and middle managers), and your shorthand should reflect this. When you add in the two groups into which you'll be placing the entities, free trade and venture capital, you'll be all set to move on to the rules. Here's what a simple but effective blueprint for this game might look like:

VP   MM
KN   JLMO

FT   VC

BIRTHDAY PARTY: LINKING

> Six children—Edel, Francie, Gillian, Holly, James, and Kayli—attend a birthday party. Three of the children are in nursery school, two are in first grade, and one is in second grade. Each child eats either pizza or a sandwich at the party. No child eats both kinds of food. The following must obtain:

Nothing fancy here, so just get the characters down on the page and some shorthand for the grade information as well:

E F G H J K
3 nurs
2 1st
1 2nd

With this blueprint in place, you'll be ready to move to the rules to learn about how the kids will be matched to the food they eat.

You can also use a grid to keep track of the characters and their characteristics. List the characters across the top, and create rows for each characteristic you need to determine. Here's how that might look in the Birthday Party game:

	E	F	G	H	J	K
Grade (NNN112)						
S/P						

Notice that we have a box for each characteristic of each character. To remind us how many students are in each grade, we listed the breakdown in the left column.

Naturally, you'll get more practice blueprinting the four full-length games we provide later in the chapter, and those in the practice test at the end of the book. For now, let's move on to the next step of the Essential Strategy.

Get the Specs: Tackling the Rules

So now we know what kind of game we're dealing with and who the characters are and what you'll be doing with them. Now it's time to tackle the rules, which specifically spell out how the characters *interact*. The rules lay down the specs that you'll need to follow when tackling each question.

Keep in mind that *the rules apply to all of the questions in the question set,* except for rare questions that specifically add a new rule or omit or modify an existing rule. In those cases, the rule change applies only to that particular question.

Some rules are complicated, and these are the ones you'll need to spend the most time learning how to handle. However, don't overlook the conventional rules that appear in many games. While these are fairly straightforward, you still need to quickly recognize their implications. Many games are ruined by careless misinterpretations of what appear on the surface to be simple rules, so it's worth taking a look at these before tackling the tough stuff.

Conventional Rules

Direct Positive

A Direct Positive rule explicitly tells you something that must be the case. Here are examples of Direct Positive rules for each of the game types discussed above, beginning with the Ordering game.

ART LECTURES: ORDERING

> Seven works of art—P, Q, R, S, T, V, and W—will be exhibited at a local gallery opening. A short lecture will be delivered by the creator of each work during the gallery opening. No two lectures will be delivered at the same time. The sequence of lectures must satisfy the following requirements:
>
> Rule: The lecture on artwork Q will be delivered fifth.

Here you'd go right ahead and place a Q under number 5 in your initial sketch. The logical implications are that Q cannot go anywhere else, and no other artwork can take space 5.

$$P \; Q \; R \; S \; T \; V \; W$$

$$\underbrace{1 \quad 2 \quad 3 \quad 4 \quad \underset{Q}{5} \quad 6 \quad 7}$$

In Ordering games, a special case of this rule can occur when a character is directly assigned to either end of the sequence, since that creates additional implications. For example, if a rule stated that the lecture on artwork S must be delivered first, then the additional implication is that no lecture precedes the lecture on S, and that S's lecture does not come after any others. Conversely, if S's lecture was assigned to space 7, no lecture can come after S's, and S's lecture cannot come before any others. Note also that a Direct Positive rule can be stated in the negative, for example: "No lecture is delivered later in the week than the lecture on artwork K." Different wording, same result. We know exactly in this case where lecture K is—last, which means seventh. Any rule that allows you to write a character directly into your blueprint is a Direct Positive.

Let's now see what a Direct Positive would look like in the context of our Choosing game.

MAGGIE'S COURSES: CHOOSING

Maggie must select exactly three introductory courses for the upcoming semester. The available introductory courses are biology, communications, English, French, history, literature, and philosophy. Her selection must accord with the following conditions:

Rule: Maggie will select French.

In this case you'd go right ahead and put an F into one of the three slots in your blueprint. The logical implication is that only two spots remain to be filled.

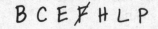

Let's try the same with our Placing game.

ECONOMIC SEMINARS: PLACING

The participants of two economic seminars, one on free trade and one on venture capital, are to be assigned from among six company employees—Jobson, King, Lee, Manute, Nora, and Orson. King and Nora are vice presidents; the rest of the employees are middle managers. Each employee must participate in at least one seminar. The following rules govern the assignment of employees to seminars:

Rule: Lee will participate in the seminar on free trade.

This tells you to place an L in the free trade column. Nothing in the introduction to this game suggests that employees must only participate in one seminar, so we can't tell yet whether Lee participates in venture capital as well. But we do know that at least one middle manager participates in free trade, since Lee is defined as such in the intro.

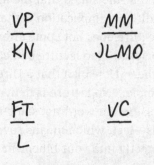

Now let's wrap up Direct Positives with our Linking scenario.

BIRTHDAY PARTY: LINKING

> Six children—Edel, Francie, Gillian, Holly, James, and Kayli—attend a birthday party.
> Three of the children are in nursery school, two are in first grade, and one is in second grade.
> Each child eats either pizza or a sandwich at the party. No child eats both kinds of food. The
> following must obtain:
>
> Rule: Gillian eats a sandwich.

If you were keeping track of the information using a table, you'd place a check
in the box intersecting G and S. If you're using a list instead, you'd simply write
an S above or below G in your cast of characters. Since the game stipulates that
each child eats either pizza or a sandwich, the implication of this rule is that
Gillian does not eat pizza.

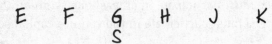

TAKE
AWAY

> Direct Positive rules and their implications are fairly simple, but they are
> often used as the starting point for longer chains of reasoning. Don't
> overlook them or underestimate their importance.

Direct Negative

A Direct Negative rule explicitly tells you something that CANNOT be the case.
Here are examples of Direct Negatives for each of the major game types, based
on the same game introductions utilized above.

ART LECTURES: ORDERING

> Seven works of art—P, Q, R, S, T, V, and W—will be exhibited at a local gallery opening.
> A short lecture will be delivered by the creator of each work during the gallery opening. No
> two lectures will be delivered at the same time. The sequence of lectures must satisfy the
> following requirements:
>
> Rule: The lecture on artwork Q will not be delivered fifth.

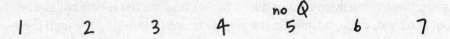

Writing "no Q" above the fifth slot in your blueprint for this Ordering game
would suffice to represent this rule. This tells us that Q must be somewhere else.
Sometimes the negative will include multiple spots in the sequence. For example: "The lecture on artwork Q will not be delivered second or fifth."

Moving on, you generally won't see a Direct Negative in a Choosing game, since
there would be no reason to include a character in the game that can never be
chosen. For example, in the game in which Maggie is to choose three of the seven

available courses, it would make no sense to see a rule that says "Maggie will not choose literature." If she can never choose it, why include literature in the first place? Direct Negative rules do apply perfectly well, however, to Placing games.

ECONOMIC SEMINARS: PLACING

The participants of two economic seminars, one on free trade and one on venture capital, are to be assigned from among six company employees—Jobson, King, Lee, Manute, Nora, and Orson. King and Nora are vice presidents; the rest of the employees are middle managers. Each employee must participate in at least one seminar. The following rules govern the assignment of employees to seminars:

<u>Rule:</u> Lee will not participate in the seminar on free trade.

Since each employee must participate in at least one seminar, this rule allows you to deduce that Lee must participate in the venture capital seminar.

TAKE AWAY

Turn negatives into positives whenever possible! When told what CANNOT be true of a particular character, see if you can bounce that information off the other game parameters to deduce something that MUST be true.

You may come across Direct Negative rules in Linking games as well.

BIRTHDAY PARTY: LINKING

Six children—Edel, Francie, Gillian, Holly, James, and Kayli—attend a birthday party. Three of the children are in nursery school, two are in first grade, and one is in second grade. Each child eats either pizza or a sandwich at the party. No child eats both kinds of food. The following must obtain:

<u>Rule:</u> Gillian does not eat a sandwich.

Following the advice to turn negatives into positives, you'd deduce that Gillian must therefore eat pizza, since sandwich and pizza are her only options.

Again, these conventional rules aren't rocket science, but if you bollix one up, you'll be in for a tough time. So it's definitely worth thinking through these basic implications before tackling the tougher stuff. We continue our discussion of conventional rules with a slightly more complex variety: rules that impose relationships between characters.

Positive Relationship

A Positive Relationship rule creates a positive link between two characters or aspects in the game. Here are examples of positive relationships for each of the major game types, again beginning with Ordering.

ART LECTURES: ORDERING

Seven works of art—P, Q, R, S, T, V, and W—will be exhibited at a local gallery opening. A short lecture will be delivered by the creator of each work during the gallery opening. No two lectures will be delivered at the same time. The sequence of lectures must satisfy the following requirements:

Rule: The lecture on artwork Q will be delivered immediately before or immediately after the lecture on artwork V.

This rule creates a "cluster" out of characters Q and V. The word "immediately" tells us that these two characters must be right next to each other somewhere in the sequence, although we don't yet know in what order. "QV or VQ" is an effective way to shorthand this common Ordering rule. Note that we also don't know where in the ordering this cluster will appear (first and second? fourth and fifth? sixth and seventh? etc.), but the fact that it takes up a definite two-slot portion of real estate will certainly come into play in your solution to many questions.

> **TAKE AWAY**
>
> Clusters can consist of two, three, and even four characters. Many games test your ability to space out such clusters among the other characters without violating other rules.

Another common Positive Relationship Ordering rule specifies the exact number of spaces between two characters. For example:

Rule: Exactly two lectures will be delivered between the lecture on artwork Q and the lecture on artwork V.

Here's how you can shorthand this:

$$Q \_\_ \_\_ V$$
$$V \_\_ \_\_ Q$$

Yet another common Positive Relationship Ordering rule forces characters before or after other characters but does not specify the distance between them. Check out an example on the next page.

Rule: The lecture on artwork Q will come after the lecture on artwork V.

In this case, we can deduce for sure that Q can't be first and V can't be last. Beyond that, we don't know how many lectures come between them. The rule is satisfied as long as V is before Q. Using "..." is a good way to represent this:

$$V \ldots Q$$

As we'll see later on, it's possible to form helpful deductions when more than one rule like this shares a common character.

Choosing games are not good candidates for simple Positive Relationship rules. We'll see how the characters in Choosing games interact positively and negatively when we get to Conditional rules. But let's move on to Placing games.

ECONOMIC SEMINARS: PLACING

The participants of two economic seminars, one on free trade and one on venture capital, are to be assigned from among six company employees—Jobson, King, Lee, Manute, Nora, and Orson. King and Nora are Vice Presidents; the rest of the employees are middle managers. Each employee must participate in at least one seminar. The following rules govern the assignment of employees to seminars:

Rule: Jobson and Manute will each attend exactly one seminar and will attend that seminar together.

This tells us that J and M will be together at exactly one seminar, but it does not tell us which one. However, as soon as we see Jobson somewhere, we'd have to place Manute there too, and vice versa. In addition, this implies that J and M cannot attend the other seminar.

Now let's check out this kind of rule in our Linking scenario.

BIRTHDAY PARTY: LINKING

Six children—Edel, Francie, Gillian, Holly, James, and Kayli—attend a birthday party. Three of the children are in nursery school, two are in first grade, and one is in second grade. Each child eats either pizza or a sandwich at the party. No child eats both kinds of food. The following must obtain:

Rule: At least one first grader eats pizza.

There are two first graders, and this rule sets up a positive relationship between one of those first graders and pizza. Note that this leaves open the possibility that the other first grader eats pizza too. If the test makers wished to close off that possibility, they would have written "*Exactly* one first grader eats pizza."

Much as in Logical Reasoning and Reading Comprehension, precision of language is a key component to Logic Games. Failing to grasp the difference between "at least" and "exactly" spells doom in this section.

By now you probably sense that where there are positives, there are likely to be negatives, and you wouldn't be mistaken in that assumption. Which brings us to our next category . . .

Negative Relationship

A Negative Relationship rule creates a negative link between two characters or aspects in the game. As always, this is best understood in the context of examples, so here goes.

ART LECTURES: ORDERING

> Seven works of art—P, Q, R, S, T, V, and W—will be exhibited at a local gallery opening. A short lecture will be delivered by the creator of each work during the gallery opening. No two lectures will be delivered at the same time. The sequence of lectures must satisfy the following requirements:
>
> Rule: The lecture on artwork Q will not be delivered immediately before or immediately after the lecture on artwork V.

This rule creates the *opposite* of a cluster: space between characters. "No QV or VQ" would suffice to shorthand this rule and would serve as a quick reminder that these two characters will never occupy adjacent spaces. This means that as soon as we know where one of them is, we know one or two places where the other character CANNOT be: one spot off limits if the known character appears at either end of the ordering and two spots off limits if the known character appears in the interior of the ordering, with a space to the right and left of it. Knowing the location of one of the characters could therefore be used to determine where that other character *could* be, or at least to narrow down the possibilities.

Characters in Choosing games may be characterized by Negative Relationships, such as in the following scenario.

MAGGIE'S COURSES: CHOOSING

> Maggie must select exactly three introductory courses for the upcoming semester. The available introductory courses are biology, communications, English, French, history, literature, and philosophy. Her selection must accord with the following conditions:
>
> Rule: Maggie will not select French if she selects English.

Order doesn't matter in a Choosing game, so we can simply shorthand this rule as "No FE." The implications are that if she chooses French, she can't choose

English, and if she chooses English, she can't choose French. It *is* possible, however, for her to reject both.

It's time to get negative about Placing. Consider the following.

ECONOMIC SEMINARS: PLACING

The participants of two economic seminars, one on free trade and one on venture capital, are to be assigned from among six company employees—Jobson, King, Lee, Manute, Nora, and Orson. King and Nora are vice presidents; the rest of the employees are middle managers. Each employee must participate in at least one seminar. The following rules govern the assignment of employees to seminars:

<u>Rule:</u> Jobson and Manute will not attend a seminar together.

This tells us that anywhere J is, M cannot be, and vice versa. Since J and M must both appear *somewhere*, we can infer from this rule that each one attends exactly one seminar. That's because if either attended both, they would have to be together in at least one of them, in opposition to the rule. Note that we can't tell yet which employee attends which seminar. "No JM" will serves as a good enough reminder until we receive more information that allows us to place them definitively.

Let's bring this rule category to a close with our final game type, Linking.

BIRTHDAY PARTY: LINKING

Six children—Edel, Francie, Gillian, Holly, James, and Kayli—attend a birthday party. Three of the children are in nursery school, two are in first grade, and one is in second grade. Each child eats either pizza or a sandwich at the party. No child eats both kinds of food. The following must obtain:

<u>Rule:</u> No first grader eats pizza.

In a simple Linking game like this one, a Negative Relationship rule translates easily into a Positive rule. Since there are only two food choices, eliminating pizza as an option for first graders means that both first graders must eat sandwiches. In more complicated games, negative rules still can be turned into positive statements, even if it doesn't result in a definite deduction. For example, if the food choices included macaroni, then the implication of this negative rule would be that each first grader must eat either a sandwich or macaroni.

> **TAKE AWAY**
>
> It bears repeating: Whether dealing with a Direct Negative rule, Negative Relationship rule, or any other negative element of the more complex rules to come, always try to turn negatives into positives. Negatives are nice, if that's all you can get. But when you can turn negatives into positives, that's when the games break wide open. Knowing what *is* is more powerful than knowing what *isn't*.

Number Rules

It's very important to understand the numbers that govern each game. Sometimes numerical information is included in the game introduction, while other times it's provided in the rules themselves. Let's work through some typical examples of Number rules, again beginning with the Ordering game type.

ART LECTURES: ORDERING

Seven works of art—P, Q, R, S, T, V, and W—will be exhibited at a local gallery opening. A short lecture will be delivered by the creator of each work during the gallery opening. No two lectures will be delivered at the same time. The sequence of lectures must satisfy the following requirements:

Rule: At least four lectures are delivered after the lecture delivered on artwork Q.

With seven lectures total, you'd be expected to take this to its logical conclusion: Q's lecture must be delivered first, second, or third. Any later would violate the rule. Again, notice how they tell you one thing but fully expect you to derive something more concrete from it.

Now take a look at how numbers may influence a Choosing game.

MAGGIE'S COURSES: CHOOSING

Maggie must select exactly three introductory courses for the upcoming semester. The available introductory courses are biology, communications, English, French, history, literature, and philosophy. Her selection must accord with the following conditions:

Here very important numerical information is provided in the first sentence of the introduction itself, strictly defining the parameters of the game. Maggie must choose exactly three of the available seven courses.

Numbers often come into play in Placing games too.

ECONOMIC SEMINARS: PLACING

The participants of two economic seminars, one on free trade and one on venture capital, are to be assigned from among six company employees—Jobson, King, Lee, Manute, Nora, and Orson. King and Nora are vice presidents; the rest of the employees are middle managers. Each employee must participate in at least one seminar. The following rules govern the assignment of employees to seminars:

<u>Rule:</u> Exactly three middle managers will participate in the venture capital seminar.

Very helpful information, since there are exactly four middle managers total in the game. Since Jobson, Lee, Manute, and Orson are the only middle managers, this rule tells us that three of them will participate in the venture capital semi-nar while the other must sit in on free trade. No doubt some of the questions will play off this breakdown, which you'll need to manipulate in various ways depending on information presented in the other rules or the question stems.

Let's see an example of how numbers may influence a Linking game.

BIRTHDAY PARTY: LINKING

Six children—Edel, Francie, Gillian, Holly, James, and Kayli—attend a birthday party. Three of the children are in nursery school, two are in first grade, and one is in second grade. Each child eats either pizza or a sandwich at the party. No child eats both kinds of food. The following must obtain:

<u>Rule:</u> There are more second graders who eat pizza than first graders who eat pizza.

The birthday party game contains numerical information right in the introduc-tion which, when combined with this number rule, yields a valuable Game Breaker (something we'll discuss in greater depth when we get to Step 3). There is only one second grader in the game, so the only way that *more* second grad-ers than first graders can eat pizza is if *no first graders eat pizza*. So should you write down "No first grade pizza"? No! Since there's only pizza and sandwiches in this game, "no pizza" means "sandwiches." So the full implication of this number rule is that the lone second grader must eat pizza, while both first grad-ers eat sandwiches.

TAKE AWAY

Always drive the information as far as it will go! People who do this usually do well on Logic Games, for the simple reason that this is one of the major things that's tested: the ability to recognize proper logical implications.

Of course, Number rules come in all shapes and sizes, and you'll be seeing plenty of them in the pages ahead. Now, however, it's time to turn our attention to the more complicated rules standing between you and Logic Games success.

While you're expected to instinctively understand the types of conventional rules discussed to this point, there are other kinds of rules that require a bit more brainpower. Let's jump right in with Positive Conditionals.

Complex Rules

Positive Conditional

Positive Conditional rules consist of if/then statements and statements that can be translated into if/then statements. These tend to give many test takers trouble. Let's see how these work, beginning with the same Ordering game we've been using throughout.

ART LECTURES: ORDERING

> Seven works of art—P, Q, R, S, T, V, and W—will be exhibited at a local gallery opening. A short lecture will be delivered by the creator of each work during the gallery opening. No two lectures will be delivered at the same time. The sequence of lectures must satisfy the following requirements:
>
> Rule: If the lecture on artwork Q is third, then the lecture on artwork V is fifth.

In our discussion of if/then statements in the Logical Reasoning chapter, we invoked a technique called reverse and negate (referred to by some as the "contrapositive"). Here's how it works:

The statement "If X, then Y" is logically equivalent to the statement "If NOT Y, then NOT X." We first reverse the order of the characters in the statement, and then we negate both terms to form a statement that means the same as the original.

Try it out in the case of the Ordering rule above: First reverse the terms to get "If V fifth, then Q third." Then (and make sure to do this second step!), negate both to get "If V is NOT fifth, then Q is NOT third." Is that logically equivalent to the original? You bet—for the simple reason that Q third requires V fifth. If V is not fifth, yet Q is *still* third, then we'd be in violation of the rule. Here's how you might shorthand this on the page:

If Q3, then V5
If V NOT 5, then Q NOT 3

Now let's consider a rule that's a bit more complicated.

> Rule: If the lecture on artwork Q is third, then the lecture on artwork V is fifth and the lecture on artwork S is seventh.

In this case, if Q is third, then two specific things must happen. What would violate this rule? If *either* thing didn't happen while Q was third—that is, if V is NOT fifth and/or S is NOT seventh. Either occurrence, by itself, is enough to violate the rule. So here's how we could shorthand both the rule and its logical implications:

$$\text{If Q3, then V5 and S7}$$
$$\text{If V NOT 5 or S NOT 7, then Q NOT 3}$$

Consider one last variation on this theme:

> Rule: If the lecture on artwork R is second and the lecture on artwork T is fourth, then the lecture on artwork W is fifth.

In this case, a combination of two conditions causes a third event to occur. This means that if this third event does *not* occur, then the original *combination* cannot occur either. That means that either part of the combination could happen without the other, or that neither part could occur, which is fine too. The only thing that couldn't happen is both occurring if the third event is missing. We can note this as follows:

$$\text{If R2 and T4, then W5}$$
$$\text{If W NOT 5, then NOT BOTH R2 and T4}$$

We can apply the same type of reasoning to our Choosing game scenario.

MAGGIE'S COURSES: CHOOSING

> Maggie must select exactly three introductory courses for the upcoming semester. The available introductory courses are biology, communications, English, French, history, literature, and philosophy. Her selection must accord with the following conditions:
>
> Rule: Biology is included in any group of courses selected that includes history.

An interesting thing to note from this rule is that not every conditional statement actually contains the words *if* and *then*. Sometimes, as in this case, these words are implied. First translate the rule into proper if/then form: Including biology anytime history is included essentially means that if history is included, then biology is included. The reverse and negate technique works for any conditional statement, regardless of game type, so we can apply it here to derive the rule's logical equivalent: If no biology, then no history. Here are both statements in shorthand form:

$$\text{If H, then B}$$
$$\text{If NO B, then NO H}$$

Now work through the Positive Conditional in our trusty Placing game.

ECONOMIC SEMINARS: PLACING

The participants of two economic seminars, one on free trade and one on venture capital, are to be assigned from among six company employees—Jobson, King, Lee, Manute, Nora, and Orson. King and Nora are vice presidents; the rest of the employees are middle managers. Each employee must participate in at least one seminar. The following rules govern the assignment of employees to seminars:

Rule: If Nora participates in the seminar on free trade, then Jobson participates in the seminar on venture capital.

Here's the shorthand of the original rule, plus the result of reverse and negate:

$$\text{If N ft, then J vc}$$
$$\text{If J NOT vc then N NOT ft}$$

Since the only seminars are free trade and venture capital, we can take this one step further:

$$\text{If J ft, then N vc}$$

Hopefully you're getting the hang of working with Positive Conditionals. Let's try one more example in the context of our Linking scenario.

BIRTHDAY PARTY: LINKING

Six children—Edel, Francie, Gillian, Holly, James, and Kayli—attend a birthday party. Three of the children are in nursery school, two are in first grade, and one is in second grade. Each child eats either pizza or a sandwich at the party. No child eats both kinds of food. The following must obtain:

Rule: If James eats pizza, Francie is in nursery school.

Here's the shorthand of the original rule, plus the result of reverse and negate:

$$\text{If J pizza, then F nurs}$$
$$\text{If F NOT nurs, then J NOT pizza}$$

Sounds reasonable, but you'd be negligent to leave it at that. "Not nursery school" means first or second grade, and "not pizza" means "sandwich," so this last statement can be rewritten in the positive as:

$$\text{If F 1st or 2nd, then J sandwich}$$

With this info under our belts, how nice would it be for a question to place Francie in first or second grade, and then ask what must be true? "James does not eat pizza" would be a fine answer to allow us to cash in on this work. Or the question might ask what CANNOT be true, in which case "James eats pizza" would get the point. Anyway, we're getting a bit ahead of ourselves, since cashing in comes after we've dissected the rules *and* tried our best to Search for Game Breakers, Step 3 of our Essential Strategy. But you can see where we're heading. Let's get back to the present discussion with a look at the next complex rule type—Negative Conditionals.

Negative Conditional

Negative Conditional rules also consist of if/then statements and statements that can be translated into if/then statements. However, unlike Positive Conditionals, these specify that when one thing happens, another thing *doesn't* happen. Here are some examples for each of the major game types.

ART LECTURES: ORDERING

> Seven works of art—P, Q, R, S, T, V, and W—will be exhibited at a local gallery opening. A short lecture will be delivered by the creator of each work during the gallery opening. No two lectures will be delivered at the same time. The sequence of lectures must satisfy the following requirements:
>
> Rule: If the lecture on artwork Q is third, then the lecture on artwork V is not fifth.

The key to using reverse and negate for Negative Conditional rules is to remember that two negatives make a positive. In the Ordering rule above, the negation of "V NOT fifth" is "V fifth." So here's how we can shorthand the rule, and its logical implication:

$$\text{If Q3, then V NOT 5}$$
$$\text{If V5, then Q NOT 3}$$

Let's apply this to one of the more complicated Ordering rules discussed earlier:

> Rule: If the lecture on artwork R is second and the lecture on artwork T is fourth, then the lecture on artwork W is not fifth.

Here's a shorthanded version of the rule plus the result when we apply reverse and negate:

$$\text{If R2 and T4, then W NOT 5}$$
$$\text{If W5, then NOT BOTH R2 and T4}$$

Try the next one based on our Choosing game intro.

MAGGIE'S COURSES: CHOOSING

Maggie must select exactly three introductory courses for the upcoming semester. The available introductory courses are biology, communications, English, French, history, literature, and philosophy. Her selection must accord with the following conditions:

Rule: If biology is selected, history is not selected.

Here's the rule and its logical equivalent in shorthand form:

$$\text{If B, then No H}$$
$$\text{If H, then NO B}$$

Notice that in this case the upshot is that biology and history can never be included together in the group of courses Maggie selects.

Now try it with Placing.

ECONOMIC SEMINARS: PLACING

The participants of two economic seminars, one on free trade and one on venture capital, are to be assigned from among six company employees—Jobson, King, Lee, Manute, Nora, and Orson. King and Nora are vice presidents; the rest of the employees are middle managers. Each employee must participate in at least one seminar. The following rules govern the assignment of employees to seminars:

Rule: If Nora participates in the seminar on free trade, then Jobson does not participate in the seminar on venture capital.

Here's the shorthand of the original rule, plus the result of reverse and negate:

$$\text{If Nft, then J NOT vc}$$
$$\text{If Jvc, then N NOT ft}$$

Since in this case free trade and venture capital are the only two seminars, we can take this one step further:

$$\text{If Nft, then Jft}$$
$$\text{If Jvc, then Nvc}$$

Bring it on home for Negative Conditionals with the Linking scenario . . .

BIRTHDAY PARTY: LINKING

> Six children—Edel, Francie, Gillian, Holly, James, and Kayli—attend a birthday party. Three of the children are in nursery school, two are in first grade, and one is in second grade. Each child eats either pizza or a sandwich at the party. No child eats both kinds of food. The following must obtain:
>
> Rule: If James eats pizza, Francie is not in nursery school.

Here's the shorthand of the original rule, plus the result of reverse and negate:

> If J pizza, then F NOT nurs
> If F nurs, then J NOT pizza

Can we take this one step further as well? Yup, and we should since it's always best to gather as much positive information as possible. "Not nursery school" means first or second grade. "Not pizza" means "sandwich." So here's our final understanding of this rule:

> If J pizza, then F 1st or 2nd
> If F nurs, then J sand

Unless

Some rules are built around the word *unless*. On the LSAT, you might see a rule indicating that a certain thing can't happen *unless* something else happens. Here's an example.

MAGGIE'S COURSES: CHOOSING

> Maggie must select exactly three introductory courses for the upcoming semester. The available introductory courses are biology, communications, English, French, history, literature, and philosophy. Her selection must accord with the following conditions:
>
> Rule: Biology is not selected unless history is selected.

To say that biology is not selected unless history is selected is the same as saying that biology requires history:

> If B, then H

To which we can now apply reverse and negate:

> If NO H, then NO B

Notice that the selection of history does not *guarantee* the selection of biology—it merely makes it possible. There's no equivalency beginning "If H . . ." because if history is selected, biology *may* be selected, but it need not be. All we know for sure from this "unless" rule are the two if/then statements listed above.

Either

Some rules contain the word *either*. Here are a few examples to chew on for the Ordering and Choosing game varieties.

ART LECTURES: ORDERING

Seven works of art—P, Q, R, S, T, V, and W—will be exhibited at a local gallery opening. A short lecture will be delivered by the creator of each work during the gallery opening. No two lectures will be delivered at the same time. The sequence of lectures must satisfy the following requirements:

Rule: The lecture on artwork T is either first or sixth.

The implications are that if some lecture beside T's lecture is first, T's must be sixth, and if some lecture beside T's lecture is sixth, T's must be first.

Here's another way *either* can be used in an Ordering rule:

Rule: Either the lecture on artwork T or the lecture on artwork V must be third.

In this case, it makes sense to jot down T/V above the third slot in your blueprint. As soon as you see one of those characters in some other spot, you can pencil the other character into spot 3.

Now see how *either* plays out in the context of a Choosing example.

MAGGIE'S COURSES: CHOOSING

Maggie must select exactly three introductory courses for the upcoming semester. The available introductory courses are biology, communications, English, French, history, literature, and philosophy. Her selection must accord with the following conditions:

Rule: Either communications or philosophy will be selected.

That means that a group with communications but not philosophy is okay. A group with philosophy but not communications is also okay. A group with *both* communications *and* philosophy is *also okay.*

Wait a minute—that seems counterintuitive to many, since the rule seems to say that we need either one or the other. However, on the LSAT the idea "but not both" will be included in the rule if the intention is that both characters cannot be included in the group. The only thing that violates the rule as stated above is a group of chosen courses that includes *neither* communications nor philosophy.

If you're having trouble interpreting a rule, think about what scenarios would *violate* that rule. That should help you zero in on what the rule really means and how it will play out throughout the game.

Only If

An "only if" statement can be turned into an if/then statement by placing the "then" after the "only" term. For example, consider the following Placing rule.

ECONOMIC SEMINARS: PLACING

The participants of two economic seminars, one on free trade and one on venture capital, are to be assigned from among six company employees—Jobson, King, Lee, Manute, Nora, and Orson. King and Nora are vice presidents; the rest of the employees are middle managers. Each employee must participate in at least one seminar. The following rules govern the assignment of employees to seminars:

<u>Rule:</u> Orson participates in the seminar on free trade only if King participates in the seminar on venture capital.

There are two parts of an "only if" statement: the part attached to the "only if" phrase (here, K vc) and the other condition in the statement (here, O ft). This other condition—in this case, Orson joining free trade—relies on the "only if" condition. Here, that means that if Orson participates in free trade, then King must participate in venture capital; the "only if" phrase in the statement demands this. So we can turn this "only if" statement into a standard if/then statement, like so:

$$\text{If O ft, then K vc}$$

In fact, we can even derive a general rule from this: For any "only if" statement, throw an "if" in front of the other condition and a "then" in front of the condition associated with the "only if" phrase and you'll end up with a valid statement in the form of "If X, then Y." It sounds confusing, but go back to look how we applied this rule to the example above and it should eventually click. The beauty of restating the "only if" statement as an if/then statement is that now we can apply reverse and negate to yield yet another valid statement:

$$\text{If K NOT vc, then O NOT ft}$$

Do we stop there? No! Remember to translate negatives into positives whenever possible. Since the only choices in this game are free trade and venture capital, we can get rid of the two NOTs:

$$\text{If K ft, then O vc}$$

That's a lot of information derived from a seemingly innocuous "only if" rule, but that's what Logic Games success is all about.

If and Only If

What if we add an "if" to the "only if" statement? Let's use the same Placing rule to find out.

ECONOMIC SEMINARS: PLACING

> The participants of two economic seminars, one on free trade and one on venture capital, are to be assigned from among six company employees—Jobson, King, Lee, Manute, Nora, and Orson. King and Nora are vice presidents; the rest of the employees are middle managers. Each employee must participate in at least one seminar. The following rules govern the assignment of employees to seminars:
>
> Rule: Orson participates in the seminar on free trade if and only if King participates in the seminar on venture capital.

The interpretation of the "only if" part of the rule remains the same as what we just deduced:

$$\text{If O ft, then K vc}$$
$$\text{If K ft, then O vc}$$

However, we must also take the "if" part into account:

$$\text{If K vc, then O ft}$$

Using reverse and negate and translating negatives to positives yields:

$$\text{If O vc, then K ft}$$

Here's the difference: The "only if" rule allows for the possibility that King and Orson participate together in the seminar on venture capital. The "*if and only if*" version of the rule does not allow for this possibility. It forces these two employees to split up, no matter what. The test makers don't use "if and only if" very often, but they have in the past, and nothing stops them from doing so in the future. Your confidence will increase when you go into the test feeling as if you're ready for anything they may throw your way.

That does it for Step 2, Get the Specs. The specs of the game are mainly spelled out in the rules, although some important specifications, especially number information, may be included in the introduction as well. The line between what we call Conventional and Complex rules may blur in cases. For example, some Conditional rules may become simple to you with practice, while a Number rule may throw you for a loop. Don't get hung up in the terminology—just study the categories above until these kinds of rules discussed, and their logical equivalencies, make sense and become second nature to you. Hopefully, even the toughest of rules will seem conventional to you by test day. The examples above cover the majority of rule scenarios you'll come across, but you'll likely encounter variations and combinations as well. You'll get plenty of practice working with rules from the eight games in this book. Extend what you learn from this section, and from those eight games, to every practice game you try.

Search for Game Breakers

As we discussed, we've added an extra step between tackling the introduction and the rules and tackling the questions. Now that you've created your blueprint and mapped out the specs of the game by analyzing the rules individually, the next important step is to combine the rules to form deductions: additional conditions not explicitly stated but that nonetheless must be true based on the given information. We call such deductions "Game Breakers" because of their ability to break the game wide open. Game Breakers come in three major varieties:

- Standard Combinations

- Number Crunching

- Restricted Possibilities

Let's get some practice with each.

Standard Combinations

Some rules link up fairly easily. For example, consider the following two rules:

If X is selected, then Y is selected.

If Y is selected, then Z is not selected.

Now, they don't come right out and say it, but it must be true that selecting X means NOT selecting Z. This is a simple matter of putting two and two together.

TAKE AWAY | Whenever you form a deduction, add it to your list of shorthanded rules. A valid deduction applies throughout the entire game exactly as if it were a given rule.

Now try one on your own. Consider the following game setup. Combine the rules to deduce as much additional information as you can.

> Six children—Edel, Francie, Gillian, Holly, James, and Kayli—attend a birthday party.
> Three of the children are in nursery school, two are in first grade, and one is in second grade.
> Each child eats either pizza or a sandwich at the party. No child eats both kinds of food. The
> following must obtain:
> > Francie and James are in the same grade.
> > No first grader eats a sandwich.
> > Exactly two nursery school children eat pizza.
> > James does not eat pizza.

Rule 4, a Direct Negative, is the best place to start.

> **TAKE AWAY**
>
> You don't have to tackle the rules in the order in which they're presented.
> It's better to begin with the most concrete rule first, because it's easier to
> build the rest of the rules around that definite information.

If James does not eat pizza, **James must eat a sandwich.** Rule 1 contains James
too, so let's go there next.

> **TAKE AWAY**
>
> Pay careful attention when more than one rule contains the same
> character. That's a clue that Game Breakers may be lurking in a
> combination of those rules.

If Francie and James are in the same grade, that must be nursery school or first
grade, since there's only one second grader. But Rule 2 says that no first grader
eats a sandwich, and we've already determined from Rule 4 that James *does* eat
a sandwich. So **Francie and James must be in nursery school.** Rule 3 then allows us to determine that **Francie must eat pizza,** since James must be the one
nursery school sandwich eater, leaving Francie and one other child as the two
nursery school pizza eaters.

Notice how we've already pinned down the complete status of two of the six
children, before even getting to the questions. Having this extra information at
the start will definitely make the game much easier. A standard combination of
rules led us to these Game Breakers.

Number Crunching

We've seen already (including in the previous example) how working the numbers of the game can lead to new and important information. Number rules may
appear in the game's introduction, or in the indented rules. Wherever you see
numerical information, see if you can push it further.

Consider the following game setup. See if you can crunch the numbers to yield new information.

ECONOMIC SEMINARS: PLACING

The participants of two economic seminars, one on free trade and one on venture capital, are to be assigned from among six company employees—Jobson, King, Lee, Manute, Nora, and Orson. King and Nora are vice presidents; the rest of the employees are middle managers. Each employee must participate in at least one seminar. The following rules govern the assignment of employees to seminars:

Jobson does not participate in the same seminar as Manute.

There is at most one vice president participating in each seminar.

If King participates in a seminar, Lee participates in that seminar.

There is exactly one more middle manager than vice president at the seminar on venture capital.

The introduction indicates that there are exactly two vice presidents, King and Nora. We can combine this with Rule 2 to deduce that King and Nora cannot attend a seminar together. "At most one VP in each" means that two VPs at a single seminar is a no-no. So King attends one seminar, while Nora attends the other. Rule 3 involves King, so it makes sense to look there next. Wherever King is, Lee is. So now for starters we have KL on one side, and N on the other. It doesn't matter that we don't yet know exactly which seminars these people attend.

TAKE AWAY

In Placing games, knowing who must and must not be placed together can be just as important as knowing where they are. Drive the information forward in any way you can.

The fact that we know exactly how many VPs are at each seminar (one) sheds a whole new light on Rule 4: It allows us to determine that there must be exactly two middle managers at the venture capital seminar. This fact that may yield a point all on its own, but it will also no doubt be of help in answering all of the questions. Any time rules involve numbers, drive the information as far as you can. Often, games that seem wide open get pretty well defined after you crunch the numbers.

Restricted Possibilities

In cases in which only two options are possible (such as when a character can go in only one of two spots), it's worth your while to check out what happens in each case. In the best case scenario, you'll be able to create two options of the game's universe, leaving very little up in the air. Here's the game we were just working on, except that we've made a small change in the opening paragraph. Find the difference and then take the information as far as you can.

> The participants of two economic seminars, one on free trade and one on venture capital, are to be assigned from among six company employees—Jobson, King, Lee, Manute, Nora, and Orson. King and Nora are vice presidents; the rest of the employees are middle managers. Each employee must participate in exactly one seminar. The following rules govern the assignment of employees to seminars:
>
> Jobson does not participate in the same seminar as Manute.
>
> There is at most one vice president participating in each seminar.
>
> If King participates in a seminar, Lee participates in that seminar.
>
> There is exactly one more middle manager than vice president at the seminar on venture capital.

Did you see the difference? Now each employee participates in exactly one seminar. Let's see where that takes us. We already concluded that there must be exactly three participants in the venture capital seminar (one vice president and two middle managers). But if each employee is in only one seminar, then the other three employees must be in the free trade seminar.

Some test takers would stop their search for Game Breakers at this point and move on to the questions, and some may even do fairly well on the game. But the best Logic Games practitioners would recognize an opportunity to drive the information even further.

We just discovered through Number Crunching that King, Lee, and one other employee must participate in one of the seminars, while Nora and the remaining two employees must participate in the other. Since there are only two seminars, there are only two ways we can do this: Place King in free trade or place Nora in free trade. Let's see what happens in the first case:

Possibility 1: K ft

Now we can incorporate Rule 1. We have to split up Jobson and Manute, and there's only one space left in free trade, so one of them must go there while the other must attend venture capital. We don't know which is which yet, but notice what this reveals: Orson, the only employee left, must take the final spot alongside Nora in venture capital. So Possibility 1 boils down to this:

Possibility 1: K ft

Pretty good. We now know everything that happens when King is the VP in free trade, except for the placement of J and M. The only other possible option is to place Nora in free trade, and the same scenario plays out.

Possibility 2: N ft

FT
N O (J/M)

VC
K L (J/M)

The possibilities are restricted to these two scenarios. In both cases, Nora must be with Orson, which by extension means that Orson cannot be with King or Lee. Armed with all of these Game Breakers, the questions should now fall very quickly. Even a difficult question would merely require checking the new information given in that specific question against the restricted possibilities set forth in the two options.

Combining rules, crunching the numbers, and boiling down the possibilities are three powerful ways to uncover Game Breakers. Not every game contains them, but when Game Breakers are available, finding them can turn a killer game into cake.

You may be wondering how long you should look for Game Breakers before going to the questions. It's a tough issue. You don't want to miss major deductions like the ones you've just seen. But you can't spend all day looking for stuff that isn't there.

Here's the best approach: Look for the important kinds of Game Breakers you've just seen: Standard Combinations, Number Crunching, and Restricted Possibilities. Then hit the questions. Here's one more rule of thumb: Games that have pretty simple setups are less likely to have big Game Breakers. So if a game seems very easy at first glance, it is less likely to have Game Breakers that make it even easier. However, a game that looks like an absolute killer probably has some Game Breakers waiting to be found. Spend more time up front on the killer games. After a while you'll get a sense for when you've spent enough time looking for Game Breakers. That's just one benefit you'll get from practicing the skills you learn in this book.

Cash In: Tackling the Questions

We're finally at the point of answering those darned questions! Whew! The purpose of all the preliminary analysis in Steps 1 through 3 is, of course, to cash in—to rack up points by answering the questions accurately and efficiently. The better you handle the rules, and the more Game Breakers you discover, the easier the questions will be. But first we have a few things to cover regarding the basics of dealing with Logic Games questions.

New Info

You'll find that many questions provide *new information*, which you are expected to add to what you already know about the game. Most often, these questions begin with the word *if.* Here are some examples based on the games discussed above:

If Maggie does not select history or literature, then . . .

If Nora participates in the seminar on venture capital, then . . .

If Gillian is not in the same grade as Holly, then . . .

If the lecture on artwork P is sixth, then . . .

New information provided in a question stem applies to that question only. Do not carry it over to other questions. Only the rules and any Game Breakers you derive from those rules apply throughout the entire game. When you see a question that includes new info, make a copy of your sketch for use in that one question only. You don't want to mark up your blueprint with info that only applies to one question. It only takes a few seconds to recopy your sketch. Put the new information into your new copy and see where it takes you.

No Info

Some questions do not contain new information. Questions that ask what must, could, or cannot be true, without providing the kind of information in the examples above, test your basic understanding of the scenario and the rules. If you've discovered Game Breakers or plotted out a Restricted Possibility scenario, you should be able to knock off these questions quickly because you've already done the work!

The Suitability Question

Nearly all logic games contain a question that asks you to pick out the one acceptable ordering or arrangement of characters from among the five choices. In these, only one of the choices will satisfy every rule and thus form a suitable scenario. The fastest way to approach such "Suitability" questions is to work backward from the rules. That is, begin with the first rule and test that against all the choices, crossing off the ones that don't conform. When you've finished checking all the rules, only one choice will be left standing.

Try out the method above to answer the question on the next page.

ART LECTURE: ORDERING

Seven works of art—P, Q, R, S, T, V, and W—will be exhibited at a local gallery opening. A short lecture will be delivered by the creator of each work during the gallery opening. No two lectures will be delivered at the same time. The sequence of lectures must satisfy the following requirements:

    The lecture on artwork R is delivered second or sixth.

    The lecture on artwork T is delivered fourth.

    The lecture on artwork S is delivered at some point after the lecture on artwork V.

    The lecture on artwork P is delivered either immediately before or immediately after the lecture on artwork W.

Which one of the following could be an accurate list of artwork lectures delivered in order from first to last?

    (A) Q, V, P, T, W, R, S

    (B) Q, V, W, P, T, R, S

    (C) S, R, Q, T, P, W, V

    (D) V, R, S, T, W, P, Q

    (E) W, P, R, T, V, Q, S

Take the rules one at a time, scanning the choices for orderings that do not conform. Here's what you should have found:

Choice **E** violates Rule 1 by placing R third.

Choice **B** violates Rule 2 by placing T fifth.

Choice **C** violates Rule 3 by placing S before V.

Choice **A** violates Rule 4 by splitting up P and W.

D remains and is therefore the correct answer to this common Suitability question.

TAKE AWAY

There is no need to double-check the right answer. If you've applied the rules properly to eliminate the other four choices, the one that remains must contain a suitable ordering. Developing confidence in your work will help you save time. You'll be surprised how a few seconds gained here and there really add up.

THE REAL DEAL: PRACTICE SET

It's time to apply what you've learned to four real, previously administered LSAT logic games. Try each game on your own, and then thoroughly study the explanations that follow.

Game 1

(PrepTest 46, Section 4, Qs. 1–6)

<u>Questions 1–6</u>

Exactly six guideposts, numbered 1 through 6, mark a mountain trail. Each guidepost pictures a different one of six animals—fox, grizzly, hare, lynx, moose, or porcupine. The following conditions must apply:

The grizzly is pictured on either guidepost 3 or guidepost 4.

The moose guidepost is numbered lower than the hare guidepost.

The lynx guidepost is numbered lower than the moose guidepost but higher than the fox guidepost.

1. Which one of the following could be an accurate list of the animals pictured on the guideposts, listed in order from guidepost 1 through guidepost 6?

   (A) fox, lynx, grizzly, porcupine, moose, hare
   (B) fox, lynx, moose, hare, grizzly, porcupine
   (C) fox, moose, grizzly, lynx, hare, porcupine
   (D) lynx, fox, moose, grizzly, hare, porcupine
   (E) porcupine, fox, hare, grizzly, lynx, moose

2. Which one of the following animals CANNOT be the one pictured on guidepost 3?

   (A) fox
   (B) grizzly
   (C) lynx
   (D) moose
   (E) porcupine

3. If the moose is pictured on guidepost 3, then which one of the following is the lowest numbered guidepost that could picture the porcupine?

   (A) guidepost 1
   (B) guidepost 2
   (C) guidepost 4
   (D) guidepost 5
   (E) guidepost 6

4. If guidepost 5 does not picture the moose, then which one of the following must be true?

   (A) The lynx is pictured on guidepost 2.
   (B) The moose is pictured on guidepost 3.
   (C) The grizzly is pictured on guidepost 4.
   (D) The porcupine is pictured on guidepost 5.
   (E) The hare is pictured on guidepost 6.

5. Which one of the following animals could be pictured on any one of the six guideposts?

   (A) fox
   (B) hare
   (C) lynx
   (D) moose
   (E) porcupine

6. If the moose guidepost is numbered exactly one higher than the lynx guidepost, then which one of the following could be true?

   (A) Guidepost 5 pictures the hare.
   (B) Guidepost 4 pictures the moose.
   (C) Guidepost 4 pictures the porcupine.
   (D) Guidepost 3 pictures the lynx.
   (E) Guidepost 3 pictures the porcupine.

Game 1: Guided Explanation

Animal Guideposts

Step 1: Create a Blueprint. The fact that there are six numbered guideposts with a different picture on each tells us this is a straightforward Ordering game. The standard Ordering sketch consists simply of the numbers in order from left to right on the page, with the characters who will fill those spaces off to the side:

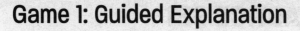

Step 2: Get the Specs.

Rule 1. This is nearly a Direct Positive rule, limiting G's possibilities to spots 3 and 4. We can build this rule right into our sketch using arrows from G to the numbers 3 and 4.

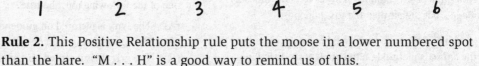

Rule 2. This Positive Relationship rule puts the moose in a lower numbered spot than the hare. "M . . . H" is a good way to remind us of this.

> **TAKE AWAY**
>
> Use dots between entities in Ordering rules to indicate that one character is lower in the ordering than another character, although you don't know *how much* lower.

Rule 3. This is a compound rule that provides two different pieces of relational information. The lynx has a relationship with both the moose and the fox—lower than one but higher than the other. Be careful to get the order right: "F . . . L . . . M" does the trick.

Step 3: Search for Game Breakers. The fact that both Rules 2 and 3 mention the moose suggests that these rules are ripe for a standard combination, and indeed combining them yields a four-character "F . . . L . . . M . . . H" cluster that must always fit somewhere within the six available spaces.

It's likely that many people spotted this deduction, but what separates the best gamers from the rest is asking the follow-up question: *Where can this cluster go?* It's worth looking into, especially since character G is restricted to one of two spots. So let's see what happens in each case.

Possibility 1: G 3rd

If G is third, F cannot come after G since that wouldn't leave enough room at the end for the LMH cluster that must follow F. So F must be first or second. If F is second, then LMH must be fourth, fifth, and sixth respectively, forcing free agent P into space 1.

> "Free agents" are characters with few or no restrictions. They will often be the ones used to round out arrangements after every other entity is placed.

TAKE AWAY

The other possibility in this G3 option is that F is first, in which case the LMH cluster and free agent P will fill out the ordering in numerous possible ways.

Possibility 2: G 4th

If G is fourth, F can't be fifth, sixth, or even third, since we still need to place LMH after F. So once again, F must be first or second, while LMH and free agent P vie for the other spots.

Analyzing the two options, you know a lot about how the characters will be arranged. For example, no matter what, *F must be 1 or 2. H must be 5 or 6,* and so on. You don't have to write down all the combinations, but knowing that you have a big cluster to place will make the questions much easier.

Here's what we have to work with heading into the questions:

Possibility 1: G 3rd

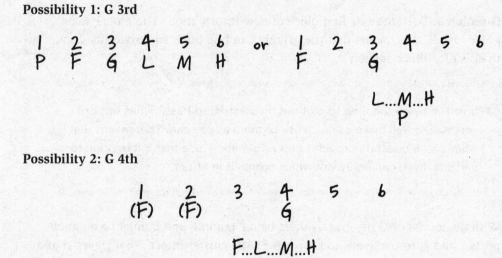

Possibility 2: G 4th

Step 4: Cash In.

Question 1: A. Apply the Suitability technique discussed earlier. Rule 1 takes out choice **B**, which improperly places the grizzly in spot 5. Rule 2 kills **E**, which has the moose numbered higher than the hare. **C** violates the first part of Rule 3, while **D** violates the second part. **A** remains and is correct.

 TAKE AWAY — Even when you've plotted out a Restricted Possibilities scenario, scanning the choices for rule violations is still an efficient and quick way to tackle the Suitability question.

Question 2: A. Here's your reward for plotting out the options and noticing that in both cases the fox must be in either the first or second spot. F can't be 3, which gives us a quick and easy point for this question.

 TAKE AWAY — When no new information is provided in a question stem, that's a good hint that deductions are possible from the setup information alone. If you've correctly worked out the Game Breakers, expect to pick up at least one five-second point as a reward for this good work. Don't second guess yourself thinking "That was too easy—I must have done something wrong . . ." The truth is that you did something *right* by thinking through the relevant issues up front.

Question 3: D. Here's our first piece of new information: The moose is on guidepost 3. This means that the grizzly can't be on 3, so Possibility 2 must be in effect for this question.

TAKE AWAY — If you've taken the time to plot out the Restricted Possibilities options, you may as well make as much use of them as you can. That means that whenever a question provides new information, use that information to first see if you can figure out which option is in effect.

With the moose on 3 the grizzly must be on 4, and F and L must be on guideposts 1 and 2, respectively, to keep our FLMH cluster intact. That leaves H and free agent P to float between spots 5 and 6. The lowest the porcupine could be is fifth, with the hare bringing up the rear, so **D** is correct.

Question 4: A. Next we're told that the moose can't be fifth, so let's bounce that information off the options. The first scenario in Possibility 1 forces M squarely into that forbidden spot, so that's off limits. The other possibility, with F in spot 1 and G in 3, has more flexibility, so let's try that. M can't be second, because L must come between F and M. M can never be sixth, because H must follow M, and the question stem says M can't be fifth. So the only place for M is fourth, with L second and H and P floating between spots 5 and 6:

1	2	3	4	5	6
F	L	G	M	(H)	(P)

As it happens, knowing that this arrangement is possible eliminates all four wrong choices. So if you checked the choices at this point, you could pick **A**. But if you didn't see that, you could still quickly work through Possibility 2. In that option, G is fourth, so for M to come after G, M would have to be fifth with H sixth—no good. So M must be before G. With F and L necessarily preceding M, the only way to get M before G would be if the ordering started out with FLM, again leaving H and P to float between the last two spots:

1	2	3	4	5	6
F	L	M	G	(H)	(P)

Checking the choices against these two possibilities, we see that the lynx must be in the second spot no matter what, choice **A**. The rest of the choices all could be true, but they need not be.

> **TAKE AWAY**
>
> Don't be afraid to plot out multiple possible orderings if need be. It doesn't take too long to work through the possibilities if you resolve yourself to do it. What does eat up time is hesitating and wondering what to do next, or wondering whether it will be worth it to pursue a certain line of reasoning. Keep moving forward at all times.

Question 5: E. This one's another "gimme" for anyone who put thought into the restrictions placed on each character—and more important, the lack of restrictions placed on the porcupine. All along we've been saying that P is a "free agent," and here we pick up a quick and easy point from this realization. F, L, M, and H are limited by their respective places in that cluster, while G is strictly limited by Rule 1 to guidepost 3 or 4. Porcupine gets the point for this one, choice **E**.

Question 6: A. The new information in this one establishes that LM must be slotted in as a pair, so naturally we turn to our options to see how this might be done. The first scenario of Possibility 1 satisfies this mandate already, so get that down on the page. The second scenario in Possibility 1, with F first and G third, allows for the LM cluster as long as L goes fourth and M goes fifth. That forces H sixth, leaving P to take the second spot. Now check Possibility 2, where G is fourth. The LM cluster can't go in spaces 5 and 6, since that would leave no room for H. Since F must always precede L, the only way to satisfy the stem in this case would be to put F first with L second and M third, leaving H and P to float between remaining slots 5 and 6. That exhausts the possibilities, so we can now simply compare the choices against these three scenarios:

1	2	3	4	5	6
P	F	G	L	M	H

1	2	3	4	5	6
F	P	G	L	M	H

1	2	3	4	5	6
F	L	M	G	(H)	(P)

The third of these possible orderings shows that the hare could be fifth, so **A** is correct. Check the other choices against the possibilities above, and you'll see that they are all impossible.

TAKE AWAY

In "could be true" questions, all of the wrong choices must be impossible.

TAKE AWAY

The answers to Logic Games questions are objectively correct, so once you find one that works, even if it's choice **A**, you don't have to waste time checking the others. Develop the confidence to make your selection, and move on.

Okay, see how things go with "Friends in Photos" on the following page.

Game 2

(PrepTest 45, Section 3, Qs. 13–17)

Note: The questions in this set have been renumbered for the purpose of this exercise.

<u>Questions 1–5</u>

An album contains photographs picturing seven friends: Raimundo, Selma, Ty, Umiko, Wendy, Yakira, Zack. The friends appear either alone or in groups with one another, in accordance with the following:

Wendy appears in every photograph that Selma appears in.

Selma appears in every photograph that Umiko appears in.

Raimundo appears in every photograph that Yakira does not appear in.

Neither Ty nor Raimundo appears in any photograph that Wendy appears in.

1. Which one of the following could be a complete and accurate list of the friends who appear together in a photograph?

   (A) Raimundo, Selma, Ty, Wendy
   (B) Raimundo, Ty, Yakira, Zack
   (C) Raimundo, Wendy, Yakira, Zack
   (D) Selma, Ty, Umiko, Yakira
   (E) Selma, Ty, Umiko, Zack

2. If Ty and Zack appear together in a photograph, then which one of the following must be true?

   (A) Selma also appears in the photograph.
   (B) Yakira also appears in the photograph.
   (C) Wendy also appears in the photograph.
   (D) Raimundo does not appear in the photograph.
   (E) Umiko does not appear in the photograph.

3. What is the maximum number of friends who could appear in a photograph that Yakira does not appear in?

   (A) six
   (B) five
   (C) four
   (D) three
   (E) two

4. If Umiko and Zack appear together in a photograph, then exactly how many of the other friends must also appear in that photograph?

   (A) four
   (B) three
   (C) two
   (D) one
   (E) zero

5. If exactly three friends appear together in a photograph, then each of the following could be true EXCEPT:

   (A) Selma and Zack both appear in the photograph.
   (B) Ty and Yakira both appear in the photograph.
   (C) Wendy and Selma both appear in the photograph.
   (D) Yakira and Zack both appear in the photograph.
   (E) Zack and Raimundo both appear in the photograph.

Game 2: Guided Explanation

Friends in Photos

Step 1: Create a Blueprint. The appearance of friends "either alone or in groups" suggests that the action of this game will involve selecting from among the seven characters to form an acceptable collection of friends. Here, the group is gathered for a photo, but it could just as easily be to receive an award, to take on an assignment—anything really. The important thing is to notice that this is a Choosing game and to adopt the proper mindset for it. We're given no numerical information as to how many friends are chosen, other than "one or more." Nor are the friends differentiated in any way. So the best we can do for an initial sketch is to get the characters down on the page and move on to see what the rules will do with them.

R   S   T   U   W   Y   Z

Step 2: Get the Specs. You can think about Choosing games in terms of who's in and who's out, which are the basic issues the rules will concern. Let's check them out.

Rule 1: Wendy appearing everywhere that Selma appears is a Positive Conditional in disguise. What it really means, in true if/then conditional form, is "If S, then W." Applying the reverse and negate technique yields "If NOT W, then NOT S."

TAKE AWAY

Translate formal logic statements into if/then form whenever possible. Not only will that make the rule easier to work with, but it will also allow you to apply reverse and negate to form its logical equivalent which may be tested directly or lead to you the deductions you'll need to pick up points.

Rule 2: The same reasoning applies here, this time concerning Selma and Umiko: The proper translation, and its reverse and negate companion, are "If U, then S" and "If NOT S, then NOT U."

Rule 3: Same idea, but with a slight twist: the "not" at the end. The valid translation is "If NOT Y, then R." Reverse and negate yields "If NOT R, then Y."

Rule 4: This one is a compound Negative Conditional, so handle it carefully. "If W, then NOT T and NOT R." The logical equivalent of this is formed once again by reversing and negating the terms: "If T or R or both, then NOT W."

TAKE AWAY

Remember that negating a negative yields a positive.

Step 3: Search for Game Breakers. Our search for Game Breakers—deductions that blow the game wide open—should be fruitful, considering that there is a significant overlap of characters among the rules. Selma appears in Rules 1 and 2. Raimundo appears in Rules 3 and 4. And Wendy appears in Rules 1 and 4. Did you make the most of the combination opportunities? Let's put it all together.

We saw from Rule 2 that U requires S, and from Rule 1 that S requires W. Combining those yields "If U → S → W." Note that S can be included without U, and W can be included without S or U. Moving on, Rule 4 tells us the consequence of W is no T or R, so we can expand our logical chain to read: "If U → S → W → NO T, NO R." To that we can add the logical equivalent of Rule 3, which we saw to be the addition of Y to any group that does not have R. Adding this long chain of deductions to the other logical equivalencies we derived from the rules puts us in a powerful position to pick up five points. Here's what we have to work with heading into the questions:

If U → S → W → NO T, NO R → Y

If NO S, then NO U

If NO W, then NO S and NO U

If NO Y, then R

If NO R, then Y

If T or R or both, then NO W, NO S, NO U

Notice that the inclusion of U triggers the most repercussions, while Z is not included in any rule or deduction, making this character our free agent.

TAKE AWAY

Stay aware of each character's level of involvement in the game. In some cases, this knowledge will help lead you in the right direction.

Step 4: Cash In.

Question 1: B. While we're armed with tons of information, what we really need for that information to be useful is for something to set it in motion. As for our standard Suitability question, it makes sense to stick to our method and check the choices directly against each rule. Choices **D** and **E** have Selma without Wendy, in direct violation of Rule 1. No choices violate Rule 2. For Rule 3, we need to focus on photos without Yakira—in this case, choices **A** and **E**. But we already eliminated **E**, so we don't have to check that one again.

In a Suitability question, you only need one reason to eliminate a choice. Once you see that a choice violates a rule, clearly cross off that choice and don't visit it again.

A satisfies Rule 3 by including Raimundo in the absence of Yakira, so we move on. **A** and **C** violate Rule 4, leaving choice **B** as the acceptable group of friends for the photo.

Question 2: E. Ty and Zack are in for this one, so let's see where that leads us. A quick glance at our completed sketch reminds us that "If T or R, then NO W, NO S, NO U." Choice **E** gets the point. Boom.

Many LSAT test takers stress out over the Logic Games section and feel a need to rush through the setup to get to the questions as quickly as possible. However, the best Logic Games players know that the games are usually won up front with the discovery of Game Breakers. The time taken to scope those out is repaid in spades by 10-second questions like this one.

Question 3: D. Simply use the statements in the final sketch to follow the chain of deductions set off by "NO Y": No Y means R is included, which in turn means no W, no S, and no U. That leaves T and free agent Z, either of whom can join R in an acceptable photo. So without Y, the group must include R, and it could include T and Z but no one else. Three is therefore the maximum number of people in a picture without Y, choice **D**.

Question 4: B. This one is another breeze, thanks to the work we did up front. Umiko is our most powerful trigger:

$$\text{If } U \rightarrow S \rightarrow W \rightarrow NO\ T,\ NO\ R \rightarrow Y$$

So if U and Z are in the picture, the picture must consist of U, Z, S, W, and Y—everyone except T and R. That means three more besides U and Z, choice **B**.

Question 5: A. This one is more difficult because it's fairly vague. We're told only the number of people in the photo (three), not any of the specific people in it. First, check to see if any character *cannot* be part of a three-person photo. Umiko can't, since choosing Umiko means definitely choosing S, W, and Y as well. So we can cross off U. Since this is a "could be true EXCEPT" question, it makes sense to scan the choices to see if one of them includes U. If so, that will be our answer.

> In "could be true EXCEPT" questions, the right answer is something that *must be false*. As soon as you spot something that is impossible, check the choices for that thing.

TAKE AWAY

Unfortunately, Umiko is not mentioned in any choices, but it was definitely worth a shot. While it didn't pay off here, proactive maneuvers like the one just described will often help you short-circuit a killer question. Here, we'll have to try out the choices one by one until we discover a scenario that cannot result in exactly three friends chosen.

A: Returning as always to our deductions listed on the page, we see that including S forces us to include W and Y as well. Adding Z to the mix, as choice **A** stipulates, is therefore impossible if the picture is to contain exactly three friends. **A** is therefore correct, and for the sake of time you wouldn't need to check the others. For the record, here are possible groups of three for the wrong choices:

B: T, Y, Z

C: S, W, Y

D: Y, Z, W

E: Z, R, T

TAKE AWAY

Employ a hierarchy of methods when approaching each Logic Games question. Start with whatever will provide the answer in the easiest manner possible. When you've deduced anything new at all based on a question's new information, check the choices to see if this new info is enough to answer the question. Expect more difficult questions to require additional steps. In some cases, you'll simply need to test out the choices one by one.

TAKE AWAY

Logic Games choices are objectively correct or incorrect. There is no wiggle room. Develop the confidence in your gaming abilities to mark correct choices without double-checking and second guessing.

The next game's sure to make you hungry. Try your hand at a little something we call "Lunch Trucks and Buildings."

(PrepTest 43, Section 4, Qs. 18–22)

Note: The questions in this set have been renumbered for the purpose of this exercise.

Questions 1–5

Each of exactly six lunch trucks sells a different one of six kinds of food: falafel, hot dogs, ice cream, pitas, salad, or tacos. Each truck serves one or more of exactly three office buildings: X, Y, or Z. The following conditions apply:

The falafel truck, the hot dog truck, and exactly one other truck each serve Y.

The falafel truck serves exactly two of the office buildings.

The ice cream truck serves more of the office buildings than the salad truck.

The taco truck does not serve Y.

The falafel truck does not serve any office building that the pita truck serves.

The taco truck serves two office buildings that are also served by the ice cream truck.

1. Which one of the following could be a complete and accurate list of each of the office buildings that the falafel truck serves?

    (A) X
    (B) X, Z
    (C) X, Y, Z
    (D) Y, Z
    (E) Z

2. For which one of the following pairs of trucks must it be the case that at least one of the office buildings is served by both of the trucks?

    (A) the hot dog truck and the pita truck
    (B) the hot dog truck and the taco truck
    (C) the ice cream truck and the pita truck
    (D) the ice cream truck and the salad truck
    (E) the salad truck and the taco truck

3. If the ice cream truck serves fewer of the office buildings than the hot dog truck, then which one of the following is a pair of lunch trucks that must serve exactly the same buildings as each other?

    (A) the falafel truck and the hot dog truck
    (B) the falafel truck and the salad truck
    (C) the ice cream truck and the pita truck
    (D) the ice cream truck and the salad truck
    (E) the ice cream truck and the taco truck

4. Which one of the following could be a complete and accurate list of the lunch trucks, each of which serves all three of the office buildings?

    (A) the hot dog truck, the ice cream truck
    (B) the hot dog truck, the salad truck
    (C) the ice cream truck, the taco truck
    (D) the hot dog truck, the ice cream truck, the pita truck
    (E) the ice cream truck, the pita truck, the salad truck

5. Which one of the following lunch trucks CANNOT serve both X and Z?

    (A) the hot dog truck
    (B) the ice cream truck
    (C) the pita truck
    (D) the salad truck
    (E) the taco truck

Game 3: Guided Explanation

Lunch Trucks and Buildings

Step 1: Create a Blueprint. The main clue to the action of this game is the fact that there are two sets of characters: food trucks and the buildings that they serve. This is therefore a Linking game in which we're asked to match the trucks to buildings in accordance with the rules. One good way to visualize the truck/building relationships is to create a table with the trucks across the top and the buildings down the side, like so:

	F	H	I	P	S	T
X						
Y						
Z						

TAKE AWAY

A table works particularly well for Linking games containing two sets of characters. If there are more than two sets of characters in a game, a list may be more helpful.

To use the table, simply put a ✓ in the appropriate box to indicate when a truck does serve a particular building and an X when it doesn't. It is worth noting that each truck must serve one or more buildings, which means that we can never have three X's in any truck's column.

Step 2: Get the Specs.
Rule 1: This rule contains two Direct Positive pieces of information: F serves Y, and H serves Y. Build those right into your table with check marks in the appropriate boxes. We're also told that exactly one more truck will serve Y, so write "exactly 3" next to the Y row to remind yourself of this.

TAKE AWAY

When shorthanding number rules, make sure to distinguish between "exactly" and "at least." The test makers often employ both, and you may get mixed up later on in the game if you don't carefully notate such rules up front.

Rule 2: A pure number rule: Writing "exactly 2" above the F row in the table will serve just fine. Chances are that you couldn't help combining that already with the big check mark in the F/Y box, leading to the realization that truck F must serve building X or building Z, but not both.

> Even though we break the Logic Games method down into discrete steps, it's never too early to start making deductions. Build anything you realize along the way into your overall conception of the game.

TAKE AWAY

Rule 3: For this one you'll need to jot down a reminder under or to the side of the table: Something along the lines of "I more than S" will suffice. But did you take it one step further? For this rule to hold, the ice cream truck cannot serve only one building, nor can the salad truck serve all three. So it must be true that the ice cream truck serves two or three buildings, while the salad truck serves one or two. Add that information to your sketch. Don't just write down the information you're given in the rules—ask yourself what it all *means*. Always take numerical information as far as you can.

Rule 4: Here's a Direct Negative rule that we can build right into our sketch by placing an X in the T/Y box.

Rule 5: The falafel and pita trucks must serve different buildings, so indicate that under your table. You may be chomping at the bit to deduce more at this point, which is fine, but we'll get to that after considering the final rule.

Rule 6: This rule links the taco and ice cream trucks, and there's virtually no way of dealing with the rule without connecting this information to what you've already learned about the taco truck in Rule 4. Which is to say that it's high time that we scoped out our Game Breakers.

> Don't be intimidated by a large number of rules! The more information they give you up front, the more you have to work with. It's often the games with very little information that turn out to be the toughest, since those contain the most ambiguity.

TAKE AWAY

Step 3: Search for Game Breakers. We already noted how F must serve X or Z, but not both, which is derived from a combination of Rules 1 and 2. You should have also combined Rules 4 and 6: The taco truck does not serve Y, but it does serve two buildings served by the ice cream truck. These two buildings served by both the ice cream and taco trucks can therefore only be buildings X and Z. The taco truck is now fully determined. Rules 1 and 5 combine to tell us that the pita truck cannot serve building Y, since the falafel truck serves Y and that truck has no buildings in common with the pita truck.

That's a pretty good amount of information to begin with, so it's time to move on to the questions.

Here's our final table to consult:

	exactly 2 F	H	2 or 3 I	P	1 or 2 S	T
X			✓			✓
exactly 3 Y	✓	✓		X		X
Z			✓			✓

I more than S

F and P different

Step 4: Cash In.

Question 1: D. We begin with a Suitability question that applies to only one truck, F. Rule 1, which specifies that F serves Y, immediately rules out choices **A**, **B**, and **E**. Rule 2 states that F serves exactly two trucks, killing **C**. That leaves **D** as the answer to this fairly standard first question.

TAKE AWAY

Even if you have only a minute or two left for the final game of the section, there will usually be at least one straightforward question that you can answer from the rules alone, without even setting up the entire game. Try to at least pick up the Suitability question if you find yourself in this situation.

Question 2: C. The hardest thing about this one is deciphering the question stem, so handle with care. Essentially, they're looking for a pair of trucks that must have at least one building in common. Our Game Breakers lead us in the right direction. We saw that I must serve both X and Z, and that P cannot serve Y. So P must serve either X or Z and therefore must serve at least one of the same buildings as I, choice **C**.

If you didn't come up with these Game Breakers, or didn't think to apply them in this way, you still could have gotten the point by simply testing out the pairs in each choice:

A and **B**: If the hot dog truck serves only Y, it need not serve any of the same buildings as the pita or taco trucks.

D and **E**: Given our deduction that the taco truck always serves only X and Z, if the salad truck serves only Y, and the ice cream truck serves only X and Z, then all is well and the salad truck doesn't have to overlap with either the ice cream truck or the taco truck.

TAKE
AWAY

Try out the choices when you have to, but look for a faster way first, especially if you were successful in discovering Game Breakers up front.

Question 3: E. Next we get another number rule, this time comparing the number of buildings served by trucks I and H. Once again our Game Breakers come to the rescue. Since we've already deduced that the ice cream truck serves X and Z, the only way for the hot dog truck to outdo that would be if the ice cream truck does not serve Y, while the hot dog truck serves all three. The salad truck would then need to serve Y, to get Y up to its three-truck mandate stated in Rule 1. Since the ice cream truck serves exactly two buildings, the salad truck serves only one (Rule 3), and so the salad truck serves only Y. Here's how things would look under these circumstances:

		exactly 2 F	H	2 or 3 I	P	1 or 2 S	T
	X		✓	✓		X	✓
exactly 3	Y	✓	✓	X	X	✓	X
	Z		✓	✓		X	✓

TAKE
AWAY

Don't be afraid to add information to your master sketch for the sake of one question. Simply erase it before moving on to the next question. Since you need a way to tell which ✓s and X's are permanent, you may wish to circle that information in your sketch or distinguish it in some other manner so that you don't confuse it with your question specific notation.

Now we can see that the ice cream and taco trucks must serve identical buildings, choice **E**.

Question 4: A. Next we're looking for a complete list of all of the trucks that can serve all three buildings. That means that any truck that can serve all the buildings must be included in the correct choice, while any truck that cannot serve all three must not be included in the correct choice. We know from Rule 2 that F can't be in this list, but a quick scan reveals that F is not included in any choices. Our deduction that the pita truck can't serve building Y bears more fruit, as it allows us to chop choices **D** and **E**. Rule 4 kills choice **C** directly. And our "1 or 2" indication above the salad truck (derived from Rule 3's stipulation that the ice cream truck serves more buildings than the salad truck) does away with **B**, leaving **A** as the correct choice.

Question 5: C. Which truck can't serve both X and Z? The falafel truck can't, because it's already serving Y and must serve exactly two buildings, which, as we've seen, means exactly one of X and Z. Unfortunately the falafel truck is not one of the choices. However, this reasoning does lead us in the right direction. Rule 5 states that the pita and falafel trucks can't serve any of the same buildings, and since the falafel truck must serve X or Z, the pita truck can't serve both of those buildings without causing a violation. **C** is correct. As for the others:

A: The hot dog truck can serve all three buildings, no problem.

B and **E:** We deduced early on that both the ice cream and taco trucks must serve both X and Z, as our final sketch readily indicates.

D: The salad truck can't serve all three buildings, but it can serve X and Z as long as the ice cream truck serves all three buildings to satisfy Rule 3.

Okay, that does it for our trucks and buildings. We move now from food to chess. Why not? Logic games can involve virtually any topic, so there's no reason why a little chess match might not play a role in your legal aspirations. See what you can make of the final game in this chapter, "Chess Tournament."

Game 4

(PrepTest 45, Section 3, Qs. 7–12)

Note: The questions in this set have been renumbered for the purpose of this exercise.

Questions 1–6

Exactly six people—Lulu, Nam, Ofelia, Pachai, Santiago, and Tyrone—are the only contestants in a chess tournament. The tournament consists of four games, played one after the other. Exactly two people play in each game, and each person plays in at least one game. The following conditions must apply:

  Tyrone does not play in the first or third game.
  Lulu plays in the last game.
  Nam plays in only one game and it is not against Pachai.
  Santiago plays in exactly two games, one just before and one just after the only game that Ofelia plays in.

1. Which one of the following could be an accurate list of the contestants who play in each of the four games?

    (A) first game: Pachai, Santiago; second game: Ofelia, Tyrone; third game: Pachai, Santiago; fourth game: Lulu, Nam
    (B) first game: Lulu, Nam; second game: Pachai, Santiago; third game: Ofelia, Tyrone; fourth game: Lulu, Santiago
    (C) first game: Pachai, Santiago; second game: Lulu, Tyrone; third game: Nam, Ofelia; fourth game: Lulu, Nam
    (D) first game: Nam, Santiago; second game: Nam, Ofelia; third game: Pachai, Santiago; fourth game: Lulu, Tyrone
    (E) first game: Lulu, Nam; second game: Santiago, Tyrone; third game: Lulu, Ofelia; fourth game: Pachai, Santiago

2. Which one of the following contestants could play in two consecutive games?

    (A) Lulu
    (B) Nam
    (C) Ofelia
    (D) Santiago
    (E) Tyrone

3. If Tyrone plays in the fourth game, then which one of the following could be true?

    (A) Nam plays in the second game.
    (B) Ofelia plays in the third game.
    (C) Santiago plays in the second game.
    (D) Nam plays a game against Lulu.
    (E) Pachai plays a game against Lulu.

4. Which one of the following could be true?

    (A) Pachai plays against Lulu in the first game.
    (B) Pachai plays against Nam in the second game.
    (C) Santiago plays against Ofelia in the second game.
    (D) Pachai plays against Lulu in the third game.
    (E) Nam plays against Santiago in the fourth game.

5. Which one of the following is a complete and accurate list of the contestants who CANNOT play against Tyrone in any game?

    (A) Lulu, Pachai
    (B) Nam, Ofelia
    (C) Nam, Pachai
    (D) Nam, Santiago
    (E) Ofelia, Pachai

6. If Ofelia plays in the third game, which one of the following must be true?

    (A) Lulu plays in the third game.
    (B) Nam plays in the third game.
    (C) Pachai plays in the first game.
    (D) Pachai plays in the third game.
    (E) Tyrone plays in the second game.

Game 4: Guided Explanation

Chess Tournament

Step 1: Create a Blueprint. This game features six people to be filtered into four chess games, which immediately suggests a Placing element. The fact that each person is to join a game tells us that we're not interested in selecting the participants, as we would in a Choosing game, because they're *all* to be selected. The question is, *Where do they go?* Think of the chess games as groups, each containing two characters. The fact that the games are played "one after the other" also suggests a possible Ordering aspect, which we should keep an eye on as well. We can represent the two people per game format like so, including, of course, the characters off to the side:

There's lots of number information in the introduction, so let's sort it out. Four games with two players each means there are eight spots to be filled by the six people. Each person plays in at least one game, so that will take up six of the eight spots. Two spots are left, which means either one person plays in three games while everyone else plays in just one, or two people play in two games while the other four play once each. Maybe this issue will be further clarified by the rules, maybe not; we'll have to wait and see.

TAKE AWAY

> Don't leave the blueprint phase until you think through all of the number information you're given in the introduction. Numbers play a big part in how the game will play out.

Step 2: Get the Specs. The introduction answered the "how many in each group" question: two per game, which makes sense. As always, the rules will flesh out the rest of the scenario.

Rule 1: This Direct Negative rule tells us where Tyrone *can't* go: 1 or 3. There's no reason why you shouldn't write that right into your sketch. And you know the drill by now—turn the negative into a positive. The most concrete information conveyed by this rule is that Tyrone must play in game 2 or 4, and possibly both, as we've already deduced that at least someone must play more than once.

Rule 2: A Direct Positive is always a welcome sight. Place an L right into one of the spaces in game 4.

Rule 3: Well, now we know that Nam is not a repeat player, and we also know she cannot be placed in the same game as Pachai. "NO NP" is one way to remind yourself of this restriction.

Rule 4: This one gives us three pieces of information in one.

> When a rule presents numerous pieces of information, take it one piece at a time—otherwise you may get overwhelmed.

First, we find out that Santiago plays in exactly two games. Building on our numerical observations above, this tells us that exactly one other person must play in exactly two games, while everyone else plays in only one.

> When you work through the introduction, think through the possible parameters of the game. Then use the rules to narrow down those possibilities as far as you can.

Next we're told by Rule 4 that Santiago's games flank Ofelia's one and only game. So Ofelia cannot be the other two-gamer, nor can Santiago and Ofelia ever play each other. And notice what else this means: It means that the order of the games is important. In other words, this is not merely a Placing game but rather a Placing/Ordering Combination game. We need to be concerned not only about placing people together in games but also about sequencing these pairs from one to four. We can represent the Ordering element of Rule 4 as "SOS."

> **TAKE AWAY**
>
> Combination games include elements of multiple game types. Here we have a Placing/Ordering combo, but you may also see other variations, such as Linking/Ordering, Choosing/Ordering, and Choosing/Linking. After you've learned how to deal with the four individual game types, you shouldn't be intimidated if the test makers hit you with a Combination game.

Okay, do we move right to the questions now, having considered each rule individually? Of course not! As always, we take the time to see if we can combine the rules in any meaningful ways. That is, we move on to the Game Breakers stage.

Step 3: Search for Game Breakers. SOS is a pretty large cluster, considering that we're dealing with only a four-slot ordering. In fact, there's only two ways to incorporate this cluster into the sequence, and hopefully you explored each option. SOS can fit either in spaces 1 through 3, or spaces 2 through 4, which means we may have a Restricted Possibilities scenario on our hands. Let's see what happens in each case.

Possibility 1: SOS = 1-2-3. In this scenario, one person is situated for sure in each game: S in 1, O in 2, S in 3, and L in 4. T must be in 2 or 4, but we can't tell where. That leaves N and P to place, depending on where T goes. One of T, L, or P will be the other player besides S that plays twice, but again, there's too much up in the air to know for sure.

Possibility 2: SOS = 2-3-4. This option is better defined. We begin by placing S in 2, O in 3, and S with L in 4, closing that game off to anyone else. That means that T must play against S in game 2, to satisfy Rule 1. With nowhere else to go, T is done. Now comes the matter of placing N and P, who, remember, can't play each other. With the spaces remaining, one of them must play in game 1, while the other must play against O in game 3. Write this information right into your blueprint.

All that's left is the other spot in game 1. S, O, and T are finished, so they can't go there. If N plays in game 1, then P can't play in that game, nor can N play herself, of course, so L must play in 1. If P plays in game 1, N can't play with P in that game, which once again forces L into game 1. No matter what, L must play in game 1 in this second option.

So here are the two options of this Restricted Possibilities scenario:

Possibility 1

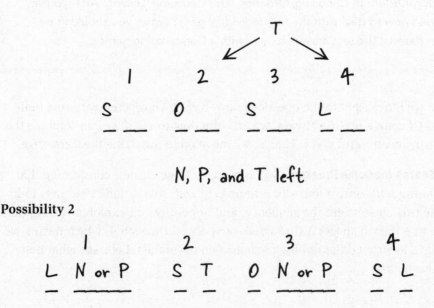

Possibility 2

Any condition that places us in Possibility 2 will be a blessing, since that scenario is almost totally defined. Possibility 1 contains more ambiguity but would still make for a good start to any question. The questions are not bad at all if you have these options plotted out in advance. Naturally, it's a bit more dicey if you don't.

Step 4: Cash In.

Question 1: A. Use the standard technique for this Suitability question: Scan the choices to see which violate each rule. Rule 1 knocks out **B**, which inappropriately places T third. Rule 2 takes care of **E**, which fails to place L last. The first part of Rule 3 kills both **C** and **D**, both of which assign Nam to two different games. Only **A** remains, so it gets the point.

> Sometimes you won't even need all the rules to eliminate all the bad choices in a Suitability question. When only one choice remains, pick it and move on.

Question 2: A. Here we're asked who could play in two consecutive games, and simply knowing our characters gets us pretty much all the way there. Neither S nor O can play in consecutive games without violating the SOS mandate of Rule 4, while T, at most, can play in games 2 and 4. So choices **C**, **D**, and **E** can be tossed right off the bat. **B** fails as well, since Nam is allowed to play in only one game. So the winner by default is Lulu, choice **A**. Should you try to construct an arrangement that proves that Lulu can play in consecutive games, just to make sure? No! If the other choices can't work, choice **A** *must* work, and it must therefore be correct.

> The hardest part of the Logic Games section for many test takers is time pressure. You must save time wherever you can to have a shot at finishing the section, and one good way to do that is to have faith in your work and select a choice without testing it when you're sure the other choices are wrong.
>
> Notice that we're two questions in and haven't yet needed to consult our Restricted Possibilities scenarios. Does that mean setting them up was a waste of time? Absolutely not. You should expect that some questions will test only a basic understanding of the game's action and rules, and that soon enough harder questions will appear that benefit from the work you did up front.

Question 3: A. In this one Tyrone plays in the fourth game, which automatically puts us in Possibility 1 territory. That's because in Possibility 2, the fourth chess game is populated by Santiago and Lulu.

In games containing Restricted Possibilities scenarios, often the most important thing is to figure out which option is operative for each of the questions. Sometimes both will be in play, while other times only one will apply to the situation at hand.

Now we simply need to place T in game 4 in Possibility 1 and compare the choices against that scenario. **A** is the only one that's possible.

Question 4: A. Here we're given no new information, so we'll have to compare the choices against the options in search of something that could be true.

A: Possibility 2 pits L against either N or P in game 1, so we have our winner already.

For the record:

B: N can never play P, thanks to Rule 3.

C: S can never play against O, thanks to Rule 4.

D: S plays third in Possibility 1, and O plays third in Possibility 2. There can therefore never be a PL matchup in that spot.

E: L plays in the fourth game in both possibilities, so an NS showdown in game 4 is impossible.

Hey, that's four A's in a row! They can't do that, can they? Well, they can, and they just did. Don't listen to the various bits of LSAT gossip floating around regarding stuff you have no control over, like answer choice patterns. If they want to put seven A's in a row, who's going to stop them? Just focus on each question individually, and don't look for shortcuts where none exist. Logic, not tricks, is what produces the best scores.

Question 5: C. Who can't play Tyrone? Back to our possibilities: Let's go ahead and cross off anyone who *can* play Tyrone. Whoever's left will be our answer.

Work the questions in whatever manner is easiest. If the test makers phrase a question in the negative, turn it around to the positive if that makes more sense to you.

In Possibility 1, T can play O in game 2 and/or L in game 4, so neither Ofelia nor Lulu can be part of the answer. Already we can cross off **A**, **B**, and **E**. Nam is in both of the remaining choices, so there's no need to check her. The only question left is whether Pachai or Santiago is the other person who can't play Tyrone, since these are the people mentioned in choices **C** and **D**, respectively. A quick glance at Possibility 2 shows T playing S in game 2, so P must be the person in addition to Nam who can't play Tyrone, choice **C**.

TAKE AWAY

Strive to employ effective answer choice strategy. If you've eliminated some choices, and a certain character is included in all of the remaining choices, that character must be part of the right answer, so there's no need to investigate that one. Look for differences among the remaining choices, and use those differences to determine the most effective way to test for the right choice.

Question 6: E. Ofelia playing in game 3 lands us squarely in Possibility 2. We like Possibility 2 because it's nearly complete. What must be true? T playing with S in game 2, something we discovered a long time ago. **E** gets the point to round out this very doable Combination game.

LOGIC GAMES SUMMARY

It will take some practice for the strategies and techniques to sink in, but you're probably already on your way to a higher Logic Games score. You'll get more practice with the four games in the practice test at the end of the book, and you should, of course, apply and hone your Logic Games techniques on as many practice games as necessary until you've mastered this challenging section. And who knows? You may be surprised at how often during your legal education and career you come up against scenarios that make you stop and think *"Hey, that's just like a logic game . . ."*

## Chapter 3

READING COMPREHENSION

or

The Good, the Bad, and the Ugly

Let's take it in reverse order.

The Ugly

Well . . . it's Reading Comprehension. Sure, some like it, but many others are hard pressed to find a less appealing, more tortuous standardized test item type. While some people actually do logic games for enjoyment, no one whips through a Reading Comp passage on the nuances of Iroquois governing principles by the pool to while away the time on a sunny afternoon. Even Logical Reasoning is not without its charms, with its colorful characters, occasionally humorous flaws, and short, entertaining dialogues. But Reading Comp? Same old, same old since first grade—just much, much harder. Been there, done that, not fun.

The Bad

Obvious enough: long, often excruciatingly boring passages, accompanied by difficult, esoteric questions. In first grade you thought *Dick and Jane* was bad; now you get a heaping helping of "Critical Legal Studies" or "the migratory patterns of hummingbirds" or some such nonsense. But wait, it's not all bad . . .

The Good

Despite their variety of topics, Reading Comp passages are all pretty much the same underneath. You will therefore learn a unified approach that you'll apply to every passage you face. The topics are predictable, so you can find many sources to practice with the kinds of passages you'll see on test day. Further, no outside knowledge is required. Some test takers forget that everything they need to answer the questions is right there in the passage—that is, that it's an *open-book test.* The answers are in front of you, and we'll teach you not only how to find them but how to *anticipate* them in some cases as well. Finally, Reading Comp is directly relevant to your legal academic and professional career. Let's face it, long boring reading passages are what law (and certainly law school) is all about. For those who accept the realities of becoming and being a lawyer, Reading Comp preparation offers an opportunity not only to increase their LSAT scores and bag better schools but to get a head start on their legal careers as well. And that ain't bad—or ugly.

Okay, so we're no Knute Rockne (college football coach famous for motivational speeches), but we'd like to see *him* hype Reading Comprehension. Anyway, that's the pep talk part of our program. Let's get down to business.

OVERVIEW

What It Is

The LSAT contains one scored Reading Comp section consisting of four passages, each roughly 450 words long and containing 5 to 8 questions, for a total of 26 or 27 questions to be completed in 35 minutes. The section usually contains one humanities passage, one social science passage, one natural science passage, and one law passage. Some passages are argumentative—that is, the author takes a stand on the subject under discussion. Others are purely descriptive. Some passages include the viewpoints of numerous characters; others present only the author's views on some person, event, or phenomenon. In general, the questions test your understanding of:

- What the author *does*

- What the passage *says*

- How the passage is *constructed*

Why It Is

As already discussed, it's not too difficult to see the relevance of Reading Comp to the study and practice of law. There's no way around it—law is about using the written and spoken word to describe and regulate human experience. Your prospective law school admission officers and professors want to know how well you understand what you read.

Your Motivation

In addition to the motivational points from the previous page (translation: *it doesn't suck as bad as it seems*), Reading Comprehension accounts for more than one quarter of your total LSAT score. As a bonus, you'll learn how to analyze dense complicated prose in a way that's bound to help you later on in law school.

GAMEPLAN

As with the other two sections, we provide you with a specialized gameplan to ensure you maximize your score and your study time is efficient. Here's how we organized the chapter:

- **X-ray of a Typical Reading Comprehension Passage:** First we'll get familiar with the components of the Reading Comp package: the directions, the passage, and the question set.

- **Essential Elements:** There are seven core elements that you will need to extract from each Reading Comp passage to succeed on the section. You'll learn the key points to focus on in each paragraph and will get practice spotting these elements in four paragraphs of a sample passage.

- **Essential Strategy:** Next you'll be introduced to a general strategy that you'll follow for every Reading Comp passage. The method will be demonstrated in the context of actual passages.

- **Question Types:** There are eight common Reading Comp question types, and we'll go over every one and detail the specific issues and traps you might meet up with on test day.

- **The New Paired Passages:** Here we'll go over the new Reading Comp passage type that asks you to compare and contrast two passages on the same topic. We'll also revisit the Essential Strategy, retailored to work with the paired passages, as well as the special question types that accompany paired passages on the new LSAT.

- **The Real Deal:** Here you'll apply what you've learned to two real LSAT Reading Comp passages. Afterward you can also reinforce what you've learned by working on four more Reading Comp passages in the practice test at the end of the book.

Let's get started.

X-RAY OF A TYPICAL READING COMPREHENSION PASSAGE

If you've come this far in your academic life, it would be a miracle indeed if you didn't know what a Reading Comprehension passage looked like—in fact, the aforementioned *Dick and Jane* was probably your first taste of one way back in elementary school. But there are still a few things worth pointing out to get you acclimated to LSAT-style Reading Comp, so let's take a quick tour through the following passage to establish some terminology. Note that this is a standard passage; three of the four Reading Comp question sets you see will be based on a long passage like this. The other question set will accompany a pair of shorter passages on the same topic, a format we'll cover in a special section later in the chapter. Don't worry about reading the passage in depth or answering the questions at this point—we guarantee you'll get more than your fill of "Mumford on Art" before long.

Common to most interpretations of the role of art is the notion that art correlates directly with the environmental characteristics of its period of origin. If we understand technology not only as a practical set of techniques and machines but also as an evolving dominant ideology of the modern age, it follows that we should witness an infiltration of technology

(5) into art not just in terms of the tools and processes at artists' disposal but also in terms of technology's influence on art's place within society. The latter supposition has been explored by American writer and critic Lewis Mumford during various stages of his prolific career.

Mumford posited an integrative role of medieval art corresponding to the unity of life characteristic of this pre-technological period. Medieval citizens, he argued, did not

(10) attend the theater, concert hall, and museum as activities unto themselves as we do but rather witnessed a fusion of music, painting, sculpture, architecture, and drama in unified religious ceremonies that incorporated people into the shared social and spiritual life of the community. Integral to this phenomenon was the non-repeatability of the experience—live musicians, specially commissioned scores, unique paintings and sculptures, and inimitable

(15) speakers filling incomparable cathedrals with exhortation and prayer. Everything in the artist's repertoire was brought to bear to ensure maximum receptivity to the political, social, and religious teachings at the heart of this medieval spectacle.

Mumford further speculated that the mass production of text and images from the sixteenth century forward ultimately disrupted the unity exemplified by the medieval

(20) experience, and with it the role of art as a testament to and reinforcement of that unity. He believed that modern communication technologies encourage the fragmentation of time, the dissociation of event and space, and the degradation of the symbolic environment via an endless repetition of cultural elements. The result is the oft-commented-upon "alienating" experience of modern life.

(25) A new aesthetic orientation emerged to express this new reality. Art turned inward to focus on man's struggle against a bureaucratized, impersonal, technological civilization. Mumford readily admits that the dissociation of the artist from communal obligations greatly expanded the realm of artistic possibilities; freed from its integrative purpose, art was set loose to traverse previously inappropriate realms of psychology and individualism

(30) in startling new ways. However, the magnificent innovation born of this freedom has been somewhat hindered by art's apprenticeship to the dominant force of the technological milieu: the market. Out of necessity, money has replaced muse as motivation for many artists, resulting in the art world of today: a collection of "industries," each concerned with nothing loftier than its own perpetuation. Mumford testified admirably to a unity of art

(35) greater than the sum of its parts. Despite modern art's potential, it is reasonable to infer the converse: that the individual arts of our technological landscape are diminished in isolation.

1. Which one of the following most accurately expresses the main point of the passage?

(A) Modern technology contains both practical and ideological elements.
(B) Mumford has demonstrated the evolution of medieval unity into modern alienation.
(C) Mumford's analyses support the idea that technology has influenced the function and quality of modern art.
(D) Technology has placed new tools at the disposal of modern artists.
(E) Most cultural institutions have been adversely affected by advances in modern communication technologies.

2. The author indicates that Mumford believed which one of the following regarding modern communication technologies?

(A) Modern communication technologies play a part in engendering alienation.
(B) Modern communication technologies represent a unifying force in society.
(C) Modern communication technologies are the only factors degrading the symbolic environment.
(D) Modern communication technologies were invented to express the new aesthetic orientation that has arisen in the modern period.
(E) No culture experienced the fragmentation of time before the advent of modern communication technologies.

3. Which one of the following most accurately describes the organization of the material presented in the passage?

(A) A theory is put forward, a specific means of testing the theory is outlined, and obstacles to carrying out the test are detailed.
(B) A consequence of accepting a particular definition is proposed, the validity of that proposal is affirmed, and a judgment based on that affirmation is stated.
(C) A supposition is introduced, a speculation regarding that supposition is described, and further speculations are detailed that counter the original supposition.
(D) An interpretation is offered, expert testimony opposing that interpretation is provided, and a consequence of that testimony is explored.
(E) A question is raised, and evidence from one time period and then another time period is presented to deem the question unanswerable.

4. Which one of the following can most reasonably be inferred from the passage?

(A) Modern religious ceremonies never make use of specially commissioned scores.
(B) Most artists are grateful to be relieved of their communal obligations.
(C) Only art that turns inward is suitable to express dissatisfaction with one's social and cultural environment.
(D) Medieval life was generally not alienating and impersonal.
(E) Mumford did not investigate the tools and processes at the disposal of modern artists.

5. The author's primary purpose in the passage is to

(A) outline an effect of a feature of modern society
(B) recommend a solution to a cultural problem
(C) bolster a critic's speculations with supporting evidence
(D) describe the major difference between two historical periods
(E) advocate for a change in society's modes of communication

The "passage," of course, is the long, fairly complex story consisting of four paragraphs. Notice the line numbers to the left of the paragraphs; these are sometimes mentioned in the questions to direct your attention to a specific part of the passage. As mentioned, passages are usually somewhere around 450 words in length and usually contain three to five paragraphs, although you'll occasionally come across a passage with two.

The "question set" usually consists of five to eight multiple-choice questions that follow the passage—in this case, questions 1–5. Unlike in Logical Reasoning, where each question usually has its own passage, all the questions of a Reading Comp set are based on the same passage. As in Logical Reasoning, each question contains five choices, and we'll discuss how to distinguish the correct choice from the imposters.

Before moving on, let's check in with the directions, so you'll never have to waste time with them again.

Directions: Each passage in this section is followed by a group of questions to be answered on the basis of what is stated or implied in the passage. For some of the questions, more than one of the choices could conceivably answer the question. However, you are to choose the best answer; that is, the response that most accurately and completely answers the question, and blacken the corresponding space on your answer sheet.

Notice the same caveat that we discovered in the Logical Reasoning directions: the admission that some choices may seem pretty darn close, but only the *really, really* right answer will get the point. Again, this highlights just how close some of the wrong choices may sound, which makes it all the more important to learn the subtle distinctions that set the credited choices apart. We'll get to all that shortly, but let's begin at the beginning with the real beasts of this section, the passages.

ESSENTIAL ELEMENTS

The most effective way to attack a Reading Comp passage is to create a *detailed synopsis* as you read. To do this efficiently in a timed situation, you will need to quickly identify seven "Essential Elements" as you research each paragraph.

Before you panic, let us state at the outset that it's not necessary, or even recommended, that you write down these Essential Elements. Sure, you may certainly jot down a few notes in the margins if you find that helpful, but by and large Essential Elements represent things you need to learn to focus on *reflexively*. The only quiz that counts comes after the passage, not after each paragraph. But if you get in the habit of searching for and recognizing these elements, you'll be able to read the passage and answer the questions strategically.

Here are the seven Essential Elements you need to extract from each and every paragraph you read:

1. Giveaways

2. Purpose

3. Players/Extras

4. Main Point

5. Author Behavior

6. Author Opinion

7. Passage Main Idea

Essential Element #1

Giveaways

Essentially, giveaways are the clues that tip you off to the other Essential Elements in our list. These are words and phrases that reek of importance—that is, they indicate things like the author's opinion and the passage's main idea and purpose. For example, the phrase "The critics' contention is therefore misguided . . ." tips us off to a number of important things. First, it tells us that the author's purpose is not merely to describe something but also to refute the assertions of others. If we understand the critics' contention, we now have a leg up on what the author *doesn't* believe, which in turn will lead us closer to what she does believe; that is, her main point.

Giveaways also include signal clues, words or phrases that highlight the passage's structure, thus making it easier to follow the author's ideas. For example, words and phrases like *in addition* and *moreover* tell us that more of the same is upcoming, whereas *however* and *on the other hand* alert us to expect a shift of some kind in focus or opinion. Some giveaways, such as *most importantly, primarily,* and *significantly* suggest that the author is placing extra emphasis on some issue or idea. Anything that's important to the author should be important to you.

Essential Element #2

Purpose

Reading Comp passages do not contain extraneous information. Every paragraph plays a role in the passage as a whole. Just as each passage has an overall purpose, each paragraph of the passage has a purpose as well—a reason for being there. For example, consider a passage whose main point is that the Harlem Renaissance helped contribute to the development and emergence of influential black writers in the 1970s. The individual paragraphs that make up the passage will all play a distinct and indispensable role in telling this story. One paragraph may lay the groundwork by introducing what the Harlem Renaissance was, while another may focus on writers of the 1970s. Ultimately, the paragraphs work together to express the author's main point. Some questions ask for the purpose of a particular paragraph in the context of the passage as a whole. Focusing on the purpose of *every* paragraph not only will help you answer such paragraph purpose questions when they arise but will also keep you on the trail of the passage's main idea.

Essential Element #3
Players/Extras

Reading Comp passages often include numerous characters, and some questions test your ability to keep them straight. "Players" are subjects that figure significantly in the drama. "Extras" are minor characters or elements that add spice to the story but aren't the main focus. You may not know in the first half of the passage who falls into which group, but you must be able to differentiate players from extras by the end. Questions often focus on players, while many wrong choices exaggerate the importance of extras.

In some passages, the author may be the only main player, while in other passages all kinds of players may be involved in the story. When that's the case, it's a safe bet that at least some questions will test your ability to keep the players straight and to distinguish them from the less important extras.

Essential Element #4
Main Point

The main point of a paragraph is the overriding idea that the author is attempting to establish in that paragraph. Each paragraph establishes this point, which will combine with the main points of the other paragraphs to create the passage's overall main idea. You will need to summarize the main point of each paragraph as you go along to keep the author's ideas and intentions in focus.

Essential Element #5
Author Behavior

The author's behavior refers to what the author actually *does* in each paragraph. Using the Harlem Renaissance example, the author may, as we mentioned, simply describe in one paragraph what it was. She may also do no more than describe the relationship between the Harlem Renaissance and black literature of the 1970s. If plain old description is the order of the day, then correct answer choices in certain questions will reflect that, while wrong choices will try to paint the author as more assertive or combative. So it pays to take note of how the author behaves in each paragraph—that is, to pin down exactly what she's doing. Perhaps the author of the Harlem Renaissance passage was out to disprove prior theories regarding the subject. In that case, "refute" or "dismiss" would better reflect her behavior in certain paragraphs. Or perhaps in one paragraph she makes a prediction of what might happen in the future regarding the actual or perceived impact of the Harlem Renaissance—again, something worth noting. Maybe she offers a proposal concerning the matter. All of these possibilities represent different approaches an author may take. You'll keep a very close watch on what kind of behavior is evidenced in each paragraph.

Essential Element #6

Author Opinion

This one is closely tied to author behavior. Some authors merely describe situations, events, or phenomena, while others go the extra step of offering an opinion of their own. LSAT test makers are quite keen on testing whether you know the difference. So as you read each paragraph, keep an eye out for whether the author takes a stand or merely relays information. Doing so will enable you to eliminate wrong answer choices that assert an authorial opinion where there is none, and vice versa.

Essential Element #7

Passage Main Idea

Identifying the first six Essential Elements will enable you to formulate a working notion of the passage's main idea, but the passage's main idea will likely remain tentative until the very end. At this time you'll have a pretty good idea of the main reason the author put pen to paper (or bytes to disk, as is more likely the case today). However, you'll need to modify the passage's main idea as you progress through the passage.

As you should see by now, the seven Essential Elements are by no means mutually exclusive. They're very closely related, so uncovering one will often lead you to others. The goal, of course, is to arrive at a comprehensive yet very specific understanding of the passage. Notice that you're not out to understand every single detail but rather to understand the kinds of things *you're likely to be asked about*. When you've mastered the art of seeing each paragraph in terms of the elements described above, you will have taken a huge step toward improving your Reading Comp score.

MINING THE ESSENTIAL ELEMENTS

Extracting Essential Elements from Reading Comp passages takes practice, so let's work through the four paragraphs of the X-ray passage you saw earlier. Read the first paragraph carefully, and see what you can take out of it in terms of the seven Essential Elements we've just discussed. Then compare your paragraph synopsis to ours.

Common to most interpretations of the role of art is the notion that art correlates directly with the environmental characteristics of its period of origin. If we understand technology not only as a practical set of techniques and machines but also as an evolving dominant ideology of the modern age, it follows that we should witness an infiltration of technology into art not just in terms of the tools and processes at artists' disposal but also in terms of technology's influence on art's place within society. The latter supposition has been explored by American writer and critic Lewis Mumford during various stages of his prolific career.

- **Giveaways:** The construction "If we understand . . . it follows that . . ." sets up the idea that based on a certain definition of technology, a certain result should follow. Pay careful attention when an author says something *should* happen, especially at the beginning of the passage. The word "prolific" suggests a slight touch of admiration for Mumford—at the very least, the author thinks he's no slouch.

- **Purpose:** Part of the purpose of every first paragraph is to introduce the passage's topic, which in this case is the "infiltration of technology into art." We know this thanks to the giveaway above in which the author states that a certain result should follow from a particular definition. The "If we understand . . . it follows that . . ." sentence construction suggests what will be the author's main concern in the passage: the influence of technology on art's place in the world. By mentioning someone who has explored this issue, the final sentence of the paragraph serves to introduce a possible player in the passage whom we should keep an eye on.

TAKE AWAY

Your key task in the first paragraph is to grasp the general scenario. As you get better at reading the passages, you'll also be able to anticipate the likely directions a passage may take based on its introduction. Keep in mind that there are only a limited number of passage structures that LSAT authors employ.

- **Players/Extras:** Lewis Mumford. We need to see how things play out, but when a theory or supposition is introduced early on in the first paragraph (technology's supposed effect on art) and someone who has explored that issue is mentioned, chances are that person will be a player.

- **Main Point:** The author introduces a topic (technology's influence on art) and then someone who has studied that topic. There's a long way to go, but for now we can simply describe the main point of this first paragraph in those terms: Mumford has explored the way technology has influenced art. We don't need to get any more specific than that at this point; we'll see where things go from here soon enough.

- **Author Behavior:** The author is making a prediction of what should follow from a specific interpretation. This usually indicates that some sort of test of the prediction will occur.

- **Author Opinion:** Nothing much to speak of, unless we count the author's interpretation of technology as an opinion. Perhaps a whole passage could be structured around this interpretation, but that's doubtful here since the author seems to be more concerned with what follows from this particular understanding. So we'll reserve judgment for now regarding authorial opinion.

- **Passage Main Idea:** Too soon to tell, but it's reasonable to anticipate, based on the giveaway discussed above, that seeing whether the technology/art prediction is correct might be the focus of the passage. The passage may deal mainly with Mumford's examination of the issue or may veer in a different direction; again, it's too early to know.

Sometimes the passage's main idea is evident up front. Other times, the situation is pretty wide open following the first, and even second, paragraph. Don't stress over the passage's main idea so early on, but of course you need to be receptive to indications of it anywhere they appear.

TAKE AWAY

Don't be overwhelmed by the amount of stuff it appears there is to know about a single paragraph. We present you with very comprehensive paragraph synopses based on our seven Essential Elements to teach you how to reflect on the kinds of issues that lead to points, but we don't expect you to reproduce such a lengthy analysis for every paragraph. The point is to learn to think through these kinds of issues quickly and instinctively as you proceed through the passage.

TAKE AWAY

Now try the second paragraph:

Mumford posited an integrative role of medieval art corresponding to the unity of life characteristic of this pre-technological period. Medieval citizens, he argued, did not attend the theater, concert hall, and museum as activities unto themselves as we do but rather witnessed a fusion of music, painting, sculpture, architecture, and drama in unified religious ceremonies that incorporated people into the shared social and spiritual life of the community. Integral to this phenomenon was the non-repeatability of the experience—live musicians, specially commissioned scores, unique paintings and sculptures, and inimitable speakers filling incomparable cathedrals with exhortation and prayer. Everything in the artist's repertoire was brought to bear to ensure maximum receptivity to the political, social, and religious teachings at the heart of this medieval spectacle.

- **Giveaways:** "Mumford posited . . . " connects this paragraph to the last line of paragraph 1 and indicates, as we may have expected, that this paragraph will detail facts of Mumford's exploration of the issue at hand.

- **Purpose:** As just indicated by the giveaway, the purpose is to tell us what Mumford thought about the whole thing. But there's a surprise: The paragraph seems to veer off topic. The astute reader will immediately notice the difference between the technology issue of the first paragraph and this description of the "pre-technological" medieval period and infer that this paragraph serves to present some kind of contrast. This might not become fully evident until the next paragraph, but this kind of anticipation is part of the "comprehension" this section tests.

- **Players/Extras:** Mumford, who shows up again in the second paragraph, appears to be a player. The medieval situation, citizens, and artists he describes may be extras or players; we'll have to wait and see.

- **Main Point:** In "pre-technological" medieval days art was "integrative"; it corresponded to a "unity of life." Most of the paragraph consists of examples of how this was so—it brought about community, was used for teaching values, etc.—but these are details you can return to later if need be. The main point simply has to do with the fact that art in medieval times was integral and tied in to society in many ways.

- **Author Behavior:** There's nothing other than plain old description. Skip for now.

- **Author Opinion:** No sign of opinion here at all. The author merely presents Mumford's take on medieval art, without providing any commentary of her own.

- **Passage Main Idea:** This paragraph doesn't add to our previous tentative notion of the passage's main idea, and it reinforces the conjecture, discussed above, that this paragraph serves as a contrast. It will somehow contribute to the "technology's influence on art" prediction that the author appears to want to test, but by itself it doesn't get us any further along. We can tolerate a bit of ambiguity, secure in the knowledge that each paragraph *must* contribute logically to the passage's main idea. We just need to read a bit further to piece it all together.

TAKE AWAY

Reading Comp passages commonly contain contrasts. Here, we sense from paragraph 1 that the main issue has something to do with technology and art, but then we get a long paragraph on a *pre*-technological period. This apparent detour may confuse the average test taker who's focusing only on details, not context and structure. But there *must* be a reason for this paragraph; it *has* to relate somehow to what came before. And the most logical reason to delve into pre-technological days is to present a contrast that will somehow highlight the author's main concern—the influence of technology on art.

Moving on, see what you can make of the third paragraph.

> Mumford further speculated that the mass production of text and images from the sixteenth century forward ultimately disrupted the unity exemplified by the medieval experience, and with it the role of art as a testament to and reinforcement of that unity. He believed that modern communication technologies encourage the fragmentation of time, the dissociation of event and space, and the degradation of the symbolic environment via an endless repetition of cultural elements. The result is the oft-commented-upon "alienating" experience of modern life.

- **Giveaways:** *Mumford, Mumford, Mumford . . .** Anyhow, no complaints here—the opening phrase "Mumford further speculated . . ." tells us we've got a continuation of Mumford's account upcoming. "He believed that . . ." in the middle of the paragraph indicates we're still learning about Mumford, not the author. The phrase "modern communication technologies" suggests that we're finally getting to the prediction raised in paragraph 1.

- **Purpose:** To continue Mumford's account, bringing things up-to-date with the modern period and thus, as just mentioned, getting to the heart of the matter—technology's influence on art.

- **Players/Extras:** No changes. It's clear by now that Mumford is a major player. The medieval experience seems to be an important element of the passage, but one that leads to something bigger as the focus shifts to the modern day.

- **Main Point:** Mass production of text and images (a form of technology) changed the medieval experience and with it the function of art in society. The paragraph ends with ways that modern technologies cause alienation, which seems to be a transition into the final paragraph. We can return to these details if need be. For now, "technology bad for society" will suffice.

- **Author Behavior:** Just run-of-the-mill description.

- **Author Opinion:** Still no indication of an opinion on the part of the author.

- **Passage Main Idea:** We're finally closing in on the main point now. The passage began with the idea that technology should have an impact on art's function, and now we find out that because of certain tech advances, art no longer testifies to or reinforces societal unity because, well, there is none to speak of. Poor us. But it's not end of story yet, with the longest paragraph yet to go.

---

* Whined to the tune of "Marsha, Marsha, Marsha . . .," Jan Brady's lament at living in the shadow of her older, more glamorous sister on *The Brady Bunch*.

Context is crucial. Notice how the main idea of paragraph 3 helps solidify our understanding of paragraph 2; not just regarding what it says but why it's there at all. Paragraph 3 relates even better to paragraph 1, which sets out the question regarding technology and art in the first place, a question just beginning to be answered now. And we should expect that this paragraph also sets the stage for the finale in paragraph 4.

Okay, time to bring it on home with paragraph 4:

> A new aesthetic orientation emerged to express this new reality. Art turned inward to focus on man's struggle against a bureaucratized, impersonal, technological civilization. Mumford readily admits that the dissociation of the artist from communal obligations greatly expanded the realm of artistic possibilities; freed from its integrative purpose, art was set loose to traverse previously inappropriate realms of psychology and individualism in startling new ways. However, the magnificent innovation born of this freedom has been somewhat hindered by art's apprenticeship to the dominant force of the technological milieu: the market. Out of necessity, money has replaced muse as motivation for many artists, resulting in the art world of today: a collection of "industries," each concerned with nothing loftier than its own perpetuation. Mumford testified admirably to a unity of art greater than the sum of its parts. Despite modern art's potential, it is reasonable to infer the converse: that the individual arts of our technological landscape are diminished in isolation.

- **Giveaways:** "A new aesthetic orientation emerged to express this new reality." This whole first sentence screams "main point time coming up!" as it relates a new kind of art ("new aesthetic orientation") with the alienating results of technology ("this new reality"). This segment—"Mumford readily admits . . . greatly expanded the . . . possibilities . . . however"—is quite telling, as it indicates that something good may have come out of the situation, yet even that good thing has been hampered by some other negatives. Another giveaway worth noticing is the phrase "Mumford testified admirably . . . ." "Hindered" and "diminished in isolation" are excellent indicators of the author's assessment of modern art. The entire final sentence is important, especially "it is reasonable to infer . . . ," which suggests that an opinion of the author is finally forthcoming.

- **Purpose:** To draw a conclusion regarding the societal change documented in the previous two paragraphs, and to fulfill the promise to investigate the prediction introduced in paragraph 1.

- **Players/Extras:** Mumford makes a few cameos, but we get the sense (especially from the giveaway "it is reasonable to infer . . .") that the author has stepped forward to drive the main point home. The author is therefore the major player in this final paragraph, offering an opinion on the art/technology issue discussed throughout the passage.

- **Main Point:** Art needed to change to deal with the alienating form of modern life brought on by technological advances. While this introduced the promise of great innovation, by and large art is "diminished" in its modern, less unified, more isolated form.

- **Author Behavior:** Still mainly descriptive, although the author does take a position by the end.

- **Author Opinion:** The author's opinion is sounded in the middle of the paragraph and comes through especially clearly in the final sentence. As is often the case, the opinion that emerges in the final paragraph forms a large part of the passage's overall main idea, which we can now state with finality as our last Essential Element.

- **Passage Main Idea:** Technology is a big part of modern culture; therefore it should influence how art functions in society. And in fact, it does, by creating a new form of existence that requires a new kind of art, one that the author finds promising yet "hindered" and "diminished." This point is developed with the aid of Mumford's analyses and especially the contrast he charted between the art of modern times and that of the pre-technological medieval period.

So, why do we care about all this context, purpose, and passage structure stuff again? Because those are the kinds of things the questions ask about. Points, remember? LSAT score moving closer to 180 and further from 120? Better law school? Better career? More money? Making your parents proud? Proving your worth to the world? Whatever—we all have our reasons. Let's stick with the first one: We care about context, purpose, and passage structure because those are things that Reading Comp questions ask about.

ESSENTIAL STRATEGY

Before we get to our four-step method for approaching the questions in a standard non–Paired Passages question set, it's imperative to first understand that all of the questions will fall under one of two categories:

- Big Picture questions

- Content questions

Big Picture questions: These questions are just like they sound: big picture. Big Picture questions test your understanding of the author's main idea, the author's main reason for writing the passage, the author's attitude toward someone or something, the author's methods of constructing the passage, and the organizational techniques employed by the author to get his or her point across. Reading Comp question sets *always* include certain standard Big Picture questions that test your understanding of the very issues we discussed at length previously—that is, the Essential Elements.

Content questions: These are those questions that focus on the details and specifics. Some ask about particular facts in the passage, and some ask you to form inferences or deductions based on these specific facts. In any case, they are distinct from the Big Picture questions described above. Content issues should take a back seat to Big Picture issues, both during your attack on the passage and while answering the questions. As you'll see, not every nitty-gritty detail you encounter will be tested in a question. So it does make sense to focus intently on Big Picture issues and skim past complex details, focusing on those *only when required to do so by a question*. Let's turn our attention to the Essential Strategy now.

Perform the following steps for every Reading Comp passage you face:

Step 1: Scout the Territory. Yes, another military metaphor, but we think it applies perfectly well. In LSAT as in war, it helps to know in advance what you're up against. Quickly scan the question stems in the question set attached to the passage. Do this *before* attacking the passage. This will enable you to determine important things up front—the number and kind of questions types. If you see, for example, that Big Picture questions dominate the question set, you'll be less tempted to get bogged down in details and more likely to focus especially hard on Essential Elements. As for Content questions, take note of paragraphs and specific details that are tested directly by certain questions. You may find it helpful to underline clue words that indicate definite tested issues and mark in the passage any line number or paragraph specifically referred to in a question.

Step 2: Mine the Essential Elements. The next step is to attack the passage by extracting the Essential Elements from each paragraph in the manner highlighted in the previous section. There are no moral victories for simply making your way from the first word to the last, as that doesn't guarantee that you've assimilated the information you'll need to get points.

Step 3: Divide and Conquer. Here's where a proper attack on the passage pays off. If you've extracted the Essential Elements, you should be able to knock off the Big Picture questions quickly and confidently. Since these author-based questions are all related and accord with the Essential Elements you've focused on in Step 2, it makes sense to answer these as a group, even though that means skipping around in the question set. Content questions focus on passage specifics, and we recommend answering these after you've tried all the Big Picture questions. In the next section you'll learn to distinguish between Big Picture and Content questions and will learn strategies for tackling the question types that constitute each category.

Step 4: Mine the Experience. As always, this step is included as a reminder to extract test day lessons from every passage and question you face. How can you get the most out of the Reading Comp passages you work through in your preparation stage? The best thing you can do is review them thoroughly and meticulously. Use the following questions to guide your analysis.

- Did "Scouting the Territory" help direct my attack on the passage?

- Did I extract the Essential Elements from each paragraph?

- What Essential Elements did I miss in my paragraph synopses?

- Did I focus too much attention on details during my attack on the passage?

- Did I successfully extract the main idea and primary purpose by the end of the passage?

- Did I "Divide and Conquer" effectively? That is, did I do the questions in the most efficient order?

- Did I use my understanding of the author's tone and behavior not only to lead me to correct choices but also to eliminate wrong ones?

- Did I recognize and eliminate the common wrong answer types that appear consistently throughout the Reading Comp section?

These are just some of the issues that should guide your review of your Reading Comp performance. Don't get discouraged if you can't at first produce stellar answers to every question in this list—that's what practice is for. Optimally, you'll see a tight connection between satisfactory answers to these questions and an improvement in your Reading Comp performance. If you find yourself struggling down the road, return to these questions to pinpoint where the difficulty may lie.

Okay, here's where things stand: You've learned about the Reading Comp section and the kinds of skills it tests. You've seen a sample passage and have learned about and gotten practice with the Essential Elements you should extract from each paragraph. Then you picked up the Essential Strategy that you'll employ in each passage. Later, you'll have a chance to put this all together to tackle two actual LSAT Reading Comp passages, but first let's take a closer look at the kinds of questions you'll face.

QUESTION TYPES

The table on the next page summarizes the nine main Reading Comp question types, arranged in the two categories we've discussed, Big Picture and Content. We'll cover each question type in the order in which they appear. Take a few minutes to familiarize yourself with them now.

Category/Question Type	Your Task	Percentage of Section
Big Picture		
1. Main Point	Recognize the overriding idea of the passage.	15%
2. Primary Purpose	Recognize the reason why the author wrote the passage.	8%
3. Paragraph Purpose	Understand the function of a paragraph in the context of the passage as a whole.	5%
4. Attitude	Recognize the author's tone or belief regarding a person, thing, or issue.	8%
5. Organization	Recognize how the passage is constructed.	6%
Content		
6. Fact	Understand what the author says about a specific detail in the passage.	20%
7. Inference	Recognize statements suggested by the information provided in the passage.	14%
8. Author Agreement	Recognize a statement consistent with the author's belief about a specific issue.	12%
9. Detail Purpose	Understand the reason why the author cites a specific example.	12%

Note: Percentages are accurate at the time of publication and may vary slightly from test to test.

In the "Real Deal" section to come, we'll work through all the steps of the Essential Strategy in the context of two real LSAT passages, but first you'll learn to apply Step 3, Divide and Conquer, to each of the nine question types listed above. As a prelude to that discussion, let's take a quick look at common wrong answer types, since eliminating those will play a large part in your success.

Common Traps for All Question Types

There are six main types of wrong choices you'll encounter in Reading Comprehension, and the good news is that you've already studied four of them in Logical Reasoning.

- **Irrelevant:** These answer choices focus on outside issues not mentioned anywhere in the passage.

- **Twister:** A twister distorts some fact or issue discussed in the passage.

- **Overreach:** These wrong answer choices blow a passage issue out of proportion, often employing extreme language characterized by such words as *only, all, always, never,* and the like.

- **Opposite:** These answer choices present the reverse of what the passage states or implies.

In addition, there are two more wrong answer types specific to Reading Comp:

- **Mish-Mash:** These inappropriately combine passage elements in a way not intended or suggested by the author. Mish-mash choices are tempting because the things they mention "are in there somewhere." However, that's not good enough. Because Reading Comp passages are so chockablock with details, the test makers have plenty of fodder to work with to combine passage elements in answer choices in ways that *sound* appealing. Many of the resulting conglomerations, however, don't correspond to what the author actually says or implies.

- **Retrieval Error:** These choices focus on something from the wrong part of the passage; for example, the wrong paragraph, person, group, event, or time period. A brilliant LSAT instructor from Manhattan dubbed this kind of wrong choice "Retrieval Error." That's what happens when you venture into a place in search of one thing, only to come out with something else. Picture a burglar entering a bank and coming out with a lit stick of dynamite instead of the bag of gold. Or a fireman bursting out of a burning house with the crib instead of the baby. They've retrieved the wrong thing. In the same vein, if you venture into the passage in search of a right answer and instead come out with an irrelevancy from the wrong part of the passage, you've fallen victim to a Retrieval Error of your own.

You'll see examples of these common traps as we explore each question type. We'll work through each type in the context of the passage we analyzed earlier, so refamiliarize yourself with that now and then proceed to our discussion of the first Big Picture question type, Main Point.

Common to most interpretations of the role of art is the notion that art correlates directly with the environmental characteristics of its period of origin. If we understand technology not only as a practical set of techniques and machines but also as an evolving dominant ideology of the modern age, it follows that we should witness an infiltration of technology
(5) into art not just in terms of the tools and processes at artists' disposal but also in terms of technology's influence on art's place within society. The latter supposition has been explored by American writer and critic Lewis Mumford during various stages of his prolific career.

Mumford posited an integrative role of medieval art corresponding to the unity of life characteristic of this pre-technological period. Medieval citizens, he argued, did not
(10) attend the theater, concert hall, and museum as activities unto themselves as we do but rather witnessed a fusion of music, painting, sculpture, architecture, and drama in unified religious ceremonies that incorporated people into the shared social and spiritual life of the community. Integral to this phenomenon was the non-repeatability of the experience—live musicians, specially commissioned scores, unique paintings and sculptures, and inimitable
(15) speakers filling incomparable cathedrals with exhortation and prayer. Everything in the artist's repertoire was brought to bear to ensure maximum receptivity to the political, social, and religious teachings at the heart of this medieval spectacle.

Mumford further speculated that the mass production of text and images from the sixteenth century forward ultimately disrupted the unity exemplified by the medieval
(20) experience, and with it the role of art as a testament to and reinforcement of that unity. He believed that modern communication technologies encourage the fragmentation of time, the dissociation of event and space, and the degradation of the symbolic environment via an endless repetition of cultural elements. The result is the oft-commented-upon "alienating" experience of modern life.

(25) A new aesthetic orientation emerged to express this new reality. Art turned inward to focus on man's struggle against a bureaucratized, impersonal, technological civilization. Mumford readily admits that the dissociation of the artist from communal obligations greatly expanded the realm of artistic possibilities; freed from its integrative purpose, art was set loose to traverse previously inappropriate realms of psychology and individualism
(30) in startling new ways. However, the magnificent innovation born of this freedom has been somewhat hindered by art's apprenticeship to the dominant force of the technological milieu: the market. Out of necessity, money has replaced muse as motivation for many artists, resulting in the art world of today: a collection of "industries," each concerned with nothing loftier than its own perpetuation. Mumford testified admirably to a unity of art
(35) greater than the sum of its parts. Despite modern art's potential, it is reasonable to infer the converse: that the individual arts of our technological landscape are diminished in isolation.

1. Main Point (Big Picture)

Most passages contain some form of Main Point question, which tests whether you have extracted from the passage the most essential idea the author is trying to get across. It usually shows up toward the beginning of the question set, but if you've done your work with the Essential Elements, the Main Point question is a good candidate to start with no matter where in the question set it appears.

Tackling Main Point Questions

Use the Essential Elements. A key component of Essential Elements is keeping track of the Main Point of each paragraph, culminating in a solid understanding of the passage's overall main idea by the time you reach the end. If you've done this work effectively, the Main Point question should pose no special problem, since you've basically contemplated this issue well in advance of tackling the question itself.

Think Globally. Reading Comp Main Point questions are closely tied to Logical Reasoning Main Point questions, so the strategies you learned to handle those certainly come into play here. There we encouraged you to think *globally,* which means to separate what the author is ultimately getting at (the main point) from what she uses to get there (evidence). In the Logical Reasoning Main Point discussion we said, "Remember that anything that leads to a larger issue cannot be the *main* point. The correct choice should have a satisfying, 'end of story' feel to it; settle for nothing less." This advice applies equally well here.

Hear Ye, Hear Ye . . . Just as in Logical Reasoning, the correct choice to a Main Point question should sound like an appropriate headline if the passage were a newspaper article; again, not as exciting or snappy, but true to the passage's essence.

Pay Your Respects. Again harking back to Essential Elements, there are reasons we differentiate players from extras, not the least of which is to chop choices that ignore the former in favor of the latter. Don't dis the players! Eliminate any main point choices that omit the passage's main character or central subject.

Find the Middle Ground. Some Main Point answer choices are too narrow, and some too broad, to reflect the true gist of the passage. As in the story of Goldilocks, the correct answer must be *just right*. Avoid overly narrow choices that focus on minor issues and overly broad choices that expand the scope of the passage beyond the author's main concern.

Spot the Traps. Overreach choices are common in Main Point questions, for the reason alluded to above: Some choices try to blow up some minor character or idea into Main Point material while ignoring the central players and features of the passage. In some cases these represent Retrieval Errors as well, since they retrieve a detail of the passage and attempt to masquerade it as the overriding point. Keep your eye out for Twister choices that distort the main point and Irrelevant choices that focus on issues that go beyond the scope of the passage.

Practice: Main Point

Use the guidelines above to work through this typical Main Point question.

> Which one of the following most accurately expresses the main point of the passage?
>
> (A) Modern technology contains both practical and ideological elements.
> (B) Mumford has demonstrated the evolution of medieval unity into modern alienation.
> (C) Mumford's analyses support the idea that technology has influenced the function and quality of modern art.
> (D) Technology has placed new tools at the disposal of modern artists.
> (E) Most cultural institutions have been adversely affected by advances in modern communication technologies.

Remember, by the time you begin working on the questions, you've already performed Steps 1 and 2 of our Essential Strategy—that is, you've already Scouted the Territory and Mined the Essential Elements.

In the guided explanations in this section of the chapter, we pick up with Step 3: Divide and Conquer. The "Divide" part of this step concerns separating the Big Picture from the Content questions to tackle the questions in the most effective order. The "Conquer" part, of course, is about answering the questions correctly.

Step 3: Divide . . . Main Point is the biggest of the Big Picture issues, and we tracked it throughout our attack on the passage, so it makes sense to handle a question like this first no matter where in the question set it appears. In accordance with our mission to extract Essential Elements from this passage, we followed the main point of each paragraph and then put it all together as the passage's main idea at the conclusion of paragraph 4. That puts us in a fine position to knock this one down.

. . . and Conquer. The passage begins with a question about the relationship between technology and art and makes its way back to that issue with a definitive conclusion on the matter in the final paragraph. We also designated Lewis Mumford a major player who's featured in all four paragraphs. So any choice that omits either the tech/art issue or Mumford can't represent the main point here. **C** is the only choice that contains all of the passage's relevant elements, and it matches the main idea we delineated in the end. The author concludes that technology influences the nature of art by creating a different kind of society to which art must adapt. She finds the quality "diminished." Finally, she relies upon Mumford's investigations to develop her position, so the first part of the choice is right on. **C** is correct.

TAKE AWAY

Scour the passage for players. If some person or group is important enough in the passage, the odds are very good that the correct choice will mention that character.

A and **D** both play off small points in the introduction to the passage's topic in the first paragraph; that is, they're both too narrow to suffice as the main point of the passage. **A**'s most obvious failing is that it ignores the major subject of the passage, art. **D** does deal with both technology and art but focuses on what the author mentions as a side issue. The author admits that technology has given artists new tools but immediately goes on to express interest in a different idea—"technology's influence on art's place within society." That's what the remainder of the passage is about.

B is true—the passage *does* describe Mumford's theory on how medieval unity evolved into modern alienation. But this exists to support a larger point about art and technology. Thinking globally, we'd have to conclude that **B** contains supporting material that would fail hands down as a headline for this passage.

A choice must be more than just true to be the main point of the passage.

E is an Overreach choice that's way too broad to represent the main point here. It also ignores the main player and the main subject, the relationship between technology and art.

Step 4: Mine the Experience. As always, strive to get as much out of every question and passage you attempt. We won't bother repeating this step, but do remain aware of its significance. Use the list of analysis questions provided earlier to review your performance and make the most of your practice time.

2. Primary Purpose (Big Picture)

Primary Purpose questions ask for the main reason why the author wrote the passage. Here are some things to keep in mind when tackling this question type.

Tackling Primary Purpose Questions

Use the Essential Elements. If you properly extracted the purpose from each paragraph, as the Essential Elements strategy encourages you to do, you should have little problem coming up with the overriding purpose by the time you get to the end of the passage. Moreover, your focus on the author's behavior, combined with your incessant search for the author's overriding main point, will also help you here since nothing that conflicts with the author's behavior or main point can be correct for a Primary Purpose question.

Go with What You Know. If the question set contains a Main Point question, and if you've dispensed with that one handily, you can probably use that knowledge to help you answer the Primary Purpose question since these two question types are so closely related. In most cases, the primary purpose will be a general restatement of the method used to arrive at the main point. In the simplest scenario, the primary purpose is *to establish the main point*. For example, if the main point of a passage is that Harriet Tubman overcame numerous obstacles to help people escape slavery before the Civil War, the primary purpose might be "to demonstrate the significant achievements of a nineteenth-century American hero." Even in more difficult cases, the primary purpose cannot and will not run counter to any part of the main idea.

Make the Match. The choices in Primary Purpose questions are usually stated in general terms, so you should go right ahead and use your Matching technique from Logical Reasoning to match the generalities of the choices to the specifics of the passage. As you may recall, this technique requires you to demand a precise correspondence between the words of the choice you select and the elements found in the passage. Nothing less will do. If any word or phrase of an answer choice does not match what's in the passage, that choice must be wrong no matter how close the rest of it sounds.

Don't hesitate to apply any technique you picked up in Logical Reasoning here in Reading Comp; there are, after all, many similarities between these sections. Conversely, there's no reason why your practice forming paragraph synopses by extracting Essential Elements from each paragraph can't help you better interpret Logical Reasoning passages. As we've been stressing throughout, the LSAT is a *synergistic* experience, with much overlap between its various components. Those who recognize and utilize that unity do better in the long run.

Know the Full Story. Beware of choices that describe what the author does in only one specific part of the passage. The correct choice must cover the author's complete intention.

Use Your Imagination. If you're unsure of a Primary Purpose answer choice, try envisioning what the passage would have to look, feel, and sound like for that choice to be correct. Then determine whether this imaginary passage matches the one on the page. If it does, that choice is correct. If it doesn't, that choice is wrong. You'll see an example of this strategy in the guided explanation that follows the question below.

Scan the Verbs. Immediately eliminate choices containing verbs that clash with the author's behavior or the overall tone of the passage. If, for example, the author's approach you identified during your consideration of the Essential Elements is strictly expository and informative, then you should quickly cross off choices containing words like *argue, dispute,* or *prove*. In this way, you can narrow the choices down to the few remaining verbs consistent with the author's purpose in writing the passage.

Spot the Traps. Beware of Overreach choices that ascribe too much to what the author is trying to accomplish in the passage. Twister choices that distort the author's intentions are also common to this question type. And, as indicated above, watch out for choices that accurately describe what the author does in one part of the passage but that don't encompass the entire story. We can think of these as Retrieval Errors, choices that attempt to encompass the author's overriding purpose but emerge from the passage with only part of it.

Practice: Primary Purpose

Now try your hand at the following Primary Purpose question.

The author's primary purpose in the passage is to

(A) outline an effect of a feature of modern society
(B) recommend a solution to a cultural problem
(C) bolster a critic's speculations with supporting evidence
(D) describe the major difference between two historical periods
(E) advocate for a change in society's modes of communication

Divide . . . Sometimes the Main Point question comes first in a question set, while its partner in crime, the Primary Purpose question, comes last. No matter—it makes sense to jump right to the Primary Purpose question immediately after Main Point, no matter where in the question set it appears. Think about it: You've just analyzed the passage, focusing very closely on the author's main ideas and purpose in writing. Then you've picked up one point for those efforts—the Main Point question—so why not bag another while you're at it? Soon enough you'll be mired in other issues, including the specifics of the Content questions. But while you're in Big Picture mode, you may as well dispense of the Primary Purpose question if one is included in the set.

Skipping around the Reading Comp question set may seem alien to you, but it's the best way to take control of the section. Your only alternative is to run through the questions in the order in which they're presented, which is not arranged for your convenience. In fact, how many things on the LSAT *are* structured for your convenience? Here's how many: zero. So why should you assume that the best order to tackle Reading Comp questions (or Logic Games questions, for that matter) is the order in which they appear? If you're having trouble with Reading Comp, a new approach may be just the thing you need.

. . . and Conquer. The choices are stated in general terms, as they often are in Primary Purpose questions, so let's jump right in and meticulously match the specifics of each to what we've picked up from the passage.

A presents a perfect match. Technology is the feature of modern society under consideration, and its influence on art, the main focus of the passage, is the "effect" to which the choice refers. So **A** is correct. As for the others:

B: The author laments what she perceives to be the degradation of modern art, but she proposes no solutions to this or any other cultural problem.

C: "Here's what Mumford says, and here's evidence to show that he's correct" would have to be the main thing we get in this passage for **C** to be correct. "Here's what Mumford says, and here's how it supports my take on art and technology" is more like it. This is an example of how to use the "imagine a passage" strategy discussed earlier.

D fails on two main counts. First, while the author, via Mumford, does outline a difference between the medieval and modern periods, nothing suggests the difference she discusses is the *major* difference between them. So this choice has a definite Twister element to it. Second, even if we ignore this bait and switch, as we've come to call it in Logical Reasoning, the difference cited is intended to support a larger point about technology's influence on art. The author did not write this passage *primarily* to compare the medieval world to the modern, despite the fact that that comparison does play a part in the passage. So aside from the Twister element, this choice is also too narrow to encompass the author's full objective.

E is a classic Overreach. In following the author's behavior throughout the passage, we found that she spent most of her time describing things and only in the end ventured the opinion that modern art has suffered somewhat from changes in technology. Nowhere does she come close to *advocating* anything, let alone a change in communication techniques.

> **TAKE AWAY**
>
> Remember to pay careful attention to the verbs in Primary Purpose answer choices. "Advocate" is too strong to describe the author's behavior in this passage, but even "recommend" in choice **B** and "bolster" in choice **C** exaggerate the author's intention.

3. Paragraph Purpose (Big Picture)

Paragraph Purpose questions ask just that—the purpose of a paragraph in the context of the passage as a whole. These should be a welcome sight if you've tracked this Essential Element carefully during your attack on the passage. Nothing fancy here in the way of strategy, as you'll mostly rely on the work you've already done in Step 2 of the Essential Strategy.

Tackling Paragraph Purpose Questions

Use the Essential Elements. You should get in the habit of noting the purpose of every paragraph you read, but Scouting the Territory during Step 1 might alert you to be especially vigilant when it comes to a specific paragraph singled out in a question. The function of a particular paragraph may not become fully evident until you've read the entire passage; remember, paragraphs don't exist in a vacuum but as components of the author's overall purpose, which may not be fully evident until the end.

Spot the Traps. Don't be surprised to come across some Retrieval Errors here—choices that describe the function of some *other* paragraph in the passage. Avoid Twister choices that distort the function of the paragraph in question and Overreach choices that exaggerate what the paragraph was written to accomplish. You may even encounter Opposite choices that totally reverse the purpose of the paragraph in question. For example, if a paragraph exists to refute an earlier assertion, an Opposite choice may state that the paragraph serves to support or affirm previous claims. In the same vein, eliminate choices that clash with the author's overall tone and opinion, since nothing that contradicts the author's general purpose or demeanor can suffice to describe her intentions in a single paragraph.

Practice: Paragraph Purpose

Keeping our passage analysis in mind, try your hand at the following Paragraph Purpose question.

> Which one of the following most accurately describes the author's purpose in the second paragraph of the passage?
>
> (A) to offer an alternative to the theory presented in the preceding paragraph
> (B) to offer speculations concerning art that will help to refute a proposition presented later in the passage
> (C) to introduce evidence that will provide the grounds for demonstrating that a theory proposed later in the passage is unsound
> (D) to show that a critic's hypotheses regarding the past are irrelevant to that critic's speculations regarding the future
> (E) to provide the basis for a contrast that will underlie an argument concerning modern art developed in subsequent paragraphs

Divide . . . Paragraph Purpose questions follow nicely on the heels of Main Point and Primary Purpose questions, since they require the same kind of Big Picture thinking you've engaged in during your paragraph analyses in Step 2 of the Essential Strategy. So try to tackle this type early on if one appears in the question set, no matter where the test makers choose to place it.

. . . and Conquer. We discussed in our paragraph 2 synopsis how the seeming detour into the pre-technological world must serve some purpose, and that that purpose is to provide a contrast to the alienating influence of technology on the modern world. In the remainder of the passage, the author contrasts art's role in an integrative medieval community with art's role in our alienating, modern technological civilization to advance her argument regarding the influence of technology on art. The description in paragraph 2 of medieval society and art thus serves as the basis of this contrast which does, as **E** puts it, underlie the author's argument concerning modern art.

> In Step 1 of the Essential Strategy, you would notice that this question specifically deals with paragraph 2, so it makes sense during Step 2 to put extra effort into the initial analysis of that paragraph. Still, don't hesitate to return to the passage to quickly review what you learned and to make sure that you understand this paragraph in the context of the entire passage.

TAKE AWAY

A: If anything, the discussion in paragraph 2 builds on the previous discussion, so there's no alternative there.

B and **C** are Opposite choices. The speculations and evidence concerning art in paragraph 2 don't refute but rather lay the foundation for what comes later.

D suggests that paragraph 2 serves to illustrate the lack of continuity in the thought of Lewis Mumford. But the author has no problem with Mumford. Mumford made different judgments about different times, but so what? Mumford's theory of medieval times is certainly consistent with his thoughts on modernity, and in any case the paragraph doesn't exist to highlight the coherence of Mumford's analysis but rather to support the point the author is trying to make about art. So this one most resembles a Twister choice.

4. Attitude (Big Picture)

Attitude questions ask about what the author thinks about a specific person, thing, issue, or situation described in the passage. They're usually fairly short, but that doesn't always mean they're easy. Here are some pointers on how to go about them.

Tackling Attitude Questions

Use the Essential Elements. Again, your focus on the author's behavior while attacking each paragraph of the passage will greatly come to your aid, since such a study tells you much about the author's overall attitude. Also, the giveaways you extract play a large role here, since these are words or phrases that specifically key you in to the author's beliefs. Be on the lookout for words or phrases that clash with the giveaways you discover during your attack on the passage.

Get in the Ballpark. There are three general ways an author may feel about something: positively, negatively, or neutral. It helps to first slot the author's attitude into one of these three categories. This preliminary assessment will often help you to eliminate at least one choice, maybe more.

Use Your Imagination. Just as in Primary Purpose questions when you used your imagination to conjure up a passage that might fit a particular choice to see if that choice matched the passage, here you can imagine what the situation in question would need to sound like for a choice under consideration to be correct. For example, suppose a question asks for the author's attitude on a recommendation put forth in the passage, and you're considering a choice containing the phrase "unconcealed skepticism." Ask yourself what "unconcealed skepticism" would sound like in the context of this particular recommendation, and then see whether that is in fact what you get in the passage. Say the author indicates that the recommendation in question may very well work but merely suggests that a better option may be available. This attitude would not accord very well with the phrase "unconcealed skepticism," nor of course would any situation in which the author actually champions the recommendation. However, language outwardly lambasting the recommendation or those who made it would fit the bill. To test for "unconcealed skepticism," you would do well to imagine a passage in which the author essentially says something along the line of "that recommendation is the stupidest thing I ever heard." If this imaginary passage matches the one in front of you, then "unconcealed skepticism" would make for a fine choice. If not, you'd need to cross it off and look elsewhere.

Spot the Traps. Overreach choices in Attitude questions exaggerate the author's overall demeanor or feeling about a particular issue. For example, say that an author argues that the revision of a medical theory in light of newly discovered evidence will help to better predict the onset of childhood diabetes. An Overreach choice might describe the author as downright hostile toward the current theory, when in fact he merely argues that while mostly valid and helpful, it can be made better. Even more blatant are Opposite choices, which assign a tone to the author's attitude or mode of presentation that flat-out contradicts the tone of the passage.

Practice: Attitude

See how you make out on this typical Attitude question.

> Which one of the following most accurately describes the author's attitude toward modern art as expressed in the passage?
>
> (A) unqualified derision
> (B) bemused indifference
> (C) reserved disappointment
> (D) boundless optimism
> (E) mild puzzlement

Divide . . . The author's attitude is closely tied to her main point and primary purpose, so there's every reason to believe that the thinking we've been doing along these lines will help us through any Attitude questions the set contains too. Moreover, Attitude questions are typically short, and the more quick points we get under our belt up front, the better we feel about ourselves, and the more time it leaves for the tough stuff. So when divvying up your tasks, it pays to turn your attention to Attitude questions, if any, after bagging any Main Point, Primary Purpose, and Paragraph Purpose questions in the set.

. . . and Conquer. You'll recall that no authorial attitude really emerged in this passage until the fourth paragraph, where the excellent giveaways "hindered" and "diminished in isolation" were our first hints as to the author's feelings about modern art. These giveaways rule out "totally positive" as the author's attitude, which kills **D**, and they show that she's more than "neutral," too, which allows us to toss **B** as well. Having discarded these choices quickly for failing to even get in the ballpark, we can now turn our attention to the negatively tinged choices.

E fails on account of "puzzlement." Is the author really puzzled? It doesn't seem so, considering that she's just spent an entire passage explaining to us the mechanism that has led to modern art's diminishment. If we use the "imagination" technique described above, we'd try to envision what an author puzzled about the quality of modern art might sound like. Whatever that might be, it isn't what we get here, so we can dispose of **E**. The author's stance on this is simply too assured to qualify as "puzzled."

One way to get through the Reading Comp section on time is to make as many "quick kills" as possible. In Primary Purpose questions you can scan for and quickly chop choices containing inappropriate verbs. In Attitude questions, you can use the "Ballpark" technique to do the same.

That leaves **A** and **C**, which differ mainly in the author's degree of negativity. Using your imagination again, you might ask yourself: What does "unqualified derision" sound like? Well, kind of like this: "THIS SUCKS! IT REALLY, RE-ALLY, SUCKS!! No two ways about it . . . IT SUCKS!!" In fact, our mild-mannered author (you know we tracked her behavior throughout for a reason, and she always seemed pretty matter-of-fact in her presentation) actually has some *positive* things to say about the change that has taken place, despite its overall negative impact: It "greatly expanded the realm of artistic possibilities"; "art was set loose" to cover new ground in "startling new ways"; and even the thing that has been "somewhat hindered" (notice the qualifier "somewhat," which by itself works against **A**'s "unqualified derision") is referred to as a "magnificent innovation." So, putting it all together, she thinks modern art is worse off, despite great promise. "Reserved disappointment" best matches this attitude toward modern art, so **C** is the answer we seek.

5. Organization (Big Picture)

Organization questions ask how the passage is put together, which means that they're not much different from Logical Reasoning Method questions. So naturally you'll want to take advantage of the skills you developed in that section to help you with these. The mechanics of these aren't particularly tricky, but the wording of the choices, often lengthy, can pose some problems. Here are a few strategies to keep in mind.

Tackling Organization Questions

Use the Essential Elements. Your careful work on the paragraph-by-paragraph synopses should help you to get a grip on the passage's overall structure, especially if you gave adequate consideration to how the paragraphs relate to one another. The purposes of the paragraphs, taken together, form a roadmap of how the passage is constructed, so again the Essential Elements you identify up front play a major role in helping you to answer the last of our Big Picture questions.

Make the Match. The same skills that you use to match choices in Logical Reasoning Method questions to the passage can be used here to find the choice that perfectly accords with the passage's organization. Don't be intimidated by the general wording of the choices. Match the elements of each choice meticulously to your conception of the passage's structure developed during your passage analysis. Carefully test out each element of the choices until the one capturing the proper organization emerges.

Spot the Traps. Irrelevant choices contain things that simply aren't in the passage, things that come out of left field. For example, the test makers may throw the word *prediction* into a choice when no prediction appears in the passage. Since passages are organized to achieve the author's purpose, you may come across Opposite choices that suggest some purpose of the author that runs counter to what the passage is organized to accomplish, or Twister choices that distort the passage structure in some way. By and large, though, wrong choices in Organization questions usually reference things that just aren't there, so if you rely on your Matching skills, you should be able to eliminate wrong choices with confidence.

Practice: Organization

Take a shot at the following Organization question, and then, as always, thoroughly review the guided explanation.

> Which one of the following most accurately describes the organization of the material presented in the passage?
>
> (A) A theory is put forward, a specific means of testing the theory is outlined, and obstacles to carrying out the test are detailed.
> (B) A consequence of accepting a particular definition is proposed, the validity of that proposal is affirmed, and a judgment based on that affirmation is stated.
> (C) A supposition is introduced, a speculation regarding that supposition is described, and further speculations are detailed that counter the original supposition.
> (D) An interpretation is offered, expert testimony opposing that interpretation is provided, and a consequence of that testimony is explored.
> (E) A question is raised, and evidence from one time period and then another time period is presented to deem the question unanswerable.

Divide . . . If you've succeeded in extracting the Essential Elements during your passage analysis, the passage's structure should be fairly clear in your mind. You can tackle the Organization question (if one appears) anytime after Main Point and Primary Purpose, but in any case you should do it before the Content questions that take you out of Big Picture mode and plunge you into the specifics of the passage. Again, it's best to handle the Big Picture questions first while those issues are foremost in your mind and save the more detail-oriented stuff for later.

. . . and Conquer. We've carefully tracked the purpose of each paragraph, so now let's reap the reward.

A: Is a theory put forward? Sure—the author's notion that "we should witness an infiltration of technology into art" in numerous ways. But the author never veers off into any kind of discussion of how to test the theory or, even further afield, obstacles to such a test. The testing and obstacles stuff is simply Irrelevant to this passage—not there.

B: Is a particular definition presented? Yes. The author defines technology as both a practical set of techniques and an evolving dominant ideology. Is a consequence of accepting this definition proposed? Yes again. The author says that if we view technology in this particular light, something should follow—namely, a particular relationship between technology and art. Is that proposed consequence affirmed? Yup. The next few paragraphs describe, with Mumford's help, this very issue of technology's influence over art. We've come this far—it would be a damn shame for it to fall to pieces now, and it doesn't. A judgment (art has been diminished through this process) is rendered in the end.

TAKE AWAY

Just because the technique for dealing with Organization questions is pretty straightforward doesn't mean these questions are cake. Often the very general wording of the choices complicates things significantly. But if you hang in there, you'll find that all the elements of the correct choice *do* match the structure of the passage and also that some of the wrong choices will contain obvious mismatches, making them quick kills.

C: The words *supposition* and *speculation* aren't so egregious to raise red flags right off the bat, as there certainly is a lot of supposing and speculating going on in the beginning. We'll even let "further speculations are detailed" slide, since Mumford does offer speculations in bulk. But we can't be as forgiving of the phrase "*counter* the original supposition," since no big turnaround occurs. The original supposition that technology should influence art in a particular way is affirmed, not countered, which means that this one ventures into Opposite territory.

D falls for the same basic reason, as no opposition to an interpretation appears in the passage. The closest we get to "expert testimony" are Mumford's theories, which serve to support the author's overall point.

E: It's fair to deem the initial inquiry a "question," as the author basically sets up the question of whether technology's infiltration into art pans out as she supposes it should based on her conception of technology. Moreover, evidence from both the medieval and modern periods *is* provided in the course of the passage in the hopes of investigating this issue. This one breaks down over the phrase "deeming the question unanswerable." The question *is* answered (technology does indeed affect art), and a value judgment based on this answer (art is diminished) is asserted.

That does it for the five Big Picture question types, so we turn out attention now to the Content question types testing your understanding of the passage's details. It's not that Content questions are necessarily more difficult than Big Picture questions; indeed, some may be easier, depending of course on your understanding of the passage. But as we've stressed throughout, you can't be tested on every detail in the passage, so it's wise to not waste much time fully understanding every single nuance—you can, and should in many cases, look back at the passage to answer questions about specific issues. But you'll nearly always be asked the kinds of Big Picture questions discussed earlier, which you can prepare for in your initial read-through by tracking the Essential Elements in the manner described. Having done so, and having knocked those off to the best of your ability, you'll be ready to dig deeper into the guts of the passage to deal with the four question types in the Content category. Let's begin with Fact questions.

6. Fact (Content)

You've heard the expression "a fact's a fact," and that's nowhere more true than in LSAT Reading Comp. Facts are merely the things the author asserts, and some questions test whether you understand them. Some call these "Detail" questions or "Explicit Text" questions, but we'll just stick to precisely what they are: facts stated somewhere in the passage. Fact questions often contain language such as "According to the passage . . ." or "The author indicates . . ." Here are some tips on how to deal with Fact questions.

Tackling Fact Questions

Retrace Your Steps. One of the things to do when Scouting the Territory during Step 1 is to take note of passage details tested in specific questions. For example, consider the question stem of the question you'll try next:

> The author indicates that Mumford believed which one of the following regarding modern communication technologies?

The question alerts you to pay a bit of extra attention to any Mumford/modern technology text you happen upon in the passage. A notation (such as an asterisk in the margins or underlining the relevant text) may help you to relocate material associated with this issue in the event that you need to reread this material in greater detail to help you select an answer.

TAKE AWAY

You may be wondering at this point when it's appropriate to look back at the passage to answer questions. Some advocate going back to the passage to find, or at least verify, the answer to every question in the set. However, we believe this is not necessary if you've successfully extracted and thought through a passage's Essential Elements. Your focus on the author's actions, intentions, attitudes, and overriding points should allow you to bag at least a few "quick kills" on Big Picture questions right out of the box, without looking back. This is how you make up the time spent analyzing the passage, and why we recommend attempting the Big Picture questions first. Content questions, on the other hand, almost always require passage checking, especially since we recommend that you don't get too bogged down in the passage details during your first read-through. You may also find the confidence to answer some Content questions based solely on your memory of the passage, and that's okay too. But if you have any doubt, go back to the relevant passage text to confirm your selection.

Focus Your Efforts. If you do go back to the passage, reread the text pertaining to the fact in question, specifically in light of what the question asks you to determine.

TAKE AWAY

Notice again the benefit implied by this Divide and Conquer approach that has you focus on Big Picture issues instead of the intricacies of details. If you try to understand every detail during your first read-through, you're going to end up spending a lot of extra time comprehending stuff that offers no reward in the end. *Remember, not every detail in the passage is tested in the question set.* And even for those that are, you're better off revisiting the relevant passage material with the definite knowledge of what it is about that material the test makers want you to understand.

Spot the Traps. As we're sure you know, facts are very malleable—just look at what politicians and pundits do with them every day. Facts may be distorted or exaggerated, which mean you should beware of Twister and Overreach choices. Also don't be surprised to come across Irrelevant choices that miss the point entirely or Retrieval Error choices that deal with a passage detail other than the one alluded to in the question.

Practice: Fact

Now try this Fact question on your own.

> The author indicates that Mumford believed which one of the following regarding modern communication technologies?
>
> (A) Modern communication technologies play a part in engendering alienation.
> (B) Modern communication technologies represent a unifying force in society.
> (C) Modern communication technologies are the only factors degrading the symbolic environment.
> (D) Modern communication technologies were invented to express the new aesthetic orientation that has arisen in the modern period.
> (E) No culture experienced the fragmentation of time before the advent of modern communication technologies.

Divide . . . "The author indicates" tells us we're dealing with a Fact question, so the answer is stated right in the passage itself. Fact questions are good candidates to tackle after you've dispensed of all the Big Picture questions. They're generally the most straightforward of the Content questions because they give you a definite starting point—the detail being tested, sometimes even aided by a line reference telling you where in the passage to find it. Some of the other Content questions aren't as forthcoming, so consider tackling the Fact questions immediately after the Big Picture questions are out of the way.

. . . and Conquer. Mumford's view on modern communication technologies appears in paragraph 3.

> Thinking through the Big Picture issues of structure and organization, and using that knowledge to answer Big Picture questions, will often help you to locate the information you need to answer Content questions.

TAKE AWAY

Now you have a choice: You can automatically return to that part of the passage to quickly review it before attempting the question, or if you're confident that you remember something about Mumford's view on this matter, you can scan through the choices trying to eliminate a few that sound off-base. Either way, it's likely you'll want to look back at the detail at some point, if nothing else, to confirm your selection. The author tells us that Mumford believed that modern communication technologies fragment time, dissociate events and space, and degrade the symbolic environment resulting in the alienating experience of modern life. **A** captures this notion best.

> The answers to some Fact questions are merely paraphrases of the text.

TAKE AWAY

THE NEW LSAT

B is an Opposite choice. Mumford thought that modern communication technologies have diminished the kind of societal unity exhibited in the Middle Ages.

C is an Overreach. While Mumford believes that these technologies degrade the symbolic environment, nothing suggests that he thinks they're the *only* things to do so.

D reverses cause and effect, at least as far as the author sees things. The author states that a new aesthetic orientation emerged to express the new reality created by the disintegrating effects of modern communication technologies. **D** gets it backward. Moreover, this choice subtly shifts the focus to an assertion of the author, as opposed to a belief of Mumford, which means a Retrieval Error is in play as well.

TAKE
AWAY

> We slated cause and effect as one of your Logical Reasoning Essential Concepts, but it's not limited to that section alone. Take advantage of the synergistic nature of the test. If you have a good grasp of cause and effect, and are hip to the ways in which the test makers play around with it, you're less likely to fall for a wrong choice like this.

E: Just because Mumford believed that modern communication technologies have this fragmentation effect doesn't mean he necessarily thinks this is the *first time in history* a society has experienced this. Perhaps other things bring about the same effect. This choice takes Mumford's beliefs too far, which can only mean one thing: Overreach.

7. Inference (Content)

Inference questions are similar to the Inference questions in Logical Reasoning. They ask you to make reasonable deductions based on the passage text—that is, to recognize things suggested by the text or that must be true yet are not stated explicitly in the passage. Sometimes Inference questions require you to combine statements to form valid inferences, but often they are simply derived from closely paraphrasing the text and understanding the author's or other characters' feelings about the issues discussed in the passage. They almost never contain formal logic elements, so all in all they are not as strict as Logical Reasoning Inference questions. Still, all your practice with those should help you with these. Here are some guidelines to get you on your way.

Tackling Inference Questions

Locate the Topic. Sometimes you'll be asked to form an inference regarding a specific topic mentioned in the question stem. In those cases, locate and carefully reread passage material concerning that topic before testing the choices.

Let the Choices Be Your Guide. When no specific reference is provided, use the choices to lead you to the relevant issues and sections of the passage. Reread those sections, and test the choices accordingly.

Use the Essential Elements. While Essential Elements concerning Big Picture issues don't come into play directly here, the correct answer to an Inference question must still closely accord with the tone of the passage and the general demeanor and the opinions of the author. If a choice sounds far afield from what you know of the author and her overriding ideas, it's likely that that choice is wrong.

Stay in Line. A good Reading Comp inference must satisfy the same general conditions as a good Logical Reasoning inference: It must be strongly supported by the facts, be in line with the overall tone of the passage, and entail no unwarranted suppositions.

Negate and Destroy. This is our trusty Logical Reasoning technique that's used to confirm or eliminate wrong answer choices. If negating the choice you believe to be correct results in something that in some way contradicts the facts of the passage, chances are that choice is correct. Conversely, if nothing seriously goes awry when you negate a choice, then that choice probably doesn't contain the inference you seek.

Spot the Traps. Much like the wrong choices in Logical Reasoning Inference questions, the wrong choices in Reading Comp Inference questions are mostly populated by Twisters, Opposites, and Overreaches. Also keep an eye out for Mish-Mashes—choices that inappropriately relate two or more passage elements—and Irrelevant choices that bring in issues from left field.

> Mish-Mash choices can be tricky, because they're built from familiar-sounding passage material. Remember, just because something in a choice is "in there"—that is, is recognizable from the passage—doesn't necessarily make it true. Similarly, just because two elements of the passage appear together in a choice doesn't mean that those elements can be combined in any old way.

**TAKE
AWAY**

Practice: Inference

Use the tips above to work through the following Inference question.

Which one of the following can most reasonably be inferred from the passage?

(A) Modern religious ceremonies never make use of specially commissioned scores.
(B) Most artists are grateful to be relieved of their communal obligations.
(C) Only art that turns inward is suitable to express dissatisfaction with one's social and cultural environment.
(D) Medieval life was generally not alienating and impersonal.
(E) Mumford did not investigate the tools and processes at the disposal of modern artists.

Divide . . . Generally worded Inference questions like the one above simply ask "what can be inferred from the passage," and thus give no indication of where in the passage the right answer will be found. These can cumbersome, since you'll need to follow multiple trails to test choices referring to issues scattered all over the passage. Even if the question is not difficult, it may still entail a lot of work to find the correct choice. Moreover, *understanding* facts is generally less overwhelming than *deducing from* facts, which strengthens the case for tackling Fact questions before Inference questions. Overall then, it's generally best to save these for near the end of the question set.

. . . and Conquer. We have no clue as to where the answer will be found, so we'll simply have to attack the choices one by one.

A: *Modern* religious ceremonies are Irrelevant—we're told nothing about those, so we can't determine where the music for those ceremonies comes from.

> **TAKE AWAY**
>
> Take note of how the test makers form wrong choices. Because special scores were commissioned for medieval religious ceremonies, the test makers assume (rightly so, we're sure) that at least some people will jump to the conclusion that such scores aren't commissioned for modern ceremonies. But nothing supports this contention.

B: Irrelevant again. We don't know whether modern artists are even aware of the paradigm shift that Mumford outlines, or if they are, that they care.

C centers around the idea of necessity. While the passage does suggest that inward-turning art is effective at expressing dissatisfaction with one's environment, nothing suggests that it is *necessary* for this purpose—that is, that it's the *only way* to express this angst. This choice is therefore too extreme to be inferred, which qualifies it as an Overreach.

D is inferable. The author contrasts the unity and communal spirit of medieval life (both aided and expressed by the arts) with the impersonal alienation of modern times. It is thus inferable that medieval life was not generally alienating and impersonal, even if the author never quite states that directly. Try negate and destroy: What if medieval life *was* generally alienating and impersonal? The contrast established between the Middle Ages and modernity would then fall apart, seriously damaging the thrust of the author's argument. This confirms that choice **D** is strongly suggested in the passage.

E: We know what Mumford *did* investigate; as for what he *didn't*, there's no way to tell.

> **TAKE AWAY**
>
> Unknowables, discussed at length in Logical Reasoning, play a part in Reading Comp too.

8. Author Agreement (Content)

Author Agreement is a special form of Inference question. These questions ask you to find the choice containing an idea to which the author would likely subscribe, so there is an element of deduction at work here. They're distinct from Fact questions because they're based on the author's *implied* beliefs that are not explicitly stated in the passage. Sometimes, as in the practice question below, they ask you to deduce what the author might believe regarding a new situation described in the question stem. Here are some tips to keep in mind for this type.

Tackling Author Agreement Questions

Locate the Topic. The same issue we discussed regarding Inference questions applies here: A specific topic may be stated in the question stem, and it may not. If it is, locate and reread the passage material concerning that topic before testing the choices.

Let the Choices Be Your Guide. In other cases, no specific topic is provided in the stem. Instead, you'll see some form of the open-ended question "With which one of the following would the author be most likely to agree?" Again, you'd have no choice but to follow the lead of the choices.

Use the Essential Elements. Having studied the author's behavior, opinions, and motivations in depth, use that knowledge to infer her position on related matters. Just as we saw with standard Inference questions, the correct answer to an Author Agreement question must also closely conform to the demeanor and opinions of the author. In fact, in some cases you may have such a good grasp of the author's beliefs that you may not need to return to the passage to test the choices—the correct one may jump off the page at you.

Spot the Traps. Be on the lookout for Overreach, Twister, and Opposite wrong choices that exaggerate, distort, or even flat-out contradict the beliefs of the author. Also beware of Retrieval Errors that attempt to attribute a belief to the author that actually belongs to some other character in the passage or that describes the author's attitude toward some *other* issue in the passage, not the one referenced in the stem.

Practice: Author Agreement

Now see what you can make of the following Author Agreement question.

A twentieth-century painting depicting isolated, anonymous people as cogs in a vast mechanized infrastructure would most likely be viewed by the author as

(A) reprehensible for bringing about the state of the affairs that it purports to criticize
(B) a response consistent with a state of cultural disintegration
(C) the only viable mechanism for dealing with the underlying realities of an impersonal, bureaucratized world
(D) an example of the depiction of the unity of life
(E) a faulty representation of the psychology of modern citizens

Divide . . . Other than handling these after the Big Picture questions, there's no one place in the pecking order that these definitely belong. Some may be comfortable tackling these right after the Big Picture questions, while the focus is still on the opinions and methods of the author. Others may prefer getting the Fact questions under their belt before trying this type. After getting some practice with all the types, you'll likely discover what works best for you.

. . . and Conquer. We're offered a new scenario—outside information, as it were—and asked what the author might think about it. Of course, the trick is to build on what we already know about the author's beliefs. This author discusses the new modern aesthetic orientation that has emerged to express the new reality of an alienating, mechanized, technological civilization. The painting cited in the question stem represents a good example of the inward-turning art the author describes, so we can reasonably infer she would find this painting consistent with the modern cultural disintegration outlined in paragraph 3. That's what we get in correct choice **B**. Let's see what's wrong with the others:

A: According to the author, modern art is a *reaction to,* not a *cause of,* the current state of affairs, so the author wouldn't fault the painting for bringing about anything.

TAKE AWAY

We saw in choice **D** of the practice Fact question how cause and effect, something we studied at length in the Logical Reasoning chapter, pops up even here in Reading Comp. Be sensitive to words or phrases such as "bringing about" that may suggest cause and effect. Moreover, when cause and effect *is* in play, check to see whether the causation flows in the right direction. This choice pulls the old switcheroo, which places it firmly in the Opposite camp.

C is a big-time Overreach. The author certainly considers art of the type described in the question stem as one way people deal with the realities of the modern world, but nothing suggests that she believes this is the *only* viable reaction.

TAKE AWAY

Extreme-sounding words like *only, always, never,* and the like often signal classic Overreaches in both Reading Comp and Logical Reasoning answer choices.

D: The first problem here is that this choice refers to one of Mumford's beliefs, while we're seeking the author's buy-in. While technically qualifying as a Retrieval Error, it isn't especially egregious since the author's beliefs are fairly well aligned with Mumford's. So it's excusable if you missed the faulty attribution here. However, the Opposite part of the story can't be ignored: A painting depicting the isolation of a mechanized world would be considered by both Mumford and the author as the direct opposite of art expressing "the unity of life."

E: On the contrary, the author seems to believe that the new form of modern art accurately captures the psychological state of modern alienation. She may not be particularly happy that art has come to this, but she believes it does reflect the current reality. **E** is therefore another Opposite choice containing a notion that we would *not* expect the author to support.

9. Detail Purpose (Content)

This final kind of Content question asks for the purpose of some specific detail in the passage; not what the detail *says* (which would make it a Fact question), but *why* the author chose to include it. But for the fact that this question type revolves around a specific detail in the passage, we might actually consider it a Big Picture question because of how much it concerns the author's purpose. Similar to your Paragraph Purpose approach, you'll make use of the Essential Elements to get you in the right frame of mind, only now you'll focus on the purpose of a detail instead of the entire paragraph. As usual, an understanding of the common traps associated with this question type will come into play as well. Here are the strategies that will win you the point.

Tackling Detail Purpose Questions

Locate the Topic. You'll always be given a specific issue to focus on, so the first step is to find the relevant passage material. Your work during Step 1, Scouting the Territory, already alerted you to the importance of the detail in question, giving you the chance to highlight it in some way for later reference. (We'll talk more about specific Scouting the Territory strategies in our analysis of the Real Deal passages later in the chapter.) Of course, if you're given a specific line reference for the detail in question, use it.

Let Context Be Your Guide. When you've located the detail in question, analyze it in terms of its function. Any time you're asked about the purpose of something in the passage, be it a paragraph or a specific element, you must think in terms of *context*—that is, how it relates to everything around it. That means going beyond the simple question of *what* is said, to the more complicated issue of *why* it's said. Doing that, once again, is helped by the work you've already performed.

Use the Essential Elements. Your continual analysis of the author's purpose and behavior in Step 2 of our Essential Strategy should help you get into the ballpark and eliminate any choices that contradict the author's overall intention. Even though you're focusing on the purpose of a particular detail in the passage, nothing that goes against the author's general purpose or demeanor can suffice to describe her reason for including that detail. Having studied the author's behavior, opinions, and motivations in depth, see if you can eliminate some choices right off the bat based on your general understanding of the author's intentions gleaned during your initial passage attack.

Spot the Traps. Watch out for Retrieval Errors—choices that focus on or describe the purpose of some *other* element in the passage. Furthermore, the test makers always have recourse to a wide range of distortions and exaggerations when it comes to describing the author's purpose. Therefore, stay on the lookout for

Twister, Overreach, and Opposite choices, as well as Mish-Mashes that inappropriately relate other elements of the passage to the element in question.

Practice: Detail Purpose

Now try your hand at this Detail Purpose question.

> The author discusses the non-repeatability inherent in medieval citizens' experience of art in lines 13–15 primarily in order to
>
> (A) support Mumford's contention that medieval citizens attended art events in isolation
> (B) support the assertion that medieval life was characterized by alienation
> (C) suggest the medieval disdain for the fragmentation of time and the dissociation of event and space
> (D) demonstrate Mumford's belief that social and religious teachings infused medieval ceremonies
> (E) describe an orientation toward art that Mumford believes will be compromised by modern technology

Divide . . . While Scouting the Territory during Step 1 of the Essential Strategy, you'll notice that a question deals with this "non-repeatability" issue, so a little extra attention to this detail would be warranted during your attack on the passage in Step 2. If you understand that material reasonably well at this time, and have a good sense as to why it is included, you would be justified in tackling this question any time after the Big Picture questions. If, however, you are thrown by that material, holding off on the question until the end would be the wiser move.

. . . and Conquer. "Non-repeatable" is the way Mumford characterized the artistic elements of the medieval religious experience. The words "live," "specially commissioned," "unique," and "inimitable" all reinforce the idea that the music, paintings, sculpture, architecture, and drama of religious ceremonies were all one-of-a-kind experiences not to be exactly repeated in the future. But *why* does the author make this point? We determined in our passage analysis that this paragraph exists to present a contrast to modern civilization, which, we're told in paragraph 3, is characterized by the exact opposite: "an endless repetition of cultural elements." The "non-repeatability" claim therefore serves to present a kind of art—unique, nonstandardized, nonrepetitive—that Mumford goes on to argue is compromised by modern communication technologies. **E** is correct.

A and **B** have it backward, which means that they fall into the Opposite category. Mumford argues that the medieval arts were not isolated but integrated into the life of the community, and that medieval life was characterized by unity, as opposed to the alienation of modern times discussed later in the passage. So these two choices go beyond distorting the author's intention—they assert the exact opposite of it. **B** also qualifies as a bona fide Retrieval Error derived from the wrong part of the passage. It tries to suck you in based on the fact that alienation *is* discussed somewhere—just not in the context of the detail in question.

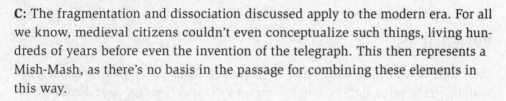

There are only so many ways that answer choices go astray. Learning to spot these common traps will make your life (at least the LSAT part of it) a lot easier.

TAKE
AWAY

C: The fragmentation and dissociation discussed apply to the modern era. For all we know, medieval citizens couldn't even conceptualize such things, living hundreds of years before even the invention of the telegraph. This then represents a Mish-Mash, as there's no basis in the passage for combining these elements in this way.

D is another Mish-Mash choice. The assertion that the artistic elements of medieval ceremonies were what the author calls "non-repeatable" speaks to the way that medieval audiences experienced the arts as a unique totality, not one by one in isolation. Nothing about this demonstrates Mumford's claim regarding the social and religious teachings of these ceremonies—that is, the *content* of this artistic spectacle. The claim in the final sentence of paragraph 2 regarding these teachings bears no direct relation to the "non-repeatability" issue raised earlier in the paragraph.

You may not need to return to the passage to answer every Content question. If you execute Step 2 correctly, some questions may be answerable from your overall grasp of the passage. Certainly look back to the passage when you need to, but also look to save time when you can. If you're confident about a choice, select it and move on.

TAKE
AWAY

Stay on Your Toes

The question types discussed in this part of the chapter make up the bulk of the questions you'll see in the Reading Comp section. However, you should be aware that there are some other kinds of questions that the test makers may throw at you from time to time. For example, they may borrow from their Logical Reasoning bag-o'-tricks and give you a Strengthen/Weaken the Argument challenge to chew on. In those cases, simply apply your Logical Reasoning skills to the relevant material, and you should be fine. (See pages 33–41.) You may also occasionally come across what we call an "Extension" question—a question that asks you to apply your understanding of the passage to a new external situation not mentioned by the author. You'll get some practice with this type in the Real Deal section to come.

But before we get to that, let's take a look at the most recent addition to the LSAT, Paired Passages.

THE NEW PAIRED PASSAGES

In June 2007, LSAC added a wrinkle to the Reading Comp section, which it calls "Comparative Reading." We'll refer to it as "Paired Passages" in order to highlight its distinguishing feature: two short passages instead of one long one.

What It Is

One of the four Reading Comp question sets will be based on two short passages written on the same subject, labeled, cleverly enough, Passage A and Passage B. The subject matter will fall into one of the four usual categories: humanities, law, social science or natural science.

The ideas in one passage will in some way relate to the ideas in the other. Some pairs may contain conflicting viewpoints, but even these may contain points of agreement and complementary elements. The relationship between the passages may be nuanced. For example, one passage may explore a generalization, while the other discusses a specific case to which that generalization applies. The authors do not interact directly; that is, they don't respond to each other. The passages exist independently, even though they share a common topic.

Together, the two short passages will be roughly the length of a standard long passage—about 450 words—and the question set accompanying them will contain somewhere around seven questions. A few of those questions may refer to a single passage, which means they'll be just like the question types we discussed earlier. We call these "Passage-Specific" questions. However, the majority of the questions in the set—"Comparison" questions—will focus on the relationship between the two passages.

Why It Is

LSAC says that the change is "a result of extensive research." Uh, okay—thanks for sharing. It does go on to say that the purpose of Comparative Reading is to assess the skills necessary to synthesize information from multiple texts, such as the ability to recognize and evaluate comparisons, contrasts, and generalizations. That said, it's not hard to see how the ability to compare two sides of a story is relevant to the study and practice of law. After all, our legal system is based on an adversarial approach that pits various interpretations of events and situations against each other. It appears that the test makers have adopted this comparative reading format as an attempt to re-create that dynamic.

Your Motivation

It's likely that some unprepared LSAT test takers may not even know about this relatively new Reading Comp item type, so acing the Paired Passage question set provides yet another opportunity to edge out your competition.

PAIRED PASSAGES ESSENTIAL STRATEGY

Because of the difference in format, we'll need to modify our Reading Comp Essential Strategy to handle these most effectively.

Step 1: Scout the Territory. Instead of distinguishing Big Picture questions from Content questions, your basic task in this initial step will be to locate any Passage-Specific questions among the question set. Remember, most questions in the set will be Comparison questions that you won't be able to answer until you've read both passages, but if you note the Passage-Specific issues up front, you can keep your eye out for them.

Step 2: Mine the Essential Elements of Passage A. You still need to extract the relevant information from each passage to answer the questions, so your focus on the Essential Elements discussed earlier in the chapter remains the same. First focus on passage A, paying special attention to the tested issues of Passage-Specific questions that you highlighted in Step 1.

Step 3: Divide and Conquer Passage A Questions. When you finish analyzing passage A, answer all questions pertaining only to that passage. It makes sense to tackle those Passage-Specific questions while passage A is still fresh in your mind.

Step 4: Mine the Essential Elements of Passage B. Extract the relevant information that will allow you to answer any Passage-Specific questions based on passage B. However, you must also gear up at this point for the Comparison questions, so as you analyze passage B, take note of how the author's purpose, style, tone, and opinions compare with those of passage A.

Step 5: Divide and Conquer Passage B Questions. When you finish analyzing passage B, answer the questions that pertain only to that passage.

Step 6: Divide and Conquer Comparison Questions. Relational thinking is generally more difficult than direct analysis, so the Comparison questions usually require a higher level of abstract thought. We therefore advise that you hold off on the Comparison questions until after you've finished all of the Passage-Specific questions. You can tackle them in order, or in any order that seems efficient to you. In the next section, we provide specific advice and practice on the kinds of Comparison questions you're likely to see.

Step 7: Mine the Experience. As always, we implore you to milk each practice passage for all of the test day lessons it provides.

It may seem like a lot of things to do, but basically you're repeating the same steps you've learned already for two different passages, and then hitting the Comparison questions that refer to both. You'll have an opportunity to try out the full method on the practice test at the end of the book, but for now let's focus specifically on the major thing that sets this passage type apart, Comparison questions.

Tackling Comparison Questions on Paired Passages

Comparison questions require you to think through the *relationship* between the information in both passages and to consider both passages before answering.

Read Proactively. Since the majority of questions you'll face in a Paired Passage set will be Comparison questions, it makes sense to begin preparing for them during your analysis of passage B. Things you should watch out for include:

- Central topic of both passages

- Points of disagreement

- Points of agreement

- Details common to both passages

- Similarities and differences in style, tone, and structure

Mix and Match. Some Comparison questions ask how the specifics of one passage relate to the specifics of the other, or for one author's take on a detail from the other passage. In these, home in on the elements being compared and search for the choice that addresses the relevant issues. Use your Logical Reasoning Matching skills to meticulously compare each choice to the subject in question. The wrong choices may present extraneous issues, or the author's view on an entirely different topic than the one under consideration. And speaking of wrong choices . . .

Spot the Traps. The wrong answers in Comparison questions fall into the same categories as the ones you've seen already—Overreach, Twister, Opposite, etc.—although they do tend to vary depending on what kind of Comparison question is at hand. The most effective way to learn how to spot these is to see them in context, so let's move on to some practice questions that illustrate the most common types of Comparison questions and the kinds of wrong choices they contain.

Practice: Comparison

The following Paired Passage set is adapted from the "Mumford on Art" passage discussed earlier in the chapter. Read and compare the passages, and then use the sample questions that follow to learn about the common types of Comparison questions.

Passage A

The role of medieval art corresponded to the unity of life characteristic of this pre-technological period. Medieval citizens did not attend the theater, concert hall, and museum as activities unto themselves as we do but rather witnessed a fusion of music, painting, sculpture, architecture, and drama in unified religious ceremonies that incorporated people
(5) into the shared social and spiritual life of the community. Integral to this phenomenon was the non-repeatability of the experience. Everything in the artist's repertoire was brought to bear to ensure maximum receptivity to the political, social, and religious teachings at the heart of this medieval spectacle.

The mass production of text and images from the sixteenth century forward ultimately
(10) disrupted the unity exemplified by the medieval experience, and with it, the role of art as a testament to and reinforcement of that unity. Modern communication technologies encourage the fragmentation of time, the dissociation of event and space, and the degradation of the symbolic environment via an endless repetition of cultural elements. The result is the oft-commented upon "alienating" experience of modern life. A new aesthetic
(15) orientation emerged to express this new reality. Individual arts, no longer indispensable elements of a superbly integrated communal expression, ventured off in their own directions, each concerned with nothing loftier than its own perpetuation. The medieval art world exemplified a unity greater than the sum of its parts. Compared with this majestic tapestry, the arts infusing our modern technological landscape are diminished in isolation.

Passage B

(20) The Middle Ages was characterized by an interrelationship among the arts that intensely dramatized the communal spirit of towns and villages and reinforced the cohesion that dominated the social sphere. Live musicians, specially commissioned scores, unique paintings and sculptures, and inimitable speakers filling incomparable cathedrals with exhortation and prayer coalesced into a vast display of societal expression. Despite the
(25) grandeur of this totality, the extent to which medieval artists longed to give free rein to individualistic visions is evidenced by the explosion of artistic creativity following the detachment of art from the communal sphere following the rise of technology as the dominant milieu of the modern age.

In response to this new social reality, modern art has turned inwards to focus on man's
(30) struggle against a bureaucratized, impersonal, technological civilization. The dissociation of art from communal obligations has greatly expanded the realm of artistic possibilities. Freed from its integrative purpose, modern art is set loose to traverse previously inappropriate realms of psychology and individualism in startling new ways. The magnificent innovation born of this freedom is evidenced in such diverse forms as Braque's Cubism, Debord's
(35) Lettrism, and Schoenberg's twelve-tone compositions. The huge social changes brought about by the spectacular rise of modern technology has both freed the artist and once again demonstrated art's enduring power to illuminate the human condition.

QUESTION 1: CENTRAL TOPIC

The two passages will likely contain different perspectives but will always be written on the same general subject. Chances are you'll be asked to recognize the topic that's central to both, or the general issue the passages are written to address. In some cases, the choices will be written in the form of questions, like so:

1.   Which one of the following questions is central to both passages?

   (A)   In what ways have modern artists illuminated the realm of psychology?
   (B)   To what extent have artists contributed to the invention of new technologies?
   (C)   How do modern communication technologies engender alienation?
   (D)   How has modern art been influenced by technological advancements?
   (E)   In what ways did the arts combine in the religious ceremonies of the medieval community?

Both passages state that technological advancement led to social upheavals, distancing art from its traditional role in medieval society and leading to drastic changes in the art forms of the modern world. One author thinks these changes are good, the other bad, but both authors are concerned with the question of how modern art has been influenced by technology, choice **D**.

A describes an issue discussed only in passage B, while choice **E** deals with something explicitly mentioned only in passage A. In any case, how the arts combined is hardly the central issue in either passage.

TAKE AWAY

Some wrong choices in a Central Topic Comparison question will mention something contained in only one passage, so keep your eye out for issues irrelevant to one (or even both) passages.

B is an Opposite choice, since both authors are concerned with the reverse relationship, the effect of technology on art. **C** makes no mention of the main subject of both passages, art.

QUESTION 2: AGREEMENT

Just because the passages are generally written from different standpoints doesn't mean there can't be certain points of agreement. For example, the two authors may rely on the same assumptions or agree on a specific fact yet use that fact to support different conclusions. As you analyze passage B, stay alert to any such similarities that may exist between the passages, such as the one highlighted in the following question.

2.   It can be inferred from the passage that both authors hold which one of the following views?

   (A)   Changes in social conditions can affect the ways in which the members of a society express themselves.
   (B)   Communication technologies have had a greater impact on modern society than have other kinds of new technologies.
   (C)   Art forms operating in isolation from one another are inferior to art forms operating in tandem.
   (D)   Some medieval artists desired to express themselves in ways that were not sanctioned by their society.
   (E)   Art is a significant binding force in modern society.

Both authors agree that technological advancements caused societal changes from medieval to modern society and that those changes influenced the orientation of art. Since artists are members of society and expression is a central component of art, choice **A** qualifies as a point of agreement. Notice how **A** is worded generally enough to accord with the thinking of both authors.

B: Neither passage compares the impact of communication technologies with the impact of other kinds of new technologies.

C, if anything, leans the other way. The author of passage A thinks that modern art forms are "diminished in isolation," while the author of passage B thinks that "freed from its integrative purpose," modern art has been characterized by "magnificent, startling innovation." So the authors would more likely disagree, not agree on **C**.

> Agreement questions often contain Opposite choices on which the two author would *disagree*, so the skills you develop to handle Logical Reasoning Disagreement questions may well come in handy here too. Those skills relate even more directly to the next question type we'll cover which tests specifically for points of disagreement.

TAKE AWAY

D: The notion of artists' desires is reflected only in passage B, so the opinion of passage A's author regarding this subject is unknowable.

> Irrelevant wrong choices appear in many different Comparison questions, since choices commonly focus on issues not considered by one or both authors.

TAKE AWAY

E: If we changed "modern" to "medieval" we'd have a winner, since both authors emphasize the role of art in contributing to the communal spirit of the Middle Ages. But neither author appears to believe that art serves the same function in modern times.

QUESTION 3: DISAGREEMENT

While there may be some points of agreement between the two passages, it's fairly certain that there will be points of disagreement and elements of conflict. So keep your eye out for ways in which the author of each passage takes exception to the facts or opinions presented in the other passage. Use the techniques we discussed to handle Logical Reasoning Disagreement questions: First pinpoint the choices that contain an issue relevant to both passages. Then test those choices for conflicting viewpoints. Let's try out this approach on question 3:

3. The authors of the two passages would be most likely to disagree over

(A) whether current artists use modern technology to create their works
(B) whether modern art has benefited from recent changes in social conditions
(C) the extent to which a spirit of community prevailed during the Middle Ages
(D) whether artists had a significant effect on the medieval community
(E) which modern art forms explore subjects previously considered inappropriate for artistic expression

A and E: While both passages consider how societal changes brought about by technological advances influenced the artistic orientation, neither says anything about artists actually *using* technology to create their works, so choice **A** fails the test for relevance. **E** does as well, since only passage B mentions some modern art forms that explore previously forbidden territories. So we can cut these two choices off the bat and consider the others in greater depth.

B: The author of passage A argues that the alienating experience of modern life has produced a new aesthetic orientation characterized by art forms that are "diminished in isolation." So that author thinks that modern art has suffered from changes in social conditions; the shift from a communal experience to an alienating one. The author of passage B agrees that such social changes have come about, but praises the art forms that emerged as liberating, innovative, and powerful. So the two authors would most likely disagree on the sentiment expressed in **B**.

TAKE
AWAY

In some cases, the Disagreement question will be a direct offshoot of the Central Topic question. Here, question 1 concerns the single question the two authors are intent on exploring, while question 3 concerns *the answers they give.*

C is a statement that both authors would agree with, as they both speak to the communal spirit and shared social life of the medieval community. Likewise, both authors agree on the unifying role that art played in cementing the social cohesion of the Middle Ages, so they would likely agree on **D** as well.

TAKE
AWAY

Just as you may come across Opposite choices in Agreement questions (statements on which the authors would *disagree*), eliminate points of agreement that represent Opposite choices in Disagreement questions.

QUESTION 4: METHOD

You may be asked to compare the ways in which the authors structure their arguments or the methods they use to advance their positions. Author behavior, one of our Essential Elements for Reading Comp, comes in especially handy in such questions, as do the techniques you learned to handle Logical Reasoning Method questions. Give Method question 4 a shot and then compare your thinking to ours.

---

4. Which one of the following most accurately describes the relationship between the arguments presented in the two passages?

   (A) Passage A outlines a function of medieval art which passage B denies.
   (B) Passage A cites facts regarding a previous society, while passage B employs evidence only from the modern period.
   (C) Passage A exposes a central assumption regarding technology that weakens the main point of passage B.
   (D) Passage A relies on evidence that passage B calls into question.
   (E) Passage A references the historical phenomenon described in passage B but draws a different conclusion regarding its effect.

As we've seen in previous questions, there's a good deal of synergy between the passages. Both cite the communal spirit of the medieval period, the role that art played in contributing to that spirit, and the distancing of art from communal obligations following societal changes brought on by technological innovations. The passages are therefore in accordance regarding the function of medieval art and both cite facts regarding a previous society, eliminating choices **A** and **B**. Moreover, the authors are on the same page regarding technology, so **C** isn't correct either.

E has it right: The authors both describe how social changes caused individual arts to switch from serving a communal, integrative function to existing on their own. However, from this same evidence (which allows us to chop choice **D**), they come to drastically different conclusions. The first author thinks modern art suffered from this historical change, while the second author thinks it flourished.

QUESTION 5: TONE

You may be asked to recognize how the style of writing and tone of passage A compare with the style and tone of passage B. There are many ways in which the passages can differ on this count. For example, some passages may be mostly descriptive, while others are more argumentative. Noting the behavior of each author will help, much as it helps you answer Method questions. Use the following question to check out some examples of possible tones you may encounter, and see if you can pick out the choice that fits the bill here.

---

5. Which one of the following best characterizes the tone displayed in the two passages?

   (A) Passage A is accusatory while passage B is hesitant.
   (B) Passage A is objective while passage B is emotional.
   (C) Passage A is nonpartisan while passage B is argumentative.
   (D) Passage A is critical while passage B is laudatory.
   (E) Passage A is impassioned while passage B is noncommittal.

D is correct. As we've seen, the author of passage A finds fault with modern forms of art, concluding that they are "diminished in isolation," while the author of passage B says only positive things about modern art.

The right answer to a Tone Comparison question will be consistent with everything you've learned regarding the relationship between the passages. The major difference is that the choices are worded more generally.

A: "Accusatory" is too strong to describe the viewpoint in passage A, while "hesitant" understates the firmness of the position put forth in passage B.

B: Both passages contain objective analyses. Moreover, passage B cannot be properly described as "emotional" just because it contains a clear argument, firmly stated.

C and **E:** "Nonpartisan" and "noncommittal" imply taking no sides. Each author clearly weighs in with an opinion, so these choices are incorrect.

QUESTION 6: ANALOGY

This may be the most challenging Comparison question you may face, asking you to choose the answer containing a pair of things that mimics the relationship between the two passages. The pair can be a pair of titles, a pair of documents, or a pair of whatever the test makers can think of that mirrors the connection between passages A and B. Sound familiar? Yup—it's like Parallel Reasoning from the Logical Reasoning section. It's no cakewalk there, and it's certainly no cakewalk here, but Analogy questions are doable if you approach them systematically and not get intimidated by the length of the answer choices. The following question will familiarize you with this difficult question type and provide some pointers on how to go about it.

6. The relationship between which one of the following pairs of documents is most analogous to the relationship between passage A and passage B?

(A) a medical report that discusses the potential side effects of a new heart medication; a hospital record documenting a recent increase in heart-related fatalities

(B) an editorial arguing that measures to curb inflation will stifle economic expansion; an economist's article that encourages increased entrepreneurship among members of the middle class

(C) a business essay stating that the recent differentiation of responsibilities among company departments enhances the functionality of each department; a consultant's analysis maintaining that a trend toward intra-departmental independence in businesses causes a decrease in each department's productivity

(D) an agricultural study that warns that current population trends will severely strain the nation's food supply; a census report that cites statistics indicating that the population is increasing more slowly than it increased in the previous decade

(E) a think tank's article defending the efforts of interest groups in the face of concerns regarding the influence of such groups on the political process; a political scientist's essay that explains the necessity for politically-minded interest groups within a democratic society

The relationship between the passages basically boils down to this: They take similar evidence concerning a societal change and run in different directions with it regarding the effect of this change on a specific societal element (art). That's an effective starting point when tackling the intimidating choices. Only the documents in **C** mirror this relationship. They both start with a common phenomenon (the trend toward interdepartmental independence within companies), but part company regarding its *effect*. The business essay says it makes departments function better, while the consultant says it makes them function worse. Same fact, different conclusion—just like in the passages.

> For Parallel Reasoning questions, we advise that you characterize the conclusion of the original argument before venturing off into the choices. Similarly, in Analogy Comparison questions, it helps to characterize the relationship between the passages in general terms before looking at the choices in order to get a sense of what the relationship you seek will sound like. That should help you blow past at least a few of the lengthy choices, leaving more time to analyze the rest.

TAKE AWAY

Of the wrong choices, only **E** contains a common underlying phenomenon agreed upon by the authors of both documents—both the think tank and the political scientist seem to agree that interest groups play some role in the political process. However, they appear to be on the same side of the fence on the issue, unlike the authors of passages A and B. The other wrong choices don't even get that far, since not one contains a pair of documents based on the same underlying premise. The pair in choice **A** concerns different issues, and are related only by the fact that both deal with the heart. The documents in **B** don't conflict, since the editorialist posits a cause and effect relationship while the article writer makes a recommendation. **D** also lacks the element of pro and con found in the original, since the slower increase cited by the census report is not inconsistent with the agricultural study's warning that food may become scarce. After all, the population is still rising according to the census, just not as quickly.

The previous questions should give you an excellent idea of what to expect in the Paired Passages question set. Remember that an actual Paired Passage set would include Passage-Specific questions as well. You'll get practice handling a complete Paired Passage question set on the practice test at the end of the book. But now let's move on to get some Real Deal practice on standard passages, which, after all, still make up three-fourths of the Reading Comp section.

Now try the following two actual released full-length passages and question sets. Give yourself 10 to 12 minutes or so for each, a little longer than the average time allotted per passage. Work through the explanations that follow each passage to evaluate your performance and solidify your understanding of the entire approach.

THE REAL DEAL: PRACTICE SET

Passage 1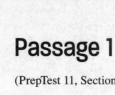

(PrepTest 11, Section 3, Qs. 22–27)

Note: The questions in this set have been renumbered for the purpose of this exercise.

Although surveys of medieval legislation, guild organization, and terminology used to designate different medical practitioners have demonstrated that numerous medical specialties were recognized
(5) in Europe during the Middle Ages, most historians continue to equate the term "woman medical practitioner," wherever they encounter it in medieval records, with "midwife." This common practice obscures the fact that, although women were not
(10) represented on all levels of medicine equally, they were represented in a variety of specialties throughout the broad medical community. A reliable study by Wickersheimer and Jacquart documents that, of 7,647 medical practitioners in France during the
(15) twelfth through fifteenth centuries, 121 were women; of these, only 44 were identified as midwives, while the rest practiced as physicians, surgeons, apothecaries, barbers, and other healers.

While preserving terminological distinctions
(20) somewhat increases the quality of the information extracted from medieval documents concerning women medical practitioners, scholars must also reopen the whole question of why documentary evidence for women medical practitioners comprises
(25) such a tiny fraction of the evidence historians of medieval medicine usually present. Is this due to the limitations of the historical record, as has been claimed, or does it also result from the methods historians use? Granted, apart from medical licenses,
(30) the principal sources of information regarding medical practitioners available to researchers are wills, property transfers, court records, and similar documents, all of which typically underrepresent women because of restrictive medieval legal
(35) traditions. Nonetheless, the parameters researchers choose when they define their investigations may contribute to the problem. Studies focusing on the upper echelons of "learned" medicine, for example, tend to exclude healers on the legal and social fringes
(40) of medical practice, where most women would have been found.

The advantages of broadening the scope of such studies are immediately apparent in Pelling and Webster's study of sixteenth-century London.
(45) Instead of focusing solely on officially recognized and licensed practitioners, the researchers defined a medical practitioner as "any individual whose occupation is basically concerned with the care of the sick." Using this definition, they found primary
(50) source information suggesting that there were 60 women medical practitioners in the city of London in 1560. Although this figure may be slightly exaggerated, the evidence contrasts strikingly with that of Gottfried, whose earlier survey identified only
(55) 28 women medical practitioners in all of England between 1330 and 1530.

Finally, such studies provide only statistical information about the variety and prevalence of women's medical practice in medieval Europe. Future
(60) studies might also make profitable use of analyses developed in other areas of women's history as a basis for exploring the social context of women's medical practice. Information about economic rivalry in medicine, women's literacy, and the control of
(65) medical knowledge could add much to our growing understanding of women medical practitioners' role in medieval society.

1. Which one of the following best expresses the main point of the passage?

(A) Recent studies demonstrate that women medical practitioners were more common in England than in the rest of Western Europe during the Middle Ages.

(B) The quantity and quality of the information historians uncover concerning women's medical practice in medieval Europe would be improved if they changed their methods of study.

(C) The sparse evidence for women medical practitioners in studies dealing with the Middle Ages is due primarily to the limitations of the historical record.

(D) Knowledge about the social issues that influenced the role women medical practitioners played in medieval society has been enhanced by several recent studies.

(E) Analyses developed in other areas of women's history could probably be used to provide more information about the social context of women's medical practice during the Middle Ages.

2. Which one of the following is most closely analogous to the error the author believes historians make when they equate the term "woman medical practitioner" with "midwife"?

(A) equating pear with apple
(B) equating science with biology
(C) equating supervisor with subordinate
(D) equating member with nonmember
(E) equating instructor with trainee

3. It can be inferred from the passage that the author would be most likely to agree with which one of the following assertions regarding Gottfried's study?

(A) Gottfried's study would have recorded a much larger number of women medical practitioners if the time frame covered by the study had included the late sixteenth century.
(B) The small number of women medical practitioners identified in Gottfried's study is due primarily to problems caused by inaccurate sources.
(C) The small number of women medical practitioners identified in Gottfried's study is due primarily to the loss of many medieval documents.
(D) The results of Gottfried's study need to be considered in light of the social changes occurring in Western Europe during the fourteenth and fifteenth centuries.
(E) In setting the parameters for his study, Gottfried appears to have defined the term "medical practitioner" very narrowly.

4. The passage suggests that a future study that would be more informative about medieval women medical practitioners might focus on which one of the following?

(A) the effect of social change on the political and economic structure of medieval society
(B) the effect of social constraints on medieval women's access to a medical education
(C) the types of medical specialties that developed during the Middle Ages
(D) the reasons why medieval historians tend to equate the term "women medical practitioner" with midwife
(E) the historical developments responsible for the medieval legal tradition's restrictions on women

5. The author refers to the study by Wickersheimer and Jacquart in order to

(A) demonstrate that numerous medical specialties were recognized in Western Europe during the Middle Ages
(B) demonstrate that women are often underrepresented in studies of medieval medical practitioners
(C) prove that midwives were officially recognized as members of the medical community during the Middle Ages
(D) prove that midwives were only a part of a larger community of women medical practitioners during the Middle Ages
(E) prove that the existence of midwives can be documented in Western Europe as early as the twelfth century

6. In the passage, the author is primarily concerned with doing which one of the following?

(A) describing new methodological approaches
(B) revising the definitions of certain concepts
(C) comparing two different analyses
(D) arguing in favor of changes in method
(E) chronicling certain historical developments

Passage 1: Guided Explanation

Women Medical Practitioners

So how did things go with the exciting world of women medical practitioners? This is a very typical social science passage, presenting one author's examination of an aspect of a society at a particular time. The one you'll work through after this is a natural science passage. You'll see more examples of these types, as well as of the other two passage types, humanities and law, later in the practice test at the end of the book. But first things first. Let's review this passage, beginning with the first step of our Essential Strategy.

Step 1: Scout the Territory. Scanning the stems for Big Picture questions reveals typical Main Point and Primary Purpose questions bookending the set in questions 1 and 6, respectively. This is fairly common and reinforces your mission of extracting the Essential Elements from each paragraph that will directly help you bag these points.

As for the Content category, question 3 is an Author Agreement question based around a character, Gottfried, so you may wish to underline Gottfried as a reminder to pay some extra attention to the author's thoughts about him or her. Question 5 is a Detail Purpose question, and you may also wish to underline the long, strange names for future reference—chances are you'll recognize those when you hit them in the passage. Question 4 is a standard Inference question— nothing surprising there. Finally, question 2 is a rare Extension question that you're probably best off saving for last.

TAKE AWAY

Notice that there are no out-and-out Fact questions in this passage; rare, but it does happen. We preview the stems to find out these sorts of things, to take note of specific tested issues, and to set the stage for our attack on the passage.

Step 2: Mine the Essential Elements. Let's start digging.

Paragraph 1 Essential Elements

- **Giveaways:** The passage opens with the popular contrast signal word "although," an immediate sign that the author is likely to present one side of a story and then another. And true to form, the long first sentence does set up an opposition: The word "midwife" is commonly used to describe all medieval women medical practitioners, yet there were lots of medical specialties recognized in the Middle Ages. "This common practice obscures the fact that . . ." indicates that the author has a problem with this, and the fact being obscured is introduced with the help of yet another "although" in sentence 2: Women actually participated in many medical specialties, suggesting that they were not only midwives, as so often described.

- **Purpose:** To introduce a common interpretation and the belief, supported by a study, that that interpretation is wrong.

- **Players/Extras:** The author cites a study by Wickersheimer and Jacquart, and we don't know yet whether these people and their study will take center stage or whether they'll fade from view.

- **Main Point:** Medieval women practiced a wide range of medical activities, but historians seem to think that "woman medical practitioner" means "midwife"; this despite a study showing that only a little more than a third of women medical practitioners were actually midwives.

- **Author Behavior:** The author seems on the attack; people are wrong about something, and he has the evidence to prove it. So there's a bit more than plain description going on here so far.

- **Author Opinion:** Yes. The practices of the historians cited does injustice to medieval women practitioners; they did more than just midwifing.

- **Passage Main Idea:** It's too soon to tell where this will all end up, but we have the foundation, so let's move on.

> Use paragraph 1 to lay the foundation for your understanding of the passage. Don't obsess on nailing down the main point so early; it often doesn't show up until later on. Be patient; all will be revealed in due time.
>
> **TAKE AWAY**

Paragraph 2 Essential Elements

- **Giveaways:** The phrase "scholars must also reopen . . ." is important because it shows the author calling on certain people to do a certain thing, which tells us a lot about author purpose.

> Giveaways are called giveaways because they give things away—important things like *why the author wrote the passage in the first place*. You can already tell from this phrase alone that any choices in a Big Picture question containing neutral-sounding verbs such as *describing* or *relating* must be wrong; this author goes further than that.
>
> **TAKE AWAY**

"Is this due to . . . or does it also result from . . . ?" shows the author considering various possibilities to explain a phenomenon. The "granted . . . nonetheless" construction suggests the author is admitting a point, yet presenting additional evidence that challenges that consideration or shows it to be unimportant. Yeah, the author grants that restrictive medieval legal conditions contribute somewhat to the lack of documentation regarding women medical practitioners. But the word "nonetheless" signals that, to the author, the range of the researchers' parameters in conducting the studies is a more pressing concern.

- **Purpose:** To raise a question, explore some possible answers to it, and support one particular answer with evidence.

- **Players/Extras:** Wickersheimer and Jacquart make no reappearance, so we can safely assume they are passage extras. Nor does anyone else enter the story, so we can infer that so far the author is the only player to consider.

- **Main Point:** The reason so little is known about medieval women medical practitioners is partly because records were not generally kept for medieval women to begin with, but more important, because researchers are at fault in the way they define their investigations of this topic.

- **Author Behavior:** Still on the attack. In paragraph 1, the author accuses historians of obscuring a fact via a common interpretation, one that the author refutes with evidence. Here, the author finds fault with the way in which researchers look into the question of medieval women medical practitioners. This too is backed up with evidence that shows that the categories they establish do not include many women who should be represented as medical people.

- **Author Opinion:** Yes. The historians are wrong in large part because of faulty methodology.

- **Passage Main Idea:** Still too soon to tell. Obviously, the author is on the historians' case, first for what they've gotten wrong and then for why they got it wrong. It may continue in this manner, or it may veer off into other territory; we'll just have to wait and see. But we don't have to wait long . . .

Paragraph 3 Essential Elements

- **Giveaways:** "The advantages of broadening the scope of such studies . . ." is a huge clue as to the author's main intention here. Having laid out the problem (equating "women medical practitioners" with "midwife" distorts the reality of the situation), and the main cause of the problem (historical studies of medical practitioners exclude certain categories where most women practitioners would be found), the author speaks of *rectifying* the problem by reversing the cause—that is, by broadening the scope of the studies so that the women in this case are accurately represented. The first few words define the tone and purpose of this paragraph.

- **Purpose:** To show that enlarging the categories studied yields dramatically different results.

- **Players/Extras:** Pelling, Webster, and Gottfried make the same kind of cameos as Wickersheimer and Jacquart did back in paragraph 1. They're there to supply evidence for the author's argument but are not players in the true sense of the word, confirmed by the fact that they're not heard from again. We can begin to conclude that this is the author's show, with the nameless historians bearing the brunt of his broadside in the background. However, we should still pay special heed to Gottfried, based on our scouting report from Step 1 revealing a point at stake concerning this character.

- **Main Point:** Broadening the definition of medical people shows that far more medieval women qualify as medical practitioners than has usually been considered the case. Looking at it the new way, there were twice as many women medical practitioners in one city in one year alone as traditional accounts reported in all of England in the course of 200 years. That's a big difference.

- **Author Behavior:** More than just pointing out the problem, the author mentions a possible solution and shows what a difference that solution makes. The author continues to be active and engaged—no mere objective reporting here.

- **Author Opinion:** Yes. Broadening the scope of the studies is a good thing, highlighted by the giveaway discussed earlier: "The advantages . . . are immediately apparent . . ."

- **Passage Main Idea:** Now we're on to something, as the author makes a recommendation; namely, that the historians change their methodology to give medieval women medical practitioners their due. But there's still one paragraph to go, so surprises may yet lurk.

> Stay alert until the end of the passage; don't tune out halfway through, figuring that you've heard the majority of the important stuff and are now just taking in the filler. The stuff at the end may be important material that the author uses to seal the deal.

TAKE AWAY

Paragraph 4 Essential Elements

- **Giveaways:** "Finally" is always a nice word, since it signals that the end is near. But we pretty much knew that anyway. Still, it tells us that another distinct point is likely coming up. The opposition between "such studies" (only statistical) and "future studies" (analyses in other areas of women's history) indicates yet one more change the author would make: gathering "information" that "could add much."

- **Purpose:** To show one more way that the current studies are lacking and propose a new and important line of inquiry.

- **Players/Extras:** The author turns out to be the only player in this one. The few honorable mentions are just extras he uses to make his case.

- **Main Point:** The way historians currently study medieval women medical practitioners over-relies on statistics, and it would be better if future studies took other factors into account that shed light on the social context contributing to medieval women's role in medicine.

- **Author Behavior:** Still criticizing, still proposing. But in a nice way, of course—the LSAT is by and large a family-friendly test.

- **Author Opinion:** Yup, this is one opinionated author. He started from the get-go with an attack on the way historians have treated this topic, and he continues to heap criticism in each successive paragraph. This one is no exception. The opinion in this final paragraph is encapsulated in the passage's main idea—and speaking of which, here it is:

- **Passage Main Idea:** By now the passage's full main idea should be evident, and it consists of an amalgamation of each paragraph's main point. The way historians look at the issue of medieval women medical practitioners is faulty. It would be better if they broadened the scope of their studies and also took other factors besides mere statistics into account. With that basic understanding under our belts, we're armed and ready for the questions—Big Picture first.

TAKE AWAY

It bears repeating: If you focus properly on Big Picture issues while reading the passage, it makes sense to tackle the Big Picture questions while the iron is hot (mixed metaphor notwithstanding).

Step 3: Divide and Conquer. Now that we've done all this preliminary work on the passage, let's use what we've learned to knock down the questions.

Divide . . . Main Point question are great candidates to tackle right out of the box, while the Big Picture issues are still fresh in your head.

REAL DEAL

1. Which one of the following best expresses the main point of the passage?

   (A) Recent studies demonstrate that women medical practitioners were more common in England than in the rest of Western Europe during the Middle Ages.

   (B) The quantity and quality of the information historians uncover concerning women's medical practice in medieval Europe would be improved if they changed their methods of study.

   (C) The sparse evidence for women medical practitioners in studies dealing with the Middle Ages is due primarily to the limitations of the historical record.

   (D) Knowledge about the social issues that influenced the role women medical practitioners played in medieval society has been enhanced by several recent studies.

   (E) Analyses developed in other areas of women's history could probably be used to provide more information about the social context of women's medical practice during the Middle Ages.

. . . and Conquer. We've just recounted the passage's main idea, so let's pit our analysis against what the choices have to offer.

A: Irrelevant. There's no comparison between England and Western Europe in the passage, so **A**'s out on that count alone. More significantly, it ignores the author's main call for a change in methodology.

B hits the nail on the head. It includes the idea of medieval women medical practitioners (the main subject of the passage), the author's critique of the historians' current treatment of this topic, and the author's call for historians to change their methods to create a more accurate portrayal of these practitioners.

C is a Retrieval Error, focusing on a mere detail in paragraph 2. Yes, the author does admit that part of the sparse evidence on this topic stems from limitations of the historical record, but immediately goes on to state and investigate a bigger culprit, faulty methodology.

D is a Twister choice (or you can call it a Mish-Mash, if you prefer). The author mentions social issues as a good source for *future* studies, not as something that has been documented in recent studies.

E is a nice recap of paragraph 4, as you should have recognized from your synopsis. But it ignores the gist of the previous three paragraphs. Being too narrow is therefore the culprit here.

Divide . . . And now on to Main Point's partner in crime, Primary Purpose. Why not, right? When a passage includes both a Main Point and Primary Purpose question, you should do them at the same time because they generally focus on the same Big Picture issues, even if that means tackling the questions in an order of your own making. So let's move right to question 6.

6. In the passage, the author is primarily concerned with doing which one of the following?

    (A) describing new methodological approaches
    (B) revising the definitions of certain concepts
    (C) comparing two different analyses
    (D) arguing in favor of changes in method
    (E) chronicling certain historical developments

. . . and Conquer. Our attack on the passage included an in-depth consideration of why this author wrote this passage, so let's go right to the choices.

D hits on all cylinders, fully mirroring the purpose points made above. Tracking the author's behavior throughout the passage, we noted time and again how the author does more than "describe" or "chronicle": He's arguing from the outset, so the verbs in choices **A** and **E** are off-base, effectively killing those choices.

TAKE AWAY

Always check the verbs in Primary Purpose questions. The easiest way to axe a Primary Purpose choice is to see that it begins with a verb that clashes with the author's behavior.

If you missed this, you may have been tempted by **A** because it does speak to the major issue of method. However, this author does more than just describe the method historians use to speak of medieval women medical practitioners; he actively criticizes that method and recommends a change. That's why **D** is correct. As for **B**, the author does show how the definition of medical practitioner has been revised in certain studies, but does not spend the majority of the passage revising the definition of "certain concepts." The revision applies to a category of people and is part of the larger issue of a change in methodology. Finally, the author did not write the passage merely to compare analyses (**C**), although that does happen in spots. Again, the passage is structured as an argument, and the correct choice here must reflect that.

TAKE AWAY

Notice the correspondence between the correct answers to questions 1 and 6: Both include the central idea of changing methods. If you had trouble with question 1, you may have used your answer to question 6 to help you see the light. Or you may have simply used question 6 to confirm your selection of choice **B** in question 1. Either way, you can see how these questions work together and how you might benefit from doing them consecutively.

Divide . . . As we noted earlier, there are no straightforward Fact questions in this set, but Detail Purpose questions combine Big Picture issues of authorial purpose with the specifics of a Fact question. So on the heels of Main Point and Primary Purpose, and with no other Big Picture questions in sight, it makes sense to try question 5 next.

5. The author refers to the study by Wickersheimer and Jacquart in order to

(A) demonstrate that numerous medical specialties were recognized in Western Europe during the Middle Ages

(B) demonstrate that women are often underrepresented in studies of medieval medical practitioners

(C) prove that midwives were officially recognized as members of the medical community during the Middle Ages

(D) prove that midwives were only a part of a larger community of women medical practitioners during the Middle Ages

(E) prove that the existence of midwives can be documented in Western Europe as early as the twelfth century

. . . and Conquer. Why mention W and J?

> **TAKE AWAY**
>
> Hey, Logic Games isn't the only place where shorthand may be helpful. If you'd abbreviate these lengthy names if they showed up in a Logic Game, why not here? It ain't much, but anything that eases your mental burden is a plus, especially considering the cumulative effect of deep concentration over multiple hours of testing.

W and J are mentioned in paragraph 1, the authors of what the passage author considers to be a "reliable" study. And we've noted during our synopsis of this paragraph that W and J are extras, thrown in to help support the author's case. They, remember, were the ones who showed that only around a third of documented women medical practitioners were actually midwives. The author uses this evidence to reinforce the oddness of the fact that historians tend to equate the term "woman medical practitioner" with "midwife." As we already noted, the author uses W and J's study to show that medieval women medical practitioners took many other forms besides midwife, choice **D**.

A: Retrieval Error. The surveys mentioned in the first sentence, not W and J's study, demonstrated the existence of numerous medical specialties in Europe. The choice also says "Western Europe," while the passage says "Europe," another minor inconsistency. But the major problem in this choice is that it focuses on the wrong thing.

B is a Twister choice, one that distorts the author's use of the detail in question. W and J *do* suggest that medieval women were underrepresented as medical practitioners: 121 out of 7,647 certainly isn't a great showing. But the author doesn't focus on this issue. He's concerned with how many out of the 121 were midwives and how many did other things.

C and **E**, like **B**, miss the point of the author's *use* of the study and therefore qualify as Twister choices as well. Sure, the study *does* prove that midwives existed in Europe in the twelfth century (**E**), and by extension, that "midwife" was an officially recognized occupation in the Middle Ages. But this is not why the author cites the study. The *proportion* of midwives among all women medical practitioners is what's important to him. He uses the study to demonstrate, by way of the 44/121 ratio, that women medical practitioners were not just midwives—they did other things too.

> **TAKE AWAY**
>
> In Detail Purpose questions, be careful not to answer based simply on what the detail says or implies but rather on what the author *does* with that detail. In this kind of question, "true" does not necessarily mean "correct."

Divide . . . Where to now? Well, we have three questions left, and here's where divvying up the question set according to your own preferences should pay off. We said earlier that it's probably best to leave the complex and unusual Extension question for last, but it's a toss up between the remaining Inference and Author Agreement questions. Question 3 is obviously an Author Agreement question and has the helpful Gottfried reference, which at least gives us a good handle on *where* to search for the answer, so let's try that one next.

REAL DEAL

3. It can be inferred from the passage that the author would be most likely to agree with which one of the following assertions regarding Gottfried's study?

    (A) Gottfried's study would have recorded a much larger number of women medical practitioners if the time frame covered by the study had included the late sixteenth century.
    (B) The small number of women medical practitioners identified in Gottfried's study is due primarily to problems caused by inaccurate sources.
    (C) The small number of women medical practitioners identified in Gottfried's study is due primarily to the loss of many medieval documents.
    (D) The results of Gottfried's study need to be considered in light of the social changes occurring in Western Europe during the fourteenth and fifteenth centuries.
    (E) **In setting the parameters for his study, Gottfried appears to have defined the term "medical practitioner" very narrowly.**

TAKE AWAY

Don't get too hung up on the question order—there's no absolute right way to divide up the question set. We provide you with general guidelines, such as tackling the Big Picture questions first, but when it comes down to the nitty-gritty of answering the Content questions, go with an order that works best for you.

. . . and Conquer. It may help to brush up on Gottfried in paragraph 3, although it's possible that you learned all you needed to know about him or her in your first read-through, having slated this up front as a tested issue. In any case, Gottfried is the researcher who, using the old definitions, classified far fewer women as medical practitioners than did Pelling and Webster. The giveaway we discussed (the "apparent advantages" of Pelling and Webster's study, in the eyes of the author) helps us to see that the author sides with the more broadly defined Pelling/Webster study over the Gottfried study. It's reasonable to infer therefore that the author thinks that Gottfried suffers from the main problem he's outlining: a faulty methodology that defines medical practitioners too narrowly. Choice **E** best captures this idea. For practice, let's see how the others go awry.

A: Only 28 women medical people in *200* years? There's nothing to suggest that the low number is due to an insufficient time frame and that adding another 70 years to the tally would change it much.

B and **C** speak to issues potentially related to the "limitations of the historical record," which the author mentions briefly before turning his attention to the main issue: the parameters used by historians to define medical practitioners. It's therefore more likely that the author believes that the small number in Gottfried's study results from the limited definition rather than factors such as the ones cited in **B** and **C**. The author drops the "historical record" issue before Gottfried hits the scene, so these have a Retrieval Error feel to them.

D is a combo Retrieval Error/Mish-Mash, trying to combine Gottfried's results with the new issue of future sociological studies brought up for the first time in paragraph 4.

> Notice how we haven't even gotten to the single question dealing with paragraph 4, and yet we've already seen a couple of wrong choices derived from the issue of "social context" discussed in the final paragraph. Keep in mind that information is included in the passage not just as support for the right answers but also as *fodder for the wrong ones*. Here, this social context business has Retrieval Error written all over it.

TAKE AWAY

Divide . . . As we're saving the complicated Extension question for last, it's high time we lock horns with Inference question 4.

REAL DEAL

4. The passage suggests that a future study that would be more informative about medieval women medical practitioners might focus on which one of the following?

    (A) the effect of social change on the political and economic structure of medieval society
    (B) the effect of social constraints on medieval women's access to a medical education
    (C) the types of medical specialties that developed during the Middle Ages
    (D) the reasons why medieval historians tend to equate the term "women medical practitioner" with midwife
    (E) the historical developments responsible for the medieval legal tradition's restrictions on women

. . . and Conquer. As mentioned above, we've already heard about this "future studies, social context" thing in some wrong choices; now we finally get an actual question about it. Clearly question 4 relates to paragraph 4, and our job is to figure out which of the situations in the choices best accords with the author's idea of a "profitable use of analyses developed in other areas of women's history." Luckily, he provides an example of what he means: He'd like information on things like women's literacy and the control of medical knowledge.

A, C, and **E** are all too broad, entirely ignoring the main issue of women's place within the medical community.

D employs a nifty little bait and switch, to borrow some lingo from Logical Reasoning, changing the focus to medieval historians. Which leaves only **B**. Indeed, social context certainly includes the effects of social constraints, and the issue of "women's access to a medical education" is very related to the passage's phrase

3

READING COMPREHENSION
The Real Deal: Practice Set

THE NEW LSAT

243

"control of medical knowledge." So it's reasonable to infer that **B** represents the kind of future study the author has in mind.

Develop your ability to paraphrase. Some answers in Reading Comp (and Logical Reasoning, for that matter) are derived very closely from the passage text.

Divide . . . Question 2 remains, and notice how they placed this difficult question very early in the question set—pretty discouraging for those who got stumped on it. This question has "save me for last—or at least toward the end" written all over it. It's Reading Comp's version of Parallel Reasoning: a question we call "Extension" because it asks you to extend your understanding beyond the passage itself to recognize some situation that corresponds to a particular passage element. Looking for an analogous external situation can be pretty daunting, which is why we saved it for last. Having finished with the others, let's have a look at it now.

2. Which one of the following is most closely analogous to the error the author believes historians make when they equate the term "woman medical practitioner" with "midwife"?

(A) equating pear with apple
(B) equating science with biology
(C) equating supervisor with subordinate
(D) equating member with nonmember
(E) equating instructor with trainee

. . . and Conquer. We're asked for an error that mimics the author's pet peeve— the equation of "woman medical practitioner" with "midwife." In Logical Reasoning we discussed Parallel Flaw questions, which ask you to find a situation among the choices that contains the same flaw as the situation described in the passage. Much like in those, your best bet here is to characterize the flaw in general terms and then look for the choice that matches that characterization.

So just what mistake does the author think is at work here? It's a group-subgroup issue: Midwives (subgroup) *are* women medical practitioners (larger group), but not all women medical practitioners are midwives. In the same way, biology (subgroup) is a science (larger group), but not all sciences are biology. So equating science with biology is a form of the same mistake, and **B** is correct. All of the other choices fail to reproduce the proper group-subgroup division evident in the original example and correct choice **B**.

Pears and apples (**A**) are both a kind of fruit. One is not a subset of the other. Supervisors and subordinates (**C**) are distinct kinds of employees. The same goes for members and nonmembers (**D**) and instructors and trainees (**E**). One may certainly mix up the representatives of any of these pairs, but the mistake would not involve confusing a broad group for a category within that group.

> **TAKE AWAY**
>
> The Extension/Parallel Reasoning connection is yet another example of LSAT synergy on display. And notice also that there's a bit of formal logic in here, what with the "all X are Y, but not all Y are X" structure. Use any strategy or technique you pick up in any part of your preparation wherever on the test it may apply.

Step 4: Mine the Experience. Don't forget to put in the proper amount of time and effort to consolidate everything you learned from this passage. You need not do it now—maybe coming back to this one in a few hours or a few days will give you a fresh perspective and help you get as much out of it as possible. But at some point go back over this entire passage with the help of the Mine the Experience analysis questions provided earlier in the chapter.

Ready for more? When you're ready for another one, try the science passage that comes next. Don't be intimidated by the complex wording or technical-sounding processes described. Use the reading strategies we've been discussing to distill the Essential Elements. Don't let yourself get overly bogged down in details. Here's a hint: The passage is structured around a cause-and-effect mechanism (as are many science passages), so keep your eye out for that. Do the best you can, and then rejoin us for guided explanations when you're done.

Passage 2

(PrepTest 12, Section 3, Qs. 21–27)

Note: The questions in this set have been renumbered for the purpose of this exercise.

How does the brain know when carbohydrates have been or should be consumed? The answer to this question is not known, but one element in the explanation seems to be the neurotransmitter
(5) serotonin, one of a class of chemical mediators that may be released from a presynaptic neuron and that cause the transmission of a nerve impulse across a synapse to an adjacent postsynaptic neuron. In general, it has been found that drugs that selectively
(10) facilitate serotonin-mediated neurotransmission tend to cause weight loss, whereas drugs that block serotonin-mediated transmission often have the opposite effect: they often induce carbohydrate craving and consequent weight gain.

(15) Serotonin is a derivative of tryptophan, an amino acid that is normally present at low levels in the bloodstream. The rate of conversion is affected by the proportion of carbohydrates in an individual's diet: carbohydrates stimulate the secretion of insulin,
(20) which facilitates the uptake of most amino acids into peripheral tissues, such as muscles. Blood tryptophan levels, however, are unaffected by insulin, so the proportion of tryptophan in the blood relative to the other amino acids increases when carbohydrates are
(25) consumed. Since tryptophan competes with other amino acids for transport across the blood–brain barrier into the brain, insulin secretion indirectly speeds tryptophan's entry into the central nervous system where, in a special cluster of neurons, it is
(30) converted into serotonin.

The level of serotonin in the brain in turn affects the amount of carbohydrate an individual chooses to eat. Rats that are allowed to choose among synthetic foods containing different proportions of
(35) carbohydrate and protein will normally alternate between foods containing mostly protein and those containing mostly carbohydrate. However, if rats are given drugs that enhance the effect of serotonin, the rats' carbohydrate intake is reduced. On the
(40) other hand, when rats are given drugs that interrupt serotonin-mediated neurotransmission, their brains fail to respond when carbohydrates are eaten, so the desire for them persists.

In human beings a serotoninlike drug, *d*-fenfluramine,
(45) (which releases serotonin into brain synapses and then prolongs its action by blocking its reabsorption into the presynaptic neuron), selectively suppresses carbohydrate snacking (and its associated weight gain) in people who crave carbohydrates. In contrast,
(50) drugs that block serotonin-mediated transmission or that interact with neurotransmitters other than serotonin have the opposite effect: they often induce carbohydrate craving and subsequent weight gain. People who crave carbohydrates report
(55) feeling refreshed and invigorated after eating a carbohydrate-rich meal (which would be expected to increase brain serotonin levels). In contrast, those who do not crave carbohydrates become sleepy following a high-carbohydrate meal. These findings suggest
(60) that serotonin has other effects that may be useful indicators of serotonin levels in human beings.

1. Which one of the following best states the main idea of the passage?

    (A) The body's need for carbohydrates varies with the level of serotonin in the blood.

    (B) The body's use of carbohydrates can be regulated by the administration of serotoninlike drugs.

    (C) The role of serotonin in regulating the consumption of carbohydrates is similar in rats and in humans.

    (D) The body's desire for carbohydrates can be influenced by serotonin or serotoninlike drugs.

    (E) Tryptophan initiates a chain of events that regulates the body's use of carbohydrates.

2. The term "rate" (line 17) refers to the rate at which

    (A) serotonin is produced from tryptophan

    (B) carbohydrates are taken into the body

    (C) carbohydrates stimulate the secretion of insulin

    (D) insulin facilitates the uptake of amino acids into peripheral tissues

    (E) tryptophan enters the bloodstream

3. It can be inferred that a person is likely to crave carbohydrates when

(A) the amount of insulin produced is too high
(B) the amount of serotonin in the brain is too low
(C) more tryptophan than usual crosses the blood–brain barrier
(D) neurotransmission by neurotransmitters other than serotonin is interrupted
(E) amino acids other than tryptophan are taken up by peripheral tissues

4. The information in the passage indicates that if human beings were given a drug that inhibits the action of serotonin, which one of the following might be expected to occur?

(A) Subjects would probably show a preference for carbohydrate-rich snacks rather than protein-rich snacks.
(B) Subjects would probably become sleepy after eating a carbohydrate-rich meal.
(C) Subjects would be more likely to lose weight than before they took the drug.
(D) Subjects' blood tryptophan levels would probably increase.
(E) Subjects' desire for both carbohydrates and proteins would increase.

5. The primary purpose of the second paragraph in the passage is to

(A) provide an overview of current research concerning the effect of serotonin on carbohydrate consumption
(B) contrast the role of tryptophan in the body with that of serotonin
(C) discuss the role of serotonin in the transmission of neural impulses
(D) explain how the brain knows that carbohydrates should be consumed
(E) establish a connection between carbohydrate intake and the production of serotonin

6. It can be inferred that after a person has taken *d*-fenfluramine, he or she will probably be

(A) inclined to gain weight
(B) sleepy much of the time
(C) unlikely to crave carbohydrates
(D) unable to sleep as much as usual
(E) likely to secrete more insulin than usual

7. The author's primary purpose is to

(A) defend a point of view
(B) correct a misconception
(C) assess conflicting evidence
(D) suggest new directions for investigation
(E) provide information that helps explain a phenomenon

Passage 2: Guided Explanation

Craving Carbs

Science got you down? If so, you're not alone. Many LSAT test takers fear, dread, and loathe the Reading Comp science passage. But that's just not necessary. The method we've been outlining is specifically geared to helping you handle dense, complicated passages, including science—or, for that matter, law passages that are often even ghastlier. No matter what the details may be like, the Big Picture issues remain fairly consistent: The author describes, argues, compares, or refutes; uses examples for specific reasons; organizes the passage in a particular way; agrees with some things, disagrees with others; and so on. So we go about it just the same as any other passage, only even *more* insistent on not getting bogged down in details. Speaking of which, our scouting report will tell us exactly how many specific details will be tested, as well as other important tidbits to keep in mind as we venture off into the passage.

Step 1: Scout the Territory. Once again we get both a Main Point and Primary Purpose question, numbers 1 and 7, respectively, a gift for those who learn to nail the Big Picture issues up front. On top of those, there's a Paragraph Purpose question (number 5), so we should put some kind of indication next to paragraph 2 to remind us that this paragraph is a tested issue.

TAKE
AWAY

> Shorthand comes in extremely handy (no pun intended) in Logic Games, but nothing says you can't mark up the page in Logical Reasoning and Reading Comp too, if it helps. Don't go crazy with it, but an occasional asterisk, underline, or some other form of notation can serve as an effective reminder.

That does it for the Big Picture questions. Question 2 is a straight Fact question containing a helpful line reference. You might want to go right to that line and underline the word "rate" as a reminder that a point depends on that detail. Question 4 is not as obliging, and it may be too long and complicated to try to figure out at this point, but "the passage indicates that" suggests that this is probably another Fact question whose answer will be found in some place where the author discusses serotonin. The remaining two questions are Inference questions. "Crave carbohydrates" is a good clue in question 3, and "*d*-fenfluramine" is an eye-catcher in question 6. Underlining or circling those words in these questions would not be out of place—anything to remind you what's important and by extension, what's *not*.

Previewing the question stems, like everything else, is a skill that will take time to develop. But when you have it down, you should be able to get a good sense of the tested issues in roughly 20–30 seconds.

Step 2: Mine the Essential Elements.

Paragraph 1 Essential Elements

- **Giveaways:** "How does the brain know . . . ?" A question raised right off the bat is a pretty good indicator of the author's interests. The answer to the question the author raises is not known, but "one element seems to be serotonin." All of this leads nicely into the author's purpose.

- **Purpose:** To explore a scientific question.

- **Players/Extras:** There are no people here; the brain's function in carbohydrate intake seems to be the focus. Serotonin is a likely candidate as a player, highlighted as it is in the giveaway discussed above.

- **Main Point:** While it's not known exactly how the brain knows when carbs have been or should be consumed, the process has something to do with serotonin.

We noticed that question 4 deals specifically with serotonin, and in fact the answer to that question can be found in the facts given at the end of this paragraph. It may be helpful to note this information for later reference.

- **Author Behavior:** Factual, informative, well-behaved. Nothing unusual for a science passage, most of which are pretty explanatory in nature.

- **Author Opinion:** Nothing to speak of at this point. So far the author is just describing some findings regarding a scientific phenomenon.

- **Passage Main Idea:** Same as the main point above. This is all we have to work with so far, so don't obsess over the passage's overall main idea just yet. It's early; this can go in lots of different directions.

Paragraph 2 Essential Elements

- **Giveaways:** We know from Step 1 that the "rate" discussed here is a tested issue, as is the function of the paragraph as a whole. Careful attention should be given to these issues. Serotonin reappears in the first word of the paragraph, and "is a derivative of tryptophan" tells us where serotonin comes from. The fact that the rate in question is "affected by the proportion of carbohydrates in an individual's diet" is easy enough to understand, even if the rest of the details in the paragraph are not.

TAKE
AWAY

This is an excellent example of how knowing what's important can help you to zero in on key information and skim past the rest. There are a lot of complicated things in this paragraph, and most of them we don't need to know if we pick up on this single "rate" detail and the general purpose of the paragraph overall.

- **Purpose:** To discuss where serotonin comes from, and what that has to do with the main topic of the passage: carbohydrates and the brain.

- **Players/Extras:** Serotonin and carbohydrates are shaping up to be players here, discussed for the second straight paragraph, but it's too soon to tell how important tryptophan and insulin will be. They may be extras making cameos in this paragraph alone.

- **Main Point:** We don't need to go into too much depth here. It's okay to just keep in mind that the amount of serotonin that's derived from tryptophan has something to do with the amount of carbs present. We can always come back to figure this out further if we need to—and we do know we'll at least have to answer one question on that "rate of conversion" business. But we may already know everything we need to know about that.

- **Author Behavior:** Descriptive, predictable.

- **Author Opinion:** No, just presenting facts.

- **Passage Main Idea:** Keep it simple! Despite all the scientific details in this paragraph, remember, there's only one Fact question about it and one Big Picture question asking for the paragraph's overall purpose. And we've already considered those issues in enough depth for now. As for the passage's main idea, it still seems to be something about how serotonin, the brain, and carbohydrates interrelate.

Paragraph 3 Essential Elements
- **Giveaways:** The phrase "serotonin in the brain . . . affects the amount of carbohydrate . . ." tells us the author's keeping to the same train of thought. The rat example appears to support the relationship the author presents, and the contrast signal words "however" and "on the other hand" keep the discussion moving along, indicating what happens in various circumstances.

- **Purpose:** To further illustrate the relationship between serotonin and carbohydrates.

- **Players/Extras:** Serotonin and carbohydrates are now firmly established as the stars of this show. Rats make an appearance, but just as an example that the author uses to illustrate the relationship she describes.

- **Main Point:** Again, despite all the detail, the author is still pretty much talking about the same old thing, and it's summarized nicely in the paragraph's first sentence: Serotonin levels affect the amount of carbs people eat.

Sometimes the paragraph's first sentence—often referred to as the "topic sentence"—will tell you just that: the overall topic of the paragraph. Then the rest of the paragraph will go on to support that point or illustrate it in some way.

- **Author Behavior/Author Opinion:** No surprises. By now we know this is not an argumentative passage. The author merely relays facts about a biological process. You should be salivating by now in anticipation of the Primary Purpose question. Assuming that nothing changes dramatically, any choice containing a verb stronger than *outline, explain,* or *describe,* for example, can be quickly and confidently tossed.

- **Passage Main Idea:** The story pretty much remains the same: There's a relationship between the amount of serotonin in the brain and the amount of carbs eaten and craved.

Again, don't try to get every detail perfectly straight in your mind; you're not writing a bio-chem dissertation or taking the MCAT (entrance test for medical school). Get the basics down, and move on to the questions. You can always look back at the passage when you need to.

Paragraph 4 Essential Elements

- **Giveaways:** Here's the mention of the *d*-word that is the subject of question 6, and we find out it's a drug that triggers serotonin and keeps it active, producing the usual effects on body carbs. It's the same as with the rats: more serotonin, fewer carbs. "In contrast" is a nice giveaway reaffirming that the opposite holds as well: Blocking serotonin causes carb cravings and weight gain. The author reports more findings regarding carbohydrate cravings, with both sides of the story again highlighted by the signal phrase "in contrast." But we know from our scouting report in Step 1 that *d*-fenfluramine is the tested issue, and that shows up in the beginning of the paragraph. There's therefore no sense belaboring the stuff at the end, since there doesn't seem to be a question about it.

TAKE
AWAY

The best Reading Comp practitioners develop a keen sense of what in the passage is important and, by extension, what's not. They allow their scouting report from Step 1 of the Essential Strategy to guide their attack on the passage. Many who struggle with Reading Comp treat every sentence—in fact, every word—equally, assuming that if they understand everything, they'll be able to answer any question thrown their way. The successful test taker knows this is a waste of time and effort, since only a limited number of questions appear, and they're right there on the page for consultation. They understand that the goal is not to become an expert on the passage; the goal is to answer the questions that appear. Scouting the Territory up front makes that task much easier.

- **Purpose:** To further relate the specifics of the serotonin/carbohydrate connection.

- **Players/Extras:** Same; no surprises.

- **Main Point:** The effects of serotonin already described can be triggered through the use of certain drugs.

- **Author Behavior:** Mild-mannered description.

- **Author Opinion:** No, just reporting facts.

- **Passage Main Idea:** Same as what we've already said, although this paragraph adds a bit on the drug thing. There's a relationship between the amount of serotonin in the brain and the amount of carbs eaten and craved: more serotonin, less carb craving. Less serotonin, more carb craving. An inverse relationship—not so terrible.

TAKE
AWAY

Bulletin from the Department of Redundancy Department: LSAT passages are often repetitive; redundant, if you will, like the title of this bulletin. Authors certainly don't introduce new ideas in every line, and whole paragraphs often contain the same ideas expressed in slightly different ways or from slightly different angles. If you read for main ideas and primary purposes, you'll be less likely to be overwhelmed by the sheer word count as you recognize the repetitive nature of these passages.

Step 3: Divide and Conquer. Okay, Steps 1 and 2 are in the bag, so it's time for the payoff, Step 3.

Divide . . . You should know the drill by now: Big Picture questions first, beginning with Main Point, which is often situated conveniently as the first question in the set (one of the few conveniences, incidentally, granted by the test makers).

1. Which one of the following best states the main idea of the passage?

    (A) The body's need for carbohydrates varies with the level of serotonin in the blood.
    (B) The body's use of carbohydrates can be regulated by the administration of serotoninlike drugs.
    (C) The role of serotonin in regulating the consumption of carbohydrates is similar in rats and in humans.
    (D) The body's desire for carbohydrates can be influenced by serotonin or serotoninlike drugs.
    (E) Tryptophan initiates a chain of events that regulates the body's use of carbohydrates.

. . . and Conquer. No need to spend a lot of time on the right answer here, as we've been developing it throughout our analysis. Choice **D** contains all the relevant elements, describing serotonin's influence on our craving for carbs. Every paragraph dealt with that issue in some form or another. Mentioning "serotonin-like drugs" is a nice touch to make paragraph 4 feel included.

> **TAKE AWAY**
>
> While the proper passage analysis leads nicely to **D**, you should still spend a good amount of time during your preparation analyzing why the wrong choices are wrong. Why? Because as we've noted throughout, the same kinds of wrong choices appear again and again, and the best way to recognize them on test day is to study them every chance you get.

A is a Twister: Serotonin is in the brain, not, as far as we know, the blood. It's tryptophan that's in the blood.

B: Retrieval Error: The drug issue comes up only in the final paragraph, so the main point cannot focus exclusively on this to the exclusion of serotonin itself.

C: Retrieval Error II: We deemed rats extras in this passage. They have no business being featured in the passage's main point.

E: Retrieval Error III: Tryptophan, another extra, is more important than serotonin? Our major player is missing in action in this one, so no go.

> **TAKE AWAY**
>
> Why do we strive to separate passage players from passage extras? Among other reasons, to quickly kill choices like **C** and **E**, which confuse one for the other.
>
> As you can see, this question is a veritable Retrieval Error extravaganza. Every paragraph of the passage focuses in some way on the serotonin-carbohydrate relationship. If you delve into the passage in search of the main idea, you'd have to come back with something reflecting this dynamic duo. **B** goes in and comes out with drugs-carbs. **C** goes in and emerges with rats-humans. **E** takes the plunge and returns bearing tryptophan-carbs. All crib, no baby. (If you miss the reference, see the Retrieval Error description in the Common Traps section earlier in the chapter.)

Divide . . . Yup—just like in the previous passage, and in all passages going forward, we're going to knock Main Point and Primary Purpose off in one fell swoop. We'll skip down to question 7 then.

7. The author's primary purpose is to

(A) defend a point of view
(B) correct a misconception
(C) assess conflicting evidence
(D) suggest new directions for investigation
(E) provide information that helps explain a phenomenon

. . . and Conquer. We've already discussed how any verb stronger than *describe* simply won't cut it as the purpose of our mild-mannered author. That kills **A** and **B** right off the bat. There's no defense of anything, and no correction of anything—just plain old description. Make it a priority to learn what the test makers mean by the words they use. The verbs in this question's choices sound so simple *yet have very precise meanings*. **A** "defense" of something implies an argument against opponents. A "correction" requires another point of view. The passage contains neither of these things, so **A** and **B** can't be correct.

TAKE AWAY

When you're confident that a verb in a Primary Purpose choice doesn't work, don't even read the rest of the choice. It's a waste of time. And time on the LSAT is precious.

Now, "defend" and "correct" may most obviously contradict the author's behavior here, but "assess" and "suggest" come in a close second. For fun, let's let those slide on the verb front and see what else **C** and **D** have to offer. Turns out . . . not much. There's no conflicting evidence that the author is trying to evaluate, nor does the author say (as does the author of "Women Medical Practitioners") that "here's a promising direction for continued study."

TAKE AWAY

One reason we chose these passages for this practice set is because of the contrast in tone and authorial intention. Compare "Women Medical Practitioners" to this passage and note the differences in style, tone, and overall purpose. Review the Main Point and Primary Purpose questions in both to reinforce how these passages differ and how the questions and correct choices reflect that difference.

That leaves **E**, and notice how the correct choice contains the blandest, most innocuous verb phrase of the bunch: "provide information." Sure it's pretty boring, but that's exactly what (and all) this author does. What about the rest? "Explain a phenomenon?" You bet: how serotonin influences the way the body craves carbs.

Divide . . . Okay, one more Big Picture question to knock down, and, being of the Paragraph Purpose variety, we should have a pretty good handle on it from our Essential Elements efforts in Step 2. After all, we assess the purpose of every paragraph as a matter of course and even gave extra special attention to paragraph 2 thanks to our initial scouting report. So let's strike while the iron is hot and jump right to question 5:

5. The primary purpose of the second paragraph in the passage is to

    (A) provide an overview of current research concerning the effect of serotonin on carbohydrate consumption
    (B) contrast the role of tryptophan in the body with that of serotonin
    (C) discuss the role of serotonin in the transmission of neural impulses
    (D) explain how the brain knows that carbohydrates should be consumed
    (E) establish a connection between carbohydrate intake and the production of serotonin

. . . and Conquer. So what's paragraph 2 doing in there, besides just taking up a lot of space? Here's how we described its purpose in our Essential Elements synopsis: "To discuss where serotonin comes from and what that has to do with the main topic of the passage: carbohydrates and the brain." In one place, the author discusses how the serotonin production process "is affected by the proportion of carbohydrates in an individual's diet." Later on, we find out that a certain proportion of chemicals also increases when carbs are consumed, with a direct effect on serotonin levels. So **E** most clearly states the function of this paragraph—to establish the serotonin/carbohydrate connection. Let's see how the wrong choices go astray:

A: Retrieval Error, wrong paragraph variety. This is what seems to happen in paragraph 3, but paragraph 2 focuses on the reverse: how carb intake affects the production of serotonin.

Again, notice how cause and effect is featured prominently not only in this science passage but in its question set as well. We studied cause and effect as a Logical Reasoning Essential Concept. As we see here (and in the previous passage too), it can play a large role in Reading Comp as well.

B's a Twister: The author does not contrast the roles of tryptophan and serotonin. She merely shows how the latter is derived from the former.

C's a Mish-Mash, Retrieval Error, or combination of both—take your pick. Neural impulses are discussed in paragraph 1.

D overstates the case, referring to the question posed in the first sentence of the passage—a question that the author admits has not yet been fully answered. The rest of the passage explores what the author calls "one element in the explanation." Paragraph 2 can't be said to accomplish the impossible—that is, explain what is not yet known.

Divide . . . Now that the Big Picture questions are out of the way (and have helped to solidify our grasp of the passage), it's time for the Fact questions. Question 2 is a good candidate to tackle next: It's short, it provides a line reference, and we've already put some thought into this issue after noting in Step 1 that "rate" in paragraph 2 is a tested issue.

2. The term "rate" (line 17) refers to the rate at which

    (A) serotonin is produced from tryptophan
    (B)   carbohydrates are taken into the body
    (C)   carbohydrates stimulate the secretion of insulin
    (D)   insulin facilitates the uptake of amino acids into peripheral tissues
    (E)   tryptophan enters the bloodstream

. . . and Conquer. "Rate" here refers to the "rate of conversion," which we hear about immediately following the idea that serotonin is a derivative of tryptophan. In this case then, "derivative of" means "converted into," an idea reinforced in the last five words of the paragraph. So the rate of conversion here refers to how fast tryptophan is converted into serotonin. **A** says the same thing, in a slightly different way.

All the other choices all describe things that *influence* the rate of conversion, but we're asked what this rate of conversion *is* in the first place.

This question is essentially a translation challenge. Understanding logical equivalencies is a prominent feature of Logic Games, but you get a taste of it here in Reading Comp.

Divide . . . Let's now dispose of the other Fact question, question 4, before trying the two Inference questions:

---

4. The information in the passage indicates that if human beings were given a drug that inhibits the action of serotonin, which one of the following might be expected to occur?

    (A) **Subjects would probably show a preference for carbohydrate-rich snacks rather than protein-rich snacks.**
    (B) Subjects would probably become sleepy after eating a carbohydrate-rich meal.
    (C) Subjects would be more likely to lose weight than before they took the drug.
    (D) Subjects' blood tryptophan levels would probably increase.
    (E) Subjects' desire for both carbohydrates and proteins would increase.

. . . and Conquer. "Inhibits serotonin" is our clue here, and we find out what happens when serotonin is inhibited—that is blocked, prevented from working—right at the end of the first paragraph. When drugs "block serotonin-mediated transmission . . . they often induce carbohydrate craving and subsequent weight gain." In plain language: People crave carbs and get fat. **C** is thus an Opposite choice.

The rat studies described in paragraph 3 add the issue of protein to the mix, which shows up in choices **A** and **E**. **A** is the better choice because the rat example showed that inhibiting serotonin alters the carb/protein intake ratio, making the rats more likely to desire more carbs. So it seems reasonable that people given the drug would desire carbs over protein.

Note that this question is actually a Fact/Inference hybrid. While it's based on definite information given in the passage, there's a touch of deduction required to recognize the likely result of the drug and, most important, to distinguish between **A** and **E**.

TAKE
AWAY

B is another Opposite choice that gets it all backward. The drug would likely cause carbohydrate cravings, and paragraph 4 says that people craving carbs will feel *refreshed*, not tired, after consuming a carbohydrate-rich meal.

D is incorrect because we're never told that blood tryptophan levels increase but rather that the *tryptophan to amino acid ratio* increases under certain conditions that decrease the amount of amino acids in the blood.

Some questions simply contain difficult answer choices, and you're best off if you don't need to give them much attention or respect. How could that be? Well, if you're confident in a choice that you think works fine, you don't have to struggle *justifying the failures* of the others. This business about the difference between an increase in tryptophan and an increase in the tryptophan–amino acids *proportion* could be pretty confusing. However, if you have confidence in choice **A**, you shouldn't let choice **D** bog you down.

Divide . . . We're left with the two Inference questions, questions 3 and 6, both identified by the standard phrase "It can be inferred . . ." You can do them in either order, although it's reasonable to guess that question 3 might be easier since it harps on the same old issue concerning the causes of carb cravings, the very thing we've been studying throughout. So let's try that one first.

3. It can be inferred that a person is likely to crave carbohydrates when

    (A)   the amount of insulin produced is too high
    (B)   the amount of serotonin in the brain is too low
    (C)   more tryptophan than usual crosses the blood–brain barrier
    (D)   neurotransmission by neurotransmitters other than serotonin is interrupted
    (E)   amino acids other than tryptophan are taken up by peripheral tissues

. . . and Conquer. The causes of carb cravings should be cemented in your head by now, but if not, you can always revisit our trusty final sentence of paragraph 1, which tells us that people crave carbs when serotonin is blocked. This idea alone is enough to distinguish **B** from the pack. Low serotonin, high carb craving. Period.

This question illustrates another reason not to fear the science passage. Often, difficult passages come with easy- to medium-level questions. Conversely, beware of passages that you breeze through—these often contain some killer questions. Just one more way for the test makers to confuse the uninitiated and keep test takers off balance. Question 3 is merely another question that harps on the major relationship established in the passage. And as we discussed above, the wrong choices are likely more difficult to deal with than the right one, flinging terminology left and right in an effort to provide a smokescreen for the fairly straightforward correct choice, **B**.

A: The passage states that carbohydrates stimulate the production of insulin. If anything, the idea that *too much* insulin would make one crave carbs seems counter-intuitive. But there's no need to nitpick over whether this is an Opposite choice or not—as long as you recognize that there's no support for it in the passage.

C, however, does have a serious Opposite ring to it, if we follow it through (which hopefully you *didn't* on the strength of your confidence in **B**). More tryptophan crossing the blood-brain barrier should result in more serotonin produced, which should in turn *decrease* the craving for carbohydrates.

D is a bit fuzzy, since it speaks of drugs interrupting neurotransmitters other than serotonin, while the passage talks about drugs interacting with neurotransmitters other than serotonin. Does the interaction cause interruption? Don't know. If we understand interacting as the opposite of interrupting, then this choice gets it backward; we'd expect carb cravings to decrease under the condition stated in **D**. So we must be content to conclude that if anything, **D** seems to lean in the wrong direction, and even if not, there's nothing positive to suggest that it's inferable.

E is less ambiguous in its backwardness than **D**, which is to say it's more clearly an Opposite wrong choice if we understand the process outlined in paragraph 2. Carbohydrates in the diet lead to the intake of amino acids other than tryptophan into peripheral tissues, which in turn causes an increase in the percentage of tryptophan in the blood relative to other amino acids. This situation ultimately facilitates tryptophan's conversion into serotonin, the very thing that reduces carb cravings. Bottom line: **E** would result in lower carb cravings, not higher.

> **TAKE AWAY**
>
> It bears repeating that the strength of choice **B** here obviates the need to go nuts with the details of the complicated process described in paragraph 2. Part of achieving LSAT mastery is learning which battles to fight. You can't fight them all. Convincing yourself why **E** is wrong (and in the process having to master the amino acid/tryptophan nightmare to do so) should take a backseat to convincing yourself that **B** is right.

Divide . . . One to go, so no choice in the matter remains. Question 6, up to bat.

6. It can be inferred that after a person has taken *d*-fenfluramine, he or she will probably be

   (A) inclined to gain weight
   (B) sleepy much of the time
   (C) unlikely to crave carbohydrates
   (D) unable to sleep as much as usual
   (E) likely to secrete more insulin than usual

. . . and Conquer. The drug *d*-fenfluramine is discussed at the beginning of paragraph 4, where we find out (after all that complicated jargon in the parentheses) that this drug suppresses carb snacking. If you know what "suppresses" means (holds back, constrains, keeps in check), choice **C** should jump off the page fairly quickly.

TAKE AWAY

Sometimes the test makers test nothing more than your ability to find the right information. Here, that meant wading through all the distracting terms in the parentheses and getting to the crux of the matter: *d*-fenfluramine suppresses carb cravings. It's a very small step from that to choice **C**.

A: Opposite: The drug suppresses not only carb snacking but its "associated weight gain" as well.

B and **D** are Twisters: They deal with sleepiness, something discussed later in the paragraph concerning the issue of how carb cravings, or lack thereof, affect how people feel after eating a high-carb meal. We can't tell how the drug in question affects this process, if at all.

E: One final Opposite choice to finish things off: Since the drug suppresses carb cravings, we would expect a lesser amount of carbs in the body, leading to a *decrease* in insulin secretion.

TAKE AWAY

You may have noticed a plethora of Opposite choices, or choices that at least lean in the wrong direction. These are very common in passages describing complicated mechanisms or processes. Opposite choices test whether you truly understand the causal relationships described. But even when the process is complex, focusing on the major elements is enough to answer most questions. In many of the questions in this set, the complexity of the passage is given a full airing via the *wrong choices,* while the right answers are not terribly difficult because they stick closely to the main relationship described throughout the passage: serotonin down, carb craving up.

Step 4: Mine the Experience. Take a break and return to this passage and the guided explanations later on to reinforce what you've learned.

READING COMPREHENSION SUMMARY

If you're a Reading Comp natural, keep doing what you're doing—you can't argue with success. The tips, strategies, and techniques we've presented in this chapter will provide you with extra ammo to add to an already effective approach. If, on the other hand, Reading Comp is one of your weak spots, try working with the Essential Strategy we've outlined to get you over the hump. Remember, it takes practice. To start with, you'll find a full Reading Comp section with four new passages to work on in the practice test at the end of the book. Use those to solidify your Reading Comp approach and to put yourself in the best position possible to ace this section on test day.

## Chapter 4

THE WRITING SAMPLE

or

... You Must Be Kidding!

So, you've been in the testing center for nearly four hours. You've endured Logic Games, Reading Comprehension, two Logical Reasoning sections, and one extra unscored section, to boot. *What more could they possibly want from you?* Just a little sample. No, not blood—writing. One final task stands between you and the partying you deserve. This chapter will teach you what you need to know to finish off your LSAT in style.

OVERVIEW

What It Is

The Writing Sample is an unscored 35-minute writing exercise that's administered as the last section of the LSAT. You are asked to choose between two plausible alternatives and construct a written argument supporting your choice. There is no right or wrong answer; either option can be plausibly defended. You'll be judged not on which option you choose but on how well you support your position. No outside knowledge is required to form your response.

Your task is to demonstrate an ability to establish a clear, logical, and persuasive position in writing. Your response will be photocopied and sent to every law school to which you apply as part of your application. You'll be given scrap paper to plan your response and two sides of paper to write it.

The admissions officers reading these essays understand the time constraints you're under and do not expect your magnum opus. A well-constructed, well-reasoned first draft is what you're after.

You may come across Argument prompts in practice tests from test-prep books prior to 2007. This was a format the LSAC tried out in the 2005–2006 period, but it was discontinued in June 2007. Those tests also contain Decision prompts, which is the format that remains on the test and the one treated in this chapter.

Why It Is

Next to reading, writing is the most time-consuming activity in law school, and the law is, of course, codified in written form. Your ability to write is therefore a relevant part of your law school qualifications.

Your Motivation

The word *unscored* makes the Writing Sample the least inspiring section of the LSAT. Faced with the formidable challenges of the multiple-choice sections, why waste valuable prep time on something that doesn't even count toward your final score?

For one thing, it's a required part of the test. Moreover, there is evidence that many law schools *do* actually consider these. A 2006 LSAC survey asked 157 law schools how often they used the Writing Sample to evaluate a candidate's qualifications for law school. The results belie the popular belief that "no one ever reads these things." Seventy percent of the schools surveyed reported that they occasionally, frequently, or always read them, while only a paltry 7 percent or so admitted to ignoring them entirely. And it's well known that those schools that *do* read the essays often use them to differentiate between two otherwise identical candidates—that is, to tip the scales in borderline cases.

So the bottom line is that you should take the Writing Sample seriously because it could make a difference. In addition, any practice you get arguing for a position is bound to help you down the road at law school, where you'll be asked to argue countless cases, and where your writing most certainly *will* be scored.

Enough said. Let's hit the gameplan.

GAMEPLAN

Once again we provide you with a gameplan to maximize your study time. Here's what you'll see in the following pages:

- **X-ray of a Typical Writing Sample Prompt:** First we'll familiarize you with the basics of the Writing Sample: the situation, the criteria, the alternatives, and the directions.

- **Essential Strategy:** We'll get right to an effective method for constructing your essay.

- **Practice Essay and Sample Response:** Next, you'll have the opportunity to write an essay and compare your response to a sample essay we provide.

X-RAY OF A TYPICAL WRITING SAMPLE PROMPT

Take a look through this sample essay prompt so that we can establish some terminology. Don't worry about formulating a response just yet—you'll have a chance to do that soon enough.

> Acadia Stevens, an environmental activist, is weighing her publishing options for her first book, *EcoBalance: Sustainability in the 21st Century.* She has received a publishing offer from a medium-size publisher, Second City Press, but is considering publishing the book herself as an e-book distributed via Internet downloads. Write an essay in which you argue for one option over the other, keeping in mind the following two criteria:
>
> - Acadia wants *EcoBalance* to have an impact on the environmental movement.
> - Acadia wants *EcoBalance* to generate sufficient profits to subsidize her research and conservation activities.
>
> Second City Press, located in Chicago, publishes mainly poetry and short fiction stories but has published nonfiction books as well. Its "How-To" series on gardening and home improvement has sold upward of 45,000 copies in the last year and ranks among the most popular of its kind. Second City's readership is based mainly in the Midwestern United States. Acadia's friend Laurel, who is the sister-in-law of Second City's editor in chief, introduced *EcoBalance* to Second City. Second City publishes the works of ten to fifteen new authors each year and sponsors extensive book tours for its most popular writers. For exclusive rights to the book, Second City has offered Acadia a $10,000 flat fee plus royalties amounting to 5 percent of retail sales. Second City plans to sell the book for $19.95 in bookstores and does not offer books for sale online.
> Acadia is an active and well-known participant in many environmental websites, including a site called OnePlanet.net, to which she contributes a weekly column on conservation efforts worldwide. OnePlanet receives roughly 25,000 page views per week and is linked to over 20 other websites devoted to social issues. Acadia lectures widely on conservation issues in the United States and abroad and is a frequent guest on public access television and radio programs. An e-commerce research company indicates successful e-books selling in the $30 to $40 price range in popular subjects such as investing and financial management but insignificant sales for fiction e-books even at a price point as low as $2.50. There are no financially successful environmental e-books currently offered on the Internet. Acadia would offer her e-book at a price point of $5.99.

The first paragraph contains the "situation," which describes a decision that needs to be made by a person, organization, or any other decision-making entity. The decision will be between two possible courses of action, also mentioned in the situation.

The situation is followed by two "criteria"—considerations that you need to take into account when making your argument for the option you select. The criteria are offset by bullet points. These are followed by in-depth descriptions of the two competing alternatives, which provide you with evidence to make your case.

Let's now take a look at exactly what the test makers tell us to do with all this information. First they provide "General Directions," which describe the overall purpose and specifications of the writing task. Then they provide specific directions directly preceding the essay prompt you'll respond to. These specific directions are called simply "Directions." Let's take a look at the general directions first. Since they're fairly long, we'll comment en route.

General Directions:

You will have 35 minutes in which to plan and write an essay on the topic inside. Read the topic and the accompanying directions carefully. You will probably find it best to spend a few minutes considering the topic and organizing your thoughts before you begin writing.

Translation: You're up the creek if you don't think a bit about the topic and get your thoughts in order before putting pen to paper. (The "accompanying directions" they refer to are the specific directions discussed separately on the next page.)

General Directions (continued):

In your essay, be sure to develop your ideas fully, leaving time, if possible, to review what you have written. **Do not write on a topic other than the one specified. Writing on a topic of your own choice is not acceptable.**

Translation: Don't invent and defend your own alternative in order to be clever, and don't write about how you spent your summer vacation.

General Directions (continued):

No special knowledge is required or expected for this writing exercise.

Translation: We're not going to ask you to explain the mechanics of photosynthesis or choose between a structuralist and post-structuralist interpretation of history. The choice presented is one that any literate person on the planet should be able to understand.

General Directions (continued):

Law schools are interested in the reasoning, clarity, organization, language usage, and writing mechanics displayed in your essay. How well you write is more important than how much you write.

Translation: Your position should be backed by evidence and should be clear and well structured. Your writing style will be taken into account. Merely filling up space doesn't win you any points. An excellent response need not take up every available line.

> ### General Directions (continued):
> Confine your essay to the blocked, lined area on the front and back of the separate writing sample response sheet. Only that area will be reproduced for law schools. Be sure that your writing is legible.

Translation: You have a front and back of a piece of paper to work with. Don't write more than that, and try to keep it neat.

That does it for the general directions. Here are the specific directions they provide:

> <u>**Directions:**</u> The scenario presented below describes two choices, either one of which can be supported on the basis of the information given. Your essay should consider both choices and argue <u>for</u> one and <u>against</u> the other, based on the two specified criteria and the facts provided. There is no "right" or "wrong" choice: a reasonable argument can be made for either.

Translation: Either choice is defensible, and you should write about both alternatives when arguing your case. In other words, don't just say why your choice is best; also say what it is that you believe makes the other choice inferior.

Okay, that's a fairly good amount of background information. Let's now take a look at a method for constructing your essay.

ESSENTIAL STRATEGY

Step 1: Scope the Situation. Analyze the situation and make sure you have a solid understanding of the alternatives presented. Then read the two bullet-pointed criteria and the descriptions of the alternatives. Select the choice that you find *easier* to defend, regardless of the one you may choose yourself in real life. While one option may appeal to you more from an aesthetic or practical standpoint, you may find the other easier to defend logically in writing. Don't spend more than a couple of minutes making your decision! Remember, both options represent plausible, defensible scenarios.

Step 2: Outline Your Response. When you've made your selection, use the scrap paper provided to outline your response. Allow yourself roughly five to seven minutes to create your outline. Don't worry about grammar or writing mechanics at this point; simply focus on getting your ideas down on paper. You will do this by listing the major points you will be making in abbreviated form. As for structure, plan to devote one long paragraph, or at most two short paragraphs, to each option. Include an introductory and concluding sentence. Here's an example of an effective essay format that you may wish to employ.

- **Introductory sentence:** Clear statement of the option you chose.

- **Paragraph 1:** Advantages of the option you selected.

- **Paragraph 2:** Disadvantages of the other option.

- **Concluding sentence:** Restate your decision and provide appropriate closure.

The introductory and concluding sentences can stand alone or be part of the first and last paragraphs, respectively. Either of the main body paragraphs can also be split into two shorter paragraphs. In any event, you should be able to establish your position in two to four paragraphs. You need not follow the exact structure stated above, but it is a good idea to have a reliable essay structure in mind going into the exercise. Since the prompts are totally formulaic (i.e., always a situation with two alternatives and two criteria), there's no reason why you can't decide the organization of your response in advance.

Your outline should include at least two advantages of your selection and at least one disadvantage of the alternative not selected. Jot these ideas down on your scrap paper in shorthand form. Don't flesh them out yet—that's what the writing stage is for. Your outline should serve as a blueprint for the points you wish to make and should help to keep your essay on track.

Step 3: Write Your Response. The writing stage entails fleshing out, in proper Standard Written English, the points you conceptualized in Steps 1 and 2. Step 3 will naturally take up the bulk of the 35 minutes. Strive to complete Steps 1 and 2 in about 10 minutes total, which will give you roughly 20 to 22 minutes to write while still leaving a few minutes to proofread your essay at the end. Here are some important points to keep in mind to execute Step 3 effectively.

- Don't rework your position during Step 3—there's simply no time to repeat your earlier work. Step 3 is all about *communicating the ideas you've committed to discussing*. Most incoherent essays result from blending Step 3 with Steps 1 and 2—that is, from reconceptualizing the argument on the fly while writing.

- Come out swinging by telling the reader immediately which choice you find superior. Establish a confident tone—don't be wishy-washy. That being said, don't be afraid to mention a minor strength of the alternative you didn't choose to show that you see all the angles.

- Conversely, you'll do yourself proud by citing a potential weakness of the option you're defending, as long as you *downplay* this weakness to demonstrate that the positives outweigh this one negative.

- Follow your outline and try not to get sidetracked.

- Finish strong with a restatement of the choice you find superior.

Step 4: Proofread Your Essay. Save three minutes or so at the end to look over your essay. Check spelling and grammar and fix any mistakes you find. A neat cross-out and rewrite is preferable to an egregious mistake. Just make sure your essay isn't littered with sloppy revisions to the point that it's difficult to read.

A Note on Style

You should make an attempt to vary your sentence structure to keep the essay engaging. And while it can't hurt to demonstrate a solid vocabulary. . .

. . . don't submit to a compulsion to evidence your estimable and irrepressible loquaciousness in an endeavor to astonish your future academic compatriots into acknowledging the vital, indisputable, and inevitable advisability of acceding to your fervent desire to obtain entrance to their legal institution.

In other words, avoid sentences like that—it sounds pretentious and increases the risk that you and your logic will get lost in the wordiness. Use language that's appropriate to make your case. Avoid overly complex sentences, and don't get carried away with flowery embellishments. Thirty-five minutes is not enough time to create the next Great American Masterpiece, but it is enough time to construct a clear and persuasive essay in support of a position. Use the vocabulary you have to the fullest, but don't try to squeeze in big words that you may not know how to use correctly. Finally, try your best to write neatly. It won't help your chances if admissions officers can't read what you wrote.

Common Essay Traps

In the children's book *The Bear Scouts,* the bear cubs learn all about how *not* to camp out by carefully observing one blunder after another by their self-proclaimed leader, Papa Bear. In a similar vein, long-time Writing Sample watchers have derived a whole host of "don'ts" from numerous analyses of sub-par essays. We've recommended things you should do in your essay. Here are some things you *shouldn't*:

Don't restate the situation. Your readers know the deal and want to know what you make of it, not how well you can copy it. Get right to the point with a strong statement of choice.

Don't restate information from the prompt word for word. Your readers are interested in how well you *interpret* the facts, not how well you *repeat* them.

Don't overextend your vocabulary. Use language that you know you can use well.

Don't go off topic. Keep each paragraph focused on the merits (or lack thereof) of one alternative, which will keep the essay organized and help the reader follow your train of thought.

Don't shortchange the discussion of the unchosen alternative. Showing why the option you didn't choose is inferior to the one you did adds considerable weight to your argument.

Don't over-rely on the first person. While writing "I" or "me" is acceptable every now and then, don't litter your essay with these words and don't use them when they add nothing to the essay, such as "I think that Acadia should publish with Second City Press." "Acadia should publish with Second City Press" makes the same point and is more concise.

Don't try to fill up every line at all costs. You can use up the two pages you're given if you have time and your argument requires it, but don't assume that doing so will necessarily result in a better essay. You may be better off putting extra time into the preparation phase, even if that results in a shorter response.

When you're feeling up to cranking out a practice essay, give it a shot in the next section.

ESSAY PRACTICE

Use the Essential Strategy to construct a response to the following essay topic. Give yourself 35 minutes to evaluate, outline, write, and proofread. Make sure to avoid the common traps just discussed. Then review the sample response and analysis that follows.

Acadia Stevens, an environmental activist, is weighing her publishing options for her first book, *EcoBalance: Sustainability in the 21st Century.* She has received a publishing offer from a medium-size publisher, Second City Press, but is considering publishing the book herself as an e-book distributed via Internet downloads. Write an essay in which you argue for one option over the other, keeping in mind the following two criteria:

- Acadia wants *EcoBalance* to have an impact on the environmental movement.
- Acadia wants *EcoBalance* to generate sufficient profits to subsidize her research and conservation activities.

Second City Press, located in Chicago, publishes mainly poetry and short fiction stories but has published nonfiction books as well. Its "How-To" series on gardening and home improvement has sold upward of 45,000 copies in the last year and ranks among the most popular of its kind. Second City's readership is based mainly in the Midwestern United States. Acadia's friend Laurel, who is the sister-in-law of Second City's editor in chief, introduced *EcoBalance* to Second City. Second City publishes the works of ten to fifteen new authors each year and sponsors extensive book tours for its most popular writers. For exclusive rights to the book, Second City has offered Acadia a $10,000 flat fee plus royalties amounting to 5 percent of retail sales. Second City plans to sell the book for $19.95 in bookstores and does not offer books for sale online.

Acadia is an active and well-known participant in many environmental websites, including a site called OnePlanet.net, to which she contributes a weekly column on conservation efforts worldwide. OnePlanet receives roughly 25,000 page views per week and is linked to over 20 other websites devoted to social issues. Acadia lectures widely on conservation issues in the United States and abroad and is a frequent guest on public access television and radio programs. An e-commerce research company indicates successful e-books selling in the $30 to $40 price range in popular subjects such as investing and financial management, but insignificant sales for fiction e-books even at a price point as low as $2.50. There are no financially successful environmental e-books currently offered on the Internet. Acadia would offer her e-book at a price point of $5.99.

Sample Response

Here is one possible response to the Writing Sample prompt. Peruse (good LSAT essay word, by the by) the outline and essay and then check out the analysis that follows.

Sample Outline

par 1 — intro
- e-book better
- her audience already online

par 2 — self-pub
- disadvantage: no track record, data not so good, BUT:
1) she could be first, and already well placed in market;
2) good platform to promote from — web, speaking, etc.
- global cause, global audience
- her audience not scared by Net

par 3 — 2nd city
- limited reach
- advance IS nice, but future money??
- support from company?? no guarantee: many other writers; possibly only offered b/c of personal / family connection
- "how-to" ¦ sounds good, BUT translate for Acadia?? gardening (popular) vs. environment (niche)
- recap: e-book better

Sample Essay

Acadia is best off independently publishing an e-book on the Internet. She has worked hard to build an online audience that is specifically interested in the subject of her book and could sell the book directly to this niche audience using the very mechanism through which they've come to know her and her cause. Her potential buyers are not limited to those who read her column but also include readers of websites linked to OnePlanet as well as users of the other online communities she frequents.

The fact that there is no proven track record for an environmental e-book is a double-edged sword: Some authors would be scared away, while an established authority like Acadia might rightfully consider it a golden opportunity to pioneer a new distribution model. While the e-commerce data look daunting, Acadia is well-positioned to blaze a new trail since her web presence and speaking and media engagements already provide a solid international platform from which to promote her product. Her global cause deserves a global audience, which is why the Internet provides the best forum to maximize the impact of her work. Online viral marketing techniques have generated explosive results for other small-scale endeavors and could work wonders for a motivated and passionate person like Acadia. The resultant financial success of the book can help her continue her environmental pursuits, as desired. Finally, while some might argue that the public isn't ready for books in digital form, those interested in societal reform are generally forward-thinking people who visualize change as a matter of course and are therefore not likely to be put off by a digital format.

Second City, with its regional readership and lack of online sales capabilities, would limit the reach of Acadia's message and the money she can earn from the book in the long run. The $10,000 advance is nice, but there may not be much in royalties after that. Although the $19.95 price point is higher than the e-book's price, Acadia will only see 5% of that money, or less than a dollar per copy. Second City would need to sell a very large number of books for Acadia to achieve her financial goals, and there's no guarantee that the company will be as motivated to promote the book as she would be herself. To be sure, the 45,000 "How-To" copies sold sounds like a lot, but that's for a whole series of books on a subject presumably more popular than environmental sustainability. Second City promotes its popular titles, but who's to say what it will do with a niche book possibly taken on only as a favor to a relative? Add to the equation 10 or more other new writers to deal with, and the prospect of Second City really getting behind "EcoBalance" seems even more risky. Acadia thus has a better chance of success if she remains loyal to her constituency and pursues online the identifiable, captive niche market that she has already worked to develop.

Sample Response Analysis

Overall, this writer does a fairly good job of arguing his position; his essay would make a fine addition to his law school application. Note that an effective essay need not be as long or as comprehensive as this sample response, which is intended to highlight the kinds of points you might wish to include and an acceptable way to state them. Also remember that you needn't have chosen the e-book alternative—either option is defensible. Here are a few positive aspects of the response that you should try to emulate in your essay.

Content

The essay begins with a clear, no-nonsense statement of choice and ends with a powerful reaffirmation of the desirability of the chosen alternative. The writer interprets the facts in light of the criteria motivating Acadia rather than simply restating the information in the prompt. Notice especially the consideration and subsequent dismissal in the second paragraph of two potential drawbacks to the alternative the writer selects. The writer acknowledges that there's no proven track record for an environmental e-book and that some people may not be ready for digital books, but he goes on to provide credible reasons why these potential drawbacks are in fact not serious objections to the e-book plan. In the same way, the writer mentions and dismisses a couple of seeming benefits of the Second City option amid an overall rejection of that alternative.

All of these examples suggest a nuanced approach to the problem and demonstrate that the writer is considering the problem on numerous levels. Sure, the writer may to some extent assume the financial success of the e-book to demonstrate the prospect of satisfying the second criterion, but the admissions officers reading these things have no doubt seen more egregious blunders. Overall, the reasoning employed in the essay is pretty solid.

Style, Grammar, and Word Choice

Stylistically, the writing is capable, and the author doesn't attempt to dazzle the reader with language beyond his capability. He uses appropriate signal words and phrases to transition between ideas, such as *while, finally, although, to be sure,* and *thus.* The essay is well organized and coherent. Of course it's not perfect, but perfection really isn't attainable in 35 minutes. Your goal is simply to fashion a response that will help and not hinder your chances of being accepted to law school. If you follow the Essential Strategy and avoid the common essay traps, you should do just fine.

WRITING SAMPLE SUMMARY

Yes, it's true that no one's primary LSAT concern is the Writing Sample, and no LSAT instructor worth his salt would advise spending anywhere near the amount of prep time on this section as on the scored multiple-choice sections. Still, admission to law school remains incredibly competitive, and you need to make the most of every opportunity to set your candidacy apart. LSAC practice PrepTests contain sample essay prompts, so complete as many practice essays as necessary to make sure you're comfortable with this section of the test. Then, when test day rolls around, the Writing Sample at the end won't distract you from acing what comes before, and it might very well provide the icing on your application cake.

## Chapter 5

LSAT PRACTICE TEST

This chapter contains a practice test that you should use to apply and reinforce the concepts, strategies, and techniques you've learned throughout this book. While the ability to answer questions individually is the basic building block of LSAT success, you also need to be able to answer the questions in the time provided. Your score therefore depends not only on how well you handle the various question types you've learned about, but also on how successfully you manage the sections overall. So before jumping into the practice test, take note of the following section management tips to learn how to work strategically with the time you're given.

SECTION MANAGEMENT

You've learned all the skills you need to answer every question on the LSAT, but that doesn't mean that you need to attempt every single question to get your maximum possible score. While the goal is to have time to work through every question, the majority of students do better by guessing at the tough questions and spending more time on the easier ones. Almost everyone runs out of time on at least one section, and if you're going to run out of time, you may as well focus on the easier questions since all questions are worth the same amount. Here's what you need to do to make the most of your time in each section.

Know Thyself!

We invoked this wisdom of Socrates way back in the Introduction to encourage you to set a realistic scoring goal. To develop your personalized section management strategy, first figure out how many correct answers you need to reach your target score. Use the scoring scale following the test in this chapter to get a sense of how many correct answers you need overall. Then break that number down by section, keeping in mind that there are usually around 24–26 Logical Reasoning questions, 26–28 Reading Comprehension questions, and 22 Logic Games questions. Be realistic in determining your score goals. Setting your goals too high can force you to struggle with questions that will just waste your time.

Going for It All

You may find that to achieve your scoring goal you need to have a shot at each question. If so, it still makes sense to attempt the easiest questions in each section first and save the hardest for last. (*Easiest*, of course, means easiest *for you*—this varies among test takers.) In Logical Reasoning, that means holding off on the questions that you have historically had difficulty with during your preparation; only you can pinpoint which ones those are. In Logic Games, it means doing the toughest game last—again, toughest for you, because the game types that pose problems for you, if any, may be different from those that throw other people for a loop. Same for Reading Comp: Save what promises to be the hardest passage for the end, after you've racked up points and confidence on the others. For example, maybe you hate science passages, or maybe you're a whiz with the physical sciences and have trouble with humanities passages instead. Think through these issues in advance. But even knowing your strengths and weaknesses, how do you figure out which of the four games or reading passages to postpone? Simple—take a quick look through the Logic Games and Reading Comp sections before jumping into the first game or passage. Don't read entire passages or begin setting up the games; just preview those sections to locate the most promising place to start and to note material that may be best attempted at the end.

> **TAKE AWAY**
>
> Although you can't move *between* sections, you're allowed to skip around *within* sections. You need not tackle the material in the order presented. Handling the questions in the most optimal order *for you* is one more way to take control of the test.

Easing Your Burden

When you estimate the points you need to reach your target score, you may find that you can achieve your goal without tackling the toughest questions at all. On most academic tests, getting 70 percent correct is barely passing. On the LSAT that hit rate puts you ahead of most of your competition. Here are some tips in case you decide that you can afford to lighten your load and not attempt every question.

Logical Reasoning

In Logical Reasoning, many people avoid Parallel Reasoning and Formal Logic questions. They can take a long time and they can be tough. That doesn't mean you have to skip all of them—some are easier than others. However, hard questions can come from any question type, so the best strategy is to give a fair shot at most of the questions but to move on if you really don't see what's going on. Most of the wasted time in Logical Reasoning comes from struggling with questions longer than you should. Often students narrow a question down to two choices and then spend minutes staring at it. Just pick one and move on. Skip the tough ones and don't fight to the death on any question.

Logic Games

In Logic Games, your scoring goals may enable you to avoid the toughest game entirely. If you can, scan all four games when the section begins and start with the easiest one—something you should do no matter what. Skipping an entire game is possible, but also consider skipping or guessing on killer questions within games. That way you may get to all four games but still not labor through every question, focusing instead on the easier ones in each. Some questions require you to work out scenarios for all of the choices. Spending two minutes there isn't as valuable as getting a shot at the easier questions of another game.

Reading Comprehension

In Reading Comprehension, see if you can skip the toughest passage. If you can, scan for it at the start of the section. Also consider skipping tougher questions from the passages you handle. For example, Extension questions often give students trouble because they require applying information from the passage to new situations not discussed in the passage. Again, any question type could pose a problem, so be prepared to take your best guess if a question isn't going well. In Reading Comp, also beware of narrowing a question down to two choices and then staring at them forever. Move on.

It's common to have difficulty managing your time when you first take the test. So as you practice, especially as test day gets close, make sure you practice not only your question answering skills but also your time management skills. Eventually, you'll be comfortable and confident even ignoring the toughest questions or making educated—or even uneducated—guesses on the questions you don't get to. But remember . . .

> **No matter what, never leave an answer blank!** There's no wrong answer penalty on the LSAT, so take your shot. If you don't get to some questions, guess. You have nothing to lose.

TAKE AWAY

HOW TO USE THIS TEST

Making the best use of this test depends on where you are in your LSAT preparation. If you're just beginning, consider checking out the Logic Games hints on pages 306–307 to give you a leg up on that section. You may also wish to work on one Logic Game, one Reading Comprehension passage, and three to five Logical Reasoning questions at a time before consulting the explanations. You need not obsess over timing guidelines at this stage, but do stay conscious of roughly how long it takes to work through the questions in each section. Mine the experience, as always, as you build your way toward taking full-length practice tests later.

If you're in the middle stage of your preparation, read the Logic Games hints on pages 306–307 only if you're having trouble with that section, or get stuck on a particular game. Take each section in its entirety and then stop to work through the explanations. Pay attention to our section management tips, and try to adhere to the timing guidelines. It's okay, however, to give yourself a little extra time to complete a section if necessary.

If you're in the final stage of your preparation, take all four sections as a simulated testing experience, allowing yourself one 10-minute break in the middle. Try the Logic Games section without reading the hints on pages 306–307. (If you still have trouble with the games, you can always try them again later on after checking out the hints.) Strictly observe timing guidelines and do your best to implement the section management strategies.

Okay, it's go time. Decide which approach works best for you at this stage of the game, and then have at it. Full guided explanations await you on page 310.

LSAT
Practice Test

SECTION I

Time—35 minutes

25 Questions

Directions: The questions in this section are based on the reasoning contained in brief statements or passages. For some questions, more than one of the choices can conceivably answer the question. However, you are to choose the best answer; that is, the response that most accurately and completely answers the question. You should not make assumptions that are by commonsense standards implausible, superfluous, or incompatible with the passage. After you have chosen the best answer, blacken the corresponding space on your answer sheet.

1.   Zack: A new study has reported that moderately overweight people have a lower chance of early death than do thin people. This is dangerous. First, there is no way to know in the immediate future whether the claim is accurate; such beliefs often persist for years before they are retracted in light of new evidence. Second, regardless of the claim's accuracy, it obscures the fact that a lower chance of early death is not synonymous with good health. The majority of moderately overweight people will no doubt view these findings as a license to discontinue diets and put aside concern for their weight.

Zoe: It is true that overweight people will respond to the claim regardless of a confirmation of its accuracy. Moreover, it is likely that some people who are more than moderately overweight will be encouraged by the study to view their condition with less concern than warranted. However, most moderately overweight people have already come to terms with and accepted their weight, so this group will mainly use the study to validate preexisting beliefs.

On the basis of their statements, Zack and Zoe are committed to disagreeing with each other about whether

(A)   the majority of moderately overweight people have a lower chance of early death than do the majority of thin people
(B)   some people who are more than moderately overweight will act on their interpretation of the study as if it pertains to them
(C)   the study poses the potential for misinterpretation among overweight people
(D)   the study will encourage the majority of moderately overweight people to alter how they conceive of their weight
(E)   a lower chance of early death means the same thing as good health

2.   Professor Vessent: In order for our department to remain popular among students and continue to receive the funding it needs, it must recruit new "star" professors to its graduate program. Star professors are expert academics who are known to the general public through appearances in the mass media. The Dean has repeatedly promised to match any offer on the market to lure available star professors to this department. However, this promise is clearly false, as the eminently qualified Katerina Goodrich was just hired by Westerton College at a salary far exceeding that which she was offered here.

Which one of the following is an assumption that the argument requires?

(A)   Continued funding for the department depends on it remaining popular among students.
(B)   Recruiting star professors to its graduate program will ensure that the department receives the funding it needs.
(C)   Katerina Goodrich is an expert academic known to the general public through appearances in the mass media.
(D)   The amount of funding the department receives is greater than the salary that the Dean offered to Katerina Goodrich.
(E)   Katerina Goodrich was among the candidates the Dean targeted when he promised to lure star professors to the department.

GO ON TO THE NEXT PAGE.

3. Most laptop computers are slower, contain smaller hard drives, and are less powerful than their desktop counterparts. In addition, they usually cost more than desktop models. College students would therefore predominantly buy desktop computers instead of laptops, if not for the fact that many professors require the use of the smaller portable laptops in class.

Which one of the following, if true, most weakens the argument?

(A) A growing number of colleges provides students with access to large computer facilities containing both desktop and laptop computers.

(B) Many college students primarily used desktop computers before coming to college.

(C) Some college professors do not require the use of laptops in class.

(D) Most colleges provide software to students that can be used on both laptop and desktop computers.

(E) Many college students share small dorm rooms and do not have enough space for multiple desktop computers.

4. Since 1997, paleontologists have discovered the fossilized remains of four species of snakes with legs. Some researchers have concluded that one of these species, *Pachyrhachis problematicus*, is the most primitive snake and that it evolved in water, since the fossil was found in marine rock and shows evidence of a flattened tail optimized for swimming. Other researchers, however, point to *Pachyrhachis problematicus's* advanced teeth to dispute the claim that *Pachyrhachis* is the most primitive snake. These researchers propose the most recently discovered legged species, the land-dwelling *Najash rionegrini*, as the world's first snake.

It can be inferred from the information above that some researchers do not believe that

(A) a snake fossil has been found in marine rock since 1997

(B) the earliest snake species had legs

(C) *Pachyrhachis problematicus* had a tail optimized for swimming

(D) the teeth of *Pachyrhachis problematicus* were less advanced than those of *Najash rionegrini*

(E) legged snake species have been discovered since 1997

5. Entrepreneur: Since people are inherently averse to unfamiliarity, all new technologies initially meet with massive resistance. As a case in point, upon first introduction all successful communication technologies were scoffed at by experts and even the industries they eventually revolutionized right up until the very moment such "hare-brained schemes" morphed into essential accoutrements of modern life. Our revolutionary electronic publishing venture has been turned down by the first twenty companies we approached, a sure sign that our venture is guaranteed to succeed.

Which one of the following best describes the flaw in the argument above?

(A) It does not outline precisely how the product in question will revolutionize the electronic publishing industry.

(B) It assumes without warrant that certain new technologies can overcome massive amounts of initial resistance to one day become essential elements of modern life.

(C) It considers a factor inextricably associated with successful technological ventures as a factor that brings about the success of technological ventures.

(D) It does not identify specific essential accoutrements of modern life that began by being rejected as "hare-brained schemes."

(E) It implies that experts and business leaders were foolish for initially rejecting ideas that would one day revolutionize entire industries.

GO ON TO THE NEXT PAGE.

6. People who complain about the high cost of traveling should make all of their purchases using credit cards that award airline miles for every purchase charged to the card. One can fly for free to predetermined selected destinations after accumulating the requisite number of miles, thus saving money in the long run.

Each of the following, if true, would cast doubt on the likelihood that fully enacting the recommendation above will have the stated effect EXCEPT:

(A) The rules regarding how the accumulated miles may be exchanged are more restrictive than the rules for similar promotions offered by hotels.

(B) People make many more purchases than they normally would when trying to accumulate credit card airline miles.

(C) The predetermined selected destinations to which free flights may be obtained via exchange for credit card airline miles are much more exotic and expensive than the destinations people visit when purchasing tickets normally.

(D) People attempting to accumulate credit card airline miles toward a free flight tend to purchase the first brand they encounter when searching for a particular product when they otherwise would have comparison shopped for bargains.

(E) People attempting to accumulate credit card airline miles toward a free flight tend to purchase expensive items that they do not need in order to attain the requisite number of miles.

7. Incompetence causes workers to perform inferior work. In addition, some incompetent people do not recognize their own incompetence, which causes them to reject the feedback and assistance that would enable them to improve the quality of their work.

The situation described above conforms most closely to which one of the following propositions?

(A) A behavior that causes negative repercussions may sometimes bring about positive outcomes that outweigh the negative repercussions of the behavior.

(B) A consequence of a phenomenon may in some cases be compounded by a secondary effect of that same phenomenon.

(C) The rejection of valuable recommendations may prove to be the difference between a negative outcome and the best possible outcome.

(D) When a character trait of a particular worker results in the performance of inferior work, that worker should be assigned less demanding responsibilities.

(E) An inferior project based on a faulty premise will be made worse by any attempt to incorporate a conflicting premise into the project.

8. Lisa has earned enough music credits at Bingville University to make her eligible to declare a music minor. Randi must also be eligible to declare a music minor at Bingville University, since she has earned more music credits at that university than Lisa and the only factor determining eligibility to declare a music minor at Bingville University is the number of music credits earned.

Which one of the following arguments is most similar in its pattern of reasoning to the argument above?

(A) Dasha has enough money to buy the item she desires from the candy store. Since Jessie has more money than Dasha, Jessie must also have enough money to buy the item she desires from the candy store.

(B) Last night The Shambles sold out a 10,000-seat arena. Since tonight's concert by The Shambles is in a venue with a capacity of only 500 people, The Shambles will sell out tonight's concert as well.

(C) Allyson's new house costs less than her previous house. Since Allyson had enough money to make a down payment on her previous house, she will have enough money to make a down payment on her new house.

(D) Marvin, who has an advanced degree, has been an excellent tutor for Joshua. Since Sybil has one more advanced degree than Marvin, she will be an even better tutor for Joshua.

(E) The Northwest Water Treatment Plant purifies a sufficient amount of water to satisfy the water needs of Reedbrook. Since the Southeast Water Treatment Plant purifies more water than does the Northwest Water Treatment Plant, the Southeast Water Treatment Plant must also be capable of providing enough purified water to satisfy the water needs of Reedbrook.

9. Alcohol dehydrogenase (ADH), an enzyme found in the liver and the stomach, breaks down alcohol before it reaches the bloodstream. It does this by converting ethanol, a toxic substance in alcohol, to acetaldehyde, another toxic substance, which is then further converted into harmless acetic acid. If one consumes alcohol at a rate faster than that which ADH can detoxify it, intoxication will result from alcohol entering the bloodstream. ADH is four times more active in men than in women.

Which one of the following is most strongly supported by the information above?

(A) A woman who consumes three alcoholic drinks in the course of an evening will experience intoxication.

(B) Men who consume alcohol are four times less likely to experience intoxication than are women who consume alcohol.

(C) A woman with an above-average quantity of acetaldehyde in her system must have recently consumed alcohol.

(D) An equivalent dose of alcohol will likely intoxicate a typical woman more than a typical man.

(E) People with ADH deficiencies will have an excess of ethanol in their bloodstreams.

GO ON TO THE NEXT PAGE.

10. Ernie: When professional basketball players sprain their ankles, they receive immediate treatment by the best doctors with access to the most up-to-date and comprehensive medical technologies. Moreover, their rehabilitation regimens are state of the art as well, since the teams have a large vested interest in accelerating the healing process. Despite this abundant attention, which "average" people like me most certainly lack, it is not unusual for professional basketball players' ankle injuries to take three months to fully heal. It is therefore untrue that the fact that my ankle injury took three months to fully heal is proof that I did not take adequate care of my injury.

The answer to which one of the following questions would be most useful in evaluating Ernie's argument?

(A) How severe was Ernie's ankle injury as compared with that of the ankle injuries to professional basketball players he describes?

(B) Is the medical treatment afforded to professional basketball players better than that afforded to other professional athletes?

(C) Do injured professional athletes have a greater vested interest in accelerating the healing process than do injured "average" people like Ernie?

(D) Has any professional basketball player suffered an ankle injury that took longer than three months to fully heal?

(E) Is the medical treatment afforded to professional athletes available to anyone who is not a professional athlete?

11. Educational consultant: Students struggling in traditional public schools are often reassigned to special education classes, when home schooling may in fact be a better alternative. Many dismiss such non-mainstream educational approaches out of hand. However, not only do home-schooled children receive the specific individual attention they require, but they also avoid the emotional hardships and social stigmas that often burden students forced to participate in traditional special education programs. This danger is especially prevalent among special education students with low self-esteem.

The educational consultant's statements best support which one of the following?

(A) Traditional special education classes are a better option than home schooling for struggling students who do not suffer from low self-esteem.

(B) Any nontraditional educational approach is superior to special education classes when it comes to helping struggling students succeed academically.

(C) Struggling students may benefit from nontraditional schooling options.

(D) Traditional schooling generally does not provide individual attention to students with low self-esteem.

(E) Traditional schooling is less effective than home schooling for most students.

12. Anthropologist: One of the wonders of nature is the ant's uncanny ability to balance duty toward its colony with the satisfaction of its individual needs. We would do well to look to this achievement as the basis for a more just social arrangement. Humans, both blessed and cursed with higher-order intelligence and autonomy, have yet to come close to realizing such balance between societal needs and individual strivings. This is because as soon as we gain power of any kind, we seek to use it to our personal advantage which inevitably (although often unintentionally) works to the detriment of the greater good. This tendency, however, is culturally driven and not instinctual, so a change in social relations is clearly attainable.

The author is mainly arguing that

(A) humans use power to seek and gain advantages over one another

(B) humans would ultimately be happier if they were more like ants in many respects

(C) humans would benefit from a better balance between individual and societal needs

(D) because the human tendency to seek personal advantage to the detriment of the greater good is instinctual, it is not possible to alter social relations

(E) humans have employed higher-order intelligence in both positive and negative ways

13. Anyone who works hard is respected by at least one other person. Since all those who respect someone are well-liked, it must be true that whoever works hard is well-liked.

The conclusion above is valid if which one of the following is assumed?

(A) Only people who do not work hard respect no one.

(B) Everyone who respects at least one person respects everyone.

(C) Whoever respects everyone works hard.

(D) Whoever is well-liked respects at least one other person.

(E) Only people who do not work hard are respected by at least one other person.

GO ON TO THE NEXT PAGE.

14. Probiotics are beneficial bacteria contained in fermented foods. One probiotic, *Lactobacillus reuteri*, is believed to help prevent gastrointestinal infections and provide overall health benefits. For 45 days, 100 randomly chosen test group subjects were given one drink a day containing *Lactobacillus reuteri,* while another 100 control group subjects were given one drink a day containing placebos. At the end of the study, all test group subjects were tested to determine their reactions to *Lactobacillus reuteri.* Within this group, 45 percent of those working night shifts exhibited a positive reaction to *Lactobacillus reuteri,* while only 16 percent of those working day shifts exhibited a positive reaction to the bacteria. These data demonstrate that *Lactobacillus reuteri* benefited more night-shift workers than day-shift workers.

The reasoning in the argument is most vulnerable to the criticism that it

(A) fails to specify the physical advantages derived from a positive reaction to *Lactobacillus reuteri*

(B) assumes without justification that no one in the control group benefited from the study

(C) distinguishes between two subgroups of a larger group participating in the study

(D) omits key information that would allow the conclusion to be verified

(E) provides no information on the effectiveness of *Lactobacillus reuteri* relative to the effectiveness of other probiotics

15. A study conducted by the Regional Educational Statistics Board (RESB) found the dropout rate among high school students from 1999 to 2002 to be 2.7 percent. However, the census bureau for the same region reported the high school dropout rate during the same period to be 5.2 percent.

Which one of the following, if true, best resolves the apparent discrepancy above?

(A) RESB reported certain students who left high school to be home schooled as graduates since they passed a high school certification exam, while the census bureau reported such students as dropouts.

(B) The census bureau included in its report statistics on elementary and junior high school dropout rates, while RESB did not.

(C) The high schools included in RESB's study were identical to the high schools studied by the census bureau.

(D) The census bureau report indicates that the high school dropout rate between 1999 and 2001 was approximately 2.7 percent, but rose dramatically in 2002 due to a severe economic downturn in the region during that year.

(E) When factoring in the number of high school dropouts who eventually returned to high school and received high school diplomas since 2002, the census bureau dropout rate mirrored that found by RESB.

16. College Dean: While of course this university requires tuition fees in order to operate, our professors gear the classroom experience to satisfy only one mandate: producing educated and enlightened citizens. Therefore, accusations that our students dictate their courses' subject matter and manner of presentation to get the most of their education expenditures, akin to consumers in the marketplace, is patently false. Moreover, critics making this charge fail to realize that students benefit immensely when academic programs and courses are geared specifically to appeal to their intellectual interests and optimal modes of receiving information.

The Dean's argument is flawed because it

(A) contains conflicting premises

(B) fails to demonstrate that courses not geared to appeal to students' intellectual interests might interest some students anyway

(C) does not provide evidence that the courses at the Dean's university are superior in quality to courses at similar universities

(D) employs different meanings of the word "consumer" when referring to the university setting as opposed to the marketplace

(E) criticizes students for engaging in a behavior based only on evidence that they have been accused of engaging in that behavior

17. Memmie: Children today are growing up in a toxic atmosphere of environmental contaminants. Their living space includes ever-increasing amounts of pesticides, air pollution, and food additives, not to mention simple dust and pollen. This toxic environment is responsible for the huge increase in childhood diseases such as asthma and bronchitis.

Bunny: Quite the opposite! Our society's recent mania for health and cleanliness, characterized by increases in immunizations and disinfectants and an unwillingness to allow children to interact hands-on with our natural surroundings, has compromised children's immune systems, which require early and abundant contact with contaminants in order to develop properly. Weaker immune systems have led to a greater incidence of childhood diseases.

The conversation most strongly suggests that Memmie and Bunny disagree over whether

(A) children's interaction with the environment affects the incidence of childhood diseases

(B) the environment to which children are exposed has become more sanitary

(C) the increase in the incidence of childhood asthma is more related to environmental contaminants than is the increase in the incidence of childhood bronchitis

(D) the incidence of childhood diseases is on the rise

(E) children's immune systems have been negatively affected by changes in their interaction with the environment

GO ON TO THE NEXT PAGE.

18. Signals originating in the pons—a structure at the base of the brain—trigger rapid eye movement (REM) sleep, and ultimately enter the cerebral cortex, the part of the brain that collects and interprets information from the outside world. Infants and young children, who learn at a much faster rate than adults, experience much longer periods of REM sleep. Moreover, studies have shown that people deprived of REM sleep have difficulty assimilating new knowledge and skills attained while awake, while those deprived of non-REM sleep while receiving a normal amount of REM sleep do not experience a similar change in their retention capabilities. It is therefore likely that the pons plays a role in the learning process.

Which one of the following best describes the role played in the argument by the claim that infants and young children learn at a much faster rate than adults and experience much longer periods of REM sleep?

(A) It is a subsidiary conclusion supported by preceding information provided in the argument.

(B) It is one of two independent pieces of evidence that taken together help to establish the argument's conclusion.

(C) It provides information about REM sleep that contradicts a later assertion meant to undermine the argument's conclusion.

(D) It provides the sole support for the argument's conclusion regarding the likely role that REM sleep plays in the learning process.

(E) It provides the basis for understanding the assertion about REM sleep that immediately follows it and upon which the argument's conclusion is primarily based.

19. If all of Seacliff's beachfront houses are worth more than two million dollars, then Seacliff would be ranked as one of the ten most desirable localities in the nation. Every beachfront house sold in Seacliff in the past three years has sold for more than two million dollars, so Seacliff must be ranked as one of the ten most desirable localities in the nation.

Which one of the following exhibits the same logical flaw exhibited in the argument above?

(A) If a newspaper relies on advertising revenue to survive, then it must have a large readership to attract advertisers. The *Daily Gazette* does not have a large readership, so it will not survive.

(B) Bowlarama earns above-average profits any month that all local members of the Southeast Bowling Association bowl at the alley. Bowlarama must have earned above-average profits this month, since all of the captains of the local Southeast Bowling Association teams bowled there this month.

(C) The Newton Chief of Police will resign if any of the town's recent scandals is revealed to the public. The chief of police will resign next month, since a local reporter has become aware that a Newton police officer illegally searched a house without a warrant.

(D) If Comtech Industries introduces a new digital camera this year, Comtech will receive significant publicity in business journals. Comtech has recently received significant publicity in business journals, so it must have introduced a new digital camera this year.

(E) Some registered independents in Clarksdale will not vote for Sapienza for city council. Since all registered independents in Clarksdale will vote in the upcoming city council election, Sapienza will not be elected unanimously to the city council.

20. Art professor: A mundane work of art merely encapsulates in a new mode the fully formed thought of another, while an inspired work of art expresses at least some part of its creator's individuality. In addition, some inspired works of art are works of genius. However, whereas the essence of a common inspired art work is always at least partially derived from other influences, the essence of a work of genius is purely original.

If all of the art professor's statements are true, which one of the following must be false?

(A) All artists wish to express their own individuality.

(B) The essence of no mundane work of art is original.

(C) The portfolio of a single artist contains both a mundane work of art and a work of genius.

(D) The majority of artists base their work on the fully formed thoughts of others.

(E) The essence of every inspired work of art is derivative.

GO ON TO THE NEXT PAGE.

21. It is stylistically permissible to append the phrase "and so on" only to a statement containing a list clearly not intended to represent an inclusive account of the situation depicted by the statement.

Based on the principle above, which one of the following statements is not stylistically permissible?

(A) Barre University grants scholarships for many kinds of individual student achievement, including grades, extracurricular activities, community involvement, and so on.

(B) Gerunds are formed by adding "ing" to the end of a verb, such as changing "talk" to "talking," "run" to "running," "fight" to "fighting," and so on.

(C) Music is employed in numerous commercial settings; for example, in movies, on TV shows, in advertisements, and so on.

(D) Nominees at The Third Annual Fowler Awards for best male performance in an independent feature film are Jordan Kurtiss, Stuart Kohm, Matthew Bolowitz, and so on.

(E) Douzaglou Tennis Academy focuses on numerous aspects of the game: serves, volleys, backhands, and so on.

22. Editorialist: Some political commentators contend that campaign finance reform is necessary in order to validate future elections, since money has become a deciding factor in elections and in the absence of limitations on campaign contributions, election winners will often be the candidates that accumulate the most financial support. This erroneous contention overlooks the fact that opinion polls have clearly demonstrated that the majority of people believe that candidates of the two major parties, who have received the most campaign contributions in recent elections, have received roughly an equal number of such contributions.

Which one of the following does NOT point out a flaw in the editorialist's reasoning?

(A) It equates the number of campaign contributions with the amount of money obtained from those contributions.

(B) It restricts the electoral field in such a way that fails to address the political commentators' contention.

(C) It assumes without warrant the accuracy of public perception of campaign contributions.

(D) It allows for the possibility that even a small difference in financial contributions might still decide elections.

(E) It presumes without justification that the absence of inequality in campaign funding will ensure the validity of future elections.

23. Arlene must take a class this semester to satisfy her college's physical education requirement. She cannot take swimming because it meets at the same time as her upper-level physics class. One reason that she cannot take racquetball is because she has not yet taken the prerequisite course necessary for participation in that class. Arlene must therefore take canoeing this semester, the only other intermediate-level physical education class offered besides swimming and racquetball.

Which one of the following is an assumption on which the argument depends?

(A) Arlene will not be required to take another physical education class at college after completing a physical education class this semester.

(B) Students at Arlene's college are not permitted to take advanced-level classes and intermediate-level classes during the same semester.

(C) Arlene has satisfied all prerequisite courses necessary to participate in swimming.

(D) The physical education requirement cannot be satisfied by anything other than an intermediate-level physical education class.

(E) It would be possible for Arlene to take racquetball this semester if she had satisfied all of the prerequisites for that class.

GO ON TO THE NEXT PAGE.

24. Richie: U.S. law prohibits the fraudulent mutilation of currency in circulation. However, according to the same law it is not illegal to mutilate currency that has been legally removed from circulation. It is therefore legal to mutilate the pennies that I use to create the jewelry and belt buckles that I sell online, since I have soldered these coins together and they therefore cannot reenter the monetary system.

Louise: That is incorrect, because your rendering the coins unavailable by incorporating them into decorative objects does not meet the condition you believe would exonerate you from a charge of illegal mutilation.

Which one of the following most accurately describes the argumentative technique used by Louise to object to Richie's argument?

(A) suggesting that Richie has misapplied a key term used in his argument

(B) arguing that Richie has failed to demonstrate that it may in some cases be permissible to make decorative objects out of mutilated coins removed from circulation

(C) implying that Richie has inappropriately argued that there may be instances in which currency mutilation is legal

(D) demonstrating that Richie has failed to establish that no coins used for decorative purposes can ever reenter the monetary system

(E) showing that Richie has fraudulently misinformed his customers as to the legality of mutilating the pennies contained in the objects they purchase from him online

25. A strong belief in progress during an age of technological innovation enhances citizens' feelings of nationalism, which in turn increases the public's interest in national affairs. Nineteenth-century America was characterized by large-scale technological innovation, and during the course of that century the New England region of the country experienced a marked increase in the number of candidates seeking public office. It is therefore likely that a strong belief in progress contributed to the increase in New Englanders seeking public office.

Which one the following, if true, most strengthens the argument above?

(A) Some European countries experienced rising nationalism during the technologically progressive years of the Industrial Revolution.

(B) The number of candidates for public office is positively correlated with the level of public interest in national affairs.

(C) A country's citizens tend to pay more attention to national affairs whenever nationalism in that country is high.

(D) Historical records indicate an increasing opposition to the policies of the national government among nineteenth-century New Englanders.

(E) Numerous Asian countries are characterized by a strong public interest in national affairs.

STOP

**IF YOU FINISH BEFORE TIME IS CALLED, YOU MAY CHECK YOUR WORK ON THIS SECTION ONLY.
DO NOT WORK ON ANY OTHER SECTION IN THE TEST.**

SECTION II

Time—35 minutes

22 Questions

Directions: Each group of questions in this section is based on a set of conditions. In answering some of the questions, it may be useful to draw a rough diagram. Choose the response that most accurately and completely answers each question and blacken the corresponding space on your answer sheet.

Questions 1–6

An orchestra performs exactly five compositions during the course of a classical concert. The compositions—performed in order from first to fifth—are selected from the works of six composers: Franck, Haydn, Mozart, Ravel, Smetana, and Vivaldi. The following conditions apply:

  If the orchestra performs a composition by Ravel, it will perform a composition by Franck immediately following the performance of a composition by Vivaldi.

  If the orchestra performs a composition by Mozart, it will perform compositions by Franck first and fifth.

  The orchestra will not perform a composition by Vivaldi unless it also performs at least one composition by Smetana.

  If the orchestra performs a composition by Haydn, it will perform a composition by Ravel third.

1. Which one of the following could be a complete and accurate list of the composers of the compositions performed during the concert, from first to last?

    (A) Franck, Mozart, Vivaldi, Franck, Smetana
    (B) Haydn, Ravel, Smetana, Vivaldi, Franck
    (C) Smetana, Franck, Vivaldi, Smetana, Ravel
    (D) Smetana, Smetana, Vivaldi, Vivaldi, Franck
    (E) Vivaldi, Franck, Ravel, Haydn, Haydn

2. If the orchestra performs a composition by Haydn later than it performs a composition by Vivaldi, then which one of the following could be false?

    (A) The orchestra performs a composition by Franck earlier than it performs a composition by Ravel.
    (B) The orchestra performs a composition by Haydn later than it performs a composition by Franck.
    (C) The orchestra performs a composition by Ravel later than it performs a composition by Vivaldi.
    (D) The orchestra performs a composition by Smetana earlier than it performs a composition by Haydn.
    (E) The orchestra performs a composition by Vivaldi earlier than it performs a composition by Smetana.

3. The orchestra CANNOT perform compositions from which one of the following pairs of composers during the concert?

    (A) Franck and Ravel
    (B) Haydn and Mozart
    (C) Haydn and Smetana
    (D) Mozart and Smetana
    (E) Mozart and Vivaldi

4. If the orchestra performs a composition by Ravel, which one of the following must be true?

    (A) The orchestra performs exactly one composition by Franck.
    (B) The orchestra does not perform any compositions by Haydn.
    (C) The orchestra does not perform any compositions by Mozart.
    (D) The orchestra performs exactly one composition by Smetana.
    (E) The orchestra performs exactly two compositions by Vivaldi.

5. If the fifth composition is the only composition the orchestra performs by Vivaldi, then which one of the following must be true?

    (A) The orchestra performs a composition by Franck immediately before it performs a composition by Smetana or Vivaldi.
    (B) The orchestra performs a composition by Haydn earlier than it performs a composition by Vivaldi.
    (C) The orchestra performs a composition by Smetana immediately before it performs a composition by Franck or Vivaldi.
    (D) The orchestra performs a composition by Vivaldi immediately after it performs a composition by Franck.
    (E) The orchestra performs a composition by Vivaldi immediately after it performs a composition by Smetana.

6. If the orchestra performs the compositions of exactly two composers during the concert, how many different pairs of composers could be the pair whose works are performed?

    (A) one
    (B) two
    (C) three
    (D) four
    (E) five

GO ON TO THE NEXT PAGE.

Questions 7–11

Dr. Schazzie visits six patients—Freid, Helbing, Jayar, Randall, Toot, and Yorkel—during hospital rounds one morning. He visits the patients one at a time in order from first to sixth, in accordance with the following conditions:

Dr. Schazzie visits Toot at some time before he visits Yorkel.

Dr. Schazzie visits both Helbing and Yorkel at some time before he visits Freid.

Dr. Schazzie visits Jayar immediately before or immediately after he visits Randall.

7. Which one of the following is an acceptable partial ordering of Dr. Schazzie's patient visits?

   (A) Freid: fourth; Randall: fifth; Jayar: sixth
   (B) Helbing: first; Freid: third; Randall: sixth
   (C) Jayar: first; Toot: second; Helbing: fourth
   (D) Toot: third; Yorkel: fourth; Freid: fifth
   (E) Toot: fourth; Yorkel: fifth; Helbing: sixth

8. If Dr. Schazzie visits Toot fourth, then which one of the following must be true?

   (A) Dr. Schazzie visits Freid fifth.
   (B) Dr. Schazzie visits Helbing third.
   (C) Dr. Schazzie visits Jayar first.
   (D) Dr. Schazzie visits Randall second.
   (E) Dr. Schazzie visits Yorkel fifth.

9. How many patients are there, any one of whom could be the third patient that Dr. Schazzie visits?

   (A) two
   (B) three
   (C) four
   (D) five
   (E) six

10. If Dr. Schazzie visits exactly two patients before Yorkel, then which one of the following must be true?

    (A) Dr. Schazzie visits either Jayar or Randall fifth.
    (B) Dr. Schazzie visits Jayar at some time before he visits Freid.
    (C) Dr. Schazzie visits Jayar fourth or fifth.
    (D) Dr. Schazzie visits Randall fifth or sixth.
    (E) Dr. Schazzie visits Toot at some time before he visits Helbing.

11. If Dr. Schazzie visits Freid immediately before or immediately after he visits Jayar, then which one of the following must be true?

    (A) Dr. Schazzie visits Freid fourth.
    (B) Dr. Schazzie visits Freid sixth.
    (C) Dr. Schazzie visits Jayar fifth.
    (D) Dr. Schazzie visits Toot third.
    (E) Dr. Schazzie visits Yorkel third.

GO ON TO THE NEXT PAGE.

Questions 12–16

Each of five journalists—Jotty, Kieran, Laughlan, Ming, and Piper—is assigned to cover at least one of the following topics for a local newspaper: finance, national affairs, and sports. Exactly two journalists will cover each topic. The following conditions must apply:

Jotty does not cover any topic that Laughlan covers.

If Kieran covers a topic, then Ming also covers that topic.

Piper covers sports if and only if she also covers national affairs.

12. Which one of the following could be an accurate matching of topics to the journalists who cover them?

(A) finance: Jotty, Ming; national affairs: Laughlan, Piper; sports: Kieran, Piper

(B) finance: Jotty, Piper; national affairs: Laughlan, Ming; sports: Kieran, Ming

(C) finance: Kieran, Ming; national affairs: Jotty, Piper; sports: Ming, Piper

(D) finance: Kieran, Ming; national affairs: Laughlan, Piper; sports: Jotty, Ming

(E) finance: Laughlan, Piper; national affairs: Kieran, Ming; sports: Jotty, Laughlan

13. Which one of the following must be true?

(A) Either Jotty or Ming covers more than one topic.

(B) Either Kieran or Laughlan covers more than one topic.

(C) Either Kieran or Piper covers more than one topic.

(D) Either Laughlan or Ming covers more than one topic.

(E) Either Ming or Piper covers more than one topic.

14. If Kieran does not cover finance, then which one of the following must be true?

(A) Jotty covers sports.

(B) Kieran covers sports.

(C) Laughlan covers finance.

(D) Ming covers national affairs.

(E) Piper covers national affairs.

15. Which one of the following would make it possible to precisely determine all six assignments of journalists to the topics they cover?

(A) Jotty and Ming cover national affairs.

(B) Jotty and Piper cover finance.

(C) Kieran and Ming cover finance.

(D) Kieran and Ming cover sports.

(E) Laughlan and Piper cover finance.

16. If Laughlan does not cover any topic that Piper covers, then each of the following could be true EXCEPT:

(A) Kieran covers sports.

(B) Laughlan covers national affairs.

(C) Ming covers national affairs.

(D) Ming covers sports.

(E) Piper covers sports.

GO ON TO THE NEXT PAGE.

On a Saturday afternoon, Master Prensabi's students perform exactly five Tae Kwon Do demonstrations. Each student performs as a member of exactly one of three teams: Team Green Belt, Team Red Belt, or Team Yellow Belt. Exactly one team performs each demonstration, and no two demonstrations are performed at the same time. One team has eight students, another has ten students, and the other has sixteen students. Each team performs at least once, and the composition of each team remains constant throughout the course of the demonstrations. The teams perform in accordance with the following conditions:

Sixteen students perform the third demonstration.

The same number of students performs the fourth and fifth demonstrations.

Team Red Belt performs more demonstrations than Team Yellow Belt.

Team Yellow Belt has more students than Team Red Belt.

17. Which one of the following could be a complete and accurate list of teams performing the demonstrations, in order from first to fifth?

(A) Team Green Belt, Team Yellow Belt, Team Green Belt, Team Red Belt, Team Red Belt

(B) Team Red Belt, Team Green Belt, Team Yellow Belt, Team Green Belt, Team Red Belt

(C) Team Red Belt, Team Yellow Belt, Team Yellow Belt, Team Red Belt, Team Red Belt

(D) Team Yellow Belt, Team Red Belt, Team Red Belt, Team Green Belt, Team Green Belt

(E) Team Yellow Belt, Team Yellow Belt, Team Green Belt, Team Red Belt, Team Red Belt

18. Team Red Belt CANNOT perform which one of the following demonstrations?

(A) first
(B) second
(C) third
(D) fourth
(E) fifth

19. If Team Yellow Belt performs the first demonstration, then which one of the following must be true?

(A) Team Green Belt has ten students.
(B) Team Green Belt performs the second demonstration.
(C) Team Red Belt has ten students.
(D) Team Red Belt performs the fourth demonstration.
(E) Team Yellow Belt has sixteen students.

20. Which one of the following CANNOT be true?

(A) Ten students perform the first demonstration.
(B) Sixteen students perform the second demonstration.
(C) Eight students perform the fourth demonstration.
(D) Ten students perform the fourth demonstration.
(E) Sixteen students perform the fifth demonstration.

21. Which one of the following could be true?

(A) Team Green Belt performs the first and fourth demonstrations.
(B) Team Red Belt performs the first and fifth demonstrations.
(C) Team Red Belt performs fewer than two demonstrations.
(D) Team Yellow Belt performs the fourth demonstration.
(E) Team Yellow Belt performs the fifth demonstration.

22. If Team Green Belt performs the fourth demonstration, then which one of the following must be true?

(A) Team Green Belt performs exactly one demonstration.
(B) Team Green Belt has ten students.
(C) Exactly one demonstration is performed by the team with eight students.
(D) Exactly two demonstrations are performed by the team with ten students.
(E) Eight students perform the fifth demonstration.

STOP

**IF YOU FINISH BEFORE TIME IS CALLED, YOU MAY CHECK YOUR WORK ON THIS SECTION ONLY.
DO NOT WORK ON ANY OTHER SECTION IN THE TEST.**

SECTION III

Time—35 minutes

25 Questions

<u>Directions:</u> The questions in this section are based on the reasoning contained in brief statements or passages. For some questions, more than one of the choices can conceivably answer the question. However, you are to choose the <u>best</u> answer; that is, the response that most accurately and completely answers the question. You should not make assumptions that are by commonsense standards implausible, superfluous, or incompatible with the passage. After you have chosen the best answer, blacken the corresponding space on your answer sheet.

1. Only a small subgroup of all philosophers believes that humankind primarily exists in a dimension other than time and space, while the majority of people cannot conceptualize existing otherwise. Philosophers constitute a very small percentage of the population. If the subgroup of philosophers is correct, it follows that even a smaller percentage of humans than the percentage represented by philosophers primarily exists in a dimension other than time and space.

    The argument above relies on which one of the following questionable techniques?

    (A) It considers a theory that would be universal if true as applying only to those who propound it.
    (B) It fails to explain how it is possible to primarily exist in a dimension other than time and space.
    (C) It trades off an ambiguous meaning with respect to the concept of existence.
    (D) It links, without justification, the views of the majority of philosophers with the views of the majority of the population.
    (E) It draws a conclusion regarding the number of people existing in a particular form from statistical data concerning percentages.

2. Every jewel displayed in the primary display case of Rothbard's jewelry store has been recently appraised. A diamond, a ruby, and an emerald are displayed in Rothbard's primary display case. None of Rothbard's jewels that has been recently appraised is on sale.

    If the statements above are true, which one of the following must also be true on the basis of them?

    (A) No jewel in Rothbard's store besides the ones displayed in the primary display case has been recently appraised.
    (B) Rothbard will not put any jewel on sale that has been recently appraised.
    (C) Neither the ruby nor the emerald displayed in Rothbard's primary display case is on sale.
    (D) The diamond, ruby, and emerald are not the only jewels displayed in Rothbard's primary display case.
    (E) Only jewels that are on sale are displayed in Rothbard's primary display case.

3. Psychology professor: All of the funding for research provided to the Graduate Department of Psychology in the upcoming fiscal year will come from psychoanalytic foundations. Since all of these foundations favor a Freudian orientation, it is unlikely that anything other than a Freudian interpretation of psychoanalytic issues will be reflected in the research generated by the department in the coming year.

    Which one of the following, if true, most strengthens the psychology professor's argument?

    (A) Researchers are more likely to make significant discoveries if they are funded by sponsors who share their orientation.
    (B) Researchers generally gear their investigations to accord with the underlying orientation of their sponsors.
    (C) Foundations in fields other than psychology sponsor research for one fiscal year at a time to evaluate the results before committing more money to a given project.
    (D) Psychology researchers tend to be fiercely independent and aggressive defenders of their findings.
    (E) Roughly as many psychoanalytic foundations maintain a Freudian orientation as those that do not.

4. Info Trek, a large and successful traditional media company, will never satisfy the prerequisites for success in its new media venture since the necessary resources, inspiration, and good fortune required for success in that industry are not attainable by the company in its quest to thrive in the new media environment.

    Which one of the following most accurately describes a flaw in the reasoning above?

    (A) It employs evidence identical to that which it seeks to establish.
    (B) It employs evidence that leads to a conclusion opposite of the one it seeks to establish.
    (C) It assumes without justification that established media companies may wish to launch new media ventures.
    (D) It relies upon a nonrepresentative sample of successful companies.
    (E) It confuses factors that are necessary for success in a new media venture with those that would guarantee success in such a venture.

GO ON TO THE NEXT PAGE.

5. A Citizens Action Committee of a small metropolitan area has created a Social Responsibility Indicator (SRI) to judge whether corporations in that area operate in accordance with the needs of the community. While tangible components of the indicator such as the faithful execution of pension plans and adherence to environmental regulations accurately reflect corporations' level of social responsibility, SRI ratings are also influenced by intangible factors such as the perception of a corporation's good will. Therefore, a corporation with a high SRI rating may not in fact be socially responsible.

The argument above relies on which one of the following assumptions?

(A) Corporations with low SRI ratings exhibit little good will.

(B) Perception of a corporation's good will does not always reflect that corporation's level of social responsibility.

(C) Good will is a larger component of SRI ratings than is adherence to environmental regulations.

(D) Good will is the only intangible factor associated with a corporation's success.

(E) SRI ratings can never accurately reflect a corporation's level of social responsibility.

6. Political advocacy groups have recently called for extensive background checks into the lives of all political candidates in order to eliminate any incentive a candidate may have to falsify his or her personal or professional records. While sound in theory, this recommendation has virtually no chance of achieving its objective, due to the sheer number of local and national candidates and the impossibility of deriving reliable interpretations from candidate data even if they could be gathered.

The argument proceeds by

(A) questioning the desirability of implementing a course of action

(B) discounting a proposal on the basis of its impracticality

(C) demonstrating that the two main drawbacks to a plan are logically inconsistent

(D) using the fact that a specific proposal cannot succeed to argue that no proposal can address the problem under consideration

(E) implying that overcoming either of two possible obstacles to a measure under consideration would make implementation of the measure feasible

7. Father: Growing up, I ate the same children's breakfast cereals that my five-year-old and seven-year-old daughters eat today. It gives me a pleasant feeling of continuity to see my children experience activities from my own childhood, including the ritual of eating cereal with milk as part of a balanced breakfast. But now experts are warning that these cereals may compromise children's health. When I was a child thirty five years ago, I ate those cereals nearly every day, and no doctor or nutritionist ever suggested that they may be unhealthy. Moreover, I am a relatively healthy adult, and my children show no adverse effects from consuming these cereals. Therefore, the recommendation that my children should limit their intake of these cereals is groundless.

Each of the following, if true, weakens the argument EXCEPT:

(A) Children today eat substantially larger portions of children's cereals than they did thirty five years ago.

(B) Sugar, a substance detrimental to children's health, comprises a much higher percentage of today's children's cereals than it did thirty five years ago.

(C) Research investigating the adverse effects of children's cereals on children's health has been conducted consistently over the last 35 years.

(D) Relatively healthy adults who consumed children's cereals on a regular basis growing up would be healthier today had they not done so.

(E) Health detriments stemming from the regular consumption of children's cereals do not become manifest until children become teenagers.

8. Many music instructors employ the Suzuki Technique, a method that encourages children to acquire musical "literacy" much in the same way they learn to speak. In both instances, children are encouraged to assimilate what they hear and combine sounds into increasingly complex arrangements. While certainly innovative and effective, an over-reliance on this technique diminishes a music student's facility for developing important traditional skills such as reading music and playing scales.

Which one of the following best expresses the main point of the passage?

(A) The Suzuki Technique mimics the way in which children acquire language.

(B) Music teachers should rely primarily on traditional instruction to teach music to children.

(C) Reading music and playing scales are important components of a musical education.

(D) The Suzuki Technique is a popular form of musical instruction.

(E) Music students benefit most from a combination of the Suzuki Technique and traditional instruction.

GO ON TO THE NEXT PAGE.

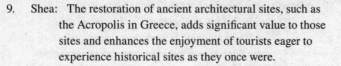

9. Shea: The restoration of ancient architectural sites, such as the Acropolis in Greece, adds significant value to those sites and enhances the enjoyment of tourists eager to experience historical sites as they once were.

    Melia: I disagree. Restorations may resemble original sites on a superficial level but lack the context and nuances to reflect historical reality.

    The dialogue most supports the claim that Shea and Melia disagree with each other about whether

    (A)   restoring an ancient site can result in a structure that resembles the original
    (B)   the Acropolis in Athens has been restored
    (C)   restoring ancient sites increases the revenues of the tourist industries containing such sites
    (D)   restoring ancient sites results in accurate representations of history
    (E)   context and nuances contribute to the historical reality of architectural sites

10. Victoria: The originators of logic and democracy, the ancient Greeks, were unable to achieve a full understanding of ethics. Modern democracies rely on numerous ethical systems but have also failed to grasp the true essence of ethics. Full comprehension in the matter of ethics is therefore clearly unattainable.

    The argument above is flawed because Victoria equates what has been misunderstood

    (A)   with what has been understood
    (B)   in the past with what has been misunderstood today
    (C)   about ethics with what has been understood about logic and democracy
    (D)   with what can never be understood
    (E)   once with what has been misunderstood many times

11. As people grow older and more mature, they often find that the moral values of their youth conflict with new opinions and understandings of the world afforded by wisdom and experience. However, at the same time such people are often loathe to express their new worldviews through their actions lest they appear to others to contradict their former moral code. This should be discouraged, as it results in people acting against their better judgment merely to preserve the image of a defunct identity.

    The argument conforms most closely to which one of the following principles?

    (A)   When two moral codes conflict in the assessment of a situation, the one that yields the most effective course of action should be followed.
    (B)   The values of old age should take precedence over the values of youth.
    (C)   Worldviews that encourage dangerous behavior should be altered to encompass more moderate values.
    (D)   One should not express one's moral code through actions if doing so entails the risk of altering one's public persona.
    (E)   The appearance of moral consistency should not take precedence over actual beliefs as a basis for guiding one's actions.

12. Most injury-causing accidents occur in the home, and one of the most common of such injuries involves accidental knife wounds. Surprisingly, research into the records of the Fairlawn General Emergency Room indicate far more people treated for knife wounds inflicted by dull knives than knife wounds inflicted by sharp knives.

    Each of the following, if true, could explain the surprising finding cited above EXCEPT:

    (A)   People at home tend to be much more careful when handling sharp knives than when handling dull knives.
    (B)   People received at the Fairlawn General Emergency Room suffering from knife wounds inflicted by sharp knives are immediately transferred to an independent special trauma unit for treatment.
    (C)   The severity of injuries from knife wounds inflicted by dull knives treated at the Fairlawn General Emergency Room is generally equal to the severity of the injuries from knife wounds inflicted by sharp knives treated at the same facility.
    (D)   Due to a public safety awareness campaign, dull knives greatly outnumber sharp knives in the homes of Fairlawn residents.
    (E)   Sharp knives tend to produce a clean cut when involved in a home-related accident, whereas dull knives produce a more jagged cut, making it more difficult to stem the flow of blood.

GO ON TO THE NEXT PAGE.

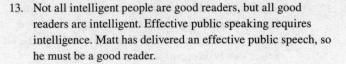

13. Not all intelligent people are good readers, but all good readers are intelligent. Effective public speaking requires intelligence. Matt has delivered an effective public speech, so he must be a good reader.

The flawed pattern of reasoning in which one of the following is most similar to that exhibited in the argument above?

(A) All light bulbs contain filaments, but not all things containing filaments are light bulbs. All objects containing filaments glow when heated. Salma owns a glowing object, so Salma must own a light bulb.

(B) Not all machines are computers, but all computers are some kind of machine. Producing quality special effects requires the use of specialized computers. Behroush wants to produce quality special effects for his documentary on space exploration, so Behroush will have to use some kind of machine.

(C) Some people with vision are not successful, but all successful people have vision. Vision is necessary to develop a viable business plan. Jacqui must be successful, because she has developed a viable business plan.

(D) To be accomplished, an actress must train for at least two years. Amanda is an actress who has trained for three years, so she must be accomplished.

(E) Not all diplomats are politicians, but all politicians are expected to be diplomatic. Dylan wishes to be known as an exceptional politician, so Dylan should seek the reconciliation of the warring factions in his party.

14. Enrico: The automobile is the technology that most shaped twentieth-century America. Before the automobile, most people lived in agrarian communities with strong ties to family and the land. The automobile made it possible, and then necessary, for many people to commute to jobs outside of their immediate communities, a development which spurred the growth of overcrowded cities surrounded by vast suburban landscapes. Moreover, the absence of one, and often two parents from the home environment during the long work day ultimately led to the breakdown of the family and the loss of centuries-old traditions.

Helen: The specific effects you cite are correct. However, the Internet has revolutionized the way information is packaged, transmitted, sought and received, and no technology influences a society more than one that alters that society's means of communication.

The conversation provides the strongest grounds for holding that Enrico and Helen disagree over whether

(A) the automobile caused a loss of tradition in twentieth-century America

(B) the Internet has altered the means of communication in twentieth-century America

(C) the Internet has had a greater influence on twentieth-century America than has the automobile

(D) new technologies have the power to shape a society

(E) other technologies besides the automobile and the Internet have played a role in shaping twentieth-century America

GO ON TO THE NEXT PAGE.

15. Due to a blight affecting country X's cocoa crop, the total revenue from that country's cocoa exports decreased 45 percent in 2003 from the total revenue generated by cocoa exports in 2002. However, the average revenue for cocoa exports per cocoa-exporting company in country X was the same in 2003 as it was in 2002.

    If the statements above are true, which one of the following must also be true?

    (A) The blight destroyed 45 percent of country X's cocoa crop.
    (B) The blight affected cocoa more than any other crop in country X.
    (C) No company in country X generated more revenue from cocoa exports in 2003 than it generated from cocoa exports in 2002.
    (D) The total combined revenue of all of country X's industries was less in 2003 than it was in 2002.
    (E) Fewer companies in country X exported cocoa in 2003 than did so in 2002.

16. Alcohol, while seeming to stimulate the senses at the time of consumption, in fact depresses the central nervous system and in the long run deadens one's experience of the world. Studies have shown that alcoholics are over 50 percent more likely than non-alcoholics to suffer from depression. It can be concluded from this evidence that alcohol's effect on the central nervous system contributes to the onset of depression.

    Which one of the following, if true, most weakens the argument above?

    (A) Many alcoholics first began consuming excess quantities of alcohol in order to cope with depression.
    (B) Some non-alcoholics have experiences that depress their central nervous systems.
    (C) The majority of depressed people are not alcoholics.
    (D) Most alcoholics did not suffer from depression before they began consuming excess amounts of alcohol.
    (E) Rehabilitated alcoholics are more likely to have successful careers than are non-rehabilitated alcoholics.

17. Town resident: Both Mabel and Jasper were seen fleeing the vicinity of a burning abandoned building. Since Jasper owns a lucrative insurance policy on the building, the police should disregard Mabel and investigate only Jasper as a potential arsonist.

    Which one of the following principles, if valid, most helps to justify the town resident's reasoning?

    (A) The desire to commit a crime often indicates a desire to commit multiple crimes.
    (B) One with the motivation to commit a potential crime is more likely than others to have committed that crime.
    (C) The act of fleeing the scene of a potential crime strongly suggests that all those so fleeing are in fact guilty of committing a crime.
    (D) When a crime has been committed, the police should focus their investigation first on the main perpetrator of the crime and later on possible accomplices.
    (E) A fire should be investigated as a potential arson only if the burning structure is covered by a lucrative insurance policy.

GO ON TO THE NEXT PAGE.

18. While many comics exhibit traditional intelligence as measured by academic testing, many comics do not. However, lack of such traditional intelligence is not an obstacle to successful comedy, as evidenced by the fact that skilled comics make us laugh because of their ability to communicate life's foibles in a way that is fresh, resonant, and surprising. A successful comedy career is thus not dependent on traditional intelligence.

Which one of the following is NOT assumed in the argument above?

(A) Traditional intelligence is not required for any other aspect of a successful comedy career besides an ability to make people laugh.

(B) It is not necessary to have traditional intelligence in order to perceive life's foibles.

(C) Traditional intelligence is not required to communicate life's foibles in a way that is fresh, resonant, and surprising.

(D) The most financially successful comedians are those who best communicate life's foibles in a way that is fresh, resonant, and surprising.

(E) Traditional intelligence is accurately reflected in the results of academic testing.

19. Dr. Nolan: Advances in emergency cardiovascular treatments between 1986 and 2006 have led to a significant decrease in the number of heart attacks in the U.S. resulting in fatalities. However, the incidence of heart disease in the U.S. rose dramatically during that same period.

Which one of the following, if true, would best resolve the seemingly paradoxical situation described above?

(A) Similar medical technologies invented between 1986 and 2006 have helped to shorten the recovery time for heart attack victims.

(B) The treatment advances were spurred by increases in heart disease prior to 1986 due largely to harmful changes in diet and lack of exercise among a significant percentage of the American population.

(C) The incidence of heart disease among non-risk groups fell between 1986 and 2006.

(D) People who survive heart attacks are classified for the rest of their lives as having heart disease due to the damage suffered by the heart during the attack.

(E) The severity of heart attacks has increased between 1986 and 2006.

20. Business school advertisement: A career in financial sales can be both rewarding and profitable. Statistics show that this field has the highest percentage of "Type A" personalities compared to all other industries. People with Type A personalities are assertive, confident, and successful. So come study at Brighton Business Institute and begin developing your Type A personality today!

The reasoning in the advertisement is flawed in that it overlooks the possibility that

(A) people with personality types other than Type A can lead rewarding lives

(B) some financial salespeople do not have Type A personalities

(C) Brighton Business Institute has graduated people who have not gone on to successful careers in financial sales

(D) personality type largely determines one's choice of career and level of success in it

(E) personality types may be altered significantly through education

21. Foreign correspondent: There has been a significant deterioration in the relations of the region's two leading powers, as indicated by the recent cessation of negotiations between the two countries in regard to the disputed territory. Tension between these two countries has historically led to large-scale regional instability. If the negotiations do not resume, it is very likely that war will erupt within the next few months.

Which one of the following best describes the role played in the foreign correspondent's argument by the assertion that relations between the two countries have significantly deteriorated?

(A) It is speculation that is subsequently discounted in the development of the argument's main point.

(B) It is the main conclusion that the argument seeks to establish based on the likelihood of a conditional circumstance.

(C) It is an intermediate conclusion that serves as evidence for the argument's main conclusion.

(D) It is the reason presented for a source of conflict described in the argument.

(E) It is one of two unrelated conclusions drawn in the argument.

GO ON TO THE NEXT PAGE.

22. Things that are passé never inspire admiration, but chivalry is admired by most people. It follows that chivalry is not passé.

The reasoning in the argument above is most closely paralleled by that in which one of the following?

(A) Janice is usually on time to school except for days following her night shift at the ice cream store. Janice did not work the night shift at the ice cream store last night, so it would be unusual if she were late to school today.

(B) This truck must not be reliable, because reliable trucks must be able to be driven at least 100,000 miles without requiring serious repairs.

(C) Mitchell's fraternity is not on probation, since most fraternities on probation have been issued behavioral warnings and Mitchell's fraternity has never been issued a behavioral warning.

(D) Economic downturns are never a cause for celebration. While some people benefit financially from such events, most people are adversely affected.

(E) Benjamin is not impulsive, because while impulsive people do not deliberate, Benjamin often practices deliberation.

23. Nutritionist: Candy containing processed sugar and artificial sweeteners is much more readily available to children than it ever has been. Children today have more money and less parental oversight than in the past, increasing their opportunities to obtain the kinds of candy that, consumed in abundance, cause childhood weight and health problems. Moreover, everyone from teachers to relatives to strangers on the street seek to gain the affection of children through candy. Candy companies, of course, play a role in encouraging consumption by constantly expanding the kinds of candies available, and the venues from which to purchase them. These factors, coupled with a culture of permissiveness, are significant contributors to the recent increase in childhood obesity.

Which one of the following, if true, would most strengthen the argument?

(A) Internal documents of industry-leading candy companies indicate that marketing their products to children is among their primary objectives.

(B) There is a significant correlation between the availability and excess consumption of candy among children.

(C) Teenagers eat as much candy as younger children but are just as likely to become obese.

(D) Children of parents who carefully supervise the amount of candy their children consume are still sometimes offered candy at school and from other adults.

(E) Children consuming less than the national average of candy consumption in their age group are 35 percent less likely to suffer from diet-related health problems.

GO ON TO THE NEXT PAGE.

24. A security camera recorded the actions of a single masked thief as he perpetrated last week's Swindale Museum robbery. Kendrick is not aware of the museum's security system, while Mason, who is aware of the security system, is close friends with the building's security manager, Yarden. Kendrick possesses both the cunning and the audacity to conceptualize the robbery, but perpetrating the robbery required knowledge of a secret code to deactivate the building's security system.

Which one of the following follows most logically from the statements above?

(A) It is impossible for a single person to have both conceptualized and perpetrated the Swindale Museum robbery.

(B) Kendrick neither conceptualized nor perpetrated the Swindale Museum robbery.

(C) Kendrick may have conceptualized but did not perpetrate the Swindale Museum robbery.

(D) Mason may have perpetrated but did not conceptualize the Swindale Museum robbery.

(E) Yarden revealed the museum's secret security code to the perpetrator of the Swindale Museum robbery.

25. Alcoholics who have stopped drinking but not participated in a 12-step program cannot be fully recovered, because full recovery requires resolution of the psychological conditions that lead to and reinforce alcohol addiction.

The argument above assumes that

(A) the psychological conditions associated with alcohol addiction cannot be resolved outside of a 12-step program

(B) any alcoholic participating in a 12-step program will achieve full recovery

(C) 12-step programs equally address the psychological conditions that lead to alcohol addiction and those that reinforce it

(D) the conditions that lead to an alcoholic's full recovery are identical to those that lead an alcoholic to stop drinking

(E) participation in a 12-step program must be independent of the resolution of psychological conditions underpinning alcoholism in order for full recovery to occur

STOP

**IF YOU FINISH BEFORE TIME IS CALLED, YOU MAY CHECK YOUR WORK ON THIS SECTION ONLY.
DO NOT WORK ON ANY OTHER SECTION IN THE TEST.**

SECTION IV

Time—35 minutes

28 Questions

Directions: Each passage in this section is followed by a group of questions to be answered on the basis of what is stated or implied in the passage. For some of the questions, more than one of the choices could conceivably answer the question. However, you are to choose the best answer; that is, the response that most accurately and completely answers the question, and blacken the corresponding space on your answer sheet.

While clear-cut guidelines exist to delineate and adjudicate blatant cases of copyright infringement, the legal implications of appropriating copyrighted materials into new forms of art and social commentary are much less clearly defined.
(5) In such cases, the Fair Use provision of Article 107 of U.S. copyright law can provide some guidance. Fair use provides an exception to copyright restrictions, allowing one to copy, publish, or distribute without permission partial (or in some cases even entire) copyrighted works for purposes such as
(10) criticism, comment, news reporting, teaching, scholarship, or research.

Not surprisingly, copyright holders have difficulty condoning any unlicensed use of their works. Fair use proponents counter that to prevent artists and critics from
(15) freely reusing cultural sounds, objects, and iconography would flout basic democratic principles, stifle creativity, and lead to cultural stagnation. Such restrictions, they believe, would severely limit the opportunity to engage those who create and consume mainstream culture in meaningful
(20) dialogue.

Judges generally consider four factors when evaluating fair use claims. The first is the purpose and character of the use, such as whether the product incorporating the material will be used in a non-profit, educational, or commercial environment.
(25) Within this category, judges look favorably on "transformative" uses, those involving radical alterations of the material's original intent. The second consideration is the nature of the work used. For example, judges generally favor the fair use of non-fiction over fiction, and of scholarly works for
(30) which quoting is expected. The third factor concerns the amount used; the lower the proportion of the original whole, the more likely fair use will be granted. However, the more central the used portion is to the spirit of the original work, the lower the chance of a fair use ruling. The fourth factor
(35) considers the effect on the value of the original; that is, the extent to which the new product will directly compete with the copyrighted work in the marketplace.

There are no hard-line rules regarding how and in what proportion judges apply the four factors to fair use
(40) determinations. Moreover, fair use is not an affirmative protection—like, for example, the right to public assembly— but rather a defense that one can appeal to only after a charge has been brought. Individuals averse to the pressure and expense of legal confrontations often decide not to invoke
(45) their fair use privilege, essentially constituting a form of self-censorship. Capitalizing on this hesitancy, many well-funded

copyright holders have launched aggressive attacks on fair use attempts through near-automatic issuances of cease-and-desist letters, regardless of legal merit. Nonetheless, fair
(50) use provides a necessary restraint on otherwise unbounded copyright privileges, and remains a powerful legal instrument should artists and social commentators choose to invoke it.

1. Which one of the following most accurately states the main point of the passage?

(A) Due to opposition from well-funded copyright holders, fair use will never be successfully employed by a majority of cultural innovators who wish to appropriate copyrighted materials.

(B) Fair use ensures the right of cultural innovators to appropriate copyrighted materials for purposes of art and social commentary.

(C) While there are four factors generally considered in fair use determinations, there are currently no hard-line rules regarding how these factors are applied to specific cases.

(D) Despite obstacles hindering its application, fair use provides the legal means by which artists and social commentators may incorporate copyrighted materials into their works.

(E) Content creators seek unbounded copyright privileges and do not under any circumstances condone the unlicensed use of their works.

2. The author of the passage would most likely agree with each of the following statements EXCEPT:

(A) Most attempts by copyright holders to prevent unlicensed use of their works do not have legal merit.

(B) Invoking in advance and then successfully employing a fair use defense requires courage on the part of cultural innovators.

(C) Not all artists and social commentators fully realize the works they initially set out to produce.

(D) The protection offered by fair use is not as strictly defined as some other legal protections.

(E) At least some of the factors that judges evaluate to make fair use determinations are subject to multiple levels of interpretation.

GO ON TO THE NEXT PAGE.

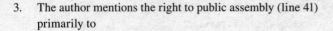
3. The author mentions the right to public assembly (line 41) primarily to

(A) suggest that two kinds of legal protection that differ in one respect are similar in another respect

(B) distinguish laws with hard-line interpretations from those with more flexible interpretations

(C) establish that appealing to affirmative protections is preferable to reacting to lawsuits only after charges have been brought

(D) provide an example of a right that can be defended only after one has been accused of breaking the law

(E) illustrate by means of contrast a limitation in the fair use provision

4. An artwork that appropriates copyrighted materials but that is considered by a court to be so transformative that it does not threaten the value of the original work in the marketplace best illustrates how

(A) fair use determinations depend largely on the temperament and biases of judges

(B) findings regarding one factor that judges consider in making fair use determinations may negate findings regarding another factor

(C) the four factors judges generally consider in rendering fair use determinations are not mutually exclusive

(D) no hard-line rules exist regarding the way in which judges apply the four relevant factors to fair use determinations

(E) combining the factors evaluated in fair use determinations is an effective way to uphold democratic principles and promote creativity

5. With respect to the prospect of the successful employment of the fair use defense, the author of the passage can most accurately be described as

(A) mildly perplexed

(B) exceedingly assured

(C) brazenly defiant

(D) cynically suspicious

(E) cautiously optimistic

6. According to the passage, self-censorship results when

(A) politicians who would otherwise criticize the behavior of well-funded copyright holders choose not to do so for fear of losing political support

(B) artists and social commentators who would otherwise appropriate cultural objects to create new works choose not to do so for fear of legal repercussions

(C) lawyers choose not to advise clients as to their fair use privileges because they are wary of entangling their clients in protracted and costly litigation

(D) artists and social commentators choose not to explore certain subjects because there is no way to do those subjects justice without appropriating cultural materials

(E) artists and social commentators refuse to make fair use a subject of their works for fear of being embroiled in legal confrontations

7. According to the information in the passage, which one of the following situations best exemplifies a transformative use of a work?

(A) Scenes from a television program from the 1970's are shown on a television special with the permission of the original producers in order to commemorate the program and highlight its originality.

(B) A small urban film center screens a silent film obtained from a public domain website containing works no longer afforded copyright protection.

(C) Clips from a copyrighted television newscast are interspersed with commercials in rapid succession in a documentary exploring the symbiotic relationship between news and advertising.

(D) An independent filmmaker shoots scenes from a subway station during a morning rush hour to use as part of a satirical exposé of the working world.

(E) A political science professor shows a documentary on the 1992 U.S. presidential election to her class in order to complement a unit she is teaching on electoral politics.

8. The author's primary purpose in the passage is to

(A) discourage copyright holders from erecting unwarranted and illegal obstacles to necessary forms of cultural innovation

(B) delineate the mechanisms of a legal provision and encourage its utilization

(C) outline a way in which artists and social commentators can reuse cultural sounds, objects, and iconography while avoiding all accusations of copyright infringement

(D) explain the four factors that judges generally consider when evaluating fair use claims

(E) show how copyright holders attempt to discourage people from exploiting a loophole in copyright law

GO ON TO THE NEXT PAGE.

Literary audiences have traditionally favored writers whose works appear to spring from the richness of lived experience. Ernest Hemingway and Jack London come to mind as semi-mythic action figures who documented their experiences

(5) in art. Next to the travails of nineteenth-century Russian novelist Fyodor Dostoyevsky, the adventures of even these lively American writers pale in comparison. Dostoyevsky was arrested for treason against the state, kept in solitary confinement for ten months, tried and condemned to death,

(10) and brought to the scaffold only to have his execution stayed at the last moment by an order of the Czar delivered dramatically on horseback. To say that his life was as dark and dramatic as the books he wrote is no mere marketing gimmick, no ritual of hyperbole characterizing the incessant

(15) and obligatory hype announcing the release of every modern novel and Hollywood spectacular.

Considering such a biography, it is commonplace to emphasize the direct link between Dostoyevsky's life and his novels. This view is not without merit: Dostoyevsky suffered

(20) greatly, and he wrote with great power and passion about the prospect of attaining redemption through suffering. Years of communing with hardened criminals in a Siberian prison yielded passages of penetrating insights into the criminal mind. Dostoyevsky suffered from a destructive gambling

(25) addiction and debilitating epileptic seizures, maladies he imparted to some of his characters. He faithfully and poignantly reproduced in his writing his most harrowing personal experience: the excruciating moments awaiting execution and the confused euphoria following its sudden,

(30) seemingly miraculous annulment.

However, the popular view of Dostoyevsky as a pre-eminent example of the synergistic relation between the artist and his work tends to obscure the contradictions that inevitably infuse even the most coherent artist's life.

(35) As Dostoyevsky himself taught via brilliantly realistic character portrayals, each human being consists of a labyrinth of internal inconsistencies, competing desires, and mysterious motivations that belie the notion of a completely unified personality. One of Dostoyevsky's most

(40) vital insights concerns the individual's struggle to bring his contradictory being into harmony with the world. The fact that Dostoyevsky himself fused his being with his art to a near miraculous extent does not suggest the absence of contradiction between the two. He was, by fellow Russian

(45) writer Ivan Turgenev's account, an odious and obstinate individual who nonetheless managed to portray the highest human types in characters such as Prince Myshkin in *The Idiot* and Alyosha in *The Brothers Karamazov*. In his writings Dostoyevsky vehemently challenged rationality

(50) as the supreme guide to human affairs, yet in his life he strove to perfect an ultra-rational gambling methodology to alleviate his crushing financial difficulties. Far from masking his brilliance, such contradictions reveal the fallible human behind it, making Dostoyevsky's accomplishments all

(55) the more remarkable.

9. Which one of the following most accurately expresses the main point of the passage?

(A) Both synergy and conflict characterize the relationship between the life Dostoyevsky lived and the novels he wrote.

(B) With great power and passion, Dostoyevsky demonstrated the need for individuals to resolve inner conflicts and attempt to achieve harmony with the world.

(C) People who emphasize a direct link between Dostoyevsky's life and his novels fail to recognize that contradictions in his life made his achievements possible.

(D) Dostoyevsky deserves the distinction of semi-mythic action figure more than American writers such as Jack London and Ernest Hemingway.

(E) The numerous contradictions between Dostoyevsky's life and works overshadow the near miraculous degree to which he managed to fuse his being with his art.

10. Which one of the following can be most reasonably inferred regarding those who see Dostoyevsky as a completely unified personality?

(A) They fail to accord to him certain human qualities that he instilled in his own fictional characters.

(B) They believe Dostoyevsky's unified personality to be the primary source of his travails.

(C) They dismiss the notion that personal experience can be effectively encapsulated in art.

(D) They consider it miraculous that Dostoyevsky achieved a unified personality despite having an odious character.

(E) They believe that there are other such unified personalities in fields other than literature.

11. The passage as a whole can most accurately be described as

(A) a portrayal of the travails of a pre-eminent nineteenth century Russian novelist

(B) an argument concerning the relationship between an artist's life and works

(C) an attempt to reconcile the events of a writer's life with the themes of his books

(D) an examination of the ways in which contradiction may be used as a literary device

(E) a refutation of the traditional judgments of literary audiences

GO ON TO THE NEXT PAGE.

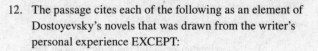
12. The passage cites each of the following as an element of Dostoyevsky's novels that was drawn from the writer's personal experience EXCEPT:

(A) characters suffering from epilepsy or an addiction to gambling
(B) perceptive observations on criminal psychology
(C) the possibility of achieving redemption through suffering
(D) the sudden and dramatic reversal of a death sentence
(E) the experience of isolation brought on by solitary confinement

13. Which one of the following most accurately describes the organization of the material presented in the passage?

(A) The biography of an author is presented, the likely repercussions of leading such a life are explored, and the accomplishments of the author in question are put forward.
(B) A predisposition of a particular audience is cited, and a popular view regarding that predisposition is refuted.
(C) The conditions of an writer's life are summarized, a likely perception based on those conditions is stated and reinforced, and an alternative approach is proposed and supported.
(D) A theory concerning the relationship between an author's life and works is stated, the writer's biography is contrasted with the lives of other writers to support the theory, and a conclusion regarding the value of the writer's works is presented.
(E) A writer's judgment regarding the events of his life is cited, a common emphasis based on that judgment is summarized, and the role of contradiction in relation to that writer's accomplishments is explored and dismissed.

14. It can be inferred from the passage that the author would most likely agree with which one of the following statements?

(A) Most Russian writers considered Dostoyevsky an odious and obstinate individual.
(B) Contradictions between an artist's life and art are necessary for that artist to bring his or her being into harmony with the world.
(C) Critics of Dostoyevsky should take into account the contradictions between his life and his art before assessing the value of his novels.
(D) The tendency to romanticize writers has helped propagate the image of Dostoyevsky as a perfectly unified personality, despite evidence detailing disparities between his life and works.
(E) Dostoyevsky's literary accomplishments are best illustrated by his challenge to rationality and portrayals of the highest human types.

15. Which one of the following most accurately describes the author's purpose in referring to Turgenev's view of Dostoyevsky?

(A) to demonstrate the incongruity between Dostoyevsky's actual personality and the perception of him among the reading public
(B) to show that even an odious and obstinate person is incapable of creating characters other than those of the highest human type
(C) to lend credence to the idea that emphasizing the synergy between Dostoyevsky's life and works is not without merit
(D) to support the claim that the relationship between Dostoyevsky's life and art was not free from contradiction
(E) to provide evidence for the assertion that Dostoyevsky created characters noted for internal inconsistencies, competing desires, and mysterious motivations

GO ON TO THE NEXT PAGE.

Impulsivity describes a range of ill-conceived behaviors characterized by rapid, unplanned reactions to stimuli often resulting in undesirable consequences. Impulsivity is a factor in attention deficit hyperactivity disorder (ADHD), mania,
(5) and addiction. Researchers utilizing functional magnetic resonance imaging (fMRI) have proposed a neurobiological explanation for this condition. fMRI tracks increases in blood flow to areas of the brain engaged in neural activities, allowing researchers to pinpoint regions responsible for
(10) those activities. In one study, adolescents with ADHD and others without ADHD were placed in a magnetic resonance imaging device and asked to press a button when any letter but X was flashed on a screen. This tested their ability to suppress the impulse to press the button when an X was
(15) displayed after a long string of other letters. The adolescents with ADHD demonstrated poorer impulse control than the non-ADHD subjects. Moreover, compared with those of the non-ADHD adolescents, the fMRI results of the ADHD adolescents indicated less activation of neuronal tissues
(20) in the frontal striatal regions known as the caudate and putamen. After taking an anti-impulsivity drug, the ADHD adolescents performed better, with a corresponding increase in caudate and putamen activity. Since the drug significantly increases the level of dopamine in the brain, the researchers
(25) hypothesized that impulsivity may involve atypical dopamine transmission in the striatal circuitry.

Other scientists have proposed a radically different explanation. Experimenting with blue jays, they concluded that animals may be hard-wired for impulsivity thanks to
(30) inborn foraging instincts conditioning them to favor small short-term benefits over potentially larger long-term rewards. These researchers theorize that early humans, exhibiting a similar foraging instinct, benefited in the long-run from unhesitating behavior averse to delayed satisfaction; that is,
(35) they see impulsivity as a trait that enhanced the survival of early humans. In modern society, however, the deferment of satisfaction often yields more positive outcomes than instant gratification in many areas: education, investment, entry-level employment, to name a few. The researchers speculate that
(40) only in the modern age has innate impulsivity become a detriment.

Both camps attempt to explain the recent significant increase in impulsivity disorders. Supporters of the foraging thesis argue that the "get it now, pay later" mentality of
(45) modern consumer society has unleashed our impulsivity instinct, somewhat successfully stifled in more restrictive conservative eras. Neurobiologists speculate that alterations in the environment have influenced neurochemical brain transmissions, thus increasing the population's susceptibility
(50) to impulsivity. It is, however, possible that the supposed increase in impulsivity merely reflects an increase in the means of detecting the condition. Whether there has in fact been an increase in impulsivity, the neurobiological and foraging theories may not be mutually exclusive. While there
(55) may exist a species-wide survival-based tendency toward impulsivity, neurobiological factors may exacerbate the condition in certain individuals.

16. Which one of the following most accurately summarizes the main point of the passage?

(A) While the neurochemical and foraging theories taken together adequately explain the cause of impulsivity, neither theory on its own explains the recent increase in the number of impulsivity disorders.

(B) Improvements in medical technologies such as fMRI have enabled scientists to determine that impulsivity is caused by atypical dopamine transmissions in the brain.

(C) While both evolutionary and neurochemical factors may contribute to impulsivity, whether or not there has been a recent increase in the incidence of the disorder remains unclear.

(D) Despite the fact that two theories plausibly explain the causes of impulsivity, researchers are no closer to discovering a cure for the disorder.

(E) Even though it appears that the incidence of impulsivity is on the rise, in actuality improvements in the means of detecting the disease are responsible for this supposed increase.

17. It can be inferred from the passage that the author would most likely agree with which one of the following statements?

(A) If two studies propose radically different explanations for the same disorder, it is necessary to conduct further studies in order to achieve consensus on a single correct explanation for that disorder.

(B) The incidence of impulsivity is on the rise because of environmental changes that have affected the way chemicals are transmitted in the brain.

(C) The performance of adolescents without ADHD on the drill described in the study in the first paragraph of the passage would improve after taking an anti-impulsivity drug.

(D) The findings of a study are not necessarily invalidated by the findings of an alternative study documenting a different potential cause of the same phenomenon.

(E) A recent increase in the number of conditions characterized by impulsivity has made it more difficult to detect the disorder.

GO ON TO THE NEXT PAGE.

18. The author of the passage most likely discusses the deferment of satisfaction in lines 36–39 primarily in order to

(A) support the contention that inborn foraging instincts may potentially hard-wire species for impulsivity

(B) provide evidence for the hypothesis that a previous evolutionary advantage may be responsible for the modern incidence of the disorder under consideration

(C) provide background information regarding the reason why impulsivity may be a factor in ADHD, mania, and addiction

(D) demonstrate that a survival trait that provided advantages to early humans continues to benefit modern humans as well

(E) illustrate how one theory regarding the cause of a modern disorder attempts to refute a previously-stated theory concerning the cause of that disorder

19. The passage cites which one of the following as a potential explanation for the recent increase in impulsivity disorders?

(A) drugs that significantly increase the level of dopamine in the caudate and putamen

(B) evolutionary adaptations in neurochemical brain transmissions that predispose individuals to impulsive behavior

(C) a large decrease in potential sources of instant gratification

(D) neurochemical deficiencies affecting the activation of neuronal tissues in the frontal striatal regions of the brain

(E) a modern outlook that encourages people to indulge materialistic desires

20. Which one of the following sequences most accurately and completely corresponds to the presentation of the material in the passage?

(A) a presentation of a hypothesis; an analysis of two mechanisms utilized to test that hypothesis; a reconciliation of the results collected from the tests

(B) an examination of two contrasting studies; an explanation of the superiority of one of those studies; a call for measures to be enacted to implement the suggestions recommended by the superior study

(C) a description of a dysfunctional behavior; a critique of two studies attempting to explain that behavior; a proposal for a new classification of that behavior

(D) a discussion of a phenomenon; a presentation of two lines of inquiry concerning the causes of that phenomenon; argumentation regarding the need for further studies into that phenomenon

(E) an introduction of a condition; a discussion of two theories regarding the cause and recent proliferation of that condition; a speculation regarding the plausibility of the two theories

21. The passage cites which one of the following as a finding of the study described in paragraph 1?

(A) Increased impulse control is correlated with increased activation of neuronal tissues in the frontal striatal regions.

(B) Adolescents without ADHD were better able than adolescents with ADHD to correctly press the button when letters other than X were flashed on the screen.

(C) No regions of the subjects' brains besides the caudate and putamen exhibited increased blood flow characteristic of neural activity during either phase of the study.

(D) After taking the anti-impulsivity drug, ADHD adolescents demonstrated better impulse control than did the non-ADHD adolescents.

(E) An excess of dopamine in the striatal circuitry may contribute to the onset of an impulsivity disorder.

GO ON TO THE NEXT PAGE.

Passage A

In *Orality and Literacy*, Walter Ong hypothesized that the dissociative effect of writing on purely oral cultures is mitigated by electronic forms of communication such as television and computer networks. This established what
(5) he called "secondary orality," an electronic-based interweaving of oral and literary traditions creating spontaneous interactive societies reminiscent of pre-literate tribal cultures. Citing Ong and fellow media theorist Marshall McLuhan, some Native Americans argue that traditional
(10) tribal customs and narratives, replicated online, can foster vibrant Native American Internet communities. They further warn that failure to establish a Native American presence online will allow illegitimate parties to appropriate tribal traditions and define the tribal experience
(15) according to their own self-interests.

Native American critics counter that significant enough differences exist between their inherited modes of primary orality and the electronic world of secondary orality to severely limit the possibilities of fostering an online tribal
(20) culture. First, they believe that online virtual communities are incapable of creating and sustaining the human attachments necessary to grant narratives meaning and power. Moreover, whereas in traditional Native American cultures members' personalities are subsumed by the tribal
(25) identity, online forum participants exist first and foremost as individuals seeking environments in which to express that pre-existing individuality. The critics concede that electronic technologies may be useful tools for projecting Native American culture outwards to a broader audience, but
(30) maintain that these tools cannot supplant traditional means of tribal acculturation.

Passage B

The rise of the Internet as a social and economic force has reinvigorated interest in the ideas of 1960's media theorist Marshall McLuhan, who predicted an electronically
(35) interconnected "global village" characterized by a worldwide reversion to the modes and structures of tribalism. Not surprisingly, the reference to tribalism has intrigued the Native American community, prompting vigorous debate concerning whether, how, and to what extent a Native
(40) American presence can be constructed online.

While the Internet is a supreme conveyor of information, information must be applied in the context of ceremony in order to produce genuine community. Ceremony requires live participation in an actual locale. A stable
(45) setting ensures a shared history and unspoken cultural understandings among participants in Native American dialogues. These factors dictate how stories are told, to what purposes they aspire, the proper relationship between storyteller and audience, and the acceptable evolution of
(50) traditional tales to ensure their relevance to the lives of tribe members. The power of the myths, metaphors, and moral teachings inherent in such storytelling is proportionally weakened by each level of mediation introduced into the

dialogue. In the end, the global village represents only
(55) *pseudo*-tribalism: the conundrum of a worldwide tribe characterized by homogenization and the effacement of local identities. The opposite is required for the continued vitality of Native American narratives: the immediacy of and immersion into what tribal members refer to as "the
(60) sacredness of place."

22. Both passages are primarily concerned with the

(A) influence of McLuhan's and Ong's theories on the rise of the Internet as a social and economic force
(B) transition between primary and secondary orality and the effect of that transition on the creation of online communities
(C) viability of establishing an online Native American community
(D) effect of Native American traditions and narratives on the global village
(E) role of ceremony in establishing genuine community among tribal groups

23. The two passages differ in that only one

(A) includes a concession that a specific kind of technology may have a useful function
(B) details reasons why the narratives of a particular culture may not be fully reproducible on the Internet
(C) expresses the viewpoint that societies should remain static in order to maintain their vitality
(D) suggests the existence of opposing viewpoints regarding an issue
(E) presents arguments from two sides of a debate

GO ON TO THE NEXT PAGE.

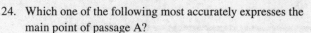
24. Which one of the following most accurately expresses the main point of passage A?

(A) Speculations from Ong's *Orality and Literacy* have helped justify the belief of some Native Americans that they should represent their culture online.

(B) The desire of some Native Americans to expand their culture via the Internet is supported by certain media theories but opposed by other members of tribal communities.

(C) Ong's theory of secondary orality helps to explain the effects that writing and forms of electronic communication have had on societies characterized by purely oral cultures.

(D) The Internet does not provide an adequate setting to replicate the ceremonial elements necessary for genuine Native American societies to flourish.

(E) The debate between Native Americans regarding the desirability of constructing an online presence for tribal cultures has reached an insurmountable impasse.

25. Which one of the following statements is most strongly supported by both passages?

(A) Ong's theory of secondary orality was derived from McLuhan's conception of the global village.

(B) Some media theories have been formulated with the intention of helping cultural groups create online identities.

(C) There is disagreement regarding the extent to which media theories effectively support the establishment of a cultural presence online.

(D) Ong's theory of secondary orality has provided greater support for establishing an online Native American presence than has McLuhan's theory of the global village.

(E) The promise of the Internet is understood in essentially the same way by all parties to the debate concerning the feasibility of establishing an online Native American presence.

26. The author of passage B would most likely believe that the virtual communities mentioned in line 20 of passage A

(A) lack what tribal members refer to as the sacredness of place

(B) suffice as foundations for establishing genuine meanings in the myths and metaphors of Native American narratives

(C) are responsible for the recent interest among some Native Americans in the theories of McLuhan

(D) were envisioned by McLuhan as vehicles by which to spread awareness of tribal cultures

(E) serve audiences united by shared histories and unspoken cultural understandings

27. The conundrum described in passage B (lines 55–57) is characterized by a conflict between

(A) metaphors employed in Native American narratives and their intended moral teachings

(B) McLuhan's conception of the global village and Ong's theory of secondary orality

(C) tribal ceremonies and the sacredness of place

(D) unique tribal identities and a homogenous global culture

(E) supporters and opponents of establishing an online Native American presence

28. The notion that electronic communication technologies may be useful in one way but not in another is shared by

(A) the author of passage A and the author of passage B

(B) the author of passage B and the Native Americans of passage B

(C) McLuhan and Ong

(D) the critics of virtual communities in passage A and the author of passage B

(E) the supporters of online Native American communities in passage A and those intrigued by McLuhan's reference to tribalism in passage B

STOP

IF YOU FINISH BEFORE TIME IS CALLED, YOU MAY CHECK YOUR WORK ON THIS SECTION ONLY.
DO NOT WORK ON ANY OTHER SECTION IN THE TEST.

LOGIC GAMES HINTS

If you're near the beginning of your preparation or are having trouble with the logic games on the practice test, the following tips may help you get started.

Game 1: Classical Concert

- There are two distinct tasks to keep in mind—make sure you're clear on what they are.

- Look for Standard Combination Game Breakers, paying special attention to rules containing the same characters.

- The inclusion of one particular character goes a long way in determining the rest. See if you can spot this influential "star."

Game 2: Doctor Visits

- The setup does not provide an opportunity to schedule any one character with certainty. Focus on the *relationships* created by the rules.

- Try sketching out the relationships vertically, placing patients visited earlier higher in your sketch than patients visited later. Use lines to connect the patients who have definite "earlier than" or "later than" relationships.

- Keep an open mind about Helbing and the Jayar/Randall cluster. Those patients may have greater flexibility in the ordering than you think.

Game 3: Journalism Topics

- Be careful of Rule 2; it works in one direction only.

- Consider Rule 3 carefully. The game will not work if you don't properly interpret the "if and only if" statement. If you're unsure of how to handle this kind of rule, look back at the "Get the Specs" section of Logic Games in Chapter 2.

- The correct interpretation of Rule 3 limits the way Piper may be assigned her topics. Try to construct a Restricted Possibilities scenario based around Piper's possible placements. After placing Piper, situating Kieran is a big factor in determining the possibilities.

Game 4: Tae Kwon Do Demonstrations

- Pay careful attention to the numbers that govern the game. There are only two possible breakdowns regarding the number of demonstrations the teams perform, and an important Game Breaker emerges from this realization.

- It's possible to create a Restricted Possibilities scenario, but Number Crunching and Standard Combinations work as well to reveal the deductions you need to succeed.

- Be careful with Rules 3 and 4; it's easy to get them confused. Notice that they are *not* talking about the same thing.

- If you determine a team that *cannot* perform a particular demonstration, make sure to turn that negative into a positive determination of who *must* perform that demonstration.

ANSWER KEY

SECTION I (Logical Reasoning)

1.	D	8.	E	15.	A	22.	E
2.	C	9.	D	16.	A	23.	D
3.	E	10.	A	17.	B	24.	A
4.	D	11.	C	18.	B	25.	B
5.	C	12.	C	19.	B		
6.	A	13.	A	20.	E		
7.	B	14.	D	21.	D		

SECTION II (Logic Games)

1.	D	8.	E	15.	A	22.	D
2.	D	9.	D	16.	E		
3.	B	10.	A	17.	A		
4.	C	11.	C	18.	C		
5.	C	12.	B	19.	D		
6.	C	13.	E	20.	E		
7.	A	14.	D	21.	B		

SECTION III (Logical Reasoning)

1.	A	8.	E	15.	E	22.	E
2.	C	9.	D	16.	A	23.	B
3.	B	10.	D	17.	B	24.	C
4.	A	11.	E	18.	D	25.	A
5.	B	12.	C	19.	D		
6.	B	13.	C	20.	D		
7.	C	14.	C	21.	C		

SECTION IV (Reading Comprehension)

1.	D	8.	B	15.	D	22.	C
2.	A	9.	A	16.	C	23.	E
3.	E	10.	A	17.	D	24.	B
4.	C	11.	B	18.	B	25.	C
5.	E	12.	E	19.	E	26.	A
6.	B	13.	C	20.	E	27.	D
7.	C	14.	D	21.	A	28.	D

Calculating Your Score

You can add up the number of questions you got right on all four sections and convert it to a 120–180 score using the table below. Keep in mind that this score is just a rough estimate. The only completely accurate predictors of your current scoring level are the scoring scales provided with official LSAC PrepTests, so make sure you take some of those in the week or two before the test to gauge where you stand.

Score	Lowest	Highest
180	98	100
179	97	97
178	96	96
177	95	95
176	94	94
175	93	93
174	92	92
173	91	91
172	90	90
171	89	89
170	87	88
169	86	86
168	85	85
167	83	84
166	82	82
165	81	81
164	80	80
163	78	79
162	77	77
161	75	76
160	74	74
159	72	73
158	70	71
157	69	69
156	67	68
155	66	66
154	64	65
153	62	63
152	61	61
151	59	60

Score	Lowest	Highest
150	57	58
149	55	56
148	54	54
147	53	53
146	51	52
145	50	50
144	48	49
143	46	47
142	45	45
141	44	44
140	42	43
139	41	41
138	39	40
137	38	38
136	36	37
135	34	35
134	33	33
133	31	32
132	30	30
131	29	29
130	28	28
129	26	27
128	25	25
127	23	24
126	22	22
125	21	21
124	20	20
123	18	19
122	17	17
121	16	16
120	0	15

SECTION I: ANSWERS & GUIDED EXPLANATIONS

Logical Reasoning

Question 1: The Zack and Zoe Show

1. Zack: A new study has reported that moderately overweight people have a lower chance of early death than do thin people. This is dangerous. First, there is no way to know in the immediate future whether the claim is accurate; such beliefs often persist for years before they are retracted in light of new evidence. Second, regardless of the claim's accuracy, it obscures the fact that a lower chance of early death is not synonymous with good health. The majority of moderately overweight people will no doubt view these findings as a license to discontinue diets and put aside concern for their weight.

    Zoe: It is true that overweight people will respond to the claim regardless of a confirmation of its accuracy. Moreover, it is likely that some people who are more than moderately overweight will be encouraged by the study to view their condition with less concern than warranted. However, most moderately overweight people have already come to terms with and accepted their weight, so this group will mainly use the study to validate preexisting beliefs.

    On the basis of their statements, Zack and Zoe are committed to disagreeing with each other about whether

    (A)   the majority of moderately overweight people have a lower chance of early death than do the majority of thin people
    (B)   some people who are more than moderately overweight will act on their interpretation of the study as if it pertains to them
    (C)   the study poses the potential for misinterpretation among overweight people
    (D)   **the study will encourage the majority of moderately overweight people to alter how they conceive of their weight**
    (E)   a lower chance of early death means the same thing as good health

Grill the Interrogator. Sounds like a morning radio program with hosts Zack and Zoe going at it. It is, of course, merely a Disagreement question. And these two don't just disagree—they're *committed* to doing so. It's very touching that in an age when so many people are afraid of commitment, at least some people still commit to arguing with each other. Anyhow, let's get to the debate, keeping our usual Disagreement issues in mind as we strive to pinpoint the conflict.

Attack the Passage. The study claims that moderately overweight people suffer from early death less than thin people. Zack has two problems with this: First, it may not be true. But even if it is, Zack is afraid that people will equate the lesser chance of early death with good health and therefore lose incentive to lose weight, a prospect Zack finds dangerous. Zoe agrees that people will react to the study regardless of proof of its accuracy, so there's one issue already we might reasonably expect to show up in a wrong choice. And she brings up a different negative not mentioned by Zack: namely, the prospect that people who are *more* than moderately overweight will inappropriately take heart from the study as well. Since this last assertion goes beyond Zack's analysis, we might reasonably expect this notion to rear its head in a wrong choice as well.

> In Disagreement questions, take note of who cares about what as you make your way through the dialogue. The wrong choices are often populated by points of agreement and issues only addressed by one speaker.

TAKE AWAY

However, Zoe asserts, most moderately overweight people (and notice that this is precisely the group that Zack speaks of in his conclusion) will use the study for nothing more than reinforcing what they already believe. So the sticking point appears to concern the effect the study will have on a specific group: the majority of moderately overweight people. That's enough to hit the choices.

Work the Choices. Since we know the group that's common to both arguments, it makes sense to scan for choices discussing that group.

> Scan the choices in Disagreement questions whenever you come out of your attack on the passage with an idea of what the right answer may entail. When both speakers concern themselves with the same group, that's a good clue that the right answer may center around that group.

TAKE AWAY

Only **A** and **D** mention the majority of moderately overweight people, so let's try those first, matching the specifics of those choices to the actual dialogue.

A has two problems. First, it speaks of the *study* in terms of the majority of moderately overweight people, when in fact this idea of the majority comes from Zack and Zoe's interpretations of the study's effect. In other words, the study itself doesn't compare the majority of moderately overweight people to the majority of thin people, so **A** is off-base from the get-go. Moreover, even if we overlook this subtle switch, neither speaker is prepared to accept the study's findings without further proof; they merely speculate on how those who *do* accept the findings will react.

D: The issue seems on target—behavior the study will encourage among moderately overweight people—so let's Quiz the Speakers. Does Zack think the study will encourage the majority of moderately overweight people to alter how they conceive of their weight? Yes; he fears they will use the study to lessen their concern for their weight, believing that being moderately overweight is actually good for their health. Does Zoe think the study will affect moderately overweight people's perception of the their weight? Emphatically not. She believes that they've already come to terms with their weight and that the study will merely reinforce their current beliefs. **D** therefore properly expresses the gist of the disagreement.

Of course, in line with the ubiquitous Mine the Experience step of our Logical Reasoning Essential Strategy, check out how the rest of the wrong choices play out.

TAKE AWAY

We don't often mention Step 4 of the Logical Reasoning Essential Strategy, Mine the Experience, since it's inherent in reviewing the comprehensive guided explanations we provide. But an occasional reminder of this step is justified, since such a large part of LSAT success is contingent upon learning the right lessons from the hard work you put in. So read the explanations in this chapter carefully, including the explanations to questions you got right. As you proceed, strive to assimilate the Take Aways into your comprehensive LSAT approach.

B features an issue we flagged above that is of interest to Zoe but not to Zack. Zack's position on the reaction of people who are *more* than moderately overweight is not known.

C represents a point of agreement. Zack feels that moderately overweight people will dangerously misinterpret the study, while Zoe fears that some who are more than moderately overweight will do the same.

E: We know that Zack disagrees with the statement in **E**, but Zoe doesn't specifically address this issue, so we can't peg this as the sticking point we seek.

TAKE AWAY

Don't confuse the objective in Disagreement questions. You're not asked to find a choice with which one speaker would disagree, but rather the choice over which the two speakers disagree *with each other*.

Question 2: Star Professors

2. Professor Vessent: In order for our department to remain popular among students and continue to receive the funding it needs, it must recruit new "star" professors to its graduate program. Star professors are expert academics who are known to the general public through appearances in the mass media. The Dean has repeatedly promised to match any offer on the market to lure available star professors to this department. However, this promise is clearly false, as the eminently qualified Katerina Goodrich was just hired by Westerton College at a salary far exceeding that which she was offered here.

    Which one of the following is an assumption that the argument requires?

    (A) Continued funding for the department depends on it remaining popular among students.
    (B) Recruiting star professors to its graduate program will ensure that the department receives the funding it needs.
    (C) **Katerina Goodrich is an expert academic known to the general public through appearances in the mass media.**
    (D) The amount of funding the department receives is greater than the salary that the Dean offered to Katerina Goodrich.
    (E) Katerina Goodrich was among the candidates the Dean targeted when he promised to lure star professors to the department.

Grill the Interrogator. We're greeted by a standard Assumption stem, which tells us to switch into traditional Assumption mode. That means to be on the lookout for gaps between evidence and conclusion, bait and switches, "But what if . . . ?" scenarios, and so on.

Attack the Passage. The venerable Professor Vessent appears upset with the dean for reneging on her promise to lure "star" professors to the department. His evidence for why the dean's promise is "clearly false" centers around a new character, Katerina Goodrich, who stands out at the end of the passage like a sore thumb—or, as we've dubbed this Logical Reasoning Essential Concept, like a loose end. For Vessent's evidence to be relevant to his conclusion, Goodrich needs to be connected to the main issue of the passage, star professors.

> **TAKE AWAY**
>
> An assumption is a missing yet required piece of the passage. Whether the assumption centers around a loose end, a bait and switch, or some other gap in the argument, the correct answer will contain a statement that *connects* the passage's evidence with its conclusion.

Work the Choices. Having recognized Katerina Goodrich as a loose end, our job is to find the choice that establishes her as a "star" professor. Perhaps you came to this realization through a "But what if . . . ?" scenario: *But what if Goodrich is not a star professor?* Vessent never says she is, yet uses her example as proof that the dean is blowing hot air. Choice **C** supplies the required connection by asserting that Goodrich indeed possesses the qualifications of a star. Sure, it would be easier if the right answer explicitly stated "Goodrich is a star professor." Instead, they invoke the *definition* of a star professor, which amounts to the same thing.

A presents an Overreach. While continued funding and continued popularity among students each require the recruitment of star professors, the argument does not require that funding is contingent upon popularity. These may simply be factors influenced independently by the attainment of star professors.

B: The word *ensure* should jump out at you—it means "guarantee," a notion that's inherent in our Essential Concept necessary/sufficient conditions. Ensure means to make sufficient, but this argument concerns what is *necessary* (star profs) for the money to keep flowing. So the notion that getting the stars will guarantee continued funding is not a required part of this argument; all it does is make it *possible* by fulfilling a necessary condition.

> **TAKE AWAY**
>
> Understanding the Essential Concepts helps in many ways. Sometimes they'll lead you to the right answer. Other times they'll help you see a choice is wrong because it deals with a familiar concept that nonetheless doesn't apply to the situation at hand.

D and **E** both provide Unnecessary Clarifications that the argument can easily do without. Neither a salary/funding comparison nor the dean's wish list of candidates is relevant to Vessent's logic. If you're unsure, try the negate and destroy test on these choices and you'll see that the argument is unaffected, meaning that the facts in these choices are not necessary for the argument to stand.

Question 3: Laptops vs. Desktops

3. Most laptop computers are slower, contain smaller hard drives, and are less powerful than their desktop counterparts. In addition, they usually cost more than desktop models. College students would therefore predominantly buy desktop computers instead of laptops, if not for the fact that many professors require the use of the smaller portable laptops in class.

Which one of the following, if true, most weakens the argument?

(A) A growing number of colleges provides students with access to large computer facilities containing both desktop and laptop computers.

(B) Many college students primarily used desktop computers before coming to college.

(C) Some college professors do not require the use of laptops in class.

(D) Most colleges provide software to students that can be used on both laptop and desktop computers.

(E) Many college students share small dorm rooms and do not have enough space for multiple desktop computers.

Grill the Interrogator. We're presented with a standard Weaken the Argument stem, which tells us to shift into Critique mode and to be on the lookout for assumptions and alternatives.

Attack the Passage. Here's something most of us in the computer age can relate to—a comparison between laptops and desktops. Laptops come off worse in this showdown: slower, smaller, and weaker than their desktop counterparts. The author concludes that college students would prefer desktops but for the fact that many classes require laptops. Sounds reasonable on its face, but since this is a Weaken question, it behooves us to open up our minds to alternatives and to define an objective that the right answer must satisfy.

TAKE
AWAY

> Alternatives is one of our Logical Reasoning Essential Concepts, and for a good reason. Many questions, especially in the Strengthen/Weaken category, test your ability to envision relevant factors that arguments overlook. In the Critique question types, whenever an author flatly states that something is the case, stay alert to plausible alternative explanations, possibilities, or results.

Work the Choices. We can state our objective like so: Show me a reason why students may *not* prefer desktops over laptops, other than the fact that professors require laptops in class. **E** meets this objective by positing a plausible alternative explanation: College students simply don't have the room for them. If this is true, we'd be less likely to believe that students would opt for desktops if not for classroom laptop requirements, as the author maintains. **E** makes the conclusion appear less likely and thus qualifies as the weakener we seek.

Remember, you must always accept the answer choices in any Strengthen or Weaken question as *true*. That means you're not to determine how reasonable or valid the choices sound unto themselves but rather to evaluate each one's effect on the argument.

A, if anything, suggests that students may not need to buy either kind of computer, but we don't have enough information to make this determination. Moreover, the argument centers around the choice between two kinds of computers, and having outside access to both doesn't speak to the issue of which kind of computer students would purchase if they weren't required to use laptops in class.

Don't forget about our Logical Reasoning Essential Concept unknowables. Recognizing the boundaries of your knowledge—that is, knowing what you don't know—can help you in many ways.

B, if anything, leans in the wrong direction, as familiarity with desktops might be a plausible additional reason why students may in fact prefer desktops to laptops if professors didn't require laptops in class. Whether you see this as a bona fide Opposite choice or not, just leaning in the wrong direction disqualifies it from consideration.

C: The fact that some profs don't require laptops is Irrelevant to a conclusion based on evidence that many do.

D is a wash in the battle between laptops and desktops, since it doesn't advantage one over the other in the eyes of students and thus has no bearing on the argument. Which is to say that it's Irrelevant to the issue at hand.

Question 4: And The World's Oldest Snake Is . . .

> 4. Since 1997, paleontologists have discovered the fossilized remains of four species of snakes with legs. Some researchers have concluded that one of these species, *Pachyrhachis problematicus*, is the most primitive snake and that it evolved in water, since the fossil was found in marine rock and shows evidence of a flattened tail optimized for swimming. Other researchers, however, point to *Pachyrhachis problematicus*'s advanced teeth to dispute the claim that *Pachyrhachis* is the most primitive snake. These researchers propose the most recently discovered legged species, the land-dwelling *Najash rionegrini*, as the world's first snake.
>
> It can be inferred from the information above that some researchers do not believe that
>
> (A) a snake fossil has been found in marine rock since 1997
> (B) the earliest snake species had legs
> (C) *Pachyrhachis problematicus* had a tail optimized for swimming
> **(D) the teeth of *Pachyrhachis problematicus* were less advanced than those of *Najash rionegrini***
> (E) legged snake species have been discovered since 1997

Grill the Interrogator. "The Snake Debate" would have made for a fine title as well, but don't hold your breath since the winner isn't announced in the passage. No doubt that we're up against an Inference question here, but we're given additional information in the question stem that tells us to expect the right answer to conflict with some belief that's stated or implied in the passage. To understand what researchers *don't* believe, we first need to understand what they do believe, so let's find out.

Attack the Passage. Seems we have a mini science passage on our hands, and anyone who tries to even pronounce *Pachyrhachis problematicus* is probably wasting her time. There are only two snakes mentioned in the passage, so in true Logic Games shorthanding fashion we may as well call them *P* and *N*. The argument seems to be over whether the Adam and Eve of snakes came from species *P* or species *N*. Both species are among the four recently discovered species of legged snakes. Those who think *P* was the oldest of earth's snakes argue that it evolved in water because it had a tail made just for swimming. Notice that the detractors to this theory don't dispute this part of the evidence but rather bring up something new: *P*'s advanced teeth. Based on this, the second group of researchers propose land-dwelling *N* as the world's oldest snake. That's a good amount to go on. Let's take our understanding into the choices.

Work the Choices. D contains the contradiction we seek. If the second group of researchers argue that *P* was not the most primitive snake entirely based on evidence of its advanced teeth, and then propose *N* instead as the world's oldest snake, then it must be true that these researchers don't think that species *N* had advanced teeth. If these researchers did think *P*'s teeth were less advanced than *N*'s teeth, then their entire case falls apart since *P*'s advanced teeth is precisely the factor they cite to dethrone *P*'s claim to original snakedom. (Of course, it's not really *P*'s claim, since *P*, an ancient snake with legs, is long gone. And snakes don't make claims. But you get the point.)

A and **C:** The first group of researchers asserted that a fossil of species *P* with a tail optimized for swimming was discovered in marine rock as one of the species discovered since 1997. The second group of researchers doesn't deny any of this but rather takes the debate in a whole new direction. We therefore can infer that the first group of researchers would *agree* with **A** and **C**, and we have no proof that the second group would disagree.

B is an Opposite choice, since both groups of researchers think that the earliest snake species had legs. Some vote for *P* and some vote for *N* for earliest snake, but both are among the legged species discovered since 1997.

E is also an Opposite: Neither group denies that legged snake species have been discovered since 1997, and in fact each group chooses one of four such species as its candidate for earliest snake. Since there's only agreement on this point, **E** is also the opposite of what we seek.

Question 5: The Confidence of Failure

5.   Entrepreneur: Since people are inherently averse to unfamiliarity, all new technologies initially meet with massive resistance. As a case in point, upon first introduction all successful communication technologies were scoffed at by experts and even the industries they eventually revolutionized right up until the very moment such "hare-brained schemes" morphed into essential accoutrements of modern life. Our revolutionary electronic publishing venture has been turned down by the first twenty companies we approached, a sure sign that our venture is guaranteed to succeed.

Which one of the following best describes the flaw in the argument above?

(A)   It does not outline precisely how the product in question will revolutionize the electronic publishing industry.

(B)   It assumes without warrant that certain new technologies can overcome massive amounts of initial resistance to one day become essential elements of modern life.

(C)   It considers a factor inextricably associated with successful technological ventures as a factor that brings about the success of technological ventures.

(D)   It does not identify specific essential accoutrements of modern life that began by being rejected as "hare-brained schemes."

(E)   It implies that experts and business leaders were foolish for initially rejecting ideas that would one day revolutionize entire industries.

Grill the Interrogator. A standard Flaw question alerts us that something just ain't right with the reasoning in this one. Gather up the usual suspects—classic flaws and Essential Concepts—and we're ready to go in.

Attack the Passage. Perhaps "A Failure of Confidence" rolls off the tongue a bit better than "The Confidence of Failure" as a question title? Not when you see the strange little situation at hand. Mr. "We're Guaranteed to Succeed Because Everyone Hates Our Product So Far" Entrepreneur should be advised not to break out the bubbly quite so fast. If all it took to guarantee success was constant failure, the world would be a much happier place! (No doubt the savvy Logical Reasoning veteran in you recognized the bait and switch between *success* and *happiness* in the previous sentence, but you get the point . . .) All it takes to rain on the entrepreneur's parade is for someone to point out the difference between correlation and causation. And since cause and effect is one of your trusty Logical Reasoning Essential Concepts, we hope that someone was you. Our would-be publishing revolutionary states that something inevitably associated with every technological success story is for the new product to first be raked over the coals by experts and business leaders. Fine so far—that may or may not be true, but it's his evidence and we need to critique *where he goes with it,* not the assertion itself.

It's not your job to argue with the facts of the passage but rather the *conclusions derived from those facts.* If an author states that the moon is made of green cheese, that sounds awfully unlikely, but the LSAT is not about debunking facts that we have no way to verify. The skill under consideration is *reasoning,* which is a thought process that winds its way from evidence to conclusion. Flaws are breakdowns along that path.

The problem with the entrepreneur is that he keeps talking, ignoring the age-old adage that it's better to keep silent and be assumed a fool than to open one's mouth and remove all doubt. Here, essentially, is his point: that since getting rejected is an unavoidable stage in the development of every successful new technology, his group is *guaranteed* to succeed since they've been rejected aplenty. In other words, he argues as if a factor necessarily associated with all successful tech ventures—rejection—is in fact the *cause* of that success.

Work the Choices. If we head to the choices with cause and effect on our mind, it's not very far to choice **C**. If we substitute "correlated" for "inextricably associated," and "causes" for "brings about," we see that **C** nicely describes a common misuse of cause and effect—namely, mistaking correlation for causation.

Just because two things occur together does not necessarily mean that one causes the other.

A and **D** provide good examples of Not Obligated wrong choices: choices that correctly indicate things the author fails to do which don't, however, affect the logic. True, the author doesn't bother to indicate just how the entrepreneur's product will revolutionize its industry (**A**), but that's a step removed from whether the product's current unpopularity will guarantee its success. Nor is this issue affected by the lack of specific examples of modern accoutrements that began as technological rejects (**D**).

Don't fault the author for failing to provide a level of detail not required by the argument. Scrutinize the *logic,* not the nitty-gritty of every single detail presented.

B: The entrepreneur doesn't assume **B**; he states it flat out as part of his evidence.

E: The entrepreneur *does* tacitly insinuate the boneheadedness of the experts and business leaders who failed to recognize technologies that would totally catch on, but there's nothing wrong with that. Not a Problem is therefore the common trap represented by **E**.

Question 6: Airline Miles

6. People who complain about the high cost of traveling should make all of their purchases using credit cards that award airline miles for every purchase charged to the card. One can fly for free to predetermined selected destinations after accumulating the requisite number of miles, thus saving money in the long run.

Each of the following, if true, would cast doubt on the likelihood that fully enacting the recommendation above will have the stated effect EXCEPT:

(A) **The rules regarding how the accumulated miles may be exchanged are more restrictive than the rules for similar promotions offered by hotels.**

(B) People make many more purchases than they normally would when trying to accumulate credit card airline miles.

(C) The predetermined selected destinations to which free flights may be obtained via exchange for credit card airline miles are much more exotic and expensive than the destinations people visit when purchasing tickets normally.

(D) People attempting to accumulate credit card airline miles toward a free flight tend to purchase the first brand they encounter when searching for a particular product when they otherwise would have comparison shopped for bargains.

(E) People attempting to accumulate credit card airline miles toward a free flight tend to purchase expensive items that they do not need in order to attain the requisite number of miles.

Grill the Interrogator. Lots to grill in this long-winded stem, but essentially we're dealing with a Weaken the Argument EXCEPT question. We're also alerted to the existence of a recommendation, the effectiveness of which is the thing that will be called into question by four of the five choices. We should therefore keep an eye out for that recommendation as well.

Attack the Passage. Recommendations are often indicated by the word *should*, which is exactly what we get here. We find this word and the recommendation in the first sentence: People who don't like the high cost of travel should buy everything with credit cards to get free airline miles. The reason given is that this will save money in the long run. It sounds reasonable on its face, and unless you can predict why this may not work, this is a good opportunity to use the "define the objective" technique.

Work the Choices. Our objective is to locate choices that, if true, would imply that people *won't* in fact save money in the long run from using credit cards to get airline miles. And since it's an EXCEPT question, meaning the right answer *won't* weaken the argument, the right answer will likely be one of our usual common traps: something Irrelevant or even the Opposite of our objective. Let's evaluate the choices one by one with our objective and these common traps in mind.

A: The comparison between the restrictions of the airline promotion and restrictions put in place by hotels running similar promotions is Irrelevant to the argument because the comparison in and of itself tells us nothing about how confining the airline restrictions actually are. Perhaps the hotel restrictions aren't very severe, and the airline promotion, while more restrictive than the hotel deal, still makes it possible to save money on traveling in the manner described. There's not enough information in **A** to cast doubt on the recommendation, so **A** is correct for this Weaken EXCEPT question.

All of the other choices satisfy our objective by showing that people buying into this deal (literally, in this case) may in the final analysis lay out more money than they normally would just to take advantage of the so-called bargain. If that's the case, then the money they save on the airline miles may not offset the extra money they spend to get them. Whether they buy more things than they normally would (**B**), travel to more expensive locales (**C**), fail to comparison shop as they would have under normal circumstances (**D**), or buy unneeded expensive items just to get the "free" miles (**E**), they're spending more money than usual just to take advantage of the deal and may not save money in the end. Note that none of these scenarios absolutely *proves* that the recommendation won't work, but that's not required to weaken the argument.

> Your job in Weaken the Argument questions is to "cast doubt" on the conclusion, which means to tip the scales toward not believing in it. A valid weakener need not obliterate the conclusion, just make it less likely.

TAKE AWAY

Question 7: The Downside of Incompetence

7. Incompetence causes workers to perform inferior work. In addition, some incompetent people do not recognize their own incompetence, which causes them to reject the feedback and assistance that would enable them to improve the quality of their work.

The situation described above conforms most closely to which one of the following propositions?

(A) A behavior that causes negative repercussions may sometimes bring about positive outcomes that outweigh the negative repercussions of the behavior.

(B) A consequence of a phenomenon may in some cases be compounded by a secondary effect of that same phenomenon.

(C) The rejection of valuable recommendations may prove to be the difference between a negative outcome and the best possible outcome.

(D) When a character trait of a particular worker results in the performance of inferior work, that worker should be assigned less demanding responsibilities.

(E) An inferior project based on a faulty premise will be made worse by any attempt to incorporate a conflicting premise into the project.

Grill the Interrogator. We're told to find the proposition that best conforms to the situation in the passage, so we have a Conforming Principle question on our hands. That tells you right off the bat not to knock yourself out in search of assumptions or Essential Concepts and that matching the choices to the elements of the passage, not critiquing the logic itself, will be your main task.

Attack the Passage. The title is of course meant to be ironic since incompetence is a downside unto itself. In any case, it gets worse. Not only does incompetence cause inferior work, but it can also cause *blindness to* the inferiority of that work. In other words, some incompetent people do crappy work and are so incompetent that they don't even know their work is crappy. Failing to recognize said crappiness then causes the oblivious offenders to reject the help they need to improve. So it appears to be a situation of incompetence fueling a kind of downward spiral. Let's check the choices to find the principle that best conforms to this scenario.

Work the Choices. **B** captures the downward spiral element we've noted just above. Note how the terms of the choice perfectly match the scenario in the passage. Incompetence is the "phenomenon" under investigation. The "consequence" of that phenomenon is poor work. The "secondary effect" is the fact that incompetent people can't recognize their work as incompetent. This makes matters worse—that is, "compounds" the problem, as **B** puts it—by becoming an obstacle to future improvement. All systems go, so we have a winner.

A breaks down over "positive outcomes." Ain't nothing positive here. As we've seen, it just goes from bad to worse.

> In Matching questions, you'll often be able to eliminate choices based on a single word or phrase. That's the power of the technique—it helps you to zero in on the specifics of each choice and cut the ones that don't perfectly conform to the scenario at hand.
>
> TAKE AWAY

C has the same problem as **A** in that there's really nothing positive implied in the passage. Not only are some people incompetent, they're *so* incompetent they're incapable of recognizing it and humbly accepting advice to improve their bad work. This is pretty far from a "best possible outcome" scenario, so the choice breaks down over this phrase.

D: The first part of the principle in **D** seems to be on track, adequately describing the situation at hand. However, compensating for incompetence by easing the workload of the offender is beyond the scope of the passage, so **D** doesn't provide an appropriate match.

E shifts the problem from the worker to the project. The statement may make sense unto itself, but there's nothing in the passage about inferior projects based on faulty or conflicting premises, so **E** can't be correct.

> Your objective in a Conforming Principle question is not to find a principle that seems true or plausible, but to find the one that corresponds best to the specific situation in the passage.
>
> TAKE AWAY

Question 8: Bingville Music Minors

8. Lisa has earned enough music credits at Bingville University to make her eligible to declare a music minor. Randi must also be eligible to declare a music minor at Bingville University, since she has earned more music credits at that university than Lisa and the only factor determining eligibility to declare a music minor at Bingville University is the number of music credits earned.

Which one of the following arguments is most similar in its pattern of reasoning to the argument above?

(A) Dasha has enough money to buy the item she desires from the candy store. Since Jessie has more money than Dasha, Jessie must also have enough money to buy the item she desires from the candy store.

(B) Last night The Shambles sold out a 10,000-seat arena. Since tonight's concert by The Shambles is in a venue with a capacity of only 500 people, The Shambles will sell out tonight's concert as well.

(C) Allyson's new house costs less than her previous house. Since Allyson had enough money to make a down payment on her previous house, she will have enough money to make a down payment on her new house.

(D) Marvin, who has an advanced degree, has been an excellent tutor for Joshua. Since Sybil has one more advanced degree than Marvin, she will be an even better tutor for Joshua.

(E) **The Northwest Water Treatment Plant purifies a sufficient amount of water to satisfy the water needs of Reedbrook. Since the Southeast Water Treatment Plant purifies more water than does the Northwest Water Treatment Plant, the Southeast Water Treatment Plant must also be capable of providing enough purified water to satisfy the water needs of Reedbrook.**

Grill the Interrogator. Parallel Reasoning questions are the only ones that ask us to find a choice "most similar in its pattern of reasoning" to an argument in the passage, so we know from the outset to enter Matching mode. We also know from the lack of any reference to *flawed, erroneous,* or *questionable* reasoning that the logic in the argument is on the up-and-up. So focus exclusively on the logical structure as you make your way through the passage.

Attack the Passage. If Lisa has enough credits to qualify for music minor eligibility, and Randi has more of those credits than Lisa, then Randi must qualify for that eligibility as well. Sounds reasonable, much as we expected. The final part of sentence 2 may seem superfluous, but it actually tightens the logic a bit by discounting the possibility that eligibility relies on other factors that may bar Randi from claiming it even though she satisfies the music credit requirement. Generalizing from the situation, we can describe what's going on as follows: Since a certain amount of something is enough to bring about a result, something that's *more* than that amount must be enough too. Speaking of which, we now have enough ammo to take on the choices.

Since Parallel Reasoning questions ask you to mimic the passage's logic and not its content, it pays to rephrase the original argument in general terms. The right answer will contain the same logical mechanism that powers the original argument but will not be about the same thing. That's why it's best to relegate the specific topic to the background and focus on the underlying logic.

Work the Choices. If you're fond of the algebraic approach, you may have represented the scenario like so: X is sufficient for Y, and since Z is more than X, Z must also be sufficient for Y. Let's find the choice that precisely mimics this structure.

A: Ah, but what if the two girls desire different items? What they each desire and how much those items cost are unknowables, so it cannot be concluded under these circumstances that Jessie's in luck.

B: If we were betting folk, we might take this bet, for it sure sounds reasonable that a band that can sell out a 10,000-seater can move 500 tickets the next night. But again the Essential Concept unknowables rears its helpful head, considering that we know absolutely nothing about tonight's concert. A well-placed *probably* would go a long way toward rescuing this argument, but the unconditional, unqualified, ultra-definite conclusion that tonight's show by the Shambles *will* sell out isn't warranted based simply on evidence of the previous night's turnout. The original Bingville argument doesn't suffer from such ambiguity, so it cannot be paralleled by **B**.

C: Two important facts are missing from this argument: (1) How much money does Allyson currently have? (2) How much is the down payment on the new house compared to the down payment on the previous house? This second omission highlights a nifty little bait and switch which you hopefully picked up on: the difference between the overall cost of the two houses and the cost of their respective *down payments*. We have no way of knowing if Allyson can cover the down payment on the new house without these little tidbits of information. Just because she could swing it last time and this house is cheaper overall doesn't mean she can cover the down payment now; too many unknowables here for this conclusion to stand. There's no such ambiguity in the Bingville story, so **C** can't be its logical mirror image.

Don't expect Logical Reasoning Essential Concepts to appear only in the limelight as the featured logical element in the passage. Sometimes they're employed very subtly within answer choices. No matter where they appear, noticing them and understanding how they work will help you greatly.

D lacks the hard-nosed quantitative comparison that fuels the valid reasoning of the original. Sure, Sybil has one more advanced degree than Marvin, but we don't know that tutoring effectiveness is directly correlated with the number of advanced degrees one possesses. There may be many additional factors (personality, compatibility, subject matter knowledge, and so on) that aren't reflected entirely by the number of diplomas hanging on a wall.

One thing to notice about an argument is how much leeway it affords. If the original argument in a Parallel Reasoning question allows for absolutely no leeway, chop any choices that contain the slightest bit of wiggle room.

E contains the hard-and-fast comparison we seek. X (amount of water purified by the Northwest Plant) is sufficient for Y (satisfying the water needs of Reedbrook). Since Z (amount of water purified by the Southeast Plant) is more than X, Z must also be sufficient for Y. No leeway, no problem. **E** is correct as the parallel situation we seek.

Question 9: Steps to Intoxication

9. Alcohol dehydrogenase (ADH), an enzyme found in the liver and the stomach, breaks down alcohol before it reaches the bloodstream. It does this by converting ethanol, a toxic substance in alcohol, to acetaldehyde, another toxic substance, which is then further converted into harmless acetic acid. If one consumes alcohol at a rate faster than that which ADH can detoxify it, intoxication will result from alcohol entering the bloodstream. ADH is four times more active in men than in women.

Which one of the following is most strongly supported by the information above?

(A) A woman who consumes three alcoholic drinks in the course of an evening will experience intoxication.

(B) Men who consume alcohol are four times less likely to experience intoxication than are women who consume alcohol.

(C) A woman with an above-average quantity of acetaldehyde in her system must have recently consumed alcohol.

(D) An equivalent dose of alcohol will likely intoxicate a typical woman more than a typical man.

(E) People with ADH deficiencies will have an excess of ethanol in their bloodstreams.

Grill the Interrogator. The phrase "most strongly supported" in the question stem suggests a Standard Inference question, so there's no need to critique the argument or look for problems with it. Just follow the logic and see if you can combine the facts enough to recognize an additional supported assertion.

Attack the Passage. The passage is loaded with cause and effect relationships. ADH causes ethanol to become acetaldehyde, which then becomes harmless acetic acid. But if one imbibes too much alcohol for ADH to detoxify, alcohol will enter the blood and intoxication will result. The passage ends more with a whimper than a bang; we're merely told that ADH is four times more active in men than in women. Now why would they tell us that? Probably to lead us in the right direction. If ADH prevents intoxication, and works better in men than in women, we can begin to piece together the idea that other things being equal, alcohol may affect women more than men. Let's check the choices to see if this idea has any legs.

>
>
> **TAKE AWAY**
>
> Don't be surprised by that "left hanging" feeling you may get from some Inference passages—remember, they're often not out to convince you of something in the same manner as the question types in the Critique category. The job of an Inference passage is simply to provide you with enough information to reasonably conclude something else.

Work the Choices. **D** hits on the issue flagged above. It does make sense that an equivalent dose of alcohol will have a greater intoxicating effect in women than men, since ADH, the detoxification agent, works better in men than in women. Notice the qualified language of the choice. It says that the same amount will "likely" intoxicate a "typical" woman more than a "typical" man. With these qualifications in place, **D** is strongly supported. However, there would be trouble if the choice said the same amount will *definitely* intoxicate *any* woman more than *any* man. That would be going too far. (Check out wrong choice **A** for a good example of an improperly qualified statement.)

> **TAKE AWAY**
>
> Correct choices in Standard Inference questions must be properly qualified or risk entering Overreach territory.

A is Unknowable. First, we don't know how long it took for the woman to consume the three drinks, nor are we told the general rate at which ADH detoxifies alcohol. We also don't know that this is a *typical* woman we're talking about. For all we know, she has the ADH capacity of a typical man. With all these issues left up in the air, we can't say for sure that three drinks in the course of an evening will definitely lead the woman in question to intoxication.

B is also Unknowable, since we don't know the relative amounts that men and women typically drink. Even though men start with an ADH advantage, they may consume a greater volume of alcohol to the point where they are more likely to get intoxicated from drinking than are women.

>
>
> **TAKE AWAY**
>
> Unknowables come into play in many Logical Reasoning situations, but they are especially important as common traps in Standard Inference questions.

C hinges on a confusion between necessary and sufficient conditions. According to the passage, the alcohol breakdown process aided by ADH is sufficient to produce acetaldehyde, but we're not told that it's necessary. For all we know, there could be other reasons why excess acetaldehyde is present in one's system beside the consumption of alcohol.

E cannot be inferred because we don't know that these people lacking ADH even consume alcohol. We therefore have no reason to believe that the mere lack of ADH will cause an overabundance of ethanol in the blood, especially when we don't know how—or if—ethanol enters the blood in other ways.

Question 10: Ernie's Ankle

10. Ernie: When professional basketball players sprain their ankles, they receive immediate treatment by the best doctors with access to the most up-to-date and comprehensive medical technologies. Moreover, their rehabilitation regimens are state of the art as well, since the teams have a large vested interest in accelerating the healing process. Despite this abundant attention, which "average" people like me most certainly lack, it is not unusual for professional basketball players' ankle injuries to take three months to fully heal. It is therefore untrue that the fact that my ankle injury took three months to fully heal is proof that I did not take adequate care of my injury.

The answer to which one of the following questions would be most useful in evaluating Ernie's argument?

(A) **How severe was Ernie's ankle injury as compared with that of the ankle injuries to professional basketball players he describes?**

(B) Is the medical treatment afforded to professional basketball players better than that afforded to other professional athletes?

(C) Do injured professional athletes have a greater vested interest in accelerating the healing process than do injured "average" people like Ernie?

(D) Has any professional basketball player suffered an ankle injury that took longer than three months to fully heal?

(E) Is the medical treatment afforded to professional athletes available to anyone who is not a professional athlete?

Grill the Interrogator. Which answer would be most useful in evaluating the argument? This is a bit unusual, right? For the sake of completeness, we thought we'd include this slight variation on the Strengthen/Weaken theme. This is an offshoot of Strengthen/Weaken because that question type is so concerned with the evaluation of effects. In Strengthen/Weaken questions, we're given facts to bounce off the argument to see where that leads. Here, we're given *questions* and need to speculate on the effects of their possible answers.

TAKE AWAY

Recognizing a question that's most useful in evaluating an argument entails understanding where such an answer will lead. In other words, will the answer to that question help us decide if we believe in the conclusion more or believe in it less? We can't actually strengthen or weaken the argument since we don't know the answers to the questions posed, but we can determine whether the answer to each question, whatever it is, would be relevant to supporting or damaging the argument.

Attack the Passage. The conclusion in the final sentence, highlighted by the word *therefore,* is a bit convoluted and thus requires a bit of unpacking.

Use structural signal words like *therefore* and *thus* to help you scan to the argument's conclusion whenever possible, especially in Critique questions that deal specifically with the validity of arguments.

We're interested in evaluating the argument, so here's our objective: We're trying to figure out whether Ernie really is slacking on his treatment, as the "proof" he's trying to discount suggests, or whether the three months to heal *isn't* strange, considering that the pros, with all their advantages, take that amount of time to heal themselves. Now, Ernie includes plenty of details in his comparison between the ankle situation of "average" him and that of the pros—except, of course, the most important: How *bad* was his injury compared with theirs? Without knowing that, there's really no way of evaluating his argument. You may have come to this realization via a strategically constructed "But what if . . . ?" scenario: *But what if their injuries are so much worse than yours, Ernie? Now what do you say, hot shot?* (Okay, you can leave that last part out.)

Asking "But what if . . . ?" is a great way to envision alternatives, one of our Logical Reasoning Essential Concepts. Recognizing alternatives greatly helps us evaluate the arguments presented in these questions.

Work the Choices. We've seen in our passage analysis that the severity of Ernie's injury is relevant to his argument, since his argument hinges on whether three months of healing is a normal amount of time. He implies it definitely is fine, since even the pros take that long, and they have every advantage he doesn't. But if his injury is a minor tweak, and still takes three months to heal, while major ankle injuries of the pros take the same amount of time, then his evidence about the pros would be less likely to sway his doubters who presumably see the three-month recovery time as proof that he's not taking proper care of his ankle. Note that this doesn't mean that he is *definitely* remiss in his treatment, only that his argument under these circumstances doesn't hold up as well. Knowing the answer to the question posed in choice **A** would therefore be most helpful in determining whether Ernie is full of hot air or whether his critics should cut him some slack.

B: The relative quality of treatment enjoyed by various kinds of professional athletes is not relevant to whether Ernie is taking care of his ankle. His evidence is derived from a comparison of himself to *basketball players,* so other athletes are Irrelevant.

C first shifts the notion of vested interest in sentence 2 from the team to the players and then provides an Irrelevant comparison with the healing interests of average Joes like Ernie. Even if we knew how Ernie's desire to get better compared with the motivation level of the pros, that wouldn't tell us whether the time it took him to heal proves he slacked off on his recuperation. The incentive issue is brought up in another context, as still more evidence that pros have every advantage when it comes to treatment. Learning the answer to the question in **C** therefore doesn't help us to evaluate Ernie's claim in the final sentence.

D is Irrelevant. Ernie merely states that three months healing time is "not unusual" for the pros, which is why he uses the three-month figure as his benchmark. Whether some basketball ankle injuries have taken longer than three months to heal has no impact on his argument.

E: So what if some lucky son-of-a-gun gets the same treatment as the pros—or if no one beside professional athletes is afforded such treatment? The answer to this question is Irrelevant to whether Ernie is earnest in his recovery efforts based on the comparisons cited in the passage.

TAKE AWAY

> Don't forget about the power of a well-placed "So what?" Such cynicism, properly channeled, can help you spot and delete Irrelevant choices. Since the main test in this kind of question is one of relevance, it's not surprising that most of the wrong choices fall into the Irrelevant category.

Question 11: Home Schooling

11. Educational consultant: Students struggling in traditional public schools are often reassigned to special education classes, when home schooling may in fact be a better alternative. Many dismiss such non-mainstream educational approaches out of hand. However, not only do home-schooled children receive the specific individual attention they require, but they also avoid the emotional hardships and social stigmas that often burden students forced to participate in traditional special education programs. This danger is especially prevalent among special education students with low self-esteem.

The educational consultant's statements best support which one of the following?

(A) Traditional special education classes are a better option than home schooling for struggling students who do not suffer from low self-esteem.

(B) Any nontraditional educational approach is superior to special education classes when it comes to helping struggling students succeed academically.

(C) Struggling students may benefit from nontraditional schooling options.

(D) Traditional schooling generally does not provide individual attention to students with low self-esteem.

(E) Traditional schooling is less effective than home schooling for most students.

Grill the Interrogator. The question stem tells us to find the statement among the choices that is "best supported," which means we're in Standard Inference territory. Critique issues, such as whether the argument is any good, are off the table, nor should you expect the answer to center around a formal logic deduction.

Attack the Passage. The consultant begins with an argument in favor of home schooling over special ed for struggling public school students and immediately follows with an admission that many are averse to such non-mainstream educational options. Then some advantages of home schooling are offered, such as individual attention and social benefits that particularly help kids with low self-esteem. Do we care whether any of this is *true* or how strong this argument is? No! We just need to recognize where the information plausibly leads, and where it doesn't.

TAKE AWAY

The whole point of reading the question stem first is that it tells us what to care about when attacking the passage. When you find yourself up against a Standard Inference question, you shouldn't concern yourself with the validity of the argument or ways to make it better or worse. Instead, focus on the parameters of the passage so you can recognize what you *don't* know (unknowables) from the information given as well as statements that distort it.

It's possible that no obvious connections leapt out at you, so with the gist of the story under our belts, it's high time to hit the choices.

Work the Choices. Let's take the choices one by one, keeping the Inference common traps in mind as we evaluate how each statement stacks up against the information in the passage.

A, if anything, is an Opposite choice. The issue of low self-esteem is pretty much a red herring. True, the consultant states that home schooling is *especially* good for them, but she still suggests that home schooling is a good option for *all* struggling students. Considering the clear advocacy for home schooling, the idea that traditional special education is better for any group of kids doesn't hold any weight.

B is an Overreach. The consultant argues for one particular kind of nontraditional educational approach, home schooling, as the better option than special ed to address some academic problems. We can't infer from this that *every* nontraditional academic approach is superior to public school special education.

TAKE AWAY

When your reaction to a choice is "Whoa, not so fast!" then you can be pretty sure that you're looking at an Overreach.

C sticks very closely to the consultant's main idea and is qualified enough to count as a statement that's well supported by her argument. It's merely a general rewording of the specific case regarding struggling students who may be better off in nontraditional home school environments than in public school special ed programs.

TAKE AWAY

When you come across easy questions, don't automatically think that it must be a trick. The LSAT contains questions of all difficulty levels, which means that some will seem easy to you. Knocking off the easier ones quickly will free up time for the tough stuff.

THE NEW LSAT

D serves up an interesting Twister, attempting to combine the low self-esteem issue with the notion of individual attention. Low self-esteem is tied to the benefit of lessening social stigmas, not to the separate issue of individual attention.

E: Look out Kansas, here comes another Twister. The passage details a comparison between home schooling and special ed with regard to the optimal way to deal with *academically challenged* students. A general comparison between traditional education and home schooling in regard to *most* students goes beyond the scope of the passage. Not only does the relevant comparison from the passage get twisted into something else in this choice, the group to which it applies gets twisted as well. So we've got Overreach and Twister elements afoot. If you read the choice and immediately thought "the deal for most students is Unknowable . . . "—just as good.

TAKE AWAY

We've said it before but it bears repeating: Don't obsess or get bogged down by terminology. If what appears to you as Unknowable we call a Twister, or vice versa, don't sweat it. The point is for you to adopt the concepts and traps we teach you and apply them in your own way directly to the questions, quickly, instinctively, and effectively. At the end of the day, if you know which choices are right and which ones are wrong, that's all that matters.

Question 12: Ant Mentors

12. Anthropologist: One of the wonders of nature is the ant's uncanny ability to balance duty toward its colony with the satisfaction of its individual needs. We would do well to look to this achievement as the basis for a more just social arrangement. Humans, both blessed and cursed with higher-order intelligence and autonomy, have yet to come close to realizing such balance between societal needs and individual strivings. This is because as soon as we gain power of any kind, we seek to use it to our personal advantage, which inevitably (although often unintentionally) works to the detriment of the greater good. This tendency, however, is culturally driven and not instinctual, so a change in social relations is clearly attainable.

The author is mainly arguing that

(A) humans use power to seek and gain advantages over one another
(B) humans would ultimately be happier if they were more like ants in many respects
(C) humans would benefit from a better balance between individual and societal needs
(D) because the human tendency to seek personal advantage to the detriment of the greater good is instinctual, it is not possible to alter social relations
(E) humans have employed higher-order intelligence in both positive and negative ways

Grill the Interrogator. The phrase "mainly arguing that" tells us that Main Point is the name of the game, so don't worry yourself over whether the logic is strong or weak or which Essential Concepts may appear in the reasoning. Instead, analyze each sentence to determine its function in the passage. This analysis will eventually reveal the primary reason the author put pen to paper.

Closely interrogate each sentence of Main Point arguments. The main point can appear anywhere in the passage, including the first sentence. Stay inquisitive, continuously asking yourself "Why are you telling me this?" The author's evidence must eventually lead to what he or she is trying to get across, and that's what you'll find in the correct choice.

Attack the Passage. Sentence 1 could be titled "Ode to the Ant." This miraculous creature, says the anthropologist, balances community duty with individual satisfaction. We should follow suit, according to sentence 2, since doing so could lead to a more just social arrangement. This recommendation sounds pretty *conclusiony,* to coin a term meaning "like a conclusion."

Anything that suggests that something *should be done* is a viable candidate for main point honors.

The question is now whether this recommendation will lead to some larger point or will itself be backed up by evidence, so let's find out. We humans have yet to get this community/individual balance thing down, according to sentence 3, which includes that enigmatic "both blessed and cursed" business. We'll let that slide unless we determine later on that it's important enough to decipher.

One habit of great LSAT test takers is determining the *relevance* of written statements. Let's face it, the LSAT contains a ton of reading, and you can't exert full concentration on every single word or your brain will explode. (Well, probably not, but you may get a headache and you *will* definitely lose time.) Grilling the Interrogator is the first step in figuring out what will be important in each passage. In Main Point questions, keep your eye on the overriding issue, and try not to get distracted by specifics that may not play a role in the correct choice.

Sentence 4 explains why we can't balance individual strivings with societal betterment; we seem to use any power we gain to promote ourselves to the detriment of the community. But, as we see in the final sentence, this tendency is not instinctual but rather instilled through culture, so there is the possibility for change. Now, we must ask ourselves whether the author wrote the passage to lead to the idea that social change is possible or for some higher purpose. The recommendation in sentence 2 supersedes the notion at the end. Change being possible works as evidence for the idea that we should try to achieve the balance exemplified by the ant. On the other hand, saying that we should copy the ant does not directly support the notion that change is possible. So of the statements in the passage, the recommendation in the second sentence stands out as the main point, while the other statements serve as support. Let's move on to the choices.

Work the Choices. C best accords with the gist of the second sentence. The achievement referred to in that sentence is the ant's ability to balance individual and societal needs. As we discussed, the notion in the final sentence that social change is achievable supports the main point that we should try to attain better balance between individual and community needs in an attempt to create a more just society.

A restates evidence presented in sentence 4 detailing *why* we don't seem to balance individual strivings with social needs, while the main point revolves around the recommendation in sentence 2.

B is an Overreach. Do we want to grow antennae, sprout huge heads, and spend our entire day building mounds out of dirt? The author notes one specific way in which humans should emulate ants, so **B** takes things too far.

D bollixes up both issues in the final sentence, which says that the tendency in question is *not* instinctual and that it *is* possible to alter social relations.

E focuses on a small part of the argument that we decided to skim right past during our attack on the passage: that bit about humans being both blessed and cursed. This is a stylistic embellishment that neither recurs in the passage nor supports any other part of it, so it cannot be featured as the passage's main point.

Question 13: R-E-S-P-E-C-T . . .

13. Anyone who works hard is respected by at least one other person. Since all those who respect someone are well-liked, it must be true that whoever works hard is well-liked.

    The conclusion above is valid if which one of the following is assumed?

    (A) **Only people who do not work hard respect no one.**
    (B) Everyone who respects at least one person respects everyone.
    (C) Whoever respects everyone works hard.
    (D) Whoever is well-liked respects at least one other person.
    (E) Only people who do not work hard are respected by at least one other person.

Grill the Interrogator. We're told to find an assumption that will validate the conclusion, so keep an eye out for the missing piece of the argument.

Attack the Passage. There's not much to it, is there? However, don't let that lull you into a false sense of security, especially since there's formal logic afoot. The words *anyone, all,* and *whoever* mean "all," and "at least one other person" means "some." Let's see where all this formal logic leads.

TAKE AWAY

> A good tip-off that formal logic is featured in an argument is the presence of *all, some,* and *none* statements, regardless of how the test makers choose to word them.

The first sentence states that every hard worker has at least one respectful admirer. The second sentence begins by stating that every person who respects someone else is well-liked and then concludes that because of this, every hard worker must be well-liked. In the context of the second sentence, "hard workers" is a loose end that needs to be tied to something else to make this connection work. If all hard workers respected at least someone, then it *would* make sense to conclude that all hard workers are well-liked. But sentence 1 doesn't say this—in fact, it gets it backward, telling us that all hard workers are *respected* by at least someone. We need to know that *anyone who works hard respects at least someone else* for this argument to be complete. Let's take that notion with us into the choices.

Work the Choices. The choices are no picnic, mainly because they all represent different combinations of the same terms and therefore pretty much sound the same. However, if you know to look for something that encapsulates the idea "anyone who works hard respects at least someone," you're in much better shape. You're still not home free, unfortunately, since the correct choice is the logical equivalent of this stated in the negative. "Only people who do not work hard respect no one" means the same thing as "every hard worker respects at least someone," so **A** gets the point for this very difficult formal logic Assumption question.

> **TAKE AWAY**
>
> Every question on the LSAT is worth exactly one point, so you shouldn't belabor tough questions that you may miss anyway. If formal logic isn't your strong suit, and choices like these give you a migraine, then skip such questions and return to them if time permits. Of course, since there is no penalty for wrong answers, you should fill in a guess even if you bag the question entirely.

We can at least eliminate **B** and **D** without too much trouble since they both ignore the loose end we tagged above: hard workers. Simply knowing that the right answer has to somehow link hard workers to something else to round out the logic lets us chop these two right off the bat.

> **TAKE AWAY**
>
> Even tough questions are amenable to shortcuts. Sometimes just knowing what the right answer must involve is enough to eliminate a few choices and increase your odds if you have to guess among the rest.

C Overreaches by expanding respect for at least someone to respect for *everyone*. For all we know, there's no one who respects everyone, and even if there is, that fact still doesn't indicate that every hard worker respects at least someone, the notion we need to complete this picture.

E is wrong because it contradicts the first sentence, and nothing that goes against the passage must be assumed by it.

Question 14: Probiotics

14. Probiotics are beneficial bacteria contained in fermented foods. One probiotic, *Lactobacillus reuteri*, is believed to help prevent gastrointestinal infections and provide overall health benefits. For 45 days, 100 randomly chosen test group subjects were given one drink a day containing *Lactobacillus reuteri*, while another 100 control group subjects were given one drink a day containing placebos. At the end of the study, all test group subjects were tested to determine their reactions to *Lactobacillus reuteri*. Within this group, 45 percent of those working night shifts exhibited a positive reaction to *Lactobacillus reuteri*, while only 16 percent of those working day shifts exhibited a positive reaction to the bacteria. These data demonstrate that *Lactobacillus reuteri* benefited more night-shift workers than day-shift workers.

The reasoning in the argument is most vulnerable to the criticism that it

(A) fails to specify the physical advantages derived from a positive reaction to *Lactobacillus reuteri*

(B) assumes without justification that no one in the control group benefited from the study

(C) distinguishes between two subgroups of a larger group participating in the study

(D) omits key information that would allow the conclusion to be verified

(E) provides no information on the effectiveness of *Lactobacillus reuteri* relative to the effectiveness of other probiotics

Grill the Interrogator. The phrase "most vulnerable to the criticism" places us squarely in the Flaw camp, which warns us to be on our guard. Faced with such a long and complicated passage, it at least helps knowing up front that we're looking for a problem with the logic. Armed with our knowledge of Essential Concepts and classic flaws, we're ready to go in.

Attack the Passage. We're introduced to a beneficial kind of bacteria called *Lactobacillus reuteri*, which we will just shorten to *Lr* for the sake of convenience.

TAKE
AWAY

Logic Games isn't the only LSAT section that benefits from shorthanding. If you come across lengthy names or concepts in Logical Reasoning or Reading Comp, it pays to abbreviate those as well.

Then we get a typical study, with a test group that gets this thing, and a control group that doesn't. The reactions of the test group subjects are then analyzed, and here's where things get interesting.

Think proactively! Why do you suppose we have you read the question stem first, before the passage? We've already told you: so you know what to look for. Now think about it: This is a Flaw question, and the passage concludes with lots of numbers and percentages. That alone should raise a red flag that these results are probably the source of the logical breakdown. If this were an Inference question, the answer could come from anywhere. If it were a Method question, we'd have to consider the overall thrust of the passage. But since it's a *Flaw* question, we can confidently focus on the part that's likely to yield the answer, and in this question that's the results at the end.

A larger percentage of night-shift workers benefited from the bacteria than day-shift workers. No problem there; that's perfectly reasonable. Then the author concludes from this that *more* night-shifters benefited than day-shifters, which should remind you of the faulty reasoning in "New England Transcendentalists" back in the Flaw section of the Logical Reasoning chapter. Since we don't know how many night-shift workers there are compared to day-shift workers, we can't trust the conclusion that a greater *percentage* of beneficiaries of the bacteria necessarily leads to a greater *actual number* of beneficiaries. That's the idea to bring with us into the choices.

Work the Choices. We see from our attack on the passage that the problem here involves confusion between percentages and numbers, but we're not home free yet because no choice states that explicitly. **D,** however, gets at the issue, albeit it in a roundabout manner, by simply noting the omission of key information. The information the passage is missing is how many night-shift workers there are and how many day-shift workers there are. If we knew that, then we'd be able to verify the conclusion. Without that information, the argument's incomplete.

What makes the LSAT hard? Let us count the ways! The test makers have devised plenty of difficulties to put in your path. Even if you know, for example, that a question involves a numbers/percentages issue, the right answer may speak to an implication or facet of this that you need to recognize to get the point. Stay on your toes!

The wrong choices provide a nice assortment of common Flaw traps:

A: Not Obligated: The author need not provide the specifics of the positive reactions to draw a conclusion about the relative number of them.

B: Does No Such Thing: The control group drops out of the equation after being mentioned early on, and the author makes no assumptions regarding its members' reactions to the bacteria.

In Reading Comprehension, we distinguish between players and extras: central characters primarily involved in the action versus those mentioned only as background figures. Extras make excellent fodder for wrong choices, and the same is true in Logical Reasoning passages, as evidenced by choice **B** here.

C: Not a Problem: "Yeah, I done it—waddaya wanna make of it?" might reply our author to the accusation in **C**. The author *does* break up the test group into day-shift and night-shift workers, but there's nothing wrong with that. It's what comes *after*, the interpretation of the statistics relating to these groups, that's logically unsound.

E: Other probiotics are Irrelevant to what conclusions can be derived from this study concerning *Lactobacillus reuteri,* which means that this choice is a toss-up between Irrelevant and Not Obligated, for those keeping track at home.

Question 15: The Case of the High School Dropouts

15. A study conducted by the Regional Educational Statistics Board (RESB) found the dropout rate among high school students from 1999 to 2002 to be 2.7 percent. However, the census bureau for the same region reported the high school dropout rate during the same period to be 5.2 percent.

Which one of the following, if true, best resolves the apparent discrepancy above?

(A) **RESB reported certain students who left high school to be home schooled as graduates since they passed a high school certification exam, while the census bureau reported such students as dropouts.**

(B) The census bureau included in its report statistics on elementary and junior high school dropout rates, while RESB did not.

(C) The high schools included in RESB's study were identical to the high schools studied by the census bureau.

(D) The census bureau report indicates that the high school dropout rate between 1999 and 2001 was approximately 2.7 percent, but rose dramatically in 2002 due to a severe economic downturn in the region during that year.

(E) When factoring in the number of high school dropouts who eventually returned to high school and received high school diplomas since 2002, the census bureau dropout rate mirrored that found by RESB.

Grill the Interrogator. The phrase "resolves an apparent discrepancy" is the signal that we're up against a Paradox question. Slip into detective mode, scoping out the mystery at hand, and keep your eyes peeled for our usual Critique helpers such as assumptions, alternatives, and the other Essential Concepts.

Attack the Passage. You shouldn't have had much trouble locating the discrepancy: One group, the RESB, cites the high school dropout rate at 2.7 percent, while the census bureau puts it at 5.2. Since they're presumably talking about the same group, something's fishy. There doesn't seem to be enough information to specifically predict the problem, but we can define the objective of the correct choice as indicating how one group has employed a different methodology or interpretation, resulting in the disparate figures. That means that alternatives will probably come into play.

Work the Choices. Test the choices one by one against the objective defined above, while keeping the Paradox common traps— Irrelevant, Opposite, and Unnecessary Clarification—in mind.

A certainly points to a difference in methodology, thus satisfying the objective we stated above. But we still have to make sure that the difference would result in skewing the stats in the direction cited in the passage. And indeed it does: If RESB pegs home-schoolers as graduates, while the census bureau labels them dropouts, it makes more sense that the dropout rate determined by the census bureau would be nearly twice as high as that found by RESB. **A** is correct.

B: So what? The inclusion of elementary and junior high school dropout rates in one report but not the other does represent a difference in methodology between the two studies, but not one that's relevant to the different findings regarding *high school* dropouts.

C is an Opposite wrong choice that only deepens the mystery by discounting the alternative possibility that the two studies included different schools. If we were told that the two studies actually did survey different sets of schools within the region, then maybe we'd be on to something. But surveying *identical* schools makes us wonder *even more* why the dropout rate reported by one study is almost double the rate reported by the other.

D: "Fascinating, Captain . . . ," yet the mystery remains: Why didn't the RESB dropout figure shoot up in 2002 because of the economic consideration cited by the census bureau? **D** therefore falls into the Unnecessary Clarification camp: It enlightens us as to how the census bureau figure *came to be* but not as to why it diverges from the RESB finding.

E: What happens *after* 2002 is Irrelevant to the mystery at hand. These two organizations can produce identical reports for the rest of the century for all we care—that wouldn't explain why their reported dropout rates from 1999 to 2002 differ in the manner cited.

> Irrelevant choices make for excellent quick kills, since they often focus on things that stick out like sore thumbs—for example, *elementary* and *junior high schools* in a passage about high schools, or *beyond the year 2002* in a passage dealing with 1999 to 2002. You must bag at least a few quick kills if you're to have a shot at finishing the section on time.

TAKE AWAY

Question 16: The Dean's Defense

16. College Dean: While of course this university requires tuition fees in order to operate, our professors gear the classroom experience to satisfy only one mandate: producing educated and enlightened citizens. Therefore, accusations that our students dictate their courses' subject matter and manner of presentation to get the most of their education expenditures, akin to consumers in the marketplace, is patently false. Moreover, critics making this charge fail to realize that students benefit immensely when academic programs and courses are geared specifically to appeal to their intellectual interests and optimal modes of receiving information.

The Dean's argument is flawed because it

(A) **contains conflicting premises**

(B) fails to demonstrate that courses not geared to appeal to students' intellectual interests might interest some students anyway

(C) does not provide evidence that the courses at the Dean's university are superior in quality to courses at similar universities

(D) employs different meanings of the word "consumer" when referring to the university setting as opposed to the marketplace

(E) criticizes students for engaging in a behavior based only on evidence that they have been accused of engaging in that behavior

Grill the Interrogator. We're told flat out that the Dean's argument is flawed, which is essentially a direct command to enter Critique mode. Prepare to encounter classic flaws and/or Essential Concepts as you wade through the argument.

Attack the Passage. Whoa! This guy should be a politician, what with all that talking out of both sides of his mouth. First he says no how, no way do we let students dictate what and how we teach. Then, as if to cap off this grand assertion, he says the exact opposite: in effect, that students learn best when we gear our courses to what they want to learn and how they want to learn it. Like, pick a side, dude . . .

TAKE AWAY

Practice paraphrasing arguments by simplifying them into common language. It's easier to see the underlying logic when you cut past fancy terminology and recast the passage in your own words.

Saying opposing things while advancing a single argument constitutes a flaw, so let's see which choice captures this problem.

Work the Choices. In one of the shortest Logical Reasoning answer choices you're likely to see, **A** hits the nail (and the Dean) on the head: His premises conflict.

B: The Dean isn't obligated to go into all this. He merely states (at first, at least) that the university doesn't let students dictate subject matter. He never says that courses are specifically geared *not* to interest students, and even if he did, he need not then show that some may appeal to them anyway. He simply says that students don't dictate what's taught. The problem arises when he abruptly changes his tune at the end.

C is a combo wrong choice. The Dean is Not Obligated to provide the evidence sought in **C** because such a comparison is Irrelevant to whether the Dean's school allows its students to dictate their courses' subjects as consumers—something evidently the Dean himself can't figure out.

> Common traps often overlap, but you only need one reason to dismiss a choice. Don't obsess over shades of wrong. If any part of a choice seems fishy, chop it.

TAKE AWAY

D: The Dean Does No Such Thing; he means exactly what he says regarding the charge that students act as consumers. The analogy is apt. The question is whether it is in fact true.

E also falls into the Does No Such Thing camp, brought on by a nifty little bait and switch. The Dean never criticizes students; he criticizes the *critics* for *misrepresenting* the students' behavior.

THE NEW LSAT

Question 17: Environment Debate

17. **Memmie:** Children today are growing up in a toxic atmosphere of environmental contaminants. Their living space includes ever-increasing amounts of pesticides, air pollution, and food additives, not to mention simple dust and pollen. This toxic environment is responsible for the huge increase in childhood diseases such as asthma and bronchitis.

Bunny: Quite the opposite! Our society's recent mania for health and cleanliness, characterized by increases in immunizations and disinfectants and an unwillingness to allow children to interact hands-on with our natural surroundings, has compromised children's immune systems, which require early and abundant contact with contaminants in order to develop properly. Weaker immune systems have led to a greater incidence of childhood diseases.

The conversation most strongly suggests that Memmie and Bunny disagree over whether

(A) children's interaction with the environment affects the incidence of childhood diseases

(B) the environment to which children are exposed has become more sanitary

(C) the increase in the incidence of childhood asthma is more related to environmental contaminants than is the increase in the incidence of childhood bronchitis

(D) the incidence of childhood diseases is on the rise

(E) children's immune systems have been negatively affected by changes in their interaction with the environment

Grill the Interrogator. It's the LSAT's version of "he said, she said"—except in this case we get two she's. Disagreement is clearly the featured question type in this one, so prepare to home in on the crux of each argument so you can spot where the speakers' opinions diverge.

Attack the Passage. We begin with Memmie, whose concern isn't so unusual: Kids are growing up in the midst of a toxic stew, which she thinks is causing a huge increase in childhood diseases. Note that the second sentence of her argument isn't crucial—it simply lists the contaminants she's worried about but doesn't add much to the logic of her argument.

TAKE AWAY

Good LSAT test takers develop a feel for the parts of Logical Reasoning and Reading Comprehension passages they can afford to skim. A list that simply specifies the items of a group already mentioned makes for promising skimming material.

Bunny counterattacks immediately with her resounding "Quite the opposite!" and her position falls a bit further from the beaten track. Far from being too dirty, she argues, children's physical surroundings are *actually too clean*. Society, according to Bunny, immunizes kids, disinfects their environment, and forbids them to get their hands dirty out in nature. The problem, however, is that this mania for cleanliness compromises children's immune systems, which presumably need contact with dirt to kick start and develop properly. Bunny claims that deficient immune systems caused by this sanitary state of affairs are the reason childhood diseases are increasing. Notice the point of *agreement* between Memmie and Bunny: They both think childhood diseases are on the rise. As for disagreement, one thinks the reason childhood diseases are up is because children's environment is too clean; the other says it's because it's too dirty. Let's apply our Matching technique to the choices, using what we've gleaned from the passage.

Work the Choices. Having a good grip on the crux of the matter, you may have benefited from a quick scan of the choices. **B** hits on the major issue of environmental cleanliness, so let's test that one out first. We've already agreed that both speakers address this issue, so this choice passes our test for relevance. However, do the speakers *disagree* on whether children's environment is getting more sanitary? To answer this question, let's Quiz the Speakers. Bunny says yes: Our recent mania for cleanliness has caused children to live in a world where they avoid early and abundant contact with contaminants, so clearly Bunny thinks the world has gotten cleaner; in fact, too clean for her tastes. Memmie says no: The world is going to the dogs and getting dirtier by the minute, filled with "ever-increasing amounts" of the toxins she despises. One says yes, one says no, which means we have a winner.

> Remember the drill for testing Disagreement choices: First test for relevance, then Quiz the Speakers. If a choice hits on an issue relevant to both arguments, and the speakers' opinions on that issue diverge when you quiz them, then that choice is correct.

TAKE AWAY

A is actually a fairly subtle point of agreement. Memmie and Bunny agree that interaction with the environment has an effect on childhood diseases. What they disagree on is *what* the environment is like and *how* it affects the kids.

C: Only Memmie mentions the specific childhood diseases asthma and bronchitis, and even she doesn't distinguish between them on the level indicated in this choice.

D is the point of agreement we noted during our initial analysis of the passage. Both think the incidence of childhood diseases is on the rise. They just have different explanations for it.

E: For one thing, the immune system is a direct part of Bunny's argument, but is not mentioned by Memmie. However, even if we took Memmie's argument to imply compromised immune systems (a plausible enough link to increased childhood diseases), then Memmie would be in agreement with Bunny on this point.

Question 18: Learning and the Pons

18. Signals originating in the pons—a structure at the base of the brain—trigger rapid eye movement (REM) sleep, and ultimately enter the cerebral cortex, the part of the brain that collects and interprets information from the outside world. Infants and young children, who learn at a much faster rate than adults, experience much longer periods of REM sleep. Moreover, studies have shown that people deprived of REM sleep have difficulty assimilating new knowledge and skills attained while awake, while those deprived of non-REM sleep while receiving a normal amount of REM sleep do not experience a similar change in their retention capabilities. It is therefore likely that the pons plays a role in the learning process.

Which one of the following best describes the role played in the argument by the claim that infants and young children learn at a much faster rate than adults and experience much longer periods of REM sleep?

(A) It is a subsidiary conclusion supported by preceding information provided in the argument.

(B) It is one of two independent pieces of evidence that taken together help to establish the argument's conclusion.

(C) It provides information about REM sleep that contradicts a later assertion meant to undermine the argument's conclusion.

(D) It provides the sole support for the argument's conclusion regarding the likely role that REM sleep plays in the learning process.

(E) It provides the basis for understanding the assertion about REM sleep that immediately follows it and upon which the argument's conclusion is primarily based.

Grill the Interrogator. The phrase "the role played in the argument" tells us point blank that this is a Role question, and the nice thing about Role question stems is that they tell us exactly what part of the passage to focus on. Here, it has something to do with the learning rates and amounts of REM sleep in children versus adults, so we're set to head into the passage looking for why the author mentions this comparison.

Attack the Passage. Aaaay! It's the Pons! No wait—that's the Fonz. Our mistake. Anyhoo . . . The first sentence is about signals from a nifty little brain structure called the "pons," signals which trigger REM sleep and end up in the information-collecting center of the brain. Fascinating, but it's sentence 2 that features the issue highlighted in the question. The connection between the faster learning rates of infants and children and their longer REM sleep compared to adults isn't quite clear yet, so we'll have to reserve judgment as to its role in the passage until we gather more facts. Sentence 3 begins with the signal word "moreover," which suggests that additional information is on its way. It appears that the author is building toward something, which would suggest that the claim in question isn't the argument's conclusion. But let's see what happens.

People who lose REM sleep have trouble retaining new knowledge and skills, but losing non-REM sleep doesn't have the same effect. So a connection between REM sleep and information gathered during wakened states is emerging, but what does this have to do with the comparison between children and adults? We need the final sentence to piece that together. There we find a hypothesis concerning the pons' role in the learning process. Since REM sleeps appears to play a part in people retaining what they learn, and the pons sends signals that trigger REM, the author speculates that the pons is involved in learning. The final sentence is therefore the author's conclusion, which eliminates one possible role for the claim in question. We can now go back to that claim in sentence 2 to fit it into the overall context of the passage. Children are cited as an example of people who have more REM sleep and learn much faster than others, which supports the connection between REM and learning, which in turn supports the conclusion regarding the pons.

Work the Choices. We've at least determined that the claim in question provides support for the conclusion but is not the passage's conclusion itself, which allows us to scan the choices for quick kills. Choice **A** can be ditched, as the featured statement is not a conclusion backed by evidence of its own; the statement that precedes it says nothing about the comparison between adults and children. In addition, **C**'s "contradicts a later assertion" should clunk against your ear, since we've determined that the featured statement plays a supporting role in the argument. It also doesn't help **C**'s cause that the word *moreover* follows the statement in question, strongly suggesting that what comes next is *consistent* with the featured claim, not contradicted by it. So a general understanding of the featured statement's supportive role allows us to scan the choices and quickly narrow them down to **B**, **D**, and **E**.

B is dead on. The author begins with the pons triggering REM sleep and ends with the pons as a likely contributor to the learning process. How does he get from the first point to the second? By connecting REM to learning: first via the claim in question, that children with more REM sleep than adults are also faster learners; and then, via a separate ("independent," as the choice puts it) piece of evidence, that lack of REM sleep is associated with hampered learning while lack of non-REM sleep isn't. It all adds up to the conclusion in the final sentence, so the claim in question can rightfully be deemed one of two supporting pillars of the argument.

D has two problems. First, we've determined that the claim in question is not the only support offered; saying it is would ignore the important evidence from the studies stated in sentence 3. Secondly, the conclusion is specifically about the likely role of the *pons,* not REM sleep.

TAKE AWAY

You rightfully may not make Essential Concepts your primary focus in Construction questions, but don't be surprised if one of them, such as a bait and switch, creeps into a wrong choice. Any practice you get spotting the Essential Concepts at work is time well spent.

E: No, correct choice **B** has it right: Sentences 2 and 3 contain *independent* facts, each forging its own connection between REM and learning. The claim that children get more REM sleep and learn faster than adults doesn't explain the findings of the REM-deprivation studies, but both provide support to the hypothesis in the conclusion. Moreover, **E** inappropriately plays down the featured claim's importance in supporting the conclusion, giving the studies in sentence 3 the lion's share of credit.

Question 19: Seacliff's Houses

19. If all of Seacliff's beachfront houses are worth more than two million dollars, then Seacliff would be ranked as one of the ten most desirable localities in the nation. Every beachfront house sold in Seacliff in the past three years has sold for more than two million dollars, so Seacliff must be ranked as one of the ten most desirable localities in the nation.

    Which one of the following exhibits the same logical flaw exhibited in the argument above?

    (A) If a newspaper relies on advertising revenue to survive, then it must have a large readership to attract advertisers. The *Daily Gazette* does not have a large readership, so it will not survive.

    (B) Bowlarama earns above-average profits any month that all local members of the Southeast Bowling Association bowl at the alley. Bowlarama must have earned above-average profits this month, since all of the captains of the local Southeast Bowling Association teams bowled there this month.

    (C) The Newton Chief of Police will resign if any of the town's recent scandals is revealed to the public. The chief of police will resign next month, since a local reporter has become aware that a Newton police officer illegally searched a house without a warrant.

    (D) If Comtech Industries introduces a new digital camera this year, Comtech will receive significant publicity in business journals. Comtech has recently received significant publicity in business journals, so it must have introduced a new digital camera this year.

    (E) Some registered independents in Clarksdale will not vote for Sapienza for city council. Since all registered independents in Clarksdale will vote in the upcoming city council election, Sapienza will not be elected unanimously to the city council.

Grill the Interrogator. The phrase "exhibits the same logical flaw" is our tip-off that we're up against a Parallel Flaw question, so keep the Essential Concepts as well as classic flaws in mind as you delve into the passage.

Attack the Passage. Since there are formal logic elements present (*if/then*, *all*, *every*), we can do the math by representing the statements in algebraic form. If X (all Seacliff beach houses worth more than two million dollars), then Y (Seacliff one of ten most desirable localities). Now comes the main realization: Is the next statement equal to X? If it is, then we would simply plot out the final sentence as X, therefore Y, and the reasoning would seem airtight. But we know from the question stem that the argument is flawed, and perhaps that knowledge forced you to look more carefully into the true meaning of the second sentence. It is *not* the same as statement X from sentence 1, because it speaks not of *all* beachfront properties in Seacliff, as does sentence 1, but only those *sold in the past three years*. So in reality the argument ends like so: Z, therefore Y. Yup, we have a fancy name for that: bait and switch. That's the flaw that the correct choice will mimic. Specifically, the conclusion isn't valid because the argument switches from evidence about a whole group to evidence concerning a small subset of that group.

> A bait and switch can appear even in arguments comprising formal logic statements. Plotting out the formal logic using X's and Y's can help you spot when two things that are meant to seem identical really aren't.

Work the Choices. So we're looking for a group-to-subgroup switch, but we can employ another Parallel Reasoning strategy first to make our work even easier. Before searching for the specific flaw, we can characterize the conclusion of the original argument to help us chop any choice whose conclusion is not in the same form.

> Savvy LSAT test takers combine strategies to make their work as easy as possible. In Parallel Reasoning questions, try using the "characterize the conclusion" strategy first to narrow down the choices, and then look deeper into the choices that remain.

The conclusion in the original Seacliff argument is a statement of something that must be the case. Sounds fairly generic, but a quick scan through the choices reveals that not every argument among them follows suit. Both **A** and **E** contain conclusions concerning something that *will not happen in the future*, so neither is parallel to the original. Moreover, you may have noticed that **E** contains valid reasoning, which disqualifies it on that count as well.

TAKE AWAY

It's not unusual to come across at least one valid argument hidden among the choices in Parallel Flaw questions.

C is also future oriented, concluding that something *will* happen based on the evidence provided. Again, that may sound similar to the original, but it differs from a conclusion stating that something must currently be the case. So we're down to **B** and **D**. Now we can search for the bait and switch flaw we noticed in the original to distinguish between the final two candidates.

And there it is in **B**: Above-average profits are dependent on all local members bowling during the month, yet the evidence triggering the "must be the case" conclusion concerns only the *captains* of the local teams. Big difference, and the same kind of bait and switch that doomed the original. **B** is therefore correct. If you plotted it out algebraically, you would have found the same structure as in the original: If X (all local SBA members bowl at Bowlarama in a given month) then Y (above-average profits at Bowlarama). Z (all local SBA *captains* bowled at Bowlarama), therefore Y (above-average profits at Bowlarama).

TAKE AWAY

Don't get thrown off by a choice's sequence of statements. The order may differ from the order in the original argument while the logic matches perfectly.

Let's round things out with a look at **D**. Symbolically, it starts off fine: If X (company introduces new digital camera) then Y (company will receive significant publicity). But notice what we get next: Y (received significant publicity), therefore X (must have introduced new digital camera). There is no Z term in the equation because there's no bait and switch present. The reasoning is flawed in another familiar way: We can't simply switch the terms of an if/then statement. As you learned in the formal logic section of Chapter 1, you must both reverse and *negate* the terms of an if/then statement to form its logical equivalent. So **D** contains a flaw, but not the parallel one we seek.

Question 20: Inspiration and Genius

20. Art professor: A mundane work of art merely encapsulates in a new mode the fully formed thought of another, while an inspired work of art expresses at least some part of its creator's individuality. In addition, some inspired works of art are works of genius. However, whereas the essence of a common inspired art work is always at least partially derived from other influences, the essence of a work of genius is purely original.

If all of the art professor's statements are true, which one of the following must be false?

(A) All artists wish to express their own individuality.
(B) The essence of no mundane work of art is original.
(C) The portfolio of a single artist contains both a mundane work of art and a work of genius.
(D) The majority of artists base their work on the fully formed thoughts of others.
(E) **The essence of every inspired work of art is derivative.**

Grill the Interrogator. The direction in the question stem to find the choice that "must be false" indicates that this is a fairly strictly constructed Inference question with no leeway as to the right answer. Don't worry about Critique issues like assumptions, alternatives, and bait and switches, etc. Instead, delve into the passage looking to understand the facts so that you can recognize the choice that contradicts them.

Attack the Passage. The passage is difficult, not only because it contains formal logic elements but also because of the abstract nature of the elements under discussion. Things like *essence, inspiration, genius,* and *originality* are harder to deal with than, say, bears, lampposts, and other concrete objects. Let's take it one step at a time and try to keep it all straight. First we're told that mundane works copy the thought of others into new forms, while inspired works express some level of individuality. Then we find out that some inspired works are works of genius. Notice how "inspired works" is part of both statements, which means that we should stop to see if we can deduce anything already.

> In Inference questions, be on the lookout for repeated terms. When two statements contain the same term, see if you can combine them to form a deduction.

TAKE AWAY

The first statement regarding inspiration can be translated into "all inspired works express individuality." Since some inspired works are works of genius, we can deduce that some works expressing individuality are works of genius. Next we hear about a distinction between a common inspired work of art and a work of genius. The essence of the common kind is always partially derivative, but the essence of genius works is purely original. Now we see the concept of genius appearing in two places, so it makes sense to check those statements for a possible combination. Some inspired works are works of genius, and the essence of all works of genius is purely original. So it must be true that some inspired works (those that are works of genius) have an essence that is purely original. If that must be true, then what must be false is the opposite: that no inspired works have an essence that is purely original. Let's check the choices for something that sounds like this.

Work the Choices. And "sounds like this" turns out to be the operative phrase, since to make matters worse, while the right answer does hinge on the deduction above, it's expressed in a further paraphrased form. We're looking for "no inspired works have an essence that is purely original." **E** says the same thing, just stated in the positive since in this context "derivative" is the opposite of "purely original."

> ## TAKE AWAY
>
> Every LSAT question is worth the same amount, so if worse comes to worst you can just skip questions like this and come back to them if you have time at the end of the section. If a question is eluding you, what you *shouldn't* do is obstinately dig in to answer it at all costs, since the costs—lost time and frustration—are too high.

The wrong choices in a "must be false" question include any statement that can or must be true. Seen in that light . . .

A could be true—why not? The professor doesn't tell us what artists *wish for* but merely what characterizes certain types of art.

B: Sure, it's possible that there is no mundane work of art whose essence is original—or, stated another way, that the essence of every mundane work of art is derivative. This is possible because the passage doesn't go into the originality/derivative debate regarding mundane works.

C: Is there anything in the passage that prevents a single artist from turning out a mundane work *and* a work of genius? No; nothing indicates that the different types of art discussed are mutually exclusive, especially since the professor focuses on the various kinds of art in the world, not the specific artists who create them. So it's possible that a single artist's portfolio contains both works of junk and genius, which means **C** need not be false and therefore isn't correct.

D: The majority of art works are mundane, in other words? Sure, why not? The professor never discusses the prevalence within the art world of the different types of art he discusses, so there's no reason why **D** must be false.

> ## TAKE AWAY
>
> Even very hard questions contain some manageable wrong choices that fit into well-worn categories. Notice, for example, the presence of Unknowables in many choices here. Confidently eliminating a few choices thanks to a solid understanding of common traps improves your odds on even the toughest Logical Reasoning questions.

Question 21: A Question of Style, and so on . . .

> 21. It is stylistically permissible to append the phrase "and so on" only to a statement containing a list clearly not intended to represent an inclusive account of the situation depicted by the statement.
>
> Based on the principle above, which one of the following statements is not stylistically permissible?
>
> (A) Barre University grants scholarships for many kinds of individual student achievement, including grades, extracurricular activities, community involvement, and so on.
> (B) Gerunds are formed by adding "ing" to the end of a verb, such as changing "talk" to "talking," "run" to "running," "fight" to "fighting," and so on.
> (C) Music is employed in numerous commercial settings; for example, in movies, on TV shows, in advertisements, and so on.
> **(D) Nominees at The Third Annual Fowler Awards for best male performance in an independent feature film are Jordan Kurtiss, Stuart Kohm, Matthew Bolowitz, and so on.**
> (E) Douzaglou Tennis Academy focuses on numerous aspects of the game: serves, volleys, backhands, and so on.

Grill the Interrogator. Earlier in question 7, "The Downside of Incompetence," we saw one kind of Conforming Principle question that contains principles in the choices. The other type puts the principle in the *passage* and asks us to match it to a situation among the choices that best accords with it. These may not always be easier, but the approach is fairly straightforward: View the principle in the passage as a *rule* and then match the choices to that rule in the manner called for by the question stem. This question asks for a statement that is not stylistically permissible, so presumably that will be defined in some way. Keep your eye out for that definition.

TAKE
AWAY

Read the question stems of Principle questions carefully! You may need to find the choice that *obeys* the principle, or the one that *violates* it.

Attack the Passage. The title of this question breaks the very rule the passage propounds and should accordingly clunk against your ear. The rule is that one may only employ the phrase "and so on" to extend a list clearly intended to continue beyond the items listed. For example, according to this principle it is not okay to say "Laurie works in New York City, and so on" since there's no clear indication that Laurie works anywhere other than the Big Apple.

THE
NEW
LSAT

TAKE AWAY

When the principle is stated in the passage, it may help to work through a quick example of the rule to make sure you understand it fully before attempting to match the choices to it.

With an understanding of the principle under our belts, let's test the choices to find the one that adds an "and so on" where it shouldn't.

Work the Choices.

A: No problem here, as the list is intended to indicate the many kinds of student achievement qualifying one for scholarship eligibility. Since there may reasonably be additional forms of achievement other than the ones listed, using "and so on" is appropriate in this case.

B: The phrase "and so on" isn't out of place in **B** either, since *talking, running,* and *fighting* clearly aren't the only gerunds in the world. They're simply used as examples of the multitude of existing gerunds, so appending "and so on" to this list would be considered stylistically permissible according to the stated principle.

C also accords with the principle in the passage. While commercial settings for music include the three vehicles listed, it's reasonable to assume that this list does not include every single commercial situation where music may be used. What about video games and shopping malls and concerts and . . . well, *and so on*. Works fine, so our search continues.

D: Now why would anyone append an "and so on" to the list of nominees at an awards show? Is it clear that the list is meant to continue? No, it isn't; the list is meant to include everyone nominated for the award in question. It would be odd, for example, to hear "The nominees are Kurtiss, Kohm, Bolowitz, and, well, you get the picture . . . ," which is pretty much the impression left by the statement in **D**. According to the stated principle, "and so on" would be stylistically impermissible here. (Incidentally, our money is on Bolowitz, mainly because we just like to say . . . *Bolowitz.*)

E: Forehands, anyone? How's about conditioning? Or that pesky overhead slam? You don't need to know a lot about tennis to infer that there may be more to the game than the elements mentioned and that the list may not be intended as an inclusive account of everything taught at Douzaglou.

22. Editorialist: Some political commentators contend that campaign finance reform is necessary in order to validate future elections, since money has become a deciding factor in elections and in the absence of limitations on campaign contributions, election winners will often be the candidates that accumulate the most financial support. This erroneous contention overlooks the fact that opinion polls have clearly demonstrated that the majority of people believe that candidates of the two major parties, who have received the most campaign contributions in recent elections, have received roughly an equal number of such contributions.

Which one of the following does NOT point out a flaw in the editorialist's reasoning?

(A) It equates the number of campaign contributions with the amount of money obtained from those contributions.

(B) It restricts the electoral field in such a way that fails to address the political commentators' contention.

(C) It assumes without warrant the accuracy of public perception of campaign contributions.

(D) It allows for the possibility that even a small difference in financial contributions might still decide elections.

(E) **It presumes without justification that the absence of inequality in campaign funding will ensure the validity of future elections.**

Grill the Interrogator. We're looking for the choice that does *not* indicate a flaw in the argument? Scandalous! That means that this editorialist has committed at least four blunders in the space of two sentences, which must be some kind of world record. To say that you should approach this passage with little respect is a bit of an understatement. It's not often that everything that can go wrong *does,* so prepare to pick this passage apart. And it will be great practice too—like four Flaw questions in one.

Attack the Passage. Ironic too, isn't it, that someone peppering his argument with four flaws accuses *others* of an "erroneous contention"? Brings to mind the old adage that people living in glass houses shouldn't throw stones.

Amazingly, there's nothing particularly contentious in the first sentence. The editorialist merely describes a view of political commentators regarding campaign finance reform. It's necessary, they say, because money gives unfair advantages to those who have it, thus corrupting the political process. There's nothing off base about that idea, or the way it's presented. So all four flaws must be crammed into the final sentence, which makes the editorialist's performance even more astounding. Literally every notion in sentence 2 must have something wrong with it in order to cram so much wrong into so little space. We hear about polls, which we know aren't always accurate, and majority opinion, which we know isn't always reliable. The opinion regards two major parties, which aren't necessarily representative of the entire political process. The major parties have received an equal *number* of contributions, a subtle bait and switch from the issue in the first sentence regarding the *accumulation* of contributions, which implies the total amount received. That's a pretty good jump on the problems at hand, so let's move to the choices.

Work the Choices. Keep in mind the issues flagged above while looking for the choice that *doesn't* point to a problem with the logic.

A and **C:** Choice **A** notes the bait and switch between number and amount mentioned above. The commentators are concerned about advantages of the candidates with "the most financial support," which means in this context those with the most money. The poll, however, deals with the number of contributors, the mistake noted in **A**—and not even the *actual* number, but the *perceived* number, which exposes the flaw indicated by **C**. The conclusion the author draws against campaign finance reform requires support from real figures, not figures derived from public opinion.

B: Hey yeah . . . what about everybody else? By implying that campaign finance reform is unnecessary because the two biggies are nearly neck and neck in money, the author ignores the role money might play in disallowing others to have a fair chance to participate in the political process. The commentators aren't concerned with parity between the two major parties, but parity across the entire political spectrum. As **B** points out, by restricting his rebuttal to evidence concerning the two biggest parties, the author doesn't address the gist of the need for campaign finance reform as posed by the political commentators because it leaves open the possibility that these two, thanks to their money, will still have unfair advantages over the rest.

D exploits the editorialist's use of the word "roughly." Forgetting for a minute that he mixes up the number of contributions with the amounts derived from them (see **A**), clearly the editorialist is trying to argue that the two major parties get roughly the same amount of money, so it's wrong to say that money decides elections. But what if even that small difference allowed for by the vague use of the word "roughly" is enough to put one candidate on top? That leaves open the possibility that the commentators may still be right in asserting that whoever gets the most money wins, thereby supporting their call for reform.

E is tricky, but falls into the Does No Such Thing category and is therefore correct.

TAKE AWAY

> In NOT or EXCEPT questions, the right answer will usually contain something that normally would be considered a common trap.

The editorialist argues that campaign finance reform isn't necessary to validate future elections but doesn't extend his analysis to *other* factors that may or may not lead to valid elections. So he does not in fact presume that elections will be valid if the campaign finance issue is taken care of. His argument concerns what's *necessary* to ensure valid elections, not what's *sufficient* to guarantee valid elections.

Essential Concepts pop up in interesting places. Here the test makers use the distinction between necessary and sufficient conditions to construct an answer choice that does *not* indicate a flaw in an argument.

TAKE
AWAY

Question 23: Arlene's Class

23. Arlene must take a class this semester to satisfy her college's physical education requirement. She cannot take swimming because it meets at the same time as her upper-level physics class. One reason that she cannot take racquetball is because she has not yet taken the prerequisite course necessary for participation in that class. Arlene must therefore take canoeing this semester, the only other intermediate-level physical education class offered besides swimming and racquetball.

Which one of the following is an assumption on which the argument depends?

(A) Arlene will not be required to take another physical education class at college after completing a physical education class this semester.

(B) Students at Arlene's college are not permitted to take advanced-level classes and intermediate-level classes during the same semester.

(C) Arlene has satisfied all prerequisite courses necessary to participate in swimming.

(D) The physical education requirement cannot be satisfied by anything other than an intermediate-level physical education class.

(E) It would be possible for Arlene to take racquetball this semester if she had satisfied all of the prerequisites for that class.

Grill the Interrogator. A standard Assumption question stem alerts us to the possibility—nay, the probability!—of discovering a major gap, bait and switch, or loose end. Lock into Critique mode and keep your eyes peeled.

Attack the Passage. Ah, the many dilemmas of college life! Where to live? What parties to attend? Oh yeah—and what classes to take? That's Arlene's predicament here, accompanied by enough rules to turn this into a mini logic game. If you found yourself bogging down in the choices and limitations of each, the adjective "intermediate-level" should have been a welcome sight: a concept that comes out of nowhere that you know by the moniker loose end. Nothing was said previously about her chosen class needing to be an intermediate-level class, and since this is an Assumption question, that's exactly the kind of thing we try to scope out before hitting the choices.

Work the Choices. D gets right to the issue at hand. If you recognized "intermediate-level" as a loose end, you should have had no problem spotting the choice that ties this notion back in with the passage's evidence. The conclusion is strong and unequivocal: Arlene *must* take canoeing. Why? Well, because it's the only other intermediate-level class available beside the ones we're told she can't take. And this would make perfect sense if somewhere the author bothered to tell us that *an intermediate-level class is required*. Which he doesn't. But **D** does and therefore gets the point for filling in the hole in this argument. If you're unsure, you could always try the negate and destroy test: What if the PE requirement *can* be filled by something other than an intermediate-level class? Then, in the spirit of the old sitcom *Diff'rent Strokes*, "Whachoo talkin' 'bout, author?" would be a reasonable response to the conclusion in the final sentence, confirming **D** as the correct choice.

A hinges on an Unknowable issue: how the requirement works. Is Arlene required to take one PE class each semester? Each year? Just this year? We don't know. Nothing about what happens after this semester is required for the argument to work. Try negate and destroy: What if Arlene *is* required to take some more gym classes in the future? That doesn't affect what she must take *now*, based on what's available *now*.

B: *Advanced* classes? That's out of left field, so nothing about that is required to make the logic of this argument work. And even if they could take advanced and intermediate classes simultaneously, that wouldn't affect whether she has to take canoeing in light of the evidence provided.

C: The passage states that Arlene can't take swimming because of a scheduling conflict, which constitutes one reason why swimming is out. The argument doesn't need two reasons, so nothing about swimming prerequisites is assumed here.

E would be inferable if the phrase "One reason" at the beginning of sentence 3 read *The only reason*. It doesn't, and even if it did, we're not looking for an inference (something that must be true based on the passage's information) but rather for an assumption (something missing yet required for the argument to work).

Question 24: Currency Mutilation

24. Richie: U.S. law prohibits the fraudulent mutilation of currency in circulation. However, according to the same law it is not illegal to mutilate currency that has been legally removed from circulation. It is therefore legal to mutilate the pennies that I use to create the jewelry and belt buckles that I sell online, since I have soldered these coins together and they therefore cannot reenter the monetary system.

    Louise: That is incorrect, because your rendering the coins unavailable by incorporating them into decorative objects does not meet the condition you believe would exonerate you from a charge of illegal mutilation.

    Which one of the following most accurately describes the argumentative technique used by Louise to object to Richie's argument?

    (A) **suggesting that Richie has misapplied a key term used in his argument**
    (B) arguing that Richie has failed to demonstrate that it may in some cases be permissible to make decorative objects out of mutilated coins removed from circulation
    (C) implying that Richie has inappropriately argued that there may be instances in which currency mutilation is legal
    (D) demonstrating that Richie has failed to establish that no coins used for decorative purposes can ever reenter the monetary system
    (E) showing that Richie has fraudulently misinformed his customers as to the legality of mutilating the pennies contained in the objects they purchase from him online

Grill the Interrogator. The question is chockfull of information. First, the words *argumentative technique* alert us that this is a Method question, and a Dialogue Method question at that. In addition, we're told that Louise objects to Richie's argument, which tells us that the skills and Essential Concepts we generally employ for Critique questions may come into play.

Attack the Passage. Richie tells us that we're generally not allowed to mutilate coins but that exceptions are made for coins legally removed from circulation. He goes on to argue that it's legal to mutilate pennies for the objects he sells online because by soldering them together, there's no way they can get back into circulation. Did you see the bait and switch here? Richie plays fast and loose with the notion of legally removing coins from circulation: Just because he himself ensures the coins can't be circulated as money doesn't mean that they have been *legally* removed from the monetary system, something Louise dutiful-ly points out, albeit in a rather complicated way. If this is all there was to it, then anyone could mutilate coins and then claim that since they can't be used again, they're allowed to be mutilated! The bait and switch thus results in a neat bit of circular reasoning. Let's find the choice that best captures Louise's response.

Work the Choices. We noticed that Richie's argument hinges on a bait and switch, and **A**'s "misapplies a key term" is as good a definition of this as we're going to get. So proactively critiquing Richie's argument suggests choice **A** as a viable candidate, but we'd better match it to Louise's statement to make sure. She doesn't directly say that he's misapplied a key term but does, as **A** states, *suggest* that he has done so. She says that by merely taking the coins out of circulation himself by making them into decorative objects, Richie doesn't meet the condi-tion he himself states would ward off a charge of illegal mutilation. That condi-tion is the legal removal of the coins from circulation. Basically, Louise is saying "Who appointed *you* secretary of the treasury?" He states a circumstance under which coins may be mutilated and then fails to meet that standard himself. He has, as Louise suggests, inappropriately applied the key term "legally removed" to his own situation.

B: As far as we know Louise never doubts that it may be okay to make stuff from mutilated coins *appropriately* removed from circulation—that is, by an agency, such as the government, that has the power to do so. What she doubts is whether the coins in question can be properly deemed "removed from circulation" just be-cause *Richie* renders them unavailable by fashioning them into decorative objects.

C: Louise's issue is not that Richie asserts that currency may be legally mutilat-ed under certain circumstances. She simply doesn't believe Richie's case meets the condition he cites.

D: Louise is concerned specifically with Richie's case. She doesn't state or sug-gest that Richie is obligated to prove that no decorative coins can ever slip back into circulation. As seen above, she attacks on a different front, questioning whether it's legal for him to make his objects in the first place.

E: Richie's relationship with his customers isn't relevant to any part of Louise's argument, so **E** doesn't accurately describe her method.

When there are Flaw elements at work in a Method question, it's perfectly legitimate to use Flaw common traps such as Irrelevant, Not Obligated, or Does No Such Thing to eliminate wrong choices.

Question 25: Progress and Politics

25. A strong belief in progress during an age of technological innovation enhances citizens' feelings of nationalism, which in turn increases the public's interest in national affairs. Nineteenth-century America was characterized by large-scale technological innovation, and during the course of that century the New England region of the country experienced a marked increase in the number of candidates seeking public office. It is therefore likely that a strong belief in progress contributed to the increase in New Englanders seeking public office.

Which one the following, if true, most strengthens the argument above?

(A) Some European countries experienced rising nationalism during the technologically progressive years of the Industrial Revolution.

(B) The number of candidates for public office is positively correlated with the level of public interest in national affairs.

(C) A country's citizens tend to pay more attention to national affairs whenever nationalism in that country is high.

(D) Historical records indicate an increasing opposition to the policies of the national government among nineteenth-century New Englanders.

(E) Numerous Asian countries are characterized by a strong public interest in national affairs.

Grill the Interrogator. We get a typical Strengthen the Argument question stem, so shifting into Critique mode is in order. Be on the lookout for the usual suspects when delving into the passage: assumptions to shore up, alternatives to discount, bait and switches to overcome, and so on.

Attack the Passage. Note the general progression of causal elements in the first sentence: A strong belief in progress during a period of tech innovation leads to nationalism, which increases interest in national affairs. So far, so good.

Cause and effect is another of your Logical Reasoning Essential Concepts, so become adept at recognizing it. In general terms, causal situations are characterized by a familiar-sounding progression: "This does that, which in turn does that . . ." The test makers may use many different terms to imply cause and effect, such as *leads to*, *results in*, *causes*, *brings about*, *produces*, and *contributes to*. These all designate the same kind of causal relationship, and understanding that can help you get to the heart of even complicated situations.

Then we're given a specific example: Nineteenth-century America was one such place characterized by the tech innovation mentioned in the first sentence. Fine—still on track. Now we learn that during that period, New England saw a large increase in people seeking public office. Uh-oh, red flag! "Seeking office" is a new concept. Yeah, we know, it kind of *sounds like* "interest in national affairs"—it's not like they're bringing something totally irrelevant such as "eating lobster rolls on the French Riviera" into the picture. Nonetheless, "seeking office" is something new, and when we see in the final sentence that the author attempts to add "seeking office" into the causal chain by linking it to "belief in progress," we know we have a genuine bait and switch on our hands.

Work the Choices. We've identified the chain of causality: *belief in progress during a tech age* to *nationalism* to *public interest in national affairs* to *increases in seeking public office*. Having recognized the bait and switch from "public interest in national affairs" to "seeking office" at the end of this chain, our task in this Strengthen question is to find the choice that connects these things. **B** does this in no uncertain terms and therefore directly lends support to the argument.

TAKE AWAY

When cause and effect is in play, make sure the chain is complete and not interrupted, especially when it appears in the context of a Critique question. It may, as in this case, be interrupted by a bait and switch. If that's the case, the right answer to a Strengthen the Argument question will overcome the switch, while the right answer to a Weaken the Argument question will exploit it.

TAKE AWAY

Notice how two Essential Concepts—cause and effect and bait and switch—interact in this question. This reinforces what we stated in the Logical Reasoning chapter about the value of taking an integrated approach to this section.

A: *Other countries?*

C directly restates evidence from the passage. It does nothing to shore up the missing link between public interest in national affairs and increases in people seeking public office.

> **TAKE AWAY**
>
> Beware of choices that do nothing more than tell you what you already know! These are particularly tempting because they lead us to think "Well, it's in there somewhere . . ." That's not good enough. The right answer to a Strengthen the Argument question must go beyond the passage to help make what's in there make better sense.

D is an Opposite choice that weakens the argument by suggesting another plausible reason for the increase in New England candidates: age-old dissatisfaction with the status quo. "Throw da bums out!"—and this choice with 'em.

E: *Other countries*, again? **E** is too far afield—literally, way off in Asia—to be of any help here.

SECTION II: ANSWERS & GUIDED EXPLANATIONS

Logic Games

Game 1: Classical Concert

> <u>Questions 1–6</u>
>
> An orchestra performs exactly five compositions during the course of a classical concert. The compositions—performed in order from first to fifth—are selected from the works of six composers: Franck, Haydn, Mozart, Ravel, Smetana, and Vivaldi. The following conditions apply:
>
> If the orchestra performs a composition by Ravel, it will perform a composition by Franck immediately following the performance of a composition by Vivaldi.
>
> If the orchestra performs a composition by Mozart, it will perform compositions by Franck first and fifth.
>
> The orchestra will not perform a composition by Vivaldi unless it also performs at least one composition by Smetana.
>
> If the orchestra performs a composition by Haydn, it will perform a composition by Ravel third.

Create a Blueprint. The game starts out as a garden-variety Ordering affair, what with the five compositions "performed in order from first to fifth." However, in standard Ordering games we're told the characters we need to put in order, whereas here the compositions are "selected from the works of six composers." So first we select them, then we sequence them—which means we have a Choosing/Ordering Combination game on our hands.

TAKE
AWAY

> Make sure that you're clear on the game's action from the very beginning. Nothing gets you in deep water faster in a logic game than misinterpreting what you're asked to do. Use clues such as "in order" and "selected" to determine the game type before moving on to the rules.

No reason not to go with our traditional Ordering blueprint, with the composition numbers listed from left to right and the composers who supply the music off to the side:

F H M R S V

    1   2   3   4   5

Get the Specs.

Rule 1: We begin with a Positive Conditional rule that has a Positive Relationship aspect embedded within it, so be very careful to interpret it correctly. If R is included in the concert, then a VF cluster must appear somewhere in the concert as well: "If R, then VF."

> When the test makers use the word *immediately* in a rule, that means "right next to." If they specify "immediately *following*" or "immediately *preceding*," then you know even more.

Applying reverse and negate yields equally important information: "If NO VF, then NO R." Since this game is part Ordering and part Choosing, this latter implication can actually be broken up into several parts. It tells us that if Vivaldi is not played during the concert, OR if Franck is not played during the concert, OR even if both *are* played but aren't played back-to-back, V before F, then Ravel is out.

> Some rules come with numerous implications. Work through quick examples of what a rule means in the context of the game if you're unsure of its full meaning.

Rule 2: The next rule follows the same basic Positive Conditional form and hits on both the Choosing and Ordering aspects of the game. "If M, then F1 and F5." Reverse and negate, always applicable to if/then rules, further stipulates "If F NOT 1 or F NOT 5, then NO M." Notice that F missing from *either* spots 1 or 5 is enough to force M out of the concert.

Rule 3: Next comes a traditional "Not . . . unless" construction: "Not V unless at least one S."

> TAKE
> AWAY

> Use the rules to solidify your conception of the game. The first two if/then rules imply that not every composer must be included in the ordering, while the phrase "at least" in Rule 3 suggests that some composers may appear more than once. These are important implications, especially if you hadn't yet fully fleshed out the parameters of the game.

Unless rules are best translated into if/thens, so let's reword it: "If V, then S." Reverse and negate yields the correct implication: "If NO S, then NO V." So V needs S, but S *doesn't* need V.

Rule 4: One more Positive Conditional rule, this one combining both game actions, similar to Rule 2. If a Haydn piece is chosen for the concert, then the concert will also include a Ravel piece third: "If H, then R3." Two things can foil Haydn's inclusion, according to reverse and negate: if a Ravel composition is not played at all, or if R *is* played but not as the third piece. We can represent this in one compact phrase as "If R NOT 3, then NO H."

Search for Game Breakers. We're faced with an embarrassment of riches when it comes to places to start our search for Game Breakers, since Franck, Haydn, and Vivaldi are all mentioned in more than one rule. Rules 1 and 4 link up well to form a Standard Combination: H requires R, and R requires VF. Hey, that's four of the five already! And why not round it out with Rule 3 by adding S to the mix, since Vivaldi won't be played without at least one contribution by Smetana. So as it turns out, choosing Haydn tells us exactly who else must be selected, and even places R in spot 3 to boot:

$$\text{If H, then H R V F S, with R3}$$

> **TAKE AWAY**
>
> Remember, not all characters are created equal. "Stars" are at the center of the action and trigger a lot when activated. Expect the questions to revolve heavily around the activity of such stars. In contrast, "free agents" are much less restricted and are often used to fill in the gaps after the status of other characters has been determined.

Now, you may have taken this Haydn business even further by seeing that with R third in this circumstance, the VF cluster will have to be first and second or fourth and fifth, leaving H and S to battle it our for the remaining spots. But let's not drive ourselves crazy—no doubt we'll fire through this scenario at some point, and there's enough left up in the air that it's fine to leave it at the Game Breaker listed above.

Anything else to notice? Well, with Haydn's selection cementing the list of included composers at HRVFS, Mozart's left out in the cold. As if it's not bad enough that he burnt out, died at 37, and was buried in a pauper's grave, now Mozart gets trumped by Haydn in an LSAT logic game:

$$\text{If H, then NO M}$$

Thanks to our trusty reverse and negate technique, that also means sweet revenge for Mozart:

$$\text{If M, then NO H}$$

> **TAKE AWAY**
>
> In Choosing games, pay attention to which entities *cannot* be included in certain scenarios, since that often leads to Game Breakers or turns out to be the key to some questions.

These Standard Combination Game Breakers are bound to help us get through the questions. Speaking of which, it's time to cash in on all this good work.

Cash In.

1. Which one of the following could be a complete and accurate list of the composers of the compositions performed during the concert, from first to last?

   (A) Franck, Mozart, Vivaldi, Franck, Smetana
   (B) Haydn, Ravel, Smetana, Vivaldi, Franck
   (C) Smetana, Franck, Vivaldi, Smetana, Ravel
   (D) Smetana, Smetana, Vivaldi, Vivaldi, Franck
   (E) Vivaldi, Franck, Ravel, Haydn, Haydn

Question 1: D. If you deduced a lot up front, you were probably able to eliminate at least a few choices of this Suitability question based on those deductions. But our usual Suitability method works just as well and pretty quickly, so let's just check the rules against the choices. Rule 1 is violated by **C**, which has R accompanied by FV instead of VF. Choice **A** violates Rule 2 by including Mozart without having Franck fifth. V needs S, says Rule 3, but choice **E** begs to differ. Finally, Rule 4 is upended by choice **B**, which has the nerve of including Haydn without scheduling Ravel third. **D** remains and is correct for this typical Suitability question.

Use the Suitability question to further cement your understanding of the game. Since choice **D** is correct, it's clearly okay for a couple of composers to be represented twice and for a couple of other composers to be left out entirely. If you hadn't yet thought through such possibilities, **D** is kind enough to alert you to them. Also, remember that **D** represents an acceptable ordering, so feel free to come back and consult it later on when considering scenarios that could be true.

TAKE
AWAY

2. If the orchestra performs a composition by Haydn later than it performs a composition by Vivaldi, then which one of the following could be false?

   (A) The orchestra performs a composition by Franck earlier than it performs a composition by Ravel.
   (B) The orchestra performs a composition by Haydn later than it performs a composition by Franck.
   (C) The orchestra performs a composition by Ravel later than it performs a composition by Vivaldi.
   (D) The orchestra performs a composition by Smetana earlier than it performs a composition by Haydn.
   (E) The orchestra performs a composition by Vivaldi earlier than it performs a composition by Smetana.

Question 2: D. We're already in a position to take advantage of our main Game Breaker: the deduction that including H means including R, V, F, and S as well. So we can take the requirement that Haydn be included to mean that compositions by HRVF and S will be in the concert—all we need to do now is figure out when each is played. Rule 4 speeds us on our way by forcing R into spot 3:

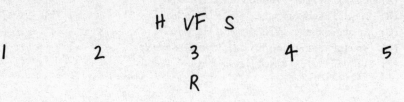

Now incorporate the other piece of new information: If H is played later than V, then the VF cluster will have to go in spots 1 and 2 respectively, leaving H and S to float between 4 and 5:

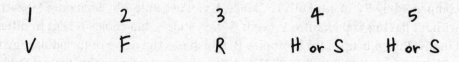

We now know as much as we're going to know, so we're ready to answer the question. We're looking for the choice that could be false. Well, the opposite of that, something that *cannot* be false, is something that must be true, so we can scan the choices for things that must be true based on the ordering above and cross them off. F is earlier than R (**A**), H is later than F (**B**), R is later than V (**C**), and V is earlier than S (**E**). Only **D** could be false since the positions for H and S in 4 and 5 aren't set in stone.

---

3. The orchestra CANNOT perform compositions from which one of the following pairs of composers during the concert?

   (A) Franck and Ravel
   (B) Haydn and Mozart
   (C) Haydn and Smetana
   (D) Mozart and Smetana
   (E) Mozart and Vivaldi

Question 3: B. This question is directly answerable from our Game Breaker, in which we deduced that Haydn and Mozart can't be included in the same concert. If you put in that work up front, then one of your rewards is this 10-second question.

If you didn't make that deduction up front, you're forced to work through the same logic now, so let's see how we might approach this strategically. We're asked for a pair of composers whose works can't both be included in the concert, and from the first two questions in the set we already have examples of concerts containing many acceptable pairs. So it behooves us to check the choices against those acceptable orderings to see if we can knock out a few choices quickly. The acceptable concert in Suitability question 1 doesn't help us, since it contains only F, S, and V, which matches none of the pairs in the choices. However, the sequence we just finished constructing in question 2 eliminates both **A** and **C** since it demonstrates that Franck and Ravel can both be included and that Haydn and Smetana can both be included as well.

> In "No Info" questions—questions that supply no new information—look back at your previous work to see if acceptable arrangements from earlier questions can help you eliminate choices. In some cases you may even wish to postpone such a question until you've worked through more scenarios against which to compare the choices.

TAKE AWAY

Only **B**, **D**, and **E** remain, and notice that they all include Mozart. That means that it must be the case—not just in this question, but throughout the game—that Mozart and some other character can't both be included in the concert. We worked this out earlier in conjunction with our Haydn Game Breaker, but let's take it from the other angle, beginning with Mozart. Since M requires F in both spots 1 and 5, that's three of the compositions already. Adding H requires also adding R, which in turn requires V and F. F is already included, but we're already over the limit with MFFHRV, and we haven't even added S to make V's presence possible. So Mozart and Haydn can never both be included in the same concert, which we deduced above when we saw that H requires a full complement of RVFS, leaving no room for M. Finally, since **B** is correct, notice this means that Mozart *could* be with Smetana (**D**) and *could* be with Vivaldi (**E**), more information to add to our growing knowledge of the game.

> If you've found a Game Breaker up front, don't be surprised when some questions fall in 10 seconds; that's as it should be, since you've essentially already done the necessary work. But if you miss Game Breakers, all is not lost since you still may discover them in the course of the questions. It may have taken you until question 3 to recognize H's influence on the game, or the incompatibility of H and M. If so, late is still better than never, and you can and should use this information for the rest of the game.

TAKE AWAY

4. If the orchestra performs a composition by Ravel, which one of the following must be true?

   (A) The orchestra performs exactly one composition by Franck.
   (B) The orchestra does not perform any compositions by Haydn.
   (C) The orchestra does not perform any compositions by Mozart.
   (D) The orchestra performs exactly one composition by Smetana.
   (E) The orchestra performs exactly two compositions by Vivaldi.

Question 4: C. The question stem asks us to throw Ravel into the mix, and the choices all speak to the issue of which composers are played and which aren't—a pure Choosing challenge.

TAKE AWAY

In Combination games, expect some questions to focus exclusively on one game action, while others focus on both. Questions 1 and 2 involved both Ordering and Choosing, but in this one we're asked only to consider the Choosing element of the game—who's in, who's out—without having to worry about their order.

So R is in, which means we need the VF cluster as well as S. That's four so far. H could be the fifth, giving us the group we discovered as our main Game Breaker. But H could be left out, opening up other possibilities. It's best to take what we know and move on to the choices.

A and **E:** We could add one more F as the final composition, giving us RVFFS, proving that neither **A** nor **E** must be true.

B: We already noted that Haydn could be included as the fifth composition. Our trusty HRVFS group proves that **B** need not be true.

C: Trying to get M in there doesn't work, since playing M means having to play at least two F's. We already have RVFS, so adding M makes RVFSM, allowing no room for M's second F required by Rule 2. So it must be true that including R means not including M, and we can pick **C** and move on.

TAKE AWAY

The right answers to Logic Games questions are objectively correct. When you find a choice that works, have the confidence to select it and move on.

D: Just for the record, RVFSS works fine to kill **D**.

Building on a strategy discussed earlier, you may have attempted to use previous work to eliminate some choices right off the bat. Since the ordering constructed for question 2 includes Ravel, you may have seen that that ordering makes it possible to eliminate choices **B** and **E** here. You should have ended up at **C** no matter what, but if you can save time in the process, all the better.

5. If the fifth composition is the only composition the orchestra performs by Vivaldi, then which one of the following must be true?

(A) The orchestra performs a composition by Franck immediately before it performs a composition by Smetana or Vivaldi.

(B) The orchestra performs a composition by Haydn earlier than it performs a composition by Vivaldi.

(C) The orchestra performs a composition by Smetana immediately before it performs a composition by Franck or Vivaldi.

(D) The orchestra performs a composition by Vivaldi immediately after it performs a composition by Franck.

(E) The orchestra performs a composition by Vivaldi immediately after it performs a composition by Smetana.

Question 5: C. Here's another question that combines both Ordering and Choosing elements, since we're told both that a Vivaldi composition is included and where in the sequence it's played. And don't blow by the word *only*! There's only one V, and it's fifth, which means we can't possibly place our VF cluster. That sets off a chain of deductions based on the results of reverse and negate discussed earlier: No possibility for VF means no R, which means no H. That leaves F, M, and S.

> **TAKE AWAY**
>
> Turn negative into positives. When you discover that certain characters cannot be included, immediately ask yourself which ones *could* or *must*.

Testing these three, we see that M is impossible as well, since M requires an F in the fifth slot, and V is there instead. That limits the possibilities for the four remaining places in the ordering to F and S. And even there we can go further by noticing that at least one S is necessary (Rule 3), while F *could* be included, but need not be. So here's what we know:

1   2   3   4   5
                    V

at least one S
F okay, but not needed

> **TAKE AWAY**
>
> Take the information you're given as far as you can. Even when the choices themselves are difficult to decipher, you have a much better chance armed with solid information derived from a valid chain of deductions.

THE NEW LSAT

We're looking for a statement that must be true based on this scenario, so let's test the choices.

A and **D:** We've determined that we don't need Franck at all. The valid ordering SSSSV eliminates **A** and **D** in one shot.

B was out as soon as we saw that H can't be included.

C must be true, regardless of whether the arrangement is SSSSV or includes any combination of F's and S's in the remaining four spots preceding V. That's because no matter what we have to get an S in there somewhere. If S is in 4, then it's immediately before V and the choice is satisfied. If S is *not* in 4, then F must be. Working backward in the same manner to spaces 3, 2, and 1, we see that somewhere an S must precede an F. Every possible scenario we concoct under these circumstances will result in a Smetana composition just before either a piece by Franck or Vivaldi.

E: As we've just seen in the discussion of correct choice **C**, F can be in spot 4 immediately preceding V, so V in 5 need not immediately follow S as long as we get at least one S into spaces 1 through 3.

---

6. If the orchestra performs the compositions of exactly two composers during the concert, how many different pairs of composers could be the pair whose works are performed?

    (A) one
    (B) two
    (C) three
    (D) four
    (E) five

Question 6: C. Start with what you already know from your work with the game to this point: Choosing H means choosing five different composers (HRVFS), and choosing R means choosing at least four (RVFS), so Haydn and Ravel can't be part of a two-composer concert. That leaves F, M, S, and V as candidates for the duo called for in the stem, so let's try out the various combinations. FM works, as long as F is at least in 1 and 5 to satisfy Rule 2. FMMMF is merely one possibility. FS works, since neither Franck nor Smetana is bogged down by any restrictions. Create any ordering you like using only these two composers and you won't violate any conditions of the game.

TAKE AWAY

Having a good sense of the game's free agents—characters relatively unrestricted in their activities—helps you to work through questions that require you to try out various possibilities.

Continuing with F's possible pairings, we see that FV is no good, since V requires S, which would bring the concert up to three composers minimum. Matching up M, we've already approved MF, so let's try MS and MV. Neither pairing is acceptable because M needs F, again bringing the composer total to three, in violation of the two-composer concert mandated by the stem. (MV is impossible also because V requires S, but you need only one valid reason to axe that pair.) The only other possible pair is SV, which is fine as evidenced by the SSSSV ordering seen in the previous question, among many other possible ways we can order S and V alone to create an acceptable concert. FM, FS, and SV are the three possible pairings for a two-composer concert, so choice **C** is correct for the final question of the set.

TAKE AWAY

Some questions are easily answered from Game Breakers or straightforward deductive work, while others require more legwork. Even after eliminating a couple of composers from consideration, we're left with no other choice but to pair up the remaining composers to see which pairs are acceptable. Don't be afraid to use your pencil to try things out when necessary; if you work systematically, you can get through it in a decent amount of time. The thing that *doesn't* work is sitting and staring at the page, afraid that you may be on the wrong track if you have to perform a few trials. The time you spend obsessing could be used to work out the possibilities and pick up the point.

Game 2: Doctor Visits

Questions 7–11

Dr. Schazzie visits six patients—Freid, Helbing, Jayar, Randall, Toot, and Yorkel—during hospital rounds one morning. He visits the patients one at a time in order from first to sixth, in accordance with the following conditions:

Dr. Schazzie visits Toot at some time before he visits Yorkel.

Dr. Schazzie visits both Helbing and Yorkel at some time before he visits Freid.

Dr. Schazzie visits Jayar immediately before or immediately after he visits Randall.

Create a Blueprint. We get six patients for six visits "in order from first to sixth," so it appears that we have an Ordering element at work again in this one. But unlike Game 1, this time Ordering is the entire story. There's no need to choose the characters to sequence, since they're already provided and the good doctor's going to hit them all—the only question is when. However, this game differs in one major respect from the Ordering games you've seen so far, so let's wait until we see the rules to determine the best way to set this up.

Get the Specs. All of the rules are in Positive Relationship form, telling us where certain characters are in relation to the others in the sequence of visits. However, since there are no hard and fast assignments of patients to visits indicated, there's more flexibility than we normally find in a standard Ordering game. We'll refer to these games as "Elastic" Ordering games because, as you'll see, the lines we use to connect the characters to each other are like elastic bands that you can mentally stretch to envision the various possible ordering scenarios. It's helpful to set these games up by positioning the characters vertically, with those earlier in the ordering above those who come later. That makes it easier to eyeball the relationships and visualize the characters occupying various slots. This will make more sense as we work through the rules and sketch out the situation, so let's do that now.

> **TAKE AWAY**
>
> Elastic Ordering games are Ordering games that focus primarily on the relationships between the characters. When you see that an Ordering game contains only Relationship rules telling you who is before and after whom in the sequence, you know you're dealing with an Elastic Ordering game that you may wish to set up vertically.

Rule 1: Toot's visit is before Yorkel's. *How much* before we don't yet know, but we can get the relationship down on the page:

Rule 2: This one provides two pieces of information, so take them one at a time. And we may as well start with Yorkel, since Yorkel's already in our sketch.

You need not wait until Step 3 of the Essential Strategy to combine rules that link up in clear ways, such as rules containing common entities. When a rule contains more than one piece of information, focus first on the part you might be able to combine with something you already know.

Yorkel is before Freid, which allows us to get Freid into our sketch, which then makes it possible to place Helbing since she too is before Freid:

Unknowables is one of our Logical Reasoning Essential Concepts, but understanding what you *don't* know comes into play here in Elastic Ordering games as well. We can deduce from our sketch already that Toot must be before Freid, but Helbing's relationship to Toot and Yorkel is thus far unknown. That's the value of the elastic bands connecting the characters—they allow us to visualize stretching H anywhere in relation to T and Y, as long as H stays above F.

Rule 3: Now comes info on J and R, and their relationship is a bit more defined. The "immediately before or immediately after" lingo locks Jayar and Randall together as a cluster, which may appear as JR or RJ in the ordering. Note, however, that no rule links either to any of the other characters, so we need to bring them into the sketch as an independent strand.

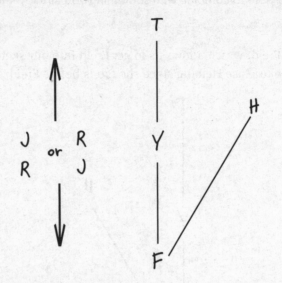

Search for Game Breakers. We've already mentioned one Game Breaker made evident by our sketch: *Toot's visit must be before Freid's,* which is a direct result of combining Rules 1 and 2. Beyond that, many orderings are possible—that's the nature of this "free-floating" type of Ordering game. Consider the Jayar/Randall cluster, for example. Those two could go before Toot, all the way in the beginning of the ordering, or way down below Freid on the back end of Schazzie's schedule. They can also end up anywhere in the middle, as long as they stay consecutive.

TAKE AWAY

In Elastic Ordering games, spend at least a few seconds mentally playing with the characters in your final sketch, stretching them into various positions before hitting the questions. Doing so will give you an idea of the possibilities and will help you avoid mistakenly assuming a character's whereabouts.

Now for the fun part—using the sketch we created to rack up points.

Cash In.

7. Which one of the following is an acceptable partial ordering of Dr. Schazzie's patient visits?

    (A) **Freid: fourth; Randall: fifth; Jayar: sixth**
    (B) Helbing: first; Freid: third; Randall: sixth
    (C) Jayar: first; Toot: second; Helbing: fourth
    (D) Toot: third; Yorkel: fourth; Freid: fifth
    (E) Toot: fourth; Yorkel: fifth; Helbing: sixth

Question 7: A. Since this Suitability question only gives us part of the ordering, we have to use what we're given to make inferences about the other slots. There's no easy way to scan the choices looking for rule violators. We have to go choice by choice, but fortunately we don't have to look far.

A: Can F be 4 while R is 5 and J is 6? Sure—that keeps J and R together as per Rule 3's mandate. But does that leave viable spots for the others? Only H, T, and Y remain, and as long as T is before Y, all is kosher in Schazzieland. **A** is therefore an acceptable partial ordering and gets the point.

B: F can never be visited third since at least three patients (H, T, and Y) come before F.

C places J and T consecutively in the first and second visits, in violation of Rule 3, which stipulates that R must be next to J in the sequence.

D: T could be visited third only if the JR cluster is visited before T while H is visited sometime later. Y could be visited next in the fourth spot. That's where **D**'s luck runs out, since with everyone officially ahead of F, Schazzie must visit F sixth, not fifth.

E: Can good old Toot be visited fourth? Actually, yeah—if J, R, and H are visited earlier. But **E** has Helbing sixth, something that can never be true since H's visit always comes before F's.

---

8.   If Dr. Schazzie visits Toot fourth, then which one of the following must be true?

    (A)   Dr. Schazzie visits Freid fifth.
    (B)   Dr. Schazzie visits Helbing third.
    (C)   Dr. Schazzie visits Jayar first.
    (D)   Dr. Schazzie visits Randall second.
    (E)   Dr. Schazzie visits Yorkel fifth.

Question 8: E. Now perhaps as soon as you saw that choice **A** works for question 7, you confidently chose it and moved on, which is as it should be. But if you were just getting your footing on this game and did make your way through all the choices, then the work you did for choice **E** in question 7 would get you on your way here. We saw in that case that the only way for T to be visited fourth was if the JR cluster and H are visited before T in spots 1 through 3. Then the only two patients left would be Y and F, who would have to take the fifth and sixth spots, respectively. Yorkel fifth is correct choice **E**.

As for the wrong choices, **A** is false because Freid must be sixth, and **B**, **C**, and **D** all could be true, but need not be because of the flexibility in arranging H, J, and R in the first three spots. For example, an ordering featuring Helbing first, Jayar second, and Randall third demonstrates that **B**, **C**, and **D** need not be true.

9. How many patients are there, any one of whom could be the third patient that Dr. Schazzie visits?

    (A) two
    (B) three
    (C) four
    (D) five
    (E) six

Question 9: D. Count 'em up is the name of the game in this one. We need to see how many patients could qualify as the third patient visited. It may seem fairly basic, but anyone who has misunderstood, for example, the flexibility inherent in the J/R cluster would certainly have trouble with much of the game, including this question. As it is, we've seen often enough—and in the previous question, in fact—how Jayar and Randall can scoot up to the top of the patient list, in either order, so there's nothing wrong with either of them being visited third if we place that cluster, first as JR and then as RJ, immediately after T or H. On the other hand, these two could come first and second, in either order, followed immediately by T or immediately by H, so both Toot and Helbing could be third as well. Not to be left out, Yorkel can join the list if Schazzie saves J and R for the middle to end of his rounds and goes with Helbing and Toot first and second, in either order, followed by Yorkel third. But we have to draw the line there, since as we've seen before, Freid must be visited fourth or later. So Schazzie can see anyone but Freid in his third visit, and **D** is correct.

10. If Dr. Schazzie visits exactly two patients before Yorkel, then which one of the following must be true?

   (A) **Dr. Schazzie visits either Jayar or Randall fifth.**
   (B) Dr. Schazzie visits Jayar at some time before he visits Freid.
   (C) Dr. Schazzie visits Jayar fourth or fifth.
   (D) Dr. Schazzie visits Randall fifth or sixth.
   (E) Dr. Schazzie visits Toot at some time before he visits Helbing.

Question 10: A. Next we get a "New Info" question, so let's follow where this new information leads. Saying that Schazzie visits exactly two patients before Yorkel is nothing more than a fancy way of saying that Yorkel's third, and if you had any doubt whether to include Yorkel in the group of patients who could be third in the previous question, a proper interpretation of this question stem should have removed that doubt.

> Make use of the clues contained in the question stems—occasionally they'll alert you to things you missed or did wrong in other questions or, conversely, will reinforce things you did right.
>
> **TAKE AWAY**

With T always visited before Y, the JR cluster must be after Y if Y is to be visited third. That's because placing the JR cluster before Y would knock Y out of the top three.

> Even when the question centers on someone else, figuring out how to place the game's clusters is often the top priority. Clusters eat up real estate in the arrangement and therefore demand your attention.
>
> **TAKE AWAY**

So J and R will be visited after Y, but to get Y into spot 3, H will have to be before Y. H or T will therefore take spots 1 and 2, in either order, while Y is third to satisfy the stem. That leaves J, R, and F in some order for visits 4, 5, and 6. Checking this understanding against the choices, we see that choice **A** must be true. Fitting the JR cluster in after Y forces F into either spaces 4 or 6, since F in 5 would split J and R in violation of Rule 3. So either J or R is fifth. All of the other choices could be true, but need not be.

11. If Dr. Schazzie visits Freid immediately before or immediately after he visits Jayar, then which one of the following must be true?

    (A) Dr. Schazzie visits Freid fourth.
    (B) Dr. Schazzie visits Freid sixth.
    (C) Dr. Schazzie visits Jayar fifth.
    (D) Dr. Schazzie visits Toot third.
    (E) Dr. Schazzie visits Yorkel third.

Question 11: C. The final question in the set requires F to be appended to one side of J, which means whichever side R isn't on. J is therefore in the middle of F and R, forming a three-visit cluster. However, we can't tell if the arrangement is FJR or RJF. Either way, though, all three of the other characters must be before F. So the FJR or RJF trio must occupy the fourth through the sixth slots. Either way J is fifth, and that's **C**. As for the others:

A, and **B:** Freid could be fourth or sixth, so both **A** and **B** could be true, but neither one must be.

D is false. The latest Toot can be visited is second, after Helbing.

E would be true if the doctor visits Helbing before Yorkel, but Helbing could be visited third while Yorkel is visited second.

TAKE AWAY

If you've done well on a game and get to a final question that seems to require a lot of work, it's okay to postpone it and return to it later if time permits. Each game consists of a mix of easy and difficult questions, so if time is a consideration you're better off seeking greener pastures elsewhere than struggling through a difficult final question of a game. Of course, if the game is going smoothly, there's no reason not to finish it off.

Game 3: Journalism Topics

Questions 12–16

Each of five journalists—Jotty, Kieran, Laughlan, Ming, and Piper—is assigned to cover at least one of the following topics for a local newspaper: finance, national affairs, and sports. Exactly two journalists will cover each topic. The following conditions must apply:

    Jotty does not cover any topic that Laughlan covers.
    If Kieran covers a topic, then Ming also covers that topic.
    Piper covers sports if and only if she also covers national affairs.

Create a Blueprint. Each element of the introduction strongly suggests Placing as the game action in this one. We have five journalists, each of whom is to cover at least one of three topics. The topics are listed, and we're told that exactly two of our five characters cover each topic. So essentially we have five characters to place into six spots, two each in finance, national affairs, and sports. So let's get our common Placing blueprint down on the page for starters:

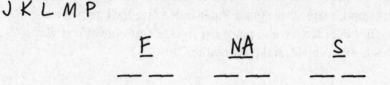

Each journalist must appear in our sketch at least once, which will take up five of the six spots. The remaining spot will have to be filled by one of the journalists taking a second turn. We therefore can deduce right from the start that exactly one journalist will cover two different topics, while the other four journalists cover a single topic.

> **TAKE AWAY**
>
> Before moving on to the rules, make sure you've taken all of the game's numerical information into account. Some games yield Game Breakers right off the bat based on the numbers provided in the introduction.

Get the Specs. Traditional Placing rules determine which characters must, can, and cannot be in which groups, and which characters must, can, and cannot be together in a group with which other characters. That's precisely what we get here:

Rule 1: Jotty and Laughlan cannot cover the same topic. NEVER JL or J ≠ L will suffice to remind us of this Negative Relationship rule.

> **TAKE AWAY**
>
> Use whatever shorthand works best for you, but try to remain consistent once you've decided how you prefer to represent each kind of rule. You don't want to burden yourself on test day with choices about how to get the info down on the page. Practice until this stage of the game is automatic.

Rule 2: Next we get a standard Positive Relationship rule. Kieran won't cover any topic unless Ming is assigned to that topic as well. But does Ming require Kieran's participation? No! Anywhere you place a K, you must place an M, but you can have an M without a K. Since the rule is in if/then format, we can and should apply reverse and negate to add to the original rule: "If K, then M. If NOT M, then NOT K."

Rule 3: This rule is probably the trickiest of the bunch, and we covered the mechanics of "if and only if" rules in Logic Games, Chapter 2. We can consider the "if" part of the rule separately from the "only if" part to derive its proper implications. "Piper covers sports *if* she also covers national affairs" means that her covering national affairs requires that she covers sports. Now consider the "only if" part: "Piper covers sports *only if* she also covers national affairs" means that her covering sports requires that she also covers national affairs. The result is that the rule works both ways. If we place Piper in NA, we have to place her in S; and if we place her in S, we have to place her in NA. One convenient way to conceptualize this is "P both NA and S, or neither."

Search for Game Breakers. Assume that you came away with the proper interpretation of Rule 3. Excellent work! But should you leave it at that? No. If you notice that a character is limited in its placement, take at least a few moments to see what happens in each case since you may be able to construct a Restricted Possibilities scenario out of that limitation. And in fact, this game is very difficult without thinking through the possibilities created by Piper's situation. If you found every question to be a tough slog, try determining now what happens in each of the Piper scenarios described above—that is, when she's in both NA and S, and when she's in neither. Take that as far as you can, and then see if what you come up with makes the questions more manageable.

Okay, here's what you might have derived as a Restricted Possibilities Game Breaker—and in this case, the moniker "Game Breaker" is well deserved, since recognizing the following options really does break the game wide open.

If we place Piper in NA and S, that means that Kieran, who needs Ming, can't be in either of those since Piper is already taking up one of the two available slots in each. So K and M must be the journalists covering finance.

Since Jotty and Laughlan need to go somewhere, they must float between national affairs and sports as Piper's companion in those. We say "float" because no further conditions determine which must be in which. All in all, then, this possibility is very well defined:

Possibility 1:

$$\underline{\text{F}} \qquad \underline{\text{NA}} \qquad \underline{\text{S}}$$
$$\text{K M} \qquad \text{P (J or L)} \qquad \text{P (J or L)}$$

The other possibility is that Piper covers neither national affairs nor sports, which means she must cover finance. That means that Kieran, who needs Ming by his side, can't cover finance and will need to pair up with Ming in either NA or S. That leaves two spots open in whichever topic the KM pair doesn't cover. Since we need to place Jotty and Laughlan somewhere, and split them up to boot, one of J and L must go with P in finance, and the other will go in the remaining group (NA or S) where the KM pair isn't. The *other* person in this re-maining group with J or L can't be either J or L; can't be P, who's only in finance in this option; and can't be K, since K needs M. So this other person can only be M. So Possibility 2 looks like this:

Possibility 2:

$$\underline{\text{F}} \qquad \underline{\text{NA}} \qquad \underline{\text{S}}$$
$$\text{P (J or L)} \qquad \text{KM or} \qquad \text{KM or}$$
$$\qquad\qquad \text{M (J or L)} \quad \text{M (J or L)}$$

Note that if the KM pair is in national affairs, then the M (J or L) pair is in sports, and vice versa. Sure, this arrangement is a bit less tidy than Possibility 1, and took a bit of work to piece together, but it yields lots of information that will help us work through the questions. And speaking of which . . .

Cash In. Nowhere is the phrase "cash in" more appropriate than when you've armed yourself with the kind of Game Breakers discussed above. If you think that the Restricted Possibilities deductive work we put in just above was too dif-ficult, annoying, or time consuming, check out how it cuts some otherwise very difficult questions down to size.

> **TAKE AWAY**
>
> Many people are averse to putting in the time to combine rules, crunch the numbers, and search for and plot out Restricted Possibilities scenarios. However, think of the time spent as time *shifted* from laboriously slogging through the questions to time spent setting yourself up for quick points. Done right, the time is not only shifted from one part of the game to another but actually *gained* in the long run, with more low-stress correct answers as a final reward.

12. Which one of the following could be an accurate matching of topics to the journalists who cover them?

   (A) finance: Jotty, Ming; national affairs: Laughlan, Piper; sports: Kieran, Piper
   (B) finance: Jotty, Piper; national affairs: Laughlan, Ming; sports: Kieran, Ming
   (C) finance: Kieran, Ming; national affairs: Jotty, Piper; sports: Ming, Piper
   (D) finance: Kieran, Ming; national affairs: Laughlan, Piper; sports: Jotty, Ming
   (E) finance: Laughlan, Piper; national affairs: Kieran, Ming; sports: Jotty, Laughlan

Question 12: B. You can employ the possibilities we charted out above, but our standard approach to Suitability questions works just as well, so let's get some more practice with that technique. Rule 1 knocks out **E**, which has Jotty and Laughlan together covering sports. Rule 2 takes care of **A**, which has Kieran without Ming covering sports. Rule 3 wipes out **D**, which has Piper in national affairs but not sports. Finally, **C** is wrong because lazy Laughlan doesn't show up for work at all in that one, and we're told up front that each journalist covers at least one topic. **B** remains and is a perfectly acceptable variation of Possibility 2 worked out on the previous page.

TAKE
AWAY

> Often the rules will knock out every choice of a Suitability question, but sometimes a choice violates a condition stated in the introduction. If you've been through all the rules and more than one choice still remains, check the intro for additional conditions you may have overlooked.

13. Which one of the following must be true?

   (A) Either Jotty or Ming covers more than one topic.
   (B) Either Kieran or Laughlan covers more than one topic.
   (C) Either Kieran or Piper covers more than one topic.
   (D) Either Laughlan or Ming covers more than one topic.
   (E) Either Ming or Piper covers more than one topic.

Question 13: E. We noticed early on that someone had to cover more than one topic for five people to fill six slots, and the possibilities we constructed show us exactly how this happens. In Possibility 1 Piper does double duty covering both national affairs and sports, while in Possibility 2 it's Ming who covers those two topics. The two possibilities also show that under no circumstances can Jotty, Kieran, or Laughlan cover more than one topic. **E** is correct.

If you missed the deductions discussed in Step 3 above, an early question like this tells you that something is up. If the wording of the choices speaks to an element that seems foreign to you, take that as a clue that there may be some aspect of the game that you've overlooked.

---

14. If Kieran does not cover finance, then which one of the following must be true?

   (A) Jotty covers sports.
   (B) Kieran covers sports.
   (C) Laughlan covers finance.
   (D) Ming covers national affairs.
   (E) Piper covers national affairs.

Question 14: D. If Kieran doesn't cover finance, then we can't be in Possibility 1, so for the sake of this question we need only consider Possibility 2.

When you've succeeded in carving out two possibilities, use the question stems of New Info questions to guide you to the possibility that's in play.

In Possibility 2, Ming covers both national affairs and sports, so **D** is correct. As for the others, **A**, **B**, and **C** could be true but need not be, while **E** must be false.

---

15. Which one of the following would make it possible to precisely determine all six assignments of journalists to the topics they cover?

   (A) Jotty and Ming cover national affairs.
   (B) Jotty and Piper cover finance.
   (C) Kieran and Ming cover finance.
   (D) Kieran and Ming cover sports.
   (E) Laughlan and Piper cover finance.

Question 15: A. Perhaps the toughest thing about this question is figuring out what it's asking. We need to find a choice that provides us with information that will shore up every journalistic assignment—that is, that will leave absolutely nothing up in the air regarding who covers what. We have no alternative but to test each choice, and luckily we don't have to look far. If Jotty and Ming cover national affairs, we're in Possibility 2 territory (since Ming covers only finance in Possibility 1). That forces our Kieran/Ming cluster into sports, leaving Piper and Laughlan to deal with finance. Everyone present and accounted for, so **A** provides the info we need to determine the precise assignments for everyone.

B and **E:** Jotty and Piper in finance is all well and good, landing us squarely in Possibility 2. This even determines that Ming will have to pair with Laughlan, but it doesn't tell us which topic those two will cover and which the Kieran/Ming team will tackle. So **B** leaves things up in the air and therefore doesn't satisfy the stem's demand for precision. Since Jotty and Laughlan are identical in terms of how they function in the game, **E** produces the same result, just substituting Laughlan for Jotty.

> **TAKE AWAY**
>
> An advanced Logic Games technique is recognizing characters that function identically in the game. Realizing that two characters are virtually identical allows you in certain cases to eliminate choices that employ them in the same way, since the correct answer can't be logically identical to any other choice in the question.

C: Kieran and Ming covering finance places us in Possibility 1, where there's variability regarding which of Jotty and Laughlan teams with Piper in national affairs and which joins her in sports.

D: Kieran and Ming in sports conjures up Possibility 2 and forces Ming into national affairs as well with either Jotty or Laughlan. However, we can't tell which will accompany her there and which will join Piper in finance.

> 16. If Laughlan does not cover any topic that Piper covers, then each of the following could be true EXCEPT:
>
>   (A) Kieran covers sports.
>   (B) Laughlan covers national affairs.
>   (C) Ming covers national affairs.
>   (D) Ming covers sports.
>   **(E) Piper covers sports.**

Question 16: E. How can we be sure of getting Laughlan away from Piper? Certainly not in Possibility 1, where Laughlan teams with Piper in either national affairs or sports, so we must once again focus our attention on Possibility 2. Keeping Laughlan and Piper apart in that option means pairing Piper with Jotty in finance, which means Ming will work with Laughlan covering one of the other two topics, with the omnipresent Kieran/Ming duo covering the remaining topic. So employing the possibilities we plotted out up front, we can quickly boil things down to:

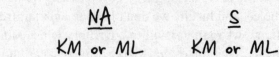

$$\underline{F} \qquad\qquad \underline{NA} \qquad\qquad \underline{S}$$
$$PJ \qquad\qquad KM\ or\ ML \qquad\qquad KM\ or\ ML$$

Now we can see that **E** has it right: Piper can't cover sports. Of course, we pretty much knew that as soon as we realized that Possibility 1 was off the table.

Here's something interesting: Even if you didn't work out the options and simply began this question by trying out choice **A**, you'd come up with an arrangement that essentially eliminates all of the wrong choices. Kieran covering sports means Ming must cover sports, which in turn means that Piper can't cover national affairs (since she'd then also need to cover sports according to Rule 3, and the KM pair is now hogging both sports spots). That would force Piper into covering finance with Jotty (thanks to the requirement in the stem), leaving Laughlan as the national affairs expert. The only journalist who could join Laughlan covering that topic is Ming. So if Kieran covers sports, **A**, **B**, **C**, and **D** must be true, leaving **E** as the choice that must be false.

> Even in difficult games, there are nifty little ways into some questions, making at least a few of them doable. Of course, you're most likely not satisfied merely with *a few doable*. You're interested in crushing the games, and the kind of deductions we worked out for this game will enable you to do just that.

TAKE AWAY

Game 4: Tae Kwon Do Demonstrations

Questions 17–22

On a Saturday afternoon, Master Prensabi's students perform exactly five Tae Kwon Do demonstrations. Each student performs as a member of exactly one of three teams: Team Green Belt, Team Red Belt, or Team Yellow Belt. Exactly one team performs each demonstration, and no two demonstrations are performed at the same time. One team has eight students, another has ten students, and the other has sixteen students. Each team performs at least once, and the composition of each team remains constant throughout the course of the demonstrations. The teams perform in accordance with the following conditions:

Sixteen students perform the third demonstration.

The same number of students performs the fourth and fifth demonstrations.

Team Red Belt performs more demonstrations than Team Yellow Belt.

Team Yellow Belt has more students than Team Red Belt.

Create a Blueprint. Prensabi . . . *Master* Prensabi. This guy needs a cameo in a James Bond film. The Master is in, and so are his students, hard at work performing a series of Tae Kwon Do demonstrations. What kind of game are we up against here? Well, consider the elements: We've got Prensabi himself, who unceremoniously drops out of sight after lending his fairly impressive name to the proceedings, so he's no factor. But we do have three different variables in play: the five demonstrations, the three teams of students (Green, Red, and Yellow), and the number of students making up each team (8, 10, and 16). This is therefore a Linking game, and our job is to match up these three variables to determine which teams, comprising how many students, perform each demonstration. We can abbreviate the teams as G, R, and Y and use a table to help us organize the match-ups:

demo	1	2	3	4	5
team (G / R / Y)					
# (8 / 10 / 16)					

There are a few additional things to notice from the setup. First, each team performs at least once, which means we can't leave out G, R, or Y entirely. In addition, at least one of the teams will have to perform more than once to fill all five demonstrations. We'll have to wait for the rules to see if this number breakdown gets any better defined.

Notice also that we don't know as of yet whether Ordering will come into play—we'll have to wait to see whether the rules contain any "before" and "after" specifications. If so, then this will be a Combination game. If not, then pure Linking will be our task.

TAKE AWAY

Get as much information as you can from the game's setup, but realize that you may have to wait until Step 2 to nail down certain particulars.

Finally, we're told that "the composition of each team remains constant throughout the course of the demonstrations." That's what's known as a "loophole closer"—something that eliminates a possible ambiguity that might disrupt the workings of the game. Here, the game doesn't work if students on one team perform a demonstration and then transfer to a different team to perform another. We're to understand that for the sake of any single question, the number of people per team remains constant. For example, if Team Green Belt has ten students in one demonstration, it will also have ten students if it performs another demonstration. This, of course, can and will change from question to question as the test makers concoct new scenarios to quiz you on. But within any single question, the number of students composing each team remains fixed.

Get the Specs.

Rule 1: A Direct Positive rule is always a welcome sight because we can drop that information right into our blueprint. Here, that means writing "16" into demo 3's column.

Rule 2: If the same number of students performs demos 4 and 5, and the composition of the teams remains constant, then *the same team* must perform demos 4 and 5.

> **TAKE AWAY**
>
> While we normally wait until Step 3 to combine the rules to scope out major Game Breakers, it's still important to derive as much information as you can from each individual rule. Determine not only what a rule *says*, but what it *means*.

Rule 3: As per the advice just above, you might stop at this point to figure out exactly how there can be more performances by Team Red than by Team Yellow, and it's fine to think through this issue at this point if the inspiration strikes. But since this is a number issue that will have a large impact on the game, we'll save it for our Game Breakers discussion, coming up right after a quick peek at Rule 4.

Rule 4: This one has the same kind of numerical feel to it as Rule 3, but it concerns a different issue—the number of students per team. And it's a bit challenging to keep it straight, since it involves the same two teams as the previous rule, this time with Yellow coming out on top of Red. It may not make for the most elegant shorthand, but "Y more students than R" may be the best way to note this rule and distinguish it from Rule 3.

> **TAKE AWAY**
>
> Shorthand pays off only when it correctly represents the game's information in simplified form. If your shorthand has to be a little less short to convey the right information, so be it. That is, don't sacrifice accuracy for brevity. You may even occasionally come across a rule that is so complicated that there's no way to simplify it without losing track of its meaning. In those cases, simply circle the rule on the page to remind yourself of its existence.

Now that we've completed our analysis of the rules, notice that there is in fact no Ordering element in this game. Sure, the demonstrations are labeled 1 through 5, but no typical Ordering issues arise, such as which teams perform before or after which other teams, and so on. The demonstrations could just as easily have been named after animals they imitate—the tiger demonstration, the dragon demonstration, and so on. So pure Linking is the name of the game.

Search for Game Breakers. This game presents an excellent opportunity to practice your Number Crunching skills. The five demonstrations must include more R's than Y's. That means that there can't be one R, since the setup tells us that each team performs at least once, meaning there must be at least one Y. With only one R in the mix, there would be no way to satisfy Rule 3 and have more Red performances than Yellow ones. Did you think through the other possible numerical scenarios? There can be two R's and one Y, leaving two G's. Or, there can be three R's, one Y, and one G. Those are the only two possible breakdowns of teams performing the demonstrations. In both cases, *there can be only one performance by Team Yellow*, which is a fairly important Game Breaker. This realization is important unto itself but can also be further combined with Rule 2.

Since there's only one Y performance, and demos 4 and 5 must be performed by the same team, neither demonstration 4 nor 5 can be performed by Team Yellow. That means that *demonstrations 4 and 5 are either both performed by Team Green or both performed by Team Red.*

It's perfectly permissible at this point to pursue a Restricted Possibilities scenario based on this new knowledge, plotting out what happens when Team Green Belt performs demos 4 and 5 and what happens when Team Red Belt does so. If you did that and it simplified the questions, great. Since we demonstrated the Restricted Possibilities strategy in our discussion of the previous game, here we're going to bang out one more Game Breaker and then use all of these deductions to blow through the questions.

This final Game Breaker comes from a combination of Rules 1 and 4. Team Yellow Belt has more students than Team Red Belt, which means Yellow cannot have the minimum number of students, 8. *Team Yellow must therefore have 10 or 16 students.* Conversely, team Red cannot have the maximum number of students and still have fewer students than Team Yellow. *So Team Red can't have 16 students* (hello, Rule 1 . . .) *and must have either 8 or 10.* Since demo 3 has 16 students according to Rule 1, that demo can't be performed by Team Red. That in turn means that *demonstration 3 must be performed by Team Green or Team Yellow.*

That's a lot to go on! It may have taken you a little while to come up with these Game Breakers (or Restricted Possibilities scenario if you went that route). But if you did this work up front, you should have found the questions very manageable with all of the following information at your fingertips:

demo	1	2	3	4	5
team (G / R / Y)			G or Y	GG or RR	
# (8 / 10 / 16)			16		

2R / 1Y / 2G

or

3R / 1Y / 1G

* only 1 Y *

Y more students than R

Y = 10 or 16

R = 8 or 10

Cash In.

17. Which one of the following could be a complete and accurate list of teams performing the demonstrations, in order from first to fifth?

    (A) **Team Green Belt, Team Yellow Belt, Team Green Belt, Team Red Belt, Team Red Belt**

    (B) Team Red Belt, Team Green Belt, Team Yellow Belt, Team Green Belt, Team Red Belt

    (C) Team Red Belt, Team Yellow Belt, Team Yellow Belt, Team Red Belt, Team Red Belt

    (D) Team Yellow Belt, Team Red Belt, Team Red Belt, Team Green Belt, Team Green Belt

    (E) Team Yellow Belt, Team Yellow Belt, Team Green Belt, Team Red Belt, Team Red Belt

Question 17: A. Since we've determined so much up front, let's check the choices against our full conception of the game. We saw from the possible numerical breakdowns that there can be only one Yellow demo (an implication of Rule 3), so **C** and **E** are out. We also saw that Team Red can't perform demo 3, since that demo is performed by a team with 16 students and Red can't have 16 students without violating Rule 4. That eliminates **D**. Choice **B** violates Rule 2, since two different teams performing demos 4 and 5 can't have the same number of students. **A** remains and is correct for this Suitability question.

18. Team Red Belt CANNOT perform which one of the following demonstrations?

    (A) first
    (B) second
    (C) third
    (D) fourth
    (E) fifth

Question 18: C. Right out of our Game Breakers—Red can't be third. Boom. (If you're just tuning in and wondering how we knew that, look back at the Game Breakers discussion or at the explanation for the previous question.)

TAKE AWAY

Don't second guess yourself and assume you've made a mistake if a question seems too easy. If you've done all the right work up front, why shouldn't you reap the rewards now?

If you didn't figure out Red's deal up front, you're forced to do it now. That's not optimal, but okay. The question will take longer, but at least when you come out of it, you'll know something new that you can apply to the rest of the game.

19. If Team Yellow Belt performs the first demonstration, then which one of the following must be true?

   (A)   Team Green Belt has ten students.
   (B)   Team Green Belt performs the second demonstration.
   (C)   Team Red Belt has ten students.
   (D)   Team Red Belt performs the fourth demonstration.
   (E)   Team Yellow Belt has sixteen students.

Question 19: D. Combine the new information with our Game Breakers to get the ball rolling. We're told that Yellow performs demo 1, and since we've deduced that Yellow performs only once, and that demo 3 must be performed by Green or Yellow, we can go right ahead and put a G for demo 3. We also deduced that 4 and 5 must be GG or RR, but GG doesn't work since that will give us three G's, an impossibility since that wouldn't allow more R's than Y's. So demos 4 and 5 must be performed by Team Red. You can stop right there and scan the choices to see if any match what we've just determined, and indeed, there it is in correct choice **D**.

For the sake of practice and discussing the wrong choices, let's see if we can also link the demos to the number of students performing them. Since Team Green performs demo 3, Green must have 16 students, leaving 10 and 8 for Teams Yellow and Red. Rule 4 takes care of this ambiguity: Yellow must have more students than Red, so it's 10 for Yellow in demo 1 and 8 for Red in demos 4 and 5. That essentially wraps up everything except for demo 2, which can be performed by either Team Red or Team Green:

demo	1	2	3	4	5
team (G / R / Y)	Y	R or G	G	R	R
# (8 / 10 / 16)	10	8 or 16	16	8	8

We can now see that **A**, **C**, and **E** must be false, while **B** merely could be true.

20. Which one of the following CANNOT be true?

   (A) Ten students perform the first demonstration.
   (B) Sixteen students perform the second demonstration.
   (C) Eight students perform the fourth demonstration.
   (D) Ten students perform the fourth demonstration.
   (E) Sixteen students perform the fifth demonstration.

Question 20: E. This No Info question gives us, as the name implies, no new information to work with, so let's proceed right to the choices to find the one that cannot be true. First we can eliminate any choice describing something we've already seen as an example in the acceptable arrangement from the Suitability question or some other matchup we've constructed in any of the previous questions. It turns out that the Suitability question is of no help, since it links teams to demos, while the choices in this question center on the number of students performing various demonstrations. But the arrangement we constructed for question 19 proves that **A** and **C** are possible, because in that one we saw a 10-student Team Yellow performing first and an 8-student Team Red performing fourth. We saw in that same question that the second demonstration could be performed by a 16-student Team Green, so **B** is possible too and therefore not the answer we seek.

For No Info questions, try to use previous work, when available, to eliminate wrong answer choices. If the question asks for something that *cannot* be true, look for previous cases that prove that certain scenarios among the choices are possible. When asked for something that *must* be true, look for cases that demonstrate exceptions.

TAKE AWAY

Having used a shortcut to eliminate three of the choices, we're down to **D** and **E** and have no choice but to test them out. You may have, however, employed some extreme cleverness by trying **E** first. Why? Because as a game element, the number 16 is more restricted than the number 10 since Rule 1 deals with the team of 16 students while no restrictions are placed on the 10-student team. Since the question is looking for something that cannot be true, the more restrictions, the better.

TAKE AWAY

When you have to test out choices, sometimes one will stand out as a better candidate than the others, and nothing says you have to test them in the order presented. When looking for something that could be true, gravitate toward free agents and less restricted characters or game elements. When looking for something that cannot be true, gravitate toward more restricted characters and game elements.

Either way, it doesn't take long to test the choices. Whenever you considered **E**, you'd see that having a 16-student team performing fifth means the same team of 16 students must also perform fourth (Rule 2) and, as always, third (Rule 1). But the only team that can perform three times is Team Red, which happens to be the one team that *can't* have 16 students, as we deduced earlier. So **E** is impossible, and correct. As for **D**, there are many ways for a 10-student team to perform fourth, and if you tried to create one, it shouldn't have taken long to prove to yourself that **D** could be true. If you tested out **E** first, however, you would have saved yourself the trouble.

---

21.   Which one of the following could be true?

(A)   Team Green Belt performs the first and fourth demonstrations.
(B)   Team Red Belt performs the first and fifth demonstrations.
(C)   Team Red Belt performs fewer than two demonstrations.
(D)   Team Yellow Belt performs the fourth demonstration.
(E)   Team Yellow Belt performs the fifth demonstration.

Question 21: B. Here we get another No Info question, this one looking for something that could be true. That means that the wrong answers all contain statements that *cannot* be true, so to test the choices we simply have to try to make them work.

TAKE
AWAY

> Knowing *how* to test the choices is sometimes half the battle. Make sure you have a good grasp of what constitutes right and wrong answers for each of the typical Logic Games question types. For example, in a "could be true" question, four of the choices must be false and thus will cause violations, while only the correct choice will be possible.

A: Green performing first and fourth means we have to tack on fifth as well to Green's workload, thanks to Rule 2. That gives us three Green performances, which we saw from our Number Crunching Game Breaker can't be because it would then be impossible for there to be more Red demos than Yellow ones. **A** doesn't work and is therefore incorrect.

B: Nothing wrong with this one. If you followed our earlier advice and looked for a previous case of this scenario, you might have found that in question 19, Red could be second, fourth and fifth. Given that there's no difference between the first and the second positions, it must also be possible for Red to be first, fourth, and fifth. If you didn't see that, it still only takes but a few seconds to confirm **B** as possible. Here's one arrangement that works:

demo	1	2	3	4	5
team (G / R / Y)	R	G	Y	R	R
# (8 / 10 / 16)	10	8	16	10	10

As long we throw Red into demo 4 to complement its appearance in demo 5, we're in good shape. You may have switched Green and Yellow in 2 and 3, and had the numbers different—it doesn't really matter as long as you come up with one acceptable arrangement in which Team Red performs first and fifth. **B** could be true and is therefore correct. As for the others:

C has been understood as a no-no ever since we crunched the numbers to form the numerical breakdowns in the Game Breaker stage. There we saw that Team Red must perform either two or three times, stemming from Rule 3 that requires more Red demos than Yellow demos.

D and **E:** We also already know from our work up front that Team Yellow can't perform demo 4 or 5, based on the same Number Crunching Game Breaker discussed in the previous choice. Since there must be more Red performances than Yellow, we deduced there can only be one Yellow performance. But 4 and 5 must be identical, so if Team Yellow performed fourth, it would have to perform fifth, and vice versa, which can't be. So 4 and 5 must be GG or RR. All of which is indicated clearly in our fleshed-out blueprint, allowing us to scrap **D** and **E** even faster than it takes to read this explanation.

> **TAKE AWAY**
>
> Our Game Breakers did all the work for us in **D** and **E,** but there is an effective strategy mentioned earlier and worth reinforcing now that's highlighted by these two choices. Notice that choices **D** and **E** are virtually identical since they both deal with Team Yellow and there's no functional difference between demonstrations 4 and 5. Sure, these two demos must be performed by the same team, with the same number of students, but that only further identifies them as equals. Now, it goes without saying that a right answer cannot be logically identical to a wrong answer. So here's another strategy to add to your growing Logic Games arsenal: When two choices are functionally interchangeable, cross them both off with confidence.

22. If Team Green Belt performs the fourth demonstration, then which one of the following must be true?

    (A) Team Green Belt performs exactly one demonstration.
    (B) Team Green Belt has ten students.
    (C) Exactly one demonstration is performed by the team with eight students.
    (D) Exactly two demonstrations are performed by the team with ten students.
    (E) Eight students perform the fifth demonstration.

Question 22: D. Once again we're presented with new information, and since this is the final question in the set, it makes sense to quickly check to see if we've come across this scenario before. Alas, no, but as mentioned above, it pays to try in order to develop good habits for test day. No matter—we have enough information under our belts (so to speak) to quickly take the new information as far as we can. Let's try it in "real time" as if we were sitting for the test, employing our Game Breakers and general knowledge of the game as we would under true testing conditions. That would go a little something like this:

Green fourth means Green fifth, so Green's done, so Yellow must be third, which means Red must be first and second. Yellow in 3 means Yellow has 16 students, but now we can't tell which of Red and Green has 8 and which has 10:

demo	1	2	3	4	5
team (G / R / Y)	R	R	Y	G	G
# (8 / 10 / 16)	8 or 10	8 or 10	16	8 or 10	8 or 10

Which MUST be true . . .? Okay:

A: *Green exactly one demo? Nope.*

B: *Green has 10 students? Not necessarily; could be 8.*

C: *Exactly one demo by the 8-student team? Nope—must be two, no matter whether Red or Green is the team with 8.*

D: *Exactly two demos by the 10-student team? Yup—no matter whether Red or Green is the team with 10.*

E: *Not even checking—D is perfect, so I'll go with that.*

Done—one minute, tops. Let's exit "real time" mode and lock down **E** for the sake of finality. **E** could be true, but need not be since Team Green performing demo 5 could have 10 students instead of 8. But remember:

TAKE AWAY

Correct Logic Games answers are *objectively correct,* which means there is no wiggle room. If you've found the right answer by doing the right work, have the confidence to mark that choice and move on to the next question, the next game, or previous questions anywhere in the section if you've come to the end of the fourth game with time to spare.

SECTION III: ANSWERS & GUIDED EXPLANATIONS

Logical Reasoning

Question 1: Extra-dimensional Existence

1. Only a small subgroup of all philosophers believes that humankind primarily exists in a dimension other than time and space, while the majority of people cannot conceptualize existing otherwise. Philosophers constitute a very small percentage of the population. If the subgroup of philosophers is correct, it follows that even a smaller percentage of humans than the percentage represented by philosophers primarily exists in a dimension other than time and space.

    The argument above relies on which one of the following questionable techniques?

    (A) **It considers a theory that would be universal if true as applying only to those who propound it.**

    (B) It fails to explain how it is possible to primarily exist in a dimension other than time and space.

    (C) It trades off an ambiguous meaning with respect to the concept of existence.

    (D) It links, without justification, the views of the majority of philosophers with the views of the majority of the population.

    (E) It draws a conclusion regarding the number of people existing in a particular form from statistical data concerning percentages.

Grill the Interrogator. "Questionable technique" lands us squarely in Flaw territory, so keep your eyes peeled for Essential Concepts and classic flaws.

Attack the Passage. This one just sounds kinds of fishy, no? The passage begins with a belief about humankind but ends with a conclusion regarding the state of only a small portion of humankind. Some philosophers believe that humankind—meaning *all* humans—exists in a dimension other than time and space. Philosophers as a group constitute a very small percentage of the population, and only some of them hold this belief in extra-dimensional existence, for lack of a better term. It would therefore be reasonable to conclude that only a very small percentage of humans hold this belief. Instead, the author concludes that only a very small percentage of the population *experience extra-dimensional existence!* No—either humans exist this way or they don't, so the mistake is shifting from the relative percentage of people *holding the belief* to the relative percentage of people *exhibiting the condition described by the belief.* Looks like we have a bait and switch on our hands, so that's the main thing to keep in mind as you head to the choices.

Work the Choices. A uses some nifty language to capture the essence of the bait and switch described above. If the belief is correct, then the phenomenon it describes must be universal. That is, it must pertain to all of humankind and not just to the small group of people who believe it. **A** is correct.

B: The passage sure does fail to explain the mechanics of this extra-dimensional existence, and it hardly seems possible that such an explanation would fit into even the longest Logical Reasoning passage. Which is to say that the author of this passage is Not Obligated to explain how the thing works in order to make the claim regarding the relative percentage of people it affects. The problem here is not how it works, but *who* it works on.

C: Equivocation? NOT! **C** describes one of our "oldie but goodie" classic flaws—using a word ambiguously to subtly shape the logic of an argument—but that's not happening here. The use of the words *exist* and *existing* remains consistent throughout.

 TAKE AWAY — A classic flaw may appear as the answer to a question or as a tricky distraction in a wrong choice. Just because you recognize a flaw described in an answer choice doesn't mean that it's necessarily the flaw exhibited in the passage.

D: Nuh-uh!—or however this universal reproach is spelled. The fancy term we give to this common trap is Does No Such Thing, which is as self-explanatory as it gets. **D** accuses the author of inappropriately linking the views of the philosophers with the views of the majority, which she simply doesn't do. In fact, we're told that the majority by and large have no idea what the philosophers are even talking about, so there's no meeting of the minds here, inappropriate or otherwise.

E: Nuh-uh!, Part II. Choice **E** appears to be fishing around for the classic mistake of confusing numbers and percentages, but that's not the problem here. The author is consistent and correct in saying that philosophers constitute a very small percentage of total humans, and that a small subgroup of those philosophers must constitute an even smaller percentage of humankind. The problem is the trait she ascribes to the latter group.

 TAKE AWAY — Even if you have difficulty understanding the answer to a Flaw question, you should be able to narrow the choices down by paying careful attention to this question type's common traps.

Question 2: Rothbard's Jewels

> 2. Every jewel displayed in the primary display case of Rothbard's jewelry store has been recently appraised. A diamond, a ruby, and an emerald are displayed in Rothbard's primary display case. None of Rothbard's jewels that has been recently appraised is on sale.
>
> If the statements above are true, which one of the following must also be true on the basis of them?
>
> (A) No jewel in Rothbard's store besides the ones displayed in the primary display case has been recently appraised.
>
> (B) Rothbard will not put any jewel on sale that has been recently appraised.
>
> **(C) Neither the ruby nor the emerald displayed in Rothbard's primary display case is on sale.**
>
> (D) The diamond, ruby, and emerald are not the only jewels displayed in Rothbard's primary display case.
>
> (E) Only jewels that are on sale are displayed in Rothbard's primary display case.

Grill the Interrogator. The question stem tells us to find a statement that must be true based on the statements in the passage, so Inference is the question type, which absolves us from tasks such as Critiquing and Matching. Prepare to piece together the facts to find another fact that can be derived from them.

Attack the Passage. The words *every* and *none* are pretty good clues that formal logic is present in this short stimulus. The first statement can be translated into if/then form: "If a jewel is displayed in the primary display case of Rothbard's jewelry store, then it has been recently appraised." We can perform reverse and negate to form another statement that means the same thing: "If a jewel has NOT been recently appraised, then it is NOT in the primary display case of Rothbard's jewelry store."

TAKE AWAY

Think through the implications of each formal logic statement you encounter. For example, when you see an if/then statement or any statement that can be translated into an if/then statement (usually via the word *all*, *every*, or *whenever*), reversing and negating the terms to form its logical equivalent should be second nature. This of course comes in plenty handy in Logic Games as well.

Even without the result of this reverse and negate, we can combine the first sentence with the second to conclude that the diamond, ruby, and emerald have been recently appraised, which in turn links up perfectly with sentence 3: Jewels that have been recently appraised are not on sale, which means that the diamond, ruby, and emerald are not on sale. That's a lot to go on, so let's see what the choices have to offer.

Work the Choices. C hits the nail on the head—or at least two-thirds of the nail. It leaves out the diamond, but that doesn't matter. We combined all three sentences to deduce that the diamond, emerald, and ruby in Rothbard's primary display case must not be on sale, so it's perfectly correct to say that neither the ruby nor the emerald is on sale. If the choice said that the ruby and emerald are the *only* jewels of Rothbard's not on sale, that would be incorrect, as the diamond is not on sale either. But as written, **C** must be true and is therefore correct.

A need not be true since nothing prohibits other jewels outside the case from being recently appraised. If we change "every" to "only" in sentence 1, then **A** would have some legs, but as written, it's not inferable.

B is incorrect because the passage merely speaks to the current status of the re-cently appraised jewels: not on sale. That's not enough to infer any hard and fast policy on the part of Rothbard regarding which jewels to put on sale. We know that no jewel of Rothbard's that has been recently appraised is on sale. *Why that is,* we just don't know.

D: No information is given as to the full contents of the primary display case. Are the three jewels mentioned in the passage the only ones in there? No way to tell.

TAKE AWAY

Unknowables is one of our Logical Reasoning Essential Concepts because of how often the test makers test your ability to recognize what you *can't* possibly determine from a set of facts. This happens particularly often in Inference questions.

E is an Opposite choice that contradicts our deduction that the diamond, ruby, and emerald in the primary display case are not on sale.

Question 3: Freudian Research

3. Psychology professor: All of the funding for research provided to the Graduate Department of Psychology in the upcoming fiscal year will come from psychoanalytic foundations. Since all of these foundations favor a Freudian orientation, it is unlikely that anything other than a Freudian interpretation of psychoanalytic issues will be reflected in the research generated by the department in the coming year.

   Which one of the following, if true, most strengthens the psychology professor's argument?

   (A) Researchers are more likely to make significant discoveries if they are funded by sponsors who share their orientation.
   (B) Researchers generally gear their investigations to accord with the underlying orientation of their sponsors.
   (C) Foundations in fields other than psychology sponsor research for one fiscal year at a time to evaluate the results before committing more money to a given project.
   (D) Psychology researchers tend to be fiercely independent and aggressive defenders of their findings.
   (E) Roughly as many psychoanalytic foundations maintain a Freudian orientation as those that do not.

Grill the Interrogator. The question stem tells us we're to find a choice that best supports a professor's conclusion, so we'll keep our eyes out for the usual ways arguments can be improved: discounting plausible alternatives, shoring up assumptions, and so on.

Attack the Passage. The argument isn't too hard to follow, as a scan of the passage quickly reveals: Because money for a psych department is coming from institutions with a Freudian orientation, the research generated by that department will be Freudian in nature. You should've noticed the bait and switch between money and orientation, since no evidence is provided as to why people supported by foundations must in their research mirror the foundations' views. A viable alternative is that they'll simply take the money and still conduct their research as they see fit.

Work the Choices. Choice **B** helps the argument by damaging the plausible alternative raised just above. It does so by pointing out that researchers generally *do* gear their research to accord with the orientation of their sponsors. With that fact in place, it's easier to believe that the department in question will in fact turn out research with a Freudian bent based on evidence that Freud's in favor at the sponsoring foundations.

> When a plausible alternative exists in a Strengthen the Argument question, look for the choice that addresses and discounts that alternative.

TAKE
AWAY

A: The *significance* of the discoveries is Irrelevant to the issue of what orientation will be followed.

C: How foundations in fields *other* than psychology function is Irrelevant to an argument dealing with the effects of funding for psychology research.

D: *Au contraire* as they say in France—or Opposite as we put it in English. Fierce independence on the part of researchers weakens the notion that the orientation of the research will mirror that of those paying for it.

E brings up another Irrelevant issue. All of the sponsoring psychoanalytic foundations are followers of Freud. The percentage of such foundations that are *not* fans of the good doctor from Vienna is beside the point.

Question 4: Info Trek's Doomed Quest

4. Info Trek, a large and successful traditional media company, will never satisfy the prerequisites for success in its new media venture since the necessary resources, inspiration, and good fortune required for success in that industry are not attainable by the company in its quest to thrive in the new media environment.

Which one of the following most accurately describes a flaw in the reasoning above?

(A) **It employs evidence identical to that which it seeks to establish.**

(B) It employs evidence that leads to a conclusion opposite of the one it seeks to establish.

(C) It assumes without justification that established media companies may wish to launch new media ventures.

(D) It relies upon a nonrepresentative sample of successful companies.

(E) It confuses factors that are necessary for success in a new media venture with those that would guarantee success in such a venture.

Grill the Interrogator. This one begins with your garden variety Flaw question stem, so be on the lookout for the classics, as well as the usual Essential Concepts.

Attack the Passage. It's short, but we already know that somewhere in this single sentence lies a fatal flaw. Perhaps if we reword the statement the problem will become evident. See if you can spot the flaw in this version of the story: "Info Trek will never achieve what's needed for success in its new media venture because it cannot get the things needed for the success of its new media venture." Mick Jagger taught that while you can't always get what you want, sometimes you get what you need. This author teaches that a company can't get what it needs because it can't get what it needs. If you said "I'll take circular reasoning for 100, Alex," you win!

TAKE AWAY

Always strive to cut past fancy wording in order to get down to the passage's essence. What sounds like fairly impressive logic may boil down to nonsense, especially in Critique questions that specifically test your nonsense detection abilities.

Work the Choices. Choice **A** presents the definition of circular reasoning: employing evidence identical to the conclusion. As we saw above, this classic flaw is precisely the problem here.

B: The only thing opposite here is this choice, which states the opposite of correct choice **A**. As we've seen, the conclusion is *identical to*, not *the opposite of*, the evidence presented.

C: The argument doesn't assume that established media companies may wish to launch new media ventures; it reports on one such specific company that has already decided to do so, so no such unjustified assumption is implicit in the argument.

D: There is no sample here to label "nonrepresentative" since the passage is about a single company, Info Trek.

E: Yes, there is an element of necessity here, as the passage speaks of factors required for success. But there's nothing about *guaranteed* success—in fact, quite the opposite. Necessity versus sufficiency is therefore not at the root of the problem.

> The test makers use Logical Reasoning Essential Concepts for more than just right answers; they also throw them into wrong choices to see who will choose them simply because of their familiarity. Just because a choice speaks to an Essential Concept doesn't mean that choice must be correct—it could be a trap.

TAKE AWAY

Question 5: Social Responsibility Indicator

5. A Citizens Action Committee of a small metropolitan area has created a Social Responsibility Indicator (SRI) to judge whether corporations in that area operate in accordance with the needs of the community. While tangible components of the indicator such as the faithful execution of pension plans and adherence to environmental regulations accurately reflect corporations' level of social responsibility, SRI ratings are also influenced by intangible factors such as the perception of a corporation's good will. Therefore, a corporation with a high SRI rating may not in fact be socially responsible.

The argument above relies on which one of the following assumptions?

(A) Corporations with low SRI ratings exhibit little good will.
(B) Perception of a corporation's good will does not always reflect that corporation's level of social responsibility.
(C) Good will is a larger component of SRI ratings than is adherence to environmental regulations.
(D) Good will is the only intangible factor associated with a corporation's success.
(E) SRI ratings can never accurately reflect a corporation's level of social responsibility.

Grill the Interrogator. We're presented with a standard Assumption question stem, so gear up for spotting the gap between the argument's evidence and conclusion.

Attack the Passage. Not a bad idea, this Social Responsibility Indicator. While tangible components play into the indicator—things you can measure like environmental friendliness—intangible things such as the public's perception of good will play into it as well. The author concludes that a high SRI rating therefore may not in fact truly indicate social responsibility. The question "Why not?" is left unanswered, so it appears that the gap in the logic occurs somewhere toward the end. It's not an easy one to pick out, however, so unless the assumption jumped out at you, the best course of action would be to test the choices in the hopes that the missing piece will reveal itself.

Work the Choices. Let's see what we can make of each choice, looking for the one that's required for the conclusion to stand.

A: Corporations with low SRI ratings are outside the scope of this argument, which concerns corporations with high ratings. But even if we grant that **A** is relevant to the accuracy of SRI ratings, **A** isn't assumed since good will is but one of many factors in SRI ratings, and the author doesn't need to establish the ways in which low SRI rating corporations missed the mark.

B: Again, it's easiest to test the choice via negate and destroy. Consider what happens if perception of a corporation's good will *always* reflects that corporation's level of social responsibility. SRI is made up only of tangible responsibility factors that can be measured and the intangible perception of good will. Therefore, if perception of good will is a perfect predictor of social responsibility, then there's no way that a high rating can be affixed to a company that is not socially responsible, and the conclusion in the final sentence falls apart. **B** is therefore a required piece of this argument. If you want to view this head on, consider it this way: Perception of good will is defined in the passage as an intangible element of SRI, in contrast to the tangible components of the indicator. If it's possible for a company to have a high SRI rating yet not be socially responsible, then the breakdown must come on the perception front, since perception of good will need not necessarily reflect actual good will in the same way that environmental regulations are either adhered to or not. For the argument to stand, therefore, it requires the premise stated in **B**.

> Notice how a single word—*perception*, in this case—can throw a monkey wrench into an argument's reasoning. Very little in a Logical Reasoning passage is superfluous, so make sure you consider every word they include since single words (and especially little words like *not* and *but*) can make a big difference.

C provides an Unnecessary Clarification that has no direct bearing on the conclusion. The relative size of the two stated components of SRI is not only Unknowable, but also Irrelevant.

D is Irrelevant as well, shifting the focus from social responsibility to success, a sure red flag. It also contains an Overreach by stating that good will is the *only* factor in this new element, success. Take your pick as to the reason to drop **D**.

E is an Overreach—the argument doesn't require such an extreme set of circumstances to be true. Even if SRI sometimes *does* accurately reflect social responsibility, that doesn't harm the conclusion that some high ratings may not in reality be deserved. The argument therefore does not rely on the notion in **E**.

Question 6: Political Background Checks

6.   Political advocacy groups have recently called for extensive background checks into the lives of all political candidates in order to eliminate any incentive a candidate may have to falsify his or her personal or professional records. While sound in theory, this recommendation has virtually no chance of achieving its objective, due to the sheer number of local and national candidates and the impossibility of deriving reliable interpretations from candidate data even if they could be gathered.

The argument proceeds by

(A)   questioning the desirability of implementing a course of action
(B)   discounting a proposal on the basis of its impracticality
(C)   demonstrating that the two main drawbacks to a plan are logically inconsistent
(D)   using the fact that a specific proposal cannot succeed to argue that no proposal can address the problem under consideration
(E)   implying that overcoming either of two possible obstacles to a measure under consideration would make implementation of the measure feasible

Grill the Interrogator. Here is no doubt one of the shortest question stems you'll see, in this case indicating a garden-variety Stand-alone Method question. Our task in these is to generalize from the text, so slip into translation mode as you venture off into the passage.

Attack the Passage. The somewhat lengthy first sentence pretty much boils down to two words: a recommendation.

> **TAKE AWAY**
>
> The reason we distinguish between Stand-alone and Dialogue Method questions is because you should approach them differently. Dialogue Method questions, while falling into the Matching category, sometimes revolve around Critique issues since one speaker usually questions the reasoning of the other. But in Stand-alone Method questions, your main task is to translate the statements into general terms.

The recommendation is offered not by the author, mind you, but by some political groups. What does the author think about it? We find out in sentence 2: It's sound in theory but doesn't have much of a chance of working in the real world. Why not? Because of that stuff at the end of the sentence, which, for our purposes, we needn't focus on. So it boils down to this: Some people recommend something, which would be nice except it won't work. In line with our Matching technique, let's meticulously match the choices to this general translation.

Work the Choices. A gets it backward because the author of the passage explicitly says that the recommendation is sound in theory, implying that he thinks it would be a good thing to check the backgrounds of politicians. He takes issue with its *feasibility*, not desirability. Which leads quite nicely into **B** . . .

B: Is there a proposal? Sure, the recommendation is a proposal of what should be done. Does the author discount it on the basis of impracticality? Yup—that's exactly what happens when the author says the plan has virtually no chance of achieving its objective. All parts present and accounted for, so **B** is correct.

C: Does the author cite two main drawbacks to a plan? We could say that: There are too many people to collect information about, and no way to analyze it all even if we could gather up all that info. Does the author assert that these drawbacks are logically inconsistent? No. If anything, they go hand in hand since the first drawback plausibly contributes to the second.

D goes beyond the scope of the argument. The author *does* argue that the recommendation is very unlikely to succeed but doesn't build on that assertion to show that there is therefore no possible way to ensure that politicians are honest about the past.

E exaggerates the optimism of the author, who states that even if we overcome the first obstacle, we'd still have the second problem to deal with. And there's no logical way to overcome the second problem without overcoming the first; if we can't gather the data in the first place, we'd never even face the obstacle of analyzing it. So the author doesn't imply that overcoming either obstacle would put the plan in the clear.

TAKE AWAY

Note that this is not the greatest of all arguments. It doesn't say, for example, *why* the volume of candidate information is too large to gather, or *why* reliable interpretations can't be derived from the mass of data if it could be collected. Certainly if this were an Assumption or Strengthen/Weaken question, these kinds of issues would be on our minds. Do we care about them here? No! Remember, shift into the right mindset for every question you face. On Stand-alone Method questions, focus primarily on *how* the author makes the argument, not on its validity.

Question 7: In Defense of Breakfast Cereals

7. Father: Growing up, I ate the same children's breakfast cereals that my five-year-old and seven-year-old daughters eat today. It gives me a pleasant feeling of continuity to see my children experience activities from my own childhood, including the ritual of eating cereal with milk as part of a balanced breakfast. But now experts are warning that these cereals may compromise children's health. When I was a child thirty five years ago, I ate those cereals nearly every day, and no doctor or nutritionist ever suggested that they may be unhealthy. Moreover, I am a relatively healthy adult, and my children show no adverse effects from consuming these cereals. Therefore, the recommendation that my children should limit their intake of these cereals is groundless.

Each of the following, if true, weakens the argument EXCEPT:

(A) Children today eat substantially larger portions of children's cereals than they did thirty five years ago.

(B) Sugar, a substance detrimental to children's health, comprises a much higher percentage of today's children's cereals than it did thirty five years ago.

(C) **Research investigating the adverse effects of children's cereals on children's health has been conducted consistently over the last 35 years.**

(D) Relatively healthy adults who consumed children's cereals on a regular basis growing up would be healthier today had they not done so.

(E) Health detriments stemming from the regular consumption of children's cereals do not become manifest until children become teenagers.

Grill the Interrogator. We see from the question stem that Weaken EXCEPT is the name of this game, which means there must be plenty of ambiguities, alternatives, or assumptions lurking in the passage. Plunge into the argument with that thought in mind.

Attack the Passage. It seems this guy has watched too many TV commercials in his life, as evidenced by his parroting the timeless "part of a balanced breakfast" spiel common to cereal ads. Anyway, that's evidently the least of his problems, considering the "Weaken EXCEPT" question stem indicating that there are at least four ways to counter what he's arguing. And that's not surprising, considering how he goes from such qualified evidence (e.g., "I'm *relatively* healthy . . . My kids *show* no adverse effects . . .") to an all out attack on the recommendation for kids to limit cereal intake, declaring it "groundless." That's a pretty big leap and likely to be a primary source of the weakeners. It's best to evaluate the choices individually in accordance with a simple defined objective: "Show me that the recommendation may actually have some merit."

Stay attuned to the *force* of the words used in the passage. Here, for example, being *relatively* healthy is part of the evidence that a recommendation is *groundless*. *Relatively* is somewhat wishy-washy, while *groundless* is anything but. A change in the force of the evidence presented to the force of the conclusion derived from that evidence constitutes a subtle yet genuine bait and switch and should be properly exploited when appearing in the context of any Critique question.

Work the Choices. Each valid weakener meets our defined objective by picking apart a different aspect of the father's vague and unconvincing evidence:

A: If kids today eat much more of these cereals than in the past (perhaps even *unbalancing* their "balanced breakfast"), the recommendation that they cut down may not be so far fetched. Perhaps the father wasn't badly affected by the cereals because he simply didn't eat as much of it.

B strongly suggests that the cereals may be unhealthier now, a fact that directly enhances the merits of the recommendation by breaking down the "it was fine then, so it's fine now" tenor of the father's argument.

D hammers away at the father's evidence that he's "relatively" healthy now—not such a ringing endorsement, especially in light of **D**'s suggestion that he would be even healthier if he had laid off the cereals. Again, this leads us in the direction of thinking that the recommendation that kids cut down their cereal intake is not as groundless as the father maintains.

E works against the part of the argument where the father claims that his kids "*show* no adverse effects" yet. If it's common for negative effects of regular cereal eating to only become noticeable during teenage years, then the fact that the father's five- and seven-year-old kids *seem* okay now may not mean that they are actually unaffected by their cereal consumption. If **E** is true, it may not be such a bad idea for them to cut back a bit now.

C, however, goes the other way by strengthening the argument. In attempting to counter the father's position, one might reasonably argue that these cereals really *were* unhealthy back in the day, but nobody checked it out back then so nobody knew. This would help damage the father's use of the fact that no doctor or nutritionist ever stepped forward to say these cereals were bad. **C** discounts this plausible attack on the father's argument by saying that researchers *have been* following this all this time, which puts the lack of warnings from doctors and nutritionists back into play. If anything, then, **C** helps the father's case and therefore gets the point for this Weaken EXCEPT question.

Question 8: The Suzuki Technique

8. Many music instructors employ the Suzuki Technique, a method that encourages children to acquire musical "literacy" much in the same way they learn to speak. In both instances, children are encouraged to assimilate what they hear and combine sounds into increasingly complex arrangements. While certainly innovative and effective, an over-reliance on this technique diminishes a music student's facility for developing important traditional skills such as reading music and playing scales.

Which one of the following best expresses the main point of the passage?

(A) The Suzuki Technique mimics the way in which children acquire language.
(B) Music teachers should rely primarily on traditional instruction to teach music to children.
(C) Reading music and playing scales are important components of a musical education.
(D) The Suzuki Technique is a popular form of musical instruction.
(E) Music students benefit most from a combination of the Suzuki Technique and traditional instruction.

Grill the Interrogator. We're asked to find the main point of the passage, so Critique issues and Essential Concepts are pretty much off the table. Focus instead on distinguishing the overriding idea from the evidence used to back it up.

Attack the Passage. Sentence 1 defines the Suzuki Technique. Chances are the passage wasn't written simply to tell us what this thing is, so remain alert to see how the author builds on this information. Sentence 2 fleshes out the Suzuki/speaking analogy, which is all well and good but still concerns nothing more than what the method is. It doesn't quite sound like an argument just yet, but that all changes in sentence 3 with the powerful contrast signal word *while*.

> **TAKE AWAY**
>
> In our discussion of Main Point questions, we advise you to "Use the Clues," which means use important signal words that telegraph where the author is going with the argument. Words and phrases like *while, however, but, despite the fact that,* and *although* denote contrast and are used to suggest that one thing and not another is really the case. When a contrast is featured in an argument, it's bound to be connected to the author's main point.

The author admits that the technique is "innovative and effective," something certainly worth noting for purposes of eliminating wrong choices that fail to recognize this admission. But the contrast signal word *while* has already tipped us off that a big *but* is coming, and here it is: Over-relying on the technique can be detrimental because it impedes traditional skills. That's the point that the introductory stuff in the beginning is leading up to; after all, the author can't knock Suzuki without first telling us what it is. We should therefore scour the choices for something along the lines of "Suzuki is generally good, but too much is overkill and bad."

Paraphrase the main point in your own words before hitting the choices. Don't expect the correct choice to match your paraphrase word for word, but having an idea in mind will not only help you spot the choice most consistent with it but also eliminate choices that wander far afield.

Work the Choices. **E** captures the gist of sentence 3. As we've seen, the author admits that Suzuki is innovative and effective but worries that if it's used *too much*, kids will miss out on some traditional instruction they need. The best expression of the main point is that a Suzuki/traditional combination is the best alternative.

A: Remember Hear Ye, Hear Ye . . . ? The right answer will sound like a good headline for the passage, and **A** fails this test. It's an Overreach that attempts to blow up the minor issue of the speaking analogy into the passage's main point. The fact that the Suzuki Technique operates much like language acquisition is background information that serves only as a foundation for the author's real assessment of Suzuki.

B is a Twister choice that perhaps even leans toward Opposite. The author asserts that teachers shouldn't *over-rely* on Suzuki, but that's not to say that they should mostly rely on traditional approaches, especially considering the positive things the author says about the Suzuki Technique earlier in the passage.

C is true, according to the author—but what about the main focus of the passage, the Suzuki Technique? That's what this thing is mainly about, so a choice that ignores Suzuki entirely cannot suffice as the passage's main point.

D is strongly suggested by the passage's first sentence, but the popularity of the method is not the central issue. If it were, why even bother to include the assessment asserted in sentence 3?

A correct answer to a Main Point question needs to be more than merely true or inferable; it must represent the main reason the author wrote the passage.

Question 9: Architectural Restorations

9. Shea: The restoration of ancient architectural sites, such as the Acropolis in Greece, adds significant value to those sites and enhances the enjoyment of tourists eager to experience historical sites as they once were.

    Melia: I disagree. Restorations may resemble original sites on a superficial level but lack the context and nuances to reflect historical reality.

    The dialogue most supports the claim that Shea and Melia disagree with each other about whether

    (A)   restoring an ancient site can result in a structure that resembles the original
    (B)   the Acropolis in Athens has been restored
    (C)   restoring ancient sites increases the revenues of the tourist industries containing such sites
    (D)   restoring ancient sites results in accurate representations of history
    (E)   context and nuances contribute to the historical reality of architectural sites

Grill the Interrogator. Shea and Melia don't see eye to eye, which can only mean that a Disagreement question is on hand. The arguments are short, so see if you can zero in on the relevant issue at the heart of the debate.

Attack the Passage. Shea says that restoring ancient architectural sites adds lots of value and enhances tourists' experience of them. Melia says no, restorations only resemble the originals on a superficial level. She thinks they lack things (nuance, context) to convey how these sites really were back in the day. Stated simply, it appears that Shea thinks restorations are valuable, while Melia thinks they're not. Let's match the choices to that idea, keeping in mind the scope of each argument to help us eliminate choices that aren't relevant to either or both positions.

Work the Choices. A quick scan may have brought you in the vicinity of the correct choice, and if not, no biggie—we should be able to dispense of the imposters fairly quickly until we find the choice that accurately reflects the sticking point.

TAKE
AWAY

> If you have a solid idea of the disagreement following your attack on the passage, scan for that idea among the choices and first test the ones that seem to relate to your notion. If you're less certain, test the choices one by one, paying close attention to the common Disagreement wrong answer types: agreement points, irrelevancies, and unknowables.

A: There seems to be agreement on the idea that restored sites can resemble the original sites. Shea argues that restorations allow tourists to "experience historical sites as they once were," which clearly suggests that she thinks there's a strong resemblance between the two. Melia, who argues against the overall value of restorations, nonetheless admits that they do resemble the originals, if only on a superficial level. Her issue is that restorations are lacking on a deeper level.

B fails the test for relevance because only Shea mentions the Acropolis specifically. Shea states that the Acropolis has been restored, and there's nothing in Melia's argument to suggest that she thinks otherwise.

C: Neither argument deals with revenues from tourism, so **C** doesn't contain the point at issue we seek.

D: The issue here seems to be in the ballpark, so let's Quiz the Speakers. Does Shea think that restoring ancient sites results in accurate representations of history? Sure, we can infer that she does since she speaks of tourists experiencing restored sites "as they once were." Does Melia think so? No way. They may look good on the surface, but they're missing important things like nuance and context, which compromises historical reality. So in regard to the issue in **D**, we'd get a yea from Shea and a nay from Melia. **D** thus effectively captures the disagreement and is correct.

E speaks directly to Melia's issues of context and nuance, issues that Shea doesn't address. For all we know, Shea *agrees* that context and nuance are important elements of historical reality and thinks that restorations such as the Acropolis possess these qualities in spades.

> Many wrong choices in Disagreement questions center on issues that one of the speakers fails to address, and some even deal with things irrelevant to both arguments. Quiz the Speakers as to their opinions on the subject of an answer choice. If either lacks an opinion on that matter, that choice can't be correct.

TAKE AWAY

Question 10: The Victoria Follies

10. Victoria: The originators of logic and democracy, the ancient Greeks, were unable to achieve a full understanding of ethics. Modern democracies rely on numerous ethical systems but have also failed to grasp the true essence of ethics. Full comprehension in the matter of ethics is therefore clearly unattainable.

The argument above is flawed because Victoria equates what has been misunderstood

(A) with what has been understood
(B) in the past with what has been misunderstood today
(C) about ethics with what has been understood about logic and democracy
(D) with what can never be understood
(E) once with what has been misunderstood many times

Grill the Interrogator. The question stem gives us more information than the fact that we're dealing with a Flaw question, although it's so specific that we really can't wrap our minds around it until we see what this "equation of misunderstanding" thing refers to. All we need to know from the start is that Victoria has botched something, big time, and we should keep our eye out for that.

TAKE AWAY

One aspect of Logical Reasoning success is asking yourself the right questions. In some cases, you'll need to combine information in the question stem with what's offered in the choices to find the choice that works.

Attack the Passage. We can boil Victoria's argument down as follows: The Greeks didn't understand ethics. We moderns don't get it either. Ethics therefore is not understandable. This logic presents a golden opportunity to think in terms of alternatives—specifically, the alternative possibility that one day someone *will* understand the essence of ethics even though no one to this point has done so. That's a good start, so let's see what the choices have to offer.

Work the Choices. The choices kind of sound the same, so bouncing them off of our lead from above is probably the best way to go.

A: Has Victoria equated what has been misunderstood with what has been understood? No, because according to her no one has been able to understand ethics, so **A** doesn't represent the source of her confusion.

B: Has Victoria equated what has been misunderstood in the past with what has been misunderstood today? Actually, yes. She does say that both the ancients and the moderns have misunderstood ethics. However, that's Not a Problem, as we label this Flaw common trap. She may be right or wrong with regard to these assertions, but she's entitled to use them as evidence. It's the conclusion that she *derives* from these assertions that goes awry.

C: Has Victoria equated what has been misunderstood about ethics with what has been understood about logic and democracy? No. Logic and democracy are mentioned merely as background information on the ancient Greeks, but they have nothing to do with the conclusion Victoria draws regarding ethics.

D: Has Victoria equated what has been misunderstood with what can never be understood? Yes. That's the gist of what we derived from our attack on the passage above. She argues that ethics will *never* be understood (full comprehension on the matter "is clearly unattainable") based on evidence that no one *yet* has understood it. Just because something hasn't been understood doesn't mean it never will be. So **D** correctly captures the gist of Victoria's mistake.

E: Has Victoria equated what has been misunderstood once with what has been misunderstood many times? No. Single as opposed to multiple misunderstandings plays no role in the argument.

Question 11: Maturing Morality

11. As people grow older and more mature, they often find that the moral values of their youth conflict with new opinions and understandings of the world afforded by wisdom and experience. However, at the same time such people are often loathe to express their new worldviews through their actions lest they appear to others to contradict their former moral code. This should be discouraged, as it results in people acting against their better judgment merely to preserve the image of a defunct identity.

The argument conforms most closely to which one of the following principles?

(A) When two moral codes conflict in the assessment of a situation, the one that yields the most effective course of action should be followed.

(B) The values of old age should take precedence over the values of youth.

(C) Worldviews that encourage dangerous behavior should be altered to encompass more moderate values.

(D) One should not express one's moral code through actions if doing so entails the risk of altering one's public persona.

(E) **The appearance of moral consistency should not take precedence over actual beliefs as a basis for guiding one's actions.**

Grill the Interrogator. The stem indicates a Conforming Principle question that asks us to match the situation in the passage to the closest principle to it among the choices. Focus on understanding the situation presented so you'll be able to meticulously match the elements of each choice to it.

Attack the Passage. The author begins with the idea that as we age and mature, our moral values mature as well. However, people often don't want to *act* on their new moral beliefs since that might make them look inconsistent. This is bad, says the author, since it basically results in people not being themselves. We need not critique the argument; we need only to find a principle that goes along with it. On to the choices.

Work the Choices. A shifts the conflict in moral codes from the conflict between youthful and mature moral beliefs to a conflict between two moral beliefs potentially applicable to a specific situation. If you didn't notice that, you may have noticed that the passage contains no element of efficiency in the application of morals. Either way, **A** doesn't conform to the situation in the passage.

TAKE AWAY

Some choices are wrong for multiple reasons, but you need only one valid reason to axe a choice. As soon as you see something that doesn't compute, cross it out and move on.

B: The author is worried about the hypocrisy that results when one possesses one set of beliefs but acts according to another. She doesn't, however, argue that one set of moral codes is *superior* to another, so **B** isn't the match we seek.

C: The notion of dangerous behavior stemming from worldviews is not present in the passage, so the principle in **C** doesn't match.

D encourages the very behavior the author warns against: people refusing to act according to their current moral beliefs because they're worried that doing so will jeopardize the identity that society has attached to them. The principle in **D** thus runs counter to the author's argument.

> TAKE AWAY
>
> Opposite choices are common in Inference and Critique questions but may appear in other question types as well. In Principle questions, don't be surprised to come across a choice that conflicts with the situation at hand.

E hits on all cylinders. The author thinks it's bad when people try to *appear* to embody certain moral beliefs in their actions when in fact their moral beliefs have changed. So the author is concerned about the "appearance of moral consistency" and does believe that that "should not take precedence over actual beliefs as a basis for guiding one's actions." The principle in **E** best matches the position taken in the passage.

Question 12: The Case of the Dull Knife Wounds

12. Most injury-causing accidents occur in the home, and one of the most common of such injuries involves accidental knife wounds. Surprisingly, research into the records of the Fairlawn General Emergency Room indicate far more people treated for knife wounds inflicted by dull knives than knife wounds inflicted by sharp knives.

    Each of the following, if true, could explain the surprising finding cited above EXCEPT:

    (A) People at home tend to be much more careful when handling sharp knives than when handling dull knives.

    (B) People received at the Fairlawn General Emergency Room suffering from knife wounds inflicted by sharp knives are immediately transferred to an independent special trauma unit for treatment.

    (C) The severity of injuries from knife wounds inflicted by dull knives treated at the Fairlawn General Emergency Room is generally equal to the severity of the injuries from knife wounds inflicted by sharp knives treated at the same facility.

    (D) Due to a public safety awareness campaign, dull knives greatly outnumber sharp knives in the homes of Fairlawn residents.

    (E) Sharp knives tend to produce a clean cut when involved in a home-related accident, whereas dull knives produce a more jagged cut, making it more difficult to stem the flow of blood.

Grill the Interrogator. A Paradox EXCEPT question offers an excellent opportunity to practice spotting resolutions to the apparent discrepancies posed in this Logical Reasoning question type. Prepare to locate the mystery at hand and to define an objective to test for viable resolutions.

Attack the Passage. The mystery isn't hard to spot, what with the word "surprisingly" tipping us off to the unusual part of our little narrative. Common sense might dictate that sharp knives would inflict more damage than dull ones, but that doesn't seem to be the case in the fair town of Fairlawn. Our objective is therefore to understand why more people would be treated at a certain emergency room for wounds from dull knives than wounds from sharp knives. Since the passage is so short and doesn't contain any obvious assumptions or Essential Concepts, let's see what the choices have to offer.

TAKE AWAY

In Paradox questions, you may come up with plausible resolutions on our own, but don't think you need to in order to handle these questions effectively. If you have a strong sense of what to test for in the choices, that's just as good.

Work the Choices. Let's take them in order, keeping the objective defined above in mind.

TAKE AWAY

When testing each Paradox choice, ask yourself "Does it all make sense now?" Usually the correct choice will be the one that returns the answer yes. In a Paradox EXCEPT question, however, the correct choice will be the one that *doesn't* clear things up.

A: If sharp knives are perceived to be dangerous, and thus people are more careful with them than with dull knives, it's easier to understand why dull-knife wound injuries may outnumber injuries from sharp knives.

B speaks to a very subtle bait and switch: Fewer sharp knife wounds *treated* at Fairlawn Emergency Room doesn't necessarily mean that fewer people with such wounds are *received* there. If Fairlawn ships out the serious sharp-knife inflicted wounds for treatment elsewhere, then the predominance of dull-knife wound *treatments* in the hospital's records wouldn't seem as surprising.

C presents its own little mystery without solving the one at hand: Why would injuries caused by dull knives be just as bad as injuries caused by sharp knives? (Choice **E**, discussed below, provides one possible reason.) While this issue may seem related to the mystery at hand, **C** doesn't get us any closer to understanding why many more dull-knife wound patients *show up for treatment in the first place.* Even if we grant the fact that the two kinds of wounds are somehow equally serious, the disproportionate number of dull-knife wounds treated at this particular emergency room would still remain unusual. **C** doesn't help clear up the mystery and is therefore correct for this Paradox EXCEPT question.

D: If home is the place where most knife accidents happen, and people who have been warned about the dangers of knives don't keep nearly as many sharp knives around as dull knives, it's less mysterious that more injuries inflicted by dull knives would be treated at the emergency room.

E presents a reason why injuries inflicted by dull knives may actually be more severe than those inflicted by sharp knives. If it's harder to stop the bleeding from a dull knife wound, that would help explain why more dull knife wound injuries are treated at Fairlawn.

Question 13: Intelligence, Speaking, and Reading

13. Not all intelligent people are good readers, but all good readers are intelligent. Effective public speaking requires intelligence. Matt has delivered an effective public speech, so he must be a good reader.

The flawed pattern of reasoning in which one of the following is most similar to that exhibited in the argument above?

(A) All light bulbs contain filaments, but not all things containing filaments are light bulbs. All objects containing filaments glow when heated. Salma owns a glowing object, so Salma must own a light bulb.

(B) Not all machines are computers, but all computers are some kind of machine. Producing quality special effects requires the use of specialized computers. Behroush wants to produce quality special effects for his documentary on space exploration, so Behroush will have to use some kind of machine.

(C) Some people with vision are not successful, but all successful people have vision. Vision is necessary to develop a viable business plan. Jacqui must be successful, because she has developed a viable business plan.

(D) To be accomplished, an actress must train for at least two years. Amanda is an actress who has trained for three years, so she must be accomplished.

(E) Not all diplomats are politicians, but all politicians are expected to be diplomatic. Dylan wishes to be known as an exceptional politician, so Dylan should seek the reconciliation of the warring factions in his party.

Grill the Interrogator. The question stem screams Parallel Flaw, so have your Essential Concepts and classic flaws at the ready as you try to find the problem with this short argument.

Attack the Passage. The first sentence contains formal logic (*not all, all*), so one way to go is to do the math and plot out the argument symbolically with X's and Y's. Not all X (intelligent people) are Y (good readers), but all Y are X. Z (effective public speaking) requires X (intelligence). M (Matt) has done Z, therefore M is Y. We can infer from a combination of sentences 1 and 2 that Matt is intelligent, but since not all intelligent people are good readers, the conclusion that Matt is a good reader doesn't follow. Now match the choices to this flawed structure to find the one that's similarly bogus.

When formal logic statements appear in a Logical Reasoning question, by all means make use of your Logic Games skills to determine what may and may not be deduced from them.

Work the Choices. Before wading into the choices in their entirety, let's see if we can chop a few on sight by comparing conclusions. The original concludes with a characteristic that a person must possess. Each answer choice centers on a person, but not all of the conclusions match the form just noted. Choice **A** speaks of something a person must *own*. Not great, but for the sake of argument we'll let that slide for now based on the idea that Salma possesses a characteristic of ownership. We won't, however, be as forgiving with **B**, which tells us what Behroush *will have to do* under certain circumstances, or **E**, which tells us what Dylan *should do*. Since these conclusions don't match the general form of the original's conclusion, we can narrow the choices down to **A**, **C**, and **D** right off the bat. If you didn't use this technique and instead evaluated **B** and **E** thoroughly, you should have found that **B** is actually valid, while **E** introduces a new term in the conclusion ("reconciliation"), something that doesn't happen in the original passage.

There may be more than one way to eliminate wrong choices, but some may be faster than others. Our "compare the conclusions" technique is quick and efficient because it allows you to zero in on a single part of each answer choice, the conclusion, to determine whether you even need to bother reading the whole thing.

Let's now test the remainders.

A: We can switch the clauses of the first sentence: Not all X (things with filaments) are Y (light bulbs), but all Y are X. Next comes "all X do Z" (glow when heated), which doesn't mirror the original's "Z requires X," so we can cut our analysis short right here and move on.

C: Not all X (people with vision) are Y (successful), but all Y are X. Z (viable business plan) requires X (vision). So far, so good. Now for the rest: J (Jacqui) has done Z, therefore J is Y. Yup, that's flawed all right. It *can* be concluded that Jacqui has vision, but because not all people with vision are successful, the conclusion "Jacqui must be successful" is flawed in the same way as "Matt must be a good reader" in the original. Same structure, same flaw, so **C** gets the point.

Sometimes testing Parallel Reasoning choices is aided by translating statements to get them in the same form as the original. That's okay *as long as you don't alter the logic.*

D: In keeping with the symbolization exercise, **D** breaks down like so: X (accomplished actress) requires Y (train at least two years). A (Amanda) has done more than Y (trained for three years). Therefore A is X. Faulty, but not parallel.

Question 14: America's Greatest Technology

14. Enrico: The automobile is the technology that most shaped twentieth-century America. Before the automobile, most people lived in agrarian communities with strong ties to family and the land. The automobile made it possible, and then necessary, for many people to commute to jobs outside of their immediate communities, a development which spurred the growth of overcrowded cities surrounded by vast suburban landscapes. Moreover, the absence of one, and often two parents from the home environment during the long work day ultimately led to the breakdown of the family and the loss of centuries-old traditions.

    Helen: The specific effects you cite are correct. However, the Internet has revolutionized the way information is packaged, transmitted, sought and received, and no technology influences a society more than one that alters that society's means of communication.

    The conversation provides the strongest grounds for holding that Enrico and Helen disagree over whether

    (A) the automobile caused a loss of tradition in twentieth-century America
    (B) the Internet has altered the means of communication in twentieth-century America
    (C) the Internet has had a greater influence on twentieth-century America than has the automobile
    (D) new technologies have the power to shape a society
    (E) other technologies besides the automobile and the Internet have played a role in shaping twentieth-century America

Grill the Interrogator. We begin with a standard Disagreement question stem, so put those Critique skills away and slip into Matching mode. We'll focus on the crux of the argument and then meticulously grill the choices to see which one best captures the essence of the conflict.

Attack the Passage. Enrico delivers a fairly passionate sermon on the earth-shattering effects of the automobile. There's no need to repeat his whole argument; suffice it to say that he provides numerous pieces of evidence to support his claim that the car was the most influential technology of the twentieth century. And Helen actually enters the conversation in agreement, at least in regard to the *effects* that Enrico cites. That's interesting information that will most likely translate into a wrong answer choice.

Take note of points of agreement even while you search for the conflict between the speakers. Points of agreement are often included among the wrong choices in Disagreement questions.

You ever get the feeling that a big *but* is coming down the pike? You should in this case, having already seen from the question stem that disagreement is the name of this game. And sure enough, Helen's amiability ends with a thud, signaled forcefully by the contrast signal word *however*. She argues that the Internet was the hot-shot technology of the twentieth century and provides her own reasons, which we need not belabor. We have enough ammo by now to check to see how the choices stack up to the debate.

Work the Choices. A quick scan shows that **C** and **E** are the only ones that involve both technologies highlighted in the dialogue, so it's worth starting with those first.

C: *Internet, automobile, influence on twentieth-century America* . . . these things all *sound* relevant to both sides of the debate, and indeed they are. So **C** passes the relevance test with flying colors. The next step is to Quiz the Speakers. Does Enrico believe that the Internet was more important to twentieth-century America than the automobile? No, he doesn't. While Enrico doesn't mention the Internet specifically, we can infer that he believes that the car was more influential than the Internet since he believes that the car was more influential than *all* other technologies of that century. Helen, on the other hand, specifically asserts that the Internet ruled century double-X. So **C** accurately captures the disagreement.

E: Let's knock off the other choice we targeted from our scan, the only other choice to seemingly get in the ballpark. Sure, **E** mentions the car and the Internet, but it begins with a big red flag: "*other* technologies." Well, neither speaker is particularly interested in which technologies merely played a role in influencing the twentieth century; they're interested in which one played the *most important* role. So **E** is Irrelevant to both arguments.

A and **D** constitute points of agreement. Helen states that the effects of the automobile that Enrico cites are correct, so we can infer that she agrees that the car caused a loss of tradition (**A**). Moreover, Enrico states that the automobile was the technology that "most shaped twentieth-century America," while Helen says that technologies that alter the way we communicate most influence a society. Both speakers therefore believe that technology can shape society (**D**); they just disagree over which twentieth-century marvel did so the most.

B: As stated above, all we know about Enrico's opinion regarding the Internet is that its influence on twentieth-century America doesn't match that of the automobile, which is inferable from his "car is number 1!" argument. Enrico's opinion regarding the specific effects of the Internet is one of many Unknowables we can take out of his dialogue with Helen, so **E** fails the relevance test.

Remember, the first test of any Disagreement answer choice is whether its subject is relevant to both sides of the debate. If a speaker's position on the issue raised in a choice is Unknowable, that choice must be wrong.

Question 15: The Cocoa Blight

15. Due to a blight affecting country X's cocoa crop, the total revenue from that country's cocoa exports decreased 45 percent in 2003 from the total revenue generated by cocoa exports in 2002. However, the average revenue for cocoa exports per cocoa-exporting company in country X was the same in 2003 as it was in 2002.

   If the statements above are true, which one of the following must also be true?

   (A) The blight destroyed 45 percent of country X's cocoa crop.
   (B) The blight affected cocoa more than any other crop in country X.
   (C) No company in country X generated more revenue from cocoa exports in 2003 than it generated from cocoa exports in 2002.
   (D) The total combined revenue of all of country X's industries was less in 2003 than it was in 2002.
   (E) Fewer companies in country X exported cocoa in 2003 than did so in 2002.

Grill the Interrogator. Here we get a "must be true" kind of Inference question, which most likely means we're dealing with a stricter situation that the "most strongly supported" Standard Inference variety. We should therefore expect the answer here to have no leeway at all. That means that formal logic may be involved, so keep your eye out for that as well.

Attack the Passage. This one would make for a good Paradox question: A blight knocked out nearly half of a country's annual cocoa revenue one year, yet the average cocoa export revenue for companies exporting cocoa in that country stayed roughly the same that year. Can this be? Sure—because total revenue from exports is not the same as average revenue per company. So there's a kind of bait and switch here, although not of the flawed variety since the author of the passage doesn't draw any kind of erroneous conclusion from the facts. The facts are not inconsistent, although they do imply another definite fact listed among the choices. Recognizing the difference between total exports and average exports is the key to spotting the inference we seek.

Work the Choices. The only way for the statements in the passage to be true is if **E** is true as well. Average export revenue per company is equal to total export revenue divided by the number of exporting companies. If total cocoa revenues decreased significantly in 2003 compared to 2002, but the average cocoa export revenue per cocoa-exporting company was the same in both years, then fewer companies must have exported cocoa in 2003 than in 2002. If you're unsure, try confirming with the negate and destroy test: What if the same number of, or more companies, exported cocoa in 2003 compared to 2002? Then the average revenue for cocoa exports per cocoa-exporting company in country X would have to fall, since the total revenue fell dramatically due to the blight. The only way the numbers gibe, therefore, is if fewer companies were in the cocoa exporting business in 2003.

TAKE AWAY

There is no actual math on the LSAT—notice how you're not expected to do any calculations here. You are, however, expected to understand the concept of average. An average equals the total divided by the number of items that add up to that total. Keeping that in mind, you can determine whether averages are properly drawn or, as in this case, what must also be true when given only part of the average equation.

A: Twister: The 45 percent figure refers to *fallen revenue.* We can't make the jump from that to infer 45 percent of *destroyed cocoa.* Looked at from another angle, how much cocoa was destroyed in the blight to account for the country losing 45 percent of cocoa export revenues is Unknowable.

B and **C:** And speaking of Unknowables, there's no information in the passage regarding *other* crops, nor any information on the actual earnings of specific companies. This passage is specifically about the cocoa crop, but it's possible that some other crop was hit harder (**B**). And just because the country lost lots of money on the whole on cocoa exports in 2003 compared to 2002 doesn't mean that some company didn't, for whatever reason, have a banner cocoa exporting year in 2003. So **C** need not be true either.

D is an Overreach attempting to expand the scope of the passage from the single cocoa industry to *all* industries in country X. Just because one component of X's economy (the cocoa-exporting industry) suffered in 2003 doesn't mean that X's overall economy was worse that year than in 2002.

TAKE AWAY

Statistics is a fertile area for misunderstanding, which explains why the wrong choices fall squarely into the Twister, Overreach, and Unknowable categories: Twister and Overreach because it's fairly easy to distort statistics and blow them out of proportion, and Unknowable because statistics often leave more issues up in the air than they actually resolve.

16. Alcohol, while seeming to stimulate the senses at the time of consumption, in fact depresses the central nervous system and in the long run deadens one's experience of the world. Studies have shown that alcoholics are over 50 percent more likely than non-alcoholics to suffer from depression. It can be concluded from this evidence that alcohol's effect on the central nervous system contributes to the onset of depression.

Which one of the following, if true, most weakens the argument above?

(A) **Many alcoholics first began consuming excess quantities of alcohol in order to cope with depression.**

(B) Some non-alcoholics have experiences that depress their central nervous systems.

(C) The majority of depressed people are not alcoholics.

(D) Most alcoholics did not suffer from depression before they began consuming excess amounts of alcohol.

(E) Rehabilitated alcoholics are more likely to have successful careers than are non-rehabilitated alcoholics.

Grill the Interrogator. We're greeted in this one with a standard Weaken question, so adopt a critical mindset as you search for alternatives, ambiguities, assumptions, and everything else in your Weaken the Argument bag o' tricks.

Attack the Passage. Hopefully you spotted the Essential Concept at the crux of this argument: cause and effect. We're told that alcohol depresses the nervous system and deadens experience, so there's a causal element at work already in the first sentence. Then we get statistical evidence that alcoholics are more likely than non-alcoholics to suffer from depression, which the author uses to draw a causal conclusion at the end: Alcohol *contributes to* depression. This conclusion seems especially reasonable in light of the earlier fact that alcohol depresses the central nervous system. However, that's not the same as suffering from the medical condition of depression. There are unknowables at work here. "Depressing the central nervous system" could instead mean making one tired, or lethargic, or irritable. Are there other possibilities regarding the relationship between alcohol use and the medical condition of depression? That thought may be enough to exit the passage and see what the choices have to offer.

Work the Choices. A provides a plausible alternative that essentially reflects the same issue captured in the Amalie example in the Essential Concepts section of the Logical Reasoning chapter: It reverses the cause and effect. If the depression came first, and the alcoholism came later as an attempt to ease the bad feelings associated with depression, then it's possible to understand the statistical evidence in sentence 2 without having it lead to the conclusion in sentence 3. **A** thus provides a valid weakener.

TAKE
AWAY

When a passage posits a causal relationship (especially in the context of any of the four Critique question types), stay open to the following alternative possibilities:

- **The two elements are not in fact causally related.** They may simply be correlated events or phenomena without one leading to the other.

- **The two elements are both caused by an independent third factor.**

- **The causation flows in the opposite direction.** That is, instead of X causing Y, as the author maintains, perhaps Y causes X. "Alcohol and Depression" offers a good example of this possibility.

B: The general experiences of non-alcoholics are Irrelevant to the conclusion here, especially since these experiences need not be alcohol-related.

C is also Irrelevant. There may be many different causes of depression, so the fact that most depressed people are not alcoholics still allows for the possibility that alcohol may contribute to depression. If the choice read "All depressed people are not alcoholics," that would contradict the second sentence, but as it stands **C** has no effect on the argument.

D essentially says the opposite of correct choice **A**, so if you see how **A** is correct, you'll probably have no problems seeing how **D** is wrong. If anything, the fact in **D** would lean toward helping the argument by at least positing a chronology that's consistent with the causal relationship asserted by the author. That is, it's easier to believe that alcohol causes depression if most alcoholics didn't become depressed until they began drinking in excess.

TAKE
AWAY

It's important to remember that weakeners don't need to kill the argument, nor do strengtheners need to prove it. It's all a matter of *tilting the argument in the right direction:* making us more or less likely to believe in the validity of the conclusion. That's the standard to keep in mind.

E: *Successful careers?* A quick kill due to irrelevancy.

Question 17: The Case of the Potential Arsonist

17. Town resident: Both Mabel and Jasper were seen fleeing the vicinity of a burning abandoned building. Since Jasper owns a lucrative insurance policy on the building, the police should disregard Mabel and investigate only Jasper as a potential arsonist.

Which one of the following principles, if valid, most helps to justify the town resident's reasoning?

(A) The desire to commit a crime often indicates a desire to commit multiple crimes.

(B) One with the motivation to commit a potential crime is more likely than others to have committed that crime.

(C) The act of fleeing the scene of a potential crime strongly suggests that all those so fleeing are in fact guilty of committing a crime.

(D) When a crime has been committed, the police should focus their investigation first on the main perpetrator of the crime and later on possible accomplices.

(E) A fire should be investigated as a potential arson only if the burning structure is covered by a lucrative insurance policy.

Grill the Interrogator. The word *principles* tells us of course that we're in Principle territory, but further clues from the question stem—"if valid, most helps to justify"—tell us just *what kind* of Principle question we're up against: Supporting Principle. The "if valid" part reminds us that Supporting Principle questions are very much like Strengthen the Argument questions, except that the answer will be in the form of a general proposition. This alerts us that traditional Critique techniques such as finding assumptions and Essential Concepts like bait and switch and loose ends may be in play, so get your critical faculties in motion.

> For every Logical Reasoning question, Step 1 is to find out what the question is asking. Why do we place such an emphasis on grilling the interrogator? It's not just to get a sneak peek at something we'll see eventually, but so that we can read each passage with the proper mindset in place.

TAKE AWAY

Attack the Passage. Not much to this story. A building is burning, and Mabel and Jasper are both seen hot-tailing it out of the area. No Citizen Medal of Honor for them, presumably. But it gets worse: Jasper actually owns a lucrative insurance policy on the building. Well, that may sound somewhat suspicious, but is it enough to warrant disregarding Mabel entirely as someone who possibly played some role in the fire? The town resident argues directly from the existence of the insurance policy to suspicion as an arsonist. That sounds reasonable enough, but there is still a bit of a gap between the motivation to commit a crime and the actual perpetration of it; after all, you can't arrest someone for holding an insurance policy. The principle we seek should narrow this gap to bolster the recommendation to ignore Mabel and focus on Jasper as a potential arsonist. Let's see which choice provides the tightening we seek.

Work the Choices. We're looking for a proposition that explicitly speaks to the idea that a potential motivation to commit a crime should play a part in who is investigated in connection with a potential crime. **B** matches all the particulars. It recognizes that we're dealing with a "potential" crime, not a definite crime, and it links up the relevant aspect of the evidence (motivation) with the conclusion to specifically target the potentially motivated suspect (Jasper) while letting another potential suspect who may have been involved (Mabel) off the hook. Armed by the principle in **B**, the resident's argument seems to carry more weight.

> **TAKE AWAY**
>
> Just as in Strengthen the Argument questions, the right answer to Supporting Principle questions aren't meant to necessarily *prove* the argument in question but to make it sound more reasonable.

A: Isn't a single conflagration enough for one town? The notion of multiple crimes plays no part in the argument, so **A** doesn't get us any closer to accepting the town resident's recommendation.

C: So high-footing it out of there implicates *all* those who flee the scene, does it? Then why not go after Mabel too? If this principle were enacted, the opposite of the town resident's recommendation would seem prudent. We'd have to suspect Mabel too.

> **TAKE AWAY**
>
> You shouldn't be surprised to see that Strengthen the Argument common traps populate the wrong choices in Supporting Principle questions, since there's so much overlap between the two question types. Opposite choices in Strengthen questions weaken the argument, while Opposite choices in Supporting Principle questions conflict with the scenario presented rather than support it.

D fails on a few counts. First, it wrongly assumes that a crime has actually been committed, when it can only at this stage be characterized as a potential crime. So the first six words of the choice immediately bring us into uncharted territory, which can never be good in any Matching question since the whole point is to match the choices to the facts in the passage. The second problem is this business about dealing with potential accomplices later on, which doesn't accord at all with the resident's idea of simply letting Mabel off scot-free.

E seems a bit extreme in limiting arson investigations to mere financial considerations, no? What about jealous lovers, hate mongers, revenge seekers, and plain old mean people who like to burn things down? Regardless of all that, this choice doesn't address the main issue of targeting Jasper to the exclusion of Mabel, who was, after all, seen fleeing the same scene at the same time. The correct principle needs to speak to the resident's specific proposal to focus on Jasper and let Mabel slide. **B** does this. **E** does not.

Question 18: Comedic Intelligence

18. While many comics exhibit traditional intelligence as measured by academic testing, many comics do not. However, lack of such traditional intelligence is not an obstacle to successful comedy, as evidenced by the fact that skilled comics make us laugh because of their ability to communicate life's foibles in a way that is fresh, resonant, and surprising. A successful comedy career is thus not dependent on traditional intelligence.

Which one of the following is NOT assumed in the argument above?

(A) Traditional intelligence is not required for any other aspect of a successful comedy career besides an ability to make people laugh.

(B) It is not necessary to have traditional intelligence in order to perceive life's foibles.

(C) Traditional intelligence is not required to communicate life's foibles in a way that is fresh, resonant, and surprising.

(D) The most financially successful comedians are those who best communicate life's foibles in a way that is fresh, resonant, and surprising.

(E) Traditional intelligence is accurately reflected in the results of academic testing.

Grill the Interrogator. The question stem instructs us to find the choice that is NOT assumed, which right off the bat tells us that there are at least four assumptions in this short argument. That's a lot of gaps to look for, so keep your eye out for holes in the argument.

> NOT and EXCEPT questions require you to do the opposite of what you would normally do. For example, a bait and switch that would normally lead you to the correct choice will in this case help you cross off a wrong choice. Conversely, a choice that you would normally eliminate as a common trap will be the one that gets the point.

TAKE AWAY

Attack the Passage. Did you notice at least a couple of bait and switches here? The author mentions comics lacking traditional intelligence to support a point about how "skilled" comics make us laugh. However, she never indicates that non-intelligent comedians are among these skilled comedians. She also argues from "successful comedy" in sentence 2 to a "successful comedy *career*" in sentence 3's conclusion. The conclusion in that final sentence attempts to sever the link between traditional intelligence and a successful comedy career, so we'll employ these bait and switches to help us home in on the assumptions necessary to bridge these gaps.

Work the Choices. A trades off the comedy/comedy *career* switch, since traditional intelligence may be necessary to have a successful career even if it isn't necessary to successfully make people laugh. Supposing that traditional intelligence *is* necessary for a successful comedy career (that is, invoking the negate and destroy test), the conclusion in the final sentence falls apart, confirming that **A** must be assumed.

B and **C** hit on the first bait and switch noted above. The author argues that traditional intelligence isn't required for successful comedy because skilled comics exploit life's foibles to make us laugh. But if only traditionally intelligent people can perceive life's foibles, and communicate them to others in fresh, resonant, and exciting ways, the author's argument falls apart. The author must therefore assume that traditional intelligence is not required to perceive and communicate life's foibles in the manner indicated.

D is an Overreach and therefore need not be assumed by the argument. The author cites the ability to communicate life's foibles in a way that is fresh, resonant, and surprising as the reason comics make us laugh. She then goes on to talk about successful comedy careers but doesn't establish any explicit connection between these two things. It therefore is not necessary that the comedians who make the *most* money are those who communicate life's foibles the *best*. **D** connects two elements—money and communication—in a way that does not affect the conclusion and is therefore correct as the choice that need NOT be assumed.

E: Perhaps you asked, "But what if traditional intelligence isn't accurately measured by the tests cited?" If you did, then **E** should have stood out as another assumption created by yet another subtle bait and switch, this one between traditional intelligence and traditional intelligence *as measured by academic testing*.

TAKE AWAY

Assumption questions are difficult to begin with and can get downright nasty when they show up as NOT questions with four assumptions lurking in the choices. Often in these cases, it's easier to spot the correct choice that is not assumed (in this case, a fairly standard Overreach in **D**) than it is to sweat out the logic of all four wrong choices.

Question 19: The Case of the Rising Heart Disease

19. Dr. Nolan: Advances in emergency cardiovascular treatments between 1986 and 2006 have led to a significant decrease in the number of heart attacks in the U.S. resulting in fatalities. However, the incidence of heart disease in the U.S. rose dramatically during that same period.

Which one of the following, if true, would best resolve the seemingly paradoxical situation described above?

(A) Similar medical technologies invented between 1986 and 2006 have helped to shorten the recovery time for heart attack victims.

(B) The treatment advances were spurred by increases in heart disease prior to 1986 due largely to harmful changes in diet and lack of exercise among a significant percentage of the American population.

(C) The incidence of heart disease among non-risk groups fell between 1986 and 2006.

(D) People who survive heart attacks are classified for the rest of their lives as having heart disease due to the damage suffered by the heart during the attack.

(E) The severity of heart attacks has increased between 1986 and 2006.

Grill the Interrogator. We're presented with a seemingly paradoxical situation to resolve, so Paradox is clearly the name of the game. As always in this question type, the first step is to locate the mystery and see if there's any kind of Essential Concept, assumption, or alternative at the heart of it.

Attack the Passage. Emergency heart treatments seem to be working, as evidenced by a significant decrease in the number of fatal heart attacks over a twenty-year period. Notice that the phrase "resulting in fatalities" means that we can't assume that there were *fewer* heart attacks in the twenty-year span indicated than there were in previous periods, only that fewer *deaths* resulted from them than before.

> It's not uncommon in Logical Reasoning for a single word or phrase to have a major impact.

TAKE AWAY

"However" at the beginning of the second sentence signals that the seeming paradox is about to be revealed, and here it is: The incidence of heart disease actually *went up* while the number of fatal heart attacks went down. That does seem strange at first glance, but hopefully it seems less strange if you zero in on the bait and switch inherent in the passage. Fatal heart attacks and heart disease sound kind of the same, and indeed may be related in a plausible way, but they're far from identical. Keep that idea in mind as we move to the choices.

Work the Choices. The objective we may assign to the correct choice is to explain how fatal heart attacks are down yet heart disease itself seems to be on the rise. Let's see how the choices respond.

A: Recovery time is Irrelevant to the mystery. Even if people recover from heart attacks sooner, the discrepancy exists between the decrease in fatal heart attacks (which of course unfortunately involve no recovery time) and the seeming increased incidence of heart disease.

B: Why the treatments were invented is Irrelevant to their effect (decrease in fatal heart attacks) and the surprising other statistic in the passage that seems to fly in the face of this effect.

TAKE
AWAY

The correct choice to a Paradox question must be relevant to all sides of the surprising issue, fact, or finding. Choices that are Irrelevant to any aspect of the paradox cannot resolve the apparent discrepancy.

C, at first glance, may appear to contradict the evidence in the final sentence regarding the increased incidence of heart disease between 1986 and 2006. However, it limits its scope to non-risk groups, so there's no contradiction between the decrease in the incidence of heart disease among this group and the dramatic increase overall. The increase may be spurred by a large number of at-risk people. In any case, this clarification doesn't impinge upon our mystery, since we still have a lot fewer fatal heart attacks occurring during a period marked by a dramatic increase in the incidence of heart disease. The mystery remains, so we keep searching.

D links the two main groups in the passage (people surviving heart attacks and people with heart disease) in a way that resolves the apparent paradox. If people who survive heart attacks are forever classified as people with heart disease, then we can see how more heart attack survivors resulting from the new emergency procedures might lead to a greater statistical incidence of heart disease overall. **D** makes the situation more understandable and is therefore correct.

E: Wow, those newfangled heart treatments must sure be hyper-charged, if fatal heart attacks are way down despite the fact that heart attacks are getting more severe. What **E** doesn't tell us, however, is what we want to know: If fatal heart attacks are down, why is heart disease up?

Question 20: Type A Personalities

20. **Business school advertisement:** A career in financial sales can be both rewarding and profitable. Statistics show that this field has the highest percentage of "Type A" personalities compared to all other industries. People with Type A personalities are assertive, confident, and successful. So come study at Brighton Business Institute and begin developing your Type A personality today!

The reasoning in the advertisement is flawed in that it overlooks the possibility that

(A) people with personality types other than Type A can lead rewarding lives
(B) some financial salespeople do not have Type A personalities
(C) Brighton Business Institute has graduated people who have not gone on to successful careers in financial sales
(D) personality type largely determines one's choice of career and level of success in it
(E) personality types may be altered significantly through education

Grill the Interrogator. Not only does the question indicate that this is a Flaw type, it also tells us that the flaw centers on an advertisement overlooking some crucial possibility. This is a strong hint that our Essential Concept alternatives will come into play, but as always in Flaw questions, keep your eye out for all the Essential Concepts and the classic flaws you've learned.

> Advertisements are fertile ground for logical flaws. Make the critical examination of ads you come across in daily life a part of your LSAT preparation.

TAKE AWAY

Attack the Passage. The ad promotes "Type A" personalities—people commonly thought of as pushy and obnoxious—as "assertive, confident, and successful." Since Type A people are found most often in financial sales positions, and financial sales can be profitable and rewarding, the ad implores people to attend Brighton Business Institute to develop their Type A personalities. There are two things going on here. First, Brighton Business Institute comes out of nowhere and right into the spotlight, which should make you suspicious of possible loose end activity. And in fact, the ad does not say, but merely assumes, that one can prepare for a career in financial sales at BBI. So there's a missing piece already that the author overlooks. Another line of attack centers around a "But what if . . .?" scenario: *But what if Type A personalities are born, not made?* In other words, it may not be possible to train someone to be Type A—Type A people may simply prefer Type A activities like financial sales. We'll keep both of these possibilities in mind as we head to the choices.

There will sometimes be more than one way to answer a question legitimately, but only one can be included among the answer choices. Follow the choices' leads to see which issue the test makers are after.

Work the Choices. Choice **D** speaks to the latter possibility we just targeted. There's a possibility that personality type affects what one chooses to do with one's life and how good one is at what one pursues. If that's the case, then the ad might be guilty of reversing cause and effect. Instead of going to school to become a Type A personality and then have a career in financial sales, **D** raises the possibility that Type A people gravitate toward financial sales because *they're already Type A*. This overlooked possibility highlights the flaw in the ad.

TAKE AWAY

Cause and effect scenarios are not always obvious, because rarely do the test makers make it easy for you by using the actual word *cause*. But when they say something "largely determines" something else, they're talking about causation.

A: The ad deals only with Type A personalities, so is Not Obligated to provide any information on the lives of *non*–Type A personalities. We can also say that this latter group is Irrelevant to the ad's reasoning.

B falls into the Does No Such Thing category. By stating its evidence in terms of percentages, the advertisement implicitly recognizes (hence, does *not* overlook) the fact that not all financial salespeople are Type A personalities.

C: The ad doesn't argue that every single BBI grad becomes a successful financial salesperson, so it's Not Obligated to address the possibility that some may not follow this route.

E: Far from overlooking the notion in **E**, the ad is based specifically around the idea that personality type can be molded through education. So we can consider **E** an Opposite choice of sorts—uncommon in Flaw questions, but not unheard of.

Question 21: Foreign Relations

21. Foreign correspondent: There has been a significant deterioration in the relations of the region's two leading powers, as indicated by the recent cessation of negotiations between the two countries in regard to the disputed territory. Tension between these two countries has historically led to large-scale regional instability. If the negotiations do not resume, it is very likely that war will erupt within the next few months.

Which one of the following best describes the role played in the foreign correspondent's argument by the assertion that relations between the two countries have significantly deteriorated?

(A) It is speculation that is subsequently discounted in the development of the argument's main point.

(B) It is the main conclusion that the argument seeks to establish based on the likelihood of a conditional circumstance.

(C) It is an intermediate conclusion that serves as evidence for the argument's main conclusion.

(D) It is the reason presented for a source of conflict described in the argument.

(E) It is one of two unrelated conclusions drawn in the argument.

Grill the Interrogator. We're after the role of the assertion indicated in the question stem, so keep an eye out for a claim of deteriorating relations between two countries to determine why the author would say such a thing.

Attack the Passage. If the featured assertion is the argument's conclusion, we would expect evidence that points to the fact that the relation in question has deteriorated, and in fact we're not disappointed: We're told right up front in the first sentence that the deterioration in relations is "indicated by the recent cessation of negotiations between the two countries in regard to the disputed territory." Since evidence follows the featured assertion, we're on the right track in suspecting that that assertion is some kind of conclusion.

> If statement 1 is an assertion of some kind, and statement 2 answers the question "Why do you say that?," then statement 1 is a conclusion and statement 2 is evidence for it.

TAKE AWAY

But now we're led down a new track, presented with a *result* of the tense relations between the two countries—regional instability—followed by a dire prediction of war if the negotiations don't resume. Getting back to the featured assertion that relations have deteriorated, it seems to be both a conclusion supported by evidence and evidence itself for a larger conclusion that they better get back to talking or war will erupt.

Work the Choices. Given what we've determined, only choice **C** reflects the dual purpose of the assertion in question. The recent cessation of negotiations is evidence supporting the featured claim that relations have deteriorated. That, however, wouldn't make the best headline for the passage since it says nothing about the prospect of war, which is really what the correspondent is out to convey.

> ## TAKE AWAY
>
> *Hear Ye, Hear Ye!*—also known as the Headline Test—can come in handy for both kinds of Construction questions, Main Point and Role. When testing whether a statement is a passage's main point, see whether it would serve as a viable headline for the passage. Only a statement that encapsulates the conclusion will work as a headline.

C has it right: The claim is an *intermediate* conclusion—that is, a conclusion of one part of the passage that itself serves as evidence for a larger point. Let's see how the wrong choices go awry.

A: The deterioration of relations is stated as fact and backed by evidence, so *speculation* is too weak a way to describe the statement in question. In addition, this information, call it what we will, is not discounted but rather used to support the conclusion in the final sentence.

B: As we've seen, the featured statement is not the argument's main conclusion but rather a subsidiary conclusion that in turn supports a larger point. The "conditional circumstance" cited in the choice refers to the "if statement" in the last sentence, which doesn't provide the basis for the statement in question—rather, the other way around.

D gets things backward. If anything, the source of conflict—the disputed territories—is the reason for the deterioration in relations.

E is close, since the statement in question *is* one of two conclusions presented in the passage. However, as we've noted, these conclusions are not unrelated. The featured statement is a preliminary conclusion, supported by evidence, that in turn goes on to support the main conclusion in the final sentence.

Question 22: It Just Smells a Little . . .

> 22. Things that are passé never inspire admiration, but chivalry is admired by most people. It follows that chivalry is not passé.
>
> The reasoning in the argument above is most closely paralleled by that in which one of the following?
>
> (A) Janice is usually on time to school except for days following her night shift at the ice cream store. Janice did not work the night shift at the ice cream store last night, so it would be unusual if she were late to school today.
>
> (B) This truck must not be reliable, because reliable trucks must be able to be driven at least 100,000 miles without requiring serious repairs.
>
> (C) Mitchell's fraternity is not on probation, since most fraternities on probation have been issued behavioral warnings and Mitchell's fraternity has never been issued a behavioral warning.
>
> (D) Economic downturns are never a cause for celebration. While some people benefit financially from such events, most people are adversely affected.
>
> **(E) Benjamin is not impulsive, because while impulsive people do not deliberate, Benjamin often practices deliberation.**

Grill the Interrogator. Here's a Parallel Reasoning question, and we're not told that the original argument is flawed so it must be valid. This means you need not trot out all your Critique tools to locate gaps or weaknesses in the argument. Prepare instead to focus your full attention on the argument's structure.

> **TAKE AWAY**
>
> There are two kinds of Parallel Reasoning passages: those with flawed reasoning, and those without flawed reasoning. **Grill the Interrogator** to see what kind of question you're up against. If the test makers don't tell you there's a flaw, there's not. Trust them on this one. Knowing whether the argument is valid will help you to get a leg up on the question.

Attack the Passage. The presence in the passage of formal logic elements like *never, most,* and *it follows that* suggests that this one may be amenable to an algebraic approach, so let's try out our technique of using letters to represent the terms. And it may help to switch the clauses of the first sentence to get that statement into a more manageable form: X (chivalry) is sometimes Y (admired). Z (passé) is never Y (admired). Therefore X (chivalry) is not Z (passé). (Hence the small jest in the title, a takeoff on the old joke "Chivalry is not dead . . . it just smells a little.") You're ready to search for that same structure among the choices.

The test makers don't always present the terms of their arguments in the most efficient order, but nothing stops you from reordering the terms to make them easier to work with as long as doing so doesn't change the logic. For example, the argument "Because of the holiday, the library will close early on Friday" is exactly the same as "The library will close early on Friday because of the holiday." Switching statements around may help you better comprehend an argument's logical flow.

Work the Choices. **A**'s conclusion, highlighted by the word "so," is that something would be *unusual*. That doesn't match the more definite "X is not Z" conclusion of the original.

B starts off promisingly with a definite "X is not Z" type of conclusion but never closes the deal since it doesn't relate the truck in question back to the 100,000-mile test. **B** is therefore missing a whole chunk of evidence present in the original.

C contains flawed reasoning. Just because *most* frats on probation have been issued warnings doesn't mean that Mitchell's frat definitely isn't on probation just because it hasn't received a warning. The "most" would need to be "all" for this argument to work, and since it doesn't work, it can't be parallel to the valid reasoning in the passage.

D: Map it out to see if it matches: X (economic downturns) leads to Y (benefit for some), but X also leads to Z (adverse effects for most). Therefore, X is never C (cause for celebration). There are more terms in this argument than in the original, and the original doesn't contrast the effects of a specific type of event. Not parallel.

E is all that's left, but let's double check to see that it matches. Do we have an "X is sometimes Y" statement? Yes: Benjamin sometimes deliberates. What about "Z is never Y"? Yes: Impulsive people never deliberate. The conclusion matches as well: X (Benjamin) is not Z (impulsive). So **E** is valid, parallel, and correct.

Parallel Reasoning questions intimidate many test takers, but the strategies you've learned can cut them down to size. However, if they still give you the heebie-jeebies, there's nothing wrong with resolving to save the Parallel Reasoning questions for last. You surely wouldn't be the first to do so, and that might be the best approach for you. Still, learning how to symbolize arguments when possible and how to characterize and match conclusions can at the very least increase your odds even if you have to guess.

23. Nutritionist: Candy containing processed sugar and artificial sweeteners is much more readily available to children than it ever has been. Children today have more money and less parental oversight than in the past, increasing their opportunities to obtain the kinds of candy that, consumed in abundance, cause childhood weight and health problems. Moreover, everyone from teachers to relatives to strangers on the street seek to gain the affection of children through candy. Candy companies, of course, play a role in encouraging consumption by constantly expanding the kinds of candies available, and the venues from which to purchase them. These factors, coupled with a culture of permissiveness, are significant contributors to the recent increase in childhood obesity.

Which one of the following, if true, would most strengthen the argument?

(A) Internal documents of industry-leading candy companies indicate that marketing their products to children is among their primary objectives.

(B) There is a significant correlation between the availability and excess consumption of candy among children.

(C) Teenagers eat as much candy as younger children but are just as likely to become obese.

(D) Children of parents who carefully supervise the amount of candy their children consume are still sometimes offered candy at school and from other adults.

(E) Children consuming less than the national average of candy consumption in their age group are 35 percent less likely to suffer from diet-related health problems.

Grill the Interrogator. Feeling in a helping mood? Hopefully you are, as this argument is in need of a bit of help, according to its stem. You know the drill: When you see a Strengthen the Argument question stem, ramp up your critical faculties in search of a gap, bait and switch, or other weakness to shore up.

Attack the Passage. Poor kids! Candy seems everywhere. Not only is there more available, kids also have more money to get it, less interference from parents, and strangers plying them with it on the street. (Whatever happened to "Don't take candy from strangers?") Add to all that the machinations of the candy companies themselves, and it's a childhood dream come true; a superabundance of candy. And wait, it gets better: There's also a "culture of permissiveness," to boot. After all these factors are listed, the idea of obesity doesn't seem so foreign—but it should. In fact, it's a loose end that literally comes out of nowhere as the last word of the passage. But why a loose end, you may ask? Certainly if you eat all that candy, it makes sense that obesity may result. Granted. But nowhere does it say that kids today are actually *eating* all this candy—all we're told is that all this extra candy is *available*. Big difference. They have their *opportunities* to consume the stuff that, *eaten in abundance,* causes weight gain, but we're never told that kids actually do eat candy in abundance. We could just as easily label the problem here as a bait and switch between *availability* of candy and *excess consumption,* leading to an unsupported conclusion, obesity. Let's see how the choices play out with this thought in mind.

TAKE AWAY

Loose ends and bait and switches are closely related. Don't worry about labeling them precisely—you don't actually get any points for using the correct terminology. As long as you recognize the kind of gap created in the passage as a *result* of these Essential Concepts, it doesn't matter what you call them, or that you call them anything at all. We employ the terminology to help you think in a certain way. Once you're thinking at that level, you'll recognize the relevant passage elements on your own terms and will use that understanding to answer the questions.

Work the Choices. Since we're to help the argument, we need to find a choice that tightens the connection between the availability of candy and its abundant consumption by kids. **B** provides this connection rather directly and in so doing makes us more likely to believe that the factors cited in the passage are indeed contributors to childhood obesity, as the author maintains.

TAKE AWAY

Don't hesitate if it seems like you can knock a question off quickly. If you've done the proper work attacking the passage in Step 2 of the Essential Strategy, there's no need to doubt yourself when you find the exact answer you seek. Saving time on questions that are easier for you frees up extra time for the more difficult questions.

A: Stop the presses! Candy companies target children? Really? Get out! Actually, aside from being common sense, this shocker is pretty well suggested in the passage already and doesn't get us any closer to supporting the claim regarding obesity since we still don't know that kids are consuming candy in abundance.

TAKE AWAY

Beware of choices that do little more than repeat some aspect of the passage's evidence.

C doesn't help the argument because we don't know the amounts of candy teenagers and younger kids eat. Maybe it's a really *small* but equal amount. In any case, this fact is too vague to help us link candy availability with obesity because, like **A**, it gets us no closer to believing that kids are actually abusing the candy.

D clarifies how the availability issue plays out for some kids whose parents are on the ball but still doesn't connect availability to actual excess consumption.

E, at best, reinforces the notion that candy isn't good for kids, but it doesn't touch on the major issue of the passage: candy availability and obesity. A trusty common trap: Irrelevant.

Question 24: The Great Museum Robbery

24. A security camera recorded the actions of a single masked thief as he perpetrated last week's Swindale Museum robbery. Kendrick is not aware of the museum's security system, while Mason, who is aware of the security system, is close friends with the building's security manager, Yarden. Kendrick possesses both the cunning and the audacity to conceptualize the robbery, but perpetrating the robbery required knowledge of a secret code to deactivate the building's security system.

Which one of the following follows most logically from the statements above?

(A) It is impossible for a single person to have both conceptualized and perpetrated the Swindale Museum robbery.

(B) Kendrick neither conceptualized nor perpetrated the Swindale Museum robbery.

(C) Kendrick may have conceptualized but did not perpetrate the Swindale Museum robbery.

(D) Mason may have perpetrated but did not conceptualize the Swindale Museum robbery.

(E) Yarden revealed the museum's secret security code to the perpetrator of the Swindale Museum robbery.

Grill the Interrogator. The phrase "follows most logically" may remind you of the "most strongly supported" terminology of Standard Inference questions, but that doesn't discount the possibility that there may be some stricter logic involved or even some formal logic elements to decipher. In any case, keep your eyes on the facts and your mind working on how they may be combined to yield the statement among the choices that's most logically inferable.

Attack the Passage. The game's afoot! For the Sherlock Holmes in you, we've got a bit of a mystery to figure out, but, as you'll see, we aren't given enough information to arrive at an airtight solution. No matter—we can still arrive at a correct answer. A museum was robbed by a single masked thief. Kendrick is smart and bold enough to think up the caper, but actually pulling it off required knowledge of a security code, and Kendrick didn't even know about the existence of the security system. That's, in fact, enough to lead us to one solid deduction—Kendrick couldn't have done it. Quick, Watson, to the choices!

Work the Choices. C contains the deduction noted above—that Kendrick could not have perpetrated the robbery because he neither knew about the need to deactivate the security system nor about the code that's required to do it. But he still may have *conceptualized* the robbery, since we're told flat out that he possesses the cunning and audacity to do so. So **C** is logically inferable, and the only thing that may be a bit confusing about it is that it comprises one definite and one nondefinite piece of information. Kendrick definitely didn't do it, but may have dreamed it up.

If an Inference choice contains two discrete ideas, evaluate them individually. Only if both are logically inferable can we deem that choice the winner.

TAKE AWAY

THE NEW LSAT

The other choices play fast and loose with the facts, creating Overreaches that infer too much from what we're told or concocting Unknowables out of the Yarden/Mason alliance.

A and **B** both Overreach. We know that Kendrick cannot have both conceptualized *and* perpetrated the robbery, but that doesn't prove that there can't be some other individual possessing the talent to both come up with and carry out the idea. So choice **A** goes too far. Similarly, nothing rules out Kendrick as the mastermind behind the plan, so it's premature to conclude that Kendrick *definitely* wasn't involved in the conceptualization of the heist.

D: The first part of **D** is copacetic, as Mason does at least know about the security system, which doesn't eliminate him as the potential perpetrator. However, we have no knowledge whatsoever regarding his possible role in conceptualization. Maybe he planned the robbery, maybe he didn't.

E further treads on Unknowable ground, trying to exploit the relationship between Mason and Yarden. The speculation that Yarden *must* have spilled the beans merely because he's friends with someone who knew about the security system would likely have Sherlock Holmes turning in his (fictional) grave.

Question 25: Recovering Alcoholics

25. Alcoholics who have stopped drinking but not participated in a 12-step program cannot be fully recovered, because full recovery requires resolution of the psychological conditions that lead to and reinforce alcohol addiction.

The argument above assumes that

(A) the psychological conditions associated with alcohol addiction cannot be resolved outside of a 12-step program

(B) any alcoholic participating in a 12-step program will achieve full recovery

(C) 12-step programs equally address the psychological conditions that lead to alcohol addiction and those that reinforce it

(D) the conditions that lead to an alcoholic's full recovery are identical to those that lead an alcoholic to stop drinking

(E) participation in a 12-step program must be independent of the resolution of psychological conditions underpinning alcoholism in order for full recovery to occur

Grill the Interrogator. A short question stem with the word "assumes" can only mean one thing—another Assumption question and the need to slip into a critical, gap-filling frame of mind.

Attack the Passage. Note how the single sentence of the passage goes from one term to another, something we'd expect when a gap exists in the argument. Hopefully you got to the "resolution of psychological conditions" part and said to yourself, "Where did *that* come from?" That's one step from recognizing that official-sounding phrase as a loose end, which is one step from using this Essential Concept to solve the problem.

Work the Choices. The loose end here is the fact that full recovery requires something that is never addressed earlier in the passage. For all we know, the resolution in question can be achieved *without* taking part in a 12-step program; nothing says it can't. If resolution of these psychological conditions *can* be achieved without the program (the negate and destroy test), then the author would have no business unequivocally asserting that alcoholics who have not participated in a 12-step program cannot be fully recovered. Perhaps they resolved their psychological conditions on their own, or with help from other quarters. The argument therefore assumes **A**: Resolution cannot happen outside the 12-step program environment.

B is an Overreach, mistaking what the author assumes to be a necessary factor in recovery (a 12-step program) for a sufficient one.

C provides an Unnecessary Clarification, since a comparison between conditions that lead to and those that reinforce alcoholism is irrelevant to the main issue regarding the requirements of recovery.

D actually goes against the grain of the passage, since the author explicitly states that ceasing to drink is not by itself sufficient for full recovery—that another condition, a 12-step program, is necessary before full recovery can be claimed. So what makes one stop drinking cannot, by this author's definition, be exactly the same thing that leads to full recovery.

E runs counter to the passage as well, since inherent in the author's argument is the notion that a 12-step program is necessary to resolve the psychological conditions underpinning alcoholism; in other words, the assumption stated in choice **A**. **E**, saying that these things must be *independent*, gets it backward.

SECTION IV: ANSWERS & GUIDED EXPLANATIONS

Reading Comprehension

Passage 1: Fair Use

Scout the Territory. We find our usual Main Point and Primary Purpose Big Picture questions on each end of the question set, so we'll look to lock down questions 1 and 8 first. The only other Big Picture question turns out to be an Attitude question in number 5, and you may benefit by underlining "successful employment of the fair use defense" as something to look out for, even though you of course don't yet know what that is.

As for the Content questions, question 2 looks somewhat sinister: an Author Agreement question with no indication whatsoever where in the passage the answer will be found. It's an EXCEPT question to boot, so it looks like a good one to postpone. However, Detail Purpose question 3 seems user-friendly thanks to the handy line reference, and you can put a small asterisk next to those lines of the passage to highlight "right to public assembly" as a tested issue. Question 4 is simply too complicated to decipher without knowing what the passage is about, so you shouldn't worry about it at this point. On the other hand, Fact question 6 looks promising thanks to a definite clue provided in the stem. Underline "self-censorship" to remind you to take special note of this detail when it appears. Question 7 looks like it might be trouble: Looking for a situation that "best exemplifies" something means we're in Extension territory, and those can be tough. In any case, a quick skim through the set gives us a good idea of what's what, and it's time to hit the passage keeping these clues in mind.

> **TAKE AWAY**
>
> The goal of Scouting the Territory is to give you a sense of what to focus on in the passage. Don't expect everything to be revealed, but look to extract a few clues from the question stems to help direct your attack on the passage.

Mine the Essential Elements. In the Reading Comprehension chapter, we identified seven Essential Elements to watch for in each paragraph and provided in-depth paragraph analyses to demonstrate the type of targeted reading that yields points. Of course, you don't have time to obsess over every paragraph *ad nauseam*, so at this stage of the game we'd like to demonstrate how to streamline this step of the Essential Strategy while still getting as much out of each paragraph as possible.

Your goal in reading the passage is to quickly pick out the key points of each paragraph—that is, to extract the things that are consistently and systematically tested in the questions.

Paragraph 1 Essential Elements

> While clear-cut guidelines exist to delineate and adjudicate blatant cases of copyright infringement, the legal implications of appropriating copyrighted materials into new forms of art and social commentary are much less clearly defined.
> (5) In such cases, the Fair Use provision of Article 107 of U.S. copyright law can provide some guidance. Fair use provides an exception to copyright restrictions, allowing one to copy, publish, or distribute without permission partial (or in some cases even entire) copyrighted works for purposes such as
> (10) criticism, comment, news reporting, teaching, scholarship, or research.

- **Giveaways:** The signal word "while" turns us on to an immediate contrast: some copyright cases are straightforward; others are not. The phrase "In such cases" refers back to non-clearly defined copyright cases, for which something called "fair use" may provide some guidance.

- **Purpose:** To introduce and define fair use, and suggest a case for which it may be useful.

- **Players/Extras:** There are no people to speak of, but fair use, mentioned twice and defined in the lengthy final sentence, seems to be the main player in the paragraph.

- **Main Point:** The fair use provision may provide exceptions to copyright restrictions in cases in which artists and social commentators want to use copyrighted materials in their works.

- **Author Behavior:** Just presenting facts so far—very descriptive.

- **Author Opinion:** Nothing yet. Just because fair use is introduced as something that may be used in certain cases to get around copyright laws doesn't mean the author is in favor of it. We'll have to wait and see what, if anything, the author thinks about this, or if she's just writing to present the facts.

- **Passage Main Idea:** Too soon to tell. Most likely the main idea will have something to do with copyright law and this fair use provision the author introduces, but we'll have to stay tuned to find out where it's all heading.

The first paragraph sets the stage, but expect that the direction the author will take will be revealed later on.

Paragraph 2 Essential Elements

> Not surprisingly, copyright holders have difficulty
> condoning any unlicensed use of their works. Fair use
> proponents counter that to prevent artists and critics from
> (15) freely reusing cultural sounds, objects, and iconography
> would flout basic democratic principles, stifle creativity, and
> lead to cultural stagnation. Such restrictions, they believe,
> would severely limit the opportunity to engage those who
> create and consume mainstream culture in meaningful
> (20) dialogue.

- **Giveaways:** "Not surprisingly" prefaces one opinion, that of copyright holders, while the word "counter" introduces the opposing viewpoint of people who believe in fair use.

- **Purpose:** To mention opposition to fair use and present another group's argument in favor of it.

- **Players/Extras:** The players here are groups: copyright holders and fair use proponents. We'll have to wait and see which, if either group, remains in the spotlight, or whether one or both drop out of sight.

TAKE AWAY

> Active reading means anticipating where the passage is likely to go with respect to each of the Essential Elements you extract. This is particularly important early in the passage when many directions are possible and the players and extras are not yet established.

- **Main Point:** People who hold copyrights don't want others to use their works unless they license them, whereas fair use supporters think the provision gives artists and critics the right to freely reuse cultural images, sounds, and objects to make new works under certain conditions.

- **Author Behavior:** Still just presenting facts.

- **Author Opinion:** None yet. So far all the author has done is tell us what fair use is and what other people think about it.

- **Passage Main Idea:** Still too soon to tell. Will the author eventually support fair use? Or oppose it? Or just keep on telling us what it is and how others feel about it? Stay tuned.

Paragraph 3 Essential Elements

> Judges generally consider four factors when evaluating fair use claims. The first is the purpose and character of the use, such as whether the product incorporating the material will be used in a non-profit, educational, or commercial environment.
> (25) Within this category, judges look favorably on "transformative" uses, those involving radical alterations of the material's original intent. The second consideration is the nature of the work used. For example, judges generally favor the fair use of non-fiction over fiction, and of scholarly works for
> (30) which quoting is expected. The third factor concerns the amount used; the lower the proportion of the original whole, the more likely fair use will be granted. However, the more central the used portion is to the spirit of the original work, the lower the chance of a fair use ruling. The fourth factor
> (35) considers the effect on the value of the original; that is, the extent to which the new product will directly compete with the copyrighted work in the marketplace.

- **Giveaways:** The first sentence sets the stage of what's to come in this long third paragraph: factors considered in fair use evaluations.

The first sentence of a paragraph is called the "topic sentence" because it often previews what's to come. If you're running short on time and have only a few minutes left to get through a whole passage, you may still get something out of it by skimming the topic sentence of each paragraph.

"The first," "the second," "the third," and "the fourth" helpfully structure the paragraph, breaking it down neatly into discussions of the four relevant fair use considerations.

- **Purpose:** To explain how fair use works.

- **Players/Extras:** This is purely about fair use—no other player emerges. Judges are mentioned a couple of times, but merely in the role of those who evaluate fair use claims.

- **Main Point:** The paragraph is solely about the mechanics of fair use, so there's no overarching point to the paragraph beyond simply explaining how the provision works. A quick skim and a general understanding of the mechanics are all that's needed here.

THE NEW LSAT

You don't have to read the entire passage in detail. Focus on the Big Picture issues and blow past details that you didn't highlight in Step 1 (Scout the Territory) of our Essential Strategy. You can return to those details later on if and when a question requires it.

- **Author Behavior:** Still in descriptive mode, nothing more.

One important thing to notice about the author's behavior is whether he or she is taking a stand, making an argument, refuting, questioning, or otherwise evaluating some thing or issue, as opposed to merely relating facts.

- **Author Opinion:** Nope—the author is still pretty much in the background. We really don't have a sense of what this author thinks about fair use because all she's done so far is tell us what it is and how it works.

- **Passage Main Idea:** We've come this far and the only overriding idea we have to work with is the notion that the fair use provision exists to ease copyright restrictions in some cases. That's essentially no different from what we learned earlier on—only fleshed out with specifics regarding the mechanics of the provision. With one more paragraph to go, we're about to find out if the author goes beyond this.

Paragraph 4 Essential Elements

> There are no hard-line rules regarding how and in what proportion judges apply the four factors to fair use
> (40) determinations. Moreover, fair use is not an affirmative protection—like, for example, the right to public assembly—but rather a defense that one can appeal to only after a charge has been brought. Individuals averse to the pressure and expense of legal confrontations often decide not to invoke
> (45) their fair use privilege, essentially constituting a form of self-censorship. Capitalizing on this hesitancy, many well-funded copyright holders have launched aggressive attacks on fair use attempts through near-automatic issuances of cease-and-desist letters, regardless of legal merit. Nonetheless, fair
> (50) use provides a necessary restraint on otherwise unbounded copyright privileges, and remains a powerful legal instrument should artists and social commentators choose to invoke it.

- **Giveaways:** The phrase "no hard-line rules" is reminiscent of the phrase "much less clearly defined" in paragraph 1, so the author seems in sentence 1 to be getting back to the ambiguity inherent in the provision. The signal word "moreover" suggests that sentence 2 will expand on this idea, and it does. Sentence 3 contains the "self-censorship" reference that we noted from our question stem analysis, so that sentence merits a detailed reading. Sentence 4 provides yet another problem with the provision, detailing aggressive attacks against fair use. And then comes the most important giveaway of all. Following this whole laundry list of fair use problems appears the word "nonetheless," signaling that despite these problems, something good may yet come of it. The rest of the last sentence finally presents the author's opinion on the matter.

- **Purpose:** To show problems inherent in fair use but to argue that fair use is *nonetheless* necessary and potentially powerful if people choose to use it.

- **Players/Extras:** Judges, individuals, and copyright holders all make cameos here, but fair use is still the star, and the author herself finally emerges to state an opinion.

- **Main Point/Author Behavior/Author Opinion/Passage Main Idea:** All of these things come together through the giveaways and purpose just noted. The author does emerge to state the opinion that fair use is a necessary and powerful instrument in the hands of artists and social commentators, should they choose to invoke it.

Divide and Conquer. With a firm grasp of the passage, it's time to knock off the questions, and you'll notice that at least the Big Picture questions should fall fairly quickly after performing the analysis above.

Divide. . . Main Point first, and there it is conveniently leading off the set.

---

1. Which one of the following most accurately states the main point of the passage?

(A) Due to opposition from well-funded copyright holders, fair use will never be successfully employed by a majority of cultural innovators who wish to appropriate copyrighted materials.

(B) Fair use ensures the right of cultural innovators to appropriate copyrighted materials for purposes of art and social commentary.

(C) While there are four factors generally considered in fair use determinations, there are currently no hard-line rules regarding how these factors are applied to specific cases.

(D) Despite obstacles hindering its application, fair use provides the legal means by which artists and social commentators may incorporate copyrighted materials into their works.

(E) Content creators seek unbounded copyright privileges and do not under any circumstances condone the unlicensed use of their works.

. . . and Conquer. The author's opinion and the passage's main idea should be fresh in your mind on the heels of mining paragraph 4's Essential Elements. There we saw the author finally took a stand in favor of fair use, despite the problems with it. **D** comes closest to this notion.

A is too negative to describe a passage that ends on a positive note.

THE NEW LSAT

B: "Ensures the right" is a bit too strong, since the author makes clear that fair use, fraught with ambiguities, is far from a surefire solution. So you may have chopped **B** as an Overreach. Even if you overlooked that, **B** only gets at a small part of the story, leaving out both the problems encountered by those seeking to use fair use and the author's eventual support of it.

C and **E** constitute Retrieval Errors. **C** attempts to expand paragraph 3 and the first line of paragraph 4 into the main idea of the passage, while **E** does the same for content creators' absolute protection of their works. Both choices are *true,* but there's more to the passage than the facts they present.

Divide . . . We now continue in Big Picture mode to dispense of the Primary Purpose question.

8. The author's primary purpose in the passage is to

   (A) discourage copyright holders from erecting unwarranted and illegal obstacles to necessary forms of cultural innovation
   (B) delineate the mechanisms of a legal provision and encourage its utilization
   (C) outline a way in which artists and social commentators can reuse cultural sounds, objects, and iconography while avoiding all accusations of copyright infringement
   (D) explain the four factors that judges generally consider when evaluating fair use claims
   (E) show how copyright holders attempt to discourage people from exploiting a loophole in copyright law

. . . and Conquer. Up until the powerful word *nonetheless* at the end of paragraph 4, we may have reasonably concluded that the author's purpose was to bore us to death with facts about fair use. And perhaps she accomplished this purpose, in any case. But as we saw above, her purpose takes a new turn in the final sentence of the passage where she advocates for the employment of fair use, despite the difficulties she cites. Any choice that doesn't reflect this element of advocacy can't be correct. Choices **C** and **D** fall on this count, since ultimately the author is out to do more than merely "outline" or "explain." (You may have also pegged **C** as an Overreach, as the author doesn't advocate using fair use to avoid *all accusations of copyright infringement,* but rather to circumvent charges of infringement in cases appropriately covered by the provision such as commentary and criticism.)

B begins in the same fashion, and if "delineate" were the only verb in the choice, it too would fail for the same reason as **C** and **D**. But "encourage its utilization" is more than enough to complete the picture, so **B** has it right. The author does spend much time telling us what the fair use provision is all about, and then encourages artists and social commentators to use it.

A and **E** are Retrieval Errors that focus too heavily on copyright holders. The author doesn't write primarily to illuminate *their* motives or persuade *them* to not be so stringent, but rather to rally those who would use their works for art and commentary to make use of a legal tool at their disposal. Nor is "loophole" the best word to describe fair use, but we need not quibble with that since **E** has a bigger problem in mistaking the main focus of the passage.

> **TAKE AWAY**
>
> If you've properly mined the passage's Essential Elements, then you should experience a natural transition between finishing off the passage and knocking off the Main Point and Primary Purpose questions.

Divide . . . There's only one more Big Picture question in the set, so let's turn to the Attitude question next.

5. With respect to the prospect of the successful employment of the fair use defense, the author of the passage can most accurately be described as

   (A) mildly perplexed
   (B) exceedingly assured
   (C) brazenly defiant
   (D) cynically suspicious
   (E) cautiously optimistic

. . . and Conquer. We're asked for the author's take on the prospect of employing the fair use defense successfully. The final sentence of the passage is the place to look, since it is there, and there alone, that we hear about the author's opinion on *anything*. The author says that the fair use provision is *necessary* and could be *powerful* if people go ahead and use it, despite potential obstacles (its ambiguity, the possibility of receiving cease-and-desist letters, etc.). So that sounds positive, but with qualifications, for after all, the author admits there's some serious opposition to using the provision. It's therefore reasonable to say that the author is optimistic, but cautiously so. That's why **E** is correct and why **B,** ignoring all the obstacles and caveats, goes too far.

> **TAKE AWAY**
>
> The first step in an Attitude question is to get in the ballpark, determining whether the tone is positive, negative, or neutral.

A: There is no sense of confusion on the part of the author, who appears to have a firm grasp of the issues.

C: The author wouldn't qualify as brazen (bold, brash) or defiant. In fact, she barely surfaces at all until the final paragraph; not exactly a sign of audacity. She voices her opinion in a reasoned, qualified way. So **C** Overreaches.

D suggest a sense of paranoia not evident in any part of the passage. The author may be wary or cautious, but is neither *cynical* nor *suspicious* regarding the prospects of utilizing fair use.

Divide . . . Now that the Big Picture questions are out of the way, Fact question 6 is a fine place to go next, especially if you underlined or circled "self-censorship" in paragraph 4.

> **TAKE AWAY**
>
> The work you do during Step 1 of the Essential Strategy, Scout the Territory, sets you up for answering the questions in Step 3. When Fact questions provide line references or include specific terminology from the passage, take careful note of those things when you come to them in the passage. That gives you a head start in answering those questions.

6. According to the passage, self-censorship results when

    (A) politicians who would otherwise criticize the behavior of well-funded copyright holders choose not to do so for fear of losing political support
    (B) artists and social commentators who would otherwise appropriate cultural objects to create new works choose not to do so for fear of legal repercussions
    (C) lawyers choose not to advise clients as to their fair use privileges because they are wary of entangling their clients in protracted and costly litigation
    (D) artists and social commentators choose not to explore certain subjects because there is no way to do those subjects justice without appropriating cultural materials
    (E) artists and social commentators refuse to make fair use a subject of their works for fear of being embroiled in legal confrontations

. . . and Conquer. The third sentence of paragraph 4 tells us what constitutes self-censorship: when individuals who fear legal confrontations consciously decide not to make use of their fair use privileges. The individuals referred to are inferably the people the author discusses throughout the passage who could and should utilize fair use—artists and social commentators who would like to appropriate cultural materials. So according to the author, self-censorship occurs when such people choose not to appropriate cultural objects in the way they would wish, out of fear of legal repercussions. **B** is correct.

> **TAKE AWAY**
>
> The right answers to Fact questions don't repeat the passage's text word for word; usually, a bit of paraphrasing is necessary. Here, the passage says "individuals," and correct choice **B** requires that we figure out which individuals the author means.

A: *Politicians?* Irrelevant. Quick kill.

C is a Twister: We're told that individuals censor themselves by not invoking fair use due to fear of legal confrontations, not that *lawyers* are afraid of entangling clients in long and costly litigation. (And besides, aren't lawyers the ones who *like* long and costly litigation?)

D may be the result *after* the individuals in question have been scared off and have thus engaged in the self-censorship the author mentions, but choosing to ditch projects for lack of appropriated materials is not what the author means by self-censorship. Again, that involves failing to utilize fair use privileges.

E distorts the idea of artists using fair use to produce their works into the idea of artists producing works *about* fair use. Classic Twister.

Divide . . . "User friendly" was how we described question 3, so let's dispose of this Detail Purpose question next.

3. The author mentions the right to public assembly (line 41) primarily to

    (A) suggest that two kinds of legal protection that differ in one respect are similar in another respect
    (B) distinguish laws with hard-line interpretations from those with more flexible interpretations
    (C) establish that appealing to affirmative protections is preferable to reacting to lawsuits only after charges have been brought
    (D) provide an example of a right that can be defended only after one has been accused of breaking the law
    (E) illustrate by means of contrast a limitation in the fair use provision

. . . and Conquer. Move right to the cited lines if necessary and reread the bit about the right to public assembly.

> Remember, Detail Purpose questions ask not *what* the author means by something, but *why* he or she mentions that thing at all.

TAKE
AWAY

The structure of the highlighted sentence suggests that the right to public assembly is intended to provide an example of something that fair use is *not*; specifically, an affirmative protection. So the author is using this example to present a contrast of sorts. Choice **E** speaks of contrast, but we better make sure the rest of **E** pans out. Does the author use the contrast to point to a limitation in fair use? Yes; we can infer that from the way she describes fair use as a "defense that one can appeal to *only after a charge has been brought*." That certainly doesn't sound as good as an *affirmative protection*; a law that directly allows people to do something such as assemble in public. **E** therefore pinpoints the purpose of this detail.

A: The author describes no similarity between fair use and the right to public assembly. Moreover, fair use is deemed a defense, not a protection, so this choice fails on that count as well.

B is a Retrieval Error that focuses on a different element of the passage, the distinction made early on between clearly-defined laws and those with looser, more flexible interpretations.

C would be correct for a passage focusing on the advantages of affirmative protections over after-the-fact defenses, but that's not what we get here. The "right to public assembly" bit is provided in order to shed light on the applicability of fair use. It's not mentioned to help the author make a general argument for the superiority of one kind of legal vehicle over another.

D: Opposite: The right to public assembly is presented as an example of an affirmative protection. *Fair use* is defined as a right that can be defended only after a charge has been brought.

Divide . . . Five down, three to go—and none of them particularly seem to be crowd-pleasers. We should, however, know enough about this author's opinions by now to take a shot at Author Agreement question 2, so let's head there next.

TAKE
AWAY

> Toward the end of a question set, there's no right or wrong order to attempt the questions. The order in which you do the questions is entirely up to you, and the goal is to knock off the easier ones (easier *for you*, that is) first. You might even decide to answer the easiest five or six questions in each question set, in which case you'd guess on the remaining few and move on to another passage. Those who achieve their target scores are those who take control of the test.

2. The author of the passage would most likely agree with each of the following statements EXCEPT:

    (A) **Most attempts by copyright holders to prevent unlicensed use of their works do not have legal merit.**
    (B) Invoking in advance and then successfully employing a fair use defense requires courage on the part of cultural innovators.
    (C) Not all artists and social commentators fully realize the works they initially set out to produce.
    (D) The protection offered by fair use is not as strictly defined as some other legal protections.
    (E) At least some of the factors that judges evaluate to make fair use determinations are subject to multiple levels of interpretation.

. . . and Conquer. Since this is an EXCEPT question, each wrong choice will contain a statement that the author would agree with. The right answer will contain something the author will either *disagree* with or something about which we can't determine her opinion.

In all scored sections of the LSAT, knowing what the question asks allows you to determine in advance what the right answers and wrong choices will look like, sound like, or do.

With no clues to guide us, we'll simply have to test the choices one by one.

A seems too extreme to attribute to our mild-mannered author. Sure, she appears to believe that copyright holders with a "no-how, no-way under any circumstances" view toward appropriation should lighten up when it comes to others making fair use of their works when appropriate. But to say that she thinks that *most* attempts by copyright holders to protect their works have no basis appears to go too far. Since we're looking for the choice that the author is least likely to agree with, we'll flag this one as a good possibility but still check the others to be sure.

B: The author details the risks of costly, stressful legal confrontations that accompany the utilization of the fair use provision, so she understands the fears that keep some would-be cultural innovators from relying on this defense. It's therefore reasonable to believe that the author thinks that appropriating materials based on the right of fair use, and then actually using the defense successfully if and when challenged requires courage on the part of cultural innovators.

C: The author asserts that some of the individuals she discusses engage in self-censorship rather than face the risks inherent in invoking their fair use privileges. It's therefore inferable that she'd agree that some artists and commentators fall short of realizing their creative visions.

D: The passage begins with a distinction between clear-cut copyright cases and those "less clearly defined" cases that may be amenable to fair use defenses. Right off the bat, then, we get the sense that the author thinks that fair use is not as strictly defined as some other legal protections. This notion is reinforced in paragraph 3, where the author makes it clear that many considerations are weighed in fair use determinations, and that there is leeway concerning how judges interpret the various factors. Finally, the author distinguishes between the right to public assembly as a proactive, definite right, compared to the take your chances, reactive element of the fair use defense. Each of these examples suggest that the author would agree that fair use is fraught with more ambiguity than are some other legal protections.

E: Paragraph 3 provides examples of multiple levels of interpretation concerning the four factors discussed. This is especially clear with regard to the third factor, which states that the lower the proportion of the original work that is used, the better the chance for a fair use ruling. This, however, is also subject to the centrality of the used portion to the spirit of the original, which qualifies as an additional level of interpretation. So it's reasonable to conclude that the author would agree that some of the factors can be interpreted on numerous levels.

Since **B**, **C**, **D**, and **E** pan out, we can go with our original instinct and select choice **A** as the winner here.

Divide . . . Questions 4 and 7 remain, and we could attempt either one next. Perhaps one looks friendlier to you than the other? If so, great. Our general rule of thumb is to save Extension questions for last, since those require us to consider issues beyond the scope of the passage and can be tricky for that reason. So let's try question 4 next.

---

4. An artwork that appropriates copyrighted materials but that is considered by a court to be so transformative that it does not threaten the value of the original work in the marketplace best illustrates how

    (A) fair use determinations depend largely on the temperament and biases of judges
    (B) findings regarding one factor that judges consider in making fair use determinations may negate findings regarding another factor
    (C) the four factors judges generally consider in rendering fair use determinations are not mutually exclusive
    (D) no hard-line rules exist regarding the way in which judges apply the four relevant factors to fair use determinations
    (E) combining the factors evaluated in fair use determinations is an effective way to uphold democratic principles and promote creativity

---

. . . and Conquer. This one doesn't fall neatly into one particular category, but it's probably closest to Inference since we need to infer what's illustrated by a hypothetical example. The clues in the stem are *transformative* and *the value of the original work,* both of which lead us to paragraph 3. Transformative works are discussed in the context of the first factor that judges consider in fair use evaluations, while the value of original works is the subject of the fourth. So here we have a case in which one factor concerning the fair use evaluation of a specific artwork seems to influence how the court interprets a different factor in regards to that work. It's not easy to precisely predict what this illustrates, but it's enough to head into the choices with a notion that synergy between factors may influence the court's ruling. Another way of saying this is that the four factors discussed in paragraph 3 are not mutually exclusive, choice **C**.

A: Nowhere in paragraph 3 does the author suggest that personal biases or the temperament of judges come into play in fair use determinations, nor does the hypothetical case presented in the question stem imply that these factors are at work either. It's simply a matter of one factor influencing another, regardless of the personal beliefs of judges.

B is an Opposite choice. The situation described shows how the factors can work together, not negate one another.

D serves up a Mish-Mash, attempting to graft the first sentence of paragraph 4 onto the situation described in the stem. The fact that the four factors may work together does not illustrate the lack of hard-line rules in fair use determinations.

E: Good things come in pairs, and evidently so too do Mish-Mashes. The choice starts out on point, since the situation in the stem most certainly is about combining the fair use factors. But it's downhill from there, as this is inexplicably related to the topics of democracy and creativity mentioned in passing long before in paragraph 2. Call it a Retrieval Error instead of a Mish-Mash if you prefer, as long as you see why it's wrong.

Divide . . . Last, and least desirable for some, is Extension question 7. It would be fine if you decided at this point that you'd had enough of the exciting world of fair use, and were ready for a new passage. For our purposes here, we'll work through it to finish this one off.

7. According to the information in the passage, which one of the following situations best exemplifies a transformative use of a work?

    (A) Scenes from a television program from the 1970's are shown on a television special with the permission of the original producers in order to commemorate the program and highlight its originality.
    (B) A small urban film center screens a silent film obtained from a public domain website containing works no longer afforded copyright protection.
    (C) Clips from a copyrighted television newscast are interspersed with commercials in rapid succession in a documentary exploring the symbiotic relationship between news and advertising.
    (D) An independent filmmaker shoots scenes from a subway station during a morning rush hour to use as part of a satirical exposé of the working world.
    (E) A political science professor shows a documentary on the 1992 U.S. presidential election to her class in order to complement a unit she is teaching on electoral politics.

. . . and Conquer. We're back to the issue of transformative works, so head back to paragraph 3 if you need to brush up on what this means. Luckily, we're given a handy definition: the use of a copyrighted work is considered transformative if it radically alters the material's original intent. Bootlegging copies of *Casablanca* and selling it on street corners presumably wouldn't qualify. We're asked to find a situation that would count as transformative, so let's test the choices with this definition in mind.

You can treat Extension questions like Logical Reasoning Matching questions: Meticulously match each choice to the issue at hand looking for the one that accords in every respect.

A: To commemorate is to remember and celebrate something, so re-running clips from an old TV show to commemorate it wouldn't count as a radical alteration of the material. In addition, permission is *granted*, which also takes us out of fair use territory, since fair use is utilized only in cases in which material is unlicensed and appropriated into new forms of art and social commentary.

B: No copyright, no problem. The fair use defense is employed only when copyright infringement is charged. Also, there's no element of alteration here, since the film center is presumably screening the film as is.

C passes the test that **B** fails—the work under consideration *is* copyrighted. So far so good. Is it appropriated into a new work of art or social commentary? Sure; a documentary exploring the relationship between news and advertising counts as social commentary. One final test: Does the use constitute a radical alteration of the original material? Yes again: Newscasts and commercials are not normally edited in rapid succession and woven into an educational documentary. So **C** meets every criteria and therefore qualifies as an example of a transformative work. Just to be certain, let's check the remaining two choices to see if either one looks better.

TAKE AWAY

You should check every choice in Reading Comp questions, unless you're low on time and need to get in and out of questions in a hurry. When a question asks for the best example of something, that leaves open the possibility that one choice could work somewhat well while another fits the bill even better. Checking the other choices can reinforce your original instinct, or, occasionally, prevent you from making a mistake.

D: Someone shooting his own footage is not beholden to any copyright restrictions, so the situation depicted in **D** doesn't qualify in any way as a transformative use of copyrighted material.

E presents a scenario in which someone is presumably using copyrighted material for a purpose of her own, but it doesn't reach the standard of "radical alteration" since the professor seems to be screening the documentary as is without changing it into a *new form* of art or social commentary. Replaying something in its original form doesn't meet the author's definition of transformative.

Mine the Experience. Let's review what it means to mine the experience of working through a Reading Comp practice passage. Think through the following questions for this passage and the other passages in this section when evaluating your performance.

- Did "Scouting the Territory" help direct my attack on the passage?

- Did I extract the Essential Elements from each paragraph?

- What Essential Elements did I miss in my paragraph synopses?

- Did I focus too much attention on details during my attack on the passage?

- Did I successfully extract the main idea and primary purpose by the end of the passage?

- Did I "Divide and Conquer" effectively? That is, did I do the questions in the most efficient order?

- Did I use my understanding of the author's tone and behavior to not only lead me to correct choices but also to eliminate wrong ones?

- Did I recognize and eliminate the common wrong answer types that appear consistently throughout the Reading Comp section?

Passage 2: Dostoyevsky

Scout the Territory. A quick glance through the question set reveals a typical Main Point challenge in question 9 and a slightly reworded Primary Purpose question asking us to characterize the passage in question 11. Question 13, an Organization question, rounds out the Big Picture questions, so as always we'll keep our eye on these global issues as we make our way through each paragraph.

The Content questions are fairly standard: Inference in 10, a Fact EXCEPT question in 12, Author Agreement in 14, and Detail Purpose in 15. It's worth noting that there are no line or paragraph references in the set, but there are a few specific references among the Content questions that you might want to underline and pay special attention to when you come across them in the passage: Dostoyevsky as a *unified personality* (question 10), elements of Dostoyevsky's novels *drawn from personal experience* (question 12), and *Turgenev's view* of Dostoyevsky (question 15).

TAKE AWAY

Don't be intimidated by specific references in the question stems; of course you're not expected to understand anything about those things until you read the passage. The point is to recognize the *tested issues* in advance so that you can spend extra time on those few specific passage details while blowing past the rest.

TAKE AWAY

Notice how a quick scouting report can give you a preview of the likely Players in the passage. Dostoyevsky is mentioned three times in the question stems alone, which is a pretty good hint as to who this one's going to be about.

Mine the Essential Elements.

Paragraph 1 Essential Elements

> Literary audiences have traditionally favored writers whose works appear to spring from the richness of lived experience. Ernest Hemingway and Jack London come to mind as semi-mythic action figures who documented their experiences
> (5) in art. Next to the travails of nineteenth-century Russian novelist Fyodor Dostoyevsky, the adventures of even these lively American writers pale in comparison. Dostoyevsky was arrested for treason against the state, kept in solitary confinement for ten months, tried and condemned to death,
> (10) and brought to the scaffold only to have his execution stayed at the last moment by an order of the Czar delivered dramatically on horseback. To say that his life was as dark and dramatic as the books he wrote is no mere marketing gimmick, no ritual of hyperbole characterizing the incessant
> (15) and obligatory hype announcing the release of every modern novel and Hollywood spectacular.

- **Giveaways:** The fact that the adventures of the famed Hemingway and London "pale in comparison" to those of Dostoyevsky is the first indication that the author finds Dostoyevsky remarkable, at least in some respects.

- **Purpose:** The majority of the paragraph is taken up with the laundry list of Dostoyevsky's bad luck, ranging from solitary confinement to Siberia, with a near execution thrown in for good measure. Serious stuff. The paragraph exists to make the point alluded to in the final sentence: that Dostoyevsky's life was dark and dramatic.

- **Players/Extras:** Dostoyevsky is the main player; Hemingway and Jack London appear to be extras mentioned to highlight just how far out there Dostoyevsky really was. We'll keep our eyes open to see if the Americans reappear.

- **Main Point:** Dostoyevsky's life was dark and dramatic, and that ain't just whistling Dixie.

TAKE AWAY

Notice how establishing the main point of the first paragraph still leaves things pretty wide open, since introductions like this can lead in many different directions. Keep the question "where are you going with all this?" firmly in mind every step of the way, until the true main idea of the passage emerges.

- **Author Behavior:** Mainly the author behaves like a narrator relaying the facts of a writer's life. We'll see if things heat up later on.

- **Author Opinion/Passage Main Idea:** The "pale in comparison" giveaway mentioned above is a subtle clue that the author is impressed with Dostoyevsky, or at least respectful of what he had to go through in his life. We'll have to wait and see where things go from here.

Paragraph 2 Essential Elements

> Considering such a biography, it is commonplace to
> emphasize the direct link between Dostoyevsky's life and his
> novels. This view is not without merit: Dostoyevsky suffered
> (20) greatly, and he wrote with great power and passion about the
> prospect of attaining redemption through suffering. Years of
> communing with hardened criminals in a Siberian prison
> yielded passages of penetrating insights into the criminal
> mind. Dostoyevsky suffered from a destructive gambling
> (25) addiction and debilitating epileptic seizures, maladies he
> imparted to some of his characters. He faithfully and
> poignantly reproduced in his writing his most harrowing
> personal experience: the excruciating moments awaiting
> execution and the confused euphoria following its sudden,
> (30) seemingly miraculous annulment.

- **Giveaways:** "Considering such a biography" is a nice transition that tells us that paragraph 2 is going to build on what we learned about Dostoyevsky's tough times in paragraph 1. "This view is not without merit" indicates that the author believes in the validity of the argument cited in the first sentence regarding the connection between Dostoyevsky's life and novels—at least to a point. Why not totally? Someone who's whole hog behind an idea doesn't generally express his support by saying the idea is *not without merit*. You probably wouldn't say that the most beautiful woman in the room *is not without certain beauty . . .*; you'd say she's beautiful. So we'll keep our eye on this potentially lukewarm support. Meanwhile, the colon after "merit" suggests that reasons why the author thinks this view may be sound are forthcoming, and indeed the rest of the paragraph consists of such examples.

Use anything you can to help you unlock the author's meaning and purpose, including the grammatical signals the author employs. A colon indicates that examples or clarifications of an idea just stated are coming up next.

TAKE AWAY

- **Purpose:** To introduce a common view regarding Dostoyevsky and to provide examples of why this view may be justified. You may have recognized in this list of examples the elements of Dostoyevsky's novels and personal experience asked about in question 12.

- **Players/Extras:** It's all about Dostoyevsky. No sight of Hemingway or London, pretty much confirming their status as extras.

- **Main Point:** Because Dostoyevsky had such a hard life, many people tend to see a link between his life and his books, an idea the author presumably thinks is not totally crazy.

- **Author Behavior/Author Opinion:** The author relays a common view and presents examples supporting it, so there's a hint at an opinion in the making. However, there's nothing extreme yet in the author's manner or viewpoint.

- **Passage Main Idea:** So far we've heard about Dostoyevsky's travails, and a belief engendered by those travails which the author seems to agree with. But the longest paragraph of the passage is yet to come, so we'll have to hold out to see where this thing ends up.

Paragraph 3 Essential Elements

> However, the popular view of Dostoyevsky as a pre-
> eminent example of the synergistic relation between the
> artist and his work tends to obscure the contradictions
> that inevitably infuse even the most coherent artist's life.
> (35) As Dostoyevsky himself taught via brilliantly realistic
> character portrayals, each human being consists of a
> labyrinth of internal inconsistencies, competing desires,
> and mysterious motivations that belie the notion of a
> completely unified personality. One of Dostoyevsky's most
> (40) vital insights concerns the individual's struggle to bring his
> contradictory being into harmony with the world. The fact
> that Dostoyevsky himself fused his being with his art to
> a near miraculous extent does not suggest the absence of
> contradiction between the two. He was, by fellow Russian
> (45) writer Ivan Turgenev's account, an odious and obstinate
> individual who nonetheless managed to portray the highest
> human types in characters such as Prince Myshkin in *The
> Idiot* and Alyosha in *The Brothers Karamazov*. In his
> writings Dostoyevsky vehemently challenged rationality
> (50) as the supreme guide to human affairs, yet in his life he
> strove to perfect an ultra-rational gambling methodology
> to alleviate his crushing financial difficulties. Far from
> masking his brilliance, such contradictions reveal the fallible
> human behind it, making Dostoyevsky's accomplishments all
> (55) the more remarkable.

- **Giveaways:** As far as clues go, they don't get much bigger than this: "However . . ." Talk about linguistic economy! In the space of a single word, the author casts doubt on the notion that the examples just provided tell the whole story—especially following on the heels of the fairly qualified phrase "not without merit" from paragraph 2. Following the first sentence through, we see that the view introduced in paragraph 2, while valid to some extent, nonetheless "tends to obscure contradictions" between Dostoyevsky's life and art, contradictions we hear more about later in the paragraph. The final sentence in its entirety constitutes an important giveaway, speaking volumes regarding the author's respect for Dostoyevsky's accomplishments.

- **Purpose:** To propose a limitation of the common view in question, and to promote Dostoyevsky's legacy in spite of the limitation of this view.

- **Players/Extras:** Turgenev, a fellow Russian writer, and Prince Myshkin and Alyosha, characters created by Dostoyevsky, all make cameos in the paragraph, but the main focus is still on Dostoyevsky himself, who we can say with certainty at this point is the only true player in the passage.

- **Main Point:** Dostoyevsky achieved remarkable synergy between his life and works, but not the perfect synergy that some people like to believe since contradictions also existed between his life and the novels he wrote. Still, that fact doesn't diminish his brilliance but rather makes his accomplishments all the more impressive.

- **Author Behavior/Author Opinion/Passage Main Idea:** The author takes a stand, coming to the opinion mentioned just above as the main point, which doubles as the passage's main idea.

> **TAKE AWAY**
>
> You'll notice that by the end of the passage, the author's behavior, opinion, and main point of the final paragraph often coalesce into the passage's main idea. The seven Essential Elements that we encourage you to track should come together to provide you with what you need to answer the Big Picture questions.

Divide and Conquer. And speaking of Big Picture questions, those are naturally the ones we'll look to knock off first.

Divide . . . You'll find the Main Point question where it's often found, right at the beginning of the set. Question 9's up first.

9. Which one of the following most accurately expresses the main point of the passage?

(A) **Both synergy and conflict characterize the relationship between the life Dostoyevsky lived and the novels he wrote.**

(B) With great power and passion, Dostoyevsky demonstrated the need for individuals to resolve inner conflicts and attempt to achieve harmony with the world.

(C) People who emphasize a direct link between Dostoyevsky's life and his novels fail to recognize that contradictions in his life made his achievements possible.

(D) Dostoyevsky deserves the distinction of semi-mythic action figure more than American writers such as Jack London and Ernest Hemingway.

(E) The numerous contradictions between Dostoyevsky's life and works overshadow the near miraculous degree to which he managed to fuse his being with his art.

. . . and Conquer. The author doesn't discount the popular view regarding the link between Dostoyevsky's life and works—indeed, he says that Dostoyevsky "fused his being with his art to a near miraculous extent." And if he wanted to disavow the popular view entirely, he wouldn't have gone out of his way to support the general merit of this view with numerous examples in paragraph 2. Instead, he's trying to take it down a notch; trying to show that while there *was* a remarkable amount of synergy between Dostoyevsky's life and works, it didn't reach the epic proportions that some would have us believe. The author tries to complete the story by suggesting that there were also contradictions. Choice **A** comes closest to capturing the main idea.

B: One part Retrieval Error, one part Mish-Mash: The "power and passion" bit is from paragraph 2, while achieving harmony with the world is an idea from paragraph 3. In any case, these tidbits don't add up to the main idea, which revolves around the main issues of synergy and contradiction.

C: The author states that the contradictions between Dostoyevsky's life and art don't detract from his accomplishments, and even make them seem more remarkable. That's not to say that the author believes that these contradictions *enabled* his achievements.

TAKE AWAY

> Cause and effect is a Logical Reasoning Essential Concept, but understanding the ins and outs of causal relationships can help you in Reading Comp, too.

D harks back to our "extras" Jack London and Ernest Hemingway, who aren't important enough figures to be included in the main idea. The author didn't write all of this to merely compare Dostoyevsky to his American counterparts.

E gets it backward. The author believes that the popular view of the synergy between Dostoyevsky's life and art overshadows the contradictions between those things, not that the contradictions overshadow the popular view.

Divide . . . It isn't quite worded the same, but functionally question 11 is very much like a Primary Purpose question, so we'll head there next.

TAKE AWAY

> The LSAT is very formulaic, but stay alert to the various ways questions may be worded. To say, for example, that the passage can be *described* as a portrayal of the travails of a Russian writer is identical to saying that the author's *purpose* is to portray the travails of a Russian writer.

11. The passage as a whole can most accurately be described as

    (A) a portrayal of the travails of a pre-eminent nineteenth century Russian novelist
    (B) an argument concerning the relationship between an artist's life and works
    (C) an attempt to reconcile the events of a writer's life with the themes of his books
    (D) an examination of the ways in which contradiction may be used as a literary device
    (E) a refutation of the traditional judgments of literary audience

. . . and Conquer. Our passage analysis has given us a broad idea of the reason this passage was written, so let's evaluate the choices one by one, using our "Make the Match" technique.

A covers paragraph 1, and only paragraph 1. Too narrow, so eliminate.

B hits on the main issue discussed at length in paragraphs 2 and 3 and featured in our analysis of the passage's Essential Elements. The author argues that the popular view of the relationship between Dostoyevsky's life and works needs to be supplemented by an understanding of the contradictions between those things.

C: In paragraph 2, the author does provide evidence that the events of Dostoyevsky's life influenced the contents of his novels, but the passage moves beyond that to show that this fact, defined as the "popular view," isn't the whole story.

D is a Twister. The author discusses contradiction mainly in the context of the conflict between Dostoyevsky's life and the works he produced. Dostoyevsky's *use of contradiction* as a literary device isn't discussed. Even if you focused on Dostoyevsky's understanding that individuals have conflicting natures, that's still a small point that doesn't encompass the passage as a whole.

E Overreaches, focusing on the literary audiences mentioned in the first sentence. It leaves out the main character, a writer, and the main theme, the relationship between his life and works. You may have been thinking Twister as well, since the author doesn't set out to absolutely refute the popular view (he in fact provides evidence for its validity), but to modify it with additional information.

Divide . . . We move next to the final Big Picture question we noted in Step 1, Organization question 13.

13. Which one of the following most accurately describes the organization of the material presented in the passage?

   (A) The biography of an author is presented, the likely repercussions of leading such a life are explored, and the accomplishments of the author in question are put forward.

   (B) A predisposition of a particular audience is cited, and a popular view regarding that predisposition is refuted.

   (C) The conditions of an writer's life are summarized, a likely perception based on those conditions is stated and reinforced, and an alternative approach is proposed and supported.

   (D) A theory concerning the relationship between an author's life and works is stated, the writer's biography is contrasted with the lives of other writers to support the theory, and a conclusion regarding the value of the writer's works is presented.

   (E) A writer's judgment regarding the events of his life is cited, a common emphasis based on that judgment is summarized, and the role of contradiction in relation to that writer's accomplishments is explored and dismissed.

. . . and Conquer. In the Reading Comp chapter we outlined a three-prong approach to tackling Organization questions: Use the Essential Elements; Make the Match; and Spot the Traps. A quick recap of each paragraph's purpose gets the ball rolling: The author discussed Dostoyevsky's hardships; then introduced and supported a view that stems from that biography; then supplemented that theory with an additional consideration. Let's use that understanding to help us make the match and avoid the traps.

A: Yes, a biography of an author *is* presented, but the choice breaks down over "likely repercussions of leading such a life." The author focuses on a likely perception *of others* based on the author leading such a life (the "popular view"), not on the consequences to Dostoyevsky himself of his travails.

B: The so-called "popular view" is not based on the predisposition of audiences cited in the first sentence, but on the kind of life Dostoyevsky led. And as we've seen earlier, *refute* is a bit strong considering that the author spends a whole paragraph extolling the valid part of the popular view. He merely argues that this view obscures a more nuanced view of the situation.

TAKE AWAY

It's not uncommon for the test makers to hammer away on the same issue in numerous places within the question set, especially regarding a nuanced point that they expect a certain number of test takers to miss.

C: The passage does begin with a summary of a writer's life, and a likely perception (again, the "popular view") is stated based on those conditions. This view is then reinforced by the examples provided in paragraph 2. The author then proposes that people should also consider the contradictions between Dostoyevsky's life and works that were exhibited in addition to the remarkable synergy he achieved, and supports this alternative approach by the examples provided in paragraph 3. We have a winner.

D: Dostoyevsky is compared with London and Hemingway to highlight the exceptional circumstances of Dostoyevsky's life, not to support a theory concerning the main theme of the passage.

E: The author doesn't discuss Dostoyevsky's view of his own life, so we can chop this choice on that count alone.

TAKE AWAY

Reading Comp Organization questions are similar to Logical Reasoning Matching questions in that every element of the choice must work. As soon as you see anything in a choice that doesn't jibe, eliminate it.

Divide . . . That brings us to the Content questions. Fact question 12 wants to know what elements of Dostoyevsky's life were encapsulated in his novels, which leads us nicely to paragraph 2. This is therefore a good question to try next.

There is no definitive right order in which to work through the set, especially after you've taken care of the Big Picture questions. But a question that strongly suggests where in the passage you may find the answer may be more user-friendly than more general questions containing no such clues.

---

12. The passage cites each of the following as an element of Dostoyevsky's novels that was drawn from the writer's personal experience EXCEPT:

   (A) characters suffering from epilepsy or an addiction to gambling
   (B) perceptive observations on criminal psychology
   (C) the possibility of achieving redemption through suffering
   (D) the sudden and dramatic reversal of a death sentence
   (E) the experience of isolation brought on by solitary confinement

---

. . . and Conquer. The author states in paragraph 1 that Dostoyevsky was kept in solitary confinement following his arrest, but this event is not mentioned in paragraph 2 as something from Dostoyevsky's life that he depicted in his novels. The other four choices are explicitly mentioned in the second paragraph as elements of his life that he wrote about in his books. **E** is therefore the odd man out here, which makes it correct for this EXCEPT question.

Divide . . . The mention of Turgenev in the stem of question 15 tells us exactly where in the passage the answer to that question will lie, and hopefully you paid some extra attention to Turgenev after noticing him as a tested issue during your initial scan of the question set. So let's make Detail Purpose question 15 our next order of business.

---

15. Which one of the following most accurately describes the author's purpose in referring to Turgenev's view of Dostoyevsky?

   (A) to demonstrate the incongruity between Dostoyevsky's actual personality and the perception of him among the reading public
   (B) to show that even an odious and obstinate person is incapable of creating characters other than those of the highest human type
   (C) to lend credence to the idea that emphasizing the synergy between Dostoyevsky's life and works is not without merit
   (D) to support the claim that the relationship between Dostoyevsky's life and art was not free from contradiction
   (E) to provide evidence for the assertion that Dostoyevsky created characters noted for internal inconsistencies, competing desires, and mysterious motivations

---

. . . and Conquer. Why does the author tell us what Turgenev thought of Dostoyevsky? A quick look back at the detail is in order.

Dostoyevsky, according to Turgenev, was a revolting and stubborn person, yet portrayed in his works characters embodying the highest human ideals. This information appears in the passage immediately following the assertion that there was contradiction between Dostoyevsky's being and his art. Turgenev's opinion of Dostoyevsky is therefore provided as part of an example supporting the author's contention that contradiction existed between Dostoyevsky's life and works, choice **D**.

A: Twister: The author supplies no evidence that Dostoyevsky *wasn't* odious and obstinate, as Turgenev maintained. Turgenev's depiction therefore isn't provided to contrast the perception of Dostoyevsky's personality with the reality of what he was really like.

B is difficult to decipher, but appears to be saying that even an odious and obstinate person can only create characters of the highest human type. Not only does this make little sense, but the author's purpose seems to be the opposite: to illustrate the contradiction inherent in the fact that such a revolting person can create such characters *at all*.

C is a Retrieval Error. The detail in question supports the notion of contradiction, not synergy. The evidence referred to in **C** is found in paragraph 2, not where Turgenev appears in paragraph 3.

E is a Retrieval Error as well. It refers to Dostoyevsky's insight regarding human contradiction mentioned earlier in paragraph 3, whereas Turgenev's view of Dostoyevsky, expressed later in the paragraph, relates to the *author's theory* regarding *Dostoyevsky's* contradictions.

Divide . . . We're left with one Inference and one Author Agreement question, which you can do in either order. There's no foolproof way to figure out which might be easier, and if you're planning on getting to both in any case, there's no need to obsess over which to tackle first. We'll go with Inference question 10 since it provides a bit more to go on in the stem, which may help lead us to the relevant part of the passage.

10. Which one of the following can be most reasonably inferred regarding those who see Dostoyevsky as a completely unified personality?

   (A) **They fail to accord to him certain human qualities that he instilled in his own fictional characters.**
   (B) They believe Dostoyevsky's unified personality to be the primary source of his travails.
   (C) They dismiss the notion that personal experience can be effectively encapsulated in art.
   (D) They consider it miraculous that Dostoyevsky achieved a unified personality despite having an odious character.
   (E) They believe that there are other such unified personalities in fields other than literature.

. . . and Conquer. The phrase "completely unified personality" appears in the second sentence of paragraph 3, so it makes sense to begin by briefly reviewing that concept.

Step 1 of our Reading Comp Essential Strategy is to Scout the Territory, which means to check the question stems in the question set for clues before delving into the passage. We do this not only to get a sense of the Big Picture/Content question breakdown but also to note the issues tested so we can better prioritize our time with respect to the passage's many details. When you see, for example, a phrase like "completely unified personality," you should underline it and keep your eye out for it as a tested issue, even though at the moment you have no idea what it means. You should then underline or circle it in the passage when you come upon it to help you locate the detail when it comes time to answer that question.

Dostoyevsky himself used character portrayals to demonstrate his view that people are inherently conflicted and filled with competing desires and mysterious motivations. He believed that people's personalities are inherently *disjointed*, not unified, and expressed this belief by creating characters in this mold. It can be inferred therefore that people who hold *him* up as a prime example of a completely unified personality fail to see in him what he instilled in his own characters, choice **A**.

B is a Mish-Mash that incorrectly attempts to cite Dostoyevsky's perceived unified personality described in paragraphs 2 and 3 as the source of his personal troubles outlined in paragraph 1.

C: Opposite: People who view Dostoyevsky as a completely unified personality see him this way precisely *because* of the extent to which he has represented his personal experience in his art. They would therefore embrace, not dismiss the notion that reflecting personal experience in art is possible.

D serves up a multiple Mish-Mash, attempting to tie people's belief in Dostoyevsky as a unified personality first with the *author's* characterization of the synergy between his life and work as "near miraculous," and then with Turgenev's characterization of Dostoyevsky as odious.

> Mish-Mashes can be tricky because they specialize in fusing passage elements together, resulting in phrases that at the very least *sound* familiar. Miraculous? Odious character? Yeah, these things are in there somewhere, but that's not good enough—they have to relate *appropriately* to the issue in question.

E: *Other* unified personalities? Fields *other than* literature? A quick kill due to irrelevancy.

Divide . . . Just one to go, so let's have at it.

14. It can be inferred from the passage that the author would most likely agree with which one of the following statements?

   (A) Most Russian writers considered Dostoyevsky an odious and obstinate individual.
   (B) Contradictions between an artist's life and art are necessary for that artist to bring his or her being into harmony with the world.
   (C) Critics of Dostoyevsky should take into account the contradictions between his life and his art before assessing the value of his novels.
   (D) The tendency to romanticize writers has helped propagate the image of Dostoyevsky as a perfectly unified personality, despite evidence detailing disparities between his life and works.
   (E) Dostoyevsky's literary accomplishments are best illustrated by his challenge to rationality and portrayals of the highest human types.

. . . and Conquer. Author Agreement question 14 offers no clues as to what the author will be agreeing with, so we have no choice but to evaluate the choices one by one, armed with everything we've learned about the author to this point. **D** is the one that works: The author describes the tendency of literary audiences to favor "semi-mythic action figures" who base their works on personal experience, which suggests an element of romanticizing such authors. This tendency, in conjunction with the harrowing story of Dostoyevsky's life, helped propagate the notion of Dostoyevsky as a perfect fusion of life and art. Many continue to believe in this "popular view" despite evidence demonstrating that contradiction existed between Dostoyevsky's life and works as well.

A is an Overreach. We know that the author thinks that Turgenev believed Dostoyevsky was a heel, but what the author thinks about how *other* Russian writers viewed Dostoyevsky is, to borrow a Logical Reasoning term, Unknowable. It therefore goes too far to say that the author thinks that *most* of Dostoyevsky's Russian colleagues viewed him as Turgenev did.

> Don't hesitate to use techniques and strategies you learn to help you handle other sections of the test wherever they may apply. As we've indicated, the LSAT is an integrated testing experience with considerable overlap between the reading and reasoning skills tested on each section.

TAKE AWAY

B: As we've seen a few times now, the author never argues that the contradiction between Dostoyevsky's life and art was responsible for his accomplishments or helped him to achieve harmony. He's actually amazed that Dostoyevsky accomplished what he did *despite* these contradictions.

> Logic Games isn't the only LSAT section where you may benefit from using prior work. There is often synergy between questions in the Reading Comp sets, too, so you should use what you learn from answering the early questions to help you with later questions when possible.

TAKE AWAY

C is Irrelevant, as critics' assessment of the value of Dostoyevsky's works isn't discussed in the passage. The main issue is to what extent his art stemmed from his life, not how good his books actually were. That would be the topic of a different passage.

E: The author never states or implies which elements of Dostoyevsky's works he believes best illustrate Dostoyevsky's accomplishments.

Mine the Experience. That's enough Russian literature for now, but when your head has cleared, don't forget to review what you've learned from this passage in order to reinforce your approach and solidify the strategies you're learning.

Passage 3: Impulsivity

Scout the Territory. In terms of the Big Picture, we get a typical Main Point question in number 16, but no Primary Purpose question, which happens. The only other Big Picture question is Organization question 20.

On the Content side, question 17 is an Author Agreement question with no clues, but Detail Purpose question 18 provides a handy line reference that we can note in the passage with an asterisk off to the side. Fact question 19 contains the specific phrase "recent increase in impulsivity disorders," which you should underline as something to watch out for, while Fact question 21 directs us right to paragraph 1 and tells us what to look for there, a study finding. That gives us a good idea of what we'll look to take out of this natural science passage, so on to Step 2.

Mine the Essential Elements.

Paragraph 1 Essential Elements

> Impulsivity describes a range of ill-conceived behaviors characterized by rapid, unplanned reactions to stimuli often resulting in undesirable consequences. Impulsivity is a factor in attention deficit hyperactivity disorder (ADHD), mania,
> (5) and addiction. Researchers utilizing functional magnetic resonance imaging (fMRI) have proposed a neurobiological explanation for this condition. fMRI tracks increases in blood flow to areas of the brain engaged in neural activities, allowing researchers to pinpoint regions responsible for
> (10) those activities. In one study, adolescents with ADHD and others without ADHD were placed in a magnetic resonance imaging device and asked to press a button when any letter but X was flashed on a screen. This tested their ability to suppress the impulse to press the button when an X was
> (15) displayed after a long string of other letters. The adolescents with ADHD demonstrated poorer impulse control than the non-ADHD subjects. Moreover, compared with those of the non-ADHD adolescents, the fMRI results of the ADHD adolescents indicated less activation of neuronal tissues
> (20) in the frontal striatal regions known as the caudate and putamen. After taking an anti-impulsivity drug, the ADHD adolescents performed better, with a corresponding increase in caudate and putamen activity. Since the drug significantly increases the level of dopamine in the brain, the researchers
> (25) hypothesized that impulsivity may involve atypical dopamine transmission in the striatal circuitry.

- **Giveaways:** "Impulsivity describes . . ." foretells a definition, and accordingly the first two sentences merely tell us what impulsivity is and in what situations it can be found. "Researchers . . . have proposed" tips us off that the passage may be based on a theory, and indeed the rest of the paragraph describes in detail the study asked about in question 21. "The researchers hypothesized . . ." reinforces the idea that the passage deals with some kind of theory.

- **Purpose:** To define a scientific condition and present a theory regarding its cause.

- **Players/Extras:** There are no specific people to speak of, but we do hear about researchers and adolescents. In addition, the adolescents who take part in the study are broken down into those with ADHD and those without, a distinction that may come into play in a Content question. But the main focus of the passage thus far is the condition of impulsivity, and the neurobiological explanation for it can be considered the star of paragraph 1.

- **Main Point:** Impulsivity is a condition present in various medical afflictions, and one theory to explain it is the neurobiological explanation.

- **Author Behavior/Author Opinion:** The author is quite objective and factual in her presentation, merely relating the theories of others. So no authorial opinion is evident yet.

- **Passage Main Idea:** Of course we don't know the passage's main idea yet, but that doesn't mean we can't begin to anticipate where the author may go from here.

> ## TAKE AWAY
>
> There are a few very common follow-ups when a theory is presented early in a Reading Comp passage. Sometimes the author goes on to support the theory, and sometimes the author goes on to refute it. In still other cases, the author will discuss one or more other theories to contrast with the first theory. Sometimes the author ventures an opinion on the theory or theories in question, and sometimes not. These are the things to be on the lookout for as you proceed further into the passage.

Paragraph 2 Essential Elements

> Other scientists have proposed a radically different explanation. Experimenting with blue jays, they concluded that animals may be hard-wired for impulsivity thanks to
> (30) inborn foraging instincts conditioning them to favor small short-term benefits over potentially larger long-term rewards. These researchers theorize that early humans, exhibiting a similar foraging instinct, benefited in the long-run from unhesitating behavior averse to delayed satisfaction; that is,
> (35) they see impulsivity as a trait that enhanced the survival of early humans. In modern society, however, the deferment of satisfaction often yields more positive outcomes than instant gratification in many areas: education, investment, entry-level employment, to name a few. The researchers speculate that
> (40) only in the modern age has innate impulsivity become a detriment.

- **Giveaways:** Sentence 1 in its entirety is the major giveaway of paragraph 2, immediately identifying the author's follow-up to paragraph 1: a different explanation for impulsivity. "The researchers theorize . . ." and "The researchers speculate . . ." provide clues as to the author's continued role as mere narrator.

- **Purpose:** To present another possible cause of impulsivity.

- **Players/Extras:** A few more anonymous researchers appear, but again the star of the paragraph is the theory presented; this time, a theory concerning the consequences of early human foraging.

- **Main Point:** The foraging instinct among early humans may have encouraged impulsive behavior as a survival mechanism, something that may explain the impulsivity phenomenon of today.

- **Author Behavior/Author Opinion:** The author is still simply relaying information about the condition in question, this time presenting the view of a different group of scientists. So far there is no evidence of authorial opinion, and we'll have to wait and see if the author continues in this manner or emerges to take a stand.

- **Passage Main Idea:** The overall main idea doesn't venture far from what we've noted already. In Big Picture terms, all we've found out so far is that impulsivity is a detrimental condition and that at least two different theories attempt to explain what causes it.

Paragraph 3 Essential Elements

> Both camps attempt to explain the recent significant increase in impulsivity disorders. Supporters of the foraging thesis argue that the "get it now, pay later" mentality of
> (45) modern consumer society has unleashed our impulsivity instinct, somewhat successfully stifled in more restrictive conservative eras. Neurobiologists speculate that alterations in the environment have influenced neurochemical brain transmissions, thus increasing the population's susceptibility
> (50) to impulsivity. It is, however, possible that the supposed increase in impulsivity merely reflects an increase in the means of detecting the condition. Whether there has in fact been an increase in impulsivity, the neurobiological and foraging theories may not be mutually exclusive. While there
> (55) may exist a species-wide survival-based tendency toward impulsivity, neurobiological factors may exacerbate the condition in certain individuals.

- **Giveaways:** Sentence 1 from the word *explain* on should have gotten your attention, since it relates specifically to the issue we underlined in question 19. And we have two explanations to choose from, given the beginnings of sentences 2 and 3: "Supporters of the foraging thesis argue that . . ."; and "Neurobiologists speculate that . . ." The next phrase—"It is, however, possible that . . ."—strongly suggests that the author might finally venture an opinion, and in fact, she goes on to offer a reason why there may not actually be an increase in the condition. In the following sentence she says that in any case, the two theories "may not be mutually exclusive," a clear statement of opinion which is clarified more specifically in the final sentence.

- **Purpose/Players/Extras:** The author accomplishes a lot in this paragraph. First, she shows how each theory attempts to explain the recent increase in impulsivity disorders. Then she questions whether that increase actually exists or is merely a result of better means of detecting the condition. She ends by speculating about how the two theories may relate. The author takes the stage in this paragraph as the main player.

- **Main Point:** Both theories may be correct in their own way, and they may together help explain the causes of impulsivity, even though the incidence of the disorder may not actually be increasing.

- **Author Behavior/Author Opinion/Passage Main Idea:** As indicated already from the discussion of the paragraph's giveaways, the author does emerge to present a speculation of her own, and the passage's main idea follows directly from the main point of this final paragraph.

> **TAKE AWAY**
>
> As you get more adept at picking out the Essential Elements, you'll find yourself combining them more and more. That's because there aren't seven *distinct* things going on in each paragraph; the Essential Elements overlap considerably. Taken together, they provide you with the knowledge you need to answer the Big Picture questions and quickly locate the relevant information to answer the rest.

Divide and Conquer. This third step is of course the focal point of our Reading Comp Essential Strategy: the time to cash in (as we say in Logic Games) on all our good work.

Divide . . . We noted back in Step 1 that there are two Big Picture questions in this group of six, so having thought through the Big Picture issues in depth, let's knock those off first, beginning with Main Point question 16.

16. Which one of the following most accurately summarizes the main point of the passage?

(A) While the neurochemical and foraging theories taken together adequately explain the cause of impulsivity, neither theory on its own explains the recent increase in the number of impulsivity disorders.

(B) Improvements in medical technologies such as fMRI have enabled scientists to determine that impulsivity is caused by atypical dopamine transmissions in the brain.

(C) While both evolutionary and neurochemical factors may contribute to impulsivity, whether or not there has been a recent increase in the incidence of the disorder remains unclear.

(D) Despite the fact that two theories plausibly explain the causes of impulsivity, researchers are no closer to discovering a cure for the disorder.

(E) Even though it appears that the incidence of impulsivity is on the rise, in actuality improvements in the means of detecting the disease are responsible for this supposed increase.

. . . and Conquer. We've seen the author emerge as a force in paragraph 3, offering her own hypothesis that the two theories may actually go hand in hand. **C** nicely captures the qualified nature of the author's speculation that the factors highlighted in both theories may contribute to impulsivity, while also noting the author's other major speculation that the supposed recent increase in the disorder may be misleading.

A and **D** can both be eliminated as Overreaches, since the author never claims that either theory, or both taken together, absolutely explain the cause of impulsivity. While the author does speculate that the two theories *may* combine to help explain the disorder, choices **A** and **D** seem a bit too certain about it. If need be, you can go deeper to eliminate these two: **A** ignores the author's point that there may in fact be no recent increase in the condition, while **D** ventures off into Irrelevant territory with its talk about a cure.

TAKE AWAY

Some choices have numerous problems, but you only need one reason to cross a choice off. Try not to overanalyze. As soon as you spot something about a choice that doesn't work for you, axe it.

B ventures off into the passage to bring back the main point and comes back only with the theory described in paragraph 1. If **B** were the main idea of the passage, there would be no reason for paragraphs 2 and 3. Classic Retrieval Error.

E twists the author's hypothesis in the final paragraph that impulsivity may not really be increasing—something the author speculates is possible. So **E** is a bit too strong, but also leaves out the main players of the passage, the two theories.

TAKE AWAY

One strategy we offer for Big Picture questions is to use your imagination; that is, envision what the passage would have to *sound like* if the choice you're considering is meant to be correct. A passage in which the main point concerns whether or not impulsivity is *on the rise* probably wouldn't need to bother with all the facts concerning its possible *cause*.

Divide . . . Now for our other Big Picture question, Organization question 20. Notice that the stem doesn't actually include the word "Organization," but a question asking about the sequence of presented material amounts to the same thing.

20. Which one of the following sequences most accurately and completely corresponds to the presentation of the material in the passage?

   (A) a presentation of a hypothesis; an analysis of two mechanisms utilized to test that hypothesis; a reconciliation of the results collected from the tests
   (B) an examination of two contrasting studies; an explanation of the superiority of one of those studies; a call for measures to be enacted to implement the suggestions recommended by the superior study
   (C) a description of a dysfunctional behavior; a critique of two studies attempting to explain that behavior; a proposal for a new classification of that behavior
   (D) a discussion of a phenomenon; a presentation of two lines of inquiry concerning the causes of that phenomenon; argumentation regarding the need for further studies into that phenomenon
   (E) an introduction of a condition; a discussion of two theories regarding the cause and recent proliferation of that condition; a speculation regarding the plausibility of the two theories

. . . and Conquer. Every element of the correct choice must accord with the structure of the passage, so be hyper critical as you look to "Make the Match."

A: The passage concerns two hypotheses, not two tests of a single hypothesis.

B first breaks down over the issue of superiority, since the author never singles out one theory as superior to the other. In addition, neither study is linked to a course of action, nor does the author call for measures to be enacted.

C begins well, considering that impulsivity *is* a dysfunctional condition that's described. However, the introduction to impulsivity is followed by a purely objective description of the two possible explanations, not a critique of them. Also, the author does not propose a new classification for impulsivity, but rather suggests that it may have a hybrid cause.

TAKE
AWAY

> One of the reasons we track the author's behavior is to help eliminate choices that distort the author's intentions. The author of this passage can't properly be described as critical, especially in the first two paragraphs where all she does is relay information.

D: The first two clauses of this choice pan out, but nowhere does the author argue for further studies.

E is correct. The author introduces the condition of impulsivity. Then a neurobiological theory and an evolutionary theory are discussed as possible causes of the condition, with a bit about what each one says about its recent proliferation. Finally, the author steps up and speculates on the plausibility of the theories, musing that maybe they work together to create the condition.

Divide . . . We located the relevant information for question 19 during our analysis of paragraph 3, which contains two different explanations given for the recent increase in impulsivity. So let's make Fact question 19 our next task.

19. The passage cites which one of the following as a potential explanation for the recent increase in impulsivity disorders?

   (A) drugs that significantly increase the level of dopamine in the caudate and putamen
   (B) evolutionary adaptations in neurochemical brain transmissions that predispose individuals to impulsive behavior
   (C) a large decrease in potential sources of instant gratification
   (D) neurochemical deficiencies affecting the activation of neuronal tissues in the frontal striatal regions of the brain
   (E) a modern outlook that encourages people to indulge materialistic desires

. . . and Conquer. It was enough in your first reading to locate the place where these possible explanations are given, since we can take a closer look now. The foraging folks speak of a consumerist mentality that has unleashed our instinct for impulsivity, which was somewhat contained in more conservative times. **E** is a fine paraphrase of this explanation.

A is a Retrieval Error, drudging up stuff about drugs and dopamine levels from paragraph 1.

B is a Mish-Mash, trying to combine the notion of evolutionary adaptations from the foraging thesis with brain transmissions from the neurobiological theory.

C, if anything, goes the other way since the foraging theorists suggest that sources of instant gratification are on the rise in a modern consumer society that encourages impulsivity.

D speaks to a premise of the neurobiological explanation for impulsivity given in paragraph 1, but isn't part of either explanation provided in paragraph 3 for the supposed *recent increase* in the disorder.

Divide . . . We may as well take care of the other Fact question in the set, so let's head back to the study in paragraph 1 to dispense with question 21.

---

21. The passage cites which one of the following as a finding of the study described in paragraph 1?

    (A) **Increased impulse control is correlated with increased activation of neuronal tissues in the frontal striatal regions.**
    (B) Adolescents without ADHD were better able than adolescents with ADHD to correctly press the button when letters other than X were flashed on the screen.
    (C) No regions of the subjects' brains besides the caudate and putamen exhibited increased blood flow characteristic of neural activity during either phase of the study.
    (D) After taking the anti-impulsivity drug, ADHD adolescents demonstrated better impulse control than did the non-ADHD adolescents.
    (E) An excess of dopamine in the striatal circuitry may contribute to the onset of an impulsivity disorder.

. . . and Conquer. Because the study is quite detailed, your best bet is probably to check the choices against the facts given in the paragraph to locate the finding the question is after.

TAKE AWAY

> The best LSAT test takers are able to tailor their techniques to specific situations at hand. In a standard Fact question, reading the entire detail in depth and then answering the question might be the best approach. But in a case like this, where the answer could come from virtually anywhere in the middle to end of paragraph 1, it may be better to work backward from the choices.

A deals with the relationship between increased impulse control and increased activation of neuronal tissues, so let's see if this is supported by the facts. The study found that the ADHD kids had poorer impulse control than the non-ADHD kids, and also showed less activation of the neuronal tissues in the frontal striatal regions. So far then there appears to be the kind of correlation cited in **A**, and it's reinforced by the fact that the better performance brought about by the drug was also accompanied by increased activity in the striatal regions indicated. **A** is correct. For the record:

B: The test was designed to see which kids had trouble resisting the urge to press the button when Xs appeared, and we know that the ADHD kids had more trouble than the others performing this task. How each group performed on the *other* letters isn't indicated.

C: Irrelevant: No information is given regarding other regions of the brain.

D: Twister: We're told that the ADHD kids improved their impulse control after receiving the drug, but not that they in fact showed *better* impulse control than the other kids.

E, if anything, reverses the implication of the study. Since the drug that helped improve impulse control also increases the brain's dopamine level, it seems more likely that a *shortage* of dopamine may contribute to the condition. Even if you didn't take it that far, there's still no evidence that too much dopamine is a problem.

Divide . . . We're down to two questions left, so let's tackle the one with the line reference since it helpfully directs us right to the relevant information. Detail Purpose question 18 is a good choice to attempt next.

18. The author of the passage most likely discusses the deferment of satisfaction in lines 36–39 primarily in order to

   (A) support the contention that inborn foraging instincts may potentially hard-wire species for impulsivity
   (B) provide evidence for the hypothesis that a previous evolutionary advantage may be responsible for the modern incidence of the disorder under consideration
   (C) provide background information regarding the reason why impulsivity may be a factor in ADHD, mania, and addiction
   (D) demonstrate that a survival trait that provided advantages to early humans continues to benefit modern humans as well
   (E) illustrate how one theory regarding the cause of a modern disorder attempts to refute a previously-stated theory concerning the cause of that disorder

. . . and Conquer. Go right to the highlighted lines and quickly review the detail in question. The author describes the researchers' notion that impulsivity may have been a good thing for early humans whose survival chances were aided by unhesitating, impulsive behavior. This is contrasted (notice the ever-helpful signal word "however") with the benefits of deferring satisfaction in modern times, illustrated by cases like education and career-building which aren't aided by the instinct for instant gratification. This all leads up to the hypothesis that impulsivity may be an early human survival trait that only in modern times has become detrimental. The purpose of the detail is therefore to help make the case that an evolutionary advantage that helped early humans survive may be the cause for what we now know as impulsivity. **B** is correct.

A: Information on the deferment of satisfaction in modern times doesn't lend support to the notion that foraging instincts may predispose species for impulsivity. If anything, the blue jays serve this purpose here, so **A** constitutes a Retrieval Error.

TAKE AWAY

Retrieval Errors occur in Detail Purpose answer choices that describe the purpose of some element of the passage other than the one in question.

C: Call it a Retrieval Error or a Mish-Mash, but **C** plucks the second sentence of paragraph 1 out of thin air to explain why the author mentions the deferment of satisfaction much later on in paragraph 2. Not only are these things unrelated, but the author in fact doesn't explain, even in paragraph 1, *why* impulsivity is a factor in the disorders cited; she merely mentions that they are.

D is a pure Opposite choice, as the example in question is used to suggest that the kind of impulsive behavior that once helped early humans survive has become a detriment today.

E: The example of deferred satisfaction isn't used to pit the foraging theory against the neurobiological theory. The two theories aren't considered together until paragraph 3, and even at that point there's no attempt to have one *refute* the other—in fact, quite the opposite, as the author speculates that the theories may actually go hand-in-hand.

Divide . . . No dividing necessary, of course, since only one question remains. So let's wrap things up with Author Agreement question 17.

17. It can be inferred from the passage that the author would most likely agree with which one of the following statements?

(A) If two studies propose radically different explanations for the same disorder, it is necessary to conduct further studies in order to achieve consensus on a single correct explanation for that disorder.

(B) The incidence of impulsivity is on the rise because of environmental changes that have affected the way chemicals are transmitted in the brain.

(C) The performance of adolescents without ADHD on the drill described in the study in the first paragraph of the passage would improve after taking an anti-impulsivity drug.

(D) The findings of a study are not necessarily invalidated by the findings of an alternative study documenting a different potential cause of the same phenomenon.

(E) A recent increase in the number of conditions characterized by impulsivity has made it more difficult to detect the disorder.

. . . and Conquer. The stem tells us nothing about where the answer may come from, so we'll just test the choices to see which would sound most reasonable to the author based on what we've learned of her behavior and opinions.

A tends to go against the author's viewpoint, since in the end she believes that the two radically different theories discussed may actually each contribute in its own way to the mystery of impulsivity. In any case, nowhere does she propose anything about further studies, so we can put **A** in the "quite doubtful" pile while we check the other choices.

B also leans in the wrong direction, in light of the author's speculation that the incidence of impulsivity may not actually be rising, but only *appearing* to rise due to better methods of detection.

C: The study doesn't investigate what would happen if non-ADHD kids were given the anti-impulsivity drug, so the author's opinion on the result is Unknowable, to again borrow an Essential Concept from Logical Reasoning.

D: The author speculates that there may be a species-wide tendency toward impulsivity, as per the foraging thesis, but that the condition may be made worse in some people by the neurobiological factors discussed in paragraph 1. This contention that the two radically different explanations may in fact not be mutually exclusive (meaning they may both be correct to some extent) allows us to infer that she would agree with **D**. To her, the existence of either explanation doesn't necessarily mean that the other explanation must be false.

E is another Opposite choice, as the author theorizes that it may be getting *easier* to detect impulsivity disorders.

> **TAKE AWAY**
>
> In Author Agreement questions that provide no starting point (that is, those that simply ask what the author would most likely agree with), see if you can make a few quick kills based on your understanding of the author's beliefs and intentions gleaned from your analysis of the Essential Elements. Then look back at the passage if need be to test the choices that remain.

Mine the Experience. That does it for the wonderful world of science. If you're leery of the natural science passage in general (and yes, you *will* see one like this on your test), look back and notice how we didn't obsess over the technical details and tried at all times to engage the passage only as much as necessary in order to answer the questions. Come back to this passage later on in your preparation, and use the "Mine the Experience" question prompts from Chapter 3 (repeated for your convenience earlier in this chapter on pages 456–457) to help you further evaluate your performance and pinpoint things you hope to improve upon going forward.

Passage 4: Native American Narratives

Scout the Territory. We finish the section with a set of Paired Passages, which means that scanning the question set for Passage-Specific questions is your task in Step 1. There are two—question 24 seeking the main point of passage A, and Fact question 27 concerning a detail from passage B. You may also notice the detail and line reference provided in question 26. Keep these tested issues in mind as you work through the passages.

Mine the Essential Elements of Passage A.

Passage A Paragraph 1 Essential Elements

> In *Orality and Literacy*, Walter Ong hypothesized that the dissociative effect of writing on purely oral cultures is mitigated by electronic forms of communication such as television and computer networks. This established what
> (5) he called "secondary orality," an electronic-based interweaving of oral and literary traditions creating spontaneous interactive societies reminiscent of pre-literate tribal cultures. Citing Ong and fellow media theorist Marshall McLuhan, some Native Americans argue that traditional
> (10) tribal customs and narratives, replicated online, can foster vibrant Native American Internet communities. They further warn that failure to establish a Native American presence online will allow illegitimate parties to appropriate tribal traditions and define the tribal experience
> (15) according to their own self-interests.

- **Giveaways:** *Hypothesized, citing,* and *argue* are important words that tell us that we're dealing with a theory that's used by some people to support a position. The phrase "vibrant Native American Internet communities" seems important as well, possibly a preview of the main subject of the passage.

- **Purpose:** To introduce a theory and outline a position based on that theory.

- **Players/Extras:** Ong and McLuhan are cited as theorists, although they may simply appear to preview the issue of what some Native Americans make of their ideas. If Ong and McLuhan drop out of sight in the next paragraph, that will confirm them as extras.

- **Main Point:** Using Ong's theory of secondary orality, some Native Americans think it's in their interest to create an online presence for their cultures.

Use your scouting report from Step 1 to your advantage! It tells you that there is no specific question concerning this confusing thing called "secondary orality," which means you shouldn't knock yourself out trying to figure out what that is. Unless a Comparison question raises this issue, chances are the only thing you need to know about secondary orality is that some Native Americans rely on it to support a position.

- **Author Behavior/Author Opinion:** The author is purely objective thus far, merely relaying the thoughts of others.

- **Passage Main Idea:** So far we have one main argument put forth, described above. We'll have to wait for paragraph 2 to see how things turn out.

Passage A Paragraph 2 Essential Elements

> Native American critics counter that significant enough differences exist between their inherited modes of primary orality and the electronic world of secondary orality to severely limit the possibilities of fostering an online tribal
> (20) culture. First, they believe that online virtual communities are incapable of creating and sustaining the human attachments necessary to grant narratives meaning and power. Moreover, whereas in traditional Native American cultures members' personalities are subsumed by the tribal
> (25) identity, online forum participants exist first and foremost as individuals seeking environments in which to express that pre-existing individuality. The critics concede that electronic technologies may be useful tools for projecting Native American culture outwards to a broader audience, but
> (30) maintain that these tools cannot supplant traditional means of tribal acculturation.

- **Giveaways:** We don't have to wait long to see where things are headed—the first four words tell us that an opposing opinion is about to emerge. Sequence clue words *first* and *moreover* help to organize the author's presentation of the critics' points. Finally, the "concede . . . but" structure of the final sentence highlights a concession on the part of the critics that they nonetheless attempt to override.

- **Purpose:** To present an argument that opposes the viewpoint put forth in paragraph 1.

- **Players/Extras:** Ong's theory receives an honorable mention, but Ong and McLuhan themselves are not mentioned again, confirming their status as "extras." The Native American critics are the stars of this paragraph.

- **Main Point:** Some Native Americans believe that while the Internet does have its place, establishing a genuine online Native American culture isn't viable because virtual communities aren't real enough to do justice to their stories. They also think that the relationship of individuals to the group is different in a live tribe as opposed to an online community.

- **Author Behavior/Author Opinion:** The author continues in her role of narrator, presenting the theories of others but not venturing an opinion of her own.

- **Passage Main Idea:** There are numerous supporting examples, but essentially the passage boils down to the idea that some Native Americans think that creating an online Native American presence is not only viable but necessary, while others believe that it's not possible or desirable.

TAKE AWAY

Many Reading Comp passages are based around contrasting viewpoints, so keep your eyes peeled for that structure. Here we get a second viewpoint even before getting to the second passage.

Divide and Conquer Passage A Questions.

Divide . . . While passage A is fresh in your mind, it makes sense to knock off the one Passage-Specific question concerning that one before immersing yourself in passage B's particulars.

24. Which one of the following most accurately expresses the main point of passage A?

    (A) Speculations from Ong's *Orality and Literacy* have helped justify the belief of some Native Americans that they should represent their culture online.

    (B) The desire of some Native Americans to expand their culture via the Internet is supported by certain media theories but opposed by other members of tribal communities.

    (C) Ong's theory of secondary orality helps to explain the effects that writing and forms of electronic communication have had on societies characterized by purely oral cultures.

    (D) The Internet does not provide an adequate setting to replicate the ceremonial elements necessary for genuine Native American societies to flourish.

    (E) The debate between Native Americans regarding the desirability of constructing an online presence for tribal cultures has reached an insurmountable impasse.

. . . and Conquer. Since we just got through analyzing this very issue, all that's left is to find the choice that best reflects our take on passage A's main point. **B** encapsulates the essential fact that some Native Americans believe in establishing an online presence, while some don't. It even throws in for good measure the fact that some media theories support the pro position.

A works nicely as the main point of paragraph 1, but oops . . . there's a paragraph 2. You might think of it as a Retrieval Error—going in for the full story, but coming out with only half.

C focuses on the speculations of role player Ong to the detriment of the main subject of passage A, Native American views on representing their culture electronically.

D seems like something the critics of paragraph 2 would agree with, but ignores the position outlined in paragraph 1. Moreover, as you'll see, this choice accords fairly well with the main point of passage B, which may have confused those who read both passages before answering this question. This provides another reason why it makes sense to take care of any Passage-Specific questions immediately after reading each individual passage.

E is an Overreach. We're told that the issue is debated, but nothing suggests that an eventual resolution is impossible.

Mine the Essential Elements of Passage B.

> When you get to passage B, focus on the same Essential Elements as always, but do so in the context of comparing each element to the content, structure, and tone of passage A. This will give you a leg up on the Comparison questions you'll see later on.

TAKE
AWAY

Passage B Paragraph 1 Essential Elements

> The rise of the Internet as a social and economic force has reinvigorated interest in the ideas of 1960's media theorist Marshall McLuhan, who predicted an electronically
> (35) interconnected "global village" characterized by a worldwide reversion to the modes and structures of tribalism. Not surprisingly, the reference to tribalism has intrigued the Native American community, prompting vigorous debate concerning whether, how, and to what extent a Native
> (40) American presence can be constructed online.

- **Giveaways:** "Native American presence...online" should jump out at you after having read passage A, suggesting that the viability of this is the subject of this passage as well.

- **Purpose:** To provide background information explaining the interest Native Americans have in constructing an online presence.

- **Players/Extras:** McLuhan makes an appearance in this one as well, but the focus again seems to be on Native Americans.

- **Main Point:** McLuhan's theory regarding tribalism has interested Native Americans in the prospect of constructing an online presence.

- **Author Behavior/Author Opinion:** Not much to speak of yet—so far the author is just introducing the topic and laying the groundwork.

- **Passage Main Idea:** As noted above, the main issue that overlaps the theme of passage A seems to be the prospect of creating a Native American presence online. We know that pro and con arguments were advanced in passage A, so we should be on guard for how this second author treats the subject.

Your job in passage B is not simply to note the main idea, but to note the central topic that it shares with passage A.

Passage B Paragraph 2 Essential Elements

> While the Internet is a supreme conveyor of information, information must be applied in the context of ceremony in order to produce genuine community. Ceremony requires live participation in an actual locale. A stable
> (45) setting ensures a shared history and unspoken cultural understandings among participants in Native American dialogues. These factors dictate how stories are told, to what purposes they aspire, the proper relationship between storyteller and audience, and the acceptable evolution of
> (50) traditional tales to ensure their relevance to the lives of tribe members. The power of the myths, metaphors, and moral teachings inherent in such storytelling is proportionally weakened by each level of mediation introduced into the dialogue. In the end, the global village represents only
> (55) *pseudo*-tribalism: the conundrum of a worldwide tribe characterized by homogenization and the effacement of local identities. The opposite is required for the continued vitality of Native American narratives: the immediacy of and immersion into what tribal members refer to as "the
> (60) sacredness of place."

- **Giveaways/Main Point/Passage Main Idea:** The first word, *while*, sets up an immediate contrast and suggests that after conceding a positive point about the Internet, the author is about to go the other way. The author then details the requirements of good Native American storytelling, suggesting that he prefers real places to online chat rooms, but it's not until the giveaway "weakened by each level of mediation" that we get a real sense of where this author is heading. The final two sentences are chock-a-bloc filled with opinion phrases showing this author to disagree with the idea that a Native American presence can be successfully crafted online.

Notice how we combined three of the Essential Elements in the analysis above. That's okay!—they're not intended to exist in a vacuum, or be robotically checked off a list. The point is for you to instinctively extract the most important and relevant information from each paragraph, and to use the Essential Elements, in tandem, as your guide. The ability to extract the Essential Elements *synergistically* is the skill you need to improve your understanding of Reading Comp passages.

It's helpful also, based on our Step 1 scouting report, to note the word *conundrum* in the second to last sentence, since we know that one question directly concerns that.

- **Purpose:** To argue a position regarding the idea of a Native American online presence introduced in the first paragraph.

- **Players/Extras:** Native American storytelling remains the key subject, but the author is the only real presence.

- **Author Behavior/Author Opinion:** As indicated by the giveaways discussed above, this author does take a stand on the issue rather than merely report the beliefs of others, as is the case in passage A. The writing is firm but not overly harsh or overbearing. The opinion, as mentioned, is that the Internet is not a viable vehicle to capture the essence and power of traditional Native American narratives.

Divide and Conquer Passage B Questions.

Divide . . . Now that we've got passage B under our belts, let's knock off the one Passage-Specific question focusing solely on that one before moving on to the Comparison questions. That puts Fact question 27 next on the agenda.

27. The conundrum described in passage B (lines 55–57) is characterized by a conflict between

    (A) metaphors employed in Native American narratives and their intended moral teachings
    (B) McLuhan's conception of the global village and Ong's theory of secondary orality
    (C) tribal ceremonies and the sacredness of place
    (D) unique tribal identities and a homogenous global culture
    (E) supporters and opponents of establishing an online Native American presence

. . . and Conquer. The author of passage B characterizes the global village as "pseudo-tribalism," and describes a contradiction that arises from what he considers to be an inauthentic tribal dynamic. The result, he says, is the strange phenomenon of a worldwide tribe in which local identities are destroyed. By calling this a "conundrum," the implication is that tribes by their very nature must have local, individual identities, so Internet culture is not appropriate for genuine tribal societies. The conflict, as correct choice **D** has it, is between unique tribal identities and a homogenous global culture.

A offers a Twister: Metaphors and moral teachings are mentioned in the same breath as elements of Native American storytelling. These elements are not in conflict with each other, but are each weakened, according to passage B, in proportion to the levels of mediation introduced into the storytelling process.

B is a Mish-Mash trap intended to snare those who had trouble separating the information in the two passages. Ong and his theory are mentioned only in passage A. This Passage-Specific question deals only with a detail from passage B.

C is an Opposite choice, since the author argues that tribal ceremonies are dependent on the sacredness of place. No conflict there.

E: The people cited in this choice do disagree regarding the viability of propagating Native American narratives online, but that's not the conflict at the heart of the *conundrum* described by the author. The conundrum is evidence raised by the author of passage B, himself an opponent of the online idea.

Divide and Conquer Comparison Questions. Now comes the majority of the questions dealing with the relationship between the two passages. You can do these in order, or divide and conquer them in any manner that works best for you. We chose the following path, but you may well have chosen a different one.

Divide . . . A Central Topic question isn't a bad place to begin the Comparison questions, so we'll tackle question 22 next.

22. Both passages are primarily concerned with the

   (A)   influence of McLuhan's and Ong's theories on the rise of the Internet as a social and economic force
   (B)   transition between primary and secondary orality and the effect of that transition on the creation of online communities
   (C)   viability of establishing an online Native American community
   (D)   effect of Native American traditions and narratives on the global village
   (E)   role of ceremony in establishing genuine community among tribal groups

. . . and Conquer. We've already scoped out the main focus of each passage and have even answered a Main Point question for passage A, so identifying the topic central to both passages shouldn't be overly taxing. **C** captures the issue at the heart of both passages, which we determined in the course of our analysis of passage B. The main topic of both passages is the creation of a Native American presence online, and both passages focus on whether or not this is possible.

A: While the theories of McLuhan and Ong are apparently consistent with what has become Internet culture, nothing in either passage suggests a link between their speculations and the rise of the Internet as a social and economic force.

B and E: Choice **B** pertains to issues discussed only in passage A, while the subject of choice **E** appears only in passage B—and even there, only as evidence for a larger point.

D reverses the relationship at the heart of both passages. The authors discuss whether Native American culture and communities can flourish on the net, not how the net is influenced by Native American culture.

> TAKE AWAY
>
> A choice need not be correct just because it contains familiar words from the passage. Read carefully to make sure the *relationship* between those familiar concepts accords with the information the author (or authors) presents.

Divide . . . While we're on the topic of synergy between the passages, why not move right to Agreement question 25? Here goes.

---

25. Which one of the following statements is most strongly supported by both passages?

    (A) Ong's theory of secondary orality was derived from McLuhan's conception of the global village.

    (B) Some media theories have been formulated with the intention of helping cultural groups create online identities.

    (C) There is disagreement regarding the extent to which media theories effectively support the establishment of a cultural presence online.

    (D) Ong's theory of secondary orality has provided greater support for establishing an online Native American presence than has McLuhan's theory of the global village.

    (E) The promise of the Internet is understood in essentially the same way by all parties to the debate concerning the feasibility of establishing an online Native American presence.

. . . and Conquer. Agreement over disagreement? That may sound a bit odd, but debate over the issue in question is recognized by both authors, so it's inferable both would agree with choice **C**. In paragraph 1 of passage A, supporters of an online Native American presence are taken with McLuhan's and Ong's ideas, citing both media theorists in support of their position. But in paragraph 2 of that same passage, other critics are described who believe the secondary orality theory doesn't support the viability of creating an online Native American presence. Similarly, the author of passage B tells how McLuhan's ideas are intriguing, "prompting vigorous debate" on whether and how a Native American presence can be constructed online. While this author weighs in on one side of the issue, he, like the author of passage 1, explicitly states that there is debate regarding what a specific media theory may mean for the prospect of creating an online Native American culture.

A attempts to connect Ong to McLuhan in a way never suggested in either passage. In fact, Ong isn't even mentioned in passage B, which kills this choice on that count alone.

B is a Twister, as we cannot infer the intentions of the media theorists mentioned from the information in the passages. All we know is how their theories have been interpreted by others.

D: We're never told by either author which theory, Ong's or McLuhan's, offers greater support to those seeking to digitize Native American culture, so **D** doesn't qualify as a point of agreement.

E goes against the grain of the passages, since both authors admit to fundamental differences of opinion regarding the value of using the Internet to promote Native traditions and narratives.

Divide . . . Let's take on Method question 23 next, which is looking for a difference in how the two authors go about making their points.

---

23. The two passages differ in that only one

 (A) includes a concession that a specific kind of technology may have a useful function
 (B) details reasons why the narratives of a particular culture may not be fully reproducible on the Internet
 (C) expresses the viewpoint that societies should remain static in order to maintain their vitality
 (D) suggests the existence of opposing viewpoints regarding an issue
 (E) presents arguments from two sides of a debate

. . . and Conquer. E is correct: While passage B suggests that there are two sides to the issue, only passage A contains actual arguments from both sides.

A: In the final sentence of passage A, the critics concede that the Internet may be useful in some ways, while in passage B the author does the same in the first sentence of paragraph 1.

B: Both passages provide reasons why the Internet may not be suitable to project Native American narratives in their genuine form. The critics supply the reasons in passage A, while the author supplies them in passage B.

C: Neither passage suggests that Native American culture should remain static. The author of passage B suggests the opposite in his reference to the "acceptable evolution of traditional tales," while neither supporters nor opponents of the online idea in passage A argue that Native American culture itself shouldn't change.

D: As we've seen, both passages suggest that there are two schools of thought within the Native American community regarding whether and how Native American culture can be represented on the net. Only passage A, however, presents actual arguments from both sides, which brings us back to **E**.

Divide . . . Of the two questions remaining, question 26 seems a bit complex, concerning the attitude of one author regarding a detail mentioned by the other. So we'll jump to question 28 next.

---

28. The notion that electronic communication technologies may be useful in one way but not in another is shared by

 (A) the author of passage A and the author of passage B
 (B) the author of passage B and the Native Americans of passage B
 (C) McLuhan and Ong
 (D) the critics of virtual communities in passage A and the author of passage B
 (E) the supporters of online Native American communities in passage A and those intrigued by McLuhan's reference to tribalism in passage B

. . . and Conquer. It turns out that the issue in this one isn't so foreign, since we saw a similar reference in choice **A** from question 23. The critics in passage A concede that "electronic technologies may be useful for projecting Native American culture outwards to a broader audience." This admission that the Internet may be good for something is similar to the admission by the author of passage B that "the Internet is a supreme conveyor of information." Both, however, immediately go on to argue that despite this positive capability, the Internet is not in the end an appropriate vehicle for capturing the vitality of true Native American culture. Choice **D** is correct.

> Don't be surprised to find some overlap among the questions in a Reading Comp set; there are, after all, only so many things they can ask you about. Use your thinking from earlier questions to help you in later ones whenever possible.

TAKE
AWAY

A: The author of passage A doesn't venture her own opinions but merely relays the opinions of others.

B: The author of passage B mentions the Native American community but doesn't tell us specifically what the members of that community think about communication technologies. All of the specific opinions in passage B come from the author.

C: If anything, Ong and McLuhan appear as early supporters of communication technologies. In any case, nothing in either passage links these theorists with the idea that such technologies *aren't* useful in certain ways.

E: Nothing suggests that the supporters of online Native American communities in passage A have anything against communication technologies; their position in fact supports the opposite supposition. Moreover, we aren't told the actual opinions of those in passage B intrigued by McLuhan's tribalism, so neither group in **E** fits the bill.

> It's always important to keep the passage's characters and their opinions straight, but this is doubly important in Paired Passage sets, which contain two authors and two sets of players and extras to keep track of.

TAKE
AWAY

Divide . . . That leaves question 26 as the final challenge of this Paired Passage set.

26. The author of passage B would most likely believe that the virtual communities mentioned in line 20 of passage A

(A) **lack what tribal members refer to as the sacredness of place**
(B) suffice as foundations for establishing genuine meanings in the myths and metaphors of Native American narratives
(C) are responsible for the recent interest among some Native Americans in the theories of McLuhan
(D) were envisioned by McLuhan as vehicles by which to spread awareness of tribal cultures
(E) serve audiences united by shared histories and unspoken cultural understandings

TAKE AWAY

Some Comparison questions are a cross between Author Agreement and Fact questions, asking you to infer what one author may think about some detail in the other passage. Noting the detail in question as a tested issue during your scouting mission in Step 1 of the Paired Passages Essential Strategy brings you one step closer to answering the question successfully.

. . . and Conquer. The author of passage B describes the virtual communities of passage A as "pseudo-tribal" communities incapable of reflecting the true ceremonial traditions of real Native American cultures. It's therefore likely that the author of passage B would think that such virtual communities lack what tribal members refer to as "the sacredness of place." **A** has it right.

B: According to the line of reasoning just stated, choice **B** represents the Opposite of what this author would think.

C: The author of passage A states that what has intrigued Native Americans was McLuhan's reference to tribalism as a characteristic of the global village. It's therefore more likely that interest in McLuhan spurred their interest in virtual communities, not the other way around.

D: The author of passage B informs us that McLuhan predicted an interconnected global village but doesn't speculate on what McLuhan thought virtual communities might be used for.

TAKE AWAY

Stay alert, both in Reading Comp and Logical Reasoning, to the difference between facts and intentions. You may be told that someone *did*, *said*, or *discovered* something, but unless you're told *why*, or what he or she expected would *result*, don't guess. In Logical Reasoning parlance, intentions and expectations in such cases are unknowable, and any choice that speculates on them without direct support will be wrong.

E, like **B,** leans in the Opposite direction. Passage B's author believes that only actual locales infused with "the sacredness of place" serve as foundations for shared histories and unspoken cultural understandings.

Mine the Experience. As always, spend a good amount of time assimilating what you've learned from this passage to help you minimize your mistakes and replicate your successes on test day. And speaking of which . . .

Go on to the next and final chapter for some final advice on how to gear up for, and get through, the fateful day.

## Chapter 6

TOP 15 LSAT TEST DAY TIPS

Hey, everyone and his grandmother has a Top *10* list of test day advice, so we figured we'd one-up 'em—actually, five-up 'em, to be precise. Here goes:

'Twas the Night Before LSAT . . .

#15: Get it together. Pack up the day before so you don't have to scramble around in the morning. Get your admission ticket, ID, nonbeeping timepiece, water, nonsugar energy snack, and sharpened No. 2 pencils all ready to go.

#14: Wind down. Runners don't run a full marathon the day *before* they run the real marathon; they rest up for the big day. Avoid cramming the day before the test. Read a book, watch a movie, hang out with friends, whatever relaxes you—but make it an early night. And speaking of which . . .

#13: Get enough sleep. Don't get into bed at 7:00 just to stare at the ceiling, but do get to bed early enough to ensure enough sleep to be alert and energetic for test day.

#12: Set two alarms. You don't want to miss the test because your alarm was set for P.M. instead of A.M.—stranger things have happened. Also, one of your alarms should be battery operated, just in case something crazy like a power outage occurs during the night. Unlikely, sure, but peace of mind will help you sleep better. Of course, if you take an afternoon test, waking up on time shouldn't be an issue.

Rise and Shine . . .

#11: Eat normally. Sure, LSAT day is special, but that doesn't mean you need to treat yourself to a special breakfast. Nerves can turn a huge bacon, egg, and cheese omelet against you—especially if you don't usually eat that kind of thing. Eat what you normally eat for breakfast; not too much, not too little. If your test is in the afternoon, still make sure to eat something before it. Bring a nonsugar snack for the break. It's a long day, and you'll need the energy.

#10: Dress for success. One word: layers. If it's hot, take some off. If it's cold, leave them on. Comfort is key.

#9: Jump-start your brain. To employ the marathon analogy again (see tip #14), runners stretch before the big event to warm up. Likewise, it helps to do a bit of reading before the test to get your mind warmed up and stretch those brain cells into shape. We're not talking Plato or Shakespeare here. Articles from a well-written newspaper, magazine, or science journal containing the same kind of sophisticated writing you'll see on the test will do.

Put on Your Game Face . . .

#8: Arrive early. Save fashionable lateness for your social life. Rushing around like a crazy person isn't the best way to start your LSAT day. If the testing center is in unfamiliar territory, you may even wish to scout it out a week or two before just to be sure you know your way. One less thing to worry about couldn't hurt.

#7: Don't sweat the small stuff. Okay, so what if it's 9 billion degrees in the testing room and that obnoxious kid from high school sits right next to you? If something potentially correctable is bothering you, by all means talk to the proctor, but if there's nothing you can do about it, *let it go*. Don't allow small annoyances to distract you from your mission.

#6: Gear up for a long haul. Some people arrive at the test center all revved up, bouncing off the walls—*the big day is finally here!* Slow down; you don't want to overheat and peak too soon. You'll get to the test site, mill about a bit, get fingerprinted, be seated, and then spend what seems like an eternity bubbling in your life story on your answer sheet. "Go time" isn't until you hear, "You may turn the page and begin work on Section 1 . . ." Which brings us to our tips for the final and most important phase of the testing experience . . .

Go Time . . .

#5: Prepare for the worst. This is by no means to say you should go in with a negative attitude, but you need to be ready to start the test with two of your least favorite sections. If that happens, you'll be prepared; if it doesn't, you'll be relieved. Win-win.

#4: Keep your focus. Maybe the woman to the right of you will appear to finish the first section in five minutes, while the guy to the left of you seems unaware that a test is even taking place. If you have a large enough group, chances are someone may even freak out and leave the room in tears. Assuming that this person isn't you, don't let it bother you. Stay focused on your objective and let the others take care of themselves.

#3: Choose your battles. Remember, every question on the LSAT is worth the same amount. No one question can hurt you unless you spend all day on it. Keep moving throughout each section. If a question isn't working for you, guess and move on. In Logic Games and Reading Comp, first tackle the games and passages that are easiest for you, no matter where in those sections they appear. Save the tough stuff for last.

#2: Stick it out. There may come a time in the last section when you'll do anything to end your agony five minutes early. Hang in there and keep applying what you've learned. True champs finish strong.

And the #1 LSAT Test Day Tip . . . Relax. If you've worked hard and prepared conscientiously, take heart from the fact that you've done all you can do. True testing terror comes from being unprepared; conversely, proper preparation breeds confidence. Nerves are normal, but how you deal with them is up to you. Channel your adrenaline positively to give you the energy you need to maintain your focus all the way through. Also remember that although the LSAT is surely important, *it's not the end of the world*. Put the event into perspective. Then do the best you can, which is the most you can ask of yourself.

FINAL THOUGHT

We began this book by telling you that the LSAT is systematic, coachable, and conquerable. Four hundred ninety-five pages later, we hope you agree. We at SparkNotes wish you the best of luck on the LSAT, and all possible success wherever that may lead. Thanks for allowing us to be part of your future.

ABOUT THE AUTHOR

Eric Goodman began his career in test preparation and instructional design soon after graduating from Cornell University. His numerous top-selling, critically acclaimed books and courses have helped tens of thousands of students master the LSAT, GMAT, GRE, and SAT. He has also authored online courses and innovative computer-based simulations in the fields of economics, corporate training, and e-commerce.

Eric lives in New York City with his wife, Cathy, and daughters, Memphis and Dasha.